Programming C# 8.0
Build Cloud, Web, and Desktop Applications

Ian Griffiths

Beijing · Boston · Farnham · Sebastopol · Tokyo

Programming C# 8.0

by Ian Griffiths

Copyright © 2020 Ian Griffiths. All rights reserved.

Printed in the United States of America.

Published by O'Reilly Media, Inc., 1005 Gravenstein Highway North, Sebastopol, CA 95472.

O'Reilly books may be purchased for educational, business, or sales promotional use. Online editions are also available for most titles (*http://oreilly.com*). For more information, contact our corporate/institutional sales department: 800-998-9938 or *corporate@oreilly.com*.

Acquisitions Editor: Tyler Ortman	**Indexer:** WordCo Indexing Services, Inc.
Development Editor: Corbin Collins	**Interior Designer:** David Futato
Production Editor: Deborah Baker	**Cover Designer:** Karen Montgomery
Copyeditor: Sonia Saruba	**Illustrator:** Rebecca Demarest
Proofreader: Christina Edwards	

December 2019:   First Edition

Revision History for the First Edition

2019-11-26:   First Release

See *http://oreilly.com/catalog/errata.csp?isbn=9781492056812* for release details.

The O'Reilly logo is a registered trademark of O'Reilly Media, Inc. *Programming C# 8.0*, the cover image, and related trade dress are trademarks of O'Reilly Media, Inc.

978-1-492-05681-2

[LSCH]

I dedicate this book to my excellent wife Deborah, and to my wonderful daughters, Hazel, Victoria, and Lyra. Thank you for enriching my life.

Table of Contents

Preface

C# has now existed for around two decades. It has grown steadily in both power and size, but Microsoft has always kept the essential characteristics intact. Each new capability is designed to integrate cleanly with the rest, enhancing the language without turning it into an incoherent bag of miscellaneous features.

Even though C# continues to be a fairly straightforward language at its heart, there is a great deal more to say about it now than in its first incarnation. Because there is so much ground to cover, this book expects a certain level of technical ability from its readers.

Who This Book Is For

I have written this book for experienced developers—I've been programming for years, and I set out to make this the book I would want to read if that experience had been in other languages, and I were learning C# today. Whereas earlier editions explained some basic concepts such as classes, polymorphism, and collections, I am assuming that readers will already know what these are. The early chapters still describe how C# presents these common ideas, but the focus is on the details specific to C#, rather than the broad concepts.

Conventions Used in This Book

The following typographical conventions are used in this book:

Italic
: Indicates new terms, URLs, email addresses, filenames, and file extensions.

`Constant width`
: Used for program listings, as well as within paragraphs to refer to program elements such as variable or function names, databases, data types, environment variables, statements, and keywords.

Constant width bold

Shows commands or other text that should be typed literally by the user. In examples, highlights code of particular interest.

Constant width italic

Shows text that should be replaced with user-supplied values or by values determined by context.

 This element signifies a tip or suggestion.

 This element signifies a general note.

 This element indicates a warning or caution.

Using Code Examples

Supplemental material (code examples, exercises, etc.) is available for download at *http://oreil.ly/Programming_Csharp*.

If you have a technical question or a problem using the code examples, please send email to *bookquestions@oreilly.com*.

This book is here to help you get your job done. In general, if example code is offered with this book, you may use it in your programs and documentation. You do not need to contact us for permission unless you're reproducing a significant portion of the code. For example, writing a program that uses several chunks of code from this book does not require permission. Selling or distributing examples from O'Reilly books does require permission. Answering a question by citing this book and quoting example code does not require permission. Incorporating a significant amount of example code from this book into your product's documentation does require permission.

We appreciate, but generally do not require, attribution. An attribution usually includes the title, author, publisher, and ISBN. For example: *Programming C# 8.0* by Ian Griffiths (O'Reilly). Copyright 2020 by Ian Griffiths, 978-1-492-05681-2.

If you feel your use of code examples falls outside fair use or the permission given above, feel free to contact us at *permissions@oreilly.com*.

O'Reilly Online Learning

For more than 40 years, *O'Reilly* has provided technology and business training, knowledge, and insight to help companies succeed.

Our unique network of experts and innovators share their knowledge and expertise through books, articles, conferences, and our online learning platform. O'Reilly's online learning platform gives you on-demand access to live training courses, in-depth learning paths, interactive coding environments, and a vast collection of text and video from O'Reilly and 200+ other publishers. For more information, please visit *http://oreilly.com*.

How to Contact Us

Please address comments and questions concerning this book to the publisher:

O'Reilly Media, Inc.
1005 Gravenstein Highway North
Sebastopol, CA 95472
800-998-9938 (in the United States or Canada)
707-829-0515 (international or local)
707-829-0104 (fax)

We have a web page for this book, where we list errata, examples, and any additional information. You can access this page at *https://oreil.ly/Programming_C_sharp* (*https://oreil.ly/Programming_C_sharp*).

Emails us with comments or technical questions at *bookquestions@oreilly.com*.

For more information about our books, courses, conferences, and news, see our website at *http://www.oreilly.com*.

Find us on Facebook: *http://facebook.com/oreilly*

Follow us on Twitter: *http://twitter.com/oreillymedia*

Watch us on YouTube: *http://www.youtube.com/oreillymedia*

Acknowledgments

Many thanks to the book's official technical reviewers: Stephen Toub, Howard van Rooijen, and Glyn Griffiths. I'd also like to give a big thank you to those who reviewed individual chapters, or otherwise offered help or information that improved this book: Brian Rasmussen, Eric Lippert, Andrew Kennedy, Daniel Sinclair, Brian Randell, Mike Woodring, Mike Taulty, Mary Jo Foley, Bart De Smet, Matthew Adams, Jess Panni, Jonathan George, Mike Larah, Carmel Eve, and Ed Freeman. Thanks in particular to endjin, both allowing me to take time out from work to write this book, and also for creating such a great place to work.

Thank you to everyone at O'Reilly whose work brought this book into existence. In particular, thanks to Corbin Collins for his support in making this book happen, and to Tyler Ortman for his support in getting this project started. Thanks also to Cassandra Furtado, Deborah Baker, Ron Bilodeau, Nick Adams, Rebecca Demarest, Karen Montgomery, and Kristen Brown, for their help in bringing the work to completion. Thanks also to Sonia Saruba's thorough copy editing, and Christina Edwards's diligent proofreading. Finally, thank you to John Osborn, for taking me on as an O'Reilly author back when I wrote my first book.

CHAPTER 1

Introducing C#

The C# programming language (pronounced "see sharp") is used for many kinds of applications, including websites, cloud-based systems, IoT devices, machine learning, desktop applications, embedded controllers, mobile apps, games, and command-line utilities. C#, along with the supporting runtime, libraries, and tools known collectively as .NET, has been center stage for Windows developers for almost two decades, but in recent years, it has also made inroads into other platforms. In June 2016, Microsoft released version 1.0 of .NET Core, a cross-platform version of .NET, enabling web apps, microservices, and console applications written in C# to run on macOS and Linux, as well as on Windows.

This push into other platforms has gone hand in hand with Microsoft's embrace of open source development. In C#'s early history, Microsoft guarded all of its source code closely,[1] but today, pretty much everything surrounding C# is developed in the open, with code contributions from outside of Microsoft being welcome. New language feature proposals are published on GitHub, enabling community involvement from the earliest stages. In 2014, the .NET Foundation (*https://dotnetfoundation.org/*) was created to foster the development of open source projects in the .NET world, and many of Microsoft's most important C# and .NET projects are now under the foundation's governance (in addition to many non-Microsoft projects). This includes Microsoft's C# compiler, which is at *https://github.com/dotnet/roslyn*, and also .NET Core, which can be found at *https://github.com/dotnet/core*, comprising the runtime, class library, and tools for creating .NET projects.

---

[1] This was true of Microsoft's previous cross-platform .NET offering. In 2008, Microsoft shipped Silverlight 2.0, which enabled C# to run inside browsers on Windows and macOS. Silverlight fought a losing battle against the improving capabilities and universal reach of HTML5 and JavaScript, but its closed source nature may not have helped its cause.

Why C#?

Although there are many ways you can use C#, other languages are always an option. Why might you choose C# over them? It will depend on what you need to do, and what you like and dislike in a programming language. I find that C# provides considerable power, flexibility, and performance, and works at a high enough level of abstraction that I don't expend vast amounts of effort on little details not directly related to the problems my programs are trying to solve.

Much of C#'s power comes from the range of programming techniques it supports. For example, it offers object-oriented features, generics, and functional programming. It supports both dynamic and static typing. It provides powerful list- and set-oriented features, thanks to Language Integrated Query (LINQ). It has intrinsic support for asynchronous programming.

More recently, C# has gained flexibility around memory management. The runtime has always provided a garbage collector (GC) that frees developers from much of the work associated with recovering memory that the program is no longer using. A GC is a common feature in modern programming languages, and while it is a boon for most programs, there are some specialized scenarios where its performance implications are problematic, so C# 7.2 (released in 2017) added various features that enable more explicit memory management, giving you the option to trade ease of development for runtime performance, but all without the loss of type safety. This enables C# to move into certain performance-critical applications that for years were the preserve of less safe languages such as C and C++.

Of course, languages do not exist in a vacuum—high-quality libraries with a broad range of features are essential. Some elegant and academically beautiful languages are glorious right up until you want to do something prosaic, such as talking to a database or determining where to store user settings. No matter how powerful a set of programming idioms a language offers, it also needs to provide full and convenient access to the underlying platform's services. C# is on very strong ground here, thanks to its runtime, the class library, and extensive third-party library support.

.NET encompasses both the runtime and the main class library that C# programs use. The runtime part is called the *Common Language Runtime* (usually abbreviated to CLR) because it supports not just C#, but any .NET language. Microsoft also offers Visual Basic, F#, and .NET extensions for C++, for example. The CLR has a *Common Type System* (CTS) that enables code from multiple languages to interoperate freely, which means that .NET libraries can normally be used from any .NET language—F# can consume libraries written in C#, C# can use Visual Basic libraries, and so on.

In addition to the runtime, there is an extensive class library. This library provides wrappers for many features of the underlying operating system (OS), but it also provides a considerable amount of functionality of its own, such as collection classes or JSON processing.

The class library built into .NET is not the whole story—many other systems provide their own .NET libraries. For example, there are extensive libraries that enable C# programs to use popular cloud services. As you'd expect, Microsoft provides comprehensive .NET libraries for working with services in its Azure cloud platform. Likewise, Amazon provides a fully featured SDK for using Amazon Web Services (AWS) from C# and other .NET languages. And libraries do not have to be associated with frameworks. There's a large ecosystem of .NET libraries, some commercial and some free and open source, including mathematical utilities, parsing libraries, and user interface (UI) components, to name just a few. Even if you get unlucky and need to use an OS feature that doesn't have any .NET library wrappers, C# offers various mechanisms for working with other kinds of APIs, such as the C-style APIs available in Win32, macOS, and Linux, or APIs based on the Component Object Model (COM) in Windows.

Finally, with .NET having been around for about two decades, many organizations have invested extensively in technology built on this platform. So C# is often the natural choice for reaping the rewards of these investments.

In summary, with C# we get a strong set of abstractions built into the language, a powerful runtime, and easy access to an enormous amount of library and platform functionality.

C#'s Defining Features

Although C#'s most superficially obvious feature is its C-family syntax, perhaps its most distinctive feature is that it was the first language designed to be a native in the world of the CLR. As the name suggests, the CLR is flexible enough to support many languages, but there's an important difference between a language that has been extended to support the CLR, and one that puts it at the center of its design. The .NET extensions in Microsoft's C++ compiler illustrate this—the syntax for using those features is visibly different from standard C++, making a clear distinction between the native world of C++ and the outside world of the CLR. But even without different syntax,[2] there would still be friction when two worlds have different ways of working. For example, if you need a dynamically resizable collection of numbers, should you use a standard C++ collection class such as vector<int>, or one from .NET such as List<int>? Whichever you choose, it will be the wrong type some

---

2 Microsoft's first set of .NET extensions for C++ resembled ordinary C++ more closely. It turned out to be confusing to use the existing syntax for something quite different from ordinary C++, so Microsoft deprecated the first system (Managed C++) in favor of the newer, more distinctive syntax, which is called C++/CLI.

of the time: C++ libraries won't know what to do with a .NET collection, while .NET APIs won't be able to use the C++ type.

C# embraces .NET, both the runtime and the class library, so these dilemmas do not arise. In the scenario just discussed, List<int> has no rival. There is no friction when using .NET's class library because it is built for the same world as C#.

The first version of C# presented a programming model that was very closely related to the underlying CLR's model. C# has gradually added its own abstractions over the years, but these have been designed to fit well with the CLR. This gives C# a distinctive feel. It also means that if you want to understand C#, you need to understand the CLR and the way in which it runs code.

Managed Code and the CLR

For years, the most common way for a compiler to work was to process source code, and to produce output in a form that could be executed directly by the computer's CPU. Compilers would produce *machine code*—a series of instructions in whatever binary format was required by the kind of CPU the computer had. Many compilers still work this way, but the C# compiler does not. Instead, it uses a model called *managed code*.

With managed code, the compiler does not generate the machine code that the CPU executes. Instead, the compiler produces a form of binary code called the *intermediate language* (IL). The executable binary is produced later, usually, although not always, at runtime. The use of IL enables features that are hard or even impossible to provide under the more traditional model.

Perhaps the most visible benefit of the managed model is that the compiler's output is not tied to a single CPU architecture. You can write a .NET component that can run on the 32-bit x86 architecture that PCs have used for decades, but that will also work well in the newer 64-bit update to that design (x64), and even on completely different architectures such as ARM. (For example, .NET Core introduced the ability to run on ARM-based devices such as the Raspberry Pi.) With a language that compiles directly to machine code, you'd need to build different binaries for each of these. But with .NET, you can compile a single component that can run on any of them, and it would even be able to run on platforms that weren't supported at the time you compiled the code if a suitable runtime became available in the future. More generally, any kind of improvement to the CLR's code generation—whether that's support for new CPU architectures, or just performance improvements for existing ones—is instantly of benefit to all .NET languages. For example, older versions of the CLR did not take advantage of the vector processing extensions available on modern x86 and x64 processors, but the current versions will now often exploit these when generating code for loops. All code running on current versions of .NET Core benefits from this, including code that was written years before this enhancement was added.

The exact moment at which the CLR generates executable machine code can vary. Typically, it uses an approach called *just-in-time* (JIT) compilation, in which each individual function is compiled the first time it runs. However, it doesn't have to work this way. There are various ways in which .NET code can be compiled *ahead of time* (AoT). There's a tool called NGen which can do this as a post-installation step. Windows Store Apps built for the *Universal Windows Platform* (UWP) use the *.NET Native* build tools, which do this earlier, as part of the build. .NET Core 3.0 adds a new tool called crossgen, which enables any .NET Core application (not just UWP apps) to use build-time native code generation. However, generation of executable code can still happen at runtime even when you use these tools[3]—the runtime's *tiered compilation* feature may choose to recompile a method dynamically to optimize it better for the ways it is being used at runtime. (It can do this whether you're using JIT or AoT.) The virtualized nature of managed execution is designed to make such things possible in a way that's invisible to your code, although it can occasionally make its presence felt through more than just performance. For example, virtualized execution leaves some latitude for when and how the runtime performs certain initialization work, and you can sometimes see the results of its optimizations causing things to happen in a surprising order.

Managed code has ubiquitous type information. The file formats dictated by the CLI require this to be present, because it enables certain runtime features. For example, .NET offers various automatic serialization services, in which objects can be converted into binary or textual representations of their state, and those representations can later be turned back into objects, perhaps on a different machine. This sort of service relies on a complete and accurate description of an object's structure, something that's guaranteed to be present in managed code. Type information can be used in other ways. For example, unit test frameworks can use it to inspect code in a test project and discover all of the unit tests you have written. This relies on the CLR's *reflection* services, which are the topic of Chapter 13.

Although C#'s close connection with the runtime is one of its main defining features, it's not the only one. There's a certain philosophy underpinning C#'s design.

Prefer Generality to Specialization

C# favors general-purpose language features over specialized ones. Over the years, Microsoft has expanded C# several times, and the language's designers always have specific scenarios in mind for new features. However, they have always tried hard to ensure that each new element they add is useful beyond these primary scenarios.

---

3 .NET Native is an exception: it does not support runtime JIT, so it does not offer tiered compilation.

For example, a few years ago Microsoft decided to add features to C# to make database access feel well integrated with the language. The resulting technology, Language Integrated Query (LINQ, described in Chapter 10), certainly supports that goal, but Microsoft achieved this without adding any direct support for data access to the language. Instead, Microsoft introduced a series of quite diverse-seeming capabilities. These included better support for functional programming idioms, the ability to add new methods to existing types without resorting to inheritance, support for anonymous types, the ability to obtain an object model representing the structure of an expression, and the introduction of query syntax. The last of these has an obvious connection to data access, but the rest are harder to relate to the task at hand. Nonetheless, these can be used collectively in a way that makes certain data access tasks significantly simpler. But the features are all useful in their own right, so as well as supporting data access, they enable a much wider range of scenarios. For example, these additions (which arrived in C# 3.0) made it very much easier to process lists, sets, and other groups of objects, because the new features work for collections of things from any origin, not just databases.

One illustration of this philosophy of generality was a language feature that was prototyped for C#, but which its designers ultimately chose not to go ahead with. The feature would have enabled you to write XML directly in your source code, embedding expressions to calculate values for certain bits of content at runtime. The prototype compiled this into code that generated the completed XML at runtime. Microsoft Research demonstrated this publicly, but this feature didn't ultimately make it into C#, although it did later ship in another of Microsoft's .NET languages, Visual Basic, which also got some specialized query features for extracting information from XML documents. Embedded XML expressions are a relatively narrow facility, only useful when you're creating XML documents. As for querying XML documents, C# supports this functionality through its general-purpose LINQ features, without needing any XML-specific language features. XML's star has waned since this language concept was mooted, having been usurped in many cases by JSON (which will doubtless be eclipsed by something else in years to come). Had embedded XML made it into C#, it would by now feel like a slightly anachronistic curiosity.

The new features added in subsequent versions of C# continue in the same vein. For example, the deconstruction and pattern matching features added in C# versions 7 and 8 are aimed at making life easier in subtle but useful ways, and are not limited to any particular application area.

C# Standards and Implementations

Before we can get going with some actual code, we need to know which implementation of C# and the runtime we are targeting. There are specifications that define language and runtime behavior for all C# implementations, as the next sidebar, "C#, the

CLR, and Standards", describes. This has made it possible for multiple implementations of C# and the runtime to emerge. At the time of writing, there are three in widespread use: .NET Framework, .NET Core, and Mono. Somewhat confusingly, Microsoft is behind all three of these, although it didn't start out that way.

C#, the CLR, and Standards

The standards body ECMA has published two OS-independent specifications that effectively define the C# language and runtime: ECMA-334 is the C# Language Specification, and ECMA-335 defines the *Common Language Infrastructure* (CLI), the virtual environment in which programs written in C# (and other .NET languages) run. Versions of these documents have also been published by the International Standards Organization as ISO/IEC 23270:2018 and ISO/IEC 23271:2012, respectively. The "2018" suggests that the C# specification is more up to date than it really is: the ECMA and ISO language standards both correspond to version 5.0 of C#. At the time of writing, ECMA is working on an updated language specification, but be aware that these particular standards are typically several years behind the state of the art. While the IEC CLI standard has an even older date, 2012 (as does ECMA-335), the runtime specifications change less often than the language, so the CLI spec is much closer to current implementations, despite the names suggesting the opposite.

ECMA-335 defines the CLI, which includes all the behavior required from the runtime (such as .NET's CLR, or the Mono runtime), and more besides. It defines not just the runtime behavior (which it calls the *Virtual Execution System*, or VES), but also the file format for executable and library files, and the Common Type System. Additionally, it defines a subset of the CTS that languages are expected to be able to support to guarantee interoperability between languages, called the Common Language Specification (CLS).

So you could say that Microsoft's CLI implementation is all of .NET rather than just the CLR, although .NET includes a lot of additional features not in the CLI specification. (For example, the class library that the CLI demands makes up only a small subset of .NET's much larger library.) The CLR is effectively .NET's VES, but you hardly ever see the term VES used outside of the specification, which is why I mostly talk about the CLR (or just *the runtime*) in this book. However, the terms CTS and CLS are more widely used, and I'll refer to them again in this book.

The Mono project was launched in 2001, and did not originate from Microsoft. (This is why it doesn't have .NET in its name—it can use the name C# because that's what the standards call the language, but .NET is a Microsoft brand name.) Mono started out with the goal of enabling Linux desktop application development in C#, but it went on to add support for iOS and Android. That crucial move helped Mono find its niche, because it is now mainly used to create cross-platform mobile device applications in C#. It was open source from the start, and has been supported by a variety of companies over its existence. At the time of writing this, Mono is under the stewardship of a company called Xamarin, and has been since 2011. Microsoft acquired Xamarin in 2016, and for now retains it as a distinct brand, positioning its Mono runtime as the way to run C# code on mobile devices.

So what about the other two implementations, both of which seem to be called .NET?

Many Microsoft .NETs (Temporarily)

For about seven years, there was only one current version of .NET at any given time, but since 2008 the picture has been less clear. This was due at first to specialized variants of .NET associated with various UI platforms coming and going, including Silverlight, several Windows Phone variants, and Windows 8's introduction of Store Applications. Though some of these are still supported, they're all dead ends except for Store Applications, which turned into Universal Windows Platform (UWP) apps. UWP has moved on to .NET Core, so these other .NET lineages are obsolete.

But even ignoring those effectively defunct forks of .NET, as I write this Microsoft still ships two current versions of .NET: the .NET Framework (Windows only, closed-source) and .NET Core (cross-platform, open source). In May of 2019, Microsoft announced that it intends to revert to a single current version in November 2020. In the long run this will reduce confusion, but in the near term it complicates matters further by introducing yet another version to be aware of.

One slightly baffling aspect of this is the minor variations in naming across the different .NETs. For the first 15 years or so, *.NET Framework* meant the combination of two things: a runtime and the class library. Its runtime was called the CLR. The class library went by various names including Base Class Library (BCL; a confusing name, because the ECMA specifications define the term "BCL" as something much narrower), or the Framework Class Library.

Today, we also have .NET Core. Its runtime is called the .NET Core Common Language Runtime (or just CoreCLR), which is a straightforward enough name: we can talk about the .NET Core CLR or the .NET Framework CLR, and it's obvious which one we mean. And throughout this book, when I talk about the CLR or the runtime without any particular qualification, it's because I'm saying something that applies to both implementations. Unfortunately, .NET Core calls its class library the .NET Core Framework (or CoreFX). This is unhelpful, because before .NET Core, the *Framework* was the combination of the CLR and the library. And just to muddy the waters further, many people at Microsoft now refer to the .NET Framework as the "desktop" framework to make it clear that they're not talking about .NET Core. (This was always confusing because plenty of people use this "desktop" version for server applications. Moreover, the first ever release of .NET Core was for the UWP, supporting only Windows applications. A year went by before Microsoft released a supported version that could do anything else.[4] And now that .NET Core 3.0 has added support on Windows for the two .NET desktop UI frameworks—Windows Presentation Foundation (WPF) and Windows Forms—most new desktop applications will target .NET Core, not the so-called .NET "desktop".) Just in case that's not all crystal clear, Table 1-1 summarizes the current situation.

Table 1-1. The names of .NET's component parts

Platform	Runtime	Class library
.NET Framework (aka .NET desktop)	.NET CLR	.NET Framework Class Library
.NET Core	.NET Core CLR	.NET Core Framework

In 2020, assuming Microsoft sticks to its plan, the names will all adjust again, with both .NET Core and .NET Framework being superseded by plain ".NET". Microsoft has not settled on definitive names for the corresponding runtime and library parts at the time of writing.

But until that time, we have two "current" versions. Each can do things the other cannot, which is why both ship concurrently. .NET Framework only runs on Windows, whereas .NET Core supports Windows, macOS, and Linux. Although this makes the .NET Framework less widely usable, it means it can support some Windows-specific features. For example, there is a section of the .NET Framework Class Library dedicated to working with Windows speech synthesis and recognition services. This isn't possible on .NET Core because it might be running on Linux, where equivalent features either don't exist or are too different to be presented through the same .NET API.

The .NET due to ship in 2020 is essentially the next version of .NET Core, just with a snappier name. .NET Core is where most of the new development of .NET has occurred for the last few years. .NET Framework is still fully supported, but is already falling behind. For example, version 3.0 of Microsoft's web application framework, ASP.NET Core, will only run on .NET Core, and not .NET Framework. So .NET Framework's retirement, and .NET Core's promotion to the one true .NET, is the inevitable conclusion of a process that has been underway for a few years.

Targeting Multiple .NET Versions with .NET Standard

The multiplicity of runtimes, each with their own different versions of the class libraries, presents a challenge for anyone who wants to make their code available to other developers. There's a package repository for .NET components at *http://nuget.org*,

---

[4] Strangely, this first, UWP-supporting release in 2015 apparently never received an official version number. The .NET Core 1.0 release is dated June 2016, about a year later.

which is where Microsoft publishes all of the .NET libraries it produces that are not built into .NET itself, and it is also where most .NET developers publish libraries they'd like to share. But which version should you build for? This is a two-dimensional question: there is the specific implementation (.NET Core, .NET Framework, Mono), and also the version (e.g., .NET Core 2.2 or 3.0, .NET Framework 4.7.2 or 4.8). And there are the older .NET variants, such as Windows Phone or Silverlight —Microsoft still supports many of these, which includes ongoing support through various libraries on NuGet. Many authors of popular open source packages distributed through NuGet also support a plethora of older framework types and versions.

Initially, people dealt with multiple versions by building multiple variants of their libraries. When you distribute .NET libraries via NuGet, you can embed multiple sets of binaries in the package targeting different flavors of .NET. However, one major problem with this is that as new forms of .NET have appeared over the years, existing libraries wouldn't run on all newer runtimes. A component written for .NET Framework 4.0 would work on all subsequent versions of .NET Framework, but not on .NET Core. Even if the component's source code was entirely compatible with .NET Core, you would need a separate version compiled to target that platform. And if the author of a library that you use hadn't provided explicit support for .NET Core, that would stop you from using it. This was bad for everyone. Component authors found themselves on a treadmill of having to churn out new variants of their component, and since that relies on those authors having the inclination and time to do this work, component consumers might find that not all of the components they want to use are available on the platform they want to use.

To avoid this, Microsoft introduced *.NET Standard*, which defines common subsets of the .NET class library's API surface area. If a NuGet package targets, say, .NET Standard 1.0, this guarantees that it will be able to to run on .NET Framework versions 4.5 or later, .NET Core 1.0 or later, or Mono 4.6 or later. And critically, if yet another variant of .NET emerges, then as long as it too supports .NET Standard 1.0, existing components will be able to run without modification, even though that new platform didn't even exist when they were written.

.NET libraries published on NuGet will target the lowest version of .NET Standard that they can if they want to ensure the broadest reach. Versions 1.1 through 1.6 gradually added more functionality in exchange for supporting a smaller range of targets. (E.g., if you want to use a .NET Standard 1.3 component on .NET Framework, it needs to be .NET Framework 4.6 or later.) .NET Standard 2.0 was a larger leap forward, and marks an important point in .NET Standard's evolution: according to Microsoft's current plans, this will be the highest version number able to run on .NET Framework. Versions of .NET Framework from 4.7.2 onward fully support it, but .NET Standard 2.1 will not run on any version of .NET Framework now or in the future. It will run on .NET Core 3.0 and .NET (i.e., future versions of .NET Core).

Future versions of Xamarin's Mono runtime are also likely to support it, but this is the end of the road for the classic .NET Framework.

What does this all mean for C# developers? If you are writing code that will never be used outside of a particular project, you will normally just target the latest version of .NET Core or, if you need some Windows-specific feature it doesn't offer, you might target .NET Framework, and you will be able to use any NuGet package that targets .NET Standard, up to and including v2.0 (which means the overwhelming majority of what's on NuGet will be available to you). If you are writing libraries that you intend to share, you should target .NET Standard instead. Microsoft's development tools choose .NET Standard 2.0 by default for new class libraries, which is a reasonable choice—you could open your library up to a wider audience by dropping to a lower version, but today, the versions of .NET that support .NET Standard 2.0 are widely available, so you would only contemplate targeting older versions if you want to support developers still using older .NET Frameworks. (Microsoft does this in most of its NuGet libraries, but you don't necessarily have to tie yourself to the same regime of support for older versions.) If you want to use certain newer features (such as the memory-efficient types described in Chapter 18), you may need to target a more recent version of .NET Standard. In any case, the development tools will ensure that you only use APIs available in whichever version of .NET Standard you declare support for.

Microsoft provides more than just a language and the various runtimes with its associated class libraries. There are also development environments that can help you write, test, debug, and maintain your code.

Visual Studio and Visual Studio Code

Microsoft offers three desktop development environments: Visual Studio, Visual Studio for Mac, and Visual Studio Code. All three provide the basic features—such as a text editor, build tools, and a debugger—but Visual Studio provides the most extensive support for developing C# applications, whether those applications will run on Windows or other platforms. It has been around the longest—for as long as C#—so it comes from the pre-open source days, and has not moved over to open source development. The various editions available range from free to eye-wateringly expensive.

Visual Studio is an Integrated Development Environment (IDE), so it takes an "everything included" approach. In addition to a fully featured text editor, it offers visual editing tools for UIs. There is deep integration with source control systems such as git, and with online systems providing source repositories, issue tracking, and other Application Lifecycle Management (ALM) features such as GitHub and Microsoft's Azure DevOps system. Visual Studio offers built-in performance monitoring and diagnostic tools. It has various features for working with applications developed for and deployed to Microsoft's Azure cloud platform. Its *Live Share* feature offers a convenient way for remote developers to work together to aid pairing or code review. It has the most extensive set of refactoring features out of the three environments described here.

In 2017 Microsoft released Visual Studio for Mac. This is not a port of the Windows version. It grew out of a product called Xamarin, a Mac-based development environment specializing in building mobile apps in C# that run on the Mono runtime. Xamarin was originally an independent product, but when, as discussed earlier, Microsoft acquired the company that wrote it, Microsoft integrated various features from the Windows version of Visual Studio when it moved the product under the Visual Studio brand.

Visual Studio Code (often shortened to VS Code) was first released in 2015. It is open source and cross platform, supporting Linux as well as Windows and Mac. It is based on the Electron platform and is written predominantly in TypeScript. (This means it really is the same program on all operating systems.) VS Code is a more lightweight product than Visual Studio: a basic installation of VS Code has little more than text editing support. However, as you open up files, it will discover downloadable extensions that, if you choose to install them, can add support for C#, F#, TypeScript, PowerShell, Python, and a wide range of other languages. (The extension mechanism is open, so anyone who wants to can publish an extension.) So although in its initial form it is less of an Integrated Development Environment (IDE) and more like a simple text editor, its extensibility model makes it pretty powerful. The wide range of extensions has led to VS Code becoming remarkably popular outside of the world of Microsoft languages, and this in turn has encouraged a virtuous cycle of even greater growth in the range of extensions.

Visual Studio offers the most straightforward path to getting started in C#—you don't need to install any extensions or modify any configuration to get up and running. So I'll start with a quick introduction to working in Visual Studio.

You can download the free version of Visual Studio, called Visual Studio Community, from *https://www.visualstudio.com/*.

Any nontrivial C# project will have multiple source code files, and in Visual Studio, these will belong to a *project*. Each project builds a single output, or *target*. The build target might be as simple as a single file—a C# project could produce an executable file or a library, for example—but some projects produce more complicated outputs. For instance, some project types build websites. A website will normally contain multiple files, but collectively, these files represent a single entity: one website. Each project's output will be deployed as a unit, even if it consists of multiple files.

Executables typically have an *.exe* file extension in Windows, while libraries use *.dll* (historically short for *dynamic link library*). .NET Core, however, puts all generated code in *.dll* files. Starting with .NET Core 3.0, it can generate a bootstrapping executable (with an *.exe* extension on Windows), but this just starts the runtime and then loads the *.dll* containing the main compiled output. .NET Framework compiles the application directly into a self-bootstrapping *.exe* (with no separate *.dll*). In either case, the only difference between the main compiled output of an application and a library is that the former specifies an application entry point. Both file types can export features to be consumed by other components. These are both examples of *assemblies*, the subject of Chapter 12.

Project files usually have extensions ending in *proj*. For example, most C# projects have a *.csproj* extension, while C++ projects use *.vcxproj*. If you examine these files with a text editor, you'll find that they usually contain XML. (That's not always true. Visual Studio is extensible, and each type of project is defined by a *project system* that can use whatever format it likes, but the built-in languages use XML.) These files describe the contents of the project and configure how it should be built. The XML format that Visual Studio uses for C# project files can also be processed by the *msbuild* tool, and also by the *dotnet* command-line tool if you've installed the .NET Core SDK, which enables you to build projects from the command line. VS Code can also work with these files.

You will often want to work with groups of projects. For example, it is good practice to write tests for your code, but most test code does not need to be deployed as part of the application, so you would typically put automated tests into separate projects. And you may want to split up your code for other reasons. Perhaps the system you're building has a desktop application and a website, and you have common code you'd like to use in both applications. In this case, you'd need one project that builds a library containing the common code, another producing the desktop application executable, another to build the website, and three more projects containing the unit tests for each of the main projects.

Visual Studio helps you work with multiple related projects through what it calls a *solution*. A solution is simply a collection of projects, and while they are usually related, they don't have to be—a solution is really just a container. You can see the currently loaded solution and all of its projects in Visual Studio's *Solution Explorer*. Figure 1-1 shows a solution with two projects. (I'm using Visual Studio 2019 here, which is the latest version at the time of writing.) Solution Explorer shows a tree view, in which you can expand each project to see its constituent files. This panel is normally open at the top right of Visual Studio, but it can be hidden or closed. You can reopen it with the View→Solution Explorer menu item.

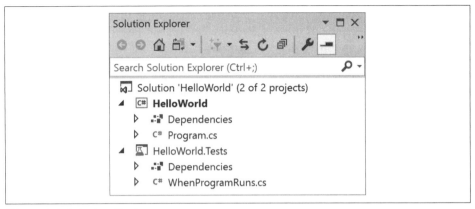

Figure 1-1. Solution Explorer

Visual Studio can load a project only if it is part of a solution. When you create a brand-new project, you can add it to an existing solution, but if you don't, Visual Studio will create one for you. If you try to open an existing project file, Visual Studio will look for an associated solution, and if it can't find one, it will create one. That's because lots of operations in Visual Studio are scoped to the currently loaded solution. When you build your code, it's normally the solution that you build. Configuration settings, such as a choice between Debug and Release builds, are controlled at the solution level. Global text searches can search all the files in the solution.

A solution is just another text file, with an *.sln* extension. Curiously, it's not an XML file—solution files use their own text-based format, although it's one that *msbuild* understands, as does VS Code. If you look at the folder containing your solution, you might also notice a *.vs* folder. (Visual Studio marks this as hidden, but if you have configured Windows File Explorer to show hidden files, as developers often do, you'll see it.) This contains user-specific settings, such as a record of which files you have open, and which project or projects to launch when starting debug sessions. That ensures that when you open a project, everything is more or less where you left it when you last worked on the project. Because these are per-user settings, you do not normally put *.vs* folders into source control.

A project can belong to more than one solution. In a large codebase, it's common to have multiple *.sln* files with different combinations of projects. You would typically have a master solution that contains every single project, but not all developers will want to work with all the code all of the time. Someone working on the desktop application in our hypothetical example will also want the shared library, but probably has no interest in loading the web project.

I'll show how to create a new project and solution, and I'll then walk through the various features Visual Studio adds to a new C# project as an introduction to the language. I'll also show how to add a unit test project to the solution.

This next section is intended for developers who are new to Visual Studio. This book is aimed at experienced developers, but does not assume any prior experience in C# or Visual Studio, so if you are already familiar with Visual Studio's basic operation, you might want to skim through this next section quickly.

Anatomy of a Simple Program

If you're using Visual Studio 2019, the simplest way to create a new project is through the "Get started" window that opens when you run it, as shown in Figure 1-2.

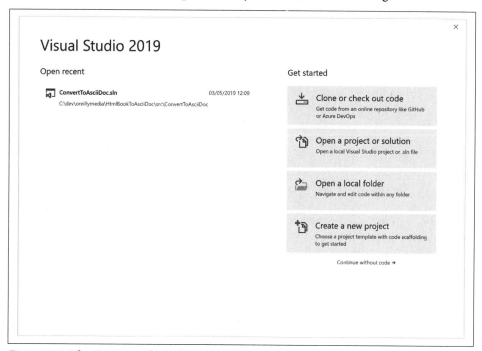

Figure 1-2. The Get started window

If you click the "Create a new project" button at the bottom right, it will open the new project dialog. Alternatively, if Visual Studio is already running (or if you're using an older version that doesn't show this "Get started" window), you can use Visual Studio's File→New→Project menu item, or if you prefer keyboard shortcuts, type Ctrl-Shift-N. Any of these actions opens the "Create a new project" dialog, shown in Figure 1-3.

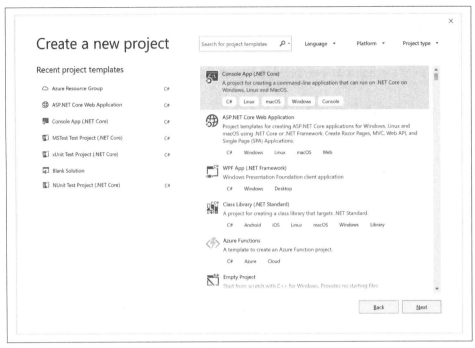

Figure 1-3. The Create a new project dialog

This window offers a list of application types. The exact set will depend on what edition of Visual Studio you have installed, and also which development workloads you chose during installation. As long as you have installed at least one of the workloads that includes C#, you should see the option to create a Console App (.NET Core). If you select this and click Next, you will see the "Configure your new project" dialog, shown in Figure 1-4.

This lets you choose a name for your new project, and also for its containing solution (which defaults to the same name). You can also choose the location on disk for the project. The Project name field affects three things. It controls the name of the *.csproj* file on disk. It also determines the filename of the compiled output. Finally, it sets the default namespace for newly created code, which I'll explain when I show the code. (You can change any of these later if you wish.)

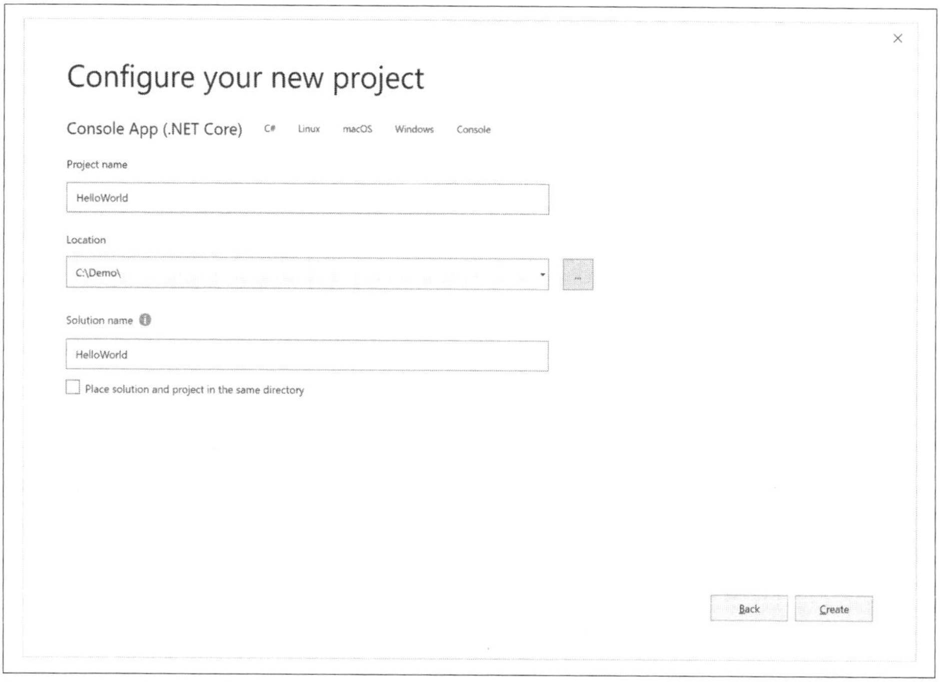

Figure 1-4. The Configure your new project dialog

Visual Studio offers a "Place solution and project in the same directory" checkbox that lets you decide how the associated solution is created. If you check it, the project and solution will have the same name and will live in the same folder on disk. But if you plan to add multiple projects to your new solution, you will typically want the solution to be in its own folder, with each project stored in a subfolder. If you leave this checkbox unchecked, Visual Studio will set things up that way, and also enable the "Solution name" text box so you can give the solution a different name from the first project, if necessary. I'm intending to add a unit test project to the solution as well as the program, so I've left the checkbox unchecked. I've set the project name to HelloWorld, and Visual Studio has set the solution name to match, which I'm happy with here. Clicking Create creates my new C# project. So I currently have a solution with a single project in it.

Adding a Project to an Existing Solution

To add a unit test project to the solution, I can go to the Solution Explorer panel, right-click on the solution node (the one at the very top), and choose Add→New Project. This opens a dialog almost identical to the one in Figure 1-3, but with the title showing "Add a new project" instead. I want to add a test project. I could scroll through the list of project types, but there are faster ways. I could type "Test" into the search box at the top of the dialog. Or, I could click on the "Project type" button at the top right, and select Test from its drop-down. Either approach will show several different test project types. If you see ones for languages other than C#, click the Language button next to the search box to filter down to just C#. Even then you'll see a few project types, because Visual Studio supports several different test frameworks. I'll choose MSTest Test Project (.NET Core).

Clicking Next opens the "Configure your new project" dialog again. This new project will contain tests for my HelloWorld project, so I'll call it HelloWorld.Tests. (Nothing demands that naming convention, by the way—I could have called it anything.) When I click OK, Visual Studio creates a second project, and both are now listed in Solution Explorer, which will look similar to Figure 1-1.

The purpose of this test project will be to ensure that the main project does what it's supposed to. I happen to prefer the style of development where you write your tests before you write the code being tested, so we'll start with the test project. To be able to do its job, my test project will need access to the code in the HelloWorld project. Visual Studio does not attempt to guess which projects in a solution may depend on which other projects. While there are only two here, even if it were capable of guessing, it would most likely guess wrong, because HelloWorld will produce an executable program, while unit test projects happen to produce a library. The most obvious guess would be that the program would depend on the library, but here we have the somewhat unusual requirement that our library (which is actually a test project) needs access to the code in our application.

Referencing One Project from Another

To tell Visual Studio about the relationship between these two projects, I right-click on the HelloWorld.Test project's Dependencies node in Solution Explorer and select the Add Reference menu item. This opens the Reference Manager dialog, which you can see in Figure 1-5. On the left, you choose the sort of reference you want—in this case, I'm setting up a reference to another project in the same solution, so I have expanded the Projects section and selected Solution. This lists all the other projects in the middle, and there is just one in this case, so I check the HelloWorld item and click OK.

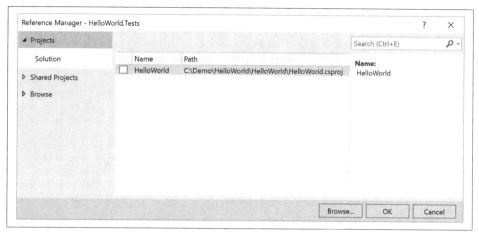

Figure 1-5. The Reference Manager dialog

Referencing External Libraries

Extensive though the .NET class library may be, it does not cover all eventualities. There are thousands of useful libraries available for .NET, many of them free. Microsoft is shipping more and more libraries separately from the main .NET class library. Visual Studio supports adding references using the NuGet system mentioned earlier. In fact, the example is already using it—although we chose Microsoft's own "MSTest" test framework that's not built into .NET. (You generally don't need unit testing services at runtime, so there's no need to build them into the class library that ships with the platform.) If you expand the Dependencies node for the HelloWorld.Tests project in Solution Explorer, and then expand the NuGet child node, you'll see various NuGet packages, as Figure 1-6 shows. (You might see higher version numbers if you try this, as these libraries are under constant development.)

You can see four test-related packages, all added for us as part of Visual Studio's test project template. NuGet is a package-based system, so rather than adding a reference to a single DLL, you add a reference to a package that may contain multiple DLLs, and any other files that may be needed to use the library.

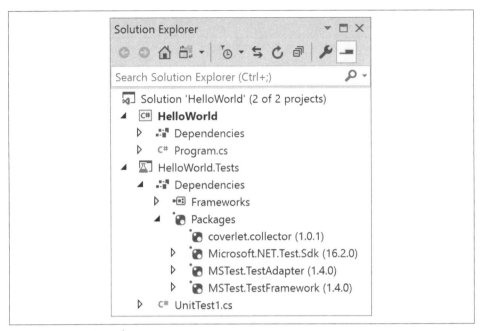

Figure 1-6. NuGet references

The public repository of packages that Microsoft runs on the *http://nuget.org* website hosts copies of all of the libraries that Microsoft does not include directly in the .NET class library, but which it nonetheless fully supports. (The testing framework used here is one example. The ASP.NET Core web framework is another.) This central NuGet repository is not just for Microsoft. Anyone can make packages available on this site, so this is where you will find the vast majority of free .NET libraries.

Visual Studio can search in the main NuGet repository. If you right-click on a project, or on its Dependencies node, and select Manage NuGet Packages, it will open the NuGet Package Manager window, shown in Figure 1-7. On the left is a list of packages from the NuGet repository. If you select Installed at the top, it will show just the packages you are already using. If you click Browse, it shows popular available packages by default, but it also provides a text box with which you can search for specific libraries.

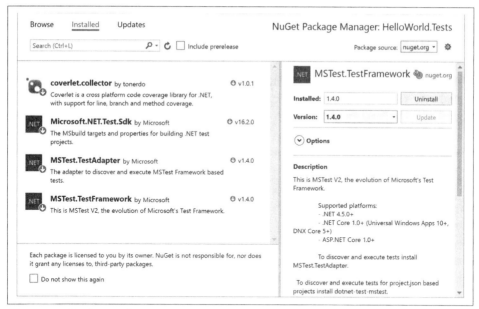

Figure 1-7. NuGet Package Manager

It is also possible to host your own NuGet repositories. For example, many companies run repositories behind their firewalls to make internally developed packages available to other employees, without having to make them publicly available. The *https://myget.org* site specializes in online hosting, and private package hosting is a feature of Microsoft's Azure DevOps and also GitHub. Or you can just host a repository on a locally accessible filesystem. You can configure NuGet to search any number of repositories in addition to the main public one.

One very important feature of NuGet packages is that they can specify dependencies on other packages. For example, if you look at the `Microsoft.NET.Test.Sdk` package in Figure 1-6, you can see from the little triangle next to it that its treeview node is expandable. Expanding it reveals that it depends on some other packages, including `Microsoft.CodeCoverage`. Because packages describe their dependencies, Visual Studio can automatically fetch all of the packages you require.

Writing a Unit Test

Now I need to write a test. Visual Studio has provided me with a test class to get me started, in a file called *UnitTest1.cs*. I want to pick a more informative name. There are various schools of thought as to how you should structure your unit tests. Some developers advocate one test class for each class you wish to test, but I like the style where you write a class for each *scenario* in which you want to test a particular class, with one method for each of the things that should be true about your code in that scenario. As you've probably guessed from the project names I've chosen, my program will only have one behavior: it will display a "Hello, world!" message when it runs. So I'll rename the *UnitTest1.cs* source file to *WhenProgramRuns.cs*. This test should verify that the program shows the required message when it runs. The test itself is very simple, but unfortunately, getting to the point where we can run this particular test is a bit more involved. Example 1-1 shows the whole source file; the test is near the end, in bold.

Example 1-1. A unit test class for our first program

```
using System;
using Microsoft.VisualStudio.TestTools.UnitTesting;

namespace HelloWorld.Tests
{
    [TestClass]
    public class WhenProgramRuns
    {
        private string _consoleOutput;

        [TestInitialize]
        public void Initialize()
        {
            var w = new System.IO.StringWriter();
            Console.SetOut(w);

            Program.Main(new string[0]);

            _consoleOutput = w.GetStringBuilder().ToString().Trim();
        }

        [TestMethod]
        public void SaysHelloWorld()
        {
            Assert.AreEqual("Hello, world!", _consoleOutput);
        }
    }
}
```

I will explain each of the features in this file once I've shown the program itself. For now, the most interesting part of this example is the SaysHelloWorld method, which defines some behavior we want our program to have. The test states that the program's output should be the "Hello, world!" message. If it's not, this test will report a failure. The test itself is pleasingly simple, but the code that sets things up for the test is a little awkward. The problem here is that the obligatory first example that all programming books are required by law to show isn't very amenable to unit testing of individual classes or methods, because you can't really test anything less than the whole program. We want to verify that the program writes a particular message to the console. In a real application, you might devise some sort of abstraction for output, and your unit tests would provide a fake version of that abstraction for test purposes. But I want my application (which Example 1-1 merely tests) to keep to the spirit of the standard "Hello, world!" example. To avoid overcomplicating the main program, I've made my test intercept console output so that I can check that the program displayed what was intended. (Chapter 15 will describe the features I'm using from the System.IO namespace to achieve this.)

There's a second challenge. Normally, a unit test will, by definition, test some isolated and usually small part of the program. But in this case, the program is so simple that there is only one feature of interest, and that feature executes when we run the program. This means my test will need to invoke the program's entry point. I could have done that by launching my HelloWorld program in a whole new process, but capturing its output would have been rather more complex than the in-process interception done by Example 1-1. Instead, I'm just invoking the program's entry point directly. In a C# application, the entry point is usually a method called Main defined in a class called Program. Example 1-2 shows the relevant line from Example 1-1, passing an empty array to simulate running the program with no command-line arguments.

Example 1-2. Calling a method

```
Program.Main(new string[0]);
```

Unfortunately, there's a problem with that. A program's entry point is typically only accessible to the runtime—it's an implementation detail of your program, and there's not normally any reason to make it publicly accessible. However, I'll make an exception here, because that's where the only code in this example will live. So to get the code to compile, we'll need to make a change to our main program. Example 1-3 shows the relevant code from the *Program.cs* file in the HelloWorld project. (I'll show the whole thing shortly.)

Example 1-3. Making the program entry point accessible

```
public class Program
{
    public static void Main(string[] args)
    {
...
```

I've added the public keyword to the start of two lines to make the code accessible to the test, enabling Example 1-1 to compile. There are other ways I could have achieved this. I could have left the class as it is, made the method internal, and then applied the InternalsVisibleToAttribute to my program to grant access just to the test suite. But internal protection and assembly-level attributes are topics for later chapters (Chapters 3 and 14, respectively), so I decided to keep it simple for this first example. I'll show the alternative approach in Chapter 14.

I'm now ready to run my test. To do this, I open Visual Studio's Unit Test Explorer panel with the Test→Windows→Test Explorer menu item. Next, I build the project with the Build→Build Solution menu. Once I've done that, the Unit Test Explorer shows a list of all the unit tests defined in the solution. It finds my SaysHelloWorld test, as you can see in Figure 1-8. Clicking on the Run All button (the double arrow at the top left) runs the test, which fails because we've only written the test so far—we've not done anything to our main program. You can see the error at the bottom of Figure 1-8. It says it was expecting a "Hello, world!" message, but the actual console output was different. (Not by much, admittedly—Visual Studio did in fact add code to my console application that shows a message. But it does not have the comma my test requires, and the w has the wrong case.)

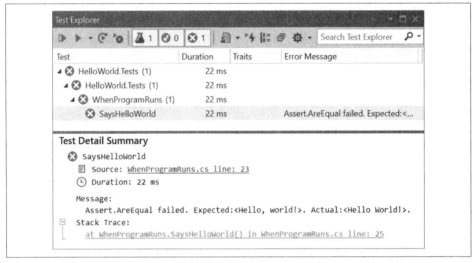

Figure 1-8. Unit Test Explorer

So it's time to look at our HelloWorld program and correct the code. When I created the project, Visual Studio generated various files, including *Program.cs*, which contains the program's entry point. Example 1-4 shows this file, including the modifications I made in Example 1-3. I will explain each element in turn, as it provides a useful introduction to some important elements of C# syntax and structure.

Example 1-4. Program.cs

```
using System;

namespace HelloWorld
{
```

```
public class Program
{
    public static void Main(string[] args)
    {
        Console.WriteLine("Hello World!");
    }
}
}
```

The file begins with a *using directive*. This is optional, but almost all source files contain one or more, and they tell the compiler which *namespaces* we'd like to use, raising the obvious question: what's a namespace?

Namespaces

Namespaces bring order and structure to what would otherwise be a horrible mess. The .NET class library contains a large number of classes, and there are many more classes out there in third-party libraries, not to mention the classes you will write yourself. There are two problems that can occur when dealing with this many named entities. First, it becomes hard to guarantee uniqueness unless either everything has a very long name, or the names include sections of random gibberish. Second, it can become challenging to discover the API you need; unless you know or can guess the right name, it's difficult to find what you need from an unstructured list of many thousands of things. Namespaces solve both of these problems.

Most .NET types are defined in a namespace. Microsoft-supplied types have distinctive namespaces. When the types are part of .NET, the containing namespaces start with System, and when they're part of some Microsoft technology that is not a core part of .NET, they usually begin with Microsoft. Libraries from other vendors tend to start with the company name, while open source libraries often use their project name. You are not forced to put your own types into namespaces, but it's recommended that you do. C# does not treat System as a special namespace, so nothing's stopping you from using that for your own types, but unless you're writing a contribution to the .NET class library that you will be submitting as a pull request to *https://github.com/dotnet/corefx*, then it's a bad idea because it will tend to confuse other developers. You should pick something more distinctive for your own code, such as your company or project name.

The namespace usually gives a clue as to the purpose of the type. For example, all the types that relate to file handling can be found in the System.IO namespace, while those concerned with networking are under System.Net. Namespaces can form a hierarchy. So the framework's System namespace doesn't just contain types. It also holds other namespaces, such as System.Net, and these often contain yet more namespaces, such as System.Net.Sockets and System.Net.Mail. These examples show that namespaces act as a sort of description, which can help you navigate the library. If you were looking for regular expression handling, for example, you might look through the available namespaces, and notice the `System.Text` namespace. Looking in there, you'd find a `System.Text.RegularExpressions` namespace, at which point you'd be pretty confident that you were looking in the right place.

Namespaces also provide a way to ensure uniqueness. The namespace in which a type is defined is part of that type's full name. This lets libraries use short, simple names for things. For example, the regular expression API includes a `Capture` class that represents the results from a regular expression capture. If you are working on software that deals with images, the term *capture* is more commonly used to mean the acquisition of some image data, and you might feel that `Capture` is the most descriptive name for a class in your own code. It would be annoying to have to pick a different name just because the best one is already taken, particularly if your image acquisition code has no use for regular expressions, meaning that you weren't even planning to use the existing `Capture` type.

But in fact, it's fine. Both types can be called `Capture`, and they will still have different names. The full name of the regular expression `Capture` class is effectively `System.Text.RegularExpressions.Capture`, and likewise, your class's full name would include its containing namespace (e.g., `SpiffingSoftworks.Imaging.Capture`).

If you really want to, you can write the fully qualified name of a type every time you use it, but most developers don't want to do anything quite so tedious, which is where the `using` directive at the start of Example 1-4 comes in. While this simple example has just one, it's common to see a list of directives here. These state the namespaces of the types a source file intends to use. You will normally edit this list to match your file's requirements. In this example, Visual Studio added `using System;` when I created the project. It chooses different sets in different contexts. If you add a class representing a UI element, for example, Visual Studio would include various UI-related namespaces in the list.

With `using` declarations like these in place, you can just use the short, unqualified name for a class. The line of code that enables my HelloWorld example to do its job uses the `System.Console` class, but because of the first `using` directive, I can refer to it as just `Console`. In fact, that's the only class I'll be using, so there's no need to add any other `using` directives in my main program.

Earlier, you saw that a project's References describe which libraries it uses. You might think that References are redundant—can't the compiler work out which external libraries we are using from the namespaces? It could if there was a direct correspondence between namespaces and either libraries or packages, but there isn't. There is sometimes an apparent connection—the popular `Newton soft.Json` NuGet package contains a *Newtonsoft.Json.dll* file that contains classes in the `Newtonsoft.Json` namespace, for example. But often there's no such connection—the .NET Framework's version of the class library includes a *System.Core.dll* file, but there is no `System.Core` namespace. So it is necessary to tell the compiler which libraries your project depends on, as well as saying which namespaces any particular source file uses. We will look at the nature and structure of library files in more detail in Chapter 12.

Even with namespaces, there's potential for ambiguity. You might use two namespaces that both happen to define a class of the same name. If you want to use that class, then you will need to be explicit, referring to it by its full name. If you need to use such classes a lot in the file, you can still save yourself some typing: you only need to use the full name once because you can define an *alias*. Example 1-5 uses aliases to resolve a clash that I've run into a few times: .NET's UI framework, the Windows Presentation Foundation (WPF), defines a `Path` class for working with Bézier curves, polygons, and other shapes, but there's also a `Path` class for working with filesystem paths, and you might want to use both types together to produce a graphical representation of the contents of a file. Just adding `using` directives for both namespaces would make the simple name `Path` ambiguous if unqualified. But as Example 1-5 shows, you can define distinctive aliases for each.

Example 1-5. Resolving ambiguity with aliases

```
using System.IO;
using System.Windows.Shapes;
using IoPath = System.IO.Path;
using WpfPath = System.Windows.Shapes.Path;
```

With these aliases in place, you can use `IoPath` as a synonym for the file-related `Path` class, and `WpfPath` for the graphical one.

Going back to our HelloWorld example, directly after the `using` directives comes a *namespace declaration*. Whereas `using` directives declare which namespaces our code will consume, a namespace declaration states the namespace in which our own code lives. Example 1-6 shows the relevant code from Example 1-4. This is followed by an opening brace ({). Everything between this and the closing brace at the end of the file will be in the `HelloWorld` namespace. By the way, you can refer to types in your own namespace without qualification, without needing a `using` directive. That's why the test code in Example 1-1 doesn't have a `using HelloWorld;` directive—it implicitly has access to that namespace because its code is inside a `namespace Hello World.Tests` declaration.

Example 1-6. Namespace declaration

```
namespace HelloWorld
{
```

Visual Studio generates a namespace declaration with the same name as your project in the source files it adds when you create a new project. You're not required to keep this—a project can contain any mixture of namespaces, and you are free to edit the namespace declaration. But if you do want to use something other than the project name consistently throughout your project, you should tell Visual Studio, because it's not just the first file, *Program.cs*, that gets this generated declaration. By default, Visual Studio adds a namespace declaration based on your project name every time you add a new file. You can tell it to use a different namespace for new files by editing the project's properties. If you right-click on the project node in Solution Explorer and select Properties, this opens the properties for the project, and if you go to the Application tab, there's a "Default namespace" text box. It will use whatever you put in there for namespace declarations of any new files. (It won't change the existing files, though.) This adds a `<RootNamespace>` property to the *.csproj* file.

Nested namespaces

As you've already seen, the .NET class library nests its namespaces, and sometimes quite extensively. Unless you're creating a trivial example, you will typically nest your own namespaces. There are two ways you can do this. You can nest namespace declarations, as Example 1-7 shows.

Example 1-7. Nesting namespace declarations

```
namespace MyApp
{
    namespace Storage
    {
        ...
    }
}
```

Alternatively, you can just specify the full namespace in a single declaration, as Example 1-8 shows. This is the more commonly used style.

Example 1-8. Nested namespace with a single declaration

```
namespace MyApp.Storage
{
    ...
}
```

Any code you write in a nested namespace will be able to use types not just from that namespace, but also from its containing namespaces without qualification. Code in Examples 1-7 or 1-8 would not need explicit qualification or `using` directives to use types either in the `MyApp.Storage` namespace or the `MyApp` namespace.

When you define nested namespaces, the convention is to create a matching folder hierarchy. If you create a project called MyApp, as you've seen, by default Visual Studio will put new classes in the `MyApp` namespace when you add them to the project. But if you create a new folder in the project (which you can do in Solution Explorer) called, say, *Storage*, Visual Studio will put any new classes you create in that folder into the `MyApp.Storage` namespace. Again, you're not required to keep this—Visual Studio just adds a namespace declaration when creating the file, and you're free to change it. The compiler does not need the namespace to match your folder hierarchy. But since the convention is supported by Visual Studio, life will be easier if you follow it.

Classes

Inside the namespace declaration, my *Program.cs* file defines a *class*. Example 1-9 shows this part of the file (which includes the `public` keywords I added earlier). The `class` keyword is followed by the name, and of course the full name of the type is effectively `HelloWorld.Program`, because this code is inside the namespace declaration. As you can see, C# uses braces ({}) to delimit all sorts of things—we already saw this for namespaces, and here you can see the same thing with the class, as well as the method it contains.

Example 1-9. A class with a method

```
public class Program
{
    public static void Main(string[] args)
    {
        Console.WriteLine("Hello World!");
    }
}
```

Classes are C#'s mechanism for defining entities that combine state and behavior, a common object-oriented idiom. But this class contains nothing more than a single method. C# does not support global methods—all code has to be written as a member of some type. So this particular class isn't very interesting—its only job is to act as the container for the program's entry point. We'll see some more interesting uses for classes in Chapter 3.

Program Entry Point

By default, the C# compiler will look for a method called Main and use that as the entry point automatically. If you really want to, you can tell the compiler to use a different method, but most programs stick with the convention. Whether you designate the entry point by configuration or convention, the method has to meet certain requirements, all of which are evident in Example 1-9.

The program entry point must be a *static method*, meaning that it is not necessary to create an instance of the containing type (Program, in this case) in order to invoke the method. It is not required to return anything, as signified by the void keyword here, although if you wish you can return int instead, which allows the program to return an exit code that the operating system will report when the program terminates. (It can also return either Task or Task<int>, enabling you to make it an async method, as described in Chapter 17.) And the method must either take no arguments at all (which would be denoted by an empty pair of parentheses after the method name) or, as in Example 1-9, it can accept a single argument: an array of text strings containing the command-line arguments.

Some C-family languages include the filename of the program itself as the first argument, on the grounds that it's part of what the user typed at the command prompt. C# does not follow this convention. If the program is launched without arguments, the array's length will be 0.

The method declaration is followed by the method body, which in this case contains code that is very nearly what we want. We've now looked at everything that Visual Studio generated for us in this file, so all that remains is to modify the code inside the braces delimiting the method body. Remember, our test is failing because our program fails to meet its one requirement: to write out a certain message to the console. This requires the single line of code shown in Example 1-10, inside the method body. This is almost exactly what's already there, it just features an extra comma and a lowercase w.

Example 1-10. Displaying a message

```
Console.WriteLine("Hello, world!");
```

With this in place, if I run the tests again, the Unit Test Explorer shows a checkmark by my test and reports that all tests have passed. So apparently the code is working. And we can verify that informally by running the program. You can do that from Visual Studio's Debug menu. The Start Debugging option runs the program in the debugger. If you run the program this way (which you can also do with the F5 keyboard shortcut), a console window will open, and you'll see it display the traditional message.

Unit Tests

Now that the program is working, I want to return to the first code I wrote, the test, because that file illustrates some C# features that the main program does not. If you go back to Example 1-1, it starts in a pretty similar way to the main program: we have some `using` directives and then a namespace declaration, the namespace being `Hello World.Tests` this time, matching the test project name. But the class looks different. Example 1-11 shows the relevant part of Example 1-1.

Example 1-11. Test class with attribute

```
[TestClass]
public class WhenProgramRuns
{
```

Immediately before the class declaration is the text `[TestClass]`. This is an *attribute*. Attributes are annotations you can apply to classes, methods, and other features of the code. Most of them do nothing on their own—the compiler records the fact that the attribute is present in the compiled output, but that is all. Attributes are useful only when something goes looking for them, so they tend to be used by frameworks. In this case, I'm using Microsoft's unit testing framework, and it goes looking for classes annotated with this `TestClass` attribute. It will ignore classes that do not have this annotation. Attributes are typically specific to a particular framework, and you can define your own, as we'll see in Chapter 14.

The two methods in the class are also annotated with attributes. Example 1-12 shows the relevant excerpts from Example 1-1. The test runner will execute any methods marked with `[TestInitialize]` once for every test the class contains, and will do so before running the actual test method itself. And, as you have no doubt guessed, the `[TestMethod]` attribute tells the test runner which methods represent tests.

Example 1-12. Annotated methods

```
[TestInitialize]
public void Initialize()
...
```

```
[TestMethod]
public void SaysHelloWorld()
...
```

There's one more feature in Example 1-1: the class contents begin with a field, shown again in Example 1-13. Fields hold data. In this case, the Initialize method stores the console output that it captures while the program runs in this _consoleOutput field, where it is available for test methods to inspect. This particular field has been marked as private, indicating that it is for its containing class's own use. The C# compiler will permit only code that lives in the same class to access this data.

Example 1-13. A field

```
private string _consoleOutput;
```

And with that, we've examined every element of a program and the test project that verifies that it works as intended.

Summary

You've now seen the basic structure of C# programs. I created a solution containing two projects, one for tests and one for the program itself. This was a simple example, so each project had only one source file of interest. Both were of similar structure. Each began with using directives indicating which types the file uses. A namespace declaration stated the namespace that the file populates, and this contained a class containing one or more methods or other members, such as fields.

We will look at types and their members in much more detail in Chapter 3, but first, Chapter 2 will deal with the code that lives inside methods, where we express what we want our programs to do.

Basic Coding in C#

All programming languages have to provide certain capabilities. It must be possible to express the calculations and operations that our code should perform. Programs need to be able to make decisions based on their input. Sometimes we will need to perform tasks repeatedly. These fundamental features are the very stuff of programming, and this chapter will show how these things work in C#.

Depending on your background, some of this chapter's content may seem very familiar. C# is said to be from the "C family" of languages. C is a hugely influential programming language, and numerous languages have borrowed much of its syntax. There are direct descendants, such as C++ and Objective-C. There are also more distantly related languages, including Java, JavaScript, and C# itself, that have no compatibility with C, but which still ape many aspects of its syntax. If you are familiar with any of these languages, you will recognize many of the language features we are about to explore.

We saw the basic elements of a program in Chapter 1. In this chapter, we will be looking just at code inside methods. As you've seen, C# requires a certain amount of structure: code is made up of statements that live inside a method, which belongs to a type, which is typically inside a namespace, all inside a file that is part of a project, typically contained by a solution. For clarity, most of the examples in this chapter will show the code of interest in isolation, as in Example 2-1.

Example 2-1. The code and nothing but the code

```
Console.WriteLine("Hello, world!");
```

Unless I say otherwise, this kind of extract is shorthand for showing the code in context inside a suitable program. So Example 2-1 is short for Example 2-2.

Example 2-2. The whole code

```
using System;

namespace Hello
{
    class Program
    {
        static void Main()
        {
            Console.WriteLine("Hello, world!");
        }
    }
}
```

Although I'll be introducing fundamental elements of the language in this section, this book is for people who are already familiar with at least one programming language, so I'll be relatively brief with the most ordinary features of the language and will go into more detail on those aspects that are particular to C#.

Local Variables

The inevitable "Hello, world!" example is missing a vital element: it doesn't really deal with information. Useful programs normally fetch, process, and produce information, so the ability to define and identify information is one of the most important features of a language. Like most languages, C# lets you define *local variables*, which are named elements inside a method that each hold a piece of information.

 In the C# specification, the term *variable* can refer to local variables, but also to fields in objects and array elements. This section is concerned entirely with local variables, but it gets tiring to keep reading the *local* prefix. So, from now on in this section, *variable* means a local variable.

C# is a *statically typed* language, which is to say that any element of code that represents or produces information, such as a variable or an expression, has a data type determined at compile time. This is different than *dynamically typed* languages, such as JavaScript, in which types are determined at runtime.[1]

The easiest way to see C#'s static typing in action is with simple variable declarations, such as the ones in Example 2-3. Each of these starts with the data type—the first two

---

1 C# does in fact offer dynamic typing as an option with its `dynamic` keyword, but it takes the slightly unusual step of fitting that into a statically typed point of view: dynamic variables have a static type of `dynamic`.

---

variables are of type `string`, followed by two `int` variables. These types represent text strings and 32-bit signed integers, respectively.

Example 2-3. Variable declarations

```
string part1 = "the ultimate question";
string part2 = "of something";
int theAnswer = 42;
int andAnotherThing;
```

The data type is followed immediately by the variable's name. The name must begin with either a letter or an underscore, which can be followed by any combination of letters, decimal digits, and underscores. (At least, those are the options if you stick to ASCII. C# supports Unicode, so if you save your file in UTF-8 or UTF-16 format, anything after the first character in an identifier can be any of the characters described in the "Identifier and Pattern Syntax" annex of the Unicode specification. This includes various accents, diacritics, and numerous somewhat obscure punctuation marks, but only characters intended for use *within* words—characters that Unicode identifies as being intended for *separating* words cannot be used.) These same rules determine what constitutes a legal identifier for any user-defined entity in C#, such as a class or a method.

Example 2-3 shows that there are a couple of forms of variable declarations. The first three variables include an *initializer*, which provides the variable's initial value, but as the final variable shows, this is optional. That's because you can assign new values into variables at any point. Example 2-4 continues on from Example 2-3 and shows that you can assign a new value into a variable regardless of whether it had an initial value.

Example 2-4. Assigning values to previously declared variables

```
part2 = " of life, the universe, and everything";
andAnotherThing = 123;
```

Because variables have a static type, the compiler will reject attempts to assign the wrong kind of data. So if we were to follow on from Example 2-3 with the code in Example 2-5, the compiler would complain. It knows that the variable called `the Answer` has a type of `int`, which is a numeric type, so it will report an error if we attempt to assign a text string into it.

Example 2-5. An error: the wrong type

```
theAnswer = "The compiler will reject this";
```

You'd be allowed to do this in dynamic languages such as JavaScript, because in those languages, a variable doesn't have its own type—all that matters is the type of the value it contains, and that can change as the code runs. It's possible to do something similar in C# by declaring a variable with type `dynamic` or `object` (which I'll describe later in "Dynamic" on page 79 and "Object" on page 80). However, the most common practice in C# is for variables to have a more specific type.

 The static type doesn't always provide a complete picture, thanks to inheritance. I'll be discussing this in Chapter 6, but for now, it's enough to know that some types are open to extension through inheritance, and if a variable uses such a type, then it's possible for it to refer to some object of a type derived from the variable's static type. Interfaces, described in Chapter 3, provide a similar kind of flexibility. However, the static type always determines what operations you are allowed to perform on the variable. If you want to use additional members specific to some derived type, you won't be able to do so through a variable of the base type.

You don't have to state the variable type explicitly. You can let the compiler work it out for you by using the keyword `var` in place of the data type. Example 2-6 shows the first three variable declarations from Example 2-3, but using `var` instead of explicit data types.

Example 2-6. Implicit variable types with the var keyword

```
var part1 = "the ultimate question";
var part2 = "of something";
var theAnswer = 40 + 2;
```

This code often misleads people who know some JavaScript, because that also has a `var` keyword that you can use in a similar-looking way. But `var` does not work the same way in C# as in JavaScript: these variables are still all statically typed. All that's changed is that we haven't said what the type is—we're letting the compiler deduce it for us. It looks at the initializers and can see that the first two variables are strings while the third is an integer. (That's why I left out the fourth variable from Example 2-3, `andAnotherThing`. That doesn't have an initializer, so the compiler would have no way of inferring its type. If you try to use the `var` keyword without an initializer, you'll get a compiler error.)

You can demonstrate that variables declared with `var` are statically typed by attempting to assign something of a different type into them. We could repeat the same thing we tried in Example 2-5, but this time with a `var`-style variable. Example 2-7 does this, and it will produce exactly the same compiler error, because it's the same mistake—we're trying to assign a text string into a variable of an incompatible type. That variable, theAnswer, has a type of int here, even though we didn't say so explicitly.

Example 2-7. An error: the wrong type (again)

```
var theAnswer = 42;
theAnswer = "The compiler will reject this";
```

Opinion is divided on how and when to use the var keyword, as the following sidebar "To var, or Not to var?" describes.

To var, or Not to var?

A variable declared with var behaves in exactly the same way as the equivalent explicitly typed declaration, which raises a question: which should you use? In a sense, it doesn't matter, because they are equivalent. However, if you like your code to be consistent, you'll want to pick one style and stick to it. Not everyone agrees on which is the "best" style.

Some developers see the extra text required for explicit variable types as unproductive "ceremony," preferring the more succinct var keyword. Let the compiler deduce the type for you, instead of doing the work yourself, or so the argument goes. It also reduces visual clutter in the code.

I take a different view, because I spend more time reading code than writing it—debugging, code review, refactoring, and enhancements seem to dominate. Anything that makes those activities easier is worth the frankly minimal time it takes to write the type names explicitly. Code that uses var everywhere slows you down, because you have to work out what the type really is in order to understand the code. Although var saved you some work when you wrote the code, that gain is quickly wiped out by the additional thought required every time you go back and look at the code. So unless you're the sort of developer who only ever writes new code, leaving others to clean up after you, the only benefit the "var everywhere" philosophy really offers is that it can look neater.

You can even use explicit types and still get the compiler to do the work: in Visual Studio, you can write the keystroke-friendly var, then press Ctrl+. to open the Quick Actions menu. This offers to replace it with the explicit type for you. (Visual Studio uses the C# compiler's API to discover the variable's type.)

That said, there are some situations in which I will use var. One is to avoid writing the name of the type twice, as in this example:

```
List<int> numbers = new List<int>();
```

We can drop the first List<int> without making this harder to read, because the name is still right there in the initializer. There are similar examples involving casts

---

and generic methods. As long as the type name appears explicitly in the variable declaration, there is no downside to using var to avoid writing the type twice.

I also use var where it is necessary. As we will see in later chapters, C# supports *anonymous types*, and as the name suggests, it's not possible to write the name of such a type. In these situations, you may be compelled to use var. (In fact, the var keyword was introduced to C# only when anonymous types were added.)

One last thing worth knowing about declarations is that you can declare and optionally initialize multiple variables in a single line. If you want multiple variables of the same type, this may reduce clutter in your code. Example 2-8 declares three variables of the same type in a single declaration.

Example 2-8. Multiple variables in a single declaration

```
double a = 1, b = 2.5, c = -3;
```

Regardless of how you declare it, a variable holds some piece of information of a particular type, and the compiler prevents us from putting data of an incompatible type into that variable. Variables are useful only because we can refer back to them later in our code. Example 2-9 starts with the variable declarations we saw in earlier examples, then goes on to use the values of those variables to initialize some more variables, and then displays the results.

Example 2-9. Using variables

```
string part1 = "the ultimate question";
string part2 = "of something";
int theAnswer = 42;

part2 = "of life, the universe, and everything";

string questionText = "What is the answer to " + part1 + ", " + part2 + "?";
string answerText = "The answer to " + part1 + ", " +
                    part2 + ", is: " + theAnswer;

Console.WriteLine(questionText);
Console.WriteLine(answerText);
```

By the way, this code relies on the fact that C# defines a couple of meanings for the + operator when it's used with strings. First, when you "add" two strings together, it concatenates them. Second, when you "add" something other than a string to the end of a string (as the initializer for answerText does—it adds theAnswer, which is a number), C# generates code that converts the value to a string before appending it. So Example 2-9 produces this output:

```
What is the answer to the ultimate question, of life, the universe, and everythi
ng?
The answer to the ultimate question, of life, the universe, and everything, is:
42
```

 In this book, text longer than 80 characters is wrapped across multiple lines to fit the page. If you try these examples, they will look different if your console windows are configured for a different width.

When you use a variable, its value is whatever you last assigned to it. If you attempt to use a variable before you have assigned a value, as Example 2-10 does, the C# compiler will report an error.

Example 2-10. Error: using an unassigned variable

```
int willNotWork;
Console.WriteLine(willNotWork);
```

Compiling that produces this error for the second line:

```
error CS0165: Use of unassigned local variable 'willNotWork'
```

The compiler uses a slightly pessimistic system (which it calls the *definite assignment* rules) for determining whether a variable has a value yet. It's not possible to create an algorithm that can determine such things for certain in every possible situation.[2] Since the compiler has to err on the side of caution, there are some situations in which the variable will have a value by the time the offending code runs, and yet the compiler still complains. The solution is to write an initializer, so that the variable always contains something, perhaps using 0 for numeric values and false for Boolean variables. In Chapter 3, I'll introduce reference types, and as the name suggests, a variable of such a type can hold a reference to an instance of the type. If you need to initialize such a variable before you've got something for it to refer to, you can use the keyword null, a special value signifying a reference to nothing.

The definite assignment rules determine the parts of your code in which the compiler considers a variable to contain a valid value and will therefore let you read from it. Writing into a variable is less restricted, but as you might expect, any given variable is accessible only from certain parts of the code. Let's look at the rules that govern this.

---

2 See Alan Turing's seminal work on computation for details. Charles Petzold's *The Annotated Turing* (John Wiley & Sons) is an excellent guide to the relevant paper.

Scope

A variable's *scope* is the range of code in which you can refer to that variable by its name. Variables are not the only things with scope. Methods, properties, types, and, in fact, anything with a name all have scope. These require broadening the definition of scope: it's the parts of your code where you can refer to the entity by its name without needing additional qualification. When I write `Console.WriteLine`, I am referring to the method by its name (`WriteLine`), but I need to qualify it with a class name (`Console`), because the method is not in scope. But with a local variable, scope is absolute: either it's accessible without qualification, or it's not accessible at all.

Broadly speaking, a variable's scope starts at its declaration and finishes at the end of its containing *block*. (The loop constructs we'll get to later cause a couple of exceptions to this rule.) A block is a region of code delimited by a pair of braces ({}). A method body is a block, so a variable defined in one method is not visible in a separate method, because it is out of scope. If you attempt to compile Example 2-11, you'll get an error complaining that `The name 'thisWillNotWork' does not exist in the current context`.

Example 2-11. Error: out of scope

```
static void SomeMethod()
{
    int thisWillNotWork = 42;
}

static void AnUncompilableMethod()
{
    Console.WriteLine(thisWillNotWork);
}
```

Methods often contain nested blocks, particularly when you work with the loop and flow control constructs we'll be looking at later in this chapter. At the point where a nested block starts, everything that is in scope in the outer block continues to be in scope inside that nested block. Example 2-12 declares a variable called `someValue` and then introduces a nested block as part of an `if` statement. The code inside this block is able to access that variable declared in the containing block.

Example 2-12. Variable declared outside block, used within block

```
int someValue = GetValue();
if (someValue > 100)
{
    Console.WriteLine(someValue);
}
```

The converse is not true. If you declare a variable in a nested block, its scope does not extend outside of that block. So Example 2-13 will fail to compile, because the `will NotWork` variable is only in scope within the nested block. The final line of code will produce a compiler error because it tries to use that variable outside of that block.

Example 2-13. Error: trying to use a variable not in scope

```
int someValue = GetValue();
if (someValue > 100)
{
    int willNotWork = someValue - 100;
}
Console.WriteLine(willNotWork);
```

This probably all seems fairly straightforward, but things get a bit more complex when it comes to potential naming collisions. C# sometimes catches people by surprise here.

Variable name ambiguity

Consider the code in Example 2-14. This declares a variable called `anotherValue` inside a nested block. As you know, that variable is only in scope to the end of that nested block. After that block ends, we try to declare another variable with the same name.

Example 2-14. Error: surprising name collision

```
int someValue = GetValue();
if (someValue > 100)
{
    int anotherValue = someValue - 100;  // Compiler error
    Console.WriteLine(anotherValue);
}

int anotherValue = 123;
```

This causes a compiler error on the first of the lines to declare `anotherValue`:

```
error CS0136: A local or parameter named 'anotherValue' cannot be declared in
  this scope because that name is used in an enclosing local scope to define a
  local or parameter
```

This seems odd. At the final line, the supposedly conflicting earlier declaration is not in scope, because we're outside of the nested block in which it was declared. Furthermore, the second declaration is not in scope within that nested block, because the declaration comes after the block. The scopes do not overlap, but despite this, we've fallen foul of C#'s rules for avoiding name conflicts. To see why this example fails, we first need to look at a less surprising example.

C# tries to prevent ambiguity by disallowing code where one name might refer to more than one thing. Example 2-15 shows the sort of problem it aims to avoid. Here we've got a variable called errorCount, and the code starts to modify this as it progresses,[3] but partway through, it introduces a new variable in a nested block, also called errorCount. It is possible to imagine a language that allowed this—you could have a rule that says that when multiple items of the same name are in scope, you just pick the one whose declaration happened last.

Example 2-15. Error: hiding a variable

```
int errorCount = 0;
if (problem1)
{
    errorCount += 1;

    if (problem2)
    {
        errorCount += 1;
    }

    // Imagine that in a real program there was a big
    // chunk of code here before the following lines.

    int errorCount = GetErrors();  // Compiler error
    if (problem3)
    {
        errorCount += 1;
    }
}
```

C# chooses not to allow this, because code that did this would be easy to misunderstand. This is an artificially short method because it's a contrived example in a book, making it easy to see the duplicate names, but if the code were a bit longer, it would be very easy to miss the nested variable declaration. Then, we might not realize that errorCount refers to something different at the end of the method than it did earlier on. C# simply disallows this to avoid misunderstanding.

But why does Example 2-14 fail? The scopes of the two variables don't overlap. Well, it turns out that the rule that outlaws Example 2-15 is not based on scopes. It is based on a subtly different concept called a *declaration space*. A declaration space is a

---

3 If you're new to C-family languages, the += operator may be unfamiliar. It is a *compound assignment* operator, described later in this chapter. I'm using it here to increase errorCount by one.

---

region of code in which a single name must not refer to two different entities. Each method introduces a declaration space for variables. Nested blocks also introduce declaration spaces, and it is illegal for a nested declaration space to declare a variable with the same name as one in its parent's declaration space. And that's the rule we've fallen foul of here—the outermost declaration space in Example 2-15 contains a variable named `errorCount`, and a nested block's declaration space tries to introduce another variable of the same name.

If that all seems a bit dry or arbitrary, it may be helpful to know *why* there's a whole separate set of rules for name collisions instead of basing it on scopes. The intent of the declaration space rules is that it mostly shouldn't matter where you put the declaration. If you were to move all of the variable declarations in a block to the start of that block—and some organizations have coding standards that mandate this sort of layout—the idea of these rules is that this shouldn't change what the code means. Clearly this wouldn't be possible if Example 2-15 were legal. And this explains why Example 2-14 is illegal. Although the scopes don't overlap, they would if you moved all variable declarations to the top of their containing blocks.

Local variable instances

Variables are features of the source code, so each particular variable has a distinct identity: it is declared in exactly one place in the source code and goes out of scope at exactly one well-defined place. However, that doesn't mean that it corresponds to a single storage location in memory. It is possible for multiple invocations of a single method to be in progress simultaneously, through recursion, multithreading, or asynchronous execution.

Each time a method runs, it gets a distinct set of storage locations to hold the local variables' values. This enables multiple threads to execute the same method simultaneously without problems, because each has its own set of local variables. Likewise, in recursive code, each nested call gets its own set of locals that will not interfere with any of its callers. The same goes for multiple concurrent invocations of a method. To be strictly accurate, each execution of a particular *scope* gets its own set of variables. This distinction matters when you use anonymous functions, described in Chapter 9. As an optimization, C# reuses storage locations when it can, so it will only allocate new memory for each scope's execution when it really has to (e.g., it won't allocate new memory for variables declared in the body of a loop for each iteration unless you put it into a situation where it has no choice), but the effect is as though it allocated new space each time.

Be aware that the C# compiler does not make any particular guarantee about where variables live (except in exceptional cases, as we'll see in Chapter 18). They might well live on the stack, but sometimes they don't. When we look at anonymous functions in later chapters, you'll see that variables sometimes need to outlive the method that declares them, because they remain in scope for nested methods that will run as call-backs after the containing method has returned.

By the way, before we move on, be aware that just as variables are not the only things to have scope, they are also not the only things to which declaration space rules apply. Other language features that we'll be looking at later, including classes, methods, and properties, also have scoping and name uniqueness rules.

Statements and Expressions

Variables give us somewhere to put the information that our code works with, but to do anything with those variables, we will need to write some code. This will mean writing *statements* and *expressions*.

Statements

When we write a C# method, we are writing a sequence of statements. Informally, the statements in a method describe the actions we want the method to perform. Each line in Example 2-16 is a statement. It might be tempting to think of a statement as an instruction to do one thing (e.g., initialize a variable or invoke a method). Or you might take a more lexical view, where anything ending in a semicolon is a statement. (And it's the semicolons that are significant here, not the line breaks, by the way. We could have written this as one long line of code and it would have exactly the same meaning.) However, both descriptions are simplistic, even though they happen to be true for this particular example.

Example 2-16. Some statements

```
int a = 19;
int b = 23;
int c;
c = a + b;
Console.WriteLine(c);
```

C# recognizes many different kinds of statements. The first three lines of Example 2-16 are *declaration statements*, statements that declare and optionally initialize a variable. The fourth and fifth lines are *expression statements*. But some statements have more structure than the ones in this example.

When you write a loop, that's an *iteration statement*. When you use the `if` or `switch` mechanisms described later in this chapter to choose between various possible actions, those are *selection statements*. In fact, the C# specification distinguishes between 13 categories of statements. Most fit broadly into the scheme of describing either what the code should do next, or, for features such as loops or conditional statements, describing how it should decide what to do next. Statements of the second kind usually contain one or more embedded statements describing the action to perform in a loop, or the action to perform when an `if` statement's condition is met.

There's one special case, though. A block is a kind of statement. This makes statements such as loops more useful than they would otherwise be, because a loop iterates over just a single embedded statement. That statement can be a block, and since a block itself is a sequence of statements (delimited by braces), this enables loops to contain more than one statement.

This illustrates why the two simplistic points of view stated earlier—"statements are actions" and "statements are things that end in semicolons"—are wrong. Compare Example 2-16 with 2-17. Both do the same thing, because the various actions we've said we want to perform remain exactly the same, and both contain five semicolons. However, Example 2-17 contains one extra statement. The first two statements are the same, but they are followed by a third statement, a block, which contains the final three statements from Example 2-16. The extra statement, the block, doesn't end in a semicolon, nor does it perform any action. In this particular example it's pointless, but it can sometimes be useful to introduce a nested block like this to avoid name ambiguity errors. So statements can be structural, rather than causing anything to happen at runtime.

Example 2-17. A block

```
int a = 19;
int b = 23;
{
    int c;
    c = a + b;
    Console.WriteLine(c);
}
```

While your code will contain a mixture of statement types, it will inevitably end up containing at least a few expression statements. These are, quite simply, statements that consist of a suitable expression, followed by a semicolon. What's a suitable expression? What's an expression, for that matter? I'd better answer that second question before coming back to what constitutes a valid expression for a statement.

Expressions

The official definition of a C# *expression* is rather dry: "a sequence of operators and operands." Admittedly, language specifications tend to be like that, but in addition to this sort of formal prose, the C# specification contains some very readable informal explanations of the more formally expressed ideas. (For example, it describes statements as the means by which "the actions of a program are expressed" before going on to pin that down with less approachable but more technically precise language.)

The quote at the start of this paragraph is from the formal definition of an expression, so we might hope that the informal explanation in the introduction will be more helpful. No such luck: it says that expressions "are constructed from operands and operators." That's certainly less precise than the other definition, but it's no easier to understand. The problem is that there are several kinds of expressions and they do different jobs, so there isn't a single, general, informal description.

It's tempting to describe an expression as some code that produces a value. That's not true for all expressions, but the majority of expressions you'll write will fit this description, so I'll focus on this for now, and I'll come to the exceptions later.

The simplest expressions are *literals*, where we just write the value we want, such as "Hello, world!" or 42. You can also use the name of a variable as an expression. Expressions can involve operators, which describe calculations or other computations to be performed. Operators have some fixed number of inputs, called *operands*. Some take a single operand. For example, you can negate a number by putting a minus sign in front of it. Some take two: the + operator lets you form an expression that adds together the results of the two operands on either side of the + symbol.

 Some symbols have different roles depending on the context. The minus sign is not just used for negation. It acts as a two-operand subtraction operator if it appears between two expressions.

In general, operands are also expressions. So, when we write 2 + 2, that's an expression that contains two more expressions—the pair of '2' literals on either side of the + symbol. This means that we can write arbitrarily complicated expressions by nesting expressions within expressions within expressions. Example 2-18 exploits this to evaluate the quadratic formula (the standard technique for solving quadratic equations).

Example 2-18. Expressions within expressions

```
double a = 1, b = 2.5, c = -3;
double x = (-b + Math.Sqrt(b * b - 4 * a * c)) / (2 * a);
Console.WriteLine(x);
```

Look at the declaration statement on the second line. The overall structure of its initializer expression is a division operation. But that division operator's two operands are also expressions. Its lefthand operand is a *parenthesized expression*, which tells the compiler that I want that whole expression (-b + Math.Sqrt(b * b - 4 * a * c)) to be the first operand of the division. This subexpression contains an addition, whose lefthand operand is a negation expression whose single operand is the variable

b. The addition's righthand side takes the square root of another, more complex expression. And the division's righthand operand is another parenthesized expression, containing a multiplication. Figure 2-1 illustrates the full structure of the expression.

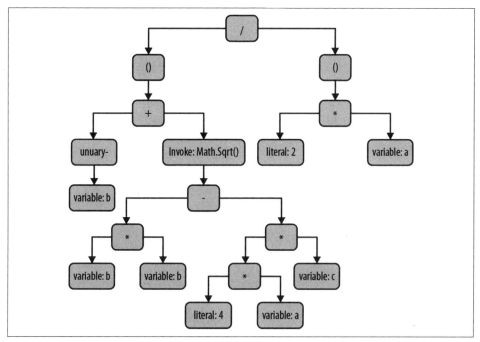

Figure 2-1. The structure of an expression

One important detail of this last example is that method invocations are a kind of expression. The `Math.Sqrt` method used in Example 2-18 is a .NET class library function that calculates the square root of its input and returns the result. What's perhaps more surprising is that invocations of methods that don't return a value, such as `Console.WriteLine`, are also, technically, expressions. And there are a few other constructs that don't produce values but are still considered to be expressions, including a reference to a type (e.g., the `Console` in `Console.WriteLine`) or to a namespace. These sorts of constructs take advantage of a set of common rules (e.g., scoping, how to resolve what a name refers to, etc.) by virtue of being expressions. However, all the non-value-producing expressions can be used only in certain specific circumstances. (You can't use one as an operand in another expression, for example.) So although it's not technically correct to define an expression as a piece of code that produces a value, the ones that do are the ones we use when describing the calculations we want our code to perform.

We can now return to the question: what can we put in an expression statement? Roughly speaking, the expression has to do something; it cannot just calculate a value. So although 2 + 2 is a valid expression, you'll get an error if you try to turn it into an expression statement by sticking a semicolon on the end. That expression calculates something but doesn't do anything with the result. To be more precise, you can use the following kinds of expressions as statements: method invocation, assignment, increment, decrement, and new object creation. We'll be looking at increment and decrement later in this chapter and we'll be looking at objects in later chapters, so that leaves invocation and assignment.

So a method invocation is allowed to be an expression statement. This can involve nested expressions of other kinds, but the whole thing must be a method call. Example 2-19 shows some valid examples. Notice that the C# compiler doesn't check whether the method call really has any lasting effect—the Math.Sqrt function is a pure function, in the sense that it does nothing other than returning a value determined entirely by its inputs. So invoking it and then doing nothing with the result doesn't really do anything at all—it's no more of an action than the expression 2 + 2. But as far as the C# compiler is concerned, any method call is allowed as an expression statement.

Example 2-19. Method invocation expressions as statements

```
Console.WriteLine("Hello, world!");
Console.WriteLine(12 + 30);
Console.ReadKey();
Math.Sqrt(4);
```

It seems inconsistent that C# forbids us from using an addition expression as a statement while allowing Math.Sqrt. Both perform a calculation that produces a result, so it makes no sense to use either in this way. Wouldn't it be more consistent if C# allowed only calls to methods that return nothing to be used for expression statements? That would rule out the final line of Example 2-19, which would seem like a good idea because that code does nothing useful. It would also be consistent with the fact that 2 + 2 also cannot form an expression statement. Unfortunately, sometimes you want to ignore the return value. Example 2-19 calls Console.ReadKey(), which waits for a keypress and returns a value indicating which key was pressed. If my program's behavior depends on which particular key the user pressed, I'll need to inspect the method's return value, but if I just want to wait for any key at all, it's OK to ignore the return value. If C# didn't allow methods with return values to be used as expression statements, I wouldn't be able to do this. The compiler has no way to distinguish between methods that make for pointless statements because they have no side effects (such as Math.Sqrt) and those that might be good candidates (such as Console.Read Key), so it allows any method.

For an expression to be a valid expression statement, it is not enough merely to contain a method invocation. Example 2-20 shows some expressions that call methods and then go on to use those as part of addition expressions. Although these are valid expressions, they're not valid expression statements, so these will cause compiler errors. What matters is the outermost expression. In both lines here, that's an addition expression, which is why these are not allowed.

Example 2-20. Errors: some expressions that don't work as statements

```
Console.ReadKey().KeyChar + "!";
Math.Sqrt(4) + 1;
```

Earlier I said that one kind of expression we're allowed to use as a statement is an assignment. It's not obvious that assignments should be expressions, but they are, and they do produce a value: the result of an assignment expression is the value being assigned to the variable. This means it's legal to write code like that in Example 2-21. The second line here uses an assignment expression as an argument for a method invocation, which shows the value of that expression. The first two WriteLine calls both display 123.

Example 2-21. Assignments are expressions

```
int number;
Console.WriteLine(number = 123);
Console.WriteLine(number);

int x, y;
x = y = 0;
Console.WriteLine(x);
Console.WriteLine(y);
```

The second part of this example assigns one value into two variables in a single step by exploiting the fact that assignments are expressions—it assigns the value of the y = 0 expression (which evaluates to 0) into x.

This shows that evaluating an expression can do more than just produce a value. Some expressions have side effects. We've just seen that an assignment is an expression, and of course it has the effect of changing what's in a variable. Method calls are expressions too, and although you can write pure functions that do nothing besides calculating their result from their input, like Math.Sqrt, many methods do something with lasting effects, such as writing data to the screen, updating a database, or launching a missile. This means that we might care about the order in which the operands of an expression get evaluated.

An expression's structure imposes some constraints on the order in which operators do their work. For example, I can use parentheses to enforce ordering. The expression 10 + (8 / 2) has the value 14, while the expression (10 + 8) / 2 has the value 9, even though both have exactly the same literal operands and arithmetic operators. The parentheses here determine whether the division is performed before or after the subtraction.[4]

However, while the structure of an expression imposes some ordering constraints, it still leaves some latitude: although both the operands of an addition need to be evaluated before they can be added, the addition operator doesn't care which operand we evaluate first. But if the operands are expressions with side effects, the order could be important. For these simple expressions, it doesn't matter because I've used literals, so we can't really tell when they get evaluated. But what about an expression in which operands call some method? Example 2-22 contains code of this kind.

Example 2-22. Operand evaluation order

```
class Program
{
    static int X(string label, int i)
    {
        Console.Write(label);
        return i;
    }

    static void Main(string[] args)
    {
        Console.WriteLine(X("a", 1) + X("b", 1) + X("c", 1) + X("d", 1));
    }
}
```

This defines a method, X, which takes two arguments. It displays the first and just returns the second. I've then used this a few times in an expression so that we can see exactly when the operands that call X are evaluated. Some languages choose not to define this order, making the behavior of such a program unpredictable, but C# does specify an order here. The rule is that within any expression, the operands are evaluated in the order in which they occur in the source. So, when the Console.WriteLine in Example 2-22, runs, it makes multiple calls to X, which calls Console.Write each time, so we see this output: abcd4.

However, this glosses over an important subtlety: what do we mean by the order of expressions when nesting occurs? The entire argument to that Console.WriteLine is

---

4 In the absence of parentheses, C# has rules of *precedence* that determine the order in which operators are evaluated. For the full (and not very interesting) details, consult the documentation, but in this example, because division has higher precedence than addition, without parentheses the expression would evaluate to 14.

one big add expression, where the first operand is X("a", 1) and the second is another add expression, which in turn has a first operand of X("b", 1) and a second operand, which is yet another add expression, whose operands are X("c", 1) and X("d", 1). Taking the first of those add expressions, which constitutes the entire argument to Console.WriteLine, does it even make sense to ask whether it comes before or after its first operand? Lexically, the outermost add expression starts at exactly the same point that its first operand starts and ends at the point where its second operand ends (which also happens to be at the exact same point that the final X("d", 1) ends). In this particular case, it doesn't really matter because the only observable effect of the order of evaluation is the output the X method produces when invoked. None of the expressions that invoke X are nested within one another, so we can meaningfully say what order those expressions are in, and the output we see matches that order. However, in some cases, such as Example 2-23, the overlapping of nested expressions can have a visible impact.

Example 2-23. Operand evaluation order with nested expressions

```
Console.WriteLine(
    X("a", 1) +
    X("b", (X("c", 1) + X("d", 1) + X("e", 1))) +
    X("f", 1));
```

Here, Console.WriteLine's argument adds the results of three calls to X; however, the second of those calls to X (first argument "b") takes as its second argument an expression that adds the results of three more calls to X (with arguments of "c", "d", and "e"). With the final call to X (passing "f") we have a total of six expressions invoking X in that statement. C#'s rule of evaluating expressions in the order in which they appear applies as always, but because there is overlap, the results are initially surprising. Although the letters appear in the source in alphabetical order, the output is "acdebf5". If you're wondering how on earth that can be consistent with expressions being evaluated in order, consider that this code starts the evaluation of each expression in the order in which the expressions start, and finishes the evaluation in the order in which the expressions finish, but that those are two different orderings. In particular, the expression that invokes X with "b" begins its evaluation before those that invoke it with "c", "d", and "e", but it finishes its evaluation *after* them. And it's that *after* ordering that we see in the output. If you find each closing parenthesis that corresponds to a call to X in this example, you'll find that the order of calls exactly matches what's displayed.

Comments and Whitespace

Most programming languages allow source files to contain text that is ignored by the compiler, and C# is no exception. As with most C-family languages, it supports two styles of *comments* for this purpose. There are *single-line comments*, as shown in Example 2-24, in which you write two / characters in a row, and everything from there to the end of the line will be ignored by the compiler.

Example 2-24. Single-line comments

```
Console.WriteLine("Say");          // This text will be ignored but the code on
Console.WriteLine("Anything");     // the left is still compiled as usual.
```

C# also supports *delimited comments*. You start a comment of this kind with /*, and the compiler will ignore everything that follows until it encounters the first */ character sequence. This can be useful if you don't want the comment to go all the way to the end of the line, as the first line of Example 2-25 illustrates. This example also shows that delimited comments can span multiple lines.

Example 2-25. Delimited comments

```
Console.WriteLine(/* Has side effects */ GetLog());

/* Some developers like to use delimited comments for big blocks of text,
 * where they need to explain something particularly complex or odd in the
 * code. The column of asterisks on the left is for decoration - asterisks
 * are necessary only at the start and end of the comment.
 */
```

There's a minor snag you can run into with delimited comments; it can happen even when the comment is within a single line, but it more often occurs with multiline comments. Example 2-26 shows the problem with a comment that begins in the middle of the first line and ends at the end of the fourth.

Example 2-26. Multiline comments

```
Console.WriteLine("This will run");     /* This comment includes not just the
Console.WriteLine("This won't");         * text on the right, but also the text
Console.WriteLine("Nor will this");     /* on the left except the first and last
Console.WriteLine("Nor this");           * lines. */
Console.WriteLine("This will also run");
```

Notice that the /* character sequence appears twice in this example. When this sequence appears in the middle of a comment, it does nothing special—comments don't nest. Even though we've seen two /* sequences, the first */ is enough to end the comment. This is occasionally frustrating, but it's the norm for C-family languages.

It's sometimes useful to take a chunk of code out of action temporarily, in a way that's easy to put back. Turning the code into a comment is a common way to do this, and although a delimited comment might seem like the obvious thing to use, it becomes awkward if the region you commented out happens to include another delimited comment. Since there's no support for nesting, you would need to add a /* after the inner comment's closing */ to ensure that you've commented out the whole range. So it is common to use single-line comments for this purpose. (You can also use the #if directive described in the next section.)

 Visual Studio can comment out regions of code for you. If you select several lines of text and type Ctrl-K followed immediately by Ctrl-C, it will add // to the start of every line in the selection. And you can uncomment a region with Ctrl-K, Ctrl-U. If you chose something other than C# as your preferred language when you first ran Visual Studio, these actions may be bound to different key sequences, but they are also available on the Edit→Advanced menu, as well as on the Text Editor toolbar, one of the standard toolbars that Visual Studio shows by default.

Speaking of ignored text, C# ignores extra whitespace for the most part. Not all whitespace is insignificant, because you need at least some space to separate tokens that consist entirely of alphanumeric symbols. For example, you can't write stati cvoid as the start of a method declaration—you'd need at least one space (or tab, newline, or other space-like character) between static and void. But with nonalphanumeric tokens, spaces are optional, and in most cases, a single space is equivalent to any amount of whitespace and new lines. This means that the three statements in Example 2-27 are all equivalent.

Example 2-27. Insignificant whitespace

```
Console.WriteLine("Testing");
Console . WriteLine(   "Testing");
Console.
   WriteLine ("Testing" )
 ;
```

There are a couple of cases where C# is more sensitive to whitespace. Inside a string literal, space is significant, because whatever spaces you write will be present in the string value. Also, while C# mostly doesn't care whether you put each element on its own line, or put all your code in one massive line, or (as seems more likely) something in between, there is an exception: preprocessing directives are required to appear on their own lines.

Preprocessing Directives

If you're familiar with the C language or its direct descendants, you may have been wondering if C# has a preprocessor. It doesn't have a separate preprocessing stage, and it does not offer macros. However, it does have a handful of directives similar to those offered by the C preprocessor, although it is only a very limited selection. Even though C# doesn't have a full preprocessing stage like C, these are known as preprocessing directives nonetheless.

Compilation Symbols

C# offers a #define directive that lets you define a *compilation symbol*. These symbols are commonly used in conjunction with the #if directive to compile code in different ways for different situations. For example, you might want some code to be present only in Debug builds, or perhaps you need to use different code on different platforms to achieve a particular effect. Often, you won't use the #define directive, though—it's more common to define compilation symbols through the compiler build settings. Visual Studio lets you configure different symbol values for each build configuration. To control this, right-click the project's node in Solution Explorer, select Properties, and in the property page that this opens, go to the Build tab. Or you can just open up the *.csproj* file and define the values you want in a <DefineConst ants> element of any <PropertyGroup>.

 The .NET SDK defines certain symbols by default. It supports two configurations, Debug and Release. It defines a DEBUG compilation symbol in the Debug configuration, whereas Release will define RELEASE instead. It defines a symbol called TRACE in both configurations. Certain project types get additional symbols. A library targeting .NET Standard 2.0 will have both NETSTANDARD and NETSTANDARD2_0 defined, for example.

Compilation symbols are typically used in conjunction with the #if, #else, #elif, and #endif directives. (#elif is short for *else if*.) Example 2-28 uses some of these directives to ensure that certain lines of code get compiled only in Debug builds. (You can also write #if false to prevent sections of code from being compiled at all. This is typically done only as a temporary measure, and is an alternative to commenting out that sidesteps some of the lexical pitfalls of attempting to nest comments.)

Example 2-28. Conditional compilation

```
#if DEBUG
    Console.WriteLine("Starting work");
#endif
    DoWork();
#if DEBUG
    Console.WriteLine("Finished work");
#endif
```

C# provides a more subtle mechanism to support this sort of thing, called a *conditional method*. The compiler recognizes an attribute defined by the .NET class libraries, called `ConditionalAttribute`, for which it provides special compile-time behavior. You can annotate any method with this attribute. Example 2-29 uses it to indicate that the annotated method should be used only when the DEBUG compilation symbol is defined.

Example 2-29. Conditional method

```
[System.Diagnostics.Conditional("DEBUG")]
static void ShowDebugInfo(object o)
{
    Console.WriteLine(o);
}
```

If you write code that calls a method that has been annotated in this way, the C# compiler will omit that call in builds that do not define the relevant symbol. So if you write code that calls this `ShowDebugInfo` method, the compiler strips out all those calls in non-Debug builds. This means you can get the same effect as Example 2-28, but without cluttering up your code with directives.

The .NET class library's `Debug` and `Trace` classes in the `System.Diagnostics` namespace use this feature. The `Debug` class offers various methods that are conditional on the DEBUG compilation symbol, while the `Trace` class has methods conditional on TRACE. If you leave the default settings for a new C# project in place, any diagnostic output produced through the `Trace` class will be available in both Debug and Release builds, but any code that calls a method on the `Debug` class will not get compiled into Release builds.

The Debug class's Assert method is conditional on DEBUG, which sometimes catches developers out. Assert lets you specify a condition that must be true at runtime, and it throws an exception if the condition is false. There are two things developers new to C# often mistakenly put in a Debug.Assert: checks that should in fact occur in all builds, and expressions with side effects that the rest of the code depends on. This leads to bugs, because the compiler will strip this code out in non-Debug builds.

#error and #warning

C# lets you choose to generate compiler errors or warnings with the #error and #warning directives. These are typically used inside conditional regions, as Example 2-30 shows, although an unconditional #warning could be useful as a way to remind yourself that you've not written some particularly important bit of the code yet.

Example 2-30. Generating a compiler error

```
#if NETSTANDARD
  #error .NET Standard is not a supported target for this source file
#endif
```

#line

The #line directive is useful in generated code. When the compiler produces an error or a warning, it normally states where the problem occurred, providing the filename, a line number, and an offset within that line. But if the code in question was generated automatically using some other file as input and if that other file contains the root cause of the problem, it may be more useful to report an error in the input file, rather than the generated file. A #line directive can instruct the C# compiler to act as though the error occurred at the line number specified and, optionally, as if the error were in an entirely different file. Example 2-31 shows how to use it. The error after the directive will be reported as though it came from line 123 of a file called *Foo.cs*.

Example 2-31. The #line directive and a deliberate mistake

```
#line 123 "Foo.cs"
    intt x;
```

The filename part is optional, enabling you to fake just line numbers. You can tell the compiler to revert to reporting warnings and errors without fakery by writing #line default.

This directive also affects debugging. When the compiler emits debug information, it takes #line directives into account. This means that when stepping through code in the debugger, you'll see the location that #line refers to.

There's another use for this directive. Instead of a line number (and optional file-name) you can write just #line hidden. This affects only the debugger behavior: when single stepping, Visual Studio will run straight through all the code after such a directive without stopping until it encounters a non-hidden #line directive (typi-cally #line default).

#pragma

The #pragma directive provides two features: it can be used to disable selected com-piler warnings, and it can also be used to override the checksum values the compiler puts into the *.pdb* file it generates containing debug information. Both of these are designed primarily for code generation scenarios, although they can occasionally be useful to disable warnings in ordinary code. Example 2-32 shows how to use a #pragma to prevent the compiler from issuing the warning that would normally occur if you declare a variable that you do not then go on to use.

Example 2-32. Disabling a compiler warning

```
#pragma warning disable CS0168
    int a;
```

You should generally avoid disabling warnings. This feature is useful in generated code because code generation can often end up creating items that are not always used, and pragmas may offer the only way to get a clean compilation. But when you're writing code by hand, it should usually be possible to avoid warnings in the first place.

Some components on NuGet supply *code analyzers*, components that get connected up to the C# compiler API, and which are given the opportunity to inspect the code and generate their own diagnostic messages. (This happens at build time, and in Vis-ual Studio, it also happens during editing, providing live diagnostics as you type. They also work live in Visual Studio Code if you enable the OmniSharp C# exten-sion.) For example, the StyleCop.Analyzers NuGet package supplies an analyzer that will warn you if any of your types' public members do not conform to Micro-soft's class library design guidelines. You can use #pragma warning directives to con-trol warnings from code analyzers, not just ones from the C# compiler. Analyzers generally prefix their warning numbers with some letters to enable you to distinguish between them—compiler warnings all start with CS and StyleCop warnings with SA, for example.

Pragmas offer special handling for the warnings you get from the *nullable references* feature added in C# 8.0. Instead of specifying a compiler- or code-analyzer-generated warning number, you can write `nullable` (e.g., `#pragma warning disable nullable`). See Chapter 3 for more details.

It's possible that future versions of C# may add other features based on `#pragma`. When the compiler encounters a pragma it does not understand, it generates a warning, not an error, on the grounds that an unrecognized pragma might be valid for some future compiler version or some other vendor's compiler.

#nullable

C# 8.0 adds a new directive, `#nullable`, which allows fine-grained control of the nullable annotation context. This is part of the *nullable references* feature described in Chapter 3. (This doesn't overlap with the nullable warning control described in the preceding section, because we get to control whether nullability annotations are enabled independently of whether warnings associated with those annotations are enabled.)

#region and #endregion

Finally, we have two preprocessing directives that do nothing. If you write `#region` directives, the only thing the compiler does is ensure that they have corresponding `#endregion` directives. Mismatches cause compiler errors, but the compiler ignores correctly paired `#region` and `#endregion` directives. Regions can be nested.

These directives exist entirely for the benefit of text editors that choose to recognize them. Visual Studio uses them to provide the ability to collapse sections of the code down to a single line on screen. The C# editor automatically allows certain features to be expanded and collapsed, such as class definitions, methods, and code blocks (a feature it calls *outlining*). If you define regions with these two directives, it will also allow those to be expanded and collapsed. This allows for outlining at both finer-grained (e.g., within a single block) and coarser-grained (e.g., multiple related methods) scales than the editor offers automatically.

If you hover the mouse over a collapsed region, Visual Studio displays a tool tip showing the region's contents. You can put text after the `#region` token. When Visual Studio displays a collapsed region, it shows this text on the single line that remains. Although you're allowed to omit this, it's usually a good idea to include some descriptive text so that people can have a rough idea of what they'll see if they expand it.

Some people like to put the entire contents of a class into various regions, because by collapsing all regions, you can see a file's structure at a glance. It might even all fit on the screen at once, thanks to the regions being reduced to a single line. On the other hand, some people hate collapsed regions, because they present speed bumps on the way to being able to look at the code and can also encourage people to put too much source code into one file.

Fundamental Data Types

.NET defines thousands of types in its class library, and you can write your own, so C# can work with an unlimited number of data types. However, a handful of types get special handling from the compiler. You saw earlier in Example 2-9 that if you have a string, and you try to add a number to it, the resulting code converts the number to a string and appends that to the first string. In fact, the behavior is more general than that—it's not limited to numbers. The compiled code works by calling the `String.Concat` method, and if you pass to that any nonstring arguments, it will call their `ToString` methods before performing the append. All types offer a `ToString` method, so this means you can append values of any type to a string.

That's handy, but it only works because the C# compiler knows about strings and provides special services for them. (There's a part of the C# specification that defines the unique string handling for the + operator.) C# provides various special services not just for strings, but also certain numeric data types, Booleans, a family of types called tuples, and two specific types called `dynamic` and `object`. Most of these are special not just to C# but also to the runtime—almost all of the numeric types (all except `BigInteger`) get direct support in intermediate language (IL), and the `bool`, `string`, and `object` types are also intrinsically understood by the runtime.

Numeric Types

C# supports integer and floating-point arithmetic. There are signed and unsigned integer types and they come in various sizes, as Table 2-1 shows. The most commonly used integer type is `int`, not least because it is large enough to represent a usefully wide range of values, without being too large to work efficiently on all CPUs that support .NET. (Larger data types might not be handled natively by the CPU and can also have undesirable characteristics in multithreaded code: reads and writes are atomic for 32-bit types,[5] but may not be for larger ones.)

---

5 Strictly speaking, this is guaranteed only for correctly aligned 32-bit types. However, C# aligns them correctly by default and you'd normally encounter misaligned data only if your code needs to call out into unmanaged code.

Table 2-1. Integer types

C# type	CLR name	Signed	Size in bits	Inclusive range
byte	System.Byte	No	8	0 to 255
sbyte	System.SByte	Yes	8	−128 to 127
ushort	System.UInt16	No	16	0 to 65,535
short	System.Int16	Yes	16	−32,768 to 32,767
uint	System.UInt32	No	32	0 to 4,294,967,295
int	System.Int32	Yes	32	−2,147,483,648 to 2,147,483,647
ulong	System.UInt64	No	64	0 to 18,446,744,073,709,551,615
long	System.Int64	Yes	64	−9,223,372,036,854,775,808 to 9,223,372,036,854,775,807

The second column in Table 2-1 shows the name of the type in the CLR. Different languages have different naming conventions and C# uses names from its C-family roots for numeric types, but those don't fit with the naming conventions that .NET has for its data types. As far as the runtime is concerned, the names in the second column are the real names—there are various APIs that can report information about types at runtime, and they report these CLR names, not the C# ones. The names are synonymous in C# source code, so you're free to use the runtime names if you want to, but the C# names are a better stylistic fit—keywords in C-family languages are all lowercase. Since the compiler handles these types differently than the rest, it's arguably good to have them stand out.

 Not all .NET languages support unsigned numbers, so the .NET class library tends to avoid them. A runtime that supports multiple languages (such as the CLR) faces a trade-off between offering a type system rich enough to cover most languages' needs, and forcing an overcomplicated type system on simple languages. To resolve this, .NET's type system, the CTS, is reasonably comprehensive, but languages don't have to support all of it. The CLS identifies a relatively small subset of the CTS that all languages should support. Signed integers are in the CLS, but unsigned ones are not. This is why you will sometimes see surprising-looking type choices, such as the Length property of an array being int (rather than uint) despite the fact that it will never return a negative value.

C# also supports floating-point numbers. There are two types: float and double, which are 32-bit and 64-bit numbers in the standard IEEE 754 formats (*http://en.wiki pedia.org/wiki/IEEE_floating_point*), and as the CLR names in Table 2-2 suggest, these correspond to what are commonly called *single-precision* and *double-precision numbers*. Floating-point values do not work in the same way as integers, so this table is a little different than the integer types table. Floating point numbers store a value and an exponent (similar in concept to scientific notation, but working in binary instead of decimal). The precision column shows how many bits are available for the value part, and then the range is expressed as the smallest nonzero value and the largest value that can be represented. (These can be either positive or negative.)

Table 2-2. Floating-point types

C# type	CLR name	Size in bits	Precision	Range (magnitude)
float	System.Single	32	23 bits (~7 decimal digits)	1.5×10^{-45} to 3.4×10^{38}
double	System.Double	64	52 bits (~15 decimal digits)	5.0×10^{-324} to 1.7×10^{308}

C# recognizes a third numeric representation called decimal (or System.Decimal in the CLR). This is a 128-bit value, so it can offer greater precision than the other formats, but it is not just a bigger version of double. It is designed for calculations that require predictable handling of decimal fractions, something neither float nor dou ble can offer. If you write code that initializes a variable of type float to 0 and then adds 0.1 to it nine times in a row, you might expect to get a value of 0.9, but in fact you'll get approximately 0.9000001. That's because IEEE 754 stores numbers in binary, which cannot represent all decimal fractions. It can handle some, such as the decimal 0.5; written in base 2, that's 0.1. But the decimal 0.1 turns into a recurring number in binary. (Specifically, it's 0.0 followed by the recurring sequence 0011.) This means float and double can represent only an approximation of the decimal value 0.1, and more generally, only a small subset of decimals can be represented completely accurately. This isn't always instantly obvious, because when floating-point numbers are converted to text, they are rounded to a decimal approximation that can mask the discrepancy. But over multiple calculations, the inaccuracies tend to add up and eventually produce surprising-looking results.

For some kinds of calculations, this doesn't really matter; in simulations or signal processing, for example, some noise and error is expected. But accountants and financial regulators tend to be less forgiving—little discrepancies like this can make it look like money has magically vanished or appeared. We need calculations that involve money to be absolutely accurate, which makes floating point a terrible choice for such work. This is why C# offers the decimal type, which provides a well-defined level of decimal precision.

 Most of the integer types can be handled natively by the CPU. (All of them can when running in a 64-bit process.) Likewise, many CPUs can work directly with float and double representations. However, none has intrinsic support for decimal, meaning that even simple operations, such as addition, require multiple CPU instructions. This means that arithmetic is significantly slower with decimal than with the other numeric types shown so far.

A decimal stores numbers as a sign bit (positive or negative) and a pair of integers. There's a 96-bit integer, and the value of the decimal is this first integer (negated if the sign bit says so) multiplied by 10 raised to the power of the second integer, which is a number in the range of 0 to 28.[6] 96 bits is enough to represent any 28-digit decimal integer (and some, but not all, 29-digit ones), so the second integer—the one representing the power of 10 by which the first is multiplied—effectively says where the decimal point goes. This format makes it possible to represent any decimal with 28 or fewer digits accurately.

When you write a literal numeric value, you can choose the type, or you can let the compiler pick a suitable type for you. If you write a plain integer, such as 123, its type will be int, uint, long, or ulong—the compiler picks the first type from that list with a range that contains the value. (So 123 would be an int, 3000000000 would be a uint, 5000000000 would be a long, etc.) If you write a number with a decimal point, such as 1.23, its type is double.

If you're dealing with large numbers, it's very easy to get the number of zeros wrong. This is usually bad and possibly very expensive or dangerous, depending on your application area. C# provides some mitigation by allowing you to add underscores anywhere in numeric literals, to break the numbers up however you please. This is analogous to the common practice in most English-speaking countries of using a comma to separate zeros into groups of 3. For example, instead of writing 5000000000, most native English speakers would write 5,000,000,000, instantly making it much easier to see that this is 5 billion and not, say, 50 billion, or 500 million. (What many native English speakers don't know is that several countries around the world use a period for this, and would write 5.000.000.000 instead, using the comma where most native English speakers would put a decimal point. Interpreting a value such as €100.000 requires you to know which country's conventions are in use if you don't want to make a disastrous financial miscalculation. But I digress.) In C# we can do something similar by writing the numeric literal as 5_000_000_000.

You can tell the compiler that you want a specific type by adding a suffix. So 123U is a uint, 123L is a long, and 123UL is a ulong. Suffix letters are case- and order-independent, so instead of 123UL, you could write 123Lu, 123uL, or any other permutation. For double, float, and decimal, use the D, F, and M suffixes, respectively.

These last three types all support a decimal exponential literal format for large numbers, where you put the letter E in the constant followed by the power. For example, the literal value 1.5E-20 is the value 1.5 multiplied by 10^{-20}. (This happens to be of

---

6 A decimal, therefore, doesn't use all of its 128 bits. Making it smaller would cause alignment difficulties, and using the additional bits for extra precision would have a significant performance impact, because integers whose length is a multiple of 32 bits are easier for most CPUs to deal with than the alternatives.

type `double`, because that's the default for a number with a decimal point, regardless of whether it's in exponential format. You could write `1.5E-20F` and `1.5E-20M` for `float` and `decimal` constants with equivalent values.)

It's often useful to be able to write integer literals in hexadecimal, because the digits map better onto the binary representation used at runtime. This is particularly important when different bit ranges of a number represent different things. For example, you may need to deal with a numeric error code that originated from a Windows system call—these occasionally crop up in exceptions. In some cases, these codes use the topmost bit to indicate success or failure, the next few bits to indicate the origin of the error, and the remaining bits to identify the specific error. For example, the COM error code E_ACCESSDENIED has the value −2,147,024,891. It's hard to see the structure in decimal, but in hexadecimal, it's easier: 80070005. The 8 indicates that this is an error, and the 007 that follows indicates that this was originally a plain Win32 error that has been translated into a COM error. The remaining bits indicate that the Win32 error code was 5 (ERROR_ACCESS_DENIED). C# lets you write integer literals in hexadecimal for scenarios like these, where the hex representation is more readable. You just prefix the number with `0x`, so in this case, you would write `0x80070005`.

You can also write binary literals by using the `0b` prefix. Digit separators can be used in hex and binary just as they can in decimals, although it's more common to group the digits by fours in these cases, e.g., `0b_0010_1010`. Obviously this makes any binary structure in a number even more evident than hexadecimal does, but 32-bit binary literals are inconveniently long, which is why we often use hexadecimal instead.

Numeric conversions

Each of the built-in numeric types uses a different representation for storing numbers in memory. Converting from one form to another requires some work—even the number 1 looks quite different if you inspect its binary representations as a `float`, an `int`, and a `decimal`. However, C# is able to generate code that converts between formats and it will often do so automatically. Example 2-33 shows some cases in which this will happen.

Example 2-33. Implicit conversions

```
int i = 42;
double di = i;
Console.WriteLine(i / 5);
Console.WriteLine(di / 5);
Console.WriteLine(i / 5.0);
```

The second line assigns the value of an `int` variable into a `double` variable. The C# compiler generates the necessary code to convert the integer value into its equivalent floating-point value. More subtly, the last two lines will perform similar conversions, as we can see from the output of that code:

```
8
8.4
8.4
```

This shows that the first division produced an integer result—dividing the integer variable i by the integer literal 5 caused the compiler to generate code that performs integer division, so the result is 8. But the other two divisions produced a floating-point result. In the second case, we've divided the double variable di by an integer literal 5. C# converts that 5 to floating point before performing the division. And in the final line, we're dividing an integer variable by a floating-point literal. This time, it's the variable's value that gets turned from an integer into a floating-point value before the division takes place.

In general, when you perform arithmetic calculations that involve a mixture of numeric types, C# will pick the type with the largest range and *promote* values of types with a narrower range into that larger one before performing the calculations. (Arithmetic operators generally require all their operands to have the same type, so if you supply operands with different types, one type has to "win" for any particular operator.) For example, double can represent any value that int can, and many that it cannot, so double is the more expressive type.[7]

C# will perform numeric conversions implicitly whenever the conversion is a promotion (i.e., the target type has a wider range than the source), because there is no possibility of the conversion failing. However, it will not implicitly convert in the other direction. The second and third lines of Example 2-34 will fail to compile, because they attempt to assign expressions of type double into an int, which is a *narrowing* conversion, meaning that the source might contain values that are out of the target's range.

Example 2-34. Errors: implicit conversions not available

```
int i = 42;
int willFail = 42.0;
int willAlsoFail = i / 1.0;
```

It is possible to convert in this direction, just not implicitly. You can use a *cast*, where you specify the name of the type to which you'd like to convert in parentheses. Example 2-35 shows a modified version of Example 2-34, where we state explicitly

---

7 Promotions are not in fact a feature of C#. There is a more general mechanism: conversion operators. C# defines intrinsic implicit conversion operators for the built-in data types. The promotions discussed here occur as a result of the compiler following its usual rules for conversions.

that we want a conversion to int, and we either don't mind that this conversion might not work correctly, or we have reason to believe that, in this specific case, the value will be in range. Note that on the final line I've put parentheses around the expression after the cast. That makes the cast apply to the whole expression; otherwise, C#'s rules of precedence mean it would apply just to the i variable, and since that's already an int, it would have no effect.

Example 2-35. Explicit conversions with casts

```
int i = 42;
int i2 = (int) 42.0;
int i3 = (int) (i / 1.0);
```

So narrowing conversions require explicit casts, and conversions that cannot lose information occur implicitly. However, with some combinations of types, neither is strictly more expressive than the other. What should happen if you try to add an int to a uint? Or an int to a float? These types are all 32 bits in size, so none of them can possibly offer more than 2^{32} distinct values, but they have different ranges, which means that each has values it can represent that the other types cannot. For example, you can represent the value 3,000,000,001 in a uint, but it's too large for an int and can only be approximated in a float. As floating-point numbers get larger, the values that can be represented get farther apart—a float can represent 3,000,000,000 and also 3,000,001,024, but nothing in between. So for the value 3,000,000,001, uint seems better than float. But what about −1? That's a negative number, so uint can't cope with that. Then there are very large numbers that float can represent that are out of range for both int and uint. Each of these types has its strengths and weaknesses, and it makes no sense to say that one of them is generally better than the rest.

Surprisingly, C# allows some implicit conversions even in these potentially lossy scenarios. The rules consider only range, not precision: implicit conversions are allowed if the target type's range completely contains the source type's range. So you can convert from either int or uint to float, because although float is unable to represent some values exactly, there are no int or uint values that it cannot at least approximate. But implicit conversions are not allowed in the other direction, because there are some float values that are simply too big—unlike float, the integer types can't offer approximations for bigger numbers.

You might be wondering what happens if you force a narrowing conversion to int with a cast, as Example 2-35 does, in situations where the number is out of range. The answer depends on the type from which you are casting. Conversion from one integer type to another works differently than conversion from floating point to integer. In fact, the C# specification does not define how floating-point numbers that are too big should be converted to an integer type—the result could be anything. But when casting between integer types, the outcome is well defined. If the two types are of different sizes, the binary will be either truncated or padded with zeros (or ones, if the source type is signed and the value is negative) to make it the right size for the target type, and then the bits are just treated as if they are of the target type. This is occasionally useful, but can more often produce surprising results, so you can choose an alternative behavior for any out-of-range cast by making it a *checked* conversion.

Checked contexts

C# defines the checked keyword, which you can put in front of either a block statement or an expression, making it a *checked context*. This means that certain arithmetic operations, including casts, are checked for range overflow at runtime. If you cast a value to an integer type in a checked context and the value is too high or low to fit, an error will occur—the code will throw a System.OverflowException.

As well as checking casts, a checked context will detect range overflows in ordinary arithmetic. Addition, subtraction, and other operations can take a value beyond the range of its data type. For integers, this causes the value to "roll over" when unchecked, so adding 1 to the maximum value produces the minimum value, and vice versa for subtraction. Occasionally, this wrapping can be useful. For example, if you want to determine how much time has elapsed between two points in the code, one way to do this is to use the Environment.TickCount property.[8] (This is more reliable than using the current date and time, because that can change as a result of the clock being adjusted, or when moving between time zones. The tick count just keeps increasing at a steady rate. That said, in real code you'd probably use the class library's Stopwatch class.) Example 2-36 shows one way to do this.

Example 2-36. Exploiting unchecked integer overflow

```
int start = Environment.TickCount;
DoSomeWork();
int end = Environment.TickCount;

int totalTicks = end - start;
Console.WriteLine(totalTicks);
```

The tricky thing about Environment.TickCount is that it occasionally "wraps around." It counts the number of milliseconds since the system last rebooted, and since its type is int, it will eventually run out of range. A span of 25 days is 2.16 billion milliseconds—too large a number to fit in an int. (.NET Core 3.0 solves this by adding a TickCount64 property, which is good for almost 300 million years. But this

---

8 A *property* is a member of a type that represents a value that can be read or modified or both; Chapter 3 describes properties in detail.

is unavailable in older versions, or any .NET Standard version available at the time I write this.) Imagine the tick count is 2,147,483,637, which is 10 short of the maximum value for int. What would you expect it to be 100 ms later? It can't be 100 higher (2,147,483,727), because that's too big a value for an int. We'd expect it to get to the highest possible value after 10 ms, so after 11 ms, it'll roll round to the minimum value; thus, after 100 ms, we'd expect the tick count to be 89 above the minimum value (which would be −2,147,483,559).

 The tick count is not necessarily precise to the nearest millisecond in practice. It often stands still for milliseconds at a time before leaping forward in increments of 10 ms, 15 ms, or even more. However, the value still rolls over—you just might not be able to observe every possible tick value as it does so.

Interestingly, Example 2-36 handles this perfectly. If the tick count in start was obtained just before the count wrapped, and the one in end was obtained just after, end will contain a much lower value than start, which seems upside down, and the difference between them will be large—larger than the range of an int. However, when we subtract start from end, the overflow rolls over in a way that exactly matches the way the tick count rolls over, meaning we end up getting the correct result regardless. For example, if the start contains a tick count from 10 ms before rollover, and end is from 90 ms afterward, subtracting the relevant tick counts (i.e., subtracting −2,147,483,558 from 2,147,483,627) seems like it should produce a result of 4,294,967,185. But because of the way the subtraction overflows, we actually get a result of 100, which corresponds to the elapsed time of 100 ms.

But in most cases, this sort of integer overflow is undesirable. It means that when dealing with large numbers, you can get results that are completely incorrect. A lot of the time, this is not a big risk, because you will be dealing with fairly small numbers, but if there is any possibility that your calculations might encounter overflow, you might want to use a checked context. Any arithmetic performed in a checked context will throw an exception when overflow occurs. You can request this in an expression with the checked operator, as Example 2-37 shows. Everything inside the parentheses will be evaluated in a checked context, so you'll see an OverflowException if the addition of a and b overflows. The checked keyword does not apply to the whole statement here, so if an overflow happens as a result of adding c, that will not cause an exception.

Example 2-37. Checked expression

```
int result = checked(a + b) + c;
```

You can also turn on checking for an entire block of code with a checked statement, which is a block preceded by the checked keyword, as Example 2-38 shows. Checked statements always involve a block—you cannot just add the checked keyword in front of the int keyword in Example 2-37 to turn that into a checked statement. You'd also need to wrap the code in braces.

Example 2-38. Checked statement

```
checked
{
    int r1 = a + b;
    int r2 = r1 - (int) c;
}
```

A checked block only affects the lines of code inside the block. If the code invokes any methods, those will be unaffected by the presence of the checked keyword—there isn't some *checked* bit in the CPU that gets enabled on the current thread inside a checked block. (In other words, this keyword's scope is lexical, not dynamic.)

C# also has an unchecked keyword. You can use this inside a checked block to indicate that a particular expression or nested block should not be a checked context. This makes life easier if you want everything except for one particular expression to be checked—rather than having to label everything except the chosen part as checked, you can put all the code into a checked block and then exclude the one piece that wants to allow overflow without errors.

You can configure the C# compiler to put everything into a checked context by default, so that only explicitly unchecked expressions and statements will be able to overflow silently. In Visual Studio, you can configure this by opening the project properties, going to the Build tab, and clicking the Advanced button. Or you can edit the *.csproj* file, adding <CheckForOverflowUnderflow>true</CheckForOverflowUnderflow> inside a <PropertyGroup>. Be aware that there's a significant cost—checking can make individual integer operations several times slower. The impact on your application as a whole will be smaller, because programs don't spend their whole time performing arithmetic, but the cost may still be nontrivial. Of course, as with any performance matter, you should measure the practical impact. You may find that the performance cost is an acceptable price to pay for the guarantee that you will find out about unexpected overflows.

BigInteger

There's one last numeric type worth being aware of: `BigInteger`. It's part of the .NET class library and gets no special recognition from the C# compiler so it doesn't strictly belong in this section of the book. However, it defines arithmetic operators and conversions, meaning that you can use it just like the built-in data types. It will compile to slightly less compact code—the compiled format for .NET programs can represent integers and floating-point values natively, but `BigInteger` has to rely on the more general-purpose mechanisms used by ordinary class library types. In theory it is likely to be significantly slower too, although in an awful lot of code, the speed at which you can perform basic arithmetic on small integers is not a limiting factor, so it's quite possible that you won't notice. And as far as the programming model goes, it looks and feels like a normal numeric type in your code.

As the name suggests, a `BigInteger` represents an integer. Its unique selling point is that it will grow as large as is necessary to accommodate values. So unlike the built-in numeric types, it has no theoretical limit on its range. Example 2-39 uses it to calculate values in the Fibonacci sequence, showing every 100,000th value. This quickly produces numbers far too large to fit into any of the other integer types. I've shown the full source of this example, including `using` directives, to illustrate that this type is defined in the `System.Numerics` namespace.

Example 2-39. Using BigInteger

```
using System;
using System.Numerics;

class Program
{
    static void Main(string[] args)
    {
        BigInteger i1 = 1;
        BigInteger i2 = 1;
        Console.WriteLine(i1);
        int count = 0;
        while (true)
        {
            if (count++ % 100000 == 0)
            {
                Console.WriteLine(i2);
            }
            BigInteger next = i1 + i2;
            i1 = i2;
            i2 = next;
        }
    }
}
```

Although `BigInteger` imposes no fixed limit, there are practical limits. You might produce a number that's too big to fit in the available memory, for example. Or more likely, the numbers may grow large enough that the amount of CPU time required to perform even basic arithmetic becomes prohibitive. But until you run out of either memory or patience, `BigInteger` will grow to accommodate numbers as large as you like.

Booleans

C# defines a type called `bool`, or as the runtime calls it, `System.Boolean`. This offers only two values: `true` and `false`. Whereas some C-family languages allow numeric types to stand in for Boolean values, with conventions such as 0 meaning false and anything else meaning true, C# will not accept a number. It demands that values indicating truth or falsehood be represented by a `bool`, and none of the numeric types is convertible to `bool`. For example, in an `if` statement, you cannot write `if (some Number)` to get some code to run only when `someNumber` is nonzero. If that's what you want, you need to say so explicitly by writing `if (someNumber != 0)`.

Strings and Characters

The `string` type (synonymous with the CLR `System.String` type) represents text. A string is a sequence of values of type `char` (or `System.Char`, as the CLR calls it), and each `char` is a 16-bit value representing a single UTF-16 *code unit*.

A common mistake is to think that each `char` represents a character. (The type's name has to share some of the blame for this.) It's often true, but not always. There are two factors to bear in mind: first, something that we might think of as a single character can be made up from multiple Unicode *code points*. (The code point is Unicode's central concept and in English at least, each character is represented by a single code point, but some languages are more complex.) Example 2-40 uses Unicode's 0301 "COMBINING ACUTE ACCENT" to add an accent to a letter to form the text cafés.

Example 2-40. Characters versus char

```
char[] chars = { 'c', 'a', 'f', 'e', (char) 0x301, 's' };
string text = new string(chars);
```

So this string is a sequence of six `char` values, but it represents text that seems to contain just five characters. There are other ways to achieve this—I could have used code point 00E9 "LATIN SMALL LETTER E WITH ACUTE" to represent that accented character as a single code point. But either approach is valid, and there are plenty of scenarios in which the only way to create the exact character required is to use this combining character mechanism. This means that certain operations on the `char` values in a string can have surprising results—if you were to reverse the order of the values, the resulting string would not look like a reversed version of the text—the acute accent would now apply to the s, resulting in śefac! (If I had used 00E9 instead of combining e with 0301, reversing the characters would have resulted in the less surprising séfac.)

Unicode's combining marks notwithstanding, there is a second factor to consider. The Unicode standard defines more code points than can be represented in a single 16-bit value. (We passed that point back in 2001, when Unicode 3.1 defined 94,205 code points.) UTF-16 represents any code point with a value higher than 65,535 as a pair of UTF-16 code units, referred to as a *surrogate pair*. The Unicode standard defines rules for mapping code points to surrogate pairs in a way that the resulting code units have values in the range 0xD800 to 0xDFFF, a reserved range for which no code points will ever be defined. (E.g., code point 10C48, "OLD TURKIC LETTER ORKHON BASH", which looks like ᱈, would become 0xD803, followed by 0xDC48.)

The .NET class library provides a `StringInfo` class that can help you deal with combining characters. .NET Core 3.0 introduces a new type `Rune` in the `System` namespace that provides various helper methods that can simplify working with multicode-unit sequences.

In summary, items that users perceive as single characters might be represented with multiple Unicode code points, and some single code points might be represented as multiple code units. Manipulating the individual `char` values that make up a `string` is therefore a job you should approach with caution.

Immutability of strings

.NET strings are immutable. There are many operations that sound as though they will modify a string, such as concatenation, or the `ToUpper` and `ToLower` methods offered by instances of the `string` type, but each of these generates a new string, leaving the original one unmodified. This means that if you pass strings as arguments, even to code you didn't write, you can be certain that it cannot change your strings.

The downside of immutability is that string processing can be inefficient. If you need to do work that performs a series of modifications to a string, such as building it up character by character, you will end up allocating a lot of memory, because you'll get a separate string for each modification. This creates a lot of extra work for .NET's garbage collector, causing your program to use more CPU time than necessary. In these situations, you can use a type called `StringBuilder`. (This type gets no special recognition from the C# compiler, unlike `string`.) This is conceptually similar to a `string`—it is a sequence of `char` values and offers various useful string manipulation methods—but it is modifiable. Alternatively, in extremely performance-sensitive scenarios, you might use the techniques shown in Chapter 18.

Formatting data in strings

C# provides a syntax that makes it easy to produce strings that contain a mixture of fixed text and information determined at runtime. (The official name for this feature is *string interpolation*.) For example, if you have local variables called name and age, you could use them in a string, as Example 2-41 shows.

Example 2-41. Expressions in strings

```
string message = $"{name} is {age} years old";
```

When you put a $ symbol in front of a string constant, the C# compiler looks for embedded expressions delimited by braces, and produces code that will insert a textual representation of the expression at that point in the string. (So if name and age were Ian and 46, respectively, the string's value would be "Ian is 46 years old".) Embedded expressions can be more complex than just variable names, as Example 2-42 shows.

Example 2-42. More complex expressions in strings

```
double width = 3, height = 4;
string info = $"Hypotenuse: {Math.Sqrt(width * width + height * height)}";
```

Interpolated strings compile into code that uses the string class's Format method (which is how this sort of data formatting was usually done in older versions of C#—string interpolation was introduced in C# 6). Example 2-43 shows code that is roughly equivalent to what the compiler will produce for Examples 2-41 and 2-42.

Example 2-43. The effect of string interpolation

```
string message = string.Format("{0} is {1} years old", name, age);
string info = string.Format(
    "Hypotenuse: {0}",
    Math.Sqrt(width * width + height * height));
```

Why not just use the underlying string.Format mechanism directly? String interpolation is much less error prone—string.Format uses position-based placeholders and it's all too easy to put an expression in the wrong place. It's also tedious for anyone reading the code to try and work out how the numbered placeholders relate to the arguments that follow, particularly as the number of expressions increases. Interpolated strings are usually much easier to read.

With some data types, there are choices to be made about their textual representation. For example, with floating-point numbers, you might want to limit the number of decimal places, or force the use of exponential notation (e.g., `1e6` instead of `1000000`). In .NET, we control this with a *format specifier*, which is a string describing how to convert some data to a string. Some data types have only one reasonable string representation, so they do not support this, but with types that do, you can pass the format specifier as an argument to the `ToString` method. For example, `System.Math.PI.ToString("f4")` formats the PI constant (which is of type `double`) to four decimal places (`"3.1416"`). There are nine built-in formats for numbers, and if none of those suits your requirements, there's also a minilanguage for defining custom formats. Moreover, different types use different format strings—as you'd expect, dates work quite differently from numbers—so the full range of available formats is too large to list here. Microsoft supplies extensive documentation of the details.

When using `string.Format`, you can include a format specifier in the placeholder; e.g., `{0:f3}` indicates that the first expression is to be formatted with three digits after the decimal point. You can include a format specifier in a similar way with string interpolation. Example 2-44 shows the age with one digit after the decimal point.

Example 2-44. Format specifiers

```
string message = $"{name} is {age:f1} years old";
```

There's one wrinkle with this: with many data types, the process of converting to a string is culture-specific. For example, as mentioned earlier, in the US and the UK, decimals are typically written with a period between the whole number part and the fractional part and you might use commas to group digits for readability, but some European countries invert this: they use periods to group digits, while the comma denotes the start of the fractional part. So what might be written as 1,000.2 in one country could be written as 1.000,2 in another.

As far as numeric literals in source code are concerned, this is a nonissue: C# uses underscores for digit grouping and always uses a period as the decimal point. But what about formatting numbers at runtime? By default, you will get conventions determined by the current thread's culture, and unless you've changed that, it will use the regional settings of the computer. Sometimes this is useful—it can mean that numbers, dates, and so on are correctly formatted for whatever locale a program runs in. However, it can be problematic: if your code relies on strings being formatted in a particular way (e.g., to serialize data that will be transmitted over a network), you may need to force a particular set of conventions. For this reason, you can pass the `string.Format` method a *format provider*, an object that controls formatting conventions. Likewise, data types with culture-dependent representations accept an optional format provider argument in their `ToString` methods. But how do you control this when using string interpolation? There's nowhere to put the format provider.

You can solve this by assigning an interpolated string into a variable of type `Formatta bleString` or `IFormattable`,[9] or you can pass it to a method that requires an argument of either of these types. When you do this, the C# compiler generates different code: instead of creating a string directly, it produces an object that enables you to take control of culture-dependent formatting. Example 2-45 illustrates this technique with the same string as Example 2-44.

Example 2-45. Format specifiers with invariant culture

```
string message = FormattableString.Invariant($"{name} is {age:f1} years old");
```

The `FormattableString` type defines two static methods, `Invariant` and `CurrentCul ture`, that each take an argument of type `FormattableString`, so by passing our interpolated string to one of these, we cause the compiler to generate code that wraps the string in a `FormattableString`.

`FormattableString` implements `IFormattable`, and that defines an extra `ToString` method that takes a format provider that it uses to format each of the placeholders in the interpolated string. The `Invariant` method that Example 2-45 uses calls that method, passing in the format provider for the *invariant culture*. This provider (which you can also obtain from the `CultureInfo.InvariantCulture` property) guarantees consistent formatting regardless of the locale in which the code runs. If you call `FormattableString.CurrentCulture`, it formats the string with the thread's current culture instead.

Verbatim string literals

C# supports one more way of expressing a string value: you can prefix a string literal with the @ symbol; e.g., `@"Hello"`. Strings of this form are called *verbatim string literals*. They are useful for two reasons: they can improve the readability of strings containing backslashes and they make it possible to write multiline string literals.

You can use @ in front of an interpolated string. This combines the benefits of verbatim literals—straightforward use of backslashes and newlines—with support for embedded expressions.

---

9 `IFormattable` is an interface. Chapter 3 describes interfaces.

In a normal string literal, the compiler treats a backslash as an escape character, enabling various special values to be included. For example, in the literal "Hello \tworld" the \t denotes a single tab character (code point 9). This is a common way to express control characters in C family languages. You can also use the backslash to include a double quote in a string—the backslash prevents the compiler from interpreting the character as the end of the string. Useful though this is, it makes including a backslash in a string a bit awkward: you have to write two of them. Since Windows uses backslashes in paths, this can get ugly, e.g., "C:\\Windows\\System32\\". A verbatim string literal can be useful here, because it treats backslashes literally, enabling you to write just @"C:\Windows\System32". (You can still include double quotes in a verbatim literal: just write two double quotes in a row: e.g., @"Hello ""world""" produces the string value Hello "World".)

Verbatim string literals also allow values to span multiple lines. With a normal string literal, the compiler will report an error if the closing double quote is not on the same line as the opening one. But with a verbatim string literal, the string can cover as many lines of source as you like.

The resulting string will use whichever line-ending convention your source code uses. Just in case you've not encountered this, one of the unfortunate accidents of computing history is that different systems use different character sequences to denote line endings. The predominant system in internet protocols is to use a pair of control codes for each line end: in either Unicode or ASCII we use code points 13 and 10, denoting a *carriage return* and a *line feed* respectively, often abbreviated to CR LF. This is an archaic hangover from the days before computers had screens, and starting a new line meant moving the teletype's print head back to its start position (carriage return) and then moving the paper up by one line (line feed). Anachronistically, the HTTP specification requires this representation, as do the various popular email standards, SMTP, POP3, and IMAP. It is also the standard convention on Windows. Unfortunately, the Unix operating system does things differently, as do most of its derivatives and lookalikes such as macOS and Linux—the convention on these systems is to use just a single line feed character. The C# compiler accepts either, and will not complain even if a single source file contains a mixture of both conventions. This introduces a potential problem for multiline string literals if you are using a source control system that converts line endings for you. For example, *git* is a very popular source control system, and thanks to its origins (it was created by Linus Torvalds, who also created Linux) there is a widespread convention of using Unix-style line endings in its repositories. However, on Windows it can be configured to convert working copies of files to a CR LF representation, automatically converting them back to LF when committing changes. This means that files will appear to use different line ending conventions depending on whether you're looking at them on a Windows system or a Unix one. (And it might even vary from one Windows system to another, because the default line handling ending is configurable. Individual users can configure the machine-wide default setting and can also set the configuration for their local clone of any repository if the repository does not specify the setting itself.) This in turn means compiling a file containing a multiline verbatim string literal on a Windows system could produce subtly different behavior than you'd see with the exact same file on a Unix system, if automatic line end conversion is enabled (which it is by default on most Windows installations of git). That might be fine—you typically want CR LF when running on Windows and LF on Unix—but it could cause surprises if you deploy code to a machine running a different OS than the one you built it on. So it's important to provide a .gitattributes file in your repositories so that they can specify the required behavior, instead of relying on changeable local settings. If you need to rely on a particular line ending in a string literal, it's best to make your .gitattributes disable line end conversions.

Tuples

C# 7.0 introduced a new language feature: support for *tuples*. These let you combine multiple values into a single value. The name tuple (which C# shares with many other programming languages that provide a similar feature) is meant to be a generalized version of words like double, triple, quadruple, and so on, but we generally call them tuples even in cases where we don't need the generality—e.g., even if we're talking about a tuple with two items in it, we still call it a tuple, not a double. Example 2-46 creates a tuple containing two int values and then displays them.

Example 2-46. Creating and using a tuple

```
(int X, int Y) point = (10, 5);
Console.WriteLine($"X: {point.X}, Y: {point.Y}");
```

That first line is a variable declaration with an initializer. It's worth breaking this down, because the syntax for tuples makes for a slightly more complex-looking declaration than we've seen so far. Remember, the general pattern for statements of this form is:

```
type identifier = initial-value;
```

That means that in Example 2-46, the type is (int X, int Y). So we're saying that our variable, point, is a tuple containing two values, both of type int, and we want to refer to those as X and Y. The initializer here is (10, 5). So when we run the example, it produces this output:

```
X: 10, Y: 5
```

If you're a fan of var, you'll be pleased to know that you can specify the names in the initializer using the syntax shown in Example 2-47, enabling you to use var instead of the explicit type. This is equivalent to Example 2-46.

Example 2-47. Naming tuple members in the initializer

```
var point = (X: 10, Y: 5);
Console.WriteLine($"X: {point.X}, Y: {point.Y}");
```

If you initialize a tuple from existing variables and you do not specify names, the compiler will presume that you want to use the names of those variables, as Example 2-48 shows.

Example 2-48. Inferring tuple member names from variables

```
int x = 10, y = 5;
var point = (x, y);
Console.WriteLine($"X: {point.x}, Y: {point.y}");
```

This raises a stylistic question: should tuple member names start with lowercase or uppercase letters? The members are similar in nature to properties, which we'll be discussing in Chapter 3, and conventionally those start with an uppercase letter. For this reason, many people believe that tuple member names should also be uppercase. To a seasoned .NET developer, that point.x in Example 2-48 just looks weird. However, another .NET convention is that local variables usually start with a lowercase name. If you stick to both of these conventions, tuple name inference doesn't look very useful. Many developers choose to accept lowercase tuple member names for tuples used purely in local variables, because it enables the use of the convenient name inference feature, using Pascal casing only for tuples that are exposed outside of a method.

Arguably it doesn't matter much, because tuple member names turn out to exist only in the eye of the beholder. Firstly, they're optional. As Example 2-49 shows, it's perfectly legal to omit them. The names just default to Item1, Item2, etc.

Example 2-49. Default tuple member names

```
(int, int) point = (10, 5);
Console.WriteLine($"X: {point.Item1}, Y: {point.Item2}");
```

Secondly, the names are purely for the convenience of the code using the tuples and are not visible to the runtime. You'll have noticed that I've used the same initializer expression, (10, 5), as I did in Example 2-46. Because it doesn't specify names, the expression's type is (int, int) which matches the type in Example 2-49, but I was also able to assign it straight into an (int X, int Y) in Example 2-46. That's because the names are essentially irrelevant—these are all the same thing under the covers. (As we'll see in Chapter 4, at runtime these are all represented as instances of a type called ValueTuple<int, int>.) The C# compiler keeps track of the names we've chosen to use, but as far as the CLR is concerned, all these tuples just have members called `Item1` and `Item2`. An upshot of this is that we can assign any tuple into any variable with the same shape, as Example 2-50 shows.

Example 2-50. Structural equivalence of tuples

```
(int X, int Y) point = (46, 3);
(int Width, int Height) dimensions = point;
(int Age, int NumberOfChildren) person = point;
```

This flexibility is a double-edged sword. The assignments in Example 2-50 seem rather sketchy. It might conceivably be OK to assign something that represents a location into something that represents a size—there are some situations in which that would be valid. But to assign that same value into something apparently representing someone's age and the number of children they have looks likely to be wrong. The compiler won't stop us though, because it considers all tuples comprising a pair of `int` values to have the same type. (It's not really any different from the fact that the compiler won't stop you assigning an `int` variable named `age` into an `int` variable named `height`. They're both of type `int`.)

If you want to enforce a semantic distinction, you would be better off defining custom types as described in Chapter 3. Tuples are really designed as a convenient way to package together a few values in cases where defining a whole new type wouldn't really be justified.

Of course, C# does require tuples to have an appropriate shape. You cannot assign an `(int, int)` into a `(int, string)`, nor into an `(int, int, int)`. However, all of the implicit conversions in "Numeric conversions" on page 63 work, so you can assign anything with an `(int, int)` shape into an `(int, double)`, or a `(double, long)`. So a tuple is really just like having a handful of variables neatly contained inside another variable.

Tuples support comparison, so you can use the `==` and `!=` relational operators described later in this chapter. To be considered equal, two tuples must have the same shape and each value in the first tuple must be equal to its counterpart in the second tuple.

Deconstruction

Sometimes you will want to split a tuple back into its component parts. Obviously you can just access each item in turn by its name (or as `Item1`, `Item2`, etc., if you didn't specify names), but C# provides another mechanism, called *deconstruction*. Example 2-51 declares and initializes two tuples and then shows two different ways to deconstruct them.

Example 2-51. Constructing then deconstructing tuples

```
(int X, int Y) point1 = (40, 6);
(int X, int Y) point2 = (12, 34);

(int x, int y) = point1;
Console.WriteLine($"1: {x}, {y}");
(x, y) = point2;
Console.WriteLine($"2: {x}, {y}");
```

Having defined `point1` and `point2`, this deconstructs `point1` into two variables, x and y. This particular form of deconstruction also declares the variables into which the tuple is being deconstructed. The alternative form is shown when we deconstruct `point2`—here, we're deconstructing it into two variables that already exist, so there's no need to declare them.

Until you become accustomed to this syntax, the first deconstruction example can seem confusingly similar to the first couple of lines, in which we declare and initialize new tuples. In those first couple of lines, the `(int X, int Y)` text signifies a tuple type with two `int` values named X and Y, but in the deconstruction line when we write `(int x, int y)` we're actually declaring two variables, each of type `int`. The only significant difference is that in the lines where we're constructing new tuples, there's a variable name before the = sign. (Also, we're using uppercase names there, but that's just a matter of convention. It would be entirely legal to write `(int x, int y) point3 = point1;`. That would declare a new tuple with two `int` values named x and y, stored in a variable named `point3`, initialized with the same values as are in `point1`. Equally, we could write `(int X, int Y) = point1;`. That would deconstruct `point` into two local variables called X and Y.)

Dynamic

C# defines a type called `dynamic`. This doesn't directly correspond to any CLR type—when we use `dynamic` in C#, the compiler presents it to the runtime as `object`, which is described in the next section. However, from the perspective of C# code, `dynamic` is a distinct type and it enables some special behavior.

With `dynamic`, the compiler makes no attempt at compile time to check whether operations performed by code are likely to succeed. In other words, it effectively disables the statically typed behavior that we normally get with C#. You are free to attempt almost any operation on a `dynamic` variable—you can use arithmetic operators, you can attempt to invoke methods on it, you can try to assign it into variables of some other type, and you can try to get or set properties on it. When you do this, the compiler generates code that attempts to make sense of what you've asked it to do at runtime.

If you have come to C# from a language in which this sort of behavior is the norm (e.g., JavaScript), you might be tempted to use `dynamic` for everything because it works in a way you are used to. However, you should be aware that there are a couple of issues with it. First, it was designed with a particular scenario in mind: interoperability with certain pre-.NET Windows components. The Component Object Model (COM) in Windows is the basis for automatability of the Microsoft Office Suite, and many other applications, and the scripting language built into Office is dynamic in nature. An upshot of this is that a lot of Office's automation APIs used to be hard work to use from C#. One of the big drivers behind adding `dynamic` to the language was a desire to improve this. As with all C# features, it was designed with broader applicability in mind and not simply as an Office interop feature. But since that was the most important scenario for this feature, you may find that its ability to support idioms you are familiar with from dynamic languages is disappointing. And the second issue to be aware of is that it is not an area of the language that is getting a lot of new work. When it was introduced, Microsoft went to considerable lengths to ensure that all dynamic behavior was as consistent as possible with the behavior you would have seen if the compiler had known at compile time what types you were going to be using. This means that the infrastructure supporting `dynamic` (which is called the Dynamic Language Runtime, or DLR) has to replicate significant portions of C# behavior. However, the DLR has not been updated much since `dynamic` was added in C# 4.0 back in 2010, even though the language has seen many new features since then. Of course, `dynamic` still works, but its capabilities represent how the language looked around a decade ago.

Even when it first appeared, it had some limitations. There are some aspects of C# that depend on the availability of static type information, meaning that `dynamic` has always had some problems working with delegates and also with LINQ. So even from the start, it was at something of a disadvantage compared to using C# as intended, i.e., as a statically typed language.

Object

The last data type to get special recognition from the C# compiler is `object` (or `System.Object`, as the CLR calls it). This is the base class of almost[10] all C# types. A variable of type `object` is able to refer to a value of any type that derives from `object`. This includes all numeric types, the `bool` and `string` types, and any custom types you can define using the keywords we'll look at in the next chapter, such as `class` and `struct`. And it also includes all the types defined by the .NET class library, with the exception of certain types that can only be stored on the stack, and which are described in Chapter 18.

---

10 There are some specialized exceptions, such as pointer types.

So `object` is the ultimate general-purpose container. You can refer to almost anything with an `object` variable. We will return to this in Chapter 6 when we look at inheritance.

Operators

Earlier you saw that expressions are sequences of operators and operands. I've shown some of the types that can be used as operands, so now it's time to see what operators C# offers. Table 2-3 shows the operators that support common arithmetic operations.

Table 2-3. Basic arithmetic operators

Name	Example
Unary plus (does nothing)	+x
Negation (unary minus)	-x
Postincrement	x++
Postdecrement	x--
Preincrement	++x
Predecrement	--x
Addition	x + y
Subtraction	x - y
Multiplication	x * y
Division	x / y
Remainder	x % y

If you're familiar with any other C-family language, all of these should seem familiar. If you are not, the most peculiar ones will probably be the increment and decrement operators. These have side effects: they add or subtract one from the variable to which they are applied (meaning they can be applied only to variables). With the postincrement and postdecrement, although the variable gets modified, the containing expression ends up getting the original value. So if x is a variable containing the value 5, the value of x++ is also 5, even though the x variable will have a value of 6 after evaluating the x++ expression. The pre- forms evaluate to the modified value, so if x is initially 5, ++x evaluates to 6, which is also the value of x after evaluating the expression.

Although the operators in Table 2-3 are used in arithmetic, some are available on certain nonnumeric types. As you saw earlier, the + symbol represents concatenation when working with strings, and as you'll see in Chapter 9, the addition and subtraction operators are also used for combining and removing delegates.

C# also offers some operators that perform certain binary operations on the bits that make up a value, shown in Table 2-4. These are not available on floating-point types.

Table 2-4. Binary integer operators

Name	Example
Bitwise negation	~x
Bitwise AND	x & y
Bitwise OR	x | y
Bitwise XOR	x ^ y
Shift left	x << y
Shift right	x >> y

The bitwise negation operator inverts all bits in an integer—any binary digit with a value of 1 becomes 0, and vice versa. The shift operators move all the binary digits left or right by the number of columns specified by the second operand. A left shift sets the bottom digits to 0. Right shifts of unsigned integers fill the top digits with 0, and right shifts of signed integers leave the top digit as it is (i.e., negative numbers remain negative because they keep their top bit set, while positive numbers keep their top bit as 0, thus remaining positive).

The bitwise AND, OR, and XOR (exclusive OR) operators perform Boolean logic operations on each bit of the two operands when applied to integers. These three operators are also available when the operands are of type `bool`. (In effect, these operators treat a `bool` as a one-digit binary number.) There are some additional operators available for `bool` values, shown in Table 2-5. The ! operator does to a `bool` what the ~ operator does to each bit in an integer.

Table 2-5. Operators for bool

Name	Example
Logical negation (also known as NOT)	!x
Conditional AND	x && y
Conditional OR	x || y

If you have not used other C-family languages, the conditional versions of the AND and OR operators may be new to you. These evaluate their second operand only if necessary. For example, when evaluating (a && b), if the expression a is false, the code generated by the compiler will not even attempt to evaluate b, because the result will be false no matter what value b has. Conversely, the conditional OR operator does not bother to evaluate its second operand if the first is true, because the result will be true regardless of the second operand's value. This is significant if the second operand's expression either has side effects (e.g., it includes a method invocation) or might produce an error. For example, you often see code like that shown in Example 2-52.

Example 2-52. The conditional AND operator

```
if (s != null && s.Length > 10)
...
```

This checks to see if the variable s contains the special value null, meaning that it doesn't currently refer to any value. The use of the && operator here is important, because if s is null, evaluating the expression s.Length would cause a runtime error. If we had used the & operator, the compiler would have generated code that always evaluates both operands, meaning that we would see a NullReferenceException at runtime if s is null; however, by using the conditional AND operator, we avoid that, because the second operand, s.Length > 10, will be evaluated only if s is not null.

 Although code of the kind shown in Example 2-52 was once common, it has gradually become much rarer thanks to a feature introduced back in C# 6.0, *null-conditional operators*. If you write s?.Length instead of just s.Length, the compiler generates code that checks s for null first, avoiding the NullReferenceException. This means the check can become just if (s?.Length > 10). Furthermore, C# 8.0 introduces a new feature in which you can indicate that certain values should never be null, which can help reduce the need for these kinds of tests for null. This is discussed in Chapter 3.

Example 2-52 tests to see if a property is greater than 10 by using the > operator. This is one of several *relational operators*, which allow us to compare values. They all take two operands and produce a bool result. Table 2-6 shows these, and they are supported for all numeric types. Some operators are available on some other types too. For example, you can compare string values with the == and != operators. (There is no built-in meaning for the other relational operators with string because different countries have different ideas about the order in which to sort strings. If you want ordered string comparison, .NET offers the StringComparer class, which requires you to select the rules by which you'd like your strings ordered.)

Table 2-6. Relational operators

Name	Example
Less than	x < y
Greater than	x > y
Less than or equal	x <= y
Greater than or equal	x >= y
Equal	x == y
Not equal	x != y

As is usual with C-family languages, the equality operator is a pair of equals signs. This is because a single equals sign means something else: it's an assignment, and assignments are expressions too. This can lead to an unfortunate problem: in some C-family languages it's all too easy to write if (x = y) when you meant if (x == y). Fortunately, this will usually produce a compiler error in C#, because C# has a special type to represent Boolean values. In languages that allow numbers to stand in for Booleans, both pieces of code are legal even if x and y are numbers. (The first means to assign the value of y into x, and then to execute the body of the if statement if that value is nonzero. That's very different than the second one, which doesn't change the value of anything, and executes the body of the if statement only if x and y are equal.) But in C#, the first example would be meaningful only if x and y were both of type bool.[11]

Another feature that's common to the C family is the conditional operator. (This is sometimes also called the ternary operator, because it's the only operator in the language that takes three operands.) It chooses between two expressions. More precisely, it evaluates its first operand, which must be a Boolean expression, and then returns the value of either the second or third operand, depending on whether the value of the first was true or false, respectively. Example 2-53 uses this to pick the larger of two values. (This is just for illustration. In practice, you'd normally use .NET's Math.Max method, which has the same effect but is rather more readable. Math.Max also has the benefit that if you use expressions with side effects, it will only evaluate each one once, something you can't do with the approach shown in Example 2-53, because we've ended up writing each expression twice.)

Example 2-53. The conditional operator

```
int max = (x > y) ? x : y;
```

---

11 Language pedants will note that it will also be meaningful in certain situations where custom implicit conversions to bool are available. We'll be getting to custom conversions in Chapter 3.

This illustrates why C and its successors have a reputation for terse syntax. If you are familiar with any language from this family, Example 2-53 will be easy to read, but if you're not, its meaning might not be instantly clear. This will evaluate the expression before the ? symbol, which is (x > y) in this case, and that's required to be an expression that produces a bool. (The parentheses are optional. I put them in to make the code easier to read.) If that is true, the expression between the ? and : symbols is used (x, in this case); otherwise, the expression after the : symbol (y here) is used.

The conditional operator is similar to the conditional AND and OR operators in that it will evaluate only the operands it has to. It always evaluates its first operand, but it will never evaluate both the second and third operands. That means you can handle null values by writing something like Example 2-54. This does not risk causing a NullReferenceException, because it will evaluate the third operand only if s is not null.

Example 2-54. Exploiting conditional evaluation

```
int characterCount = s == null ? 0 : s.Length;
```

However, in some cases, there are simpler ways of dealing with null values. Suppose you have a string variable, and if it's null, you'd like to use the empty string instead. You could write (s == null ? "" : s). But you could just use the *null coalescing* operator instead, because it's designed for precisely this job. This operator, shown in Example 2-55 (it's the ?? symbol), evaluates its first operand, and if that's non-null, that's the result of the expression. If the first operand is null, it evaluates its second operand and uses that instead.

Example 2-55. The null coalescing operator

```
string neverNull = s ?? "";
```

We could combine a null-conditional operator with the null coalescing operator to provide a more succinct alternative to Example 2-54, shown in Example 2-56.

Example 2-56. Null-conditional and null coalescing operators

```
int characterCount = s?.Length ?? 0;
```

One of the main benefits offered by the conditional, null-conditional, and null coalescing operators is that they often allow you to write a single expression in cases where you would otherwise have needed to write considerably more code. This can be particularly useful if you're using the expression as an argument to a method, as in Example 2-57.

Example 2-57. Conditional expression as method argument

```
FadeVolume(gateOpen ? MaxVolume : 0.0, FadeDuration, FadeCurve.Linear);
```

Compare this with what you'd need to write if the conditional operator did not exist. You would need an `if` statement. (I'll get to `if` statements in the next section, but since this book is not for novices, I'm assuming you're familiar with the rough idea.) And you'd either need to introduce a local variable, as Example 2-58 does, or you'd need to duplicate the method call in the two branches of the `if`/`else`, changing just the first argument. So, terse though the conditional and null coalescing operators are, they can remove a lot of clutter from your code.

Example 2-58. Life without the conditional operator

```
double targetVolume;
if (gateOpen)
{
    targetVolume = MaxVolume;
}
else
{
    targetVolume = 0.0;
}
FadeVolume(targetVolume, FadeDuration, FadeCurve.Linear);
```

There is one last set of operators to look at: the *compound assignment* operators. These combine assignment with some other operation and are available for the +, -, *, /, %, <<, >>, &, ^, |, and ?? operators. They enable you not to have to write the sort of code shown in Example 2-59.

Example 2-59. Assignment and addition

```
x = x + 1;
```

We can write this assignment statement more compactly as the code in Example 2-60. All the compound assignment operators take this form—you just stick an = on the end of the original operator.

Example 2-60. Compound assignment (addition)

```
x += 1;
```

This is a distinctive syntax that makes it very clear that we are modifying the value of a variable in some particular way. So, although those two snippets perform identical work, many developers find the second idiomatically preferable.

That's not quite a comprehensive list of operators. There are a few more specialized ones that I'll get to once we've looked at the areas of the language for which they were defined. (Some relate to classes and other types, some to inheritance, some to collections, and some to delegates. There are chapters coming up on all of these.) By the way, although I've been describing which operators are available on which types (e.g., numeric versus Boolean), it's possible to write a custom type that defines its own meanings for most of these. That's how .NET's `BigInteger` type can support the same arithmetic operations as the built-in numeric types. I'll show how this can be done in Chapter 3.

Flow Control

Most of the code we have examined so far executes statements in the order they are written and stops when it reaches the end. If that were the only possible way in which execution could flow through our code, C# would not be very useful. So, as you'd expect, it has a variety of constructs for writing loops and for deciding which code to execute based on inputs.

Boolean Decisions with if Statements

An `if` statement decides whether or not to run some particular statement depending on the value of a `bool` expression. For example, the `if` statement in Example 2-61 will execute the block statement that shows a message only if the `age` variable's value is less than 18.

Example 2-61. Simple if statement

```
if (age < 18)
{
    Console.WriteLine("You are too young to buy alcohol in a bar in the UK.");
}
```

You don't have to use a block statement with an `if` statement. You can use any statement type as the body. A block is necessary only if you want the `if` statement to govern the execution of multiple statements. However, some coding style guidelines recommend using a block in all cases. This is partly for consistency, but also because it avoids a possible error when modifying the code at a later date: if you have a nonblock statement as the body of an `if`, and then you add another statement after that, intending it to be part of the same body, it can be easy to forget to add a block around the two statements, leading to code like that in Example 2-62. The indentation suggests that the developer meant for the final statement to be part of the `if` statement's body, but C# ignores indentation, so that final statement will always run. If you are in the habit of always using a block, you won't make this mistake.

Example 2-62. Probably not what was intended

```
if (launchCodesCorrect)
    TurnOnMissileLaunchedIndicator();
    LaunchMissiles();
```

An if statement can optionally include an else part, which is followed by another statement that runs only if the if statement's expression evaluates to false. So Example 2-63 will write either the first or the second message, depending on whether the optimistic variable is true or false.

Example 2-63. If and else

```
if (optimistic)
{
    Console.WriteLine("Glass half full");
}
else
{
    Console.WriteLine("Glass half empty");
}
```

The else keyword can be followed by any statement, and again, this is typically a block. However, there's one scenario in which most developers do not use a block for the body of the else part, and that's when they use another if statement. Example 2-64 shows this—its first if statement has an else part, which has another if statement as its body.

Example 2-64. Picking one of several possibilities

```
if (temperatureInCelsius < 52)
{
    Console.WriteLine("Too cold");
}
else if (temperatureInCelsius > 58)
{
    Console.WriteLine("Too hot");
}
else
{
    Console.WriteLine("Just right");
}
```

This code still looks like it uses a block for that first else, but that block is actually the statement that forms the body of a second if statement. It's that second if statement that is the body of the else. If we were to stick rigidly to the rule of giving each if and else body its own block, we'd rewrite Example 2-64 as Example 2-65. This seems unnecessarily fussy, because the main risk that we're trying to avert by using blocks doesn't really apply in Example 2-64.

Example 2-65. Overdoing the blocks

```
if (temperatureInCelsius < 52)
{
    Console.WriteLine("Too cold");
}
else
{
    if (temperatureInCelsius > 58)
    {
        Console.WriteLine("Too hot");
    }
    else
    {
        Console.WriteLine("Just right");
    }
}
```

Although we can chain if statements together as shown in Example 2-64, C# offers a more specialized statement that can sometimes be easier to read.

Multiple Choice with switch Statements

A switch statement defines multiple groups of statements and either runs one group or does nothing at all, depending on the value of an input expression. As Example 2-66 shows, you put the expression inside parentheses after the switch keyword, and after that, there's a region delimited by braces containing a series of case sections, defining the behavior for each anticipated value for the expression.

Example 2-66. A switch statement with strings

```
switch (workStatus)
{
case "ManagerInRoom":
    WorkDiligently();
    break;

case "HaveNonUrgentDeadline":
case "HaveImminentDeadline":
    CheckTwitter();
    CheckEmail();
    CheckTwitter();
    ContemplateGettingOnWithSomeWork();
    CheckTwitter();
    CheckTwitter();
```

```
    break;

case "DeadlineOvershot":
    WorkFuriously();
    break;

default:
    CheckTwitter();
    CheckEmail();
    break;
}
```

As you can see, a single section can serve multiple possibilities—you can put several different case labels at the start of a section, and the statements in that section will run if any of those cases apply. You can also write a default section, which will run if none of the cases apply. By the way, you're not required to provide a default section. A switch statement does not have to be comprehensive, so if there is no case that matches the expression's value and there is no default section, the switch statement simply does nothing.

Unlike if statements, which take exactly one statement for the body, a case may be followed by multiple statements without needing to wrap them in a block. The sections in Example 2-66 are delimited by break statements, which causes execution to jump to the end of the switch statement. This is not the only way to finish a section —strictly speaking, the rule imposed by the C# compiler is that the end point of the statement list for each case must not be reachable, so anything that causes execution to leave the switch statement is acceptable. You could use a return statement instead, or throw an exception, or you could even use a goto statement.

Some C-family languages (C, for example) allow *fall-through*, meaning that if execution is allowed to reach the end of the statements in a case section, it will continue with the next one. Example 2-67 shows this style, and it is not allowed in C# because of the rule that requires the end of a case statement list not to be reachable.

Example 2-67. C-style fall-through, illegal in C#

```
switch (x)
{
case "One":
    Console.WriteLine("One");
case "Two":  // This line will not compile
    Console.WriteLine("One or two");
    break;
}
```

C# outlaws this, because the vast majority of case sections do not fall through, and when they do in languages that allow it, it's often a mistake caused by the developer forgetting to write a `break` statement (or some other statement to break out of the `switch`). Accidental fall-through is likely to produce unwanted behavior, so C# requires more than the mere omission of a `break`: if you want fall-through, you must ask for it explicitly. As Example 2-68 shows, we use the unloved `goto` keyword to express that we really do want one case to fall through into the next one.

Example 2-68. Fall-through in C#

```
switch (x)
{
case "One":
    Console.WriteLine("One");
    goto case "Two";
case "Two":
    Console.WriteLine("One or two");
    break;
}
```

This is not technically a `goto` statement. It is a `goto case` statement, and can be used only to jump within a `switch` block. C# does also support more general `goto` statements—you can add labels to your code and jump around within your methods. However, `goto` is heavily frowned upon, so the fall-through form offered by `goto case` statements seems to be the only use for this keyword that is considered respectable in modern society.

These examples have all used strings. You can also use `switch` with integer types, `char`, and any `enum` (a kind of type discussed in the next chapter). For many years, these were the only possibilities, because `case` labels had to be constants. But C# 7 augmented `switch` statements to support patterns in `case` labels. Patterns are discussed later in this chapter.

Loops: while and do

C# supports the usual C-family loop mechanisms. Example 2-69 shows a `while` loop. This takes a `bool` expression. It evaluates that expression, and if the result is `true`, it will execute the statement that follows. So far, this is just like an `if` statement, but the difference is that once the loop's embedded statement is complete, it then evaluates the expression again, and if it's `true` again, it will execute the embedded statement a second time. It will keep doing this until the expression evaluates to `false`. As with `if` statements, the body of the loop does not need to be a block, but it usually is.

Example 2-69. A while loop

```
while (!reader.EndOfStream)
{
    Console.WriteLine(reader.ReadLine());
}
```

The body of the loop may decide to finish the loop early with a `break` statement. It does not matter whether the `while` expression is `true` or `false`—executing a `break` statement will always terminate the loop.

C# also offers the `continue` statement. Like a `break` statement, this terminates the current iteration, but unlike `break`, it will then reevaluate the `while` expression, so iteration may continue. Both `continue` and `break` jump straight to the end of the loop, but you could think of `continue` as jumping directly to the point just before the loop's closing }, while `break` jumps to the point just after. By the way, `continue` and `break` are also available for all of the other loop styles I'm about to show.

Because a `while` statement evaluates its expression before each iteration, it's possible for a `while` loop not to run its body at all. Sometimes, you may want to write a loop that runs at least once, only evaluating the `bool` expression after the first iteration. This is the purpose of a do loop, as shown in Example 2-70.

Example 2-70. A do loop

```
char k;
do
{
    Console.WriteLine("Press x to exit");
    k = Console.ReadKey().KeyChar;
}
while (k != 'x');
```

Notice that Example 2-70 ends in a semicolon, denoting the end of the statement. Compare this with the line containing the `while` keyword in Example 2-69, which does not, despite otherwise looking very similar. That may look inconsistent, but it's not a typo. Putting a semicolon at the end of the line with the `while` keyword in Example 2-69 would be legal, but it would change the meaning—it would indicate that we want the body of the `while` loop to be an empty statement. The block that followed would then be treated as a brand-new statement to execute after the loop completes. The code would get stuck in an infinite loop unless the reader were already at the end of the stream. (The compiler will issue a warning about a "Possible mistaken empty statement" if you do that, by the way.)

C-Style for Loops

Another style of loop that C# inherits from C is the for loop. This is similar to while, but it adds two features to that loop's bool expression: it provides a place to declare and/or initialize one or more variables that will remain in scope for as long as the loop runs, and it provides a place to perform some operation each time around the loop (in addition to the statement that forms the body of the loop). So the structure of a for loop looks like this:

```
for (initializer; condition; iterator) body
```

A very common application of this is to do something to all the elements in an array. Example 2-71 shows a for loop that multiplies every element in an array by 2. The condition part works in exactly the same way as in a while loop—it determines whether the embedded statement forming the loop's body runs, and it will be evaluated before each iteration. Again, the body doesn't strictly have to be a block, but usually is.

Example 2-71. Modifying array elements with a for loop

```
for (int i = 0; i < myArray.Length; i++)
{
    myArray[i] *= 2;
}
```

The initializer in this example declares a variable called i and initializes it to 0. This initialization happens just once, of course—this wouldn't be very useful if it reset the variable to 0 every time around the loop, because the loop would never end. This variable's lifetime effectively begins just before the loop starts and finishes when the loop finishes. The initializer does not need to be a variable declaration—you can use any expression statement.

The iterator in Example 2-71 just adds 1 to the loop counter. It runs at the end of each loop iteration, after the body runs, and before the condition is reevaluated. (So if the condition is initially false, not only does the body not run, the iterator will never be evaluated.) C# does nothing with the result of the iterator expression—it is useful only for its side effects. So it doesn't matter whether you write i++, ++i, i += 1, or even i = i + 1.

A for loop doesn't let you do anything that you couldn't have achieved by writing a while loop and putting the initialization code before the loop and the iterator at the end of the loop body instead.[12] However, there may be readability benefits. A `for` statement puts the code that defines how we loop in one place, separate from the code that defines what we do each time around the loop, which might help those reading the code to understand what it does. They don't have to scan down to the end of a long loop to find the iterator statement (although a long loop body that trails over pages of code is generally considered to be bad practice, so this last benefit is a little dubious).

Both the initializer and the iterator can contain lists, as Example 2-72 shows, although in this particular case it isn't terribly useful—since all the iterators run every time around, `i` and `j` will have the same value as each other throughout.

Example 2-72. Multiple initializers and iterators

```
for (int i = 0, j = 0; i < myArray.Length; i++, j++)
...
```

You can't write a single `for` loop that performs a multidimensional iteration. If you want that, you would nest one loop inside another, as Example 2-73 illustrates.

Example 2-73. Nested for loops

```
for (int j = 0; j < height; ++j)
{
    for (int i = 0; i < width; ++i)
    {
        ...
    }
}
```

Although Example 2-71 shows a common enough idiom for iterating through arrays, you will often use a different, more specialized construct.

Collection Iteration with foreach Loops

C# offers a style of loop that is not universal in C-family languages. The `foreach` loop is designed for iterating through collections. A `foreach` loop fits this pattern:

```
foreach (item-type iteration-variable in collection) body
```

The *collection* is an expression whose type must match a particular pattern recognized by the compiler. The .NET class library's `IEnumerable<T>` interface, which we'll

---

12 A `continue` statement complicates matters, because it provides a way to move to the next iteration without getting all the way to the end of the loop body. Even so, you could still reproduce the effect of the iterator when using `continue` statements—it would just require more work.

be looking at in Chapter 5, matches this pattern, although the compiler doesn't actually require an implementation of that interface—it just requires the collection to have a `GetEnumerator` method that resembles the one defined by that interface. Example 2-74 uses `foreach` to show all the strings in an array. (All arrays provide the method that `foreach` requires.)

Example 2-74. Iterating over a collection with foreach

```
string[] messages = GetMessagesFromSomewhere();
foreach (string message in messages)
{
    Console.WriteLine(message);
}
```

This loop will run the body once for each item in the array. The *iteration variable* (`message`, in this example) is different each time around the loop and will refer to the item for the current iteration.

In one way, this is less flexible than the `for`-based loop shown in Example 2-71: a `foreach` loop cannot modify the collection it iterates over. That's because not all collections support modification. `IEnumerable<T>` demands very little of its collections —it does not require modifiability, random access, or even the ability to know up front how many items the collection provides. (In fact, `IEnumerable<T>` is able to support never-ending collections. For example, it is perfectly legal to write an implementation that will return random numbers for as long as you care to keep fetching values.)

But `foreach` offers two advantages over `for`. One advantage is subjective and therefore debatable: it's a bit more readable. But significantly, it's also more general. If you're writing methods that do things to collections, those methods will be more broadly applicable if they use `foreach` rather than `for`, because you'll be able to accept an `IEnumerable<T>`. Example 2-75 can work with any collection that contains strings, rather than being limited to arrays.

Example 2-75. General-purpose collection iteration

```
public static void ShowMessages(IEnumerable<string> messages)
{
    foreach (string message in messages)
    {
        Console.WriteLine(message);
    }
}
```

This code can work with collection types that do not support random access, such as the `LinkedList<T>` class described in Chapter 5. It can also process lazy collections that decide what items to produce on demand, including those produced by iterator functions, also shown in Chapter 5, and by certain LINQ queries, as described in Chapter 10.

Patterns

There's one last essential mechanism to look at in C#: *patterns*. A pattern describes one or more criteria that a value can be tested against. You've already seen some simple patterns in action: each `case` in a `switch` specifies a pattern. But as we'll now see, there are many kinds of patterns, and they aren't just for `switch` statements.

 Most of the pattern functionality was added to C# relatively recently. Support first appeared in C# 7.0, and most of the pattern types now available were added in C# 8.0.

The `switch` examples earlier, such as Example 2-66, all used one of the simplest pattern types: the *constant pattern*. With this pattern, you specify just a constant value, and an expression matches this pattern if it has that value. In a similar vein, Example 2-76 shows *tuple patterns*, which match tuples with specific values. These are conceptually very similar to constant patterns—the values for the individual tuple elements are all constants here. (The distinction between constant patterns and tuple patterns is largely a matter of history: before patterns were introduced, `case` labels only supported the limited set of types for which the CLR offers intrinsic support for constant values, and that list does not include tuples.)

Example 2-76. Tuple patterns

```
switch (p)
{
case (0, 0):
    Console.WriteLine("How original");
    break;

case (0, 1):
case (1, 0):
    Console.WriteLine("What an absolute unit");
    break;

case (1, 1):
    Console.WriteLine("Be there and be square");
    break;
}
```

Example 2-77 shows a more interesting kind of pattern: it uses *type patterns*. An expression matches a type pattern if it has the specified type. As you saw earlier in "Object" on page 80, some variables are capable of holding a variety of different types. Variables of type `object` are an extreme case of this, since they can hold more or less anything. Language features such as *interfaces* (discussed in Chapter 3), generics (Chapter 4), and inheritance (Chapter 6) can lead to scenarios where the static type of a variable provides more information than the anything-goes `object` type, but with some latitude for a range of possible types at runtime. Type patterns can be useful in these cases.

Example 2-77. Type patterns

```
switch (o)
{
case string s:
    Console.WriteLine($"A piece of string is {s.Length} long");
    break;

case int i:
    Console.WriteLine($"That's numberwang! {i}");
    break;
}
```

Type patterns have an interesting characteristic that constant ones do not: as well as the Boolean match/no-match common to all patterns, a type pattern produces an additional output. Each `case` in Example 2-77 introduces a variable, which the code for that `case` then goes on to use. This output is just the input, but copied into a variable with the specified static type. So that first `case` will match if o turns out to be a `string`, in which case we can access it through the s variable (which is why that `s.Length` expression compiles correctly; `o.Length` would not if o is of type `object`).

 Sometimes, you won't actually need a type pattern's output—it might be enough just to know that the input matched a pattern. In these cases you can use a *discard*: if you put an underscore (_) in the place where the output variable name would normally go, that tells the C# compiler that you are only interested in whether the value matches the type.

Some patterns do a little more work to produce their output. For example, Example 2-78 shows a *positional pattern* that matches any tuple containing a pair of `int` values and extracts those values into two variables, x and y.

Example 2-78. Positional pattern

```
case (int x, int y):
    Console.WriteLine($"I know where it's at: {x}, {y}");
    break;
```

Positional patterns are an example of a *recursive pattern*: they are patterns that contain patterns. In this case, this positional pattern contains a type pattern as each of its children. But we can mix things up, because positional patterns can contain any pattern type (including another recursive pattern, if that's what you need). In fact, that's exactly what was going on in Example 2-76—a tuple pattern is really just a special case of a positional pattern, where the children are all constant patterns. Example 2-79 shows a positional pattern with a constant pattern in the first position and a type pattern in the second.

Example 2-79. Positional pattern with constant and type patterns

```
case (0, int y):
    Console.WriteLine($"This is on the X axis, at height {y}");
    break;
```

If you are a fan of var you might be wondering if you can write something like Example 2-80. This will work, and the static types of the x and y variables here will depend on the type of the pattern's input expression. If the compiler can determine how the expression deconstructs (e.g., if the switch statement input's static type is an (int, int) tuple), then it will use this information to determine the output variables' static types. In cases where this is unknown, but it's still conceivable that this pattern could match (e.g., the input is object), then x and y here will also have type object.

Example 2-80. Positional pattern with var

```
case (var x, var y):
    Console.WriteLine($"I know where it's at: {x}, {y}");
    break;
```

 The compiler will reject patterns in cases where it can determine that a match is impossible. For example, if it knows the input type is a (string, int, bool) tuple, it cannot possibly match a positional pattern with only two child patterns, so C# won't let you try.

Example 2-80 shows an unusual case where using var instead of an explicit type can introduce a significant change of behavior. These *var patterns* differ in one important respect from the *type patterns* in Example 2-78: a *var pattern* always matches its input, whereas a *type pattern* inspects its input's type to determine at runtime whether it matches. This check might be optimized away in practice—there are cases where a type pattern will always match because its input type is known at compile time. But the only way to express in your code that you definitely don't want the child patterns in a positional pattern to perform a runtime check is to use var. So although a positional pattern containing type patterns strongly resembles the deconstruction syntax shown in Example 2-51, the behavior is quite different. Example 2-78 is in effect performing three runtime tests: is the value a 2-tuple, is the first value an int, and is the second value an int? (So it would work for tuples with a static type of (object, object), as long as each value is an int at runtime.) This shouldn't really be surprising: the point of patterns is to test at runtime whether a value has certain characteristics. However, with some recursive patterns you may find yourself wanting to express a mixture of runtime matching (e.g., is this thing a string?) combined with statically typed deconstruction (e.g., if this is a string, I'd like to extract its Length property which I believe to be of type int, and I want a compiler error if that belief turns out to be wrong). Patterns are not designed to do this, so it's best not to try to use them that way.

What if we don't need to use all of the items in the tuple? You already know one way to handle that. Since we can use any pattern in each position, we could use a type pattern with a discard in, say, the second position: (int x, int _). However, Example 2-81 shows a shorter alternative: instead of a discarding type pattern, we can use just a lone underscore. This is a *discard pattern*. You can use it in a recursive pattern any place a pattern is required, but where you want to indicate that anything will do in that particular position, and that you don't need to know what it was.

Example 2-81. Positional pattern with discard pattern

```
case (int x, _):
    Console.WriteLine($"At X: {x}. As for Y, who knows?");
    break;
```

This has subtly different semantics though: a type pattern with a discard will check at runtime that the value to be discarded has the specified type, and the pattern will only match if this check succeeds. But a discard pattern always matches, so this would match (10, 20), (10, "Foo"), and (10, (20, 30)), for example.

Positional patterns are not the only recursive ones: you can also write a *property pattern*. We'll look at properties in detail in the next chapter, but for now it's enough to know that they are members of a type that provide some sort of information, such as the string type's Length property, which provides an int telling you how many code units the string contains. Example 2-82 shows a *property pattern* that inspects this Length property.

Example 2-82. Property pattern

```
case string { Length: 0 }:
    Console.WriteLine("How long is a piece of string? Not very!");
    break;
```

This property pattern starts with a type name, so it effectively incorporates the behavior of a type pattern in addition to its property-based tests. (You can omit this in cases where the type of the pattern's input is sufficiently specific to identify the property. E.g., if the input in this case already had a static of type `string`, we could omit this.) This is then followed by a section in braces listing each of the properties that the pattern wants to inspect and the pattern to apply for that property. (These child patterns are what make this another recursive pattern.) So this example first checks to see if the input is a `string`. If it is, it then applies a constant pattern to the string's `Length`, so this pattern matches only if the input is a `string` with `Length` of 0.

Property patterns can optionally specify an output. Example 2-82 doesn't do this. Example 2-83 shows the syntax, although in this particular case it's not terribly useful because this pattern will ensure that s only ever refers to an empty string.

Example 2-83. Property pattern with output

```
case string { Length: 0 } s:
    Console.WriteLine($"How long is a piece of string? This long: {s.Length}");
    break;
```

Since each property in a property pattern contains a nested pattern, those too can produce outputs, as Example 2-84 shows.

Example 2-84. Property pattern with nested pattern with output

```
case string { Length: int length }:
    Console.WriteLine($"How long is a piece of string? This long: {length}");
    break;
```

Getting More Specific with when

Sometimes, the built-in pattern types won't provide the level of precision you need. For example, with positional patterns, we've seen how to write patterns that match, say, any pair of values, or any pair of numbers, or a pair of numbers where one has a particular value. But what if you want to match a pair of numbers where the first is higher than the second? This isn't a big conceptual leap, but there's no built-in support for this. We could detect the condition with an `if` statement of course, but it would seem a shame to have to restructure our code from a `switch` to a series of `if` and `else` statements just to make this small step forward. Fortunately we don't have to.

Any pattern in a `case` label can be qualified by adding a `when` clause. It allows a boolean expression to be included. This will be evaluated if the value matches the main part of the pattern, and the value will match the pattern as a whole only if the `when` clause is true. Example 2-85 shows a positional pattern with a `when` clause that matches pairs of numbers in which the first number is larger than the second.

Example 2-85. Pattern with when clause

```
case (int w, int h) when w > h:
    Console.WriteLine("Landscape");
    break;
```

Patterns in Expressions

All of the patterns I've shown so far appear in `case` labels as part of a `switch` statement. This is not the only way to use patterns. They can also appear inside expressions. To see how this can be useful, look first at the `switch` statement in Example 2-86. The intent here is to return a single value determined by the input, but it's a little clumsy: I've had to write four separate `return` statements to express that.

Example 2-86. Patterns, but not in expressions

```
switch (shape)
{
    case (int w, int h) when w < h: return "Portrait";
    case (int w, int h) when w > h: return "Landscape";
    case (int _, int _): return "Square";
    default: return "Unknown";
}
```

Example 2-87 shows code that performs the same job, but rewritten to use a *switch expression*. As with a `switch` statement, a `switch` expression contains a list of patterns. The difference is that whereas labels in a `switch` statement are followed by a list of statements, in a `switch` expression each pattern is followed by a single expression. The value of a `switch` expression is the result of evaluating the expression associated with the first pattern that matches.

Example 2-87. A switch expression

```
return shape switch
{
    (int w, int h) when w < h => "Portrait",
    (int w, int h) when w > h => "Landscape",
```

```
    (int _, int _) => "Square",
    _ => "Unknown"
};
```

`switch` expressions look quite different than `switch` statements, because they don't use the `case` keyword. Instead, they just dive straight in with the pattern, and then use => between the pattern and its corresponding expression. There are a few reasons for this. First, it makes `switch` expressions a bit more compact. Expressions are generally used inside other things—in this case, the `switch` expression is the value of a `return` statement, but you might also use these as a method argument or anywhere else an expression is allowed—so we generally want them to be succinct. Secondly, using `case` here could have led to confusion because the rules for what follows each `case` would be different for `switch` statements and `switch` expressions: in a `switch` statement each `case` label is followed by one or more statements, but in a `switch` expression each pattern needs to be followed by a single expression. Finally, although `switch` expressions were only added to version 8.0 of C#, this sort of construct has been around in other languages for many years. C#'s version of it more closely resembles equivalents from other languages than it would have done if the expression form used the `case` keyword.

Notice that the final pattern in Example 2-87 is a discard pattern. This will match anything, and it's there to ensure that the pattern is exhaustive; i.e., that it covers all possible cases. (It has a similar effect to a `default` section in a `switch` statement.) Unlike a `switch` statement, where it's OK for there to be no matches, a `switch` expression has to produce a result, so the compiler will warn you if your patterns don't handle all possible cases for the input type. It would complain in this situation if we were to remove that final case, assuming the `shape` input is of type `object`. (Conversely, if `shape` were of type `(int, int)` we would have to remove that final case, because the first three cases in fact cover all possible values for that type and the compiler will produce an error telling us that the final pattern will never apply.) If you ignore this warning, and then at runtime you evaluate a `switch` expression with an unmatchable value, it will throw a `SwitchExpressionException`. Exceptions are described in Chapter 8.

There's one more way to use a pattern in an expression, and that's with the `is` keyword. It turns any pattern into a boolean expression. Example 2-88 shows a simple example that determines whether a value is a tuple containing two integers.

Example 2-88. An is expression

```
bool isPoint = value is (int x, int y);
```

As with patterns in switch statements or expressions, the pattern in an is expression can extract values from its source. Example 2-89 uses the same expression as the preceding example, but goes on to use the two values from the tuple.

Example 2-89. Using the values from an is expression's pattern

```
if (value is (int x, int y))
{
    Console.WriteLine($"X: {x}, Y: {y}");
}
```

New variables introduced in this way by an is expression remain in scope after their containing statement. So in both these examples, x and y would continue to be in scope until the end of the containing block. Since the pattern in Example 2-89 is in the if statement's condition expression, that means these variables remain in scope after the body block. However, if you try to use them outside of the body you'll find that the compiler's definite assignment rules will tell you that they are uninitialized. It allows Example 2-89 because it knows that the body of the if statement will run only if the pattern matches, so in that case x and y will have been initialized and are safe to use.

Patterns in is expressions cannot include a when clause. It would be redundant: the result is a boolean expression, so you can just add on any qualification you require using the normal boolean operators, as Example 2-90 shows.

Example 2-90. No need for when in an is expression's pattern

```
if (value is (int w, int h) && w < h)
{
    Console.WriteLine($"(Portrait) Width: {w}, Height: {h}");
}
```

Summary

In this chapter, I showed the nuts and bolts of C# code—variables, statements, expressions, basic data types, operators, flow control, and patterns. Now it's time to take a look at the broader structure of a program. All code in C# programs must belong to a type, and types are the topic of the next chapter.

CHAPTER 3

Types

C# does not limit us to the built-in data types shown in Chapter 2. You can define your own types. In fact, you have no choice: if you want to write code at all, C# requires you to define a type to contain that code. Everything we write, and any functionality we consume from the .NET class library (or any other .NET library), will belong to a type.

C# recognizes multiple kinds of types. I'll begin with the most important.

Classes

Most of the types you work with in C# will be *classes*. A class can contain both code and data, and it can choose to make some of its features publicly available, while keeping others accessible only to code within the class. So classes offer a mechanism for *encapsulation*—they can define a clear public programming interface for other people to use, while keeping internal implementation details inaccessible.

If you're familiar with object-oriented languages, this will all seem very ordinary. If you're not, then you might want to read a more introductory-level book first, because this book is not meant to teach programming. I'll just describe the details specific to C# classes.

I've already shown examples of classes in earlier chapters, but let's look at the structure in more detail. Example 3-1 shows a simple class. (See the sidebar "Naming Conventions" on page 107 for information about names for types and their members.)

Example 3-1. A simple class

```
public class Counter
{
    private int _count;
```

```
    public int GetNextValue()
    {
        _count += 1;
        return _count;
    }
}
```

Class definitions always contain the `class` keyword followed by the name of the class. C# does not require the name to match the containing file, nor does it limit you to having one class in a file. That said, most C# projects make the class and filenames match by convention. In any case, class names must follow the basic rules described in Chapter 2 for identifiers such as variables; e.g., they cannot start with a number.

The first line of Example 3-1 contains an additional keyword: `public`. Class definitions can optionally specify *accessibility*, which determines what other code is allowed to use the class. Ordinary classes have just two choices here: `public` and `internal`, with the latter being the default. (As I'll show later, you can nest classes inside other types, and nested classes have a slightly wider range of accessibility options.) An internal class is available for use only within the component that defines it. So if you are writing a class library, you are free to define classes that exist purely as part of your library's implementation: by marking them as `internal`, you prevent the rest of the world from using them.

You can choose to make your internal types visible to selected external components. Microsoft sometimes does this with its libraries. The .NET class library is spread across numerous DLLs, each of which defines many internal types, but some internal features are used by other DLLs in the library. This is made possible by annotating a component with the `[assembly: InternalsVisibleTo("name")]` attribute, specifying the name of the component with which you wish to share. (Chapter 14 describes this in more detail.) For example, you might want to make every class in your application visible to a project so that you can write unit tests for code that you don't intend to make publicly available.

The `Counter` class in Example 3-1 has chosen to be `public`, but that doesn't mean it has to make everything accessible. It defines two members—a field called `_count` that holds an `int`, and a method called `GetNextValue` that operates on the information in that field. (The CLR will automatically initialize this field to 0 when a `Counter` is created.) As you can see, both of these members have accessibility qualifiers too. As is very common with object-oriented programming, this class has chosen to make the data member private, exposing public functionality through a method.

Accessibility modifiers are optional for members, just as they are for classes, and again, they default to the most restrictive option available: `private`, in this case. So I could have left off the `private` keyword in Example 3-1 without changing the meaning, but I prefer to be explicit. (If you leave it unspecified, people reading your code may wonder whether the omission was deliberate or accidental.)

Naming Conventions

Microsoft defines a set of conventions for publicly visible identifiers, which it (mostly) conforms to in its class libraries, and I usually follow them in my examples. Microsoft provides a free analyzer, FxCop, which can help enforce these conventions. You can enable this for any project by adding a reference to the `Microsoft.CodeAnal ysis.FxCopAnalyzers` NuGet package. If you just want to read a description of the rules, they're part of the design guidelines for .NET class libraries at *https://docs.micro soft.com/dotnet/standard/design-guidelines/index*.

In these conventions, the first letter of a class name is capitalized, and if the name contains multiple words, each new word also starts with a capital letter. (For historical reasons, this convention is called *Pascal casing*, or sometimes *PascalCasing* as a self-referential example.) Although it's legal in C# for identifiers to contain underscores, the conventions don't allow them in class names. Methods also use Pascal casing, as do properties. Fields are rarely public, but when they are, they use the same casing.

Method parameters use a different convention known as *camelCasing*, in which uppercase letters are used at the start of all but the first word. The name refers to the way this convention produces one or more humps in the middle of the word.

The class library design guidelines remain silent regarding implementation details. (The original purpose of these rules, and the FxCop tool, was to ensure a consistent feel across the whole public API of the .NET Framework class library. The "Fx" is short for *Framework*.) So these rules say nothing about how private fields are named. I've used an underscore prefix in Example 3-1 because I like fields to look different from local variables. This makes it easy to see what sort of data my code is working with, and it can also help to avoid situations where method parameter names clash with field names. (Microsoft uses this same convention for instance fields in .NET Core, along with `s_` and `t_` prefixes for static and thread-local fields.) Some people find this convention ugly and prefer not to distinguish fields visibly, but might choose always to access members through the `this` reference (described later) so that the distinction between variable and field access is still clear.

Fields hold data. They are a kind of variable, but unlike a local variable, whose scope and lifetime is determined by its containing method, a field is tied to its containing type. Example 3-1 is able to refer to the `_count` field by its unqualified name because fields are in scope within their defining class. But what about the lifetime? We know that each invocation of a method gets its own set of local variables. How many sets of a class's fields are there? There are a couple of possibilities, depending on how you define the field, but in this case, it's one per instance. Example 3-2 uses the Counter class from Example 3-1 to illustrate this. I've written this code in a separate class, to demonstrate that we can use the Counter class's public method from other classes.

Example 3-2. Using a custom class

```
class Program
{
    static void Main(string[] args)
    {
        var c1 = new Counter();
        var c2 = new Counter();
        Console.WriteLine("c1: " + c1.GetNextValue());
        Console.WriteLine("c1: " + c1.GetNextValue());
        Console.WriteLine("c1: " + c1.GetNextValue());

        Console.WriteLine("c2: " + c2.GetNextValue());

        Console.WriteLine("c1: " + c1.GetNextValue());
    }
}
```

This uses the new operator to create new instances of my class. Since I use new twice, I get two Counter objects, and each has its own _count field. So we get two independent counts, as the program's output shows:

```
c1: 1
c1: 2
c1: 3
c2: 1
c1: 4
```

As you'd expect, it begins counting up, and then a new sequence starts at 1 when we switch to the second counter. But when we go back to the first counter, it carries on from where it left off. This demonstrates that each instance has its own _count. But what if we don't want that? Sometimes you will want to keep track of information that doesn't relate to any single object.

Static Members

The static keyword lets us declare that a member is not associated with any particular instance of the class. Example 3-3 shows a modified version of the Counter class from Example 3-1. I've added two new members, both static, for tracking and reporting counts across all instances.

Example 3-3. Class with static members

```
public class Counter
{
    private int _count;
    private static int _totalCount;

    public int GetNextValue()
    {
        _count += 1;
        _totalCount += 1;
        return _count;
    }

    public static int TotalCount => _totalCount;
}
```

TotalCount reports the count, but it doesn't do any work—it just returns a value that the class keeps up to date, and as I'll explain in "Properties" on page 165, this makes it an ideal candidate for being a property rather than a method. The static field _total Count keeps track of the total number of calls to GetNextValue, unlike the nonstatic _count, which just tracks calls to the current instance. Notice that I'm free to use that static field inside GetNextValue in exactly the same way as I use the nonstatic _count. The difference in behavior is clear if I add the line of code shown in Example 3-4 to the end of the Main method in Example 3-2.

Example 3-4. Using a static property

```
Console.WriteLine(Counter.TotalCount);
```

This line displays 5, the sum of the two counts. To access a static member, I just write *ClassName.MemberName*. In fact, Example 3-4 uses two static members—as well as my class's TotalCount property, it uses the Console class's static WriteLine method.

Because I've declared TotalCount as a static property, the code it contains has access only to other static members. If it tried to use the nonstatic _count field or call the nonstatic GetNextValue method, the compiler would complain. Replacing _total Count with _count in the TotalCount property results in this error:

```
error CS0120: An object reference is required for the non-static field, method,
    or property Counter._count'
```

Since nonstatic fields are associated with a particular instance of a class, C# needs to know which instance to use. With a nonstatic method or property, that'll be whichever instance the method or property itself was invoked on. So in Example 3-2, I wrote either c1.GetNextValue() or c2.GetNextValue() to choose which of my two objects to use. C# passed the reference stored in either c1 or c2, respectively, as an implicit hidden first argument. You can get hold of that reference from code inside a class by using the `this` keyword. Example 3-5 shows an alternative way we could have written the first line of `GetNextValue` from Example 3-3, indicating explicitly that we believe `_count` is a member of the instance on which the `GetNextValue` method was invoked.

Example 3-5. The this keyword

```
this._count += 1;
```

Explicit member access through `this` is sometimes necessary due to name collisions. Although all the members of a class are in scope for any code in the same class, the code in a method does not share a *declaration space* with the class. Remember from Chapter 2 that a declaration space is a region of code in which a single name must not refer to two different entities, and since methods do not share theirs with the containing class, you are allowed to declare local variables and method parameters that have the same name as class members. This can easily happen if you don't use a convention such as an underscore prefix for field names. You don't get an error in this case—locals and parameters just hide the class members. But you can still get at the class members by qualifying access with `this`.

Static methods don't get to use the `this` keyword, because they are not associated with any particular instance.

Static Classes

Some classes only provide static members. There are several examples in the `System.Threading` namespace, which provides various classes that offer multithreading utilities. For example, the `Interlocked` class provides atomic, lock-free, read-modify-write operations; the `LazyInitializer` class provides helper methods for performing deferred initialization in a way that guarantees to avoid double initialization in multi-threaded environments. These classes provide services only through static methods. It makes no sense to create instances of these types, because there's no useful per-instance information they could hold.

You can declare that your class is intended to be used this way by putting the `static` keyword in front of the `class` keyword. This compiles the class in a way that prevents instances of it from being constructed. Anyone attempting to construct instances of a class designed to be used this way clearly doesn't understand what it does, so the compiler error will be a useful prod in the direction of the documentation.

You can declare that you want to be able to invoke static methods on certain classes without naming the class every time. This can be useful if you are writing code that makes heavy use of the static methods supplied by a particular type. (This isn't limited to static classes by the way. You can use this technique with any class that has static members, but it is likely to be most useful with classes whose members are all static.) Example 3-6 uses a static method (Sin) and a static property (PI) of the Math class (in the System namespace). It also uses the Console class's static WriteLine method. (I'm showing the entire source file in this and the next example because the using directives are particularly important.)

Example 3-6. Using static members normally

```
using System;

class Program
{
    static void Main(string[] args)
    {
        Console.WriteLine(Math.Sin(Math.PI / 4));
    }
}
```

Example 3-7 is exactly equivalent, but it does not qualify any of the three static members with their defining class's name.

Example 3-7. Using static members without explicit qualification

```
using static System.Console;
using static System.Math;

class Program
{
    static void Main(string[] args)
    {
        WriteLine(Sin(PI / 4));
    }
}
```

To utilize this less verbose alternative, you must declare which classes you want to use in this way with using static directives. Whereas using directives normally specify a namespace, enabling types in that namespace to be used without qualification, using static directives specify a class, enabling its static members to be used without qualification.

Reference Types

Any type defined with the class keyword will be a *reference type*, meaning that a variable of that type will not contain the data that makes up an instance of the type; instead, it can contain a *reference* to an instance of the type. Consequently, assignments don't copy the object, they just copy the reference. Example 3-8 contains almost the same code as Example 3-2, except instead of using the new keyword to initialize the c2 variable, it initializes it with a copy of c1.

Example 3-8. Copying references

```
Counter c1 = new Counter();
var c2 = c1;
Console.WriteLine("c1: " + c1.GetNextValue());
Console.WriteLine("c1: " + c1.GetNextValue());
Console.WriteLine("c1: " + c1.GetNextValue());

Console.WriteLine("c2: " + c2.GetNextValue());

Console.WriteLine("c1: " + c1.GetNextValue());
```

Because this example uses new just once, there is only one Counter instance, and the two variables both refer to this same instance. So we get different output:

```
c1: 1
c1: 2
c1: 3
c2: 4
c1: 5
```

It's not just locals that do this—if you use a reference type for any other kind of variable, such as a field or property, assignment works the same way, copying the reference and not the whole object. This is the defining characteristic of a reference type, and it is different from the behavior we saw with the built-in numeric types in Chapter 2. With those, each variable contains a value, not a reference to a value, so assignment necessarily involves copying the value. (This value copying behavior is not available for most reference types—see the next sidebar, "Copying Instances".)

Copying Instances

Some C-family languages define a standard way to make a copy of an object. For example, in C++ you can write a copy constructor, and you can overload the assignment operator; the language has rules for how these are applied when duplicating an object. In C#, some types can be copied, and it's not just the built-in numeric types. Later in this chapter you'll see how to define a *struct*, which is a custom value type. Structs can always be copied, and there is no way to customize this process: assignment just copies all the fields, and if any fields are of reference type, this just copies the reference. This is sometimes called a "shallow" copy, because it copies only the contents of the struct; it does not make copies of any of the things the struct refers to.

There is no intrinsic mechanism for making a copy of a class instance. The .NET class library defines ICloneable, an interface for duplicating objects, but this is not very widely supported. It's a problematic API, because it doesn't specify how to handle

---

objects with references to other objects. Should a clone also duplicate the objects to which it refers (a deep copy) or just copy the references (a shallow copy)? In practice, types that wish to allow themselves to be copied often just provide an ad hoc method for the job, rather than conforming to any pattern.

We can write code that detects whether two references refer to the same thing. Example 3-9 arranges for three variables to refer to two counters with the same count, and then compares their identities. By default, the == operator does exactly this sort of object identity comparison when its operands are reference types. However, types are allowed to redefine the == operator. The string type changes == to perform value comparisons, so if you pass two distinct string objects as the operands of ==, the result will be true if they contain identical text. If you want to force comparison of object identity, you can use the static object.ReferenceEquals method.

Example 3-9. Comparing references

```
var c1 = new Counter();
c1.GetNextValue();
Counter c2 = c1;
var c3 = new Counter();
c3.GetNextValue();

Console.WriteLine(c1.Count);
Console.WriteLine(c2.Count);
Console.WriteLine(c3.Count);
Console.WriteLine(c1 == c2);
Console.WriteLine(c1 == c3);
Console.WriteLine(c2 == c3);
Console.WriteLine(object.ReferenceEquals(c1, c2));
Console.WriteLine(object.ReferenceEquals(c1, c3));
Console.WriteLine(object.ReferenceEquals(c2, c3));
```

The first three lines of output confirm that all three variables refer to counters with the same count:

```
1
1
1
True
False
False
True
False
False
```

It also illustrates that while they all have the same count, only c1 and c2 are considered to be the same thing. That's because we assigned c1 into c2, meaning that c1 and c2 will both refer to the same object, which is why the first comparison succeeds. But c3 refers to a different object entirely (even though it happens to have the same value), which is why the second comparison fails. (I've used both the == and object.ReferenceEquals comparisons here to illustrate that they do the same thing in this case, because Counter has not defined a custom meaning for ==.)

We could try the same thing with int instead of a Counter, as Example 3-10 shows. (This initializes the variables in a slightly idiosyncratic way in order to resemble Example 3-9 as closely as possible.)

Example 3-10. Comparing values

```
int c1 = new int();
c1++;
int c2 = c1;
int c3 = new int();
c3++;

Console.WriteLine(c1);
Console.WriteLine(c2);
Console.WriteLine(c3);
Console.WriteLine(c1 == c2);
Console.WriteLine(c1 == c3);
Console.WriteLine(c2 == c3);
Console.WriteLine(object.ReferenceEquals(c1, c2));
Console.WriteLine(object.ReferenceEquals(c1, c3));
Console.WriteLine(object.ReferenceEquals(c2, c3));
Console.WriteLine(object.ReferenceEquals(c1, c1));
```

As before, we can see that all three variables have the same value:

```
1
1
1
True
True
True
False
False
False
False
```

This also illustrates that the int type does define a special meaning for ==. With int, this operator compares the values, so those three comparisons succeed. But object.ReferenceEquals never succeeds for value types—in fact, I've added an extra, fourth comparison here, where I compare c1 with itself, and even that fails! That surprising result occurs because it's not meaningful to perform a reference comparison with int—it's not a reference type. The compiler has to perform implicit conversions from int to object for the last four lines of Example 3-10: it has wrapped each argument to object.ReferenceEquals in something called a *box*, which we'll be looking at in Chapter 7. Each argument gets a distinct box, which is why even the final comparison fails.

There's another difference between reference types and types like int. By default, any reference type variable can contain a special value, null, meaning that the variable does not refer to any object at all. You cannot assign this value into any of the built-in numeric types (although see the next sidebar, "Nullable<T>").

Nullable<T>

.NET defines a wrapper type called Nullable<T>, which adds nullability to value types. Although an int variable cannot hold null, a Nullable<int> can. The angle brackets after the type name indicate that this is a generic type—you can plug various different types into that T placeholder—and I'll talk about those more in Chapter 4.

The compiler provides special handling for Nullable<T>. It lets you use a more compact syntax, so you can write int? instead. When nullable numerics appear inside arithmetic expressions, the compiler treats them differently than normal values. For example, if you write a + b, where a and b are both int?, the result is an int? that will be null if either operand was null, and will otherwise contain the sum of the values. This also works if only one of the operands is an int? and the other is an ordinary int.

While you can set an int? to null, it's not a reference type. It's more like a combination of an int and a bool. (Although, as I'll describe in Chapter 7, the CLR performs some tricks with Nullable<T> that sometimes makes it look more like a reference type than a value type.)

If you use the null-conditional operators described in Chapter 2 (.? and ?[*index*]) to access members with a value type, the resulting expression will be of the nullable version of that type. For example, if str is a variable of type string, the expression str.?Length has type Nullable<int> (or if you prefer, int?) because Length is of type int, but the use of a null-conditional operator means the expression could evaluate to null.

Banishing null with non-nullable references

The widespread availability of null references in programming languages dates back to 1965, when computer scientist Tony Hoare added them to the highly influential ALGOL language. He has since apologized for this invention, which he described as "my billion-dollar mistake." The possibility that a reference type variable might contain null makes it hard to know whether it's safe to attempt to perform an action with that variable. (C# programs will throw a NullReferenceException if you attempt this, which will typically crash your program. Chapter 8 discusses exceptions.) Some modern programming languages avoid the practice of allowing references to be nullable by default, offering instead some system for optional values through an explicit opt-in mechanism in the type system. In fact, as you've seen with `Nullable<T>` this is already the case for built-in numeric types (and also, as we'll see, any custom value types that you define), but until recently, nullability has not been optional for all reference type variables.

C# 8.0 introduces a significant new feature to the language that extends the type system to make a distinction between references that may be null, and ones that must not be. The feature's name is *nullable references*, which seems odd, because references have always been able to contain `null` since C# 1.0. However, the feature's name refers to the fact that in sections of code that enable this feature, nullability becomes an opt-in feature: a reference will never contain null unless it is explicitly defined as a nullable reference. At least, that's the theory.

 Enabling the type system to distinguish between nullable and non-nullable references was always going to be a tricky thing to retrofit to a language almost two decades into its life. So the reality is that C# cannot always guarantee that a non-nullable reference will never contain a `null`. However, it can make the guarantee if certain constraints hold, and more generally it will significantly reduce the chances of encountering a `NullReferenceException` even in cases where it cannot absolutely rule this out.

Making non-nullability the default is a radical change, so this feature is switched off unless you enable it explicitly. And since switching it on can have a dramatic impact on existing code, it is possible to control the feature at a fine-grained level.

C# provides two dimensions of control, which it calls the *nullable annotation context* and the *nullable warning context*. Each line of code in a C# program is associated with one of each kind of context. The default is that all your code is in a *disabled* nullable annotation context and a *disabled* nullable warning context. You can change these defaults at a project level. You can also use the `#nullable` directive to change the nullable annotation context at a more fine-grained level—a different one every line if you want—and you can control the nullable warning context at an equally precise level with a `#pragma warning` directive. So how do these two contexts work?

The nullable annotation context determines whether we get to declare the nullability of a particular use of a reference type (e.g., a field, variable, or argument). In a disabled annotation context (the default) we cannot express this, and all references are implicitly nullable. The official categorization describes these as *oblivious* to nullability, distinguishing them from references you have deliberately annotated as being nullable. However, in an enabled annotation context, we get to choose. Example 3-11 shows how.

Example 3-11. Specifying nullability

```
string cannotBeNull = "Text";
string? mayBeNull = null;
```

This should look familiar because it mirrors the syntax for nullability of built-in numeric types and custom value types. If you just write the type name, that denotes something non-nullable. If you want it to be nullable, you append a ?.

The most important point to notice here is that in an enabled nullable annotation context, the old syntax gets the new behavior, and if you want the old behavior, you need to use the new syntax. This means that if you take existing code originally written without any awareness of nullability, and you put it into an enabled annotation context, *all* reference type variables are now effectively annotated as being non-nullable, the opposite of how the compiler treated the exact same code before.

The most direct way to put code into an enabled nullable annotation context is with a `#nullable enable` directive. You can put this at the top of a source file to enable it for the whole file, or you can use it more locally, followed by a `#nullable restore` to put back the project-wide default. On its own this will produce no visible change. The compiler won't act on these annotations if the nullable warning context is disabled, and it is disabled by default. You can enable it locally with `#pragma warning enable nullable` (and `#pragma warning restore nullable` reverts to the project-wide default). You can control the project-wide defaults in the *.csproj* file by adding a `<Nullable>` property. Example 3-12 sets the defaults to an enabled nullable warning context and a disabled nullable annotation context.

Example 3-12. Specifying an enabled nullable warning context as the project-wide default

```
<PropertyGroup>
  <Nullable>warnings</Nullable>
</PropertyGroup>
```

This means that any files that do not explicitly opt into an enabled nullable annotation context will be in a disabled nullable annotation context, but that all code will be in an enabled nullable warning context unless it explicitly opts out. Other project-wide settings are `disable` (the default), `enable` (uses enabled warning and annotation contexts), and `annotations` (enables annotations, but not warnings).

If you've specified an enabled annotation context at the project level, you can use `#nullable disable` to opt out in individual files. Likewise, if you've specified either form of enabled warning context at the project level, you can opt out with `#pragma warning disable nullable`.

We have all this fine-grained control to make it easier to enable non-nullability for existing code. If you just fully enable the feature for an entire project in one step, you're likely to encounter a lot of warnings. In practice, it may make more sense to put all code in the project in an enabled warning context, but not to enable annotations anywhere to begin with. Since all of your references will be deemed *oblivious* to nullability checking, you won't yet see any warnings. You can then start to move code into an enabled annotation context one file at a time (or in even smaller chunks if you prefer), making any necessary changes.

Over time, the goal would be to get all the code to the point where you can fully enable non-nullable support at the project level.

What does the compiler do for us in code where we've fully enabled non-nullability support? We get two main things. First, the compiler uses rules similar to the definite assignment rules to ensure that we don't attempt to dereference a method without first checking to see whether it's null. Example 3-13 shows some cases the compiler will accept, and some that would cause warnings in an enabled nullable warning context, assuming that `mayBeNull` was declared in an enabled nullable annotation context as being nullable.

Example 3-13. Dereferencing a nullable reference

```
if (mayBeNull != null)
{
    // Allowed because we can only get here if mayBeNull is not null
    Console.WriteLine(mayBeNull.Length);
}

// Allowed because it checks for null and handles it
Console.WriteLine(mayBeNull?.Length ?? 0);

// The compiler will warn about this in an enabled nullable warning context
Console.WriteLine(mayBeNull.Length);
```

Second, in addition to checking whether dereferencing (use of . to access a member) is safe, the compiler will also warn you when you've attempted to assign a reference that might be null into something that requires a non-nullable reference, or if you pass one as an argument to a method when the corresponding parameter is declared as non-nullable.

Sometimes, you'll run into a roadblock on the path to moving all your code into fully enabled nullability contexts. Perhaps you depend on some component that is unlikely to be upgraded with nullability annotations in the foreseeable future, or perhaps there's a scenario in which C#'s conservative safety rules incorrectly decide that some code is not safe. What can you do in these cases? You wouldn't want to disable warnings for the entire project, and it would be irritating to have to leave the code peppered with #pragma directives. There is an alternative: you can tell the C# compiler that you know something it doesn't. If you have a reference that the compiler presumes could be null (perhaps because it came from a component that does not support non-nullability) but which you have good reason to believe will never be null, you can tell the compiler this by using the *null forgiving operator*, which you can see near the end of the second line of Example 3-14. It is sometimes known informally as the *dammit operator*, because being an exclamation mark makes it look like a slightly exasperated kind of assertion.

Example 3-14. The null forgiving operator

```
string? referenceFromLegacyComponent = legacy.GetReferenceWeKnowWontBeNull();
string nonNullableReferenceFromLegacyComponent = referenceFromLegacyComponent!;
```

You can use the null forgiving operator in any enabled nullable annotation context. It has the effect of converting a nullable reference to a non-nullable reference. You can then go on to dereference that non-nullable reference or otherwise use it in places where a nullable reference would not be allowed without causing any compiler warnings.

 The null forgiving operator does not check its input. If you apply this in a scenario where the value turns out to be null at runtime, it will not detect this. Instead, you will get a runtime error at the point where you try to use the reference.

While the null forgiving operator can be useful at the boundary between nullable-aware code and old code that you don't control, there's another way to let the compiler know when an apparently nullable expression will not in fact be null: nullable attributes. .NET defines several attributes that you can use to annotate code to describe when it will or won't return null values. Consider the code in Example 3-15. If you do not enable the nullable reference type features, this works fine, but if you turn them on, you will get a warning. (This uses a dictionary, a collection type that is described in detail in Chapter 5.)

Example 3-15. Nullability and the Try pattern—before nullable reference types

```
public static string Get(IDictionary<int, string> d)
{
    if (d.TryGetValue(42, out string s))
    {
        return s;
    }
}
```

```
        return "Not found";
}
```

With nullability warnings enabled, the compiler will complain at the `out string s`. It will tell you, correctly, that `TryGetValue` might pass a `null` through that `out` argument. (This kind of argument is discussed later; it provides a way to return additional values besides the function's main return value.) This function checks whether the dictionary contains an entry with the specified key. If it does, it will return `true`, and put the relevant value into the `out` argument, but if not, it returns `false`, and sets that `out` argument to the `null`. We can modify our code to reflect this fact by putting a `?` after the `out string`. Example 3-16 shows this modification.

Example 3-16. Nullable-aware use of the Try pattern

```
public static string Get(IDictionary<int, string> d)
{
    if (d.TryGetValue(42, out string? s))
    {
        return s;
    }

    return "Not found";
}
```

You might expect this to cause a new problem. Our `Get` method returns a `string`, not a `string?`, so how can that `return s` be correct? We just modified our code to indicate that `s` might be `null`, so won't the compiler complain when we try to return this possibly `null` value from a method that declares that it won't return `null`? But in fact this compiles. The compiler accepts this because it knows that `TryGetValue` will only set that `out` argument to `null` if it returns `false`. That means that the compiler knows that although the `s` variable's type is `string?`, it will not be `null` inside the body of the `if` statement. It knows this thanks to a nullable attribute applied to the `TryGetValue` method's definition. (Attributes are described in Chapter 14.) Example 3-17 shows the attribute in the method's declaration. (This method is part of a generic type, which is why we see `TKey` and `TValue` here and not the `int` and `string` types I used in my examples. Chapter 4 discusses this kind of method in detail. In the examples at hand, `TKey` and `TValue` are, in effect, `int` and `string`.)

Example 3-17. A nullable attribute

```
public bool TryGetValue(TKey key, [MaybeNullWhen(false)] out TValue value)
```

This annotation is how C# knows that the value might be `null` if `TryGetValue` returns `false`. Without this attribute, Example 3-15 would have compiled successfully even with nullable warnings enabled, because by writing `IDictionary<int, string>` (and not `IDictionary<int, string?>`) I am indicating that my dictionary does not permit null values. So normally, C# will assume that when a method returns a value from the dictionary, it will also produce a `string`. But `TryGetValue` sometimes has no value to return, which is why it needs this annotation. Table 3-1 describes the various attributes you can apply to give the C# compiler more information about what may or may not be `null`.

Table 3-1. Nullable attributes

Type	Usage
AllowNull	Code is allowed to supply `null` even when the type is non-nullable
DisallowNull	Code must not supply `null` even when the type is nullable
MaybeNull	Code should be prepared for this to return the `null` value even when the type is non-nullable
MaybeNullWhen	Used only with `out` or `ref` parameters; the output may be `null` if the method returns the specified `bool` value
NotNullWhen	Used only with `out` or `ref` parameters; the output may not be `null` if the method returns the specified `bool` value
NotNullIfNotNull	If you pass a non-`null` value as the argument for the parameter that this attribute names, the value returned by this attribute's target will not be `null`

These attributes have been applied to the most widely used parts of the .NET class libraries in .NET Core 3.0 to reduce the friction involved in adopting nullable references.

Moving code into enabled nullable warning and annotation contexts can provide a significant boost to code quality. Many developers who migrate existing codebases often uncover some latent bugs in the process, thanks to the additional checks the compiler performs. However, it is not perfect. There are two holes worth being aware of, caused by the fact that nullability was not baked into the type system from the start. The first is that legacy code introduces blind spots—even if all your code is in an enabled nullable annotation context, if it uses APIs that are not, references it obtains from those will be oblivious to nullability. If you need to use the null forgiving operator to keep the compiler happy, there's always the possibility that you are mistaken, at which point you'll end up with a null in what is supposed to be a non-nullable variable. The second is a bit more vexing in that you can hit it in brand-new code, even if you fully enabled this feature from the start: certain storage locations in .NET have their memory filled with zero values when they are initialized. If these locations are of a reference type, they will end up starting out with a `null` value, and there's currently no way that the C# compiler can enforce their non-nullability. Arrays have this issue. Look at Example 3-18.

Example 3-18. Arrays and nullability

```
var nullableStrings = new string?[10];
var nonNullableStrings = new string[10];
```

This code declares two arrays of strings. The first uses `string?`, so it allows nullable references. The second does not. However, in .NET you have to create arrays before you can put anything in them, and a newly created array's memory is always zero-initialized. This means that our `nonNullableStrings` array will start life full of nulls. There is no way to avoid this because of how arrays work in .NET. One way to mitigate this problem is to avoid using arrays directly. If you use `List<string>` instead (see Chapter 5), it will contain only items that you have added—unlike an array, a `List<T>` does not provide a way to initialize it with empty slots. But this will not always be possible. Sometimes you will simply need to take care that you initialize all the elements in an array.

A similar problem exists with fields in value types, which are described in the following section. If they have reference type fields, there are situations in which you cannot prevent them from being initialized to `null`. So the nullable references feature is not perfect. It is nonetheless very useful. Teams that have made the necessary changes to existing projects to use it have reported that this process tends to uncover many previously undiscovered bugs. It is an important tool for improving the quality of your code.

Although non-nullable references diminish one of the distinctions between reference types and built-in numeric types, important differences remain. A variable of type `int` is not a reference to an `int`. It contains the value of the `int`—there is no indirection. In some languages, this choice between reference-like and value-like behavior is determined by the way in which you use a type, but in C#, it is a fixed feature of the type. Any particular type is either a reference type or a *value type*. The built-in numeric types are all value types, as is `bool`, whereas a `class` is always a reference type. But this is not a distinction between built-in and custom types. You can write custom value types.

Structs

Sometimes it will be appropriate for a custom type to get the same value-like behavior as the built-in value types. The most obvious example would be a custom numeric type. Although the CLR offers various intrinsic numeric types, some kinds of calculations require a bit more structure than these provide. For example, many scientific and engineering calculations work with complex numbers. The runtime does not define an intrinsic representation for these, but the class library supports them with the `Complex` type. It would be unhelpful if a numeric type such as this behaved significantly differently from the built-in types. Fortunately, it doesn't, because it is a value type. The way to write a custom value type is to use the `struct` keyword instead of `class`.

A struct can have most of the same features as a class; it can contain methods, fields, properties, constructors, and any of the other member types supported by classes, and we can use the same accessibility keywords, such as `public` and `internal`. There are a few restrictions, but with the simple `Counter` type I wrote earlier, I *could* just replace the `class` keyword with `struct`. However, this would not be a useful transformation. Remember, one of the main distinctions between reference types (classes) and value types is that the former have identity: it might be useful for me to create multiple `Counter` objects so that I can count different kinds of things. But with value types (either the built-in ones or custom structs), the assumption is that they can be copied freely. If I have an instance of the `int` type (e.g., 4) and I store that in several fields, there's no expectation that this value has a life of its own: one instance of the number 4 is indistinguishable from another. The variables that hold values have their own identities and lifetimes, but the values that they hold do not. This is different from how reference types work: not only do the variables that refer to them have identities and lifetimes, the objects they refer to have their own identities and lifetimes independent of any particular variable.

If I add one to the `int` value 4, the result is a completely different `int` value. If I call `GetNextValue()` on a `Counter`, its count goes up by one but it remains the same `Counter` instance. So although replacing `class` with `struct` in Example 3-3 would compile, we really don't want our `Counter` type to become a struct. Example 3-19 shows a better candidate.

Example 3-19. A simple struct

```
public struct Point
{
    private double _x;
    private double _y;
    public Point(double x, double y)
    {
        _x = x;
        _y = y;
    }

    public double X => _x;
    public double Y => _y;
}
```

This represents a point in two-dimensional space. And while it's certainly possible to imagine wanting the ability to represent particular points with their own identity (in which case we'd want a class), it's perfectly reasonable to want to have a value-like type representing a point's location.

Although Example 3-19 is OK as far as it goes, it's common for values to support comparison. As mentioned earlier, C# defines a default meaning for the == operator for reference types: it is equivalent to object.ReferenceEquals, which compares identities. That's not meaningful for value types, so C# does not automatically support == for a struct. You are not strictly required to provide a definition, but the built-in value types all do, so if we're trying to make a type with similar characteristics to those, we should do this. If you add an == operator on its own, the compiler will inform you that you are required to define a matching != operator. You might think C# would define != as the inverse of ==, since they appear to mean the opposite. However, some types will return false for both operators for certain pairs of operands, so C# requires us to define both independently. As Example 3-20 shows, to define a custom meaning for an operator, we use the operator keyword followed by the operator we'd like to customize. This example defines the behavior for == and !=, which are very straightforward for our simple type.

Example 3-20. Support custom comparison

```
public static bool operator ==(Point p1, Point p2)
{
    return p1.X == p2.X && p1.Y == p2.Y;
}

public static bool operator !=(Point p1, Point p2)
{
    return p1.X != p2.X || p1.Y != p2.Y;
}

public override bool Equals(object obj)
{
    return obj is Point p2 && this.X == p2.X && this.Y == p2.Y;
}

public override int GetHashCode()
{
    return (X, Y).GetHashCode();
}
```

If you just add the == and != operators, you'll find that the compiler generates warnings recommending that you define two methods called Equals and GetHashCode. Equals is a standard method available on all .NET types, and if you have defined a custom meaning for ==, you should ensure that Equals does the same thing. Example 3-20 does this, and as you can see, it contains the same logic as the == operator, but it has to do some extra work. The Equals method permits comparison with any type, so we first check to see if our Point is being compared with another Point. I've used a type pattern to perform this check, and also to get the incoming obj argument into a variable of type Point in the case where the pattern matches. Finally, Example 3-20 implements GetHashCode, which we're required to do if we implement Equals. See the next sidebar, "GetHashCode", for details.

GetHashCode

All .NET types have a GetHashCode method. It returns an int that in some sense represents the value of your object. Some data structures and algorithms are designed to work with this sort of simplified, reduced version of an object's value. A hash table, for example, can find a particular entry in a very large table very efficiently, as long as the type of value you're searching for offers a good hash code implementation. Some of the collection classes described in Chapter 5 rely on this. The details of this sort of algorithm are beyond the scope of this book, but if you search the web for "hash table" you'll find plenty of information.

A correct implementation of GetHashCode must meet two requirements. The first is that whatever number an instance returns as its hash code, that instance must continue to return the same code as long as its own value does not change. The second requirement is that two instances that have equal values according to their Equals methods must return the same hash code. Any type that fails to meet either of these requirements might cause code that uses its GetHashCode method to malfunction. The default implementation of GetHashCode for reference types meets the first requirement but makes no attempt to meet the second—pick any two objects that use the default implementation, and most of the time they'll have different hash codes. That's fine because the default reference type Equals implementation only ever returns true if you compare an object with itself, but this is why you need to override GetHashCode if you override Equals. Value types get default implementations of GetHashCode and Equals that meet both requirements. However, these use reflection (see Chapter 13), which is slow, so you should normally write your own.

Ideally, objects that have different values should have different hash codes, but that's not always possible—GetHashCode returns an int, which has a finite number of possible values. (4,294,967,296, to be precise.) If your data type offers more distinct values, then it's clearly not possible for every conceivable value to produce a different hash code. For example, the 64-bit integer type, long, obviously supports more distinct values than int. If you call GetHashCode on a long with a value of 0, on .NET 4.0 it returns 0, and you'll get the same hash code for a long with a value of 4,294,967,297. Duplicates like these are called *hash collisions*, and they are an unavoidable fact of life. Code that depends on hash codes just has to be able to deal with these.

The rules do not require the mapping from values to hash codes to be fixed forever—they only need to be consistent for the lifetime of the process. In fact, there are good reasons to be inconsistent. Criminals who attack online computer systems sometimes try to cause hash collisions. Collisions decrease the efficiency of hash-based algorithms, so an attack that attempts to overwhelm a server's CPU will be more effective if it can induce collisions for values that it knows the server will use in hash-based lookups. Some types in the .NET class library deliberately change the way they produce hashes each time you restart a program to avoid this problem.

Because hash collisions are unavoidable, the rules cannot forbid them, which means you could return the same value (e.g., 0) from `GetHashCode` every time, regardless of the instance's actual value. Although not technically against the rules, it tends to produce lousy performance from hash tables and the like. Ideally, you will want to minimize hash collisions. That said, if you don't expect anything to depend on your type's hash code, there's not much point in spending time carefully devising a hash function that produces well-distributed values. Sometimes a lazy approach, such as deferring to a single field, is OK. Or you could defer to a tuple like Example 3-20 does, because tuples do a reasonably good job of producing a hash over all their properties. Or if you can target .NET Core 3.0 or .NET Standard 2.1 or later, you can use the `Hash Code.Combine` method.

With the code in Example 3-20 added to the struct in Example 3-19, we can run a few tests. Example 3-21 works similarly to Examples 3-9 and 3-10.

Example 3-21. Comparing struct instances

```
var p1 = new Point(40, 2);
Point p2 = p1;
var p3 = new Point(40, 2);

Console.WriteLine($"{p1.X}, {p1.Y}");
Console.WriteLine($"{p2.X}, {p2.Y}");
Console.WriteLine($"{p3.X}, {p3.Y}");
Console.WriteLine(p1 == p2);
Console.WriteLine(p1 == p3);
Console.WriteLine(p2 == p3);
Console.WriteLine(object.ReferenceEquals(p1, p2));
Console.WriteLine(object.ReferenceEquals(p1, p3));
Console.WriteLine(object.ReferenceEquals(p2, p3));
Console.WriteLine(object.ReferenceEquals(p1, p1));
```

Running that code produces this output:

```
40, 2
40, 2
40, 2
True
True
True
False
```

```
False
False
False
```

All three instances have the same value. With `p2` that's because I initialized it by assigning `p1` into it, and with `p3` I constructed it from scratch but with the same arguments. Then we have the first three comparisons, which, remember, use `==`. Since Example 3-20 defines a custom implementation that compares values, all the comparisons succeed. And all the `object.ReferenceEquals` values fail, because this is a value type, just like `int`. In fact, this is the same behavior we saw with Example 3-10, which used `int` instead of `Counter`. (Again, the compiler has generated implicit conversions here that produce boxes, which we will look at in Chapter 7.) So we have achieved our goal of defining a type with similar behavior to built-in value types such as `int`.

When to Write a Value Type

I've shown some of the differences in observable behavior between a `class` and a `struct`, but although I argued why `Counter` was a poor candidate for being a `struct`, I've not fully explained what makes a good one. The short answer is that there are only two circumstances in which you should write a value type. First, if you need to represent something value-like, such as a number, a struct is likely to be ideal. Second, if you have determined that a struct has usefully better performance characteristics for the scenario in which you will use the type, a struct may not be ideal but might still be a good choice. But it's worth understanding the pros and cons in more detail. And I will also address a surprisingly persistent myth about value types.

With reference types, an object is distinct from a variable that refers to it. This can be very useful, because we often use objects as models for real things with identities of their own. But this has some performance implications. An object's lifetime is not necessarily directly related to the lifetime of a variable that refers to it. You can create a new object, store a reference to it in a local variable, and then later copy that reference to a static field. The method that originally created the object might then return, so the local variable that first referred to the object no longer exists, but the object needs to stay alive because it's still possible to reach it by other means.

The CLR goes to considerable lengths to ensure that the memory an object occupies is not reclaimed prematurely, but is eventually freed once the object is no longer in use. This is a fairly complex process (described in detail in Chapter 7), and .NET applications can end up causing the CLR to consume a considerable amount of CPU time just tracking objects in order to work out when they fall out of use. Creating lots of objects increases this overhead. Adding complexity in certain ways can also increase the costs of object tracking—if a particular object remains alive only because it is reachable through some very convoluted path, the CLR may need to follow that path each time it tries to work out what memory is still in use. Each level of indirection you add generates extra work. A reference is by definition indirect, so every reference type variable creates work for the CLR.

Value types can often be handled in a much simpler way. For example, consider arrays. If you declare an array of some reference type, you end up with an array of references. This is very flexible—elements can be null if you want, and you're also free to have multiple different elements all referring to the same item. But if what you actually need is a simple sequential collection of items, that flexibility is just overhead. A collection of 1,000 reference type instances requires 1,001 blocks of memory: one block to hold an array of references, and then 1,000 objects for those references to refer to. But with value types, a single block can hold all the values. This simplifies things for memory management purposes—either the array is still in use or it's not, and there's no need for the CLR to check the 1,000 individual elements separately.

It's not just arrays that can benefit from this sort of efficiency. There's also an advantage for fields. Consider a class that contains 10 fields, all of type int. The 40 bytes required to hold those fields' values can live directly inside the memory allocated for an instance of the containing class. Compare that with 10 fields of some reference type. Although those references can be stored inside the object instance's memory, the objects they refer to will be separate entities, so if the fields are all non-null and all refer to different objects, you'll now have 11 blocks of memory—one for the instance that contains all the fields, and then one for each object those fields refer to. Figure 3-1 illustrates these differences between references and values for both arrays and objects (with smaller examples, because the same principle applies even with a handful of instances).

Value types can also sometimes simplify lifetime handling. Often, the memory allocated for local variables can be freed as soon as a method returns (although, as we'll see in Chapter 9, anonymous functions mean that it's not always that simple). This means the memory for local variables can often live on the stack, which typically has much lower overheads than the heap. For reference types, the memory for a variable is only part of the story—the object it refers to cannot be handled so easily, because that object may continue to be reachable by other paths after the method exits.

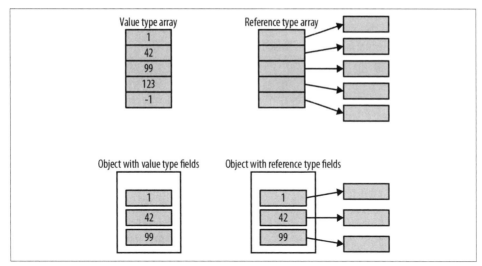

Figure 3-1. References versus values

In fact, the memory for a value may be reclaimed even before a method returns. New value instances often overwrite older instances. For example, C# can normally just use a single piece of memory to represent a variable, no matter how many different values you put in there. Creating a new instance of a value type doesn't necessarily mean allocating more memory, whereas with reference types, a new instance means a new heap block. This is why it's OK for each operation we perform with a value type —every integer addition or subtraction, for example—to produce a new instance.

One of the most persistent myths about value types says that values are allocated on the stack, unlike objects. It's true that objects always live on the heap, but value types don't always live on the stack,[1] and even in the situations where they do, that's an implementation detail, not a fundamental feature of C#. Figure 3-1 shows two coun‐ terexamples. An int value inside an array of type int[] does not live on the stack; it lives inside the array's heap block. Likewise, if a class declares a nonstatic int field, the value of that int lives inside the heap block for its containing object instance. And even local variables of value types don't necessarily end up on the stack. For example, optimizations may make it possible for the value of a local variable to live entirely inside the CPU's registers, rather than needing to go on the stack. And as you'll see in Chapters 9 and 17, locals can sometimes live on the heap.

You might be tempted to summarize the preceding few paragraphs as "there are some complex details, but in essence, value types are more efficient." But that would be a mistake. There are some situations in which value types are significantly more

---

1 There are certain exceptions, described in Chapter 18.

expensive. Remember that a defining feature of a value type is that values get copied on assignment. If the value type is big, that will be relatively expensive. For example, the .NET class library defines the Guid type to represent the 16-byte *globally unique identifiers* that crop up in lots of bits of Windows. This is a struct, so any assignment statement involving a Guid is asking to make a copy of a 16-byte data structure. This is likely to be more expensive than making a copy of a reference, because the CLR uses a pointer-based implementation for references; a pointer typically takes 4 or 8 bytes, but more importantly, it'll be something that fits naturally into a single CPU register.

It's not just assignment that causes values to be copied. Passing a value type argument to a method may require a copy. As it happens, with method invocation, it is actually possible to pass a reference to a value, although as we'll see later, it's a slightly limited kind of reference, and the restrictions it imposes are sometimes undesirable, so you may end up deciding that the cost of the copy is preferable. This is why Microsoft's design guidelines suggest that you should not make a type a struct unless it "has an instance size under 16 bytes" (a guideline that the Guid type technically violates, being exactly 16 bytes in size). But this is not a hard and fast rule—it really depends on how you will be using it, and since more recent versions of C# provide more flexibility for using values types indirectly, it is increasingly common for performance-sensitive code to ignore this restriction, and instead to take care to minimize copying.

Value types are not automatically going to be more efficient than reference types, so in most cases, your choice should be driven by the behavior you require. The most important question is this: does the identity of an instance matter to you? In other words, is the distinction between one object and another object important? For our Counter example, the answer is yes: if we want something to keep count for us, it's simplest if that counter is a distinct thing with its own identity. (Otherwise, our Counter type adds nothing beyond what int gives us.) But for our Point type, the answer is no, so it's a reasonable candidate for being a value type.

An important and related question is: does an instance of your type contain state that changes over time? Modifiable value types tend to be problematic, because it's all too easy to end up working with some copy of a value, and not the instance you meant to. (I'll show an important example of this problem later, in "Properties and mutable value types" on page 169, and another when I describe List<T> in Chapter 5.) So it's usually a good idea for value types to be immutable. This doesn't mean that variables of these types cannot be modified; it just means that to modify the variable, you must replace its contents entirely with a different value. For something simple like an int, this will seem like splitting hairs, but the distinction is important with structs that contain multiple fields, such as .NET's Complex type, which represents numbers that combine a real and an imaginary component. You cannot change the Real or Imaginary property of an existing Complex instance, because the type is immutable. And the `Point` type shown earlier works the same way. If the value you've got isn't the value you want, immutability just means you need to create a new value, because you can't tweak the existing instance.

Immutability does not necessarily mean you should write a struct—the built-in `string` type is immutable, and that's a class.[2] However, because C# often does not need to allocate new memory to hold new instances of a value type, value types are able to support immutability more efficiently than classes in scenarios where you're creating lots of new values (e.g., in a loop). Immutability is not an absolute requirement for structs—there are some unfortunate exceptions in .NET's class library. But value types should normally be immutable, so a requirement for mutability is usually a good sign that you want a class rather than a struct.

A type should only be a struct if it represents something that is very clearly similar in nature to other things that are value types. (In most cases it should also be fairly small, because passing large types by value is expensive.) For example, in the .NET class library, `Complex` is a struct, which is unsurprising because it's a numeric type, and all of the built-in numeric types are value types. `TimeSpan` is also a value type, which makes sense because it's effectively just a number that happens to represent a length of time. In the UI framework WPF, types used for simple geometric data such as `Point` and `Rect` are structs. But if in doubt, write a class.

Guaranteeing Immutability

Since C# 7.2, it has been possible to declare your intention to make a struct read-only by adding the `readonly` keyword in front of `struct`, as Example 3-22 shows. This is similar to the `Point` type shown in Example 3-19, but I've made a couple of other alterations. In addition to adding the `readonly` qualifier, I've also used read-only auto properties to reduce the clutter. I've also added a member function for reasons that will soon become clear. For a read-only type to be useful, it needs to have a constructor, a special member that initializes the fields and properties. I'll describe these in more detail later.

Example 3-22. A read-only struct

```
public readonly struct Point
{
    public Point(double x, double y)
    {
```

---

2 You wouldn't want it to be a value type, because strings can be large, so passing them by value would be expensive. In any case, it cannot be a struct, because strings vary in length. However, that's not a factor you need to consider, because you can't write your own variable-length data types in C#. Only strings and array types have variable size.

```
        X = x;
        Y = y;
    }

    public double X { get; }
    public double Y { get; }
    public double DistanceFromOrigin()
    {
        return Math.Sqrt(X * X + Y * Y);
    }
}
```

Applying the readonly keyword to a struct has two effects. First, the C# compiler
will keep you honest, preventing modification either from outside or from within. If
you declare any fields, the compiler will generate an error unless these are also
marked readonly. Similarly, if you try to define a settable auto property (described
later in this chapter), the compiler will produce an error.

Second, read-only structs enjoy certain optimizations. If in some other type you
declare a readonly field (either directly, or indirectly with a read-only auto property),
whose type is a readonly struct, the compiler may be able to avoid making a copy
of the data when something uses that field. Consider the class in Example 3-23.

Example 3-23. A read-only struct in a read-only property

```
public class LocationRecord
{
    public LocationRecord(string label, Point location)
    {
        Label = label;
        Location = location;
    }

    public string Label { get; }
    public Point Location { get; }
}
```

Suppose you had a variable r containing a reference to a LocationRecord. What
would happen if you wrote the expression r.Location.DistanceFromOrigin()? Logically, we're asking r.Location to retrieve the Point, and since Point is a value type,
that would entail making a copy of the value. Normally, C# will generate code that
really does make a copy because it cannot in general know whether invoking some
member of a struct will modify it. These are known as *defensive copies*, and they
ensure that expressions like this can't cause a nasty surprise such as changing the
value of a property or field that appears to be read-only. However, since Point is a
readonly struct, the compiler can know that it does not need to create a defensive
copy here. In this case, it would be safe for either the C# compiler or the JIT compiler

(or AoT code generator) to optimize this code by invoking `DistanceFromOrigin` directly on the value stored inside the `LocationRecord` without first making a copy.

You are allowed to use a `readonly struct` in writable fields and properties if you want to. The `readonly` keyword guarantees only that any particular value of this type will not change. If you want to overwrite an existing value with a completely different value, that's up to you.

Members

Whether you're writing a class or a struct, there are several different kinds of members you can put in a custom type. We've seen examples of some already, but let's take a closer and more comprehensive look.

With one exception (static constructors), you can specify the accessibility for all class and struct members. Just as a type can be `public` or `internal`, so can each member. Members may also be declared as `private`, making them accessible only to code inside the type, and this is the default accessibility. And, as we'll see in Chapter 6, inheritance adds three more accessibility levels for members: `protected`, `protected internal`, and `protected private`.

Fields

You've already seen that fields are named storage locations that hold either values or references depending on their type. By default, each instance of a type gets its own set of fields, but if you want a field to be singular, rather than having one per instance, you can use the `static` keyword. You can also apply the `readonly` keyword to a field, which states that it can be set only during construction, and cannot change thereafter.

The `readonly` keyword does not make any absolute guarantees. There are mechanisms by which it is possible to contrive a change in the value of a `readonly` field. The reflection mechanisms discussed in Chapter 13 provide one way, and unsafe code, which lets you work directly with raw pointers, provides another. The compiler will prevent you from modifying a field accidentally, but with sufficient determination, you can bypass this protection. And even without such subterfuge, a `readonly` field is free to change during construction.

C# offers a keyword that seems, superficially, to be similar: you can define a `const` field. However, this is designed for a somewhat different purpose. A `readonly` field is initialized and then never changed, whereas a `const` field defines a value that is invariably the same. A `readonly` field is much more flexible: it can be of any type, and its value can be calculated at runtime, which means you can define either per-instance or `static` fields as `readonly`. A const field's value is determined at compile time, which means it is defined at the class level (because there's no way for individual instances to have different values). This also limits the available types. For most reference types, the only supported `const` value is `null`, so in practice, it's normally only useful to use `const` with types intrinsically supported by the compiler. (Specifically, if you want to use values other than `null`, a `const`'s type must be either one of the built-in numeric types, `bool`, `string`, or an enumeration type, as described later in this chapter.)

This makes a `const` field rather more limited than a `readonly` one, so you could reasonably ask: what's the point? Well, although a `const` field is inflexible, it makes a strong statement about the unchanging nature of the value. For example, .NET's `Math` class defines a `const` field of type `double` called `PI` that contains as close an approximation to the mathematical constant π as a `double` can represent. That's a value that's fixed forever—thus it is a constant in a very strong sense.

When it comes to less inherently constant values, you need to be a bit careful about `const` fields; the C# specification allows the compiler to assume that the value really will never change. Code that reads the value of a `readonly` field will fetch the value from the memory containing the field at runtime. But when you use a `const` field, the compiler can read the value at compile time and copy it into the IL as though it were a literal. So if you write a library component that declares a `const` field and you later change its value, this change will not necessarily be picked up by code using your library unless that code gets recompiled.

One of the benefits of a `const` field is that it is eligible for use in certain contexts in which a `readonly` field is not. For example, if you want to use a constant pattern (Chapter 2 introduced patterns), perhaps in the label for a `case` in a `switch` statement, for example, the value you specify has to be fixed at compile time. So a constant pattern cannot refer to a `readonly` field, but you can use a suitably typed `const` field. You can also use `const` fields in the expression defining the value of another `const` field (as long as you don't introduce any circular references).

A `const` field is required to contain an expression defining its value, such as the one shown in Example 3-24.

Example 3-24. A const field

```
const double kilometersPerMile = 1.609344;
```

While mandatory for a const, this initializer expression is optional for a class's ordinary and readonly[3] fields. If you omit the initializing expression, the field will automatically be initialized to a default value. (That's 0 for numeric values, and the equivalents for other types—false, null, etc.) Structs are a bit more limited because when they are initialized implicitly, their instance fields are set to 0, so you are not allowed to write initializers for them. Structs do support initializers for noninstance fields, though (i.e., const and static fields).

If you do supply an initializer expression for a non-const field, it does not need to be evaluable at compile time, so it can do runtime work such as calling methods or reading properties. Of course, this sort of code can have side effects, so it's important to be aware of the order in which initializers run.

Nonstatic field initializers run for each instance you create, and they execute in the order in which they appear in the file, immediately before the constructor runs. Static field initializers execute no more than once, no matter how many instances of the type you create. They also execute in the order in which they are declared, but it's harder to pin down exactly when they will run. If your class has no static constructor, C# guarantees to run field initializers before the first time a field in the class is accessed, but it doesn't necessarily wait until the last minute—it retains the right to run field initializers as early as it likes. (The exact moment at which this happens has varied across releases of .NET.) But if a static constructor does exist, then things are slightly clearer: static field initializers run immediately before the static constructor runs, but that merely raises the questions: what's a static constructor, and when does it run? So we had better take a look at constructors.

Constructors

A newly created object may require some information to do its job. For example, the Uri class in the System namespace represents a *uniform resource identifier* (URI) such as a URL. Since its entire purpose is to contain and provide information about a URI, there wouldn't be much point in having a Uri object that didn't know what its URI was. So it's not actually possible to create one without providing a URI. If you try the code in Example 3-25, you'll get a compiler error.

Example 3-25. Error: failing to provide a Uri with its URI

```
Uri oops = new Uri();  // Will not compile
```

---

3 If you omit the initializer for a readonly field, you should set it in the constructor instead; otherwise it's not very useful.

The Uri class defines several *constructors*, members that contain code that initializes a new instance of a type. If a particular class requires certain information to work, you can enforce this requirement through constructors. Creating an instance of a class almost always involves using a constructor at some point,[4] so if the constructors you define all demand certain information, developers will have to provide that information if they want to use your class. So all of the Uri class's constructors need to be given the URI in one form or another.

To define a constructor, you first specify the accessibility (public, private, internal, etc.) and then the name of the containing type. This is followed by a list of parameters in parentheses (which can be empty). Example 3-26 shows a class that defines a single constructor that requires two arguments: one of type decimal, and one of type string. The argument list is followed by a block containing code. So constructors look a lot like methods, but with the containing type name in place of the usual return type and method name.

Example 3-26. A class with one constructor

```
public class Item
{
    public Item(decimal price, string name)
    {
        _price = price;
        _name = name;
    }
    private readonly decimal _price;
    private readonly string _name;
}
```

This constructor is pretty simple: it just copies its arguments to fields. A lot of constructors do no more than that. You're free to put as much code in there as you like, but by convention, developers usually expect the constructor to do very little—its main job is to ensure that the object is in a valid initial state. That might involve checking the arguments and throwing an exception if there's a problem, but not much else. You are likely to surprise developers who use your class if you write a constructor that does something nontrivial, such as adding data to a database or sending a message over the network.

Example 3-27 shows how to use a constructor that takes arguments. We just use the new operator, passing in suitably typed values as arguments.

---

4 There's an exception. If a class supports a CLR feature called *serialization*, objects of that type can be deserialized directly from a data stream, bypassing constructors. But even here, you can dictate what data is required.

Example 3-27. Using a constructor

```
var item1 = new Item(9.99M, "Hammer");
```

You can define multiple constructors, but it must be possible to distinguish between them: you cannot define two constructors that both take the same number of arguments of the same types, because there would be no way for the new keyword to know which one you meant.

Default constructors and zero-argument constructors

If you do not define any constructors at all, C# will provide a *default constructor* that is equivalent to an empty constructor that takes no arguments. And if you're writing a struct, you'll get that even if you do define other constructors.

 Although the C# specification unambiguously defines a default constructor as one generated for you by the compiler, be aware that there's another widely used meaning. You will often see the term *default constructor* used to mean any public, parameterless constructor, regardless of whether it was generated by the compiler. There's some logic to this—from the perspective of code using a class, it's not possible to tell the difference between a compiler-generated constructor, and an explicit zero-argument constructor, so if the term *default constructor* is to mean anything useful from that perspective, it can mean only a public constructor that takes no arguments. However, that's not how the C# specification defines the term.

The compiler-generated default constructor does nothing beyond the zero initialization of fields, which is the starting point for all new objects. However, there are some situations in which it is necessary to write your own parameterless constructor. You might need the constructor to execute some code. Example 3-28 sets an _id field based on a static field that it increments for each new object to give each instance a distinct ID. This doesn't require any arguments to be passed in, but it does involve running some code.

Example 3-28. A nonempty zero-argument constructor

```
public class ItemWithId
{
    private static int _lastId;
    private int _id;

    public ItemWithId()
    {
        _id = ++_lastId;
```

```
        }
}
```

There is another way to achieve the same effect as Example 3-28. I could have written a static method called GetNextId, and then used that in the _id field initializer. Then I wouldn't have needed to write this constructor. However, there is one advantage to putting code in the constructor: field initializers are not allowed to invoke the object's own nonstatic methods, but constructors are. That's because the object is in an incomplete state during field initialization, so it may be dangerous to call its nonstatic methods—they may rely on fields having valid values. But an object is allowed to call its own nonstatic methods inside a constructor, because although the object's still not fully built yet, it's closer to completion, and so the dangers are reduced.

There are other reasons for writing your own zero-argument constructor. If you define at least one constructor for a class, this will disable the default constructor generation. If you need your class to provide parameterized construction, but you still want to offer a no-arguments constructor, you'll need to write one, even if it's empty. Alternatively, if you want to write a class whose only constructor is an empty, zero-argument one, but with a protection level other than the default of public—you might want to make it private, so that only your code can create instances, for example—you would need to write the constructor explicitly even if it is empty, so that you have somewhere to specify the protection level.

Some frameworks can use only classes that provide a zero-argument constructor. For example, if you build a UI with Windows Presentation Foundation (WPF), classes that can act as custom UI elements usually need such a constructor.

With structs, zero-argument constructors work slightly differently, because value types need to support implicit initialization. When a value type is used as a field of some other type, or the element type of an array, the memory that holds the value is part of the containing object, and when you create a new object or array, the CLR always fills its memory with zeros. This means that it is always possible to initialize a value without passing any constructor arguments. So whereas C# removes the default constructor for a class when you add a constructor that takes arguments, it does not do this for a struct—even if it did hide it, you'd still be able to invoke this implicit initialization indirectly, e.g., by creating a one-element array of that type: MyStruct s = (new MyStruct[1])[0];. Since implicit initialization is always available for a struct, there would be no sense in the compiler hiding the corresponding constructor. C# doesn't let you write a zero-argument constructor for a struct because there are so many scenarios in which that constructor would not run. The CLR's zero initialization is used in most cases.

Chaining constructors

If you write a type that offers several constructors, you may find that they have a certain amount in common—there are often initialization tasks that all constructors have to perform. The class in Example 3-28 calculates a numeric identifier for each object in its constructor, and if it were to provide multiple constructors, they might all need to do that same work. Moving the work into a field initializer would be one way to solve that, but what if only some constructors wanted to do it? You might have work that was common to most constructors, but you might want to make an exception by having one constructor that allows the ID to be specified rather than calculated. The field initializer approach would no longer be appropriate, because you'd want individual constructors to be able to opt in or out. Example 3-29 shows a modified version of the code from Example 3-28, defining two extra constructors.

Example 3-29. Optional chaining of constructors

```
public class ItemWithId
{
    private static int _lastId;
    private int _id;
    private string _name;

    public ItemWithId()
    {
        _id = ++_lastId;
    }

    public ItemWithId(string name)
        : this()
    {
        _name = name;
    }
    public ItemWithId(string name, int id)
    {
        _name = name;
        _id = id;
    }
}
```

If you look at the second constructor in Example 3-29, its parameter list is followed by a colon, and then this(), which invokes the first constructor. A constructor can invoke any other constructor that way. Example 3-30 shows a different way to structure all three constructors, illustrating how to pass arguments.

Example 3-30. Chained constructor arguments

```
public ItemWithId()
    : this(null)
{
}

public ItemWithId(string name)
    : this(name, ++_lastId)
{
}

private ItemWithId(string name, int id)
{
    _name = name;
    _id = id;
}
```

The two-argument constructor here is now a sort of master constructor—it is the only one that actually does any work. The other constructors just pick suitable arguments for that main constructor. This is arguably a cleaner solution than the previous examples, because the work of initializing the fields is done in just one place, rather than having different constructors each performing their own smattering of field initialization.

Notice that I've made the two-argument constructor in Example 3-30 `private`. At first glance, it can look a bit odd to define a way of building an instance of a class and then make it inaccessible, but it makes perfect sense when chaining constructors. And there are other scenarios in which a private constructor might be useful—we might want to write a method that makes a clone of an existing `ItemWithId`, in which case that constructor would be useful, but by keeping it private, we retain control of exactly how new objects get created. It can sometimes even be useful to make all of a type's constructors `private`, forcing users of the type to go through what's sometimes called a *factory method* (a `static` method that creates an object) to get hold of an instance. There are two common reasons for doing this. One is if full initialization of the object requires additional work of a kind that is inadvisible in a constructor (e.g., if you need to do slow work that uses the asynchronous language features described in Chapter 17, you cannot put that code inside a constructor). Another is if you want to use inheritance (see Chapter 6) to provide multiple variations on a type, but you want to be able to decide at runtime which particular type is returned.

Static constructors

The constructors we've looked at so far run when a new instance of an object is created. Classes and structs can also define a static constructor. This runs at most once in the lifetime of the application. You do not invoke it explicitly—C# ensures that it runs automatically at some point before you first use the class. So, unlike an instance constructor, there's no opportunity to pass arguments. Since static constructors cannot take arguments, there can be only one per class. Also, because these are never accessed explicitly, you do not declare any kind of accessibility for a static constructor. Example 3-31 shows a class with a static constructor.

Example 3-31. Class with static constructor

```
public class Bar
{
    private static DateTime _firstUsed;
    static Bar()
    {
        Console.WriteLine("Bar's static constructor");
        _firstUsed = DateTime.Now;
    }
}
```

Just as an instance constructor puts the instance into a useful initial state, the static constructor provides an opportunity to initialize any static fields.

By the way, you're not obliged to ensure that a constructor (static or instance) initializes every field. When a new instance of a class is created, the instance fields are initially all set to 0 (or the equivalent, such as `false` or `null`). Likewise, a type's static fields are all zeroed out before the class is first used. Unlike with local variables, you only need to initialize fields if you want to set them to something other than the default zero-like value.

Even then, you may not need a constructor. A field initializer may be sufficient. However, it's useful to know exactly when constructors and field initializers run. I mentioned earlier that the behavior varies according to whether constructors are present, so now that we've looked at constructors in a bit more detail, I can finally show a more complete picture of initialization. (There will still be more to come—as Chapter 6 describes, inheritance adds another dimension.)

At runtime, a type's static fields will first be set to 0 (or equivalent values). Next, the field initializers run in the order in which they are written in the source file. This ordering matters if one field's initializer refers to another. In Example 3-32, fields a and c both have the same initializer expression, but they end up with different values (1 and 42, respectively) due to the order in which initializers run.

Example 3-32. Significant ordering of static fields

```
private static int a = b + 1;
private static int b = 41;
private static int c = b + 1;
```

The exact moment at which static field initializers run depends on whether there's a static constructor. As mentioned earlier, if there isn't, then the timing is not defined —C# guarantees to run them no later than the first access to one of the type's fields, but it reserves the right to run them arbitrarily early. The presence of a static constructor changes matters: in that case, the static field initializers run immediately before the constructor. So when does the constructor run? It will be triggered by one of two events, whichever occurs first: creating an instance, or accessing any static member of the class.

For nonstatic fields, the story is similar: the fields are first all initialized to 0 (or equivalent values), and then field initializers run in the order in which they appear in the source file, and this happens before the constructor runs. Of course, the difference is that instance constructors are invoked explicitly, so it's clear when this initialization occurs.

I've written a class called `InitializationTestClass` designed to illustrate this construction behavior, shown in Example 3-33. The class has both static and nonstatic fields, all of which call a method, `GetValue`, in their initializers. That method always returns the same value, 1, but it prints out a message so we can see when it is called. The class also defines a no-arguments instance constructor and a static constructor, both of which print out messages.

Example 3-33. Initialization order

```
public class InitializationTestClass
{
    public InitializationTestClass()
    {
        Console.WriteLine("Constructor");
    }

    static InitializationTestClass()
    {
        Console.WriteLine("Static constructor");
    }

    public static int s1 = GetValue("Static field 1");
    public int ns1 = GetValue("Non-static field 1");
    public static int s2 = GetValue("Static field 2");
    public int ns2 = GetValue("Non-static field 2");

    private static int GetValue(string message)
```

```
    {
        Console.WriteLine(message);
        return 1;
    }

    public static void Foo()
    {
        Console.WriteLine("Static method");
    }
}

class Program
{
    static void Main(string[] args)
    {
        Console.WriteLine("Main");
        InitializationTestClass.Foo();
        Console.WriteLine("Constructing 1");
        InitializationTestClass i = new InitializationTestClass();
        Console.WriteLine("Constructing 2");
        i = new InitializationTestClass();
    }
}
```

The Main method prints out a message, calls a static method defined by Initializa
tionTestClass, and then constructs a couple of instances. Running the program, I
see the following output:

```
Main
Static field 1
Static field 2
Static constructor
Static method
Constructing 1
Non-static field 1
Non-static field 2
Constructor
Constructing 2
Non-static field 1
Non-static field 2
Constructor
```

Notice that both static field initializers and the static constructor run before the call
to the static method (Foo) begins. The field initializers run before the static constructor, and as expected, they run in the order in which they appear in the source file.
Because this class includes a static constructor, we know when static initialization will
begin—it is triggered by the first use of that type, which in this example is when our
Main method calls InitializationTestClass.Foo. You can see that it happens
immediately before that point and no earlier, because our Main method manages to
print out its first message before the static initialization occurs. If this example did

not have a static constructor, and had only static field initializers, there would be no guarantee that static initialization would happen at the exact same point; the C# specification allows the initialization to happen earlier.

You need to be careful about what you do in code that runs during static initialization: it may run earlier than you expect. For example, suppose your program uses some sort of diagnostic logging mechanism, and you need to configure this when the program starts in order to enable logging of messages to the proper location. There's always a possibility that code that runs during static initialization could execute before you've managed to do this, meaning that diagnostic logging will not yet be working correctly. That might make problems in this code hard to debug. Even when you narrow down C#'s options by supplying a static constructor, it's relatively easy to trigger that earlier than you intended. Use of any static member of a class will trigger its initialization, and you can find yourself in a situation where your static constructor is kicked off by static field initializers in some other class that doesn't have a static constructor—this could happen before your Main method even starts.

You could try to fix this by initializing the logging code in its own static initialization. Because C# guarantees to run initialization before the first use of a type, you might think that this would ensure that the logging initialization would complete before the static initialization of any code that uses the logging system. However, there's a potential problem: C# guarantees only when it will *start* static initialization for any particular class. It doesn't guarantee to wait for it to finish. It cannot make such a guarantee, because if it did, code such as the peculiarly British Example 3-34 would put it in an impossible situation.

Example 3-34. Circular static dependencies

```
public class AfterYou
{
    static AfterYou()
    {
        Console.WriteLine("AfterYou static constructor starting");
        Console.WriteLine("AfterYou: NoAfterYou.Value = " + NoAfterYou.Value);
        Value = 123;
        Console.WriteLine("AfterYou static constructor ending");
    }

    public static int Value = 42;
}

public class NoAfterYou
{
    static NoAfterYou()
    {
        Console.WriteLine("NoAfterYou static constructor starting");
        Console.WriteLine("NoAfterYou: AfterYou.Value: = " + AfterYou.Value);
```

```
        Value = 456;
        Console.WriteLine("NoAfterYou static constructor ending");
    }

    public static int Value = 42;
}
```

There is a circular relationship between the two types in this example: both have static constructors that attempt to use a static field defined by the other class. The behavior will depend on which of these two classes the program tries to use first. In a program that uses AfterYou first, I see the following output:

```
AfterYou static constructor starting
NoAfterYou static constructor starting
NoAfterYou: AfterYou.Value: = 42
NoAfterYou static constructor ending
AfterYou: NoAfterYou.Value = 456
AfterYou static constructor ending
```

As you'd expect, the static constructor for AfterYou runs first, because that's the class my program is trying to use. It prints out its first message, but then it tries to use the NoAfterYou.Value field. That means the static initialization for NoAfterYou now has to start, so we see the first message from its static constructor. It then goes on to retrieve the AfterYou.Value field, even though the AfterYou static constructor hasn't finished yet. (It retrieved the value set by the field initializer, 42, and not the value set by the static constructor, 123.) That's allowed, because the ordering rules say only when static initialization is triggered, and they do not guarantee when it will finish. If they tried to guarantee complete initialization, this code would be unable to proceed —the NoAfterYou static constructor could not move forward, because the AfterYou static construction is not yet complete, but that couldn't move forward, because it would be waiting for the NoAfterYou static initialization to finish.

The moral of this story is that you should not get too ambitious about what you try to achieve during static initialization. It can be hard to predict the exact order in which things will happen.

 The Microsoft.Extensions.Hosting NuGet package provides a much better way to handle initialization problems with its Host Builder class. It is beyond the scope of this chapter, but it is well worth finding and exploring.

Deconstructors

In Chapter 2, we saw how to deconstruct a tuple into its component parts. But deconstruction is not just for tuples. You can enable deconstruction for any type you write by adding a suitable Deconstruct member, as shown in Example 3-35.

Example 3-35. Enabling deconstruction

```
public readonly struct Size
{
    public Size(double w, double h)
    {
        W = w;
        H = h;
    }

    public void Deconstruct(out double w, out double h)
    {
        w = W;
        h = H;
    }

    public double W { get; }
    public double H { get; }
}
```

C# recognizes this pattern of a method named `Deconstruct` with a list of `out` arguments (which the next section will describe in more detail) and enables you to use the same deconstruction syntax as you can with tuples. Example 3-36 uses this to extract the component values of a `Size` to enable it to express succinctly the calculation it performs.

Example 3-36. Using a custom deconstructor

```
static double DiagonalLength(Size s)
{
    (double w, double h) = s;
    return Math.Sqrt(w * w + h * h);
}
```

Types with a deconstructor can also use positional pattern matching. Chapter 2 showed how you can use a syntax very similar to deconstruction in a pattern to match tuples. Any type with a custom deconstructor can use this same syntax. Example 3-37 uses the `Size` type's custom deconstructor to define various patterns for a `Size` in a switch expression.

Example 3-37. Positional pattern using a custom deconstructor

```
static string DescribeSize(Size s) => s switch
{
    (0, 0) => "Empty",
    (0, _) => "Extremely narrow",
    (double w, 0) => $"Extremely short, and this wide: {w}",
```

```
    _ => "Normal"
};
```

Recall from Chapter 2 that positional patterns are recursive: each position within the pattern contains a nested pattern. Since `Size` deconstructs into two elements, each positional pattern has two positions in which to put child patterns. Example 3-37 variously uses constant patterns, a discard, and a type pattern.

To use a deconstructor in a pattern, C# needs to know the type to be deconstructed at compile time. This works in Example 3-37 because the input to the switch expression is of type `Size`. If a positional pattern's input is of type `object`, the compiler will presume that you're trying to match a tuple instead, unless you explicitly name the type, as Example 3-38 does.

Example 3-38. Positional pattern with explicit type

```
static string Describe(object o) => o switch
{
    Size (0, 0) => "Empty",
    Size (0, _) => "Extremely narrow",
    Size (double w, 0) => $"Extremely short, and this wide: {w}",
    Size _ => "Normal shape",
    _ => "Not a shape"
};
```

Although the compiler provides special handling for the `Deconstruct` member that these examples rely on, from the runtime's perspective, this is just an ordinary method. So this would be a good time to look in more detail at methods.

Methods

Methods are named bits of code that can optionally return a result, and that may take arguments. C# makes the fairly common distinction between *parameters* and *arguments*: a method defines a list of the inputs it expects—the parameters—and the code inside the method refers to these parameters by name. The values seen by the code could be different each time the method is invoked, and the term *argument* refers to the specific value supplied for a parameter in a particular invocation.

As you've already seen, when an accessibility specifier, such as `public` or `private`, is present, it appears at the start of the method declaration. The optional `static` keyword comes next, where present. After that, the method declaration states the return type. As with many C-family languages, you can write methods that return nothing, and you indicate this by putting the `void` keyword in place of the return type. Inside the method, you use the `return` keyword followed by an expression to specify the value for the method to return. In the case of a `void` method, you can use the `return` keyword without an expression to terminate the method, although this is optional, because when execution reaches the end of a void method, it terminates automatically. You normally only use return in a void method if your code determines that it needs to exit early.

Passing arguments by reference

Methods can return only one item directly in C#. If you want to return multiple values, you can of course make that item a tuple. Alternatively, you can designate parameters as being for output rather than input. Example 3-39 returns two values, both produced by integer division. The main return value is the quotient, but it also returns the remainder through its final parameter, which has been annotated with the out keyword. Because tuples were only introduced in C# 7, whereas out parameters have been around since the start, out crops up a lot. For example, you'll see lots of methods following a similar pattern to int.TryParse, in which the return type is a bool indicating success or failure, with the actual result being passed through an out parameter.

Example 3-39. Returning multiple values with out

```
public static int Divide(int x, int y, out int remainder)
{
    remainder = x % y;
    return x / y;
}
```

Example 3-40 shows one way to call a method with an out parameter. Instead of supplying an expression as we do with arguments for normal parameters, we've written the out keyword followed by a variable declaration. This introduces a new variable and initializes it with the value that the method returns through this out parameter. So in this case, we end up with a new variable r initialized to 1.

Example 3-40. Putting an out parameter's result into a new variable

```
int q = Divide(10, 3, out int r);
```

A variable declared in an out argument follows the usual scoping rules, so in Example 3-40, r will remain in scope for as long as q. Less obviously, r is available in the rest of the expression. Example 3-41 uses this to attempt to parse some text as an integer, returning the parsed result if that succeeds, and a fallback value of 0 if parsing fails.

Example 3-41. Using out parameter's result in the same expression

```
int value = int.TryParse(text, out int x) ? x : 0;
```

When you pass an out argument, this works by passing a reference to the local variable. When Example 3-40 calls `Divide`, and when that method assigns a value into `remainder`, it's really assigning it into the caller's `r` variable. This is an `int`, which is a value type, so it would not normally be passed by reference, and this kind of reference is limited compared to what you can do with a reference type.[5] For example, you can't declare a field in a class that can hold this kind of reference, because the local `r` variable will cease to exist when it goes out of scope, whereas an instance of a class can live indefinitely in a heap block. C# has to ensure that you cannot put a reference to a local variable in something that might outlive the variable it refers to.

 Methods annotated with the `async` keyword (described in Chapter 17) cannot have any out arguments. This is because asynchronous methods may implicitly return to their caller before they complete, continuing their execution some time later. This in turn means that the caller may also have returned before the `async` runs again, in which case the variables passed by reference might no longer exist by the time the asynchronous code is ready to set them. The same restriction applies to anonymous functions (described in Chapter 9). Both kinds of methods are allowed to pass out arguments into methods that they call, though.

You won't always want to declare a new variable for each out argument. As Example 3-42 shows, you can just write out followed by the name of an existing variable. (This was once the only way to use out arguments, so it's common to see code that declares a new variable in a separate statement immediately before using it as an out argument, even though the form shown in Example 3-40 would be simpler.)

Example 3-42. Putting an out parameter's result into an existing variable

```
int r, q;
q = Divide(10, 3, out r);
Console.WriteLine($"3: {q}, {r}");
q = Divide(10, 4, out r);
Console.WriteLine($"4: {q}, {r}");
```

---

5 The CLR calls this kind of reference a Managed Pointer, to distinguish it from the kind of reference that refers to an object on the heap. Unfortunately, C#'s terminology is less clear: it calls both of these things references.

When invoking a method with an out parameter, we are required to indicate explicitly that we are aware of how the method uses the argument. Regardless of whether we use an existing variable or declare a new one, we must use the out keyword at the call site as well as in the declaration. (Some C-family languages do not make any visual distinction between calls that pass values and ones that pass references, but the semantics are very different, so C# makes it explicit.)

Sometimes you will want to invoke a method that has an out argument that you have no use for—maybe you only need the main return value. As Example 3-43 shows, you can put just an underscore after the out keyword. This tells C# to discard the result. (This is a relatively new feature, so in older codebases, it's fairly common to see code that introduces a variable whose only job is to have somewhere to put an unwanted out result.)

Example 3-43. Discarding an out parameter's result

```
int q = Divide(10, 3, out _);
```

You should avoid using _ (a single underscore) as the name of something in C#, because it can prevent the compiler from interpreting it as a discard. If a local variable of this name is in scope, writing out _ has, since C# 1.0, indicated that you want to assign an out result into that variable, so for backward compatibility, current versions of C# have to retain that behavior. You can only use this form of discard if there is no symbol named _ in scope.

An out reference requires information to flow from the method back to the caller, so if you try to write a method that returns without assigning something into all of its out arguments, you'll get a compiler error. C# uses the *definite assignment* rules mentioned in Chapter 2 to check this. (This requirement does not apply if the method throws an exception instead of returning.) There's a related keyword, ref, that has similar reference semantics, but allows information to flow bidirectionally. With a ref argument, it's as though the method has direct access to the variable the caller passed in—we can read its current value, as well as modify it. (The caller is obliged to ensure that variables passed with ref contain a value before making the call, so in this case, the method is not required to set it before returning.) If you call a method with a parameter annotated with ref instead of out, you have to make clear at the call site that you meant to pass a reference to a variable as the argument, as Example 3-44 shows.

Example 3-44. Calling a method with a ref argument

```
long x = 41;
Interlocked.Increment(ref x);
```

There's a third way to add a level of indirection to an argument: you can apply the `in` keyword. (This was new in C# 7.2.) Whereas `out` only enables information to flow out of the method, `in` only allows it to flow in. It's like a `ref` argument, but where the called method is not allowed to modify the variable the argument refers to. This may seem redundant: if there's no way to pass information back through the argument, why pass it by reference? An `in int` argument doesn't sound usefully different than an ordinary `int` argument. In fact, you wouldn't use `in` with `int`. You only use it with relatively large types. As you know, value types are normally passed by value, meaning a copy has to be made when passing a value as an argument. The `in` keyword enables us to avoid this copy by passing a reference instead. In the past, people have sometimes used the `ref` keyword to avoid making copies of data, but this creates a risk that the method might modify the value when the caller might not want that. With `in`, we get the same in-only semantics we get when passing values the normal way, but with the potential efficiency gains of not having to pass the whole value.

You should only use `in` for types that are larger than a pointer. This is why `in int` is not useful. An `int` is 32 bits long, so passing a reference to an `int` doesn't save us anything. In a 32-bit process, that reference will be a 32-bit pointer, so we have saved nothing, and we end up with the slight extra inefficiency involved in using a value indirectly through a reference. In a 64-bit process, the reference will be a 64-bit pointer, so we've ended up having to pass more data into the method than we would have done if we had just passed the `int` directly! (Sometimes the CLR can inline the method and avoid the costs of creating the pointer, but this means that at best `in int` would cost the same as an `int`. And since `in` is purely about performance, that's why `in` is not useful for small types such as `int`.)

Example 3-45 defines a fairly large value type. It contains four `double` values, each of which is 8 bytes in size, so each instance of this type occupies 32 bytes. The .NET design guidelines have always recommended avoiding making value types this large, and the main reason for this is that passing them as arguments is inefficient. However, the availability of the `in` keyword can reduce those costs, meaning that in some cases, it might make sense to define a `struct` this large.

Example 3-45. A large value type

```
public readonly struct Rect
{
    public Rect(double x, double y, double width, double height)
    {
```

```
        X = x;
        Y = y;
        Width = width;
        Height = height;
    }

    public double X { get; }
    public double Y { get; }
    public double Width { get; }
    public double Height { get; }
}
```

Example 3-46 shows a method that calculates the area of a rectangle represented by the Rect type defined in Example 3-45. We really wouldn't want to have to copy all 32 bytes to call this very simple method, especially since it only uses half of the data in the Rect. Since this method annotates its parameter with in, no such copying will occur: the argument will be passed by reference, which in practice means that only a pointer needs to be passed—either 4 or 8 bytes, depending on whether the code is running in a 32-bit or a 64-bit process.

Example 3-46. A method with an in parameter

```
public static double GetArea(in Rect r) => r.Width * r.Height;
```

You might expect that calling a method with in parameters would require the call site to indicate that it knows that the argument will be passed by reference by putting in in front of the argument, just like we need to write out or ref at the call site for the other two by-reference styles. And as Example 3-47 shows, you can do this, but it is optional. If you want to be explicit about the by-reference invocation, you can be, but unlike with ref and out, the compiler just passes the argument by reference anyway if you don't add in.

Example 3-47. A method with an in parameter

```
var r = new Rect(10, 20, 100, 100);
double area = GetArea(in r);
double area2 = GetArea(r);
```

The in keyword is optional at the call site because defining a parameter such as in is only a performance optimization—unlike out and ref—which does not change the behavior. Microsoft wanted to make it possible for developers to introduce a source-level-compatible change in which an existing method is modified by adding in to a parameter. This is a breaking change at the binary level, but in scenarios where you can be sure people will in any case need to recompile (e.g., when all the code is under your control), it might be useful to introduce such a change for performance reasons.

Of course, as with all such enhancements you should measure performance before and after the change to see if it has the intended effect.

Although the examples just shown work as intended, in sets a trap for the unwary. It works only because I marked the struct in Example 3-45 as readonly. If instead of defining my own Rect I had used the very similar-looking struct with the same name from the System.Windows namespace (part of the WPF UI framework), Example 3-47 would not avoid the copy. It would have compiled and produced the correct results at runtime, but it would not offer any performance benefit. That's because System.Windows.Rect is not read-only. Earlier, I discussed the defensive copies that C# makes when you use a readonly field containing a mutable value type. The same principle applies here, because an in argument is in effect read-only: code that passes arguments expects them not to be modified unless they are explicitly marked as out or ref. So the compiler must ensure that in arguments are not modified even though the method being called has a reference to the caller's variable. When the type in question is already read-only, the compiler doesn't have to do any extra work. But if it is a mutable value type, then if the method to which this argument was passed in turn invokes a method on that value, the compiler generates code that makes a copy and invokes the method on that, because it can't know whether the method might modify the value. You might think the compiler could enforce this by preventing the method with the in parameter from doing anything that might modify the value, but in practice that would mean stopping it from invoking any methods on the value—the compiler cannot in general determine whether any particular method call might modify the value. (And even if it doesn't today, maybe it will in a future version of the library that defines the type.) Since properties are methods in disguise, this would make in arguments more or less unusable. This leads to a simple rule:

> You should use in only with readonly value types, because mutable value types can undo the performance benefits. (Mutable value types are typically a bad idea in any case.)

C# 8.0 adds a feature that can loosen this constraint a little. It allows the readonly keyword to be applied to members so that they can declare that they will not modify the value of which they are a member. This makes it possible to avoid these defensive copies on mutable values.

You can use the out and ref keywords with reference types too. That may sound redundant, but it can be useful. It provides double indirection—the method receives a reference to a variable that holds a reference. When you pass a reference type argument to a method, that method gets access to whatever object you choose to pass it.

While the method can use members of that object, it can't normally replace it with a different object. But if you mark a reference type argument with ref, the method has access to your variable, so it could replace it with a reference to a completely different object.

It's technically possible for constructors to have out and ref parameters too, although it's unusual. Also, just to be clear, the out or ref qualifiers are part of the method (or constructor) signature. A caller can pass an out (or ref) argument if and only if the parameter was declared as out (or ref). Callers can't decide unilaterally to pass an argument by reference to a method that does not expect it.

Reference variables and return values

Now that you've seen various ways in which you can pass a method a reference to a value (or a reference to a reference), you might be wondering whether you can get hold of these references in other ways. You can, as Example 3-48 shows, but there are some constraints.

Example 3-48. A local ref variable

```
string rose = null;
ref string rosaIndica = ref rose;
rosaIndica = "smell as sweet";
Console.WriteLine($"A rose by any other name would {rose}");
```

This example declares a variable called rose. It then declares a new variable of type ref string. The ref here has exactly the same effect as it does on a method parameter: it indicates that this variable is a reference to some other variable. Since the code initializes it with ref rose, the variable rosaIndica is a reference to that rose variable. So when the code assigns a value into rosaIndica, that value goes into the rose variable that rosaIndica refers to. When the final line reads the value of the rose variable, it will see the value that was written by the preceding line.

So what are the constraints? As you saw earlier with ref and out arguments, C# has to ensure that you cannot put a reference to a local variable in something that might outlive the variable it refers to. So you cannot use this keyword on a field. Static fields live for as long as their defining type is loaded (typically until the process exits), and member fields of classes live on the heap enabling them to outlive any particular method call. (This is also true of most structs. It is not true of a ref struct, but even those do not currently support the ref keyword on a field.) And even in cases where you might think lifetime isn't a problem (e.g., because the target of the reference is itself a field in an object) it turns out that the runtime simply doesn't support storing this kind of reference in a field, or as an element type in an array. More subtly, this also means you can't use a ref local variable in a context where C# would store the variable in a class. That rules out their use in `async` methods and iterators, and also prevents them being captured by anonymous functions (which are described in Chapters 17, 5, and 9, respectively).

Although types cannot define fields with `ref`, they can define methods that return a `ref`-style reference (and since properties are methods in disguise, a property getter may also return a reference). As always, the C# compiler has to ensure that a reference cannot outlive the thing it refers to, so it will prevent use of this feature in cases where it cannot be certain that it can enforce this rule. Example 3-49 shows various uses of `ref` return types, some of which the compiler accepts, and some it does not.

Example 3-49. Valid and invalid uses of ref returns

```
public class Referable
{
    private int i;
    private int[] items = new int[10];

    public ref int FieldRef => ref i;

    public ref int GetArrayElementRef(int index) => ref items[index];

    public ref int GetBackSameRef(ref int arg) => ref arg;

    public ref int WillNotCompile()
    {
        int v = 42;
        return ref v;
    }

    public ref int WillAlsoNotCompile()
    {
        int i = 42;
        return ref GetBackSameRef(ref i);
    }

    public ref int WillCompile(ref int i)
    {
        return ref GetBackSameRef(ref i);
    }
}
```

The methods that return a reference to an `int` that is a field, or an element in an array, are allowed, because `ref` style references can always refer *to* items inside objects on the heap. (They just can't live *in* them.) Heap objects can exist for as long as they are needed (and the garbage collector, discussed in Chapter 7, is aware of these kinds of references, and will ensure that heap objects with references pointing to their interiors are kept alive). And a method can return any of its `ref` arguments, because the caller was already required to ensure that they remain valid for the duration of the call. However, a method cannot return a reference to one of its local variables, because in cases where those variables end up living on the stack, the stack frame will cease to exist when the method returns. It would be a problem if a method could return a reference to a variable in a now-defunct stack frame.

The rules get a little more subtle when it comes to returning a reference that was obtained from some other method. The final two methods in Example 3-49 both attempt to return the reference returned by GetBackSameRef. One works, and the other does not. The outcome makes sense: WillAlsoNotCompile needs to be rejected for the same reason WillNotCompile was; both attempt to return a reference to a local variable, WillAlsoNotCompile just trying to disguise this by going through another method, GetBackSameRef. In cases like these, the C# compiler makes the conservative assumption that any method that returns a ref and which also takes one or more ref arguments might choose to return a reference to one of those arguments. So the compiler disallows the call to GetBackSameRef in WillAlsoNotCompile on the grounds that it might return a reference to the same local variable that was passed in by reference. (And it happens to be right in this case. But it would reject any call of this form even if the method in question returned a reference to something else entirely.) But it allows WillCompile to return the ref returned by GetBack SameRef because in that case, the reference we pass in is one we would be allowed to return directly.

As with in arguments, the main reason for using ref returns is that they can enable greater runtime efficiency by avoiding copies. Instead of returning the entire value, methods of this kind can just return a pointer to the existing value. It also has the effect of enabling callers to modify whatever is referred to. For example, in Example 3-49, I can assign a value into the FieldRef property, even though the property appears to be read-only. The absence of a setter doesn't matter in this case because its type is ref int, which is valid as the target of an assignment. So by writing r.FieldRef = 42; (where r is of type Referable) I get to modify the i field. Likewise, the reference returned by GetArrayElementRef can be used to modify the relevant element in the array. If this is not your intention, you can make the return type ref readonly instead of just ref. In this case the compiler will not allow the resulting reference to be used as the target of an assignment.

 You should only use ref readonly returns with a readonly struct, because otherwise you will run into the same defensive copy issues we saw earlier.

Optional arguments

You can make non-`out`, non-`ref` arguments optional by defining default values. The method in Example 3-50 specifies the values that the arguments should have if the caller doesn't supply them.

Example 3-50. A method with optional arguments

```
public static void Blame(string perpetrator = "the youth of today",
    string problem = "the downfall of society")
{
    Console.WriteLine($"I blame {perpetrator} for {problem}.");
}
```

This method can then be invoked with no arguments, one argument, or both arguments. Example 3-51 just supplies the first, taking the default for the `problem` argument.

Example 3-51. Omitting one argument

```
Blame("mischievous gnomes");
```

Normally, when invoking a method you specify the arguments in order. However, what if you want to call the method in Example 3-50, but you want to provide a value only for the second argument, using the default value for the first? You can't just leave the first argument empty—if you tried to write `Blame( , "everything")`, you'd get a compiler error. Instead, you can specify the name of the argument you'd like to supply, using the syntax shown in Example 3-52. C# will fill in the arguments you omit with the specified default values.

Example 3-52. Specifying an argument name

```
Blame(problem: "everything");
```

Obviously, you can omit arguments like this only when you're invoking methods that define default argument values. However, you are free to specify argument names when invoking any method—sometimes it can be useful to do this even when you're not omitting any arguments, because it can make it easier to see what the arguments are for when reading the code. This is particularly helpful if you're faced with an API that takes arguments of type `bool`, and it's not immediately clear what they mean. Example 3-53 constructs a `StreamReader` (described in Chapter 15), and this particular constructor takes many arguments. It's clear enough what the first two are, but the remaining three are likely to be something of a mystery to anyone reading the code, unless they happen to have committed all 11 `StreamReader` constructor overloads to memory. (The *using declaration* syntax shown here is described in Chapter 7.)

Example 3-53. Unclear arguments

```
using var r = new StreamReader(stream, Encoding.UTF8, true, 8192, false);
```

Argument names are not required here, but if we include them anyway, as Example 3-54 does, it becomes much easier to understand what the code does.

Example 3-54. Improving clarity by naming arguments

```
using var r = new StreamReader(stream, Encoding.UTF8,
  detectEncodingFromByteOrderMarks: true, bufferSize: 8192, leaveOpen: false);
```

Prior to C# 7.2, once you started naming arguments, you couldn't stop. You would not have been allowed to write the code in Example 3-55. The rationale for this limitation was that because named arguments make it possible to supply arguments in a different order than the parameters are declared, the compiler couldn't presume there was any association between argument positions and parameter positions. However, that reasoning turned out to be suspect, because even when we supply all of the arguments in order, we might still want to use argument names purely to improve clarity. So it is now possible to do as Example 3-55 does, naming the second argument to make its meaning evident, but to continue with unnamed arguments if it's clear enough what those do without naming them.

Example 3-55. Selective argument naming

```
using var w = new StreamWriter(filepath, append: true, Encoding.UTF8);
```

It's important to understand how C# implements default argument values because it has an impact on evolving library design. When you invoke a method without providing all the arguments, as Example 3-52 does, the compiler generates code that passes a full set of arguments as normal. It effectively rewrites your code, adding back in the arguments you left out. The significance of this is that if you write a library that defines default argument values like this, you will run into problems if you ever change the defaults. Code that was compiled against the old version of the library will have copied the old defaults into the call sites, and won't pick up the new values unless it is recompiled.

You will sometimes see an alternative mechanism used for allowing arguments to be omitted, which avoids baking default values into call sites: *overloading*. This is a slightly histrionic term for the rather mundane idea that a single name or symbol can be given multiple meanings. In fact, we already saw this technique with constructors —in Example 3-30, I defined one master constructor that did the real work, and then two other constructors that called into that one. We can use the same trick with methods, as Example 3-56 shows.

Example 3-56. Overloaded method

```
public static void Blame(string perpetrator, string problem)
{
    Console.WriteLine($"I blame {perpetrator} for {problem}.");
}

public static void Blame(string perpetrator)
{
    Blame(perpetrator, "the downfall of society");
}

public static void Blame()
{
    Blame("the youth of today", "the downfall of society");
}
```

In one sense, this is slightly less flexible than default argument values, because code calling the Blame method no longer has any way to specify a value for the problem argument while picking up the default perpetrator (although it would be easy enough to solve that by just adding a method with a different name). On the other hand, method overloading offers two potential advantages: it allows you to decide on the default values at runtime if necessary, and it also provides a way to make out and ref arguments optional. Those require references to local variables, so there's no way to define a default value, but you can always provide overloads with and without those arguments if you need to. And you can use a mixture of the two techniques— you might rely mainly on optional arguments, using overloads only to enable out or ref arguments to be omitted.

Variable argument count with the params keyword

Some methods need to be able to accept different amounts of data in different situations. Take the mechanism that I've used many times in this book to display information. In most cases, I've passed a simple string to Console.WriteLine, but in some cases I've wanted to format and display other pieces of information. As Example 3-57 shows, you can embed expressions in strings.

Example 3-57. String interpolation

```
Console.WriteLine($"PI: {Math.PI}. Square root of 2: {Math.Sqrt(2)}");
Console.WriteLine($"It is currently {DateTime.Now}");
var r = new Random();
Console.WriteLine(
    $"{r.Next(10)}, {r.Next(10)}, {r.Next(10)}, {r.Next(10)}");
```

As you may recall from Chapter 2, when you put a $ symbol in front of a string constant, the compiler transforms it into a call to the string.Format method (a feature known as *string interpolation*), and it replaces the nested expressions with placeholders such as {0} and {1}, which refer to the first and second arguments after the string. It is as though we had written the code in Example 3-58.

Example 3-58. String formatting

```
Console.WriteLine(string.Format(
    "PI: {0}. Square root of 2: {1}", Math.PI, Math.Sqrt(2)));
Console.WriteLine(string.Format("It is currently {0}", DateTime.Now));
var r = new Random();
Console.WriteLine(string.Format(
    "{0}, {1}, {2}, {3}",
    r.Next(10), r.Next(10), r.Next(10), r.Next(10)));
```

If you look at the documentation for `string.Format`, you'll see that it offers several overloads taking various numbers of arguments. Obviously, it offers only a finite number of overloads, but if you try it, you'll find that this is nonetheless an openended arrangement. You can pass as many arguments as you like after the string, and the numbers in the placeholders can go as high as necessary to refer to these arguments. The final line of Example 3-58 passes four arguments after the string, and even though the `string` class does not define an overload accepting that many arguments, it works.

One particular overload of the `string.Format` method takes over once you pass more than a certain number of arguments after the string (more than three, as it happens). This overload just takes two arguments: a `string` and an `object[]` array. The code that the compiler creates to invoke the method builds an array to hold all the arguments after the string, and passes that. So the final line of Example 3-58 is effectively equivalent to the code in Example 3-59. (Chapter 5 describes arrays.)

Example 3-59. Explicitly passing multiple arguments as an array

```
Console.WriteLine(string.Format(
    "{0}, {1}, {2}, {3}",
    new object[] { r.Next(10), r.Next(10), r.Next(10), r.Next(10) }));
```

The compiler will do this only with parameters that are annotated with the `params` keyword. Example 3-60 shows how the relevant `string.Format` method's declaration looks.

Example 3-60. The params keyword

```
public static string Format(string format, params object[] args)
```

The params keyword can appear only on a method's final parameter, and that parameter type must be an array. In this case it's an object[], meaning that we can pass objects of any type, but you can be more specific to limit what can be passed in.

 When a method is overloaded, the C# compiler looks for the method whose parameters best match the arguments supplied. It will consider using a method with a params argument only if a more specific match is not available.

You may be wondering why the string class bothers to offer overloads that accept one, two, or three object arguments. The presence of this params version seems to make those redundant—it lets you pass any number of arguments after the string, so what's the point of the ones that take a specific number of arguments? Those overloads exist to make it possible to avoid allocating an array. That's not to say that arrays are particularly expensive; they cost no more than any other object of the same size. However, allocating memory is not free. Every object you allocate will eventually have to be freed by the garbage collector (except for objects that hang around for the whole life of the program), so reducing the number of allocations is usually good for performance. Because of this, most APIs in the .NET class library that accept a variable number of arguments through params also offer overloads that allow a small number of arguments to be passed without needing to allocate an array to hold them.

Local functions

You can define methods inside other methods. These are called *local functions*, and Example 3-61 defines two of them. (You can also put them inside other method-like features, such as constructors or property accessors.)

Example 3-61. Local functions

```
static double GetAverageDistanceFrom(
    (double X, double Y) referencePoint,
    (double X, double Y)[] points)
{
    double total = 0;
    for (int i = 0; i < points.Length; ++i)
    {
        total += GetDistanceFromReference(points[i]);
    }
    return total / points.Length;

    double GetDistanceFromReference((double X, double Y) p)
    {
        return GetDistance(p, referencePoint);
    }
```

```
static double GetDistance((double X, double Y) p1, (double X, double Y) p2)
{
    double dx = p1.X - p2.X;
    double dy = p1.Y - p2.Y;
    return Math.Sqrt(dx * dx + dy * dy);
}
}
```

One reason for using local functions is that they can make the code easier to read by moving steps into named methods—it's easier to see what's happening when there's a method call to GetDistance than it is if we just have the calculations inline. Be aware that there can be overheads, although in this particular example when I run the Release build of this particular code on .NET Core 3.0, the JIT compiler is smart enough to inline both of the local calls here, so the two local functions vanish, and GetAverageDistanceFrom ends up being just one method. So we've paid no penalty here, but with more complex nested functions, the JIT compiler may decide not to inline. And when that happens, it's useful to know how the C# compiler enables this code to work.

The GetDistanceFromReference method here takes a single tuple argument, but it uses the referencePoint variable defined by its containing method. For this to work, the C# compiler moves that variable into a generated struct, which it passes by reference to the GetDistanceFromReference method as a hidden argument. This is how a single local variable can be accessible to both methods. Since this generated struct is passed by reference, the referencePoint variable can still remain on the stack in this example. However, if you obtain a delegate referring to a local method, any variables shared in this way have to move into a class that lives on the garbage-collected heap, which will have higher overheads. (See Chapters 7 and 9 for more details.) If you want to avoid any such overheads, you can always just not share any variables between the inner and outer methods. Starting with C# 8.0, you can tell the compiler that this is your intention by applying the static keyword to the local function, as Example 3-61 does with GetDistance. This will cause the compiler to produce an error if the method attempts to use a variable from its containing method.

Besides providing a way to split methods up for readability, local functions are sometimes used to work around some limitations with iterators (see Chapter 5) and async methods (Chapter 17). These are methods that might return partway through execution and then continue later, which means the compiler needs to arrange to store all of their local variables in an object living on the heap, so that those variables can survive for as long as is required. This prevents these kinds of methods from using certain types, such as Span<T>, described in Chapter 18. In cases where you need to use both async and Span<T>, it is common to move code using the latter into a local, non-`async` function that lives inside the `async` function. This enables the local function to use local variables with these constrained types.

Expression-bodied methods

If you write a method simple enough to consist of nothing more than a single return statement, you can use a more concise syntax. Example 3-62 shows an alternative way to write the `GetDistanceFromReference` method from "Local functions" on page 161. (As you've probably noticed, I've already used this in a few other examples.)

Example 3-62. An expression-bodied method

```
double GetDistanceFromReference((double X, double Y) p)
    => GetDistance(p, referencePoint);
```

Instead of a method body, you write => followed by the expression that would otherwise have followed the `return` keyword. This => syntax is based on the lambda syntax you can use for writing inline functions and building expression trees. These are discussed in Chapter 9.

Extension methods

C# lets you write methods that appear to be new members of existing types. *Extension methods*, as they are called, look like normal static methods, but with the `this` keyword added before the first parameter. You are allowed to define extension methods only in a static class. Example 3-63 adds a not especially useful extension method to the `string`, called `Show`.

Example 3-63. An extension method

```
namespace MyApplication
{
    public static class StringExtensions
    {
        public static void Show(this string s)
        {
            System.Console.WriteLine(s);
        }
    }
}
```

I've shown the namespace declaration in this example because namespaces are significant: extension methods are available only if you've written a `using` directive for the namespace in which the extension is defined, or if the code you're writing is defined in the same namespace. In code that does neither of these things, the `string` class will look normal, and will not acquire the `Show` method defined by Example 3-63.

However, code such as Example 3-64, which is defined in the same namespace as the extension method, will find that the method is available.

Example 3-64. Extension method available due to namespace declaration

```
namespace MyApplication
{
    class Program
    {
        static void Main(string[] args)
        {
            "Hello".Show();
        }
    }
}
```

The code in Example 3-65 is in a different namespace, but it also has access to the extension method, thanks to a using directive.

Example 3-65. Extension method available due to using directive

```
using MyApplication;

namespace Other
{
    class Program
    {
        static void Main(string[] args)
        {
            "Hello".Show();
        }
    }
}
```

Extension methods are not really members of the class for which they are defined— the string class does not truly gain an extra method in these examples. It's just an illusion maintained by the C# compiler, one that it keeps up even in situations where method invocation happens implicitly. This is particularly useful with C# features that require certain methods to be available. In Chapter 2, you saw that foreach loops depend on a GetEnumerator method. Many of the LINQ features we'll look at in Chapter 10 also depend on certain methods being present, as do the asynchronous language features described in Chapter 17. In all cases, you can enable these language features for types that do not support them directly by writing suitable extension methods.

Properties

Classes and structs can define *properties*, which are really just methods in disguise. To access a property, you use a syntax that looks like field access but ends up invoking a method. Properties can be useful for signaling intent. When something is exposed as a property, the implication is that it represents information about the object, rather than an operation the object performs, so reading a property is usually inexpensive and should have no significant side effects. Methods, on the other hand, are more likely to cause an object to do something.

Of course, since properties are just a kind of method, nothing enforces this. You are free to write a property that takes hours to run and makes significant changes to your application's state whenever its value is read, but that would be a pretty lousy way to design code.

Properties typically provide a pair of methods: one to get the value and one to set it. Example 3-66 shows a very common pattern: a property with `get` and `set` methods that provide access to a field. Why not just make the field public? That's often frowned upon, because it makes it possible for external code to change an object's state without the object knowing about it. It might be that in future revisions of the code, the object needs to do something—perhaps update the UI—every time the value changes. In any case, because properties contain code, they offer more flexibility than public fields. For example, you might want to store the data in a different format than is returned by the property, or you may even be able to implement a property that calculates its value from other properties. Another reason for using properties is simply that some systems require it—for example, some UI data binding systems are only prepared to consume properties. Also, some types do not support instance fields; later in this chapter, I'll show how to define an abstract type using an *interface*, and interfaces can contain properties, but not instance fields.

Example 3-66. Class with simple property

```
public class HasProperty .
{
    private int _x;
    public int X
    {
        get
        {
            return _x;
        }
        set
        {
            _x = value;
        }
```

```
        }
    }
```

 Inside a set accessor, value has a special meaning. It's a *contextual keyword*—text that the language treats as a keyword in certain contexts. Outside of a property you can use value as an identifier, but within a property it represents the value that the caller wants to assign to the property.

In cases where the entire body of the get is just a return statement, or where the set is a single expression statement, you can use the *expression-bodied member* syntax shown in Example 3-67. (This is very similar to the method syntax shown in Example 3-62.)

Example 3-67. Expression-bodied get and set

```
public class HasProperty
{
    private int _x;
    public int X
    {
        get => _x;
        set => _x = value;
    }
}
```

The pattern in Examples 3-66 and 3-67 is so common that C# can write most of it for you. Example 3-68 is more or less equivalent—the compiler generates a field for us, and produces get and set methods that retrieve and modify the value just like those in Example 3-66. The only difference is that code elsewhere in the same class can't get directly at the field in Example 3-68, because the compiler hides it. The official name in the language specification for this is an *automatically implemented property*, but these are typically referred to as just *auto-properties*.

Example 3-68. An auto-property

```
public class HasProperty
{
    public int X { get; set; }
}
```

Whether you use explicit or automatic properties, this is just a fancy syntax for a pair of methods. The get method returns a value of the property's declared type—an int, in this case—while the setter takes a single argument of that type through the implicit value parameter. Example 3-66 makes use of that argument to update the field. You're not obliged to store the value in a field, of course. In fact, nothing even forces you to make the `get` and `set` methods related in any way—you could write a getter that returns random values, and a setter that completely ignores the value you supply. However, just because you *can* doesn't mean you *should*. In practice, anyone using your class will expect properties to remember the values they've been given, not least because in use, properties look just like fields, as Example 3-69 shows.

Example 3-69. Using a property

```
var o = new HasProperty();
o.X = 123;
o.X += 432;
Console.WriteLine(o.X);
```

If you're using the full syntax shown in Example 3-66 to implement a property, or the expression-bodied form shown in Example 3-67, you can leave out either the `set` or the `get` to make a read-only or write-only property. Read-only properties can be useful for aspects of an object that are fixed for its lifetime, such as an identifier, or which are calculated from other properties. Write-only properties are less useful, although they can crop up in dependency injection systems. You can't make a write-only property with the auto-property syntax shown in Example 3-68, because you wouldn't be able to do anything useful with the value being set.

There are two variations on read-only properties. Sometimes it is useful to have a property that is publicly read-only, but which your class is free to change. You can define a property where the getter is public but the setter is not (or vice versa for a write-only property). You can do this with either the full or the automatic syntax. Example 3-70 shows how this looks with the latter.

Example 3-70. Auto-property with private setter

```
public int X { get; private set; }
```

If you want your property to be read-only in the sense that its value never changes after construction, you can leave out the setter entirely when using the auto-property syntax, as Example 3-71 shows.

Example 3-71. Auto-property with no setter

```
public int X { get; }
```

With no setter and no directly accessible field, you may be wondering how you can set the value of such a property. The answer is that inside your object's constructor, the property appears to be settable. (There isn't really a setter if you omit the `set`— the compiler generates code that just sets the backing field directly when you "set" the property in the constructor.) A get-only auto-property is effectively equivalent to a readonly field wrapped with an ordinary get-only property. As with fields, you can also write an initializer to provide an initial value. Example 3-72 uses both styles; if you use the constructor that takes no arguments, the property's value will be 42, and if you use the other constructor, it will have whatever value you supply.

Example 3-72. Initializing an auto-property with no setter

```
public class WithAutos
{
    public int X { get; } = 42;

    public WithAutos()
    {
    }

    public WithAutos(int val)
    {
        X = val;
    }
}
```

Sometimes it is useful to write a read-only property with a value calculated entirely in terms of other properties. For example, if you have written a type representing a vector with properties called X and Y, you could add a property that returns the magnitude of the vector, calculated from those other two properties, as Example 3-73 shows.

Example 3-73. A calculated property

```
public double Magnitude
{
    get
    {
        return Math.Sqrt(X * X + Y * Y);
    }
}
```

There is a more compact way of writing this. We could use the expression-bodied syntax shown in Example 3-67, but for a read-only property we can go one step further: you can put the => and expression directly after the property name. (This enables us to leave out the braces and the get keyword.) Example 3-74 is exactly equivalent to Example 3-73.

Example 3-74. An expression-bodied read-only property

```
public double Magnitude => Math.Sqrt(X * X + Y * Y);
```

Speaking of read-only properties, there's an important issue to be aware of involving properties, value types, and immutability.

Properties and mutable value types

As I mentioned earlier, value types tend to be more straightforward if they're immutable, but it's not a requirement. One reason to avoid modifiable value types is that you can end up accidentally modifying a copy of the value rather than the one you meant, and this issue becomes apparent if you define a property that uses a mutable value type. The Point struct in the System.Windows namespace is modifiable, so we can use it to illustrate the problem. Example 3-75 defines a Location property of this type.

Example 3-75. A property using a mutable value type

```
using System.Windows;

public class Item
{
    public Point Location { get; set; }
}
```

The Point type defines read/write properties called X and Y, so given a variable of type Point, you can set these properties. However, if you try to set either of these properties via another property, the code will not compile. Example 3-76 tries this—it attempts to modify the X property of a Point retrieved from an Item object's Location property.

Example 3-76. Error: cannot modify a property of a value type property

```
var item = new Item();
item.Location.X = 123;   // Will not compile
```

This example produces the following error:

```
error CS1612: Cannot modify the return value of 'Item.Location' because it is
not a variable
```

C# considers fields to be variables as well as local variables and method arguments, so if we were to modify Example 3-75 so that Location was a public field rather than a property, Example 3-76 would then compile, and would work as expected. But why doesn't it work with a property? Remember that properties are just methods, so Example 3-75 is more or less equivalent to Example 3-77.

Example 3-77. Replacing a property with methods

```
using System.Windows;

public class Item
{
    private Point _location;
    public Point get_Location()
    {
        return _location;
    }
    public void set_Location(Point value)
    {
        _location = value;
    }
}
```

Since Point is a value type, get_Location returns a copy. You might be wondering if we could use the ref return feature described earlier. We certainly could with plain methods, but there are a couple of constraints to doing this with properties. Firstly, you cannot define an auto-property with a ref type. Secondly, you cannot define a writeable property with a ref type. However, you can define a read-only ref property as Example 3-78 shows.

Example 3-78. A property returning a reference

```
using System.Windows;

public class Item
{
    private Point _location;

    public ref Point Location => ref _location;
}
```

With this implementation of Item, the code in Example 3-76 now works fine. (Ironically, to make the property modifiable, we had to turn it into a read-only property.)

Before ref returns were added to C# there was no way to make this work. All possible implementations of the property would end up returning a copy of the property value, so if the compiler did allow Example 3-76 to compile, we would be setting the X property on the copy returned by the property, and not the actual value in the Item object that the property represents. Example 3-79 makes this explicit, and it will in fact compile—the compiler will let us shoot ourselves in the foot if we make it sufficiently clear that we really want to. And with this version of the code, it's quite obvious that this will not modify the value in the Item object.

Example 3-79. Making the copy explicit

```
var item = new Item();
Point location = item.Location;
location.X = 123;
```

However, with the property implementation in Example 3-78, the code in Example 3-76 does compile, and ends up behaving like the code shown in Example 3-80. Here we can see that we've retrieved a reference to a Point, so when we set its X property, we're acting on whatever that refers to (the _location field in the Item in this case), rather than a local copy.

Example 3-80. Making the reference explicit

```
var item = new Item();
ref Point location = ref item.Location;
location.X = 123;
```

So it's possible to make it work, thanks to fairly recent additions to the language. But it's also easy to get it wrong. Fortunately, most value types are immutable, and this problem arises only with mutable value types.

 Immutability doesn't exactly solve the problem—you still can't write the code you might want to, such as item.Location.X = 123. But at least immutable structs don't mislead you by making it look like you should be able to do that.

Since all properties are really just methods (typically in pairs), in theory they could accept arguments beyond the implicit value argument used by set methods. The CLR allows this, but C# does not support it except for one special kind of property: an indexer.

Indexers

An *indexer* is a property that takes one or more arguments, and is accessed with the same syntax as is used for arrays. This is useful when you're writing a class that contains a collection of objects. Example 3-81 uses one of the collection classes provided by the .NET class library, List<T>. It is essentially a variable-length array, and it feels like a native array thanks to its indexer, used on the second and third lines. (I'll describe arrays and collection types in detail in Chapter 5. And I'll describe generic types, of which List<T> is an example, in Chapter 4.)

Example 3-81. Using an indexer

```
var numbers = new List<int> { 1, 2, 1, 4 };
numbers[2] += numbers[1];
Console.WriteLine(numbers[0]);
```

From the CLR's point of view, an indexer is a property much like any other, except that it has been designated as the *default property*. This concept is something of a holdover from the old COM-based versions of Visual Basic that got carried over into .NET, and which C# mostly ignores. Indexers are the only C# feature that treats default properties as being special. If a class designates a property as being the default one, and if the property accepts at least one argument, C# will let you use that property through the indexer syntax.

The syntax for declaring indexers is somewhat idiosyncratic. Example 3-82 shows a read-only indexer. You could add a `set` accessor to make it read/write, just like with any other property.[6]

Example 3-82. Class with indexer

```
public class Indexed
{
    public string this[int index]
    {
        get => index < 5 ? "Foo" : "bar";
    }
}
```

C# supports multidimensional indexers. These are simply indexers with more than one parameter—since properties are really just methods, you can define indexers with any number of parameters. You are free to use any mixture of types for the parameters.

As you may recall from Chapter 2, C# offers *null-conditional* operators. In that chapter, we saw this used to access properties and fields—e.g., `myString?.Length` will be of type `int?`—and its value will be `null` if `myString` is null, and the value of the `Length` property otherwise. There is one other form of null-conditional operator, which can be used with an indexer, shown in Example 3-83.

---

6 Incidentally, the default property has a name, because all properties are required to. C# calls the indexer property `Item`, and automatically adds the annotation indicating that it's the default property. You won't normally refer to an indexer by name, but the name is visible in some tools. The .NET class library documentation lists indexers under `Item`, even though it's rare to use that name in code.

Example 3-83. Null conditional index access

```
string? s = objectWithIndexer?[2];
```

As with the null conditional field or property access, this generates code that checks whether the lefthand part (`objectWithIndexer` in this case) is null. If it is, the whole expression evaluates to null; it only invokes the indexer if the lefthand part of the expression is not null. It is effectively equivalent to the code shown in Example 3-84.

Example 3-84. Code equivalent to null-conditional index access

```
string? s = objectWithIndexer == null ? null : objectWithIndexer[2];
```

This null-conditional index syntax also works with arrays.

Initializer Syntax

You will often want to set certain properties when you create an object, because it might not be possible to supply all relevant information through constructor arguments. This is particularly common with objects that represent settings for controlling some operation. For example, the `ProcessStartInfo` type enables you to configure many different aspects of a newly created OS process. It has 16 properties, but you would typically only need to set a few of these in any particular scenario. Even if you assume that the name of the file to run should always be present, there are still 32,768 possible combinations of properties. You wouldn't want to have a constructor for every one of those.

In practice, a class might offer constructors for a handful of particularly common combinations, but for everything else, you just set the properties after construction. C# offers a succinct way to create an object and set some of its properties in a single expression. Example 3-85 uses this *object initializer* syntax. This also works with fields, although it's relatively unusual to have writable public fields.

Example 3-85. Using an object initializer

```
Process.Start(new ProcessStartInfo
{
    FileName = "cmd.exe",
    UseShellExecute = true,
    WindowStyle = ProcessWindowStyle.Maximized,
});
```

You can supply constructor arguments too. Example 3-86 has the same effect as Example 3-85, but chooses to supply the filename as a constructor argument (because this is one of the few properties `ProcessStartInfo` lets you supply that way).

Example 3-86. Using a constructor and an object initializer

```
Process.Start(new ProcessStartInfo("cmd.exe")
{
    UseShellExecute = true,
    WindowStyle = ProcessWindowStyle.Maximized,
});
```

The object initializer syntax can remove the need for a separate variable to refer to the object while you set the properties you need. As Examples 3-85 and 3-86 show, you can pass an object initialized in this way directly as an argument to a method. An important upshot of this is that this style of initialization can be contained entirely within a single expression. This is important in scenarios that use expression trees, which we'll be looking at in Chapter 9.

There's a variation on this syntax that enables you to supply values to an indexer in an object initializer. Example 3-87 uses this to initialize a dictionary. (Chapter 5 describes dictionaries and other collection types in detail.)

Example 3-87. Using an indexer in an object initializer

```
var d = new Dictionary<string, int>
{
    ["One"] = 1,
    ["Two"] = 2,
    ["Three"] = 3
};
```

Operators

Classes and structs can define customized meanings for operators. I showed some custom operators earlier: Example 3-20 supplied definitions for == and !=. A class or struct can support almost all of the arithmetic, logical, and relational operators introduced in Chapter 2. Of the operators shown in Tables 2-3, 2-4, 2-5, and 2-6, you can define custom meanings for all except the conditional AND (&&) and conditional OR (||) operators. Those operators are evaluated in terms of other operators, however, so by defining logical AND (&), logical OR (|), and also the logical true and false operators (described shortly), you can control the way that && and || work for your type, even though you cannot implement them directly.

All custom operator implementations follow a certain pattern. They look like static methods, but in the place where you'd normally expect the method name, you instead have the operator keyword followed by the operator for which you want to define a custom meaning. After that comes a parameter list, where the number of parameters is determined by the number of operands the operator requires.

Example 3-88 shows how the binary + operator would look for the Counter class defined earlier in this chapter.

Example 3-88. Implementing the + operator

```
public static Counter operator +(Counter x, Counter y)
{
    return new Counter { _count = x._count + y._count };
}
```

Although the argument count must match the number of operands the operator requires, only one of the arguments has to be the same as the defining type. Example 3-89 exploits this to allow the Counter class to be added to an int.

Example 3-89. Supporting other operand types

```
public static Counter operator +(Counter x, int y)
{
    return new Counter { _count = x._count + y };
}

public static Counter operator +(int x, Counter y)
{
    return new Counter { _count = x + y._count };
}
```

C# requires certain operators to be defined in pairs. We already saw this with the == and != operators—it is illegal to define one and not the other. Likewise, if you define the > operator for your type, you must also define the < operator, and vice versa. The same is true for >= and <=. (There's one more pair, the true and false operators, but they're slightly different; I'll get to those shortly.)

When you overload an operator for which a compound assignment operator exists, you are in effect defining behavior for both. For example, if you define custom behavior for the + operator, the += operator will automatically work too.

The operator keyword can also define custom conversions—methods that convert your type to or from some other type. For example, if we wanted to be able to convert Counter objects to and from int, we could add the two methods in Example 3-90 to the class.

Example 3-90. Conversion operators

```
public static explicit operator int(Counter value)
{
    return value._count;
}
```

```
public static explicit operator Counter(int value)
{
    return new Counter { _count = value };
}
```

I've used the explicit keyword here, which means that these conversions are accessed with the cast syntax, as Example 3-91 shows.

Example 3-91. Using explicit conversion operators

```
var c = (Counter) 123;
var v = (int) c;
```

If you use the implicit keyword instead of explicit, your conversion will be able to happen without needing a cast. In Chapter 2 we saw that some conversions happen implicitly: in certain situations, C# will automatically promote numeric types. For example, you can use an int where a long is expected, perhaps as an argument for a method or in an assignment. Conversion from int to long will always succeed and can never lose information, so the compiler will automatically generate code to perform the conversion without requiring an explicit cast. If you write implicit conversion operators, the C# compiler will silently use them in exactly the same way, enabling your custom type to be used in places where some other type was expected. (In fact, the C# specification defines numeric promotions such as conversion from int to long as built-in implicit conversions.)

Implicit conversion operators are something you shouldn't need to write very often. You should do so only when you can meet the same standards as built-in promotions: the conversion must always be possible and should never throw an exception. Moreover, the conversion should be unsurprising—implicit conversions are a little sneaky in that they allow you to cause methods to be invoked in code that doesn't look like it's calling a method. So unless you're intending to confuse other developers, you should write implicit conversions only where they seem to make unequivocal sense.

C# recognizes two more operators: true and false. If you define either of these, you are required to define both. These are a bit of an oddball pair, because although the C# specification defines them as unary operator overloads, they don't correspond directly to any operator you can write in an expression. They come into play in two scenarios.

If you have not defined an implicit conversion to bool, but you have defined the true and false operators, C# will use the true operator if you use your type as the expression for an if statement or a do or while loop, or as the condition expression in a for loop. However, the compiler prefers the implicit `bool` operator, so this is not the main reason the `true` and `false` operators exist.

The main scenario for the `true` and `false` operators is to enable your custom type to be used as an operand of a conditional Boolean operator (either && or ||). Remember that these operators will evaluate their second operand only if the first outcome does not fully determine the result. If you want customize the behavior of these operators, you cannot implement them directly. Instead, you must define the nonconditional versions of the operators (& and |), and you must also define the `true` and `false` operators. When evaluating &&, C# will use your `false` operator on the first operand, and if that indicates that the first operand is false, then it will not bother to evaluate the second operand. If the first operand is not false, it will evaluate the second operand and then pass both into your custom & operator. The || operator works in much the same way, but with the `true` and | operators, respectively.

You may be wondering why we need special `true` and `false` operators—couldn't we just define an implicit conversion to the `bool` type? In fact we can, and if we do that instead of providing &, |, `true`, and `false`, C# will use that to implement && and || for our type. However, some types may want to represent values that are neither true nor false—there may be a third value representing an unknown state. The `true` operator allows C# to ask the question "is this definitely true?" and for the object to be able to answer "no" without implying that it's definitely false. A conversion to `bool` does not support that.

 The `true` and `false` operators have been present since the first version of C#, and their main application was to enable the implementation of types that support nullable Boolean values with similar semantics to those offered by many databases. The nullable type support added in C# 2.0 provides a better solution, so these operators are no longer particularly useful, but there are still some old parts of the .NET class library that depend on them.

No other operators can be overloaded. For example, you cannot define custom meanings for the . operator used to access members of a method, or the conditional (? :), the null coalescing (??), or the new operators.

Events

Structs and classes can declare *events*. This kind of member enables a type to provide notifications when interesting things happen, using a subscription-based model. For example, a UI object representing a button might define a `Click` event, and you can write code that subscribes to that event.

Events depend on delegates, and since Chapter 9 is dedicated to these topics, I won't go into any detail here. I'm mentioning them only because this section on type members would otherwise be incomplete.

Nested Types

The final kind of member we can define in a class or a struct is a nested type. You can define nested classes, structs, or any of the other types described later in this chapter. A nested type can do anything its normal counterpart would do, but it gets a couple of additional features.

When a type is nested, you have more choices for accessibility. A type defined at global scope can be only public or internal—private would make no sense, because that makes something accessible only from within its containing type, and there is no containing type when you define something at global scope. But a nested type does have a containing type, so if you define a nested type and make it private, that type can be used only from inside the type within which it is nested. Example 3-92 shows a private class.

Example 3-92. A private nested class

```
class Program
{
    private static void Main(string[] args)
    {
        // Ask the class library where the user's My Documents folder lives
        string path =
            Environment.GetFolderPath(Environment.SpecialFolder.MyDocuments);
        string[] files = Directory.GetFiles(path);
        var comparer = new LengthComparer();
        Array.Sort(files, comparer);
        foreach (string file in files)
        {
            Console.WriteLine(file);
        }
    }

    private class LengthComparer : IComparer<string>
    {
        public int Compare(string x, string y)
        {
            int diff = x.Length - y.Length;
            return diff == 0 ? x.CompareTo(y) : diff;
        }
    }
}
```

Private classes can be useful in scenarios like this where you are using an API that requires an implementation of a particular interface. In this case, I'm calling `Array.Sort` to sort a list of files by the lengths of their names. (This is not useful, but it looks nice.) I'm providing the custom sort order in the form of an object that implements the `IComparer<string>` interface. I'll describe interfaces in detail in the next section, but this interface is just a description of what the `Array.Sort` method needs us to provide. I've written a custom class to implement this interface. This class is just an implementation detail of the rest of my code, so I don't want to make it public. A nested private class is just what I need.

Code in a nested type is allowed to use nonpublic members of its containing type. However, an instance of a nested type does not automatically get a reference to an instance of its containing type. (If you're familiar with Java, this may surprise you. C# nested classes are equivalent to Java static nested classes, and there is no equivalent to an inner class.) If you need nested instances to have a reference to their container, you will need to declare a field to hold that, and arrange for it to be initialized; this would work in exactly the same way as any object that wants to hold a reference to another object. Obviously, it's an option only if the outer type is a reference type.

So far, we've looked only at classes and structs, but there are some other ways to define custom types in C#. Some of these are complicated enough to warrant getting their own chapters, but there are a couple of simpler ones that I'll discuss here.

Interfaces

An interface defines a programming interface. Interfaces are very often entirely devoid of implementation, but C# 8.0 adds the ability to define default implementations for some or all methods, and also to define nested types and static fields. (Interfaces cannot define nonstatic fields, though.) Classes can choose to implement interfaces. If you write code that works in terms of an interface, it will be able to work with anything that implements that interface, instead of being limited to working with one particular type.

For example, the .NET class library includes an interface called `IEnumerable<T>`, which defines a minimal set of members for representing sequences of values. (It's a generic interface, so it can represent sequences of anything. An `IEnumerable<string>` is a sequence of strings, for example. Generic types are discussed in Chapter 4.) If a method has a parameter of type `IEnumerable<string>`, you can pass it a reference to an instance of any type that implements the interface, which means that a single method can work with arrays, various collection classes provided by the .NET class library, certain LINQ features, and many other things.

An interface declares methods, properties, and events, but it doesn't have to define their bodies, as Example 3-93 shows. Properties indicate whether getters and/or setters should be present, but we have semicolons in place of the bodies. An interface is effectively a list of the members that a type will need to provide if it wants to implement the interface. Prior to C# 8.0, these method-like members were the only kinds of members interfaces could have. I'll discuss the additional member types now available shortly, but the majority of interfaces you are likely to come across today only contain these kinds of members.

Example 3-93. An interface

```
public interface IDoStuff
{
    string this[int i] { get; set; }
    string Name { get; set; }
    int Id { get; }
    int SomeMethod(string arg);
    event EventHandler Click;
}
```

Individual method-like members are not allowed accessibility modifiers—their accessibility is controlled at the level of the interface itself. (Like classes, interfaces are either public or internal, unless they are nested, in which case they can have any accessibility.) Interfaces cannot declare constructors—an interface only gets to say what services an object should supply once it has been constructed.

By the way, most interfaces in .NET follow the convention that their name starts with an uppercase I followed by one or more words in PascalCasing.

A class declares the interfaces that it implements in a list after a colon following the class name, as Example 3-94 shows. It should provide implementations of all the members listed in the interface. You'll get a compiler error if you leave any out.

Example 3-94. Implementing an interface

```
public class DoStuff : IDoStuff
{
    public string this[int i] { get { return i.ToString(); } set { } }
    public string Name { get; set; }
    ...etc
}
```

When we implement an interface in C#, we typically define each of that interface's methods as a public member of our class. However, sometimes you may want to avoid this. Occasionally, some API may require you to implement an interface that you feel pollutes the purity of your class's API. Or, more prosaically, you may already have defined a member with the same name and signature as a member required by the interface, but that does something different from what the interface requires. Or worse, you may need to implement two different interfaces, both of which define members that have the same name and signature but require different behavior. You can solve any of these problems with a technique called *explicit implementation* to define members that implement a member of a specific interface without being public. Example 3-95 shows the syntax for this, with an implementation of one of the methods from the interface in Example 3-93. With explicit implementations, you do not specify the accessibility, and you prefix the member name with the interface name.

Example 3-95. Explicit implementation of an interface member

```
int IDoStuff.SomeMethod(string arg)
{
    ...
}
```

When a type uses explicit interface implementation, those members cannot be used through a reference of the type itself. They become visible only when referring to an object through an expression of the interface's type.

When a class implements an interface, it becomes implicitly convertible to that interface type. So you can pass any expression of type `DoStuff` from Example 3-94 as a method argument of type `IDoStuff`, for example.

Interfaces are reference types. Despite this, you can implement interfaces on both classes and structs. However, you need to be careful when doing so with a struct, because when you get hold of an interface-typed reference to a struct, it will be a reference to a *box*, which is effectively an object that holds a copy of a struct in a way that can be referred to via a reference. We'll look at boxing in Chapter 7.

Default Interface Implementation

A new feature in C# 8.0 called *default interface implementation* allows you to include some implementation details in an interface definition. This relies on runtime support, so this is only available in code that targets .NET Core 3.0 or later, or .NET Standard 2.1 or later. You can supply static fields, nested types, and bodies for methods, property accessors, and the `add` and `remove` methods for events (which I will describe in Chapter 9). Example 3-96 shows this in use to define a default implementation of a property.

Example 3-96. An interface with a default property implementation

```
public interface INamed
{
    int Id { get; }
```

```
    string Name => $"{this.GetType()}: {this.Id}";
}
```

If a class chooses to implement INamed, it will only be required to provide an implementation for this interface's Id property. It can also supply a Name property if it wants to, but this is not required. If the class does not define its own Name, the definition from the interface will be used instead.

Default interface implementations provide a partial solution to a long-standing limitation of interfaces: if you define an interface that you then make available for other code to use (e.g., via a class library), adding new members to that interface could cause problems for existing code that uses it. Code that invokes methods on the interface won't have a problem because it will be blissfully unaware that new members were added, but any class that implements your interface would, prior to C# 8.0, be broken if you were to add new members. A concrete class is required to supply all the members of an interface it implements, so if the interface gets new members, formerly complete implementations will now be incomplete. Unless you have some way of reaching out to everyone who has written types that implement your interface and getting them to add the missing members, you will cause them problems if they upgrade to the new version.

You might think that this would only be a problem if the authors of code that works with an interface deliberately upgraded to the library containing the updated interface, at which point they'd have an opportunity to fix the problem. However, library upgrades can sometimes be forced on code. If you write an application that uses multiple libraries, each of which was built against different versions of some common library, then at least one of those is going to end up getting a different version of that common library at runtime than the version it was compiled against. (The poster child for this is the Json.NET library for parsing JSON. It's extremely widely used and has had many versions released, so it's common for a single application to use multiple libraries, each with a dependency on a different version of Json.NET. Only one version is used at runtime, so they can't all have their expectations met.) This means that even if you use schemes such as semantic versioning, in which breaking changes are always accompanied by a change to the component's major version number, that might not be enough to avoid trouble: you might find yourself needing to use two components where one wants the v1.0 flavor of some interface, while another wants the v2.0 edition.

The upshot of this was that interfaces were essentially frozen: you couldn't add new members over time or even across major version changes. But default interface implementations loosen this restriction: you can add a new member to an existing interface if you also provide a default implementation for it. That way, existing types that implemented the older version were able to supply a complete implementation of the updated definition, because they automatically pick up the default implementation of the newly added member without needing to be modified in any way. (There is a slight fly in the ointment, making it still sometimes preferable to use the older solution to this problem, abstract base classes: Chapter 6 describes these issues. So although default interface implementation can provide a useful escape hatch, you should still avoid modifying published interfaces if at all possible.)

In addition to providing extra flexibility for backward compatibility, the default interface implementation feature adds three more capabilities: interfaces can now define constants, static fields, and types.[7] Example 3-97 shows an interface that contains a nested constant and type.

Example 3-97. An interface with a const and a nested type

```
public interface IContainMultitudes
{
    public const string TheMagicWord = "Please";

    public enum Outcome
    {
        Yes,
        No
    }

    Outcome MayI(string request)
    {
        return request == TheMagicWord ? Outcome.Yes : Outcome.No;
    }
}
```

With non-method-like members such as these, we need to specify an accessibility, because in some cases you may want to introduce these nested members purely for the benefit of default method implementations, in which case you'd want them to be private. In this case, I want the relevant members to be accessible to all, since they form part of the API defined by this interface, so I have marked them as public. You might be looking at that nested Outcome type and wondering what's going on. Wonder no more.

---

7 In C# 8.0, you can nest class, struct, interface, and enum types in an interface. Nested delegate types are not supported.

Enums

The enum keyword declares a very simple type that defines a set of named values. Example 3-98 shows an enum that defines a set of mutually exclusive choices. You could say that this *enumerates* the options, which is where the enum keyword gets its name.

Example 3-98. An enum with mutually exclusive options

```
public enum PorridgeTemperature
{
    TooHot,
    TooCold,
    JustRight
}
```

An enum can be used in most places you might use any other type—it could be the type of a local variable, a field, or a method parameter, for example. But one of the most common ways to use an enum is in a switch statement, as Example 3-99 shows.

Example 3-99. Switching with an enum

```
switch (porridge.Temperature)
{
case PorridgeTemperature.TooHot:
    GoOutsideForABit();
    break;

case PorridgeTemperature.TooCold:
    MicrowaveMyBreakfast();
    break;

case PorridgeTemperature.JustRight:
    NomNomNom();
    break;
}
```

As this illustrates, to refer to enumeration members, you must qualify them with the type name. In fact, an enum is really just a fancy way of defining a load of const fields. The members are all just int values under the covers. You can even specify the values explicitly, as Example 3-100 shows.

Example 3-100. Explicit enum values

```
[System.Flags]
public enum Ingredients
```

```
{
    Eggs            =           0b1,
    Bacon           =          0b10,
    Sausages        =         0b100,
    Mushrooms       =        0b1000,
    Tomato          =      0b1_0000,
    BlackPudding    =     0b10_0000,
    BakedBeans      =    0b100_0000,
    TheFullEnglish  =    0b111_1111
}
```

This example also shows an alternative way to use an enum. The options in Example 3-100 are not mutually exclusive. I've used binary constants here, so you can see that each value corresponds to a particular bit position being set to 1. This makes it easy to combine them—Eggs and Bacon would be 3 (11 in binary), while Eggs, Bacon, Sausages, BlackPudding, and BakedBeans (my preferred combination) would be 103 (1100111 in binary, or 0x67 in hex).

 When combining flag-based enumeration values, we normally use the bitwise OR operator. For example, you could write Ingredi ents.Eggs|Ingredients.Bacon. Not only is this significantly easier to read than using the numeric values, but it also works well with Visual Studio's search tools—you can find all the places a particular symbol is used by right-clicking on its definition and choosing Find All References from the context menu. You might come across code that uses + instead of |. This works for some combinations, but Ingredients.TheFullEnglish + Ingredients.Eggs would be a value of 128, which doesn't correspond to anything, so it's safer to stick with |.

When you declare an enum that's designed to be combined in this way, you're supposed to annotate it with the Flags attribute, which is defined in the System namespace. (Chapter 14 will describe attributes in detail.) Example 3-100 does this, although in practice, it doesn't matter greatly if you forget, because the C# compiler doesn't care, and in fact, there are very few tools that pay any attention to it. The main benefit is that if you call ToString on an enum value, it will notice when the Flags attribute is present. For this Ingredients type, ToString would convert the value of 3 to the string Eggs, Bacon, which is also how the debugger would show the value, whereas without the Flags attribute, it would be treated as an unrecognized value and you would just get a string containing the digit 3.

With this sort of flags-style enumeration, you can run out of bits fairly quickly. By default, enum uses int to represent the value, and with a sequence of mutually exclusive values, that's usually sufficient. It would be a fairly complicated scenario that needed billions of different values in a single enumeration type. However, with 1 bit per flag, an int provides space for just 32 flags. Fortunately, you can get a little more breathing room, because you can specify a different underlying type—you can use any built-in integer type, meaning that you can go up to 64 bits. As Example 3-101 shows, you can specify the underlying type after a colon following the enum type name.

Example 3-101. 64-bit enum

```
[System.Flags]
public enum TooManyChoices : long
{
    ...
}
```

All enum types are value types, incidentally, like the built-in numeric types or any struct. But they are very limited. You cannot define any members other than the constant values—no methods or properties, for example.

Enumeration types can sometimes enhance the readability of code. A lot of APIs accept a bool to control some aspect of their behavior, but might often have done better to use an enum. Consider the code in Example 3-102. It constructs a Stream Reader, a class for working with data streams that contain text. The second constructor argument is a bool.

Example 3-102. Unhelpful use of bool

```
using var rdr = new StreamReader(stream, true);
```

It's not remotely obvious what that second argument does. If you happen to be familiar with StreamReader, you may know that this argument determines whether byte ordering in a multibyte text encoding should be set explicitly from the code, or determined from a preamble at the start of the stream. (Using the named argument syntax would help here.) And if you've got a really good memory, you might even know which of those choices true happens to select. But most mere mortal developers will probably have to reach for IntelliSense or even the documentation to work out what that argument does. Compare that experience with Example 3-103, which shows a different type.

Example 3-103. Clarity with an enum

```
using var fs = new FileStream(path, FileMode.Append);
```

This constructor's second argument uses an enumeration type, which makes for rather less opaque code. It doesn't take an eidetic memory to work out that this code intends to append data to an existing file.

As it happens, because this particular API has more than two options, it couldn't use a `bool`. So `FileMode` really had to be an `enum`. But these examples illustrate that even in cases where you're selecting between just two choices, it's well worth considering defining an `enum` for the job so that it's completely obvious which choice is being made when you look at the code.

Other Types

We're almost done with our survey of types and what goes in them. There's one kind of type that I'll not discuss until Chapter 9: delegates. We use delegates when we need a reference to a function, but the details are somewhat involved.

I've also not mentioned pointers. C# supports pointers that work in a pretty similar way to C-style pointers, complete with pointer arithmetic. (If you're not familiar with these, they provide a reference to a particular location in memory.) These are a little weird, because they are slightly outside of the rest of the type system. For example, in Chapter 2, I mentioned that a variable of type `object` can refer to "almost anything." The reason I had to qualify that is that pointers are one of the two exceptions— `object` can work with any C# data type except a pointer, or a `ref struct`. (Chapter 18 discusses the latter.)

But now we really are done. Some types in C# are special, including the fundamental types discussed in Chapter 2 and the structs, interfaces, enums, delegates, and pointers just described, but everything else looks like a class. There are a few classes that get special handling in certain circumstances—notably attribute classes (Chapter 14) and exception classes (Chapter 8)—but except for certain special scenarios, even those are otherwise completely normal classes. Even though we've seen all the kinds of types that C# supports, there's one way to define a class that I've not shown yet.

Anonymous Types

C# offers two mechanisms for grouping a handful of values together. You've already seen tuples, which were described in Chapter 2. These were introduced in C# 7.0, but there is an alternative that has been available since C# 3.0: Example 3-104 shows how to create an instance of an *anonymous type* and how to use it.

Example 3-104. An anonymous type

```
var x = new { Title = "Lord", Surname = "Voldemort" };

Console.WriteLine($"Welcome, {x.Title} {x.Surname}");
```

As you can see, we use the new keyword without specifying a type name. Instead, we just use the object initializer syntax. The C# compiler will provide a type that has one read-only property for each entry inside the initializer. So in Example 3-104, the variable x will refer to an object that has two properties, Title and Surname, both of type string. (You do not state the property types explicitly in an anonymous type. The compiler infers each property's type from the initialization expression in the same way as it does for the var keyword.) Since these are just normal properties, we can access them with the usual syntax, as the final line of the example shows.

The compiler generates a fairly ordinary class definition for each anonymous type. It is immutable, because all the properties are read-only. It overrides Equals so that you can compare instances by value, and it also provides a matching GetHashCode implementation. The only unusual thing about the generated class is that it's not possible to refer to the type by name in C#. Running Example 3-104 in the debugger, I find that the compiler has chosen the name <>f__AnonymousType0'2. This is not a legal identifier in C# because of those angle brackets (<>) at the start. C# uses names like this whenever it wants to create something that is guaranteed not to collide with any identifiers you might use in your own code, or that it wants to prevent you from using directly. This sort of identifier is called, rather magnificently, an *unspeakable name*.

Because you cannot write the name of an anonymous type, a method cannot declare that it returns one, or that it requires one to be passed as an argument (unless you use an anonymous type as an inferred generic type argument, something we'll see in Chapter 4). Of course, an expression of type object can refer to an instance of an anonymous type, but only the method that defines the type can use its properties (unless you use the dynamic type described in Chapter 2). So anonymous types are of somewhat limited value. They were added to the language for LINQ's benefit: they enable a query to select specific columns or properties from some source collection, and also to define custom grouping criteria, as you'll see in Chapter 10.

These limitations provide a clue as to why Microsoft felt the need to add tuples in C# 7.0 when the language already had a pretty similar-looking feature. However, if the inability to use anonymous types as parameters or return types was the only problem, an obvious solution might have been to introduce a syntax enabling them to be identified. The syntax for referring to tuples could arguably have worked—we can now write (string Name, double Age) to refer to a tuple type, but why introduce a whole new concept? Why not just use that syntax to name anonymous types? (Obviously we'd no longer be able to call them anonymous types, but at least we wouldn't have ended up with two confusingly similar language features.) However, the lack of names isn't the only problem with anonymous types.

As C# has been used in increasingly diverse applications, and across a broader range of hardware, efficiency has become more of a concern. In the database access scenarios for which anonymous types were originally introduced, the cost of object allocations would have been a relatively small part of the picture, but the basic concept—a small bundle of values—is potentially useful in a much wider range of scenarios, some of which are more performance sensitive. However, anonymous types are all reference types, and while in many cases that's not a problem, it can rule them out in some hyper-performance-sensitive scenarios. Tuples, on the other hand, are all value types, making them viable even in code where you are attempting to minimize the number of allocations. (See Chapter 7 for more detail on memory management and garbage collection, and Chapter 18 for information about some of the newer language features aimed at enabling more efficient memory usage.) Also, since tuples are all based on a set of generic types under the covers, they may end up reducing the runtime overhead required to keep track of loaded types: with anonymous types, you can end up with a lot more distinct types loaded. For related reasons, anonymous types would have problems with compatibility across component boundaries.

Does this mean that anonymous types are no longer of any use? In fact, they still offer some advantages. The most significant one is that you cannot use a tuple in a lambda expression that will be converted into an expression tree. This issue is described in detail in Chapter 9, but the practical upshot is that you cannot use tuples in the kinds of LINQ queries mentioned earlier that anonymous types were added to support.

More subtle is the fact that with tuples, property names are a convenient fiction, whereas with anonymous types, they are real. This has two upshots. One regards equivalence: the tuples (X: 10, Y:20) and (W:10, H:20) are considered interchangeable, where any variable capable of holding one is capable of holding the other. That is not true for anonymous types: new { X = 10, Y = 20 } has a different type than new { W = 10, H = 20 }, and attempting to pass one to code that expects the other will cause a compiler error. This difference can make tuples more convenient, but it can also make them more error prone, because the compiler looks only at the shape of the data when asking whether you're using the right type. Anonymous types can still enable errors: if you have two types with exactly the same property names and types but which are semantically different, there's no way to express that with anonymous types. (In practice you'd probably just define two normal types to deal with this.) The second upshot of anonymous types offering genuine properties is that you can pass them to code that inspects an object's properties. Many reflection-driven features such as certain serialization frameworks, or UI framework data binding, depend on being able to discover properties at runtime through reflection (see Chapter 13). Anonymous types may work better with these frameworks than tuples, in which the properties' real names are all things like Item1, Item2, etc.

Partial Types and Methods

There's one last topic I want to discuss relating to types. C# supports what it calls a *partial type declaration*. This is a very simple concept: it means that the type declaration might span multiple files. If you add the `partial` keyword to a type declaration, C# will not complain if another file defines the same type—it will simply act as though all the members defined by the two files had appeared in a single declaration in one file.

This feature exists to make it easier to write code generation tools. Various features in Visual Studio can generate bits of your class for you. This is particularly common with UIs. UI applications typically have markup that defines the layout and content of each part of the UI, and you can choose for certain UI elements to be accessible in your code. You usually achieve this by adding a field to a class associated with the markup file. To keep things simple, all the parts of the class that Visual Studio generates go in a separate file from the parts that you write. This means that the generated parts can be remade from scratch whenever needed without any risk of overwriting the code that you've written. Before partial types were introduced to C#, all the code for a class had to go in one file, and from time to time, code generation tools would get confused, leading to loss of code.

 Partial classes are not limited to code generation scenarios, so you can of course use this to split your own class definitions across multiple files. However, if you've written a class so large and complex that you feel the need to split it into multiple source files just to keep it manageable, that's probably a sign that the class is too complex. A better response to this problem might be to change your design. However, it can be useful if you need to maintain code that is built in different ways for different target platforms: you can use partial classes to put target-specific parts in separate files.

Partial methods are also designed for code generation scenarios, but they are slightly more complex. They allow one file, typically a generated file, to declare a method, and for another file to implement the method. (Strictly speaking, the declaration and implementation are allowed to be in the same file, but they usually won't be.) This may sound like the relationship between an interface and a class that implements that interface, but it's not quite the same. With partial methods, the declaration and implementation are in the same class—they're in different files only because the class has been split across multiple files.

If you do not provide an implementation of a partial method, the compiler acts as though the method isn't there at all, and any code that invokes the method is simply ignored at compile time. The main reason for this is to support code generation mechanisms that are able to offer many kinds of notifications, but where you want zero runtime overhead for notifications that you don't need. Partial methods enable this by letting the code generator declare a partial method for each kind of notification it provides, and to generate code that invokes all of these partial methods where necessary. All code relating to notifications for which you do not write a handler method will be stripped out at compile time.

It's an idiosyncratic mechanism, but it was driven by frameworks that provide extremely fine-grained notifications and extension points. There are some more obvious runtime techniques you could use instead, such as interfaces, or features that I'll cover in later chapters, such as callbacks or virtual methods. However, any of these would impose a relatively high cost for unused features. Unused partial methods get stripped out at compile time, reducing the cost of the bits you don't use to nothing, which is a considerable improvement.

Summary

You've now seen most of the kinds of types you can write in C#, and the sorts of members they support. Classes are the most widely used, but structs are useful if you need value-like semantics for assignment and arguments; both support the same member types—namely, fields, constructors, methods, properties, indexers, events, custom operators, and nested types. Interfaces are abstract, so at the instance level they support only methods, properties, indexers, and events, but with C# 8.0's new default interface implementation feature, they can now provide static fields, nested types, and default implementations for other members. And enums are very limited, providing just a set of known values.

There's another feature of the C# type system that makes it possible to write very flexible types, called generic types. We'll look at these in the next chapter.

CHAPTER 4
Generics

In Chapter 3, I showed how to write types and described the various kinds of members they can contain. However, there's an extra dimension to classes, structs, interfaces, and methods that I did not show. They can define *type parameters*, placeholders that let you plug in different types at compile time. This allows you to write just one type and then produce multiple versions of it. A type that does this is called a *generic type*. For example, the class library defines a generic class called List<T> that acts as a variable-length array. T is a type parameter here, and you can use almost any type as an argument, so List<int> is a list of integers, List<string> is a list of strings, and so on. You can also write a *generic method*, which is a method that has its own type arguments, independently of whether its containing type is generic.

Generic types and methods are visually distinctive because they always have angle brackets (< and >) after the name. These contain a comma-separated list of parameters or arguments. The same parameter/argument distinction applies here as with methods: the declaration specifies a list of parameters, and then when you come to use the method or type, you supply arguments for those parameters. So List<T> defines a single type parameter, T, and List<int> supplies a *type argument*, int, for that parameter.[1]

Type parameters can be called whatever you like, within the usual constraints for identifiers in C#. There's a common but not universal convention of using T when there's only one parameter. For multiparameter generics, you tend to see slightly more descriptive names. For example, the class library defines the

---

1 When saying the names of generic types, the convention is to use the word "of" as in "List of T" or "List of int."

`Dictionary<TKey, TValue>` collection class. Sometimes you will see a descriptive name like that even when there's just one parameter, but in any case, you will tend to see a T prefix, so that the type parameters stand out when you use them in your code.

Generic Types

Classes, structs, and interfaces can all be generic, as can delegates, which we'll be looking at in Chapter 9. Example 4-1 shows how to define a generic class. The syntax for structs and interfaces is much the same: the type name is followed immediately by a type parameter list.

Example 4-1. Defining a generic class

```
public class NamedContainer<T>
{
    public NamedContainer(T item, string name)
    {
        Item = item;
        Name = name;
    }

    public T Item { get; }
    public string Name { get; }
}
```

Inside the body of the class, I can use the type parameter T anywhere you would normally see a type name. In this case, I've used it as the type of a constructor argument, and also the `Item` property. I could define fields of type T too. (In fact I have, albeit not explicitly. The automatic property syntax generates hidden fields, so my `Item` property will have an associated hidden field of type T.) You can also define local variables of type T. And you're free to use type parameters as arguments for other generic types. My `NamedContainer<T>` could declare a variable of type `List<T>`, for example.

The class that Example 4-1 defines is, like any generic type, not a complete type. A generic type declaration is *unbound*, meaning that there are type parameters that must be filled in to produce a complete type. Basic questions, such as how much memory a `NamedContainer<T>` instance will require, cannot be answered without knowing what T is—the hidden field for the `Item` property would need 4 bytes if T were an `int`, but 16 bytes if it were a `decimal`. The CLR cannot produce executable code for a type if it does not know how the contents will be arranged in memory. So to use this, or any other generic type, we must provide type arguments. Example 4-2 shows how. When type arguments are supplied, the result is sometimes called a *constructed type*. (This has nothing to do with constructors, the special kind of member we looked at in Chapter 3. In fact, Example 4-2 uses those too—it invokes the constructors of a couple of constructed types.)

Example 4-2. Using a generic class

```
var a = new NamedContainer<int>(42, "The answer");
var b = new NamedContainer<int>(99, "Number of red balloons");
var c = new NamedContainer<string>("Programming C#", "Book title");
```

You can use a constructed generic type anywhere you would use a normal type. For example, you can use them as the types for method parameters and return values, properties, or fields. You can even use one as a type argument for another generic type, as Example 4-3 shows.

Example 4-3. Constructed generic types as type arguments

```
// ...where a, and b come from Example 4-2.
var namedInts = new List<NamedContainer<int>>() { a, b };
var namedNamedItem = new NamedContainer<NamedContainer<int>>(a, "Wrapped");
```

Each different type I supply as an argument to NamedContainer<T> constructs a distinct type. (And for generic types with multiple type arguments, each distinct combination of type arguments would construct a distinct type.) This means that NamedContainer<int> is a different type than NamedContainer<string>. That's why there's no conflict in using NamedContainer<int> as the type argument for another NamedContainer as the final line of Example 4-3 does—there's no infinite recursion here.

Because each different set of type arguments produces a distinct type, in most cases there is no implied compatibility between different forms of the same generic type. You cannot assign a NamedContainer<int> into a variable of type NamedContainer<string> or vice versa. It makes sense that those two types are incompatible, because int and string are quite different types. But what if we used object as a type argument? As Chapter 2 described, you can put almost anything in an object variable. If you write a method with a parameter of type object, it's OK to pass a string, so you might expect a method that takes a NamedContainer<object> to be happy with a NamedContainer<string>. That won't work, but some generic types (specifically, interfaces and delegates) can declare that they want this kind of compatibility relationship. The mechanisms that support this (called *covariance* and *contravariance*) are closely related to the type system's inheritance mechanisms. Chapter 6 is all about inheritance and type compatibility, so I will discuss this aspect of generic types there.

The number of type parameters forms part of an unbound generic type's identity. This makes it possible to introduce multiple types with the same name as long as they have different numbers of type parameters. (The technical term for number of type parameters is *arity*.) So you could define a generic class called, say, `Operation<T>`, and then another class, `Operation<T1, T2>`, and also `Operation<T1, T2, T3>`, and so on, all in the same namespace, without introducing any ambiguity. When you are using these types, it's clear from the number of arguments which type was meant—`Operation<int>` clearly uses the first, while `Operation<string, double>` uses the second, for example. And for the same reason, a nongeneric `Operation` class would be distinct from generic types of the same name.

My `NamedContainer<T>` example doesn't do anything to instances of its type argument, `T`—it never invokes any methods, or uses any properties or other members of `T`. All it does is accept a `T` as a constructor argument, which it stores away for later retrieval. This is also true of many generic types in the .NET class library—I've mentioned some collection classes, which are all variations on the same theme of containing data for later retrieval. There is a reason for this: a generic class can find itself working with any type, so it can presume little about its type arguments. However, it doesn't have to be this way. You can specify *constraints* for your type arguments.

Constraints

C# allows you to state that a type argument must fulfill certain requirements. For example, suppose you want to be able to create new instances of the type on demand. Example 4-4 shows a simple class that provides deferred construction—it makes an instance available through a static property, but does not attempt to construct that instance until the first time you read the property.

Example 4-4. Creating a new instance of a parameterized type

```
// For illustration only. Consider using Lazy<T> in a real program.
public static class Deferred<T>
    where T : new()
{
    private static T _instance;

    public static T Instance
    {
        get
        {
            if (_instance == null)
            {
                _instance = new T();
            }
            return _instance;
        }
```

```
        }
}
```

 You wouldn't write a class like this in practice, because the class library offers Lazy<T>, which does the same job but with more flexibility. Lazy<T> can work correctly in multithreaded code, which Example 4-4 will not. Example 4-4 is just to illustrate how constraints work. Don't use it!

For this class to do its job, it needs to be able to construct an instance of whatever type is supplied as the argument for T. The get accessor uses the new keyword, and since it passes no arguments, it clearly requires T to provide a parameterless constructor. But not all types do, so what happens if we try to use a type without a suitable constructor as the argument for Deferred<T>? The compiler will reject it, because it violates a constraint that this generic type has declared for T. Constraints appear just before the class's opening brace, and they begin with the where keyword. The new() constraint in Example 4-4 states that T is required to supply a zero-argument constructor.

If that constraint had not been present, the class in Example 4-4 would not compile—you would get an error on the line that attempts to construct a new T. A generic type (or method) is allowed to use only features of its type parameters that it has specified through constraints, or that are defined by the base object type. (The object type defines a ToString method, for example, so you can invoke that on instances of any type without needing to specify a constraint.)

C# offers only a very limited suite of constraints. You cannot demand a constructor that takes arguments, for example. In fact, C# supports only six kinds of constraints on a type argument: a type constraint, a reference type constraint, a value type constraint, notnull, unmanaged, and the new() constraint. We just saw that last one, so let's look at the rest.

Type Constraints

You can constrain the argument for a type parameter to be compatible with a particular type. For example, you could use this to demand that the argument type implements a certain interface. Example 4-5 shows the syntax.

Example 4-5. Using a type constraint

```
using System;
using System.Collections.Generic;

public class GenericComparer<T> : IComparer<T>
    where T : IComparable<T>
```

```
{
    public int Compare(T x, T y)
    {
        return x.CompareTo(y);
    }
}
```

I'll just explain the purpose of this example before describing how it takes advantage of a type constraint. This class provides a bridge between two styles of value comparison that you'll find in .NET. Some data types provide their own comparison logic, but at times, it can be more useful for comparison to be a separate function implemented in its own class. These two styles are represented by the IComparable<T> and IComparer<T> interfaces, which are both part of the class library. (They are in the System and System.Collections.Generics namespaces, respectively.) I showed IComparer<T> in Chapter 3—an implementation of this interface can compare two objects or values of type T. The interface defines a single Compare method that takes two arguments and returns either a negative number, 0, or a positive number if the first argument is respectively less than, equal to, or greater than the second. IComparable<T> is very similar, but its CompareTo method takes just a single argument, because with this interface, you are asking an instance to compare *itself* to some other instance.

Some of the .NET class library's collection classes require you to provide an IComparer<T> to support ordering operations such as sorting. They use the model in which a separate object performs the comparison, because this offers two advantages over the IComparable<T> model. First, it enables you to use data types that don't implement IComparable<T>. Second, it allows you to plug in different sorting orders. (For example, suppose you want to sort some strings with a case-insensitive order. The string type implements IComparable<string>, but that provides a case-sensitive, locale-specific order.) So IComparer<T> is the more flexible model. However, what if you are using a data type that implements IComparable<T>, and you're perfectly happy with the order that provides? What would you do if you're working with an API that demands an IComparer<T>?

Actually, the answer is that you'd probably just use the .NET feature designed for this very scenario: Comparer<T>.Default. If T implements IComparable<T>, that property will return an IComparer<T> that does precisely what you want. So in practice you wouldn't need to write the code in Example 4-5, because Microsoft has already written it for you. However, it's instructive to see how you'd write your own version, because it illustrates how to use a type constraint.

The line starting with the where keyword states that this generic class requires the argument for its type parameter T to implement IComparable<T>. Without this addition, the Compare method would not compile—it invokes the CompareTo method on an argument of type T. That method is not present on all objects, and the C# compiler allows this only because we've constrained T to be an implementation of an interface that does offer such a method.

Interface constraints are somewhat unusual. If a method needs a particular argument to implement a particular interface, you wouldn't normally need a generic type constraint. You can just use that interface as the argument's type. However, Example 4-5 can't do this. You can demonstrate this by trying Example 4-6. It won't compile.

Example 4-6. Will not compile: interface not implemented

```
public class GenericComparer<T> : IComparer<T>
{
    public int Compare(IComparable<T> x, T y)
    {
        return x.CompareTo(y);
    }
}
```

The compiler will complain that I've not implemented the IComparer<T> interface's Compare method. Example 4-6 has a Compare method, but its signature is wrong—that first argument should be a T. I could also try the correct signature without specifying the constraint, as Example 4-7 shows.

Example 4-7. Will not compile: missing constraint

```
public class GenericComparer<T> : IComparer<T>
{
    public int Compare(T x, T y)
    {
        return x.CompareTo(y);
    }
}
```

That will also fail to compile, because the compiler can't find that CompareTo method I'm trying to use. It's the constraint for T in Example 4-5 that enables the compiler to know what that method really is.

Type constraints don't have to be interfaces, by the way. You can use any type. For example, you can constrain a particular argument to always derive from a particular base class. More subtly, you can also define one parameter's constraint in terms of another type parameter. Example 4-8 requires the first type argument to derive from the second, for example.

Example 4-8. Constraining one argument to derive from another

```
public class Foo<T1, T2>
    where T1 : T2
...
```

Type constraints are fairly specific—they require either a particular inheritance relationship, or the implementation of certain interfaces. However, you can define slightly less specific constraints.

Reference Type Constraints

You can constrain a type argument to be a reference type. As Example 4-9 shows, this looks similar to a type constraint. You just put the keyword class instead of a type name. If you are using C# 8.0, and are in an enabled nullable annotation context, the meaning of this annotation changes: it requires the type argument to be a non-nullable reference type. If you specify class?, that allows the type argument to be either a nullable or a non-nullable reference type.

Example 4-9. Constraint requiring a reference type

```
public class Bar<T>
    where T : class
...
```

This constraint prevents the use of value types such as int, double, or any struct as the type argument. Its presence enables your code to do three things that would not otherwise be possible. First, it means that you can write code that tests whether variables of the relevant type are null.[2] If you've not constrained the type to be a reference type, there's always a possibility that it's a value type, and those can't have null values. The second capability is that you can use it as the target type of the as operator, which we'll look at in Chapter 6. This is really just a variation on the first feature —the as keyword requires a reference type because it can produce a null result.

---

2 This is permitted even if you used the plain class constraint in an enabled nullable annotation context. The nullable references feature does not provide watertight guarantees of non-null-ness, so it permits comparison with null.

You cannot use a nullable type such as int? (or Nullable<int>, as the CLR calls it) as the argument for a parameter with a class constraint. Although you can test an int? for null and use it with the as operator, the compiler generates quite different code for nullable types for both operations than it does for a reference type. It cannot compile a single method that can cope with both reference types and nullable types if you use these features.

The third feature that a reference type constraint enables is the ability to use certain other generic types. It's often convenient for generic code to use one of its type arguments as an argument for another generic type, and if that other type specifies a constraint, you'll need to put the same constraint on your own type parameter. So if some other type specifies a class constraint, this might require you to constrain one of your own arguments in the same way.

Of course, this does raise the question of why the type you're using needs the constraint in the first place. It might be that it simply wants to test for null or use the as operator, but there's another reason for applying this constraint. Sometimes, you just need a type argument to be a reference type—there are situations in which a generic method might be able to compile without a class constraint, but it will not work correctly if used with a value type. To illustrate this, I'll describe a scenario in which I sometimes find myself needing to use this kind of constraint.

I regularly write tests that create an instance of the class I'm testing, and that also need one or more fake objects to stand in for real objects with which the object under test wants to interact. Using these stand-ins reduces the amount of code any single test has to exercise, and can make it easier to verify the behavior of the object being tested. For example, my test might need to verify that my code sends messages to a server at the right moment, but I don't want to have to run a real server during a unit test, so I provide an object that implements the same interface as the class that would transmit the message, but which won't really send the message. This combination of an object under test plus a fake is such a common pattern that it might be useful to put the code into a reusable base class. Using generics means that the class can work for any combination of the type being tested and the type being faked. Example 4-10 shows a simplified version of a kind of helper class I sometimes write in these situations.

Example 4-10. Constrained by another constraint

```
using Microsoft.VisualStudio.TestTools.UnitTesting;
using Moq;

public class TestBase<TSubject, TFake>
    where TSubject : new()
    where TFake : class
```

```
{
    public TSubject Subject { get; private set; }
    public Mock<TFake> Fake { get; private set; }

    [TestInitialize]
    public void Initialize()
    {
        Subject = new TSubject();
        Fake = new Mock<TFake>();
    }
}
```

There are various ways to build fake objects for test purposes. You could just write new classes that implement the same interface as your real objects, but there are also third-party libraries that can generate them. One such library is called Moq (an open source project available for free from *https://github.com/Moq/*), and that's where the Mock<T> class in Example 4-10 comes from. It's capable of generating a fake implementation of any interface or of any nonsealed class. (Chapter 6 describes the sealed keyword.) It will provide empty implementations of all members by default, and you can configure more interesting behaviors if necessary. You can also verify whether the code under test used the fake object in the way you expected.

How is that relevant to constraints? The Mock<T> class specifies a reference type constraint on its own type argument, T. This is due to the way in which it creates dynamic implementations of types at runtime; it's a technique that can work only for reference types. Moq generates a type at runtime, and if T is an interface, that generated type will implement it, whereas if T is a class, the generated type will derive from it.[3] There's nothing useful it can do if T is a struct, because you cannot derive from a value type. That means that when I use Mock<T> in Example 4-10, I need to make sure that whatever type argument I pass is not a struct (i.e., it must be a reference type). But the type argument I'm using is one of my class's type parameters: TFake. So I don't know what type that will be—that'll be up to whoever is using my class.

For my class to compile without error, I have to ensure that I have met the constraints of any generic types that I use. I have to guarantee that Mock<TFake> is valid, and the only way to do that is to add a constraint on my own type that requires TFake to be a reference type. And that's what I've done on the third line of the class definition in Example 4-10. Without that, the compiler would report errors on the two lines that refer to Mock<TFake>.

---

3 Moq relies on the *dynamic proxy* feature from the Castle Project to generate this type. If you would like to use something similar in your code, you can find this at *http://castleproject.org/*.

To put it more generally, if you want to use one of your own type parameters as the type argument for a generic that specifies a constraint, you'll need to specify the same constraint on your own type parameter.

Value Type Constraints

Just as you can constrain a type argument to be a reference type, you can also constrain it to be a value type. As shown in Example 4-11, the syntax is similar to that for a reference type constraint, but with the struct keyword.

Example 4-11. Constraint requiring a value type

```
public class Quux<T>
    where T : struct
...
```

Before now, we've seen the struct keyword only in the context of custom value types, but despite how it looks, this constraint permits any of the built-in numeric types such as int, as well as custom structs.

.NET's Nullable<T> type imposes this constraint. Recall from Chapter 3 that Nullable<T> provides a wrapper for value types that allows a variable to hold either a value, or no value. (We normally use the special syntax C# provides, so we'd write, say, int? instead of Nullable<int>.) The only reason this type exists is to provide nullability for types that would not otherwise be able to hold a null value. So it only makes sense to use this with a value type—reference type variables can already be set to null without needing this wrapper. The value type constraint prevents you from using Nullable<T> with types for which it is unnecessary.

Value Types All the Way Down with Unmanaged Constraints

You can specify unmanaged as a constraint, which requires that the type argument be a value type, but also that it contains no references. Not only does this mean that all of the type's fields must be value types, but the type of each field must in turn contain only fields that are value types, and so on all the way down. In practice this means that all the actual data needs to be either one of a fixed set of built-in types (essentially, all the numeric types, bool, or a pointer) or an enum type. This is mainly of interest in interop scenarios, because types that match the unmanaged constraint can be passed safely and efficiently to unmanaged code.

Not Null Constraints

C# 8.0 introduces a new constraint type, notnull, which is available if you use the new nullable references feature. If you specify this, then either value types or non-nullable reference types are allowed.

Other Special Type Constraints

Chapter 3 described various special kinds of types, including enumeration types (enum) and delegate types (covered in detail in Chapter 9). It is sometimes useful to constrain type arguments to be one of these kinds of types. There's no special trick to this, though: you can just use type constraints. All delegate types derive from Sys tem.Delegate, and all enumeration types derive from System.Enum. As Example 4-12 shows, you can just write a type constraint requiring a type argument to derive from either of these.

Example 4-12. Constraints requiring delegate and enum types

```
public class RequireDelegate<T>
    where T : Delegate
{
}

public class RequireEnum<T>
    where T : Enum
{
}
```

This used not to work. For years, the C# compiler rather surprisingly went out of its way to forbid the use of these two types in type constraints. It was only in C# 7.3 that we have finally been able to write these kinds of constraints.

Multiple Constraints

If you'd like to impose multiple constraints for a single type argument, you can just put them in a list, as Example 4-13 shows. There are a couple of ordering restrictions: if you have a reference or value type constraint, the **class** or **struct** keyword must come first in the list. If the new() constraint is present, it must be last.

Example 4-13. Multiple constraints

```
public class Spong<T>
    where T : IEnumerable<T>, IDisposable, new()
...
```

When your type has multiple type parameters, you write one `where` clause for each type parameter you wish to constrain. In fact, we saw this earlier—Example 4-10 defines constraints for both of its parameters.

Zero-Like Values

There are certain features that all types support, and which therefore do not require a constraint. This includes the set of methods defined by the `object` base class, covered in Chapters 3 and 6. But there's a more basic feature that can sometimes be useful in generic code.

Variables of any type can be initialized to a default value. As you have seen in the preceding chapters, there are some situations in which the CLR does this for us. For example, all the fields in a newly constructed object will have a known value even if we don't write field initializers and don't supply values in the constructor. Likewise, a new array of any type will have all of its elements initialized to a known value. The CLR does this by filling the relevant memory with zeros. The exact meaning of this depends on the data type. For any of the built-in numeric types, the value will quite literally be the number 0, but for nonnumeric types, it's something else. For `bool`, the default is `false`, and for a reference type, it is `null`.

Sometimes, it can be useful for generic code to be able to set a variable to this initial default zero-like value. But you cannot use a literal expression to do this in most situations. You cannot assign `null` into a variable whose type is specified by a type parameter unless that parameter has been constrained to be a reference type. And you cannot assign the literal 0 into any such variable, because there is no way to constrain a type argument to be a numeric type.

Instead, you can request the zero-like value for any type using the `default` keyword. (This is the same keyword we saw inside a `switch` statement in Chapter 2, but used in a completely different way. C# keeps up the C-family tradition of defining multiple, unrelated meanings for each keyword.) If you write `default(`*SomeType*`)`, where *Some Type* is either a specific type or a type parameter, you will get the default initial value for that type: 0 if it is a numeric type, and the equivalent for any other type. For example, the expression `default(int)` has the value 0, `default(bool)` is `false`, and `default(string)` is `null`. You can use this with a generic type parameter to get the default value for the corresponding type argument, as Example 4-14 shows.

Example 4-14. Getting the default (zero-like) value of a type argument

```
static void ShowDefault<T>()
{
    Console.WriteLine(default(T));
}
```

Inside a generic type or method that defines a type parameter T, the expression default(T) will produce the default, zero-like value for T—whatever T may be—without requiring constraints. So you could use the generic method in Example 4-14 to verify that the defaults for int, bool, and string are the values I stated.

In cases where the compiler is able to infer what type is required, you can use a simpler form. Instead of writing default(T) you can just write default. That wouldn't work in Example 4-14 because Console.WriteLine can accept pretty much anything, so the compiler can't narrow it down to one option, but it will work in Example 4-15 because the compiler can see that the generic method's return type is T, so this must need a default(T). Since it can infer that, it's enough for us to write just default.

Example 4-15. Getting the default (zero-like) value of an inferred type

```
static T GetDefault<T>() => default;
```

And since I've just shown you an example of one, this seems like a good time to talk about generic methods.

Generic Methods

As well as generic types, C# also supports generic methods. In this case, the generic type parameter list follows the method name and precedes the method's normal parameter list. Example 4-16 shows a method with a single type parameter. It uses that parameter as its return type, and also as the element type for an array to be passed in as the method's argument. This method returns the final element in the array, and because it's generic, it will work for any array element type.

Example 4-16. A generic method

```
public static T GetLast<T>(T[] items) => items[items.Length - 1];
```

You can define generic methods inside either generic types or non-generic types. If a generic method is a member of a generic type, all of the type parameters from the containing type are in scope inside the method, as well as the type parameters specific to the method.

Just as with a generic type, you can use a generic method by specifying its name along with its type arguments, as Example 4-17 shows.

Example 4-17. Invoking a generic method

```
int[] values = { 1, 2, 3 };
int last = GetLast<int>(values);
```

Generic methods work in a similar way to generic types, but with type parameters that are only in scope within the method declaration and body. You can specify constraints in much the same way as with generic types. The constraints appear after the method's parameter list and before its body, as Example 4-18 shows.

Example 4-18. A generic method with a constraint

```
public static T MakeFake<T>()
    where T : class
{
    return new Mock<T>().Object;
}
```

There's one significant way in which generic methods differ from generic types, though: you don't always need to specify a generic method's type arguments explicitly.

Type Inference

The C# compiler is often able to infer the type arguments for a generic method. I can modify Example 4-17 by removing the type argument list from the method invocation, as Example 4-19 shows, and this doesn't change the meaning of the code in any way.

Example 4-19. Generic method type argument inference

```
int[] values = { 1, 2, 3 };
int last = GetLast(values);
```

When presented with this sort of ordinary-looking method call, if there's no nongeneric method of that name available, the compiler starts looking for suitable generic methods. If the method in Example 4-16 is in scope, it will be a candidate, and the compiler will attempt to deduce the type arguments. This is a pretty simple case. The method expects an array of some type T, and we've passed an array with elements of type int, so it's not a massive stretch to work out that this code should be treated as a call to GetLast<int>.

It gets more complex with more intricate cases. The C# specification has about six pages dedicated to the type inference algorithm, but it's all to support one goal: letting you leave out type arguments when they would be redundant. By the way, type inference is always performed at compile time, so it's based on the static type of the method arguments.

With APIs that make extensive use of generics (such as LINQ, the topic of Chapter 10), explicitly listing every type argument can make the code very hard to follow, so it is common to rely on type inference. And if you use anonymous types, type argument inference becomes essential because it is not possible to supply the type arguments explicitly.

Generics and Tuples

C#'s lightweight tuples have a distinctive syntax, but as far as the runtime is concerned, there is nothing special about them. They are all just instances of a set of generic types. Look at Example 4-20. This uses (int, int) as the type of a local variable to indicate that it is a tuple containing two int values.

Example 4-20. Declaring a tuple variable in the normal way

```
(int, int) p = (42, 99);
```

Now look at Example 4-21. This uses the ValueTuple<int, int> type in the System namespace. But this is exactly equivalent to the declaration in Example 4-20. In Visual Studio, if you hover the mouse over the p2 variable, it will report its type as (int, int).

Example 4-21. Declaring a tuple variable with its underlying type

```
ValueTuple<int, int> p2 = (42, 99);
```

One thing that C#'s special syntax for tuples adds is the ability to name the tuple elements. The ValueTuple family names its elements Item1, Item2, Item3, etc., but in C# we can pick other names. When you declare a local variable with named tuple elements, those names are entirely a fiction maintained by C#—there is no runtime representation of those at all. However, when a method returns a tuple, as in Example 4-22, it's different: the names need to be visible so that code consuming this method can use the same names. Even if this method is in some library component that my code has referenced, I want to be able to write Pos().X, instead of having to use Pos().Item1.

Example 4-22. Returning a tuple

```
public (int X, int Y) Pos() => (10, 20);
```

To make this work, the compiler applies an attribute named `TupleElementNames` to the method's return value, and this contains an array listing the property names to use. (Chapter 14 describes attributes.) You can't actually write code that does this yourself: if you write a method that returns a `ValueTuple<int, int>` and you try to apply the `TupleElementNamesAttribute` as a `return` attribute, the compiler will produce an error telling you not to use this attribute directly, and to use the tuple syntax instead. But that attribute is how the compiler reports the tuple element names.

Be aware that there's another family of tuple types in the .NET class library, `Tuple<T>`, `Tuple<T1, T2>`, and so on. These look almost identical to the `ValueTuple` family. The difference is that the `Tuple` family of generic types are all classes, whereas all the `ValueTuple` types are structs. The C# lightweight tuple syntax only uses the `ValueTuple` family. The `Tuple` family has been around in the .NET class libraries for much longer though, so you often see them used in older code that needed to bundle a set of values together without defining a new type just for that job.

Inside Generics

If you are familiar with C++ templates, you will by now have noticed that C# generics are quite different than templates. Superficially, they have some similarities, and can be used in similar ways—both are suitable for implementing collection classes, for example. However, there are some template-based techniques that simply won't work in C#, such as the code in Example 4-23.

Example 4-23. A template technique that doesn't work in C# generics

```
public static T Add<T>(T x, T y)
{
    return x + y;  // Will not compile
}
```

You can do this sort of thing in a C++ template but not in C#, and you cannot fix it completely with a constraint. You could add a type constraint requiring T to derive from some type that defines a custom + operator, which would get this to compile, but it would be pretty limited—it would work only for types derived from that base type. In C++, you can write a template that will add together two items of any type that supports addition, whether that is a built-in type or a custom one. Moreover, C++ templates don't need constraints; the compiler is able to work out for itself whether a particular type will work as a template argument.

This issue is not specific to arithmetic. The fundamental problem is that because generic code relies on constraints to know what operations are available on its type parameters, it can use only features represented as members of interfaces or shared base classes. If arithmetic in .NET were interface-based, it would be possible to define a constraint that requires it. But operators are all static methods, and although C# 8.0 has made it possible for interfaces to contain static members, there's no way for individual types to supply their own implementation—the dynamic dispatch mechanism that enables each type to supply its own interface implementation only works for instance members. This new language feature makes it possible to imagine some IArithmetic interface that defined the necessary static operator methods, and for these all to defer to instance members of the interface that did the actual work, but no such mechanism exists at the time of writing.

The limitations of C# generics are an upshot of how they are designed to work, so it's useful to understand the mechanism. (These limitations are not specific to Microsoft's CLR, by the way. They are an inevitable result of how generics fit into the design of the CLI.)

Generic methods and types are compiled without knowing which types will be used as arguments. This is the fundamental difference between C# generics and C++ templates—in C++, the compiler gets to see every instantiation of a template. But with C#, you can instantiate generic types without access to any of the relevant source code, long after the code has been compiled. After all, Microsoft wrote the generic List<T> class years ago, but you could write a brand-new class today and plug that in as the type argument just fine. (You might point out that the C++ standard library's std::vector has been around even longer. However, the C++ compiler has access to the source file that defines the class, which is not true of C# and List<T>. C# sees only the compiled library.)

The upshot of this is that the C# compiler needs to have enough information to be able to generate type-safe code at the point at which it compiles generic code. Take Example 4-23. It cannot know what the + operator means here, because it would be different for different types. With the built-in numeric types, that code would need to compile to the specialized intermediate language (IL) instructions for performing addition. If that code were in a checked context (i.e., using the checked keyword shown in Chapter 2), we'd already have a problem, because the code for adding integers with overflow checking uses different IL opcodes for signed and unsigned integers. Furthermore, since this is a generic method, we may not be dealing with the built-in numeric types at all—perhaps we are dealing with a type that defines a custom + operator, in which case the compiler would need to generate a method call. (Custom operators are just methods under the covers.) Or if the type in question turns out not to support addition, the compiler should generate an error.

There are several possible outcomes for compiling a simple addition expression, depending on the actual types involved. That is fine when the types are known to the compiler, but it has to compile the code for generic types and methods without knowing which types will be used as arguments.

You might argue that perhaps Microsoft could have supported some sort of tentative semicompiled format for generic code, and in a sense, it did. When introducing generics, Microsoft modified the type system, file format, and IL instructions to allow generic code to use placeholders representing type parameters to be filled in when the type is fully constructed. So why not extend it to handle operators? Why not let the compiler generate errors at the point at which you compile code that attempts to use a generic type instead of insisting on generating errors when the generic code itself is compiled? Well, it turns out that you can plug in new sets of type arguments at run-time—the reflection API that we'll look at in Chapter 13 lets you construct generic types. So there isn't necessarily a compiler available at the point at which an error would become apparent, because not all versions of .NET ship with a copy of the C# compiler. And in any case, what should happen if a generic class was written in C# but consumed by a completely different language, perhaps one that didn't support operator overloading? Which language's rules should apply when it comes to working out what to do with that + operator? Should it be the language in which the generic code was written, or the language in which the type argument was written? (What if there are multiple type parameters, and for each argument, you use a type written in a different language?) Or perhaps the rules should come from the language that decided to plug the type arguments into the generic type or method, but what about cases where one piece of generic code passes its arguments through to some other generic entity? Even if you could decide which of these approaches would be best, it supposes that the rules used to determine what a line of code actually means are available at runtime, a presumption that once again founders on the fact that the relevant compilers will not necessarily be installed on the machine running the code.

.NET generics solve this problem by requiring the meaning of generic code to be fully defined when the generic code is compiled, using the rules of the language in which the generic code was written. If the generic code involves using methods or other members, they must be resolved statically (i.e., the identity of those members must be determined precisely at compile time). Critically, that means compile time for the generic code itself, not for the code consuming the generic code. These requirements explain why C# generics are not as flexible as the consumer-compile-time substitution model that C++ uses. The payoff is that you can compile generics into libraries in binary form, and they can be used by any .NET language that supports generics, with completely predictable behavior.

Summary

Generics enable us to write types and methods with type arguments, which can be filled in at compile time to produce different versions of the types or methods that work with particular types. The most important use case for generics back when they were first introduced was to make it possible to write type-safe collection classes. .NET did not have generics at the beginning, so the collection classes available in version 1.0 used the general-purpose `object` type. This meant you had to cast objects back to their real type every time you extracted one from a collection. It also meant that value types were not handled efficiently in collections; as we'll see in Chapter 7, referring to values through an `object` requires the generation of *boxes* to contain the values. Generics solve these problems well. They make it possible to write collection classes such as `List<T>`, which can be used without casts. Moreover, because the CLR is able to construct generic types at runtime, it can generate code optimized for whatever type a collection contains. So collection classes can handle value types such as `int` much more efficiently than before generics were introduced. We'll look at some of these collection types in the next chapter.

CHAPTER 5

Collections

Most programs need to deal with multiple pieces of data. Your code might have to iterate through some transactions to calculate the balance of an account, for example, or display recent messages in a social media web application, or update the positions of characters in a game. In most kinds of applications, the ability to work with collections of information is likely to be important.

C# offers a simple kind of collection called an *array*. The CLR's type system supports arrays intrinsically, so they are efficient, but for some scenarios they can be too basic, so the class library builds on the fundamental services provided by arrays to provide more powerful and flexible collection types. I'll start with arrays, because they are the foundation of most of the collection classes.

Arrays

An array is an object that contains multiple *elements* of a particular type. Each element is a storage location similar to a field, but whereas with fields we give each storage slot a name, array elements are simply numbered. The number of elements is fixed for the lifetime of the array, so you must specify the size when you create it. Example 5-1 shows the syntax for creating new arrays.

Example 5-1. Creating arrays

```
int[] numbers = new int[10];
string[] strings = new string[numbers.Length];
```

As with all objects, we construct an array with the new keyword followed by a type name, but instead of parentheses with constructor arguments, we put square brackets containing the array size. As the example shows, the expression defining the size can be a constant, but it doesn't have to be—the second array's size will be determined by evaluating numbers.Length at runtime. In this case the second array will have 10 elements, because we're using the first array's Length property. All arrays have this read-only property, and it returns the total number of elements in the array.

The Length property's type is int, which means it can "only" cope with arrays of up to about 2.1 billion elements. In a 32-bit process, that's rarely a problem, because the limiting factor on array size is likely to be available address space. In 64-bit processes, larger arrays are possible, so there's also a LongLength property of type long. However, you don't see that used much, because the runtime does not currently support creation of arrays with more than 2,147,483,591 (0x7FEFFFFF) elements in any single dimension. So only rectangular multidimensional arrays (described later in this chapter) can contain more elements than Length can report. And even those have an upper limit of 4,294,967,295 (0xFFFFFFFF) elements on current versions of .NET.

 If you're using .NET Framework (and not .NET Core) you'll run into another limit first: a single array cannot normally take more than 2 GB of memory. (This is an upper limit on the size of any single object. In practice, only arrays usually run into this limit, although you could conceivably hit it with a particularly long string.) You can overcome this by adding a <gcAllowVeryLargeObjects enabled="true" /> element inside the <runtime> section of a project's *App.config* file. The limits in the preceding paragraph still apply, but those are significantly less restrictive than a 2-GB ceiling.

In Example 5-1, I've broken my normal rule of avoiding redundant type names in variable declarations. The initializer expressions make it clear that the variables are arrays of int and string, respectively, so I'd normally use var for this sort of code, but I've made an exception here so that I can show how to write the name of an array type. Array types are distinct types in their own right, and if we want to refer to the type that is a single dimensional array of some particular element type, we put [] after the element type name.

All array types derive from a common base class called System.Array. This defines the Length and LongLength properties, and various other members we'll be looking at in due course. You can use array types in all the usual places you can use other types. So you could declare a field, or a method parameter of type string[]. You can also use an array type as a generic type argument. For example, IEnumerable<int[]> would be a sequence of arrays of integers (each of which could be a different size).

An array type is always a reference type, regardless of the element type. Nonetheless, the choice between reference type and value type elements makes a significant difference in an array's behavior. As discussed in Chapter 3, when an object has a field with a value type, the value itself lives inside the memory allocated for the object. The same is true for arrays—when the elements are value types, the value lives in the array element itself, but with a reference type, elements contain only references. Each instance of a reference type has its own identity, and since multiple variables may all end up referring to that instance, the CLR needs to manage its lifetime independently of any other object, so it will end up with its own distinct block of memory. So while an array of 1,000 int values can all live in one contiguous memory block, with reference types, the array just contains the references, not the actual instances. An array of 1,000 different strings would need 1,001 heap blocks—one for the array and one for each string.

 When using reference type elements, you're not obliged to make every element in an array of references refer to a distinct object. You can leave as many elements as you like set to null, and you're also free to make multiple elements refer to the same object. This is just another variation on the theme that references in array elements work in much the same way as they do in local variables and fields.

To access an element in an array, we use square brackets containing the index of the element we'd like to use. The index is zero-based. Example 5-2 shows a few examples.

Example 5-2. Accessing array elements

```
// Continued from Example 5-1
numbers[0] = 42;
numbers[1] = numbers.Length;
numbers[2] = numbers[0] + numbers[1];
numbers[numbers.Length - 1] = 99;
```

As with the array's size at construction, the array index can be a constant, but it can also be a more complex expression, calculated at runtime. In fact, that's also true of the part that comes directly before the opening bracket. In Example 5-2, I've just used a variable name to refer to an array, but you can use brackets after any array-typed expression. Example 5-3 retrieves the first element of an array returned by a method call. (The details of the example aren't strictly relevant, but in case you're wondering, it finds the copyright message associated with the component that defines an object's type. For example, if you pass a string to the method, it will return "© Microsoft Corporation. All rights reserved." This uses the reflection API and custom attributes, the topics of Chapters 13 and 14.)

Example 5-3. Convoluted array access

```
public static string GetCopyrightForType(object o)
{
    Assembly asm = o.GetType().Assembly;
    var copyrightAttribute = (AssemblyCopyrightAttribute)
        asm.GetCustomAttributes(typeof(AssemblyCopyrightAttribute), true)[0];
    return copyrightAttribute.Copyright;
}
```

Expressions involving array element access are special, in that C# considers them to be a kind of variable. This means that as with local variables and fields, you can use them on the lefthand side of an assignment statement, whether they're simple, like the expressions in Example 5-2, or more complex, like those in Example 5-3. You can also use them with the ref keyword (as described in Chapter 3) to pass a reference to a particular element to a method, to store it in a ref local variable, or to return it from a method with a ref return type.

The CLR always checks the index against the array size. If you try to use either a negative index, or an index greater than or equal to the length of the array, the runtime will throw an IndexOutOfRangeException.

Although the size of an array is invariably fixed, its contents are always modifiable—there is no such thing as a read-only array. (As we'll see in "ReadOnlyCollection<T>" on page 245, .NET provides a class that can act as a read-only façade for an array.) You can, of course, create an array with an immutable element type, and this will prevent you from modifying the element in place. So Example 5-4, which uses the immutable Complex value type provided by .NET, will not compile.

Example 5-4. How not to modify an array with immutable elements

```
var values = new Complex[10];
// These lines both cause compiler errors:
values[0].Real = 10;
values[0].Imaginary = 1;
```

The compiler complains because the Real and Imaginary properties are read-only; Complex does not provide any way to modify its values. Nevertheless, you can modify the array: even if you can't modify an existing element in place, you can always overwrite it by supplying a different value, as Example 5-5 shows.

Example 5-5. Modifying an array with immutable elements

```
var values = new Complex[10];
values[0] = new Complex(10, 1);
```

Read-only arrays wouldn't be much use in any case, because all arrays start out filled with a default value that you don't get to specify. The CLR fills the memory for a new array with zeros, so you'll see 0, null, or `false`, depending on the array's element type. For some applications, all-zero (or equivalent) content might be a useful initial state for an array, but in some cases, you'll want to set some other content before starting to work.

Array Initialization

The most straightforward way to initialize an array is to assign values into each element in turn. Example 5-6 creates a `string` array, and since `string` is a reference type, creating a five-element array doesn't create five strings. Our array starts out with five nulls. (This is true even if you've enabled C# 8.0's nullable references feature, as described in Chapter 3. Unfortunately, array initialization is one of the holes that make it impossible for that feature to offer absolute guarantees of non-nullness.) So the code goes on to populate each array element with a reference to a string.

Example 5-6. Laborious array initialization

```
var workingWeekDayNames = new string[5];
workingWeekDayNames[0] = "Monday";
workingWeekDayNames[1] = "Tuesday";
workingWeekDayNames[2] = "Wednesday";
workingWeekDayNames[3] = "Thursday";
workingWeekDayNames[4] = "Friday";
```

This works, but it is unnecessarily verbose. C# supports a shorter syntax that achieves the same thing, shown in Example 5-7. The compiler turns this into code that works like Example 5-6.

Example 5-7. Array initializer syntax

```
var workingWeekDayNames = new string[]
    { "Monday", "Tuesday", "Wednesday", "Thursday", "Friday" };
```

You can go further. Example 5-8 shows that if you specify the type explicitly in the variable declaration, you can write just the initializer list, leaving out the `new` keyword. This works only in initializer expressions, by the way; you can't use this syntax to create an array in other expressions, such as assignments or method arguments. (The more verbose initializer expression in Example 5-7 works in all those contexts.)

Example 5-8. Shorter array initializer syntax

```
string[] workingWeekDayNames =
    { "Monday", "Tuesday", "Wednesday", "Thursday", "Friday" };
```

We can go further still: if all the expressions inside the array initializer list are of the same type, the compiler can infer the array type, so we can write just `new[]` without an explicit element type. Example 5-9 does this.

Example 5-9. Array initializer syntax with element type inference

```
var workingWeekDayNames = new[]
    { "Monday", "Tuesday", "Wednesday", "Thursday", "Friday" };
```

That was actually slightly longer than Example 5-8. However, as with Example 5-7, this style is not limited to variable initialization. You can also use it when you need to pass an array as an argument to a method, for example. If the array you are creating will only be passed into a method and never referred to again, you may not want to declare a variable to refer to it. It might be neater to write the array directly in the argument list. Example 5-10 passes an array of strings to a method using this technique.

Example 5-10. Array as argument

```
SetHeaders(new[] { "Monday", "Tuesday", "Wednesday", "Thursday", "Friday" });
```

Searching and Sorting

Sometimes, you will not know the index of the array element you need. For example, suppose you are writing an application that shows a list of recently used files. Each time the user opens a file in your application, you would want to bring that file to the top of the list, and you'd need to detect when the file was already in the list to avoid having it appear multiple times. If the user happened to use your recent file list to open the file, you would already know it's in the list, and at what offset. But what if the user opens the file some other way? In that case, you've got a filename and you need to find out where that appears in your list, if it's there at all.

Arrays can help you find the item you want in this kind of scenario. There are methods that examine each element in turn, stopping at the first match, and there are also methods that can work considerably faster if your array stores its elements in order. To help with that, there are also methods for sorting the contents of an array into whichever order you require.

The static `Array.IndexOf` method provides the most straightforward way to search for an element. It does not need your array elements to be in any particular order:

you just pass it the array in which to search and the value you're looking for, and it will walk through the elements until it finds a value equal to the one you want. It returns the index at which it found the first matching element, or −1 if it reached the end of the array without finding a match. Example 5-11 shows how you might use this method as part of the logic for updating a list of recently opened files.

Example 5-11. Searching with IndexOf

```
int recentFileListIndex = Array.IndexOf(myRecentFiles, openedFile);
if (recentFileListIndex < 0)
{
    AddNewRecentEntry(openedFile);
}
else
{
    MoveExistingRecentEntryToTop(recentFileListIndex);
}
```

That example starts its search at the beginning of the array, but you have other options. The IndexOf method is overloaded, and you can pass an index from which to start searching, and optionally a second number indicating how many elements you want it to look at before it gives up. There's also a LastIndexOf method, which works in reverse. If you do not specify an index, it starts from the end of the array and works backward. As with IndexOf, you can provide one or two more arguments, indicating the offset at which you'd like to start and the number of elements to check.

These methods are fine if you know precisely what value you're looking for, but often, you'll need to be a bit more flexible: you may want to find the first (or last) element that meets some particular criteria. For example, suppose you have an array representing the bin values for a histogram. It might be useful to find out which is the first nonempty bin. So rather than searching for a particular value, you'd want to find the first element with any value other than zero. Example 5-12 shows how to use the FindIndex method to locate the first such entry.

Example 5-12. Searching with FindIndex

```
public static int GetIndexOfFirstNonEmptyBin(int[] bins)
    => Array.FindIndex(bins, IsNonZero);

private static bool IsNonZero(int value) => value != 0;
```

My IsNonZero method contains the logic that decides whether any particular element is a match, and I've passed that method as an argument to FindIndex. You can pass any method with a suitable signature—FindIndex requires a method that takes an instance of the array's element type and returns a bool. (Strictly speaking, it takes a

`Predicate<T>`, which is a kind of delegate, something I'll discuss in Chapter 9.) Since any method with a suitable signature will do, we can make our search criteria as simple or as complex as we like.

By the way, the logic for this particular example is so simple that writing a separate method for the condition is probably overkill. For simple cases such as these, you'd almost certainly use the lambda syntax (using => to indicate that an expression represents an inline function) instead. That's also something I'll be discussing in Chapter 9, so this is jumping ahead, but I'll just show how it looks because it's rather more concise. Example 5-13 has exactly the same effect as Example 5-12, but doesn't require us to declare and write a whole extra method explicitly. (And at the time of writing this, it's also more efficient, because with a lambda, the compiler generates code that reuses the `Predicate<T>` object that it creates, whereas Example 5-12 will construct a new one each time.)

Example 5-13. Using a lambda with FindIndex

```
public static int GetIndexOfFirstNonEmptyBin(int[] bins)
    => Array.FindIndex(bins, value => value != 0);
```

As with `IndexOf`, `FindIndex` provides overloads that let you specify the offset at which to start searching, and the number of elements to check before giving up. The `Array` class also provides `FindLastIndex`, which works backward—it corresponds to `LastIndexOf`, much as `FindIndex` corresponds to `IndexOf`.

When you're searching for an array entry that meets some particular criteria, you might not be all that interested in the index of the matching element—you might need to know only the value of the first match. Obviously, it's pretty easy to get that: you can just use the value returned by `FindIndex` in conjunction with the array index syntax. However, you don't need to, because the `Array` class offers `Find` and `FindLast` methods that search in precisely the same way as `FindIndex` and `FindLastIndex`, but return the first or last matching value instead of returning the index at which that value was found.

An array could contain multiple items that meet your criteria, and you might want to find all of them. You could write a loop that calls `FindIndex`, adding one to the index of the previous match and using that as the starting point for the next search, repeating until either reaching the end of the array, or getting a result of −1, indicating that no more matches were found. And that would be the way to go if you needed to know the index of each match. But if you are interested only in knowing all of the matching values, and do not need to know exactly where those values were in the array, you could use the `FindAll` method shown in Example 5-14 to do all the work for you.

Example 5-14. Finding multiple items with FindAll

```
public T[] GetNonNullItems<T>(T[] items) where T : class
    => Array.FindAll(items, value => value != null);
```

This takes any array with reference type elements, and returns an array that contains only the non-null elements in that array.

All of the search methods I've shown so far run through an array's elements in order, testing each element in turn. This works well enough, but with large arrays it may be unnecessarily expensive, particularly in cases where comparisons are relatively complex. Even for simple comparisons, if you need to deal with arrays with millions of elements, this sort of search can take long enough to introduce visible delays. However, we can do much better. For example, given an array of values sorted into ascending order, a *binary search* can perform many orders of magnitude better. Example 5-15 examines this.

Example 5-15. Search performance and BinarySearch

```
var sw = new Stopwatch();

int[] big = new int[100_000_000];
Console.WriteLine("Initializing");
sw.Start();
var r = new Random(0);
for (int i = 0; i < big.Length; ++i)
{
    big[i] = r.Next(big.Length);
}
sw.Stop();
Console.WriteLine(sw.Elapsed.ToString("s\\.f"));
Console.WriteLine();

Console.WriteLine("Searching");
for (int i = 0; i < 6; ++i)
{
    int searchFor = r.Next(big.Length);
    sw.Reset();
    sw.Start();
    int index = Array.IndexOf(big, searchFor);
    sw.Stop();
    Console.WriteLine($"Index: {index}");
    Console.WriteLine($"Time:  {sw.Elapsed:s\\.ffff}");
}
Console.WriteLine();

Console.WriteLine("Sorting");
sw.Reset();
sw.Start();
Array.Sort(big);
```

```
sw.Stop();
Console.WriteLine(sw.Elapsed.ToString("s\\.ff"));
Console.WriteLine();

Console.WriteLine("Searching (binary)");
for (int i = 0; i < 6; ++i)
{
    int searchFor = r.Next() % big.Length;
    sw.Reset();
    sw.Start();
    int index = Array.BinarySearch(big, searchFor);
    sw.Stop();
    Console.WriteLine($"Index: {index}");
    Console.WriteLine($"Time:  {sw.Elapsed:s\\.fffffff}");
}
```

This example creates an `int[]` with 100,000,000 values. It fills it with random numbers[1] using the `Random` class, and then uses `Array.IndexOf` to search for some randomly selected values in the array. Next, it sorts the array into ascending order by calling `Array.Sort`. This lets the code use the `Array.BinarySearch` method to search for some more randomly selected values. It uses the `Stopwatch` class from the `System.Diagnostics` namespace to measure how long this all takes. (The strange-looking text in the final `Console.WriteLine` is a format specifier indicating how many decimal places I require.) By measuring such tiny steps, we're in the slightly suspect territory known as *microbenchmarking*. Measuring a single operation out of context can produce misleading results because in real systems, performance depends on numerous factors that interact in complex and sometimes unpredictable ways, so you need to take these figures with a pinch of salt. Even so, the scale of the difference in this case is pretty revealing. Here's the output from my system:

```
Initializing
1.07

Searching
Index: 55504605
Time:  0.0191
Index: 21891944
Time:  0.0063
Index: 56663763
Time:  0.0173
Index: 37441319
Time:  0.0111
Index: -1
Time:  0.0314
Index: 9344095
```

---

1 I've limited the range of the random numbers to be the same as the size of the array, because with Random's full range, the majority of searches will fail.

```
Time:  0.0032

Sorting
7.3

Searching (binary)
Index: 8990721
Time:  0.0002616
Index: 4404823
Time:  0.0000205
Index: 52683151
Time:  0.0000019
Index: -37241611
Time:  0.0000018
Index: -49384544
Time:  0.0000019
Index: 88243160
Time:  0.000001
```

It takes 1.07 seconds just to populate the array with random numbers. (Most of that time is spent generating the numbers. Filling the array with a constant value, or with the loop count, takes more like 0.1 seconds.) The IndexOf searches take varying lengths of time. The slowest was when the value being searched for was not present—the search that failed returned an index of −1, and it took 0.0314 seconds here. That's because IndexOf had to look at every single element in the array. In the cases where it found a match, it was faster, and the speed was determined by how early on it found the match. The fastest in this particular run was when it found a match after just over 9 million entries—that took 0.0032 seconds, around 10 times faster than having to look at all 100 million entries. Predictably enough, the time increases with the number of elements it has to inspect.

On average, you'd expect successful searches to take about half as long as the worst case (assuming evenly distributed random numbers), so you'd be looking at somewhere around 0.016 seconds, and the overall average would depend on how often you expect searches to fail. That's not disastrous, but it's definitely heading into problematic territory. For UI work, anything that takes longer than 0.1 seconds tends to annoy the user, so although our average speed might be fast enough, our worst case is close enough to the margin of acceptability for concern. (And, of course, you may see much slower results on low-end hardware.) While this is looking only moderately concerning for client-side scenarios, this sort of performance could be a serious problem on a heavily loaded server. If you do this much work for every incoming request, it will seriously limit the number of users each server can support.

Now look at the times for the binary search, a technique that does not look at every element. It starts with the element in the middle of the array. If that happens to be the value required, it can stop, but otherwise, depending on whether the value it found is higher or lower than the value we want, it can know instantly which half of the array the value will be in (if it's present at all). It then leaps to the middle of the remaining half, and if that's not the right value, again it can determine which quarter will contain the target. At each step, it narrows the search down by half, and after halving the size a few times, it will be down to a single item. If that's not the value it's looking for, the item it wants is missing.

 This process explains the curious negative numbers that Binary Search produces. When the value is not found, this binary chop process will finish at the value nearest to the one we are looking for, and that might be useful information. So a negative number still tells us the search failed, but that number is the negation of the index of the closest match.

Each iteration is more complex than in a simple linear search, but with large arrays it pays off, because far fewer iterations are needed. In this example, it has to perform only 27 steps instead of 100,000,000. Obviously, with smaller arrays, the improvement is reduced, and there will be some minimum size of array at which the relative complexity of a binary search outweighs the benefit. If your array contains only 10 values, a linear search may well be faster. But a binary search is the clear winner with 100,000,000 elements.

By massively reducing the amount of work, BinarySearch runs a lot faster than IndexOf. In this example, the worst case is 0.0002616 seconds (261.6 µs), which is about 12 times faster than the best result we saw with the linear search. And that first search was an unusually slow outlier;[2] the second was an order of magnitude faster, and the rest were all two orders of magnitude faster, fast enough that we're near the point where it's difficult to make accurate measurements for individual operations. So once this code is up and running, the search speeds are all under 2 µs. Perhaps most interestingly, where it found no match (producing a negative result) Array.IndexOf had its slowest result by far, but with BinarySearch, the no-match cases look pretty quick: it determines that an element is missing over 15,000 times faster than the linear search does.

Besides consuming far less CPU time for each search, this sort of search does less collateral damage. One of the more insidious kinds of performance problems that can occur on modern computers is code that is not just slow in its own right, but that causes everything else on the machine to slow down. The IndexOf search churns through 400 MB of data for each failing search, and we can expect it to trawl through

---

2 A more complex test setup reveals 261.1 µs to be an exceptional result: it appears that the first search a process performs is relatively slow. This may well be overhead unrelated to searching that affects only the first piece of code to call BinarySearch, such as JIT compilation. When the intervals get this small, you're at the limits of what microbenchmarking can usefully tell you.

an average of 200 MB for successful searches. This will tend to have the effect of flushing out the CPU's cache memory, so code and data structures that might otherwise have remained in the fast cache memory need to be fetched from main memory the next time they are required; code that uses `IndexOf` on such a large array will need to reload its world back into the cache once the search completes. And if this code shares the CPU with other code on a multithreaded server, it could also evict other threads' data from the cache, making them run slower too. `BinarySearch` needs to look at only a handful of array elements, so it will have only a minimal impact on the cache.

There's just one tiny problem: even though the individual searches were much faster, the binary search was, overall, a total performance disaster here. We have saved almost a tenth of a second on the searches, but to be able to do that, we had to spend 7.3 seconds sorting the array. A binary search works only for data that is already ordered, and the cost of getting your data into order could well outweigh the benefits. This particular example would need to do about 500 searches before the cost of sorting was outweighed by the improved search speed, and, of course, that would work only if nothing changed in the meantime that forced you to redo the sort. With performance tuning, it's always important to look at the whole scenario, and not just the microbenchmarks.

Incidentally, `Array.BinarySearch` offers overloads for searching within some subsection of the array, similar to those we saw for the other search methods. It also lets you customize the comparison logic. This works with the comparison interfaces I showed in earlier chapters. By default, it will use the `IComparable<T>` implementation provided by the array elements themselves, but you can provide a custom `IComparer<T>` instead. The `Array.Sort` method I used to put the elements into order also supports narrowing down the range and using custom comparison logic.

There are other searching and sorting methods besides the ones provided by the `Array` class itself. All arrays implement `IEnumerable<T>` (where `T` is the array's element type), which means you can also use any of the operations provided by .NET's *LINQ to Objects* functionality. This offers a much wider range of features for searching, sorting, grouping, filtering, and generally working with collections of objects; Chapter 10 will describe these features. Arrays have been in .NET for longer than LINQ, which is one reason for this overlap in functionality, but where arrays provide their own equivalents of standard LINQ operators, the array versions can sometimes be more efficient because LINQ is a more generalized solution.

Multidimensional Arrays

The arrays I've shown so far have all been one-dimensional, but C# supports two multidimensional forms: *jagged arrays* and *rectangular arrays*.

Jagged arrays

A jagged array is simply an array of arrays. The existence of this kind of array is a natural upshot of the fact that arrays have types that are distinct from their element type. Because int[] is a type, you can use that as the element type of another array. Example 5-16 shows the syntax, which is very nearly unsurprising.

Example 5-16. Creating a jagged array

```
int[][] arrays = new int[5][]
{
    new[] { 1, 2 },
    new[] { 1, 2, 3, 4, 5, 6 },
    new[] { 1, 2, 4 },
    new[] { 1 },
    new[] { 1, 2, 3, 4, 5 }
};
```

Again, I've broken my usual rule for variable declarations—normally I'd use var on the first line because the type is evident from the initializer, but I wanted to show the syntax both for declaring the variable and for constructing the array. And there's a second redundancy in Example 5-16: when using the array initializer syntax, you don't have to specify the size explicitly, because the compiler will work it out for you. I've exploited that for the nested arrays, but I've set the size (5) explicitly for the outer array to show where the size appears, because it might not be where you would expect.

The type name for a jagged array is simple enough. In general, array types have the form *ElementType*[], so if the element type is int[], we'd expect the resulting array type to be written as int[][], and that's what we see. The constructor syntax is a bit more peculiar. It declares an array of five arrays, and at a first glance, new int[5][] seems like a perfectly reasonable way to express that. It is consistent with array index syntax for jagged arrays; we can write arrays[1][3], which fetches the second of those five arrays, and then retrieves the fourth element from that second array. (This is not a specialized syntax, by the way—there is no need for special handling here, because any expression that evaluates to an array can be followed by the index in square brackets. The expression arrays[1] evaluates to an int[] array, and so we can follow that with [3].)

However, the new keyword *does* treat jagged arrays specially. It makes them look consistent with array element access syntax, but it has to twist things a little to do that. With a one-dimensional array, the pattern for constructing a new array is new *Ele mentType*[*length*], so for creating an array of five things, you'd expect to write new *ElementType*[5]. If the things you are creating are arrays of int, wouldn't you expect to see int[] in place of *ElementType*? That would imply that the syntax should be new int[][5].

That would be logical, but it looks like it's the wrong way round, and that's because the array type syntax itself is effectively reversed. Arrays are constructed types, like generics. With generics, the name of the generic type from which we construct the actual type comes before the type argument (e.g., List<int> takes the generic List<T> type and constructs it with a type argument of int). If arrays had generic-like syntax, we might expect to see array<int> for a one-dimensional array, array<array<int>> for two dimensions, and so on—the element type would come *after* the part that signifies that we want an array. But array types do it the other way around—the arrayness is signified by the [] characters, so the element type comes first. This is why the hypothetical logically correct syntax for array construction looks weird. C# avoids the weirdness by not getting overly stressed about logic here, and just puts the size where most people expect it to go rather than where it arguably should go.

 C# does not define particular limits to the number of dimensions, but there are some implementation-specific runtime limits. (Microsoft's compiler didn't flinch when I asked for a 5,000-dimensional jagged array, but the CLR refused to load the resulting program. In fact, it wouldn't load anything with more than 4,144 dimensions, and there were some performance issues with a mere 2,000.) The syntax extends in the obvious way—for example, int[][][] for the type and new int[5][][] for construction.

Example 5-16 initializes the array with five one-dimensional int[] arrays. The layout of the code should make it fairly clear why this sort of array is referred to as *jagged*: each row has a different length. With arrays of arrays, there is no requirement for a rectangular layout. I could go further. Arrays are reference types, so I could have set some rows to null. If I abandoned the array initializer syntax and initialized the array elements individually, I could have decided to make some of the one-dimensional int[] arrays appear in more than one row.

Because each row in this jagged array contains an array, I've ended up with six objects here—the five int[] arrays, and then the int[][] array that contains references to them. If you introduce more dimensions, you'll get yet more arrays. For certain kinds of work, the nonrectangularity and the large numbers of objects can be problematic, which is why C# supports another kind of multidimensional array.

Rectangular arrays

A rectangular array is a single array object that supports multidimensional indexing. If C# didn't offer multidimensional arrays, we could build something a bit like them by convention. If you want an array with 10 rows and 5 columns, you could construct a one-dimensional array with 50 elements, and then use code like `myArray[i + (5 * j)]` to access it, where `i` is the column index, and `j` is the row index. That would be an array that you had chosen to think of as being two-dimensional, even though it's really just one big contiguous block. A rectangular array is essentially the same idea, but where C# does the work for you. Example 5-17 shows how to declare and construct rectangular arrays.

 Rectangular arrays are not just about convenience. There's a type safety aspect too: `int[,]` is a different type than `int[]` or `int[,,]`, so if you write a method that expects a two-dimensional rectangular array, C# will not allow anything else to be passed.

Example 5-17. Rectangular arrays

```
int[,] grid = new int[5, 10];
var smallerGrid = new int[,]
{
    { 1, 2, 3, 4 },
    { 2, 3, 4, 5 },
    { 3, 4, 5, 6 },
};
```

As you can see, rectangular array type names use only a single pair of square brackets, no matter how many dimensions they have. The number of commas inside the brackets denotes the number of dimensions, so these examples with one comma are two-dimensional.

The initializer syntax is very similar to that for multidimensional arrays (see Example 5-16) except I do not start each row with `new[]`, because this is one big array, not an array of arrays. The numbers in Example 5-17 form a shape that is clearly rectangular, and if you attempt to make things jagged (with different row sizes) the compiler will report an error. This extends to higher dimensions. If you wanted a three-dimensional "rectangular" array, it would need to be a *cuboid*. Example 5-18 shows a cuboid array. You could think of the initializer as being a list of two rectangular slices making up the cuboid. And you can go higher, with *hypercuboid* arrays (although they are still known as rectangular arrays, regardless of how many dimensions you use).

Example 5-18. A 2×3×5 cuboid "rectangular" array

```
var cuboid = new int[,,]
{
    {
        { 1, 2, 3, 4, 5 },
```

```
        { 2, 3, 4, 5, 6 },
        { 3, 4, 5, 6, 7 }
    },
    {
        { 2, 3, 4, 5, 6 },
        { 3, 4, 5, 6, 7 },
        { 4, 5, 6, 7, 8 }
    },
};
```

The syntax for accessing rectangular arrays is predictable enough. If the second variable from Example 5-17 is in scope, we could write `smallerGrid[2, 3]` to access the final item in the array; as with single-dimensional arrays, indices are zero-based, so this refers to the third row's fourth item.

Remember that an array's `Length` property returns the total number of elements in the array. Since rectangular arrays have all the elements in a single array (rather than being arrays that refer to some other arrays), this will return the product of the sizes of all the dimensions. A rectangular array with 5 rows and 10 columns would have a `Length` of 50, for example. If you want to discover the size along a particular dimension at runtime, use the `GetLength` method, which takes a single `int` argument indicating the dimension for which you'd like to know the size.

Copying and Resizing

Sometimes you will want to move chunks of data around in arrays. You might want to insert an item in the middle of an array, moving the items that follow it up by one position (and losing one element at the end, since array sizes are fixed). Or you might want to move data from one array to another, perhaps one of a different size.

The static `Array.Copy` method takes references to two arrays, along with a number indicating how many elements to copy. It offers overloads so that you can specify the positions in the two arrays at which to start the copy. (The simpler overload starts at the first element of each array.) You are allowed to pass the same array as the source and destination, and it will handle overlap correctly: the copy acts as though the elements were first all copied to a temporary location before starting to write them to the target.

As well as the static `Copy` method, the `Array` class defines a non-static `CopyTo` method, which copies the entire array into a target array, starting at the specified offset. This method is present because all arrays implement certain collection interfaces, including `ICollection<T>` (where `T` is the array's element type), which defines this `CopyTo` method. `CopyTo` does not guarantee to handle overlap correctly when copying an array into itself, and the documentation recommends using `Array.Copy` in scenarios where you know you will be dealing with arrays—`CopyTo` is just for the benefit of general-purpose code that can work with any implementation of a collection interface.

Copying elements from one array to another can become necessary when you need to deal with variable amounts of data. You would typically allocate an array larger than initially necessary, and if this eventually fills up, you'll need a new, larger array, and you'd need to copy the contents of the old array into the new one. In fact, the `Array` class can do this for you for one-dimensional arrays with its `Resize` method. The method name is slightly misleading, because arrays cannot be resized, so it allocates a new array and copies the data from the old one into it. `Resize` can build either a larger or a smaller array, and if you ask it for a smaller one, it will just copy as many elements as will fit.

While I'm talking about methods that copy the array's data around, I should mention `Reverse`, which simply reverses the order of the array's elements. Also, while this isn't strictly about copying, the `Array.Clear` method is often useful in scenarios where you're juggling array sizes—it allows you to reset some range of the array to its initial zero-like state.

These methods for moving data around within arrays are useful for building more flexible data structures on top of the basic services offered by arrays. But you often won't need to use them yourself, because the class library provides several useful collection classes that do this for you.

List<T>

The `List<T>` class, defined in the `System.Collections.Generic` namespace, contains a variable-length sequence of elements of type `T`. It provides an indexer that lets you get and set elements by number, so a `List<T>` behaves like a resizable array. It's not completely interchangeable—you cannot pass a `List<T>` as the argument for a parameter that expects a `T[]` array—but both arrays and `List<T>` implement various common generic collection interfaces that we'll be looking at later. For example, if you write a method that accepts an `IList<T>`, it will be able to work with either an array or a `List<T>`.

Although code that uses an indexer resembles array element access, it is not quite the same thing. An indexer is a kind of property, so it has the same issues with mutable value types that I discussed in Chapter 3. Given a variable `pointList` of type `List<Point>` (where `Point` is the mutable value type in the `System.Windows` namespace), you cannot write `pointList[2].X = 2`, because `point List[2]` returns a copy of the value, and this code is effectively asking to modify that temporary copy. This would lose the update, so C# forbids it. But this does work with arrays. If `pointArray` is of type `Point[]`, `pointArray[2]` does not *get* an element, it *identifies* an element, making it possible to modify an array element's value in situ by writing `pointArray[2].X = 2`. (Since `ref` return values were added in C# 7.0, it has become possible to write indexers that work this way, but `List<T>` and `IList<T>` were created long before that.) With immutable value types such as `Complex`, this distinction is moot, because you cannot modify their values in place in any case—you would have to overwrite an element with a new value whether using an array or a list.

Unlike an array, a `List<T>` provides methods that change its size. The `Add` method appends a new element to the end of the list, while `AddRange` can add several. `Insert` and `InsertRange` add elements at any point in the list, shuffling all the elements after the insertion point down to make space. These four methods all make the list longer, but `List<T>` also provides `Remove`, which removes the first instance of the specified value; `RemoveAt`, which removes an element at a particular index; and `RemoveRange`, which removes multiple elements starting at a particular index. These all shuffle elements back down, closing up the gap left by the removed element or elements, making the list shorter.

`List<T>` uses an array internally to store its elements. This means all the elements live in a single block of memory, and it stores them contiguously. This makes normal element access very efficient, but it is also why insertion needs to shift elements up to make space for the new element, and removal needs to shift them down to close up the gap.

Example 5-19 shows how to create a `List<T>`. It's just a class, so we use the normal constructor syntax. It shows how to add and remove entries, and also how to access elements using the array-like indexer syntax. This also shows that `List<T>` provides its size through a `Count` property, a seemingly arbitrarily different name than the `Length` provided by arrays. (In fact, arrays also offer `Count`, because they implement `ICollection` and `ICollection<T>`. However, they use explicit interface implementation, meaning that you can see an array's Count property only through a reference of one of these interface types.)

Example 5-19. Using a List<T>

```
var numbers = new List<int>();
numbers.Add(123);
numbers.Add(99);
numbers.Add(42);
Console.WriteLine(numbers.Count);
Console.WriteLine($"{numbers[0]}, {numbers[1]}, {numbers[2]}");

numbers[1] += 1;
Console.WriteLine(numbers[1]);

numbers.RemoveAt(1);
Console.WriteLine(numbers.Count);
Console.WriteLine($"{numbers[0]}, { numbers[1]}");
```

Because a List<T> can grow and shrink as required, you don't need to specify its size at construction. However, if you want to, you can specify its *capacity*. A list's capacity is the amount of space it currently has available for storing elements, and this will often be different than the number of elements it contains. To avoid allocating a new internal array every time you add or remove an element, it keeps track of how many elements are in use independently of the size of the array. When it needs more space, it will overallocate, creating a new array that is larger than needed by a factor proportional to the size. This means that, if your program repeatedly adds items to a list, the larger it gets, the less frequently it needs to allocate a new array, but the proportion of spare capacity after each reallocation will remain about the same.

If you know up front that you will eventually store a specific number of elements in a list, you can pass that number to the constructor, and it will allocate exactly that much capacity, meaning that no further reallocation will be required. If you get this wrong, it won't cause an error—you're just requesting an initial capacity, and it's OK to change your mind later.

If the idea of unused memory going to waste in a list offends you, but you don't know exactly how much space will be required before you start, you could call the TrimEx cess method once you know the list is complete. This reallocates the internal storage to be exactly large enough to hold the list's current contents, eliminating waste. This will not always be a win. To ensure that it is using exactly the right amount of space, TrimExcess has to create a new array of the right size, leaving the old, oversized one to be reclaimed by the garbage collector later on, and in some scenarios, the overhead of forcing an extra allocation just to trim things down to size may be higher than the overhead of having some unused capacity.

Lists have a third constructor. Besides the default constructor, and the one that takes a capacity, you can also pass in a collection of data with which to initialize the list. You can pass any `IEnumerable<T>`.

You can provide initial content for lists with syntax similar to an array initializer. Example 5-20 loads the same three values into the new list as at the start of Example 5-19. This is the only form; in contrast to arrays, you cannot omit the `new List<int>` part when the variable declaration is explicit about the type (i.e., when you don't use `var`). Nor will the compiler infer the type argument, so whereas with an array you can write just `new[]` followed by an initializer, you cannot write `new List<>`.

Example 5-20. List initializer

```
var numbers = new List<int> { 123, 99, 42 };
```

This compiles into code that calls `Add` once for each item in the list. You can use this syntax with any type that has a suitable `Add` method and implements the `IEnumerable` interface. This works even if `Add` is an extension method. (So if some type implements `IEnumerable`, but does not supply an `Add` method, you are free to use this initializer syntax if you provide your own `Add`.)

`List<T>` provides `IndexOf`, `LastIndexOf`, `Find`, `FindLast`, `FindAll`, `Sort`, and `Binary Search` methods for finding and sorting list elements. These provide the same services as their array namesakes, although `List<T>` chooses to provide these as instance methods rather than statics.

We've now seen two ways to represent a list of values: arrays and lists. Fortunately, interfaces make it possible to write code that can work with either, so you won't need to write two sets of functions if you want to support both lists and arrays.

List and Sequence Interfaces

The .NET class library defines several interfaces representing collections. Three of these are relevant to simple linear sequences of the kind you can store in an array or a list: `IList<T>`, `ICollection<T>`, and `IEnumerable<T>`, all in the `System.Collections.Generics` namespace. There are three interfaces, because different code makes different demands. Some methods need random access to any numbered element in a collection, but not everything does, and not all collections can support that—some sequences produce elements gradually, and there may be no way to leap straight to the *n*th element. Consider a sequence representing keypresses, for example—each item will emerge only as the user presses the next key. Your code can work with a wider range of sources if you opt for less demanding interfaces.

IEnumerable<T> is the most general of collection interfaces, because it demands the least from its implementers. I've mentioned it a few times already because it's an important interface that crops up a lot, but I've not shown the definition until now. As Example 5-21 shows, it declares just a single method.

Example 5-21. IEnumerable<T> and IEnumerable

```
public interface IEnumerable<out T> : IEnumerable
{
    IEnumerator<T> GetEnumerator();
}

public interface IEnumerable
{
    IEnumerator GetEnumerator();
}
```

Using inheritance, IEnumerable<T> requires its implementers also to implement IEnumerable, which appears to be almost identical. It's a nongeneric version of IEnumerable<T>, and its GetEnumerator method will typically do nothing more than invoke the generic implementation. The reason we have both forms is that the nongeneric IEnumerable has been around since .NET v1.0, which didn't support generics. The arrival of generics in .NET v2.0 made it possible to express the intent behind IEnumerable more precisely, but the old interface had to remain for compatibility. So these two interfaces effectively require the same thing: a method that returns an enumerator. What's an enumerator? Example 5-22 shows both the generic and nongeneric interfaces.

Example 5-22. IEnumerator<T> and IEnumerator

```
public interface IEnumerator<out T> : IDisposable, IEnumerator
{
    T Current { get; }
}

public interface IEnumerator
{
    bool MoveNext();
    object Current { get; }
    void Reset();
}
```

The usage model for an IEnumerable<T> (and also IEnumerable) is that you call GetEnumerator to obtain an enumerator, which can be used to iterate through all the items in the collection. You call the enumerator's MoveNext(); if it returns false, it means the collection was empty. Otherwise, the Current property will now provide the first item from the collection. Then you call MoveNext() again to move to the next item, and for as long as it keeps returning true, the next item will be available in Current. (The Reset method is a historical artifact added to help compatibility with COM, the Windows pre-.NET cross-language object model. The documentation allows implementations to throw a NotSupportedException from Reset, so you will not normally use this method.)

 Notice that IEnumerator<T> implementations are required to implement IDisposable. You must call Dispose on enumerators once you're finished with them, because many of them rely on this.

The foreach loop in C# does all of the work required to iterate through an enumerable collection for you,[3] including generating code that calls Dispose even if the loop terminates early due to a break statement, an error, or, perish the thought, a goto statement. Chapter 7 will describe the uses of IDisposable in more detail.

IEnumerable<T> is at the heart of LINQ to Objects, which I'll discuss in Chapter 10. LINQ operators are available on any object that implements this interface.

.NET Core 3.0 and .NET Standard 2.1 add a new interface, IAsyncEnumerable<T>. Conceptually, this is identical to IEnumerable<T>: it represents the ability to provide a sequence of items. The difference is that it supports asynchronous operation. As Example 5-23 shows, this interface and its counterpart, IAsyncEnumerator<T>, resemble IEnumerable<T> and IEnumerator<T>. The main difference is the use of asynchronous programming features ValueTask<T> and CancellationToken, which Chapter 16 will describe. There are also some minor differences: there are no nongeneric versions of these interfaces, and also, there's no facility to reset an existing asynchronous enumerator (although as noted earlier, many synchronous enumerators throw a NotSupportedException if you call Reset).

Example 5-23. IAsyncEnumerable<T> and IAsyncEnumerator<T>

```
public interface IAsyncEnumerable<out T>
{
    IAsyncEnumerator<T> GetAsyncEnumerator(
        CancellationToken cancellationToken = default);
}
```

---

3 Surprisingly, foreach doesn't require any particular interface; it will use anything with a GetEnumerator method that returns an object providing a MoveNext method and a Current property. This is a historical quirk —back before generics, this was the only way to enable iteration through collections of value-typed elements without boxing. Chapter 7 describes boxing.

```
public interface IAsyncEnumerator<out T> : IAsyncDisposable
{
    T Current { get; }

    ValueTask<bool> MoveNextAsync();
}
```

You can consume an IAsyncEnumerable<T> with a specialized form of foreach loop, in which you prefix it with the await keyword. This can only be used in a method marked with the async keyword. Chapter 17 describes the async and await keywords in detail, and also the use of await foreach.

Although IEnumerable<T> is important and widely used, it's pretty restrictive. You can ask it only for one item after another, and it will hand them out in whatever order it sees fit. It does not provide a way to modify the collection, or even of finding out how many items the collection contains without having to iterate through the whole lot. For these jobs, we have ICollection<T>, which is shown in Example 5-24.

Example 5-24. ICollection<T>

```
public interface ICollection<T> : IEnumerable<T>, IEnumerable
{
    void Add(T item);
    void Clear();
    bool Contains(T item);
    void CopyTo(T[] array, int arrayIndex);
    bool Remove(T item);

    int Count { get; }
    bool IsReadOnly { get; }
}
```

This requires implementers also to provide IEnumerable<T>, but notice that this does not inherit the nongeneric ICollection. There is such an interface, but it represents a different abstraction: it's missing all of the methods except CopyTo. When introducing generics, Microsoft reviewed how the nongeneric collection types were used and concluded that the one extra method that the old ICollection added didn't make it noticeably more useful than IEnumerable. Worse, it also included a property called SyncRoot that was intended to help manage certain multithreaded scenarios, but which turned out to be a poor solution to that problem in practice. So the abstraction represented by ICollection did not get a generic equivalent, and has not been greatly missed. During the review, Microsoft also found that the absence of a general-purpose interface for modifiable collections was a problem, and so it made ICollection<T> fit that bill. It was not entirely helpful to attach this old name to a different abstraction, but since almost nobody was using the old nongeneric ICollection, it doesn't seem to have caused much trouble.

The third interface for sequential collections is IList<T>, and all types that implement this are required to implement ICollection<T>, and therefore also IEnumerable<T>. As you'd expect, List<T> implements IList<T>. Arrays implement it too, using their element type as the argument for T. Example 5-25 shows how the interface looks.

Example 5-25. IList<T>

```
public interface IList<T> : ICollection<T>, IEnumerable<T>, IEnumerable
{
    int IndexOf(T item);
    void Insert(int index, T item);
    void RemoveAt(int index);

    T this[int index] { get; set; }
}
```

Again, although there is a nongeneric IList, this interface has no direct relationship to it, even though they do represent similar concepts—the nongeneric IList has equivalents to the IList<T> members, and it also includes equivalents to most of ICollection<T>, including all the members missing from ICollection. So it would have been possible to require IList<T> implementations to implement IList, but that would have forced implementations to provide two versions of most members, one working in terms of the type parameter T, and the other using object, because that's what the old nongeneric interfaces had to use. It would also force collections to provide the nonuseful SyncRoot property. The benefits would not outweigh these inconveniences, and so IList<T> implementations are not obliged to implement IList. They can if they want to, and List<T> does, but it's up to the individual collection class to choose.

One unfortunate upshot of the way these three generic interfaces are related is that they do not provide an abstraction representing indexed collections that are read-only, or even ones that are fixed-size. While IEnumerable<T> is a read-only abstraction, it's an in-order one with no way to go directly to the *n*th value. Prior to .NET 4.5 (which introduced various new collection interfaces), the only option for indexed access was IList<T>, but that also defines methods for insertion and indexed removal, as well as mandating an implementation of ICollection<T> with its addition and value-based removal methods. So you might be wondering how arrays can implement these interfaces, given that all arrays are fixed-size.

Arrays mitigate this problem by using explicit interface implementation to hide the IList<T> methods that can change a list's length, discouraging you from trying to use them. (As you saw in Chapter 3, this technique enables you to provide a full implementation of an interface but to be selective about which members are directly visible.) However, you can store a reference to an array in a variable of type IList<T>, making those methods visible—Example 5-26 uses this to call an array's IList<T>.Add method. However, this results in a runtime error.

Example 5-26. Trying (and failing) to enlarge an array

```
IList<int> array = new[] { 1, 2, 3 };
array.Add(4);  // Will throw an exception
```

The Add method throws a NotSupportedException, with an error message stating that the collection has a fixed size. If you inspect the documentation for IList<T> and ICollection<T>, you'll see that all the members that would modify the collection are allowed to throw this error. You can discover at runtime whether this will happen for *all* modifications with the ICollection<T> interface's IsReadOnly property. However, that won't help you discover up front when a collection allows only certain changes. (For example, an array's size is fixed, but you can still modify elements.)

This causes an irritating problem: if you're writing code that does in fact require a modifiable collection, there's no way to advertise that fact. If a method takes an IList<T>, it's hard to know whether that method will attempt to resize that list or not. Mismatches cause runtime exceptions, and those exceptions may well appear in code that isn't doing anything wrong, and where the mistake—passing the wrong sort of collection—was made by the caller. These problems are not showstoppers; in dynamically typed languages, this degree of compile-time uncertainty is in fact the norm, and it doesn't stop you from writing good code.

There is a ReadOnlyCollection<T> class, but as we'll see later, that solves a different problem—it's a wrapper class, not an interface, so there are plenty of things that are fixed-size collections that do not present a ReadOnlyCollection<T>. If you were to write a method with a parameter of type ReadOnlyCollection<T>, it would not be able to work directly with certain kinds of collections (including arrays). In any case, it's not even the same abstraction—read-only is a tighter restriction than fixed-size.

.NET defines IReadOnlyList<T>, an interface that provides a better solution for representing read-only indexed collections (although it still doesn't help with modifiable fixed-sized ones). Like IList<T>, it requires an implementation of IEnumerable<T>, but it does not require ICollection<T>. It defines two members: Count, which returns the size of the collection (just like ICollection<T>.Count), and a read-only indexer. This solves most of the problems associated with using IList<T> for read-only collections. One minor problem is that because it's newer than most of the other interfaces I've described here it is not universally supported. (It was introduced in .NET 4.5 in 2012, seven years after IList<T>.) So if you come across an API that requires an IReadOnlyList<T>, you can be sure it will not attempt to modify the collection, but if an API requires IList<T>, it's difficult to know whether that's because it intends to modify the collection, or merely because it was written before IReadOnly List<T> was invented.

 Collections do not need to be read-only to implement IReadOnly List<T>—a modifiable list can easily present a read-only façade. So this interface is implemented by all arrays and also List<T>.

The issues and interfaces I've just discussed raise a question: when writing code or classes that work with collections, what type should you use? You will typically get the most flexibility if your API demands the least specific type it can work with. For example, if an IEnumerable<T> suits your needs, don't demand an IList<T>. Likewise, interfaces are usually better than concrete types, so you should prefer IList<T> over either List<T> or T[]. Just occasionally, there may be performance arguments for using a more specific type; if you have a tight loop critical to the overall performance of your application that works through the contents of a collection, you may find such code runs faster if it works only with array types, because the CLR may be able to perform better optimizations when it knows exactly what to expect. But in many cases, the difference will be too small to measure and will not justify the inconvenience of being tied to a particular implementation, so you should never take such a step without measuring the performance for the task at hand to see what the benefit might be. (And if you're considering such a performance-oriented change, you should also look at the techniques described in Chapter 18.) If you find that there is a possible performance win, but you're writing a shared library in which you want to provide both flexibility and the best possible performance, there are a couple of options for having it both ways. You could offer overloads, so callers can pass in either an interface or a specific type. Alternatively, you could write a single public method that accepts the interface but which tests for known types and chooses between different internal code paths based on what the caller passes.

The interfaces we've just examined are not the only generic collection interfaces, because simple linear lists are not the only kind of collection. But before moving on to the others, I want to show enumerables and lists from the flip side: how do we implement these interfaces?

Implementing Lists and Sequences

It is often useful to provide information in the form of either an IEnumerable<T> or an IList<T>. The former is particularly important because .NET provides a powerful toolkit for working with sequences in the form of LINQ to Objects, which I'll show in

Chapter 10. LINQ to Objects provides various operators that all work in terms of IEnumerable<T>. IList<T> is a useful abstraction anywhere that random access to any element by index is required. Some frameworks expect an IList<T>. If you want to bind a collection of objects to some kind of list control, for example, some UI frameworks will expect either an IList or an IList<T>.

You could implement these interfaces by hand, as none of them is particularly complicated. However, C# and the .NET class library can help. There is direct language-level support for implementing IEnumerable<T>, and there is class library support for the generic and nongeneric list interfaces.

Implementing IEnumerable<T> with Iterators

C# supports a special form of method called an *iterator*. An iterator is a method that produces enumerable sequences using a special keyword, yield. Example 5-27 shows a simple iterator and some code that uses it. This will display numbers counting down from 5 to 1.

Example 5-27. A simple iterator

```
public static IEnumerable<int> Countdown(int start, int end)
{
    for (int i = start; i >= end; --i)
    {
        yield return i;
    }
}

private static void Main(string[] args)
{
    foreach (int i in Countdown(5, 1))
    {
        Console.WriteLine(i);
    }
}
```

An iterator looks much like any normal method, but the way it returns values is different. The iterator in Example 5-27 has a return type of IEnumerable<int>, and yet it does not appear to return anything of that type. Instead of a normal return statement, it uses a yield return statement, and that returns a single int, not a collection. Iterators produce values one at a time with yield return statements, and unlike with a normal return, the method can continue to execute after returning a value—it's only when the method either runs to the end, or decides to stop early with a yield break statement or by throwing an exception, that it is complete. Example 5-28 shows this rather more starkly. Each yield return causes a value to be emitted from the sequence, so this one will produce the numbers 1–3.

Example 5-28. A very simple iterator

```
public static IEnumerable<int> ThreeNumbers()
{
    yield return 1;
    yield return 2;
    yield return 3;
}
```

Although this is fairly straightforward in concept, the way it works is somewhat involved because code in iterators does not run in the same way as other code. Remember, with IEnumerable<T>, the caller is in charge of when the next value is retrieved; a foreach loop will get an enumerator and then repeatedly call MoveNext() until that returns false, and expect the Current property to provide the current value. So how do Examples 5-27 and 5-28 fit into that model? You might think that perhaps C# stores all the values an iterator yields in a List<T>, returning that once the iterator is complete, but it's easy to demonstrate that that's not true by writing an iterator that never finishes, such as the one in Example 5-29.

Example 5-29. An infinite iterator

```
public static IEnumerable<BigInteger> Fibonacci()
{
    BigInteger v1 = 1;
    BigInteger v2 = 1;

    while (true)
    {
        yield return v1;
        var tmp = v2;
        v2 = v1 + v2;
        v1 = tmp;
    }
}
```

This iterator runs indefinitely; it has a while loop with a true condition, and it contains no break statement, so this will never voluntarily stop. If C# tried to run an iterator to completion before returning anything, it would get stuck here. (The numbers grow, so if it ran for long enough, the method would eventually terminate by throwing an OutOfMemoryException, but it would never return anything useful.) But if you try this, you'll find it starts returning values from the Fibonacci series immediately, and will continue to do so for as long as you continue to iterate through its output. Clearly, C# is not simply running the whole method before returning.

C# performs some serious surgery on your code to make this work. If you examine the compiler's output for an iterator using a tool such as ILDASM (the disassembler for .NET code, provided with the .NET SDK), you'll find it generates a private nested class that acts as the implementation for both the IEnumerable<T> that the method returns, and also the IEnumerator<T> that the IEnumerable<T>'s GetEnumerator method returns. The code from your iterator method ends up inside this class's Move Next method, but it is barely recognizable, because the compiler splits it up in a way that enables each yield return to return to the caller, but for execution to continue from where it left off the next time MoveNext is called. Where necessary, it will store local variables inside this generated class so that their values can be preserved across multiple calls to MoveNext. Perhaps the easiest way to get a feel for what C# has to do when compiling an iterator is to write the equivalent code by hand. Example 5-30 provides the same Fibonacci sequence as Example 5-29 without the aid of an iterator. It's not precisely what the compiler does, but it illustrates some of the challenges.

Example 5-30. Implementing IEnumerable<T> by hand

```
public class FibonacciEnumerable :
    IEnumerable<BigInteger>, IEnumerator<BigInteger>
{
    private BigInteger v1;
    private BigInteger v2;
    private bool first = true;

    public BigInteger Current => v1;

    public void Dispose() { }

    object IEnumerator.Current => Current;

    public bool MoveNext()
    {
        if (first)
        {
            v1 = 1;
            v2 = 1;
            first = false;
        }
        else
        {
            var tmp = v2;
            v2 = v1 + v2;
            v1 = tmp;
        }

        return true;
    }

    public void Reset()
    {
        first = true;
    }
```

```
public IEnumerator<BigInteger> GetEnumerator() =>
    new FibonacciEnumerable();

IEnumerator IEnumerable.GetEnumerator() => GetEnumerator();
}
```

This is not a particularly complex example, because its enumerator is essentially in either of two states—either it is running for the first time and therefore needs to run the code that comes before the loop, or it is inside the loop. Even so, this code is much harder to read than Example 5-29, because the mechanics of supporting enumeration have obscured the essential logic.

The code would get even more convoluted if we needed to deal with exceptions. You can write using blocks and finally blocks, which enable your code to behave correctly in the face of errors, as I'll show in Chapters 7 and 8, and the compiler can end up doing a lot of work to preserve the correct semantics for these when the method's execution is split up over multiple iterations.[4] You wouldn't need to write too many enumerations by hand this way before being grateful that C# can do it for you.

You don't have to return an IEnumerable<T>, by the way. If you prefer, you can return an IEnumerator<T> instead. And, as you saw earlier, objects that implement either of these interfaces also always implement the nongeneric equivalents, so if you need a plain IEnumerable or IEnumerator, you don't need to do extra work—you can pass an IEnumerable<T> to anything that was expecting a plain IEnumerable, and likewise for enumerators. If for some reason you want to provide one of these nongeneric interfaces and you don't wish to provide the generic version, you are allowed to write iterators that return the nongeneric forms directly.

One thing to be careful of with iterators is that they run very little code until the first time the caller calls MoveNext. So if you were to single-step through code that calls the Fibonacci method in Example 5-29, the method call would appear not to do anything at all. If you try to step into the method at the point at which it's invoked, none of the code in the method runs. It's only when iteration begins that you'd see your iterator's body execute. This has a couple of consequences.

The first thing to bear in mind is that if your iterator method takes arguments, and you want to validate those arguments, you may need to do some extra work. By default, the validation won't happen until iteration begins, so errors will occur later than you might expect. If you want to validate arguments immediately, you will need

---

4 Some of this cleanup work happens in the call to Dispose. Remember, IEnumerator<T> implementations all implement IDisposable. The foreach keyword calls Dispose after iterating through a collection (even if iteration was terminated by an error). If you're not using foreach and are performing iteration by hand, it's vitally important to remember to call Dispose.

to write a wrapper. Example 5-31 shows an example—it provides a normal method called Fibonacci that doesn't use yield return, and will therefore not get the special compiler behavior for iterators. This normal method validates its argument before going on to call a nested iterator method. (This also illustrates that local methods can use yield return.)

Example 5-31. Iterator argument validation

```
public static IEnumerable<BigInteger> Fibonacci(int count)
{
    if (count < 0)
    {
        throw new ArgumentOutOfRangeException("count");
    }
    return Core(count);

    static IEnumerable<BigInteger> Core(int count)
    {
        BigInteger v1 = 1;
        BigInteger v2 = 1;

        for (int i = 0; i < count; ++i)
        {
            yield return v1;
            var tmp = v2;
            v2 = v1 + v2;
            v1 = tmp;
        }
    }
}
```

The second thing to remember is that iterators may execute several times. IEnumerable<T> provides a GetEnumerator that can be called many times over, and your iterator body will run from the start each time. So even though your iterator method may only have been called once, it could run several times.

Collection<T>

If you look at types in the .NET class library, you'll find that when they offer properties that expose an implementation of IList<T>, they often do so indirectly. Instead of an interface, properties often provide some concrete type, although it's usually not List<T> either. List<T> is designed to be used as an implementation detail of your code, and if you expose it directly, you may be giving users of your class too much control. Do you want them to be able to modify the list? And even if you do, mightn't your code need to know when that happens?

The class library provides a `Collection<T>` class that is designed to be used as the base class for collections that a type will make publicly available. It is similar to `List<T>`, but there are two significant differences. First, it has a smaller API—it offers `IndexOf`, but all the other searching and sorting methods available for `List<T>` are missing, and it does not provide ways to discover or change its capacity independently of its size. Second, it provides a way for derived classes to discover when items have been added or removed. `List<T>` does not, on the grounds that it's your list so you presumably know when you add and remove items. Notification mechanisms are not free, so `List<T>` avoids unnecessary overhead by not offering them. But `Collection<T>` assumes that external code will have access to your collection, and that you will therefore not be in control of every addition and removal, justifying the overhead involved in providing a way for you to find out when the list is modified. (This is only available to the code deriving from `Collection<T>`. If you want code using your collection to be able to detect changes, the `ObservableCollection<T>` type is designed for that exact scenario.)

You typically derive a class from `Collection<T>`, and you can override the virtual methods it defines to discover when the collection changes. (Chapter 6 will discuss inheritance and overriding.) `Collection<T>` implements both `IList` and `IList<T>`, so you could present a `Collection<T>`-based collection through an interface type property, but it's common to make a derived collection type public, and to use that instead of an interface as the property type.

ReadOnlyCollection<T>

If you want to provide a nonmodifiable collection, then instead of using `Collection<T>`, you can use `ReadOnlyCollection<T>`. This goes further than the restrictions imposed by arrays, by the way: not only can you not add, remove, or insert items, but you cannot even replace elements. This class implements `IList<T>`, which requires an indexer with both a `get` and a `set`, but the `set` throws an exception. (Of course, it also implements `IReadOnlyCollection<T>`.)

If your collection's element type is a reference type, making the collection read-only does not prevent the objects to which the elements refer from being modified. I can retrieve, say, the twelfth element from a read-only collection, and it will hand me back a reference. Fetching a reference counts as a read-only operation, but now that I have got that reference, the collection object is out of the picture, and I am free to do whatever I like with that reference. Since C# does not offer any concept of a read-only reference (there's nothing equivalent to C++ `const` references), the only way to present a truly read-only collection is to use an immutable type in conjunction with `ReadOnlyCollection<T>`.

There are two ways to use ReadOnlyCollection<T>. You can use it directly as a wrapper for an existing list—its constructor takes an IList<T>, and it will provide read-only access to that. (List<T> provides a method called AsReadOnly that constructs a read-only wrapper for you, by the way.) Alternatively, you could derive a class from it. As with Collection<T>, some classes do this for collections they wish to expose via properties, and it's usually because they want to define additional methods specific to the collection's purpose. Even if you derive from this class, you will still be using it to wrap an underlying list, because the only constructor it provides is the one that takes a list.

 ReadOnlyCollection<T> is typically not a good fit with scenarios that automatically map between object models and an external representation. For example, it causes problems in types used as Data Transfer Objects (DTOs) that get converted to and from JSON messages sent over network connections, and also in object-relational mapping systems that present the contents of a database through an object model. Frameworks for these scenarios need to be able to instantiate your types and populate them with data, so although a read-only collection might be a good conceptual match for what some part of your model represents, it might not fit in with the way these mapping frameworks expect to initialize objects.

Addressing Elements with Index and Range Syntax

Whether using arrays, List<T>, IList<T>, or the various related types and interfaces just discussed, we've identified elements using simple examples such as items[0], and more generally, expressions of the form *arrayOrListExpression*[*indexExpression*]. So far, all the examples have used an expression of type int for the index, but that is not the only choice. Example 5-32 accesses the final element of an array using an alternative syntax.

Example 5-32. Accessing the last element of an array with an end-relative index

```
char[] letters = { 'a', 'b', 'c', 'd' };
char lastLetter = letters[^1];
```

This demonstrates one of two new operators introduced in C# 8.0 for use in indexers: the ^ operator and the *range operator*. The latter, shown in Example 5-33, is a pair of periods (..), and it is used to identify subranges of arrays, strings, or any indexable type that implements a certain pattern.

Example 5-33. Getting a subrange of an array with the range operator

```
int[] numbers = { 1, 2, 3, 4, 5, 6, 7 };
// Gets 4th and 5th (but not, the 3rd, for reasons explained shortly)
int[] theFourthTheFifth = numbers[3..5];
```

Expressions using the ^ and .. operators are of type Index and Range, respectively. These types are built into .NET Core 3.0 and .NET Standard 2.1. At the time of writing, Microsoft has not produced a NuGet package defining versions of these types for older targets, meaning that these new language features are only available on newer runtimes. It's possible that by the time you read this, there will be a NuGet package that makes Index and Range more widely available, since most of what they do does not depend on new underlying runtime capabilities. However, it is now Microsoft's policy that new C# language features are associated with new versions of .NET, so even if packages do emerge, the level of support on older runtimes remains to be seen.

System.Index

You can put the ^ operator in front of any int expression. It produces a Sys tem.Index, a value type that represents a position. When you create an index with ^, it is end-relative, but you can also create start-relative indexes. There's no special operator for that, but since Index offers an implicit conversion from int, you can just assign int values directly into variables of type Index, as Example 5-34 shows. You can also explicitly construct an index, as the line with var shows. The final bool argument is optional—it defaults to false—but I'm showing it to illustrate how Index knows which kind you want.

Example 5-34. Some start-relative and end-relative Index values

```
Index first = 0;
Index second = 1;
Index third = 2;
var fourth = new Index(3, fromEnd: false);

Index antePenultimate = ^3;
Index penultimate = ^2;
Index last = ^1;
Index directlyAfterTheLast = ^0;
```

As Example 5-34 shows, end-relative indexes exist independently of any particular collection. (Internally, Index stores end-relative indexes as negative numbers. This means that an Index is the same size as an int. It also means that negative end-relative values are illegal—you'll get an exception if you try to create one.) C# generates code that determines the actual element position when you use an index. If small and big are arrays with 3 and 30 elements, respectively, small[last] would return the third, and big[last] would return the thirtieth. C# will turn these into small[last.GetOffset(small.Length)] and big[last.GetOffset(big.Length)], respectively.

It has often been said that three of the hardest problems in computing are picking names for things, and off-by-one errors. At first glance, Example 5-34 makes it look like Index might be contributing to these problems. It may be vexing that the index for the third item is two, not three, but that at least is consistent with how arrays have always worked in C#, and is normal for any zero-based indexing system. But given that zero-based convention, why on earth do the end-relative indexes appear to be one-based? We denote the first element with 0 but the last element with ^1!

There are some good reasons for this. The fundamental insight is that in C#, indexes have always specified distances. When programming language designers choose a zero-based indexing system, this is not really a decision to call the first element 0: it is a decision to interpret an index as a distance from the start of an array. An upshot of this is that an index doesn't really refer to an item. Figure 5-1 shows a collection with four elements, and indicates where various index values would point in that collection. Notice that the indexes all refer to the boundaries between the items. This may seem like splitting hairs, but it's the key to understanding all zero-based index systems, and it is behind the apparent inconsistency in Example 5-34.

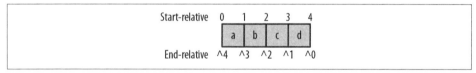

Figure 5-1. Where Index values point

When you access an element of a collection by index, you are asking for the element that *starts* at the position indicated by the index. So array[0] retrieves the single element that starts at the beginning of the array, the element that fills the space between indexes 0 and 1. Likewise, array[1] retrieves the element between indexes 1 and 2. What would array[^0] mean?[5] That would be an attempt to fetch the element that *starts* at the very end of the array. Since elements all take up a certain amount of space, an element that starts at the very end of the array would necessarily finish one position after the end of the array. In this example, four-element array, array[^0] is equivalent to array[4], so we're asking for the element occupying the space that

---

5 Since end-relative indexes are stored as negative numbers, you might be wondering whether ^0 is even legal, since the int type does not distinguish between positive and negative zero. It is allowed because, as you'll soon see, ^0 is useful when using ranges. To make this work, Index adjusts end-relative indexes by one as well as negating them, so it stores ^0 as −1, ^1 as −2, etc.

starts four elements from the start, and which ends five elements from the start. And since this is a four-element array, that's obviously not going to work.

The apparent discrepancy—the fact that `array[0]` gets the first, but we need to write `array[^1]` to get the last—occurs because elements sit between two indexes, and array indexers always retrieve the element between the index specified and the index after that. The fact that they do this even when you've specified an end-relative index is the reason those appear to be one-based. This language feature could have been designed differently: you could imagine a rule in which end-relative indexes always access the element that *ends* at the specified distance from the end, and which starts one position earlier than that. There would have been a pleasing symmetry to this, because it would have made `array[^0]` refer to the final element, but this would have caused more problems than it solved.

It would be confusing to have indexers interpret an index in two different ways—it would mean that two different indexes might refer to the same position and yet fetch different elements. In any case, C# developers are already used to things working this way. As Example 5-35 shows, the way to access the final element of an array prior to C# 8.0 was to use an index calculated by subtracting one from the length. And if you want the element before last, you subtract two from the length, and so on. As you can see, the new end-relative syntax is entirely consistent with the long-established existing practice.

Example 5-35. End-relative indexing, and pre-Index equivalents

```
int lastOld = numbers[numbers.Length - 1];
int lastNew = numbers[^1];

int penultimateOld = numbers[numbers.Length - 2];
int penultimateNew = numbers[^2];
```

One more way to think of this is to wonder what it might look like if we accessed arrays by specifying ranges. The first element is in the range 0–1, and the last is in the range ^1–^0. Expressed this way, there is clearly symmetry between the start-relative and end-relative forms. And speaking of ranges…

System.Range

As I said earlier, C# 8.0 adds two new operators for working with arrays and other indexable types. We've just looked at ^ and the corresponding Index type. The other is called the *range operator*, and it has a corresponding type, Range, also in the System namespace. A Range is just a pair of Index values, which it makes available through Start and End properties. Range offers a constructor taking two Index values, but in C# the idiomatic way to create one is with the range operator, as Example 5-36 shows.

Example 5-36. Various ranges

```
Range everything = 0..^0;
Range alsoEverything = 0..;
Range everythingAgain = ..^0;
Range everythingOneMoreTime = ..;
var yetAnotherWayToSayEverything = Range.All;

Range firstThreeItems = 0..3;
Range alsoFirstThreeItems = ..3;

Range allButTheFirstThree = 3..^0;
Range alsoAllButTheFirstThree = 3..;

Range allButTheLastThree = 0..^3;
Range alsoAllButTheLastThree = ..^3;

Range lastThreeItems = ^3..^0;
Range alsoLastThreeItems = ^3..;
```

As you can see, if you do not put a start index before the `..`, it defaults to 0, and if you omit the end it defaults to `^0` (i.e., the very start and end, respectively). The example also shows that the start can be either start-relative or end-relative, as can the end.

 The default value for `Range`—the one you'll get in a field or array element that you do not explicitly initialize—is 0..0. This denotes an empty range. While this is a natural upshot of the fact that value types are always initialized to zero-like values by default, it might not be what you'd expect given that `..` is equivalent to `Range.All`.

Since `Range` works in terms of `Index`, the start and end denote offsets, not elements. For example, consider what the range `1..3` would mean for the elements shown in Figure 5-1. In this case, both indexes are start-relative. The start index, `1`, is the boundary between the first and second elements (a and b), and the end index, `3`, is the boundary between the third and fourth elements (c and d). So this is a range that starts at the beginning of b and ends at the end of c, as Figure 5-2 shows. So this identifies a two-element range (b and c).

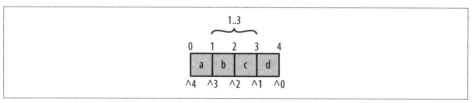

Figure 5-2. A range

The interpretation of ranges sometimes surprises people when they first see it: some expect 1..3 to represent the first, second, and third elements (or, if they take into account C#'s zero-based indexing, perhaps the second, third, and fourth elements). It can seem inconsistent at first that the start index appears to be inclusive while the end index is exclusive. But once you remember that an index refers not to an item, but to an offset, and therefore the boundary between two items, it all makes sense. If you draw the positions represented by a range's indexes as Figure 5-2 does, it becomes perfectly obvious that the range identified by 1..3 covers just two elements.

So what can we do with a Range? As Example 5-33 showed, we can use one to get a subrange of an array. That creates a new array of the relevant size and copies the values from the range into it. This same syntax also works for getting substrings, as Example 5-37 shows.

Example 5-37. Getting a substring with a range

```
string t1 = "dysfunctional";
string t2 = t1[3..6];
Console.WriteLine($"Putting the {t2} in {t1}");
```

You can also use Range with ArraySegment<T>, a value type that refers to a range of elements within an array. Example 5-38 makes a slight modification to Example 5-33. Instead of passing the range to the array's indexer, this first creates an ArraySeg ment<int> that represents the entire array, and then uses a range to get a second ArraySegment<int> representing the fourth and fifth elements. The advantage of this is that it does not need to allocate a new array—both ArraySegment<int> values refer to the same underlying array, they just point to different sections of it, and since ArraySegment<int> is a value type, this can avoid allocating new heap blocks. (Array Segment<int> has no direct support for range, by the way. The compiler turns this into a call to the segment's Slice method.)

Example 5-38. Getting a subrange of an ArraySegment<T> with the range operator

```
int[] numbers = { 1, 2, 3, 4, 5, 6, 7 };
ArraySegment<int> wholeArrayAsSegment = numbers;
ArraySegment<int> theFourthTheFifth = wholeArrayAsSegment[3..5];
```

The ArraySegment<T> type has been around since .NET 2.0 (and has been in .NET Standard since 1.0). It's a useful way to avoid extra allocations, but it's limited: it only works with arrays. What about strings? .NET Core 2.1 introduced a more general form of this concept, Span<T> (and this is also available for older versions of .NET, thanks to the System.Memory NuGet package). Just like ArraySegment<T>, Span<T> represents a subsequence of items inside something else, but it is much more flexible about what that "something else" might be. It could be an array, but it can also be a string, memory in a stack frame, or memory allocated by some library or system call entirely outside of .NET. The Span<T> type is discussed in more detail in Chapter 18, but for now, Example 5-39 illustrates its basic use (and its read-only counterpart as well).

Example 5-39. Getting a subrange of a Span<T> with the range operator

```
int[] numbers = { 1, 2, 3, 4, 5, 6, 7 };
Span<int> wholeArrayAsSpan = numbers;
Span<int> theFourthTheFifth = wholeArrayAsSpan[3..5];
ReadOnlySpan<char> textSpan = "dysfunctional".AsSpan();
ReadOnlySpan<char> such = textSpan[3..6];
```

These have much the same logical meaning as the preceding examples, but they avoid making copies of the underlying data.

We've now seen that we can use ranges with several types: arrays, strings, ArraySeg ment<T>, and Span<T>. This raises a question: does C# have a list of types that get special handling, or can we support indexers and ranges in our own types? The answers are, respectively, yes and yes. C# has some baked-in handling for arrays and strings: it knows to call specific .NET class library methods to produce subarrays and substrings. However, there is no special handling for array segments or spans: they work because they conform to a pattern. There is also a pattern to enable use of Index. If you support these same patterns, you can make Index and Range work with your own types.

Supporting Index and Range in Your Own Types

The array type does not define an indexer that accepts an argument of type Index. Nor do any of the generic array-like types shown earlier in this chapter—they all just have ordinary int-based indexers, but you can use Index with them nonetheless. As I explained earlier, code of the form col[index] will expand to col[index.GetOff set(a.Length)].[6] So all you need is an int-based indexer, and a property of type int called either Length or Count. Example 5-40 shows about the least amount of work you can possibly do to enable code to pass an Index to your type's indexer. It's not a very useful implementation, but it's enough to keep C# happy.

---

6 In cases where you use ^ directly against an int inside an array indexer (e.g., a[^i] where i is an int), the compiler generates marginally simpler code. Instead of converting i to an Index, then calling GetOffset, it will generate code equivalent to a[a.Length - i].

Example 5-40. Minimally enabling Index

```
public class Indexable
{
    public char this[int index] => (char)('0' + index);

    public int Length => 10;
}
```

 There's an even simpler way: just define an indexer that takes an argument of type Index. However, most indexable types supply an int-based indexer, so in practice you'd be overloading your indexer, offering both forms. That is not simpler, but it would enable your code to distinguish between start- and end-relative indexes. If we use either 1 or ^9 with Example 5-40, its indexer sees 1 in either case, because C# generates code that converts the Index to a start-based int, but if you write an indexer with an Index parameter, C# will pass the Index straight in. If you overload the indexer so that both int and Index forms are available, it will never generate code that calls the int index: the pattern only kicks in if no Index-specific indexer is available.

IList<T> meets the pattern's requirements (as do types that implement it, such as List<T>), so you can pass an Index to the indexer of anything that implements this. (It supplies a Count property instead of Length, but the pattern accepts either.) This is a widely implemented interface, so in practice, many types that were defined long before C# 8.0 now automatically get support for Index without needing modification. This is an example of how the pattern-based support for Index means libraries that target older .NET versions (such as .NET Standard 2.0) where Index is not available can nonetheless define types that will work with Index when used with .NET Core 3.0 or later.

The pattern for supporting Range is different: if your type supplies an instance method called Slice that takes two integer arguments, C# will allow code to supply a Range as an indexer argument. Example 5-40 shows the least a type can do to enable this, although it's not a very useful implementation. (As with Index, you can alternatively just define an indexer overload that accepts a Range directly. But again, an advantage to the pattern approach is that you can use it when targeting older versions —such as .NET Standard 2.0 that do not offer the Range or Index types—while still supporting ranges for code that targets newer versions.)

Example 5-41. Minimally enabling Range

```
public class Rangeable
{
    public int Length => 10;

    public Rangeable Slice(int offset, int length) => this;
}
```

You might have noticed that this type doesn't define an indexer. That's because this pattern-based support for expressions of the form x[1..^1] doesn't need one. It may look like we're using an indexer, but this just calls the Slice method. (Likewise, the earlier range examples with string and arrays compile into method calls.) You need the Length property (or Count) because the compiler generates code that relies on this to resolve the range's indexes. Example 5-42 shows roughly how the compiler uses types that support this pattern.

Example 5-42. How range indexing expands

```
Rangeable r1 = new Rangeable();
Range r = 2..^2;

Rangeable r2;

r2 = r1[r];
// is equivalent to
int startIndex = r.Start.GetOffset(r1.Length);
int endIndex = r.End.GetOffset(r1.Length);
r2 = r1.Slice(startIndex, endIndex - startIndex);
```

So far, all of the collections we've looked at have been linear: I've shown only simple sequences of objects, some of which offer indexed access. However, .NET provides other kinds of collections.

Dictionaries

One of the most useful kinds of collection is a dictionary. .NET offers the Dictio nary<TKey, TValue> class, and there's a corresponding interface called, predictably, IDictionary<TKey, TValue>, and also a read-only version, IReadOnlyDiction ary<TKey, TValue>. These represent collections of key/value pairs, and their most useful capability is to look up a value based on its key, making dictionaries useful for representing associations.

Suppose you are writing a UI for an application that supports online discussions. When displaying a message, you might want to show certain things about the user who sent it, such as their name and picture, and you'd probably want to avoid looking up these details every time from wherever they're stored; if the user is in conversation with a few friends, the same people will crop up repeatedly, so you'd want some sort of cache to avoid duplicate lookups. You might use a dictionary as part of this cache. Example 5-43 shows an outline of this approach. (It omits application-specific details of how the data is actually fetched and when old data is removed from memory.)

Example 5-43. Using a dictionary as part of a cache

```
public class UserCache
{
    private readonly Dictionary<string, UserInfo> _cachedUserInfo =
        new Dictionary<string, UserInfo>();

    public UserInfo GetInfo(string userHandle)
    {
        RemoveStaleCacheEntries();
        if (!_cachedUserInfo.TryGetValue(userHandle, out UserInfo info))
        {
            info = FetchUserInfo(userHandle);
            _cachedUserInfo.Add(userHandle, info);
        }
        return info;
    }

    private UserInfo FetchUserInfo(string userHandle)
    {
        // fetch info ...
    }

    private void RemoveStaleCacheEntries()
    {
        // application-specific logic deciding when to remove old entries ...
    }
}

public class UserInfo
{
    // application-specific user information ...
}
```

The first type argument, TKey, is used for lookups, and in this example, I'm using a string that identifies the user in some way. The TValue argument is the type of value associated with the key—information previously fetched for the user and cached locally in a UserInfo instance, in this case. The GetInfo method uses TryGetValue to look in the dictionary for the data associated with a user handle. There is a simpler way to retrieve a value. As Example 5-44 shows, dictionaries provide an indexer. However, that throws a KeyNotFoundException if there is no entry with the specified key. That would be fine if your code always expects to find what it's looking for, but in our case, the key will be missing for any user whose data is not already in the cache. This will probably happen rather a lot, which is why I'm using TryGetValue. As an alternative, we could have used the ContainsKey method to see if the entry exists before retrieving it, but that's inefficient if the value is present—the dictionary would end up looking up the entry twice, once in the call to ContainsKey and then again when we use the indexer. TryGetValue performs the test and the lookup as a single operation.

Example 5-44. Dictionary lookup with indexer

```
UserInfo info = _cachedUserInfo[userHandle];
```

As you might expect, we can also use the indexer to set the value associated with a key. I've not done that in Example 5-43. Instead, I've used the Add method, because it has subtly different semantics: by calling Add, you are indicating that you do not think any entry with the specified key already exists. Whereas the dictionary's indexer will silently overwrite an existing entry if there is one, Add will throw an exception if you attempt to use a key for which an entry already exists. In situations where the presence of an existing key would imply that something is wrong, it's better to call Add so that the problem doesn't go undetected.

The IDictionary<TKey, TValue> interface requires its implementations also to provide the ICollection<KeyValuePair<TKey, TValue>> interface, and therefore also IEnumerable<KeyValuePair<TKey, TValue>>. The read-only counterpart requires the latter, but not the former. These interfaces depend on a generic struct, KeyValue Pair<TKey, TValue>, which is a simple container that wraps a key and a value in a single instance. This means you can iterate through a dictionary using foreach, and it will return each key/value pair in turn.

The presence of an IEnumerable<T> and an Add method also means that we can use the collection initializer syntax. It's not quite the same as with a simple list, because a dictionary's Add takes two arguments: the key and value. However, the collection initializer syntax can cope with multiargument Add methods. You wrap each set of arguments in nested braces, as Example 5-45 shows.

Example 5-45. Collection initializer syntax with a dictionary

```
var textToNumber = new Dictionary<string, int>
{
    { "One", 1 },
    { "Two", 2 },
    { "Three", 3 },
};
```

As you saw in Chapter 3, there's an alternative way to populate a dictionary: instead of using a collection initializer, you can use the object initializer syntax. As you may recall, this syntax lets you set properties on a newly created object. It is the only way to initialize the properties of an anonymous type, but you can use it on any type. Indexers are just a special kind of property, so it makes sense to be able to set them with an object initializer. Although Chapter 3 showed this already, it's worth comparing object initializers with collection initializers, so Example 5-46 shows the alternative way to initialize a dictionary.

Example 5-46. Object initializer syntax with a dictionary

```
var textToNumber = new Dictionary<string, int>
{
    ["One"] = 1,
    ["Two"] = 2,
    ["Three"] = 3
};
```

Although the effect is the same here with Examples 5-45 and 5-46, the compiler generates slightly different code for each. With Example 5-45, it populates the collection by calling Add, whereas Example 5-46 uses the indexer. For Dictionary<TKey, TValue>, the result is the same, so there's no objective reason to choose one over the other, but the difference could matter for some classes. For example, if you are using a class that has an indexer but no Add method, only the index-based code would work. Also, with the object initializer syntax, it would be possible to set both indexed values and properties on types that support this (although you can't do that with Dictionary<TKey, TValue> because it has no writable properties other than its indexer).

The Dictionary<TKey, TValue> collection class relies on hashes to offer fast lookup. Chapter 3 described the GetHashCode method, and you should ensure that whatever type you are using as a key provides a good hash implementation. The string class works well. The default GetHashCode method is viable only if different instances of a type are always considered to have different values, but types for which that is true function well as keys. Alternatively, the dictionary class provides constructors that accept an IEqualityComparer<TKey>, which allows you to provide an implementation of GetHashCode and Equals to use instead of the one supplied by the key type itself. Example 5-47 uses this to make a case-insensitive version of Example 5-45.

Example 5-47. A case-insensitive dictionary

```
var textToNumber =
    new Dictionary<string, int>(StringComparer.InvariantCultureIgnoreCase)
{
    { "One", 1 },
    { "Two", 2 },
```

```
    { "Three", 3 },
};
```

This uses the `StringComparer` class, which provides various implementations of `ICom parer<string>` and `IEqualityComparer<string>`, offering different comparison rules. Here, I've chosen an ordering that ignores case, and also ignores the configured locale, ensuring consistent behavior in different regions. If I were using strings to be displayed, I'd probably use one of its culture-aware comparisons.

Sorted Dictionaries

Because `Dictionary<TKey, TValue>` uses hash-based lookup, the order in which it returns elements when you iterate over its contents is hard to predict and not very useful. It will generally bear no relation to the order in which the contents were added, and no obvious relationship to the contents themselves. (The order typically looks random, although it's actually related to the hash code.)

Sometimes, it's useful to be able to retrieve the contents of a dictionary in some meaningful order. You could always get the contents into an array and then sort them, but the `System.Collections.Generic` namespace contains two more implementations of the `IDictionary<TKey, TValue>` interface, which keep their contents permanently in order. There's `SortedDictionary<TKey, TValue>`, and the more confusingly titled `SortedList<TKey, TValue>`, which—despite the name—implements the `IDictionary<TKey, TValue>` interface and does not directly implement `IList<T>`.

These classes do not use hash codes. They still provide reasonably fast lookup by virtue of keeping their contents sorted. They maintain the order every time you add a new entry, which makes addition rather slower for both these classes than with the hash-based dictionary, but it means that when you iterate over the contents, they come out in order. As with array and list sorting, you can specify custom comparison logic, but if you don't supply that, these dictionaries require the key type to implement `IComparable<T>`.

The ordering maintained by a `SortedDictionary<TKey, TValue>` is apparent only when you use its enumeration support (e.g., with `foreach`). `SortedList<TKey, TValue>` also enumerates its contents in order, but it additionally provides numerically indexed access to the keys and values. This does not work through the object's indexer—that expects to be passed a key just like any dictionary. Instead, the sorted list dictionary defines two properties, `Keys` and `Values`, which provide all the keys and values as `IList<TKey>` and `IList<TValue>`, respectively, sorted so that the keys will be in ascending order.

Inserting and removing objects is relatively expensive for the sorted list because it has to shuffle the key and value list contents up or down. (This means a single insertion has $O(n)$ complexity.) The sorted dictionary, on the other hand, uses a tree data structure to keep its contents sorted. The exact details are not specified, but insertion and removal performance are documented as having $O(\log n)$ complexity, which is much better than for the sorted list.[7] However, this more complex data structure gives a sorted dictionary a significantly larger memory footprint. This means that neither is definitively faster or better than the other—it all depends on the usage pattern, which is why .NET supplies both.

In most cases, the hash-based `Dictionary<TKey, Value>` will provide better insertion, removal, and lookup performance than either of the sorted dictionaries, and much lower memory consumption than a `SortedDictionary<TKey, TValue>`, so you should use these sorted dictionary collections only if you need to access the dictionary's contents in order.

Sets

The `System.Collections.Generic` namespace defines an `ISet<T>` interface. This offers a simple model: a particular value is either a member of the set or not. You can add or remove items, but a set does not keep track of how many times you've added an item, nor does `ISet<T>` require items to be stored in any particular order.

All set types implement `ICollection<T>`, which provides the methods for adding and removing items. In fact, it also defines the method for determining membership: although I've not drawn attention to it before now, you can see in Example 5-24 that `ICollection<T>` defines a `Contains` method. This takes a single value, and returns `true` if that value is in the collection.

Given that `ICollection<T>` already provides the defining operations for a set, you might wonder why we need `ISet<T>`. But it does add a few things. Although `ICollection<T>` defines an `Add` method, `ISet<T>` defines its own subtly different version, which returns a `bool`, so you can find out whether the item you just added was already in the set. Example 5-48 uses this to detect duplicates in a method that displays each string in its input once. (This illustrates the usage, but in practice it would be simpler to use the `Distinct` LINQ operator described in Chapter 10.)

Example 5-48. Using a set to determine what's new

```
public static void ShowEachDistinctString(IEnumerable<string> strings)
{
    var shown = new HashSet<string>();  // Implements ISet<T>
```

---

7 The usual complexity analysis caveats apply—for small collections, the simpler data structure might well win, its theoretical advantage only coming into effect with larger collections.

```
    foreach (string s in strings)
    {
        if (shown.Add(s))
        {
            Console.WriteLine(s);
        }
    }
}
```

ISet<T> also defines some operations for combining sets. The UnionWith method takes an IEnumerable<T> and adds to the set all the values from that sequence that were not already in the set. The ExceptWith method removes from the set items that are also in the sequence you pass. The IntersectWith method removes from the set items that are not also in the sequence you pass. And SymmetricExceptWith also takes a sequence, and removes from the set elements that are in the sequence, but also adds to the set values in the sequence that were not previously in the set.

There are also some methods for comparing sets. Again, these all take an IEnumerable<T> argument representing the other set with which the comparison is to be performed. IsSubsetOf and IsProperSubsetOf both let you check whether the set on which you invoke the method contains only elements that are also present in the sequence, with the latter method additionally requiring the sequence to contain at least one item not present in the set. IsSupersetOf and IsProperSupersetOf perform the same tests in the opposite direction. The Overlaps method tells you whether the two sets share at least one element in common.

Mathematical sets do not define an order for their contents, so it's not meaningful to refer to the 1st, 10th, or *n*th element of a set—you can ask only whether an element is in the set or not. In keeping with this feature of mathematical sets, .NET sets do not support indexed access, so ISet<T> does not demand support for IList<T>. Sets are free to produce the members in whatever order they like in their IEnumerable<T> implementation.

The .NET class library offers two classes that provide this interface, with different implementation strategies: HashSet and SortedSet. As you may have guessed from the names, one of the two built-in set implementations does in fact choose to keep its elements in order; SortedSet keeps its contents sorted at all times, and presents items in this order through its IEnumerable<T> implementation. The documentation does not describe the exact strategy used to maintain the order, but it appears to use a balanced binary tree to support efficient insertion and removal, and to offer fast lookup when trying to determine whether a particular value is already in the list.

The other implementation, HashSet, works more like Dictionary<TKey, TValue>. It uses hash-based lookup, which can often be faster than the ordered approach, but if you enumerate through the collection with foreach, the results will not be in any useful order. (So the relationship between HashSet and SortedSet is much like that between the hash-based dictionary and the sorted dictionaries.)

Queues and Stacks

A *queue* is a list where you can only add items to the end of the list, and you can only remove the first item (at which point the second item, if there was one, becomes the new first item). This style of list is often called a first-in, first-out (FIFO) list. This makes it less useful than a List<T>, because you can read, write, insert, or remove items at any point in a List<T>. However, the constraints make it possible to implement a queue with considerably better performance characteristics for insertion and removal. When you remove an item from a List<T>, it has to shuffle all the items after the one removed to close up the gap, and insertions require a similar shuffle. Insertion and removal at the end of a List<T> is efficient, but if you need FIFO semantics, you can't work entirely at the end—you'll need to do either insertions or removals at the start, making List<T> a bad choice. Queue<T> can use a much more efficient strategy because it needs only to support queue semantics. (It uses a circular buffer internally, although that's an undocumented implementation detail.)

To add a new item to the end of a queue, call the Enqueue method. To remove the item at the head of the queue, call Dequeue, or use Peek if you want to look at the item without removing it. Both operations will throw an InvalidOperationException if the queue is empty. You can find out how many items are in the queue with the Count property.

Although you cannot insert, remove, or change items in the middle of the list, you can inspect the whole queue, because Queue<T> implements IEnumerable<T>, and also provides a ToArray method that returns an array containing a copy of the current queue contents.

A *stack* is similar to a queue, except you retrieve items from the same end as you insert them—so this is a last-in, first-out (LIFO) list. Stack<T> looks very similar to Queue<T> except instead of Enqueue and Dequeue, the methods for adding and removing items use the traditional names for stack operations: Push and Pop. (Other methods—such as Peek, ToArray, and so on—remain the same.)

The class library does not offer a double-ended queue (so there is no equivalent to the C++ deque class). However, linked lists can offer a superset of that functionality.

Linked Lists

The LinkedList<T> class provides an implementation of the classic doubly linked list data structure, in which each item in the sequence is wrapped in an object (of type LinkedListNode<T>) that provides a reference to its predecessor and its successor.

The advantage of a linked list is that insertion and removal is inexpensive—it does not require elements to be moved around in arrays, and does not require binary trees to be rebalanced. It just requires a few references to be swapped around. The downsides are that linked lists have fairly high memory overheads, requiring an extra object on the heap for every item in the collection, and it's also relatively expensive for the CPU to get to the *n*th item because you have to go to the start and then traverse *n* nodes.

The first and last nodes in a LinkedList<T> are available through the predictably named First and Last properties. You can insert items at the start or end of the list with AddFirst and AddLast, respectively. To add items in the middle of a list, call either AddBefore or AddAfter, passing in the LinkedListNode<T> before or after which you'd like to add the new item.

The list also provides RemoveFirst and RemoveLast methods, and two overloads of a Remove method that allow you to remove either the first node that has a specified value, or a particular LinkedListNode<T>.

The LinkedListNode<T> itself provides a Value property of type T containing the actual item for this node's point in the sequence. Its List property refers back to the containing LinkedList<T>, and the Previous and Next properties allow you to find the previous or next node.

To iterate through the contents of a linked list, you could, of course, retrieve the first node from the First property and then follow each node's Next property until you get a null. However, LinkedList<T> implements IEnumerable<T>, so it's easier just to use a foreach loop. If you want to get the elements in reverse order, start with Last and follow each node's Previous. If the list is empty, First and Last will be null.

Concurrent Collections

The collection classes described so far are designed for single-threaded usage. You are free to use different instances on different threads simultaneously, but a particular instance of any of these types must be used only from one thread at any one time.[8] But some types are designed to be used by many threads simultaneously, without needing to use the synchronization mechanisms discussed in Chapter 16. These are in the System.Collections.Concurrent namespace.

---

8 There's an exception to this rule: you can use a collection from multiple threads as long as none of the threads attempts to modify it.

The concurrent collections do not offer equivalents for every nonconcurrent collection type. Some classes are designed to solve specific concurrent programming problems. Even with the ones that do have nonconcurrent counterparts, the need for concurrent use without locking can mean that they present a somewhat different API than any of the normal collection classes.

The ConcurrentQueue<T> and ConcurrentStack<T> classes are the ones that look most like the nonconcurrent collections we've already seen, although they are not identical. The queue's Dequeue and Peek have been replaced with TryDequeue and TryPeek, because in a concurrent world, there's no reliable way to know in advance whether attempting to get an item from the queue will succeed. (You could check the queue's Count, but even if that is nonzero, some other thread may get in there and empty the queue between when you check the count and when you attempt to retrieve an item.) So the operation to get an item has to be atomic with the check for whether an item is available, hence the Try forms that can fail without throwing an exception. Likewise, the concurrent stack provides TryPop and TryPeek.

ConcurrentDictionary<TKey, TValue> looks fairly similar to its nonconcurrent cousin, but it adds some extra methods to provide the atomicity required in a concurrent world: the TryAdd method combines the test for the presence of a key with the addition of a new entry; GetOrAdd does the same thing but also returns the existing value if there is one as part of the same atomic operation.

There is no concurrent list, because you tend to need more coarse-grained synchronization to use ordered, indexed lists successfully in a concurrent world. But if you just want a bunch of objects, there's ConcurrentBag<T>, which does not maintain any particular order.

There's also BlockingCollection<T>, which acts like a queue but allows threads that want to take items off the queue to choose to block until an item is available. You can also set a limited capacity, and make threads that put items onto the queue block if the queue is currently full, waiting until space becomes available.

Immutable Collections

Microsoft provides a set of collection classes that guarantee immutability, and yet provide a lightweight way to produce a modified version of the collection without having to make an entire new copy. Unlike the types discussed so far in this chapter, these are not built into the part of the class library that ships with .NET, so they need a reference to the System.Collections.Immutable NuGet package.

Immutability can be a very useful characteristic in multithreaded environments, because if you know that the data you are working with cannot change, you don't need to take special precautions to synchronize your access to it. (This is a stronger guarantee than you get with IReadOnlyList<T>, which merely prevents you from modifying the collection; it could just be a façade over a collection that some other thread is able to modify.) But what do you do if your data needs to be updated occasionally? It seems a shame to give up on immutability and to take on the overhead of traditional multithreaded synchronization in cases where you expect conflicts to be rare.

A low-tech approach is to build a new copy of all of your data each time something changes (e.g., when you want to add an item to a collection, create a whole new collection with a copy of all the old elements and also the new one, and use that new collection from then on). This works, but can be extremely inefficient. However, techniques exist that can effectively reuse parts of existing collections. The basic principle is that if you want to add an item to a collection, you build a new collection that just points to the data that is already there, along with some extra information to say what has changed. It is rather more complex in practice, but the key point is that there are well-established ways in which to implement various kinds of collections so that you can efficiently build what look like complete self-contained copies of the original data with some small modification applied, without either having to modify the original data, or having to build a complete new copy of the collection. The immutable collections do all this for you, encapsulating the work behind some straightforward interfaces.

This enables a model where you're free to update your application's model without affecting code that was in the middle of using the current version of the data. Consequently, you don't need to hold locks while reading data—you might need some synchronization when getting the latest version of the data, but thereafter, you can process the data without any concurrency concerns. This can be especially useful when writing multithreaded code. The .NET Compiler Platform (often known by its codename, Roslyn) that is the basis of Microsoft's C# compiler uses this technique to enable compilation to exploit multiple CPU cores efficiently.

The System.Collections.Immutable namespace defines its own interfaces—IImmutableList<T>, IImmutableDictionary<TKey, TValue>, IImmutableQueue<T>, IImutableStack<T>, and IImutableSet<T>. This is necessary because all operations that modify the collection in any way need to return a new collection. Example 5-49 shows what this means for adding entries to a dictionary.

Example 5-49. Creating immutable dictionaries

```
IImmutableDictionary<int, string> d = ImmutableDictionary.Create<int, string>();
d = d.Add(1, "One");
d = d.Add(2, "Two");
d = d.Add(3, "Three");
```

The whole point of immutable types is that code using an existing object can be certain that nothing will change, so additions, removals, or modifications necessarily mean creating a new object that looks just like the old one but with the modification applied. (The built-in `string` type works in exactly the same way because it is also immutable—the methods that sound like they will change the value, such as `Trim`, actually return a new string.) So in Example 5-49, the variable d refers successively to four different immutable dictionaries: an empty one, one with one value, one with two values, and finally one with all three values.

If you are adding a range of values like this, and you won't be making intermediate results available to other code, it is more efficient to add multiple values in a single operation, because it doesn't have to produce a separate `IImmutableDiction ary<TKey, TValue>` for each entry you add. (You could think of immutable collections as working a bit like a source control system, with each change corresponding to a commit—for every commit you do, a version of the collection will exist that represents its contents immediately after that change.) It's more efficient to batch a bunch of related changes into a single "version" so the collections all have `AddRange` methods that let you add multiple items in one step.

When you're building a new collection from scratch, the same principle applies: it will be more efficient if you put all of the initial content into the first version of the collection, instead of adding items one at a time. Each immutable collection type offers a nested `Builder` class to make this easier, enabling you to add items one at a time, but to defer the creation of the actual collection until you have finished. Example 5-50 shows how this is done.

Example 5-50. Creating an immutable dictionary with a builder

```
ImmutableDictionary<int, string>.Builder b =
    ImmutableDictionary.CreateBuilder<int, string>();
b.Add(1, "One");
b.Add(2, "Two");
b.Add(3, "Three");
IImmutableDictionary<int, string> d = b.ToImmutable();
```

The builder object is not immutable. Much like `StringBuilder`, it is a mutable object that provides an efficient way to build a description of an immutable object.

ImmutableArray<T>

In addition to the immutable list, dictionary, queue, stack, and set types, there's one more immutable collection class that is a bit different than the rest: `ImmutableAr ray<T>`. This is essentially a wrapper providing an immutable façade around an array. It implements `IImmutableList<T>`, meaning that it offers the same services as an immutable list, but it has quite different performance characteristics.

When you call `Add` on an immutable list, it will attempt to reuse most of the data that is already there, so if you have a million items in your list, the "new" list returned by `Add` won't contain a new copy of those items—it will mostly reuse the data that was already there. However, to achieve this, `ImmutableList<T>` uses a somewhat complex tree data structure internally. The upshot is that looking up values by index in an `ImmutableList<T>` is nothing like as efficient as using an array (or a `List<T>`). The indexer for `ImmutableList<T>` has *O(log n)* complexity.

An `ImmutableArray<T>` is much more efficient for reads—being a wrapper around an array, it has *O(1)* complexity, i.e., the time taken to fetch an entry is constant, regardless of how large the collection may be. The tradeoff is that all of the `IImmutableList<T>` methods for building a modified version of the list (`Add`, `Remove`, `Insert`, `SetItem`, etc.) build a complete new array, including a new copy of any data that needs to be carried over. (In other words, unlike all the other immutable collection types, `ImmutableArray<T>` employs the low-tech approach to immutability that I described earlier.) This makes modifications very much more expensive, but if you have some data you expect to modify either rarely or not at all after the initial creation of the array, this is an excellent tradeoff, because you will only ever build one copy of the array.

Summary

In this chapter, we saw the intrinsic support for arrays offered by the runtime, and also the various collection classes that .NET provides when you need more than a fixed-size list of items. Next, we'll look at a more advanced topic: inheritance.

CHAPTER 6

Inheritance

C# classes support *inheritance*, a popular object-oriented code reuse mechanism. When you write a class, you can optionally specify a base class. Your class will derive from this, meaning that everything in the base class will be present in your class, as well as any members you add.

Classes support only single inheritance (so you can only specify one base class). Interfaces offer a form of multiple inheritance. Value types do not support inheritance at all. One reason for this is that value types are not normally used by reference, which removes one of the main benefits of inheritance: runtime polymorphism. Inheritance is not necessarily incompatible with value-like behavior—some languages manage it —but it often has problems. For example, assigning a value of some derived type into a variable of its base type ends up losing all of the fields that the derived type added, a problem known as *slicing*. C# sidesteps this by restricting inheritance to reference types. When you assign a variable of some derived type into a variable of a base type, you're copying a reference, not the object itself, so the object remains intact. Slicing is an issue only if the base class offers a method that clones the object, and doesn't provide a way for derived classes to extend that (or it does, but some derived class fails to extend it).

Classes specify a base class using the syntax shown in Example 6-1—the base type appears after a colon that follows the class name. This example assumes that a class called SomeClass has been defined elsewhere in the project, or one of the libraries it uses.

Example 6-1. Specifying a base class

```
public class Derived : SomeClass
{
}
```

```
public class AlsoDerived : SomeClass, IDisposable
{
    public void Dispose() { }
}
```

As you saw in Chapter 3, if the class implements any interfaces, these are also listed after the colon. If you want to derive from a class, and you want to implement interfaces as well, the base class must appear first, as you can see illustrated in the second class in Example 6-1.

You can derive from a class that in turn derives from another class. The `MoreDerived` class in Example 6-2 derives from `Derived`, which in turn derives from `Base`.

Example 6-2. Inheritance chain

```
public class Base
{
}

public class Derived : Base
{
}

public class MoreDerived : Derived
{
}
```

This means that `MoreDerived` technically has multiple base classes: it derives from both `Derived` (directly) and `Base` (indirectly, via `Derived`). This is not multiple inheritance because there is only a single chain of inheritance—any single class derives directly from at most one base class. (All classes derive either directly or indirectly from `object`, which is the default base class if you do not specify one.)

Since a derived class inherits everything the base class has—all its fields, methods, and other members, both public and private—an instance of the derived class can do anything an instance of the base class could do. This is the classic *is a* relationship that inheritance implies in many languages. Any instance of `MoreDerived` is a `Derived`, and also a `Base`. C#'s type system recognizes this relationship.

Inheritance and Conversions

C# provides various built-in implicit conversions. In Chapter 2, we saw the conversions for numeric types, but there are also ones for reference types. If some type `D` derives from `B` (either directly or indirectly), then a reference of type `D` can be converted implicitly to a reference of type `B`. This follows from the *is a* relationship I described in the preceding section—any instance of D is a B. This implicit conversion enables polymorphism: code written to work in terms of B will be able to work with type derived from B.

 Reference conversions are special. Unlike other conversions, they cannot change the value in any way. (The built-in implicit numeric conversions all create a new value from their input, often involving a change of representation. The binary representation of the integer 1 looks different for the float and int types, for example.) In effect, they convert the interpretation of the reference, rather than converting the reference itself or the object it refers to. As you'll see later in this chapter, there are various places where the CLR will take the availability of an implicit reference conversion into account, but will not consider other forms of conversion.

Obviously, there is no implicit conversion in the opposite direction—although a variable of type B could refer to an object of type D, there's no guarantee that it will. There could be any number of types derived from B, and a B variable could refer to an instance of any of them. Nevertheless, you will sometimes want to attempt to convert a reference from a base type to a derived type, an operation sometimes referred to as a *downcast*. Perhaps you know for a fact that a particular variable holds a reference of a certain type. Or perhaps you're not sure, and would like your code to provide additional services for specific types. C# offers four ways to do this.

We can attempt a downcast using the cast syntax. This is the same syntax we use for performing nonimplicit numeric conversions, as Example 6-3 shows.

Example 6-3. Feeling downcast

```
public static void UseAsDerived(Base baseArg)
{
    var d = (Derived) baseArg;

    // ... go on to do something with d
}
```

This conversion is not guaranteed to succeed—that's why we can't use an implicit conversion. If you try this when the baseArg argument refers to something that's neither an instance of Derived, nor something derived from Derived, the conversion will fail, throwing an InvalidCastException. (Exceptions are described in Chapter 8.)

A cast is therefore appropriate only if you're confident that the object really is of the type you expect, and you would consider it to be an error if it turned out not to be. This is useful when an API accepts an object that it will later give back to you. Many asynchronous APIs do this, because in cases where you launch multiple operations concurrently, you need some way of working out which particular one finished when you get a completion notification (although, as we'll see in later chapters, there are various ways to tackle that problem). Since these APIs don't know what sort of data you'll want to associate with an operation, they usually just take a reference of type object, and you would typically use a cast to turn it back into a reference of the required type when the reference is eventually handed back to you.

Sometimes, you will not know for certain whether an object has a particular type. In this case, you can use the as operator instead, as shown in Example 6-4. This allows you to attempt a conversion without risking an exception. If the conversion fails, this operator just returns null.

Example 6-4. The as operator

```
public static void MightUseAsDerived(Base b)
{
    var d = b as Derived;

    if (d != null)
    {
        // ... go on to do something with d
    }
}
```

Although this technique is quite common in existing code, the introduction of patterns in C# 7.0 provided a more succinct alternative. Example 6-5 has the same effect as Example 6-4: the body of the if runs only if b refers to an instance of Derived, in which case it can be accessed through the variable d. The is keyword here indicates that we want to test b against a pattern. In this case we're using a type pattern, which performs the same runtime type test as the as operator. An expression that applies a pattern with is produces a bool indicating whether the pattern matches. We can use this as the if statement's condition expression, removing the need to compare with null. And since type patterns incorporate variable declaration and initialization, the work that needed two statements in Example 6-4 can all be rolled into the if statement in Example 6-5.

Example 6-5. Type pattern

```
public static void MightUseAsDerived(Base b)
{
    if (b is Derived d)
    {
        // ... go on to do something with d
    }
}
```

In addition to being more compact, the is operator also has the benefit of working in one scenario where as does not: you can test whether a reference of type object refers to an instance of a value type such as an int. (This may seem like a contradiction—how could you have a reference to something that is not a reference type? Chapter 7 will show how this is possible.) The as operator wouldn't work because it returns null when the instance is not of the specified type, but of course it cannot do that for a value type—there's no such thing as a null of type int. Since the type pattern eliminates the need to test for null—we just use the bool result that the is operator produces—we are free to use value types.

Finally, it can occasionally be useful to know whether a reference refers to an object of a particular type, without actually wanting to use members specific to that type. For example, you might want to skip some particular piece of processing for a certain derived class. We can use the is operator for this too. If you just put the name of a type instead of a full pattern, as Example 6-6 does, it tests whether an object is of a particular type, returning true if it is, and false otherwise.

Example 6-6. The is operator

```
if (!(b is WeirdType))
{
    // ... do the processing that everything except WeirdType requires
}
```

This form of the is operator is a historical oddity. It looks very similar to the pattern-based usage, but this is not a pattern. (You can't write just the type name in any of the other places that patterns occur.) And it is redundant: we could achieve the same effect with a type pattern that discards its output. (The pattern-based version would be !(b is WeirdType _).) The only reason this nonpattern form exists is that it used to be the only form. Patterns were only introduced in C# 7.0, whereas this usage of is has been in the language from the start.

When converting with the techniques just described, you don't necessarily need to specify the exact type. These operations will succeed as long as an implicit reference conversion exists from the object's real type to the type you're looking for.[1] For example, given the Base, Derived, and MoreDerived types that Example 6-2 defines, suppose you have a variable of type Base that currently contains a reference to an instance of MoreDerived. Obviously, you could cast the reference to MoreDerived (and both as and is would also succeed for that type), but as you'd probably expect, converting to Derived would work too.

---

1 This excludes custom implicit conversions.

These four mechanisms also work for interfaces. When you try to convert a reference to an interface type reference (or test for an interface type with `is`), it will succeed if the object referred to implements the relevant interface.

Interface Inheritance

Interfaces support inheritance, but it's not quite the same as class inheritance. The syntax is similar, but as Example 6-7 shows, an interface can specify multiple base interfaces. While .NET offers only single implementation inheritance, this limitation does not apply to interfaces because most of the complications and potential ambiguities that can arise with multiple inheritance do not apply to purely abstract types. Even the addition of default interface implementations in C# 8.0 didn't change this because those don't get to add either fields or public members to the implementing type. (When a class uses a default implementation for a member, that member is accessible only through references of the interface's type.)

Example 6-7. Interface inheritance

```
interface IBase1
{
    void Base1Method();
}

interface IBase2
{
    void Base2Method();
}

interface IBoth : IBase1, IBase2
{
    void Method3();
}
```

Although *interface inheritance* is the official name for this feature, it is a misnomer—whereas derived classes inherit all members from their base, derived interfaces do not. It may appear that they do—given a variable of type `IBoth`, you can invoke the `Base1Method` and `Base2Method` methods defined by its bases. However, the true meaning of interface inheritance is simply that type that implements an interface is obliged to implement all inherited interfaces. So a class that implements `IBoth` must also implement `IBase1` and `IBase2`. It's a subtle distinction, especially since C# does not require you to list the base interfaces explicitly. The class in Example 6-8 only declares that it implements `IBoth`. But if you were to use .NET's reflection API to inspect the type definition, you would find that the compiler has added `IBase1` and `IBase2` to the list of interfaces the class implements as well as the explicitly declared `IBoth`.

Example 6-8. Implementing a derived interface

```
public class Impl : IBoth
{
    public void Base1Method()
    {
    }

    public void Base2Method()
    {
    }

    public void Method3()
    {
    }
}
```

Since implementations of a derived interface must implement all base interfaces, C#
lets you access bases' members directly through a reference of a derived type, so a
variable of type IBoth provides access to Base1Method and Base2Method, as well as
that interface's own Method3. Implicit conversions exist from derived interface types
to their bases. For example, a reference of type IBoth can be assigned to variables of
type IBase1 and IBase2.

Generics

If you derive from a generic class, you must supply the type arguments it requires.
You must provide concrete types unless your derived type is generic, in which case it
can use its own type parameters as arguments. Example 6-9 shows both techniques,
and also illustrates that when deriving from a class with multiple type parameters,
you can use a mixture, specifying one type argument directly and punting on the
other.

Example 6-9. Deriving from a generic base class

```
public class GenericBase1<T>
{
    public T Item { get; set; }
}

public class GenericBase2<TKey, TValue>
{
    public TKey Key { get; set; }
    public TValue Value { get; set; }
}

public class NonGenericDerived : GenericBase1<string>
{
```

```
}

public class GenericDerived<T> : GenericBase1<T>
{
}

public class MixedDerived<T> : GenericBase2<string, T>
{
}
```

Although you are free to use any of your type parameters as type arguments for a
base class, you cannot derive from a type parameter. This is a little disappointing if
you are used to languages that permit such things, but the C# language specification
simply forbids it. However, you are allowed to use your own type as a type argument
to your base class. And you can also specify a constraint on a type argument requiring it to derive from your own type. Example 6-10 shows each of these.

Example 6-10. Requiring a type argument to derive from the type it's applied to

```
public class SelfAsTypeArgument : IComparable<SelfAsTypeArgument>
{
    // ... implementation removed for clarity
}

public class Curious<T>
    where T : Curious<T>
{
}
```

Covariance and Contravariance

In Chapter 4, I mentioned that generic types have special rules for type compatibility,
referred to as *covariance* and *contravariance*. These rules determine whether references of certain generic types are implicitly convertible to one another when implicit
conversions exist between their type arguments.

Covariance and contravariance are applicable only to the generic
type arguments of interfaces and delegates. (Delegates are
described in Chapter 9.) You cannot define a covariant or contravariant class or struct.

Consider the simple Base and Derived classes shown earlier in Example 6-2, and look
at the method in Example 6-11, which accepts any Base. (It does nothing with it, but
that's not relevant here—what matters is what its signature says it can use.)

Example 6-11. A method accepting any Base

```
public static void UseBase(Base b)
{
}
```

We already know that as well as accepting a reference to any Base, this can also accept a reference to an instance of any type derived from Base, such as Derived. Bearing that in mind, consider the method in Example 6-12.

Example 6-12. A method accepting any IEnumerable<Base>

```
public static void AllYourBase(IEnumerable<Base> bases)
{
}
```

This requires an object that implements the IEnumerable<T> generic interface described in Chapter 5, where T is Base. What would you expect to happen if we attempted to pass an object that did not implement IEnumerable<Base>, but did implement IEnumerable<Derived>? Example 6-13 does this, and it compiles just fine.

Example 6-13. Passing an IEnumerable<T> of a derived type

```
IEnumerable<Derived> derivedItems =
    new Derived[] { new Derived(), new Derived() };
AllYourBase(derivedItems);
```

Intuitively, this makes sense. The AllYourBase method is expecting an object that can supply a sequence of objects that are all of type Base. An IEnumerable<Derived> fits the bill because it supplies a sequence of Derived objects, and any Derived object is also a Base. However, what about the code in Example 6-14?

Example 6-14. A method accepting any ICollection<Base>

```
public static void AddBase(ICollection<Base> bases)
{
    bases.Add(new Base());
}
```

Recall from Chapter 5 that ICollection<T> derives from IEnumerable<T>, and it adds the ability to modify the collection in certain ways. This particular method exploits that by adding a new Base object to the collection. That would mean trouble for the code in Example 6-15.

Example 6-15. Error: trying to pass an ICollection<T> with a derived type

```
ICollection<Derived> derivedList = new List<Derived>();
AddBase(derivedList);  // Will not compile
```

Code that uses the `derivedList` variable will expect every object in that list to be of type `Derived` (or something derived from it, such as the `MoreDerived` class from Example 6-2). But the `AddBase` method in Example 6-14 attempts to add a plain `Base` instance. That cannot be correct, and the compiler does not allow it. The call to `Add Base` will produce a compiler error complaining that references of type `ICollec tion<Derived>` cannot be converted implicitly to references of type `ICollection<Base>`.

How does the compiler know that it's not OK to do this, while the very similar-looking conversion from `IEnumerable<Derived>` to `IEnumerable<Base>` is allowed? It's not because Example 6-14 contains code that would cause a problem, by the way. You'd get the same compiler error even if the `AddBase` method were completely empty. The reason we don't get an error in Example 6-13 is that the `IEnumerable<T>` interface declares its type argument `T` as covariant. You saw the syntax for this in Chapter 5, but I didn't draw attention to it, so Example 6-16 shows the relevant part from that interface's definition again.

Example 6-16. Covariant type parameter

```
public interface IEnumerable<out T> : IEnumerable
```

That out keyword does the job. (Again, C# keeps up the C-family tradition of giving each keyword multiple jobs—we first saw this keyword in the context of method parameters that can return information to the caller.) Intuitively, describing the type argument T as "out" makes sense, in that the `IEnumerable<T>` interface only ever *provides* a T—it does not define any members that *accept* a T. (The interface uses this type parameter in just one place: its read-only `Current` property.)

Compare that with `ICollection<T>`. This derives from `IEnumerable<T>`, so clearly it's possible to get a T out of it, but it's also possible to pass a T into its `Add` method. So `ICollection<T>` cannot annotate its type argument with out. (If you were to try to write your own similar interface, the compiler would produce an error if you declared the type argument as being covariant. Rather than just taking your word for it, it checks to make sure you really can't pass a T in anywhere.)

The compiler rejects the code in Example 6-15 because T is not covariant in `ICollec tion<T>`. The terms *covariant* and *contravariant* come from a branch of mathematics called *category theory*. The parameters that behave like `IEnumerable<T>`'s T are called covariant because implicit reference conversions for the generic type work in the same direction as conversions for the type argument: Derived is implicitly convertible to Base, and since T is covariant in IEnumerable<T>, IEnumerable<Derived> is implicitly convertible to IEnumerable<Base>.

Predictably, contravariance works the other way around, and as you've probably guessed, we denote it with the in keyword. It's easiest to see this in action with code that uses members of types, so Example 6-17 shows a marginally more interesting pair of classes than the earlier examples.

Example 6-17. Class hierarchy with actual members

```
public class Shape
{
    public Rect BoundingBox { get; set; }
}

public class RoundedRectangle : Shape
{
    public double CornerRadius { get; set; }
}
```

Example 6-18 defines two classes that use these shape types. Both implement IComparer<T>, which I introduced in Chapter 4. The BoxAreaComparer compares two shapes based on the area of their bounding box—the shape whose bounding box covers the greater area will be deemed the larger by this comparison. The CornerSharpnessComparer, on the other hand, compares rounded rectangles by looking at how pointy their corners are.

Example 6-18. Comparing shapes

```
public class BoxAreaComparer : IComparer<Shape>
{
    public int Compare(Shape x, Shape y)
    {
        double xArea = x.BoundingBox.Width * x.BoundingBox.Height;
        double yArea = y.BoundingBox.Width * y.BoundingBox.Height;

        return Math.Sign(xArea - yArea);
    }
}

public class CornerSharpnessComparer : IComparer<RoundedRectangle>
{
    public int Compare(RoundedRectangle x, RoundedRectangle y)
    {
        // Smaller corners are sharper, so smaller radius is "greater" for
        // the purpose of this comparison, hence the backward subtraction.
        return Math.Sign(y.CornerRadius - x.CornerRadius);
```

```
        }
}
```

References of type `RoundedRectangle` are implicitly convertible to `Shape`, so what about `IComparer<T>`? Our `BoxAreaComparer` can compare any shapes, and declares this by implementing `IComparer<Shape>`. The comparer's type argument `T` is only ever used in the `Compare` method, and that is happy to be passed any `Shape`. It will not be fazed if we pass it a pair of `RoundedRectangle` references, so our class is a perfectly adequate `IComparer<RoundedRectangle>`. An implicit conversion from `IComparer<Shape>` to `IComparer<RoundedRectangle>` therefore makes sense, and is in fact allowed. However, the `CornerSharpnessComparer` is fussier. It uses the `Corner Radius` property, which is available only on rounded rectangles, not on any old `Shape`. Therefore, no implicit conversion exists from `IComparer<RoundedRectangle>` to `IComparer<Shape>`.

This is the reverse of what we saw with `IEnumerable<T>`. Implicit conversion is available between `IEnumerable<T1>` and `IEnumerable<T2>` when an implicit reference conversion from `T1` to `T2` exists. But implicit conversion between `IComparer<T1>` and `IComparer<T2>` is available when an implicit reference conversion exists in the other direction: from `T2` to `T1`. That reversed relationship is called contravariance. Example 6-19 is an excerpt of the definition for `IComparer<T>` showing this contravariant type parameter.

Example 6-19. Contravariant type parameter

```
public interface IComparer<in T>
```

Most generic type parameters are neither covariant nor contravariant. (They are *invariant*.) `ICollection<T>` cannot be variant, because it contains some members that accept a `T` and some that return one. An `ICollection<Shape>` might contain shapes that are not `RoundedRectangles`, so you cannot pass it to a method expecting an `ICollection<RoundedRectangle>`, because such a method would expect every object it retrieves from the collection to be a rounded rectangle. Conversely, an `ICollection<RoundedRectangle>` cannot be expected to allow shapes other than rounded rectangles to be added, and so you cannot pass an `ICollection<RoundedRec tangle>` to a method that expects an `ICollection<Shape>` because that method may try to add other kinds of shapes.

Arrays are covariant, just like `IEnumerable<T>`. This is rather odd, because we can write methods like the one in Example 6-20.

Example 6-20. Changing an element in an array

```
public static void UseBaseArray(Base[] bases)
{
    bases[0] = new Base();
}
```

If I were to call this with the code in Example 6-21, I would be making the same mistake as I did in Example 6-15, where I attempted to pass an ICollection<Derived> to a method that wanted to put something that was not Derived into the collection. But while Example 6-15 does not compile, Example 6-21 does, due to the surprising covariance of arrays.

Example 6-21. Passing an array with derived element type

```
Derived[] derivedBases = { new Derived(), new Derived() };
UseBaseArray(derivedBases);
```

This makes it look as though we could sneakily make this array accept a reference to an object that is not an instance of the array's element type—in this case, putting a reference to a non-Derived object, Base, in Derived[]. But that would be a violation of the type system. Does this mean the sky is falling?

In fact, C# correctly forbids such a violation, but it relies on the CLR to enforce this at runtime. Although a reference to an array of type Derived[] can be implicitly converted to a reference of type Base[], any attempt to set an array element in a way that is inconsistent with the type system will throw an ArrayTypeMismatchException. So Example 6-20 would throw that exception when it tried to assign a reference to a Base into the Derived[] array.

Type safety is maintained, and rather conveniently, if we write a method that takes an array and only reads from it, we can pass arrays of some derived element type and it will work. The downside is that the CLR has to do extra work at runtime when you modify array elements to ensure that there is no type mismatch. It may be able to optimize the code to avoid having to check every single assignment, but there is still some overhead, meaning that arrays are not quite as efficient as they might be.

This somewhat peculiar arrangement dates back to the time before .NET had formalized concepts of covariance and contravariance—these came in with generics, which were introduced in .NET 2.0. Perhaps if generics had been around from the start, arrays would be less odd, although having said that, even after .NET 2.0 their peculiar form of covariance was for many years the only mechanism built into the framework that provided a way to pass a collection covariantly to a method that wanted to read from it using indexing. Until .NET 4.5 introduced IReadOnlyList<T> (for which T is covariant), there was no read-only indexed collection interface in the framework, and therefore no standard indexed collection interface with a covariant type parameter. (IList<T> is read/write, so just like ICollection<T>, it cannot offer variance.)

While we're on the subject of type compatibility and the implicit reference conversions that inheritance makes available, there's one more type we should look at: object.

System.Object

The System.Object type, or object as we usually call it in C#, is useful because it can act as a sort of universal container: a variable of this type can hold a reference to almost anything. I've mentioned this before, but I haven't yet explained why it's true. The reason this works is that almost everything derives from object.

If you do not specify a base class when writing a class, the C# compiler automatically uses object as the base. As we'll see shortly, it chooses different bases for certain kinds of types such as structs, but even those derive from object indirectly. (As ever, pointer types are an exception—these do not derive from object.)

The relationship between interfaces and objects is slightly more subtle. Interfaces do not derive from object, because an interface can specify only other interfaces as its bases. However, a reference of any interface type is implicitly convertible to a reference of type object. This conversion will always be valid, because all types that are capable of implementing interfaces ultimately derive from object. Moreover, C# chooses to make the object class's members available through interface references even though they are not, strictly speaking, members of the interface. This means that references of any kind always offer the following methods defined by object: ToString, Equals, GetHashCode, and GetType.

The Ubiquitous Methods of System.Object

I've used ToString in numerous examples already. The default implementation returns the object's type name, but many types provide their own implementation of ToString, returning a more useful textual representation of the object's current value. The numeric types return a decimal representation of their value, for example, while bool returns either "True" or "False".

I discussed Equals and GetHashCode in Chapter 3, but I'll provide a quick recap here. Equals allows an object to be compared with any other object. The default implementation just performs an identity comparison—that is, it returns true only when an object is compared with itself. Many types provide an Equals method that performs value-like comparison—for example, two distinct string objects may contain identical text, in which case they will report being equal to each other. (Should you need to perform an identity-based comparison of objects that provide value-based comparison, you can use the `object` class's static `ReferenceEquals` method.) Incidentally, `object` also defines a static version of `Equals` that takes two arguments. This checks whether the arguments are `null`, returning `true` if both are `null` and `false` if only one is `null`; otherwise, it defers to the first argument's `Equals` method. And, as discussed in Chapter 3, `GetHashCode` returns an integer that is a reduced representation of the object's value, which is used by hash-based mechanisms such as the `Dictionary<TKey, TValue>` collection class. Any pair of objects for which `Equals` returns `true` must return the same hash codes.

The `GetType` method provides a way to discover things about the object's type. It returns a reference of type `Type`. That's part of the reflection API, which is the subject of Chapter 13.

Besides these public members, available through any reference, `object` defines two more members that are not universally accessible. An object has access to these members only on itself. They are `Finalize` and `MemberwiseClone`. The CLR calls the `Finalize` method to notify you that your object is no longer in use and the memory it occupies is about to be reclaimed. In C# we do not normally work directly with the `Finalize` method, because C# presents this mechanism through destructors, as I'll show in Chapter 7. `MemberwiseClone` creates a new instance of the same type as your object, initialized with copies of all of your object's fields. If you need a way to create a clone of an object, this may be easier than writing code that copies all the contents across by hand, although it is not very fast.

The reason these last two methods are available only from inside the object is that you might not want other people cloning your object, and it would be unhelpful if external code could call the `Finalize` method, fooling your object into thinking that it was about to be freed if in fact it wasn't. The `object` class limits the accessibility of these members. But they're not private—that would mean that only the `object` class itself could access them, because private members are not visible even to derived classes. Instead, `object` makes theses members *protected*, an accessibility specifier designed for inheritance scenarios.

Accessibility and Inheritance

By now, you will already be familiar with most of the accessibility levels available for types and their members. Elements marked as `public` are available to all, `private` members are accessible only from within the type that declared them, and `internal` members are available to code defined in the same component.[2] But with inheritance, we get three other accessibility options.

---

2 More precisely, the same assembly, and also friend assemblies. Chapter 12 describes assemblies.

A member marked as `protected` is available inside the type that defined it, and also inside any derived types. But for code using an instance of your type, `protected` members are not accessible, just like `private` members.

The next protection level for type members is `protected internal`. (You can write `internal protected` if you prefer; the order makes no difference.) This makes the member more accessible than either `protected` or `internal` on its own: the member will be accessible to all derived types *and* to all code that shares an assembly.

The third protection level that inheritance adds is `protected private`. Members marked with this (or the equivalent `private protected`) are available only to types that are both derived from *and* defined in the same component as the defining type.

You can use `protected`, `protected internal`, or `protected private` for any member of a type, and not just methods. You can even use nested types with these accessibility specifiers.

Although `protected` (and `protected internal`, although not `protected private`) members are not available through an ordinary variable of the defining type, they are still part of the type's public API, in the sense that anyone who has access to your classes will be able to use these members. As with most languages that support a similar mechanism, `protected` members in C# are typically used to provide services that derived classes might find useful. If you write a `public` class that supports inheritance, then anyone can derive from it and gain access to its `protected` members. Removing or changing `protected` members would therefore risk breaking code that depends on your class just as surely as removing or changing `public` members would.

When you derive from a class, you cannot make your class more visible than its base. If you derive from an `internal` class, for example, you cannot declare your class to be `public`. Your base class forms part of your class's API, so anyone wishing to use your class will also in effect be using its base class; this means that if the base is inaccessible, your class will also be inaccessible, which is why C# does not permit a class to be more visible than its base. For example, if you derive from a `protected` nested class, your derived class could be `protected`, `private`, or `protected private` but not `public`, `internal`, or `protected internal`.

> This restriction does not apply to the interfaces you implement. A `public` class is free to implement `internal` or `private` interfaces. However, it does apply to an interface's bases: a `public` interface cannot derive from an `internal` interface.

When defining methods, there's another keyword you can add for the benefit of derived types: `virtual`.

Virtual Methods

A *virtual method* is one that a derived type can replace. Several of the methods defined by `object` are virtual: the `ToString`, `Equals`, `GetHashCode`, and `Finalize` methods are all designed to be replaced. The code required to produce a useful textual representation of an object's value will differ considerably from one type to another, as will the logic required to determine equality and produce a hash code. Types typically define a finalizer only if they need to do some specialized cleanup work when they go out of use.

Not all methods are virtual. In fact, C# makes methods nonvirtual by default. The `object` class's `GetType` method is not virtual, so you can always trust the information it returns to you because you know that you're calling the `GetType` method supplied by .NET, and not some type-specific substitute designed to fool you. To declare that a method should be virtual, use the `virtual` keyword, as Example 6-22 shows.

Example 6-22. A class with a virtual method

```
public class BaseWithVirtual
{
    public virtual void ShowMessage()
    {
        Console.WriteLine("Hello from BaseWithVirtual");
    }
}
```

 You can also apply the `virtual` keyword to properties. Properties are just methods under the covers, so this has the effect of making the accessor methods virtual. The same is true for events, which are discussed in Chapter 9.

There's nothing unusual about the syntax for invoking a virtual method. As Example 6-23 shows, it looks just like calling any other method.

Example 6-23. Using a virtual method

```
public static void CallVirtualMethod(BaseWithVirtual o)
{
    o.ShowMessage();
}
```

The difference between virtual and nonvirtual method invocations is that a virtual method call decides at runtime which method to invoke. The code in Example 6-23 will, in effect, inspect the object passed in, and if the object's type supplies its own implementation of `ShowMessage`, it will call that instead of the one defined in

`BaseWithVirtual`. The method is chosen based on the actual type the target object turns out to have at runtime, and not the static type (determined at compile time) of the expression that refers to the target object.

 Since virtual method invocation selects the method based on the type of the object on which you invoke the method, static methods cannot be virtual.

Derived types are not obliged to replace virtual methods. Example 6-24 shows two classes that derive from the one in Example 6-22. The first leaves the base class's implementation of `ShowMessage` in place. The second overrides it. Note the `override` keyword—C# requires us to state explicitly that we are intending to override a virtual method.

Example 6-24. Overriding virtual methods

```
public class DeriveWithoutOverride : BaseWithVirtual
{
}

public class DeriveAndOverride : BaseWithVirtual
{
    public override void ShowMessage()
    {
        Console.WriteLine("This is an override");
    }
}
```

We can use these types with the method in Example 6-23. Example 6-25 calls it three times, passing in a different type of object each time.

Example 6-25. Exploiting virtual methods

```
CallVirtualMethod(new BaseWithVirtual());
CallVirtualMethod(new DeriveWithoutOverride());
CallVirtualMethod(new DeriveAndOverride());
```

This produces the following output:

```
Hello from BaseWithVirtual
Hello from BaseWithVirtual
This is an override
```

Obviously, when we pass an instance of the base class, we get the output from the base class's `ShowMessage` method. We also get that with the derived class that has not supplied an override. It is only the final class, which overrides the method, that produces different output. This shows that virtual methods provide a way to write polymorphic code: Example 6-23 can use a variety of types. You might be wondering why we need this, given that interfaces also enable polymorphic code. Prior to C# 8.0, one major advantage of virtual methods over interfaces was that the base class could provide an implementation that derived classes would acquire by default, supplying their own implementation only if they really needed something different. The addition of default interface implementations to the language means that interfaces can now do the same thing, although a default interface member implementation cannot define or access nonstatic fields, so it is somewhat limited compared to a class that defines a virtual function. (And since default interface implementations require runtime support, they are unavailable to code that needs to target runtimes older than .NET Core 3.0, which includes any library targeting .NET Standard 2.0 or older.) However, there is a more subtle advantage available to virtual methods, but before we can look at it, we need to explore a feature of virtual methods which at first glance even more closely resembles the way interfaces work.

Abstract Methods

You can define a virtual method without providing a default implementation. C# calls this an *abstract method*. If a class contains one or more abstract methods, the class is incomplete, because it doesn't provide all of the methods it defines. Classes of this kind are also described as being abstract, and it is not possible to construct instances of an abstract class; attempting to use the new operator with an abstract class will cause a compiler error. Sometimes when discussing classes, it's useful to make clear that some particular class is *not* abstract, for which we normally use the term *concrete class*.

If you derive from an abstract class, then unless you provide implementations for all the abstract methods, your derived class will also be abstract. You must state your intention to write an abstract class with the abstract keyword; if this is absent from a class that has unimplemented abstract methods (either ones it has defined itself, or ones it has inherited from its base class), the C# compiler will report an error. Example 6-26 shows an abstract class that defines a single abstract method. Abstract methods are virtual by definition; there wouldn't be much use in defining a method that has no body, if there were no way for derived classes to supply a body.

Example 6-26. An abstract class

```
public abstract class AbstractBase
{
    public abstract void ShowMessage();
}
```

Abstract method declarations just define the signature, and do not contain a body. Unlike with interfaces, each abstract member has its own accessibility—you can declare abstract methods as public, internal, protected internal, protected private, or protected. (It makes no sense to make an abstract or virtual method private, because the method will be inaccessible to derived types and therefore impossible to override.)

> Although classes that contain abstract methods are required to be abstract, the converse is not true. It is legal, albeit unusual, to define a class as abstract even if it would be a viable concrete class. This prevents the class from being constructed. A class that derives from this will be concrete without needing to override any abstract methods.

Abstract classes have the option to declare that they implement an interface without needing to provide a full implementation. You can't just omit the unimplemented members, though. You must explicitly declare all of its members, marking any that you want to leave unimplemented as being abstract, as Example 6-27 shows. This forces concrete derived types to supply the implementation.

Example 6-27. Abstract interface implementation

```
public abstract class MustBeComparable : IComparable<string>
{
    public abstract int CompareTo(string other);
}
```

There's clearly some overlap between abstract classes and interfaces. Both provide a way to define an abstract type that code can use without needing to know the exact type that will be supplied at runtime. Each option has its pros and cons. Interfaces have the advantage that a single type can implement multiple interfaces, whereas a class gets to specify only a single base class. But abstract classes can define fields, and can use these in any default member implementations they supply, and they also provide a way to supply default implementations that will work on runtimes older than .NET Core 3.0. However, there's a more subtle advantage available to virtual methods that comes into play when you release multiple versions of a library over time.

Inheritance and Library Versioning

Imagine what would happen if you had written and released a library that defined some public interfaces and abstract classes, and in the second release of the library, you decided that you wanted to add some new members to one of the interfaces. It's conceivable that this might not cause a problem for customers using your code.

Certainly, any place where they use a reference of that interface type will be unaffected by the addition of new features. However, what if some of your customers have written types that implement your interface? Suppose, for example, that in a future version of .NET, Microsoft decided to add a new member to the IEnumerable<T> interface.

Prior to C# 8.0, that would have been a disaster. This interface is widely used, but also widely implemented. Classes that already implement IEnumerable<T> would become invalid because they would not provide this new member, so old code would fail to compile, and code already compiled would throw MissingMethodException errors at runtime. The introduction in C# 8.0 of support for default member implementations in interfaces mitigates this: in the unlikely event that Microsoft did add a new member to IEnumerable<T>, it could supply a default implementation preventing these errors. However, there's a more subtle problem. Some classes might by chance already have had a member with the same name and signature as the newly added method. If that code is recompiled against the new interface definition, the compiler would treat that existing member as part of the implementation of the interface, even though the developer who wrote the method did not write it with that intention. So unless the existing code coincidentally happens to do exactly what the new member requires, we'd have a problem, and we wouldn't get compiler errors or warnings to alert us.

Consequently, the widely accepted rule is that you do not alter interfaces once they have been published. If you have complete control over all of the code that uses and implements an interface, you can get away with modifying the interface, because you can make any necessary modifications to the affected code. But once the interface has become available for use in codebases you do not control—that is, once it has been published—it's no longer possible to change it without risking breaking someone else's code. Default interface implementations mitigate this risk, but they cannot eliminate the problem of existing methods accidentally being misinterpreted when they get recompiled against the updated interface.

Abstract base classes do not have to suffer from this problem. Obviously, introducing new abstract members would cause exactly the same MissingMethodException failures, but introducing new virtual methods does not. (And since virtual methods have been in C# since v1, this enables you to target runtimes older than .NET Core 3.0, where default interface implementation support is unavailable.)

But what if, after releasing version 1.0 of a component, you add a new virtual method in v1.1 that turns out to have the same name and signature as a method that one of your customers happens to have added in a derived class? Perhaps in version 1.0, your component defines the rather uninteresting base class shown in Example 6-28.

Example 6-28. Base type version 1.0

```
public class LibraryBase
{
}
```

If you release this library, perhaps as a product in its own right, or maybe as part of some software development kit (SDK) for your application, a customer might write a derived type such as the one in Example 6-29. The Start method they have written is clearly not meant to override anything in the base class.

Example 6-29. Class derived from version 1.0 base

```
public class CustomerDerived : LibraryBase
{
    public void Start()
    {
        Console.WriteLine("Derived type's Start method");
    }
}
```

Since you won't necessarily get to see every line of code that your customers write, you might be unaware of this Start method. So in version 1.1 of your component, you might decide to add a new virtual method, also called Start, as Example 6-30 shows.

Example 6-30. Base type version 1.1

```
public class LibraryBase
{
    public virtual void Start() { }
}
```

Imagine that your system calls this method as part of an initialization procedure introduced in v1.1. You've defined a default empty implementation so that types derived from LibraryBase that don't need to take part in that procedure don't have to do anything. Types that wish to participate will override this method. But what happens with the class in Example 6-29? Clearly the developer who wrote that did not intend to participate in your new initialization mechanism, because that didn't exist when the code was written. It could be bad if your code calls the CustomerDerived class's Start method, because the developer presumably expects it to be called only when their code decides to call it. Fortunately, the compiler will detect this problem. If the customer attempts to compile Example 6-29 against version 1.1 of your library (Example 6-30), the compiler will warn them that something is not right:

```
warning CS0114: 'CustomerDerived.Start()' hides inherited member
'LibraryBase.Start()'. To make the current member override that implementation,
add the override keyword. Otherwise add the new keyword.
```

This is why the C# compiler requires the override keyword when we replace virtual methods. It wants to know whether we were intending to override an existing method, so that if we weren't, it can warn us about collisions. (The absence of any equivalent keyword signifying the intention to implement an interface member is why the compiler cannot detect the same problem with default interface implementation. And the reason for this absence is that default interface implementation didn't exist prior to C# 8.0.)

We get a *warning* rather than an *error*, because the compiler provides a behavior that is likely to be safe when this situation has arisen due to the release of a new version of a library. The compiler guesses—correctly, in this case—that the developer who wrote the CustomerDerived type didn't mean to override the LibraryBase class's Start method. So rather than having the CustomerDerived type's Start method override the base class's virtual method, it *hides* it. A derived type is said to hide a member of a base class when it introduces a new member with the same name.

Hiding methods is quite different than overriding them. When hiding occurs, the base method is not replaced. Example 6-31 shows how the hidden Start method remains available. It creates a CustomerDerived object and places a reference to that object in two variables of different types: one of type CustomerDerived, and one of type LibraryBase. It then calls Start through each of these.

Example 6-31. Hidden versus virtual method

```
var d = new CustomerDerived();
LibraryBase b = d;

d.Start();
b.Start();
```

When we use the d variable, the call to Start ends up calling the derived type's Start method, the one that has hidden the base member. But the b variable's type is LibraryBase, so that invokes the base Start method. If CustomerDerived had overridden the base class's Start method instead of hiding it, both of those method calls would have invoked the override.

When name collisions occur because of a new library version, this hiding behavior is usually the right thing to do. If the customer's code has a variable of type CustomerDerived, then that code will want to invoke the Start method specific to that derived type. However, the compiler produces a warning, because it doesn't know for certain that this is the reason for the problem. It might be that you *did* mean to override the method, and you just forgot to write the override keyword.

Like many developers, I don't like to see compiler warnings, and I try to avoid committing code that produces them. But what should you do if a new library version puts you in this situation? The best long-term solution is probably to change the name of the method in your derived class so that it doesn't clash with the method in the new version of the library. However, if you're up against a deadline, you may want a more expedient solution. So C# lets you declare that you know that there's a name clash, and that you definitely want to hide the base member, not override it. As Example 6-32 shows, you can use the new keyword to state that you're aware of the issue, and definitely want to hide the base class member. The code will still behave in the same way, but you'll no longer get the warning, because you've assured the compiler that you know what's going on. But this is an issue you should fix at some point, because sooner or later the existence of two methods with the same name on the same type that mean different things is likely to cause confusion.

Example 6-32. Avoiding warnings when hiding members

```
public class CustomerDerived : LibraryBase
{
    public new void Start()
    {
        Console.WriteLine("Derived type's Start method");
    }
}
```

 C# does not let you use the new keyword to deal with the equivalent problem that arises with default interface implementations. There is no way to retain the default implementation supplied by an interface and also declare a public method with the same signature. This is slightly frustrating because it's possible at the binary level: it's the behavior you get if you do not recompile the code that implements an interface after adding a new member with a default implementation. You can still have separate implementations of, say, ILibrary.Start and CustomerDerived.Start, but you have to use explicit interface implementation.

Just occasionally, you may see the new keyword used in this way for reasons other than handling library versioning issues. For example, the ISet<T> interface that I showed in Chapter 5 uses it to introduce a new Add method. ISet<T> derives from ICollection<T>, an interface that already provides an Add method, which takes an instance of T and has a void return type. ISet<T> makes a subtle change to this, shown in Example 6-33.

Example 6-33. Hiding to change the signature

```
public interface ISet<T> : ICollection<T>
{
    new bool Add(T item);
    // ... other members omitted for clarity
}
```

The ISet<T> interface's Add method tells you whether the item you just added was already in the set, something the base ICollection<T> interface's Add method doesn't support. ISet<T> needs its Add to have a different return type—bool instead of void —so it defines Add with the new keyword to indicate that it should hide the ICollec tion<T> one. Both methods are still available—if you have two variables, one of type ICollection<T> and the other of type ISet<T>, both referring to the same object, you'll be able to access the void Add through the former, and the bool Add through the latter.

Microsoft didn't have to do this. It could have called the new Add method something else—AddIfNotPresent, for example. But it's arguably less confusing just to have the one method name for adding things to a collection, particularly since you're free to ignore the return value, at which point the new Add looks indistinguishable from the old one. And most ISet<T> implementations will implement the ICollec tion<T>.Add method by calling straight through to the ISet<T>.Add method, so it makes sense that they have the same name.

Aside from the preceding example, so far I've discussed method hiding only in the context of compiling old code against a new version of a library. What happens if you have old code *compiled* against an old library but that ends up *running* against a new version? That's a scenario you are highly likely to run into when the library in question is the .NET class library. Suppose you are using third-party components that you have only in binary form (e.g., ones you've bought from a company that does not supply source code). The supplier will have built these to use some particular version of .NET. If you upgrade your application to run with a new version of .NET, you might not be able to get hold of newer versions of the third-party components— maybe the vendor hasn't released them yet, or perhaps it has gone out of business.

If the components you're using were compiled for, say, .NET Standard 1.2, and you use them in a project built for .NET Core 3.0, all of those older components will end up using the .NET Core 3.0 versions of the framework class library. .NET has a versioning policy that arranges for all the components that a particular program uses to get the same version of the framework class library, regardless of which version any individual component may have been built for. So it's entirely possible that some component, *OldControls.dll*, contains classes that derive from classes in .NET Standard 1.2, and that define members that collide with the names of members newly added in .NET Core 3.0.

This is more or less the same scenario as I described earlier, except that the code that was written for an older version of a library is not going to be recompiled. We're not going to get a compiler warning about hiding a method, because that would involve running the compiler, and we have only the binary for the relevant component. What happens now?

Fortunately, we don't need the old component to be recompiled. The C# compiler sets various flags in the compiled output for each method it compiles, indicating things like whether the method is virtual or not, and whether the method was intended to override some method in the base class. When you put the new keyword on a method, the compiler sets a flag indicating that the method is not meant to override anything. The CLR calls this the *newslot* flag. When C# compiles a method such as the one in Example 6-29, which does not specify either override or new, it also sets this same *newslot* flag for that method, because at the time the method was compiled, there was no method of the same name on the base class. As far as both the developer and the compiler were concerned, the CustomerDerived class's Start was written as a brand-new method that was not connected to anything on the base class.

So when this old component gets loaded in conjunction with a new version of the library defining the base class, the CLR can see what was intended—it can see that, as far as the author of the CustomerDerived class was concerned, Start is not meant to override anything. It therefore treats CustomerDerived.Start as a distinct method from LibraryBase.Start—it hides the base method just like it did when we were able to recompile.

By the way, everything I've said about virtual methods can also apply to properties, because a property's accessors are just methods. So you can define virtual properties, and derived classes can override or hide these in exactly the same way as with methods. I won't be getting to events until Chapter 9, but those are also methods in disguise, so they can also be virtual.

Just occasionally, you may want to write a class that overrides a virtual method, and then prevents derived classes from overriding it again. For this, C# defines the sealed keyword, and in fact, it's not just methods that can be sealed.

Sealed Methods and Classes

Virtual methods are deliberately open to modification through inheritance. A sealed method is the opposite—it is one that cannot be overridden. Methods are sealed by default in C#: methods cannot be overridden unless declared virtual. But when you override a virtual method, you can seal it, closing it off for further modification. Example 6-34 uses this technique to provide a custom ToString implementation that cannot be further overridden by derived classes.

Example 6-34. A sealed method

```
public class FixedToString
{
    public sealed override string ToString()
    {
        return "Arf arf!";
    }
}
```

You can also seal an entire class, preventing anyone from deriving from it. Example 6-35 shows a class that not only does nothing, but also prevents anyone from extending it to do something useful. (You'd normally seal only a class that does something. This example is just to illustrate where the keyword goes.)

Example 6-35. A sealed class

```
public sealed class EndOfTheLine
{
}
```

Some types are inherently sealed. Value types, for example, do not support inheritance, so structs and enums are effectively sealed. The built-in string class is also sealed.

There are two normal reasons for sealing either classes or methods. One is that you want to guarantee some particular invariant, and if you leave your type open to modification, you will not be able to guarantee that invariant. For example, instances of the string type are immutable. The string type itself does not provide a way to modify an instance's value, and because nobody can derive from string, you can guarantee that if you have a reference of type string, you have a reference to an immutable object. This makes it safe for you to use in scenarios where you do not want the value to change—for example, when you use an object as a key to a dictionary (or anything else that relies on a hash code), you need the value not to change, because if the hash code changes while the item is in use as a key, the container will malfunction.

The other usual reason for leaving things sealed is that designing types that can successfully be modified through inheritance is hard, particularly if your type will be used outside of your own organization. Simply opening things up for modification is not sufficient—if you decide to make all your methods virtual, it might make it easy for people using your type to modify its behavior, but you will have made a rod for your back when it comes to maintaining the base class. Unless you control all of the code that derives from your class, it will be almost impossible to change anything in the base, because you will never know which methods may have been overridden in derived classes, making it hard to ensure that your class's internal state is consistent at all times. Developers writing derived types will doubtless do their best not to break things, but they will inevitably rely on aspects of your class's behavior that are undocumented. So in opening up every aspect of your class for modification through inheritance, you rob yourself of the freedom to change your class.

You should be very selective about which methods, if any, you make virtual. And you should also document whether callers are allowed to replace the method completely, or whether they are required to call the base implementation as part of their override. Speaking of which, how do you do that?

Accessing Base Members

Everything that is in scope in a base class and is not private will also be in scope and accessible in a derived type. If you want to access some member of the base class, you typically just access it as if it were a normal member of your class. You can either access members through the this reference, or just refer to them by name without qualification.

However, there are some situations in which you need to state that you are explicitly referring to a base class member. In particular, if you have overridden a method, calling that method by name will invoke your override recursively. If you want to call back to the original method that you overrode, there's a special keyword for that, shown in Example 6-36.

Example 6-36. Calling the base method after overriding

```
public class CustomerDerived : LibraryBase
{
    public override void Start()
    {
        Console.WriteLine("Derived type's Start method");
        base.Start();
    }
}
```

By using the base keyword, we are opting out of the normal virtual method dispatch mechanism. If we had written just Start(), that would have been a recursive call, which would be undesirable here. By writing base.Start(), we get the method that would have been available on an instance of the base class, the method we overrode.

In this example, I have called the base class's implementation after completing my work. C# doesn not care when you call the base—you could call it as the first thing the method does, as the last, or halfway through the method. You could even call it several times, or not at all. It is up to the author of the base class to document whether and when the base class implementation of the method should be called by an override.

You can use the base keyword for other members too, such as properties and events. However, access to base constructors works a bit differently.

Inheritance and Construction

Although a derived class inherits all the members of its base class, this does not mean the same thing for constructors as it does for everything else. With other members, if they are public in the base class, they will be public members of the derived class too, accessible to anyone who uses your derived class. But constructors are special, because someone using your class cannot construct it by using one of the constructors defined by the base class.

It's obvious enough why that should be: if you want an instance of some type D, then you'll want it to be a fully fledged D with everything in it properly initialized. Suppose that D derives from B. If you were able to use one of B's constructors directly, it wouldn't do anything to the parts specific to D. A base class's constructor won't know about any of the fields defined by a derived class, so it cannot initialize them. If you want a D, you'll need a constructor that knows how to initialize a D. So with a derived class, you can use only the constructors offered by that derived class, regardless of what constructors the base class might provide.

In the examples I've shown so far in this chapter, I've been able to ignore this because of the default constructor that C# provides. As you saw in Chapter 3, if you don't write a constructor, C# writes one for you that takes no arguments. It does this for derived classes too, and the generated constructor will invoke the no-arguments constructor of the base class. But this changes if I start writing my own constructors. Example 6-37 defines a pair of classes, where the base defines an explicit no-arguments constructor, and the derived class defines one that requires an argument.

Example 6-37. No default constructor in derived class

```
public class BaseWithZeroArgCtor
{
    public BaseWithZeroArgCtor()
    {
        Console.WriteLine("Base constructor");
    }
}

public class DerivedNoDefaultCtor : BaseWithZeroArgCtor
{
    public DerivedNoDefaultCtor(int i)
    {
```

```
        Console.WriteLine("Derived constructor");
    }
}
```

Because the base class has a zero-argument constructor, I can construct it with `new BaseWithZeroArgCtor()`. But I cannot do this with the derived type: I can construct that only by passing an argument—for example, `new DerivedNoDefaultCtor(123)`. So as far as the publicly visible API of `DerivedNoDefaultCtor` is concerned, the derived class appears not to have inherited its base class's constructor.

However, it has in fact inherited it, as you can see by looking at the output you get if you construct an instance of the derived type:

```
Base constructor
Derived constructor
```

When constructing an instance of `DerivedNoDefaultCtor`, the base class's constructor runs immediately before the derived class's constructor. Since the base constructor ran, clearly it was present. All of the base class's constructors are available to a derived type, but they can be invoked only by constructors in the derived class. Example 6-37 invoked the base constructor implicitly: all constructors are required to invoke a constructor on their base class, and if you don't specify which to invoke, the compiler invokes the base's zero-argument constructor for you.

What if the base doesn't define a parameterless constructor? In that case, you'll get a compiler error if you derive a class that does not specify which constructor to call. Example 6-38 shows a base class without a zero-argument constructor. (The presence of explicit constructors disables the compiler's normal generation of a default constructor, and since this base class supplies only a constructor that takes arguments, this means there is no zero-argument constructor.) It also shows a derived class with two constructors, both of which call into the base constructor explicitly, using the base keyword.

Example 6-38. Invoking a base constructor explicitly

```
public class BaseNoDefaultCtor
{
    public BaseNoDefaultCtor(int i)
    {
        Console.WriteLine("Base constructor: " + i);
    }
}

public class DerivedCallingBaseCtor : BaseNoDefaultCtor
{
    public DerivedCallingBaseCtor()
        : base(123)
    {
```

```
        Console.WriteLine("Derived constructor (default)");
    }

    public DerivedCallingBaseCtor(int i)
        : base(i)
    {
        Console.WriteLine("Derived constructor: " + i);
    }
}
```

The derived class here decides to supply a parameterless constructor even though the base class doesn't have one—it supplies a constant value for the argument the base requires. The second just passes its argument through to the base.

 Here's a frequently asked question: *how do I provide all the same constructors as my base class, just passing the arguments straight through?* The answer is: *write all the constructors by hand.* There is no way to get C# to generate a set of constructors in a derived class that look identical to the ones that the base class offers. You need to do it the long-winded way.

At least Visual Studio can generate the code for you—if you click on a class declaration, and then click the Quick Actions icon that appears, it will offer to generate constructors with the same arguments as any nonprivate constructor in the base class, automatically passing all the arguments through for you.

As Chapter 3 showed, a class's field initializers run before its constructor. The picture is more complicated once inheritance is involved, because there are multiple classes and multiple constructors. The easiest way to predict what will happen is to understand that although instance field initializers and constructors have separate syntax, C# ends up compiling all the initialization code for a particular class into the constructor. This code performs the following steps: first, it runs field initializers specific to this class (so this step does not include base field initializers—the base class will take care of itself); next, it calls the base class constructor; and finally, it runs the body of the constructor. The upshot of this is that in a derived class, your instance field initializers will run before base class construction has occurred—not just before the base constructor body, but even before the base's instance fields have been initialized. Example 6-39 illustrates this.

Example 6-39. Exploring construction order

```
public class BaseInit
{
    protected static int Init(string message)
    {
```

```
        Console.WriteLine(message);
        return 1;
    }

    private int b1 = Init("Base field b1");

    public BaseInit()
    {
        Init("Base constructor");
    }

    private int b2 = Init("Base field b2");
}

public class DerivedInit : BaseInit
{
    private int d1 = Init("Derived field d1");

    public DerivedInit()
    {
        Init("Derived constructor");
    }

    private int d2 = Init("Derived field d2");
}
```

I've put the field initializers on either side of the constructor just to show that their position relative to nonfield members is irrelevant. The order of the fields matters, but only with respect to one another. Constructing an instance of the DerivedInit class produces this output:

```
Derived field d1
Derived field d2
Base field b1
Base field b2
Base constructor
Derived constructor
```

This verifies that the derived type's field initializers run first, and then the base field initializers, followed by the base constructor, and then finally the derived constructor. In other words, although constructor bodies start with the base class, instance field initialization happens in reverse.

That's why you don't get to invoke instance methods in field initializers. Static methods are available, but instance methods are not, because the class is a long way from being ready. It could be problematic if one of the derived type's field initializers were able to invoke a method on the base class, because the base class has performed no initialization at all at that point—not only has its constructor body not run, but its field initializers haven't run either. If instance methods were available during this phase, we'd have to write all of our code to be very defensive, because we could not assume that our fields contain anything useful.

As you can see, the constructor bodies run relatively late in the process, which is why we are allowed to invoke methods from them. But there's still potential danger here. What if the base class defines a virtual method and invokes that method on itself in its constructor? If the derived type overrides that, we'll be invoking the method before the derived type's constructor body has run. (Its field initializers will have run at that point, though. In fact, this is the main reason field initializers run in what seems to be reverse order—it means that derived classes have a way of performing some initialization before the base class's constructor has a chance to invoke a virtual method.) If you're familiar with C++, you might hazard a guess that when the base constructor invokes a virtual method, it'll run the base implementation. But C# does it differently: a base class's constructor will invoke the derived class's override in that case. This is not necessarily a problem, and it can occasionally be useful, but it means you need to think carefully and document your assumptions clearly if you want your object to invoke virtual methods on itself during construction.

Special Base Types

The .NET class library defines a few base types that have special significance in C#. The most obvious is `System.Object`, which I've already described in some detail.

There's also `System.ValueType`. This is the abstract base type of all value types, so any `struct` you define—and also all of the built-in value types, such as `int` and `bool`—derive from `ValueType`. Ironically, `ValueType` itself is a reference type; only types that derive from `ValueType` are value types. Like most types, `ValueType` derives from `System.Object`. There is an obvious conceptual difficulty here: in general, derived classes are everything their base class is, plus whatever functionality they add. So, given that `object` and `ValueType` are both reference types, it may seem odd that types derived from `ValueType` are not. And for that matter, it's not obvious how an `object` variable can hold a reference to an instance of something that's not a reference type. I will resolve all of these issues in Chapter 7.

C# does not permit you to derive explicitly from `ValueType`. If you want to write a type that derives from `ValueType`, that's what the `struct` keyword is for. You can declare a variable of type `ValueType`, but since the type doesn't define any public members, a `ValueType` reference doesn't enable anything you can't do with an `object` reference. The only observable difference is that with a variable of that type, you can assign instances of any value type into it but not instances of a reference type. Aside from that, it's identical to `object`. Consequently, it's fairly rare to see `ValueType` mentioned explicitly in C# code.

Enumeration types also all derive from a common abstract base type: System.Enum. Since enums are value types, you won't be surprised to find out that Enum derives from ValueType. As with ValueType, you would never derive from Enum explicitly—you use the enum keyword for that. Unlike ValueType, Enum does add some useful members. For example, its static GetValues method returns an array of all the enumeration's values, while GetNames returns an array with all those values converted to strings. It also offers Parse, which converts from the string representation back to the enumeration value.

As Chapter 5 described, arrays all derive from a common base class, System.Array, and you've already seen the features that offers.

The System.Exception base class is special: when you throw an exception, C# requires that the object you throw be of this type or a type that derives from it. (Exceptions are the topic of Chapter 8.)

Delegate types all derive from a common base type, System.MulticastDelegate, which in turn derives from System.Delegate. I'll discuss these in Chapter 9.

Those are all the base types that the CTS treats as being special. There's one more base type to which the C# compiler assigns special significance, and that's Sys tem.Attribute. In Chapter 1, I applied certain annotations to methods and classes to tell the unit test framework to treat them specially. These attributes all correspond to types, so when I applied the [TestClass] attribute to a class, I was using a type called TestClassAttribute. Types designed to be used as attributes are all required to derive from System.Attribute. Some of them are recognized by the compiler—for example, there are some that control the version numbers that the compiler puts into the file headers of the EXE and DLL files it produces. I'll show all of this in Chapter 14.

Summary

C# supports single implementation inheritance, and only with classes—you cannot derive from a struct at all. However, interfaces can declare multiple bases, and a class can implement multiple interfaces. Implicit reference conversions exist from derived types to base types, and generic interfaces and delegates can choose to offer additional implicit reference conversions using either covariance or contravariance. All types derive from System.Object, guaranteeing that certain standard members are available on all variables. We saw how virtual methods allow derived classes to modify selected members of their bases, and how sealing can disable that. We also looked at the relationship between a derived type and its base when it comes to accessing members, and constructors in particular.

Our exploration of inheritance is complete, but it has raised some new issues, such as the relationship between value types and references, and the role of finalizers. So, in the next chapter, I'll talk about the connection between references and an object's life cycle, along with the way the CLR bridges the gap between references and value types.

CHAPTER 7

Object Lifetime

One benefit of .NET's managed execution model is that the runtime can automate most of your application's memory management. I have shown numerous examples that create objects with the new keyword, and none has explicitly freed the memory consumed by these objects.

In most cases, you do not need to take any action to reclaim memory. The runtime provides a *garbage collector* (GC),[1] a mechanism that automatically discovers when objects are no longer in use, and recovers the memory they had been occupying so that it can be used for new objects. However, there are certain usage patterns that can cause performance issues or even defeat the GC entirely, so it's useful to understand how it works. This is particularly important with long-running processes that could run for days (short-lived processes may be able to tolerate a few memory leaks).

The GC is designed to manage memory efficiently, but memory is not the only limited resource you may need to deal with. Some things have a small memory footprint in the CLR but represent something relatively expensive, such as a database connection or a handle from an OS API. The GC doesn't always deal with these effectively, so I'll explain IDisposable, the interface designed for dealing with things that need to be freed more urgently than memory.

Value types often have completely different rules governing their lifetime—some local variable values live only for as long as their containing method runs, for example. Nonetheless, value types sometimes end up acting like reference types, and being managed by the GC. I will discuss why that can be useful, and I will explain the *boxing* mechanism that makes it possible.

---

1 The acronym GC is used throughout this chapter to refer to both the *garbage collector* mechanism and also *garbage collection*, which is what the garbage collector does.

Garbage Collection

The CLR maintains a *heap*, a service that provides memory for the objects and values whose lifetime is managed by the GC. Each time you construct an instance of a class with new, or you create a new array object, the CLR allocates a new heap block. The GC decides when to deallocate that block.

A heap block contains all the nonstatic fields for an object, or all the elements if it's an array. The CLR also adds a header, which is not directly visible to your program. This includes a pointer to a structure describing the object's type. This supports operations that depend on the real type of an object. For example, if you call GetType on a reference, the runtime uses this pointer to find out the type. (The type is often not completely determined by the static type of the reference, which could be an interface type or a base class of the actual type.) It's also used to work out which method to use when you invoke a virtual method or an interface member. The CLR also uses this to know how large the heap block is—the header does not include the block size, because the runtime can work that out from the object's type. (Most types are fixed size. There are only two exceptions, strings and arrays, which the CLR handles as special cases.) The header contains one other field, which is used for a variety of diverse purposes, including multithreaded synchronization and default hash code generation. Heap block headers are just an implementation detail, and other CLI implementations could choose different strategies. However, it's useful to know what the overhead is. On a 32-bit system, the header is 8 bytes long, and if you're running in a 64-bit process, it takes 16 bytes. So an object that contained just one field of type double (an 8-byte type) would consume 16 bytes in a 32-bit process, and 24 bytes in a 64-bit process.

Although objects (i.e., instances of a class) always live on the heap, instances of value types are different: some live on the heap, and some don't.[2] The CLR stores some value-typed local variables on the stack, for example, but if the value is in an instance field of a class, the class instance will live on the heap, and that value will therefore live inside that object on the heap. And in some cases, a value will have an entire heap block to itself.

If you're using something through a reference type variable, then you are accessing something on the heap. It's important to clarify exactly what I mean by a reference type variable, because unfortunately, the terminology is a little confusing here: C# uses the term *reference* to describe two quite different things. For the purposes of this discussion, a reference is something you can store in a variable of a type that derives from object, but not from ValueType. This does not include every in-, out-, or ref-

---

2 Value types defined with ref struct are an exception: they always live on the stack. Chapter 18 discusses these.

style method argument, nor `ref` variables or returns. Although those are references of a kind, a `ref int` argument is a reference to a value type, and that's not the same thing as a reference type. (The CLR actually uses a different term for the mechanism that supports `ref`, `in`, and `out`: it calls these *managed pointers*, making it clear that they are rather different from object references.)

The managed execution model used by C# (and all .NET languages) means the CLR knows about every heap block your code creates, and also about every field, variable, and array element in which your program stores references. This information enables the runtime to determine at any time which objects are *reachable*—that is, those that the program could conceivably get access to in order to use its fields and other members. If an object is not reachable, then by definition the program will never be able to use it again. To illustrate how the CLR determines reachability, I've written a simple method that fetches web pages from my employer's website, shown in Example 7-1.

Example 7-1. Using and discarding objects

```
public static string WriteUrl(string relativeUri)
{
    var baseUri = new Uri("https://endjin.com/");
    var fullUri = new Uri(baseUri, relativeUri);
    var w = new WebClient();
    return w.DownloadString(fullUri);
}
```

Normally, you would not use the `WebClient` type shown in Example 7-1. In most cases, you would use the newer `HttpClient` instead. I'm avoiding `HttpClient` here because it only offers asynchronous methods, which complicates variables' lifetimes.

The CLR analyzes the way in which we use local variables and method arguments. For example, although the `relativeUri` argument is in scope for the whole method, we use it just once as an argument when constructing the second `Uri`, and then never use it again. A variable is described as *live* from the first point where it receives a value up until the last point at which it is used. Method arguments are live from the start of the method until their final usage, unless they are unused, in which case they are never live. Local variables become live later; `baseUri` becomes live once it has been assigned its initial value, and then ceases to be live with its final usage, which in this example, happens at the same point as `relativeUri`. Liveness is an important property in determining whether a particular object is still in use.

To see the role that liveness plays, suppose that when Example 7-1 reaches the line that constructs the `WebClient`, the CLR doesn't have enough free memory to hold the new object. It could request more memory from the OS at this point, but it also has the option to try to free up memory from objects that are no longer in use, meaning that our program wouldn't need to consume more memory than it's already using.[3] The next section describes the process that the CLR uses when it takes that second option.

Determining Reachability

The CLR starts by determining all of the *root references* in your program. A *root* is a storage location, such as a local variable, that could contain a reference and is known to have been initialized, and that your program could use at some point in the future without needing to go via some other object reference. Not all storage locations are considered to be roots. If an object contains an instance field of some reference type, that field is not a root, because before you can use it, you'd need to get hold of a reference to the containing object, and it's possible that the object itself is not reachable. However, a reference type static field is a root reference, because the program can read the value in that field at any time—the only situation in which that field will become inaccessible in the future is when the component that defines the type is unloaded, which in most cases will be when the program exits.

Local variables and method arguments are more interesting. Sometimes they are roots, but sometimes not. It depends on exactly which part of the method is currently executing. A local variable or argument can be a root only if the flow of execution is currently inside the region in which that variable or argument is live. So, in Example 7-1, baseUri is a root reference only after it has had its initial value assigned, and before the call to construct the second Uri, which is a rather narrow window. The fullUri variable is a root reference for slightly longer, because it becomes live after receiving its initial value, and continues to be live during the construction of the WebClient on the following line; its liveness ends only once Download String has been called.

When a variable's last use is as an argument in a method or constructor invocation, it ceases to be live when the method call begins. At that point, the method being called takes over—its own arguments are live at the start (except for arguments it does not use). However, they will typically cease to be live before the method returns. This means that in Example 7-1, the object referred to by fullUri may cease to be accessible through root references before the call to DownloadString returns.

---

3 The CLR doesn't always wait until it runs out of memory. I will discuss the details later. For now, the important point is that from time to time, it will try to free up some space.

Since the set of live variables changes as the program executes, the set of root references also evolves, so that the CLR needs to be able to form a snapshot of the relevant program state. The exact details are undocumented, but the garbage collection can suspend all threads that are running managed code when necessary to guarantee correct behavior.

Live variables and static fields are not the only kinds of roots. Temporary objects created as a result of evaluating expressions need to stay alive for as long as necessary to complete the evaluation, so there can be some root references that don't correspond directly to any named entities in your code. And there are other types of root. For example, the GCHandle class lets you create new roots explicitly, which can be useful in interop scenarios to enable some unmanaged code to get access to a particular object. There are also situations in which roots are created implicitly. Interop with COM objects can establish root references without explicit use of GCHandle—if the CLR needs to generate a COM wrapper for one of your .NET objects, that wrapper will effectively be a root reference. Calls into unmanaged code may also involve passing pointers to memory on the heap, which will mean that the relevant heap block needs to be treated as reachable for the duration of the call. The CLI specification does not dictate the full list of ways in which root references come into existence, but the broad principle is that roots will exist where necessary to ensure that objects that are still in use remain reachable.

Having built up a complete list of current root references for all threads, the GC works out which objects can be reached from these references. It looks at each reference in turn, and if non-null, the GC knows that the object it refers to is reachable. There may be duplicates—multiple roots may refer to the same object, so the GC keeps track of which objects it has already seen. For each newly discovered object, the GC adds all of the instance fields of reference type in that object to the list of references it needs to look at, again discarding duplicates. (This includes hidden fields generated by the compiler, such as those for automatic properties, which I described in Chapter 3.) This means that if an object is reachable, so are all the objects to which it holds references. The GC repeats this process until it runs out of new references to examine. Any objects that it has *not* discovered to be reachable must be unreachable, because the GC is simply doing what the program does: a program can use only objects that are accessible either directly or indirectly through its variables, temporary local storage, static fields, and other roots.

Going back to Example 7-1, what would all this mean if the CLR decides to run the GC when we construct the WebClient? The fullUri variable is still live, so the Uri it refers to is reachable, but the baseUri is no longer live. We did pass a copy of base Uri into the constructor for the second Uri, and if that had held onto a copy of the reference, then it wouldn't matter that baseUri is not live; as long as there's some way to get to an object by starting from a root reference, then the object is reachable. But as it happens, the second Uri won't do that, so the first Uri the example allocates would be deemed to be unreachable, and the CLR would be free to recover the memory it had been using.

One important upshot of how reachability is determined is that the GC is unfazed by circular references. This is one reason .NET uses GC instead of reference counting (another popular approach for automating memory management). If you have two objects that refer to each other, a reference counting scheme will consider both objects to be in use, because each is referred to at least once. But the objects may be unreachable—if there are no other references to the objects, the application will not have any way to use them. Reference counting fails to detect this, so it could cause memory leaks, but with the scheme used by the CLR's GC, the fact that they refer to each other is irrelevant—the GC will never get to either of them, so it will correctly determine that they are no longer in use.

Accidentally Defeating the Garbage Collector

Although the GC can discover ways that your program could reach an object, it has no way to prove that it necessarily will. Take the impressively idiotic piece of code in Example 7-2. Although you'd never write code this bad, it makes a common mistake. It's a problem that usually crops up in more subtle ways, but I want show it in a more obvious example first. Once I've shown how it prevents the GC from freeing objects that we're not going to be using, I'll describe a less straightforward but more realistic scenario in which this same problem often occurs.

Example 7-2. An appallingly inefficient piece of code

```
static void Main(string[] args)
{
    var numbers = new List<string>();
    long total = 0;
    for (int i = 1; i < 100_000; ++i)
    {
        numbers.Add(i.ToString());
        total += i;
    }
    Console.WriteLine("Total: {0}, average: {1}",
        total, total / numbers.Count);
}
```

This adds together the numbers from 1 to 100,000 and then displays their average. The first mistake here is that we don't even need to do the addition in a loop, because there's a simple and very well-known closed-form solution for this sort of sum: n*(n +1)/2, with n being 100,000 in this case. That mathematical gaffe notwithstanding, this code does something even more stupid: it builds up a list containing every number it adds, but all it does with that list is retrieve its Count property to calculate an average at the end. Just to make things worse, the code converts each number into a string before putting it in the list. It never actually uses those strings.

Obviously, this is a contrived example, although I wish I could say I'd never encountered anything this bafflingly pointless in real programs. Sadly, I've come across genuine examples at least this bad, although they were all better obfuscated—when you encounter this sort of thing in the wild, it normally takes half an hour or so to work out that it really is doing something as staggeringly pointless as this. However, my point here is not to lament standards of software development. The purpose of this example is to show how you can run into a limitation of the GC.

Suppose the loop in Example 7-2 has been running for a while—perhaps it's on its 90,000th iteration, and is trying to add an entry to the numbers list. Suppose that the List<string> has used up its spare capacity and the Add method will therefore need to allocate a new, larger internal array. The CLR may decide at this point to run the GC to see if it can free up some space. What will happen?

Example 7-2 creates three kinds of objects: it constructs a List<string> at the start, it creates a new string each time around the loop by calling ToString() on an int, and more subtly, the List<string> will allocate a string[] to hold references to those strings. Because we keep adding new items, it will have to allocate larger and larger arrays. (That array is an implementation detail of List<string>, so we can't see it directly.) So the question is: which of these objects can the GC discard to make space for a larger array in the call to Add?

Our numbers variable remains live until the program's final statement and we're looking at an earlier point in the code, so the List<string> object it refers to is reachable. The string[] array object it is currently using must also be reachable: it's allocating a newer, larger one, but it will need to copy the contents of the old one across to the new one, so the list must still have a reference to that current array stored in one of its fields. Since that array is still reachable, every string the array refers to will also be reachable. Our program has created 90,000 strings so far, and the GC will find all of them by starting at our numbers variable, looking at the fields of the List<string> object that refers to, and then looking at every element in the array that one of the list's private fields refers to.

The only allocated items that the GC might be able to collect are old string[] arrays that the List<string> created back when the list was smaller, and which it no longer has a reference to. By the time we've added 90,000 items, the list will probably have resized itself quite a few times. So depending on when the GC last ran, it will probably be able to find a few of these now-unused arrays. But more interesting here is what it cannot free.

The program never uses the 90,000 strings it creates, so ideally, we'd like the GC to free up the memory they occupy—they will be taking up a few megabytes. We can see very easily that these strings are not used, because this is such a short program. But the GC will not know that; it bases its decisions on reachability, and it correctly determines that all 90,000 strings are reachable by starting at the `numbers` variable. And as far as the GC is concerned, it's entirely possible that the list's `Count` property, which we use after the loop finishes, will look at the contents of the list. You and I happen to know that it won't, because it doesn't need to, but that's because we know what the `Count` property means. For the GC to infer that our program will never use any of the list's elements directly or indirectly, it would need to know what `List<string>` does inside its `Add` and `Count` methods. This would mean analysis with a level of detail far beyond the mechanisms I've described, which could make garbage collections considerably more expensive. Moreover, even with the serious step up in complexity required to detect which reachable objects this example will never use, in more realistic scenarios the GC would be unlikely to be able to make predictions that were significantly better than relying on reachability alone.

For example, a much more plausible way to run into this problem is in a cache. If you write a class that caches data that is expensive to fetch or calculate, imagine what would happen if your code only ever added items to the cache and never removed them. All of the cached data would be reachable for as long as the cache object itself is reachable. The problem is that your cache will consume more and more space, and unless your computer has sufficient memory to hold every piece of data that your program could conceivably need to use, it will eventually run out of memory.

A naive developer might complain that this is supposed to be the garbage collector's problem. The whole point of GC is meant to be that I don't need to think about memory management, so why am I running out of memory all of a sudden? But, of course, the problem is that the GC has no way of knowing which objects are safe to remove. Not being clairvoyant, it cannot accurately predict which cached items your program may need in the future—if the code is running in a server, future cache usage could depend on what requests the server receives, something the GC cannot predict. So although it's possible to imagine memory management smart enough to analyze something as simple as Example 7-2, in general, this is not a problem the GC can solve. Thus, if you add objects to collections and keep those collections reachable, the GC will treat everything in those collections as being reachable. It's your job to decide when to remove items.

Collections are not the only situation in which you can fool the GC. As I'll show in Chapter 9, there's a common scenario in which careless use of events can cause memory leaks. More generally, if your program makes it possible for an object to be reached, the GC has no way of working out whether you're going to use that object again, so it has to be conservative.

That said, there is a technique for mitigating this with a little help from the GC.

Weak References

Although the GC will follow ordinary references in a reachable object's fields, it is possible to hold a *weak reference*. The GC does not follow weak references, so if the only way to reach an object is through weak references, the GC behaves as though the object is not reachable, and will remove it. A weak reference provides a way of telling the CLR, "do not keep this object around on my account, but for as long as something else needs it, I would like to be able to get access to it." Example 7-3 shows a cache that uses WeakReference<T>.

Example 7-3. Using weak references in a cache

```
public class WeakCache<TKey, TValue> where TValue : class
{
    private readonly Dictionary<TKey, WeakReference<TValue>> _cache =
        new Dictionary<TKey, WeakReference<TValue>>();

    public void Add(TKey key, TValue value)
    {
        _cache.Add(key, new WeakReference<TValue>(value));
    }

    public bool TryGetValue(TKey key, out TValue cachedItem)
    {
        WeakReference<TValue> entry;
        if (_cache.TryGetValue(key, out entry))
        {
            bool isAlive = entry.TryGetTarget(out cachedItem);
            if (!isAlive)
            {
                _cache.Remove(key);
            }
            return isAlive;
        }
        else
        {
            cachedItem = null;
            return false;
        }
    }
}
```

This cache stores all values via a WeakReference<T>. Its Add method passes the object to which we'd like a weak reference as the constructor argument for a new WeakReference<T>. The TryGetValue method attempts to retrieve a value previously stored with Add. It first checks to see if the dictionary contains a relevant entry. If it does, that entry's value will be the WeakReference<T> we created earlier. My code calls that weak reference's TryGetTarget method, which will return true if the object is still available, and false if it has been collected.

 Availability doesn't necessarily imply reachability. The object may have become unreachable since the most recent GC. Or there may not even have been a GC since the object was allocated. TryGetTar get doesn't care whether the object is reachable right now, it cares only whether the GC has detected that it is eligible for collection.

If the object is available, TryGetTarget provides it through an out parameter, and this will be a strong reference. So, if this method returns true, we don't need to worry about any race condition in which the object becomes unreachable moments later— the fact that we've now stored that reference in the variable the caller supplied via the cachedItem argument will keep the target alive. If TryGetTarget returns false, my code removes the relevant entry from the dictionary, because it represents an object that no longer exists. That's important because although a weak reference won't keep its target alive, the WeakReference<T> is an object in its own right, and the GC can't free it until I've removed it from this dictionary. Example 7-4 tries this code out, forcing a couple of garbage collections so we can see it in action. (This splits each stage into separate methods with inlining disabled because otherwise, the JIT compiler on .NET Core will inline these methods, and it ends up creating hidden temporary variables that can cause the array to remain reachable longer than it should, distorting the results of this test.)

Example 7-4. Exercising the weak cache

```
class Program
{
    static WeakCache<string, byte[]> cache = new WeakCache<string, byte[]>();
    static byte[] data = new byte[100];

    static void Main(string[] args)
    {
        AddData();
        CheckStillAvailable();

        GC.Collect();
        CheckStillAvailable();

        SetOnlyRootToNull();
        GC.Collect();
        CheckNoLongerAvailable();
    }

    [MethodImpl(MethodImplOptions.NoInlining)]
    private static void AddData()
    {
```

```
        cache.Add("d", data);
    }

    [MethodImpl(MethodImplOptions.NoInlining)]
    private static void CheckStillAvailable()
    {
        Console.WriteLine("Retrieval: " +
            cache.TryGetValue("d", out byte[] fromCache));
        Console.WriteLine("Same ref?  " +
            object.ReferenceEquals(data, fromCache));
    }

    [MethodImpl(MethodImplOptions.NoInlining)]
    private static void SetOnlyRootToNull()
    {
        data = null;
    }

    [MethodImpl(MethodImplOptions.NoInlining)]
    private static void CheckNoLongerAvailable()
    {
        byte[] fromCache;
        Console.WriteLine("Retrieval: " + cache.TryGetValue("d", out fromCache));
        Console.WriteLine("Null?  " + (fromCache == null));
    }
}
```

This begins by creating an instance of my cache class, and then adding a reference to a 100-byte array to the cache. It also stores a reference to the same array in a static field called data, keeping it reachable until the code calls SetOnlyRootToNull, which sets its value to null. The example tries to retrieve the value from the cache immediately after adding it, and also uses object.ReferenceEquals just to check that the value we get back really refers to the same object that we put in. Then I force a garbage collection, and try again. (This sort of artificial test code is one of the few situations in which you'd want to do this—see the section "Forcing Garbage Collections" on page 327 for details.) Since the data field still holds a reference to the array, the array is still reachable, so we would expect the value still to be available from the cache. Next I set data to null, so my code is no longer keeping that array reachable. The only remaining reference is a weak one, so when I force another GC, we expect the array to be collected and the final lookup in the cache to fail. To verify this, I check both the return value, expecting false, and the value returned through the out parameter, which should be null. And that is exactly what happens when I run the program, as you can see:

```
Retrieval: True
Same ref?  True
Retrieval: True
Same ref?  True
```

```
Retrieval: False
Null?  True
```

 Writing code to illustrate GC behavior means entering treacherous territory. The principles of operation remain the same, but the exact behavior of small examples changes over time. (I've had to modify some examples since previous editions of the book.) It's entirely possible that if you try these examples, you might see different behavior due to changes in the runtime since going to press.

Later, I will describe finalization, which complicates matters by introducing a twilight zone in which the object has been determined to be unreachable, but has not yet gone. Objects that are in this state are typically of little use, so by default, a weak reference will treat objects waiting for finalization as though they have already gone. This is called a *short weak reference*. If, for some reason, you need to know whether an object has really gone (rather than merely being on its way out), the `WeakRefer ence<T>` class's constructor has overloads, some of which can create a *long weak reference*, which provides access to the object even in this zone between unreachability and final removal.

Reclaiming Memory

So far, I've described how the CLR determines which objects are no longer in use, but not what happens next. Having identified the garbage, the runtime must then collect it. The CLR uses different strategies for small and large objects. (By default, it defines a large object as one bigger than 85,000 bytes.) Most allocations involve small objects, so I'll write about those first.

The CLR tries to keep the heap's free space contiguous. Obviously, that's easy when the application first starts up, because there's nothing but free space, and it can keep things contiguous by allocating memory for each new object directly after the last one. But after the first garbage collection occurs, the heap is unlikely to look so neat. Most objects have short lifetimes, and it's common for the majority of objects allocated after any one GC to be unreachable by the time the next GC runs. However, some will still be in use. From time to time, applications create objects that hang around for longer, and, of course, whatever work was in progress when the GC ran will probably be using some objects, so the most recently allocated heap blocks are likely still to be in use. This means that the end of the heap might look something like Figure 7-1, where the grey rectangles are the reachable blocks, and the white ones show blocks that are no longer in use.

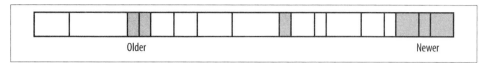

Figure 7-1. Section of heap with some reachable objects

One possible allocation strategy would be to start using these empty blocks as new memory is required, but there are a couple of problems with that approach. First, it tends to be wasteful, because the blocks the application requires will probably not fit precisely into the holes available. Second, finding a suitable empty block can be somewhat expensive, particularly if there are lots of gaps and you're trying to pick one that will minimize waste. It's not impossibly expensive, of course—lots of heaps work this way—but it's a lot costlier than the initial situation where each new block could be allocated directly after the last one because all the spare space was contiguous. The expense of heap fragmentation is nontrivial, so the CLR typically tries to get the heap back into a state where the free space is contiguous. As Figure 7-2 shows, it moves all the reachable objects toward the start of the heap, so that all the free space is at the end, which puts it back in the favorable situation of being able to allocate new heap blocks one after another in the contiguous lump of free space.

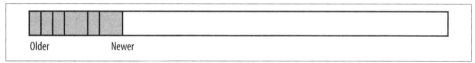

Figure 7-2. Section of heap after compaction

The runtime has to ensure that references to these relocated blocks continue to work after the blocks have moved. The CLR happens to implement references as pointers (although the CLI spec does not require this—a reference is just a value that identifies some particular instance on the heap). It already knows where all the references to any particular block are because it had to find them to discover which blocks were reachable. It adjusts all these pointers when it moves the block.

Besides making heap block allocation a relatively cheap operation, compaction offers another performance benefit. Because blocks are allocated into a contiguous area of free space, objects that were created in quick succession will typically end up right next to each other in the heap. This is significant, because the caches in modern CPUs tend to favor locality (i.e., they perform best when related pieces of data are stored close together).

The low cost of allocation and the high likelihood of good locality can sometimes mean that garbage-collected heaps offer better performance than traditional heaps that require the program to free memory explicitly. This may seem surprising, given that the GC appears to do a lot of extra work that is unnecessary in a noncollecting heap. Some of that "extra work" is illusory, however—something has to keep track of which objects are in use, and traditional heaps just push that housekeeping overhead into our code. However, relocating existing memory blocks comes at a price, so the CLR uses some tricks to minimize the amount of copying it needs to do.

The older an object is, the more expensive it will be for the CLR to compact the heap once it finally becomes unreachable. If the most recently allocated object is unreachable when the GC runs, compaction is free for that object: there are no more objects after it, so nothing needs to be moved. Compare that with the first object your program allocates—if that becomes unreachable, compaction would mean moving every reachable object on the heap. More generally, the older an object is, the more objects will be put after it, so the more data will need to be moved to compact the heap. Copying 20 MB of data to save 20 bytes does not sound like a great trade-off. So the CLR will often defer compaction for older parts of the heap.

To decide what counts as "old," the CLR divides the heap into *generations*. The boundaries between generations move around at each GC, because generations are defined in terms of how many GCs an object has survived. Any object allocated after the most recent GC is in generation 0, because it has not yet survived any collections. When the GC next runs, generation 0 objects that are still reachable will be moved as necessary to compact the heap, and will then be deemed to be in generation 1.

Objects in generation 1 are not yet considered to be old. A GC will typically occur while the code is right in the middle of doing things—after all, it runs when space on the heap is being used up, and that won't happen if the program is idle. So there's a high chance that some of the recently allocated objects represent work in progress and although they are currently reachable, they will become unreachable shortly. Generation 1 acts as a sort of holding zone while we wait to see which objects are short-lived and which are longer-lived.

As the program continues to execute, the GC will run from time to time, promoting new objects that survive into generation 1. Some of the objects in generation 1 will become unreachable. However, the GC does not necessarily compact this part of the heap immediately—it may allow a few generation 0 collections and compactions in between each generation 1 compaction, but it will happen eventually. Objects that survive this stage are moved into generation 2, which is the oldest generation.

The CLR attempts to recover memory from generation 2 much less frequently than from other generations. Research shows that in most applications, objects that survive into generation 2 are likely to remain reachable for a long time, so when one of those objects does eventually become unreachable, it's likely to be very old, as will the objects around it. This means that compacting this part of the heap to recover the memory is costly for two reasons: not only will this old object probably be followed by a large number of other objects (requiring a large volume of data to be copied), but also the memory it occupied might not have been used for a long time, meaning it's probably no longer in the CPU's cache, slowing down the copy even further. And the caching costs will continue after collection, because if the CPU has had to shift megabytes of data around in old areas of the heap, this will probably have the side effect of flushing other data out the CPU's cache. Cache sizes can be as small as 512 KB at the low-power, low-cost end of the spectrum, and can be over 30 MB in high-end, server-oriented chips, but in the midrange, anything from 2 MB to 16 MB of cache is typical, and many .NET applications' heaps will be larger than that. Most of the data the application had been using would have been in the cache right up until the generation 2 GC, but would be gone once the GC has finished. So when the GC completes and normal execution resumes, the code will run in slow motion for a while until the data the application needs is loaded back into the cache.

Generations 0 and 1 are sometimes referred to as the *ephemeral* generations, because they mostly contain objects that exist only for a short while. The contents of these parts of the heap will often be in the CPU's cache because they will have been accessed recently, so compaction is not particularly expensive for these sections. Moreover, because most objects have a short lifetime, the majority of memory that the GC is able to collect will be from objects in these first two generations, so these are likely to offer the greatest reward (in terms of memory recovered) in exchange for the CPU time expended. So it's common to see several ephemeral collections per second in a busy program, but it's also common for several minutes to elapse between successive generation 2 collections.

The CLR has another trick up its sleeve for generation 2 objects. They often don't change much, so there's a high likelihood that during the first phase of a GC—in which the runtime detects which objects are reachable—it would be repeating some work it did earlier, because it will follow exactly the same references and produce the same results for significant subsections of the heap. So the CLR will sometimes use the OS memory protection services to detect when older heap blocks are modified. This enables it to rely on summarized results from earlier GC operations instead of having to redo all of the work every time.

How does the GC decide to collect just from generation 0, rather than also collecting from 1 or even 2? Collections for all three generations are triggered by using up a certain amount of memory. So, for generation 0 allocations, once you have allocated some particular number of bytes since the last GC, a new GC will occur. The objects that survive this will move into generation 1, and the CLR keeps track of the number of bytes added to generation 1 since the last generation 1 collection; if that number exceeds a threshold, generation 1 will be collected too. Generation 2 works in the same way. The thresholds are not documented, and in fact they're not even constant; the CLR monitors your allocation patterns and modifies these thresholds to try to find a good balance for making efficient use of memory, minimizing the CPU time spent in the GC, and avoiding the excessive latency that could arise if the CLR waited a very long time between collections, leaving huge amounts of work to do when the collection finally occurs.

This explains why, as mentioned earlier, the CLR doesn't necessarily wait until it has actually run out of memory before triggering a GC. It may be more efficient to run one sooner.

You may be wondering how much of the preceding information is of practical significance. After all, the bottom line would appear to be that the CLR ensures that heap blocks are kept around for as long as they are reachable, and that some time after they become unreachable, it will eventually reclaim their memory, and it employs a strategy designed to do this efficiently. Are the details of this generational optimization scheme relevant to a developer? They are insofar as they tell us that some coding practices are likely to be more efficient than others.

The most obvious upshot of the process is that the more objects you allocate, the harder the GC will have to work. But you'd probably guess that without knowing anything about the implementation. More subtly, larger objects cause the GC to work harder—collections for each generation are triggered by the amount of memory your application uses. So bigger objects don't just increase memory pressure, they also end up consuming more CPU cycles as a result of triggering more frequent GCs.

Perhaps the most important fact to emerge from an understanding of the generational collector is that the length of an object's lifetime has an impact on how hard the GC must work. Objects that live for a very short time are handled efficiently, because the memory they use will be recovered quickly in a generation 0 or 1 collection, and the amount of data that needs to be moved to compact the heap will be small. Objects that live for an extremely long time are also OK, because they will end up in generation 2. They will not be moved about often, because collections are infrequent for that part of the heap. Furthermore, the CLR may be able to use the OS memory manager's write detection feature to manage reachability discovery for old objects more efficiently. However, although very short-lived and very long-lived objects are handled efficiently, objects that live long enough to get into generation 2 but not much longer are a problem. Microsoft occasionally describes this occurrence as a *mid-life crisis*.

If your application has a lot of objects making it into generation 2 that go on to become unreachable, the CLR will need to perform collections on generation 2 more often than it otherwise might. (In fact, generation 2 is collected only during a *full collection*, which also collects free space previously used by large objects.) These are usually significantly more expensive than other collections. Compaction requires more work with older objects, but also, more housekeeping is required when disrupting the generation 2 heap. The picture the CLR has built up about reachability within this section of the heap may need to be rebuilt, and the GC will need to disable the write detection used to enable that while it compacts the heap, which incurs a cost. There's a good chance that most of this part of the heap will not be in the CPU's cache either, so working with it can be slow.

Full garbage collections consume significantly more CPU time than collections in the ephemeral generations. In UI applications, this can cause delays long enough to be irritating for the user, particularly if parts of the heap had been paged out by the OS. In server applications, full collections may cause significant blips in the typical time taken to service a request. Such problems are not the end of the world, of course, and as I'll describe later, the CLR offers some mechanisms to mitigate these kinds of issues. Even so, minimizing the number of objects that survive to generation 2 is good for performance. You would need to consider this when designing code that caches interesting data in memory—a cache aging policy that failed to take the GC's behavior into account could easily behave inefficiently, and if you didn't know about the perils of middle-aged objects, it would be hard to work out why. Also, as I'll show later in this chapter, the midlife crisis issue is one reason you might want to avoid C# destructors where possible.

I have left out some heap operation details, by the way. For example, I've not talked about how the GC typically dedicates sections of the address space to the heap in fixed-size chunks, nor the details of how it commits and releases memory. Interesting though these mechanisms are, they have much less relevance to how you design your code than an awareness of the assumptions that a generational GC makes about typical object lifetimes.

There's one last thing to talk about on the topic of collecting memory from unreachable objects. As mentioned earlier, large objects work differently. There's a separate heap called, appropriately enough, the *Large Object Heap* (LOH), and the CLR uses this for any object larger than 85,000 bytes.[4] That's just the object itself, not the sum total of all the memory an object allocates during construction. An instance of the GreedyObject class in Example 7-5 would be tiny—it needs only enough space for a single reference, plus the heap block overhead. In a 32-bit process, that would be 4 bytes for the reference and 8 bytes of overhead, and in a 64-bit process it would be twice as large. However, the array to which it refers is 400,000 bytes long, so that would go on the LOH, while the GreedyObject itself would go on the ordinary heap.

Example 7-5. A small object with a large array

```
public class GreedyObject
{
    public int[] MyData = new int[100000];
}
```

---

4 .NET Core provides a configuration setting that lets you change this threshold.

It's technically possible to create a class whose instances are large enough to require the LOH, but it's unlikely to happen outside of generated code or highly contrived examples. In practice, most LOH heap blocks will contain arrays and possibly strings.

The biggest difference between the LOH and the ordinary heap is that the GC does not usually compact the LOH, because copying large objects is expensive. (Applications can request that the LOH be compacted at the next full GC. But applications that do not explicitly request this will never have their LOH compacted in current CLR implementations.) It works more like a traditional C heap: the CLR maintains a list of free blocks and decides which block to use based on the size requested. However, the list of free blocks is populated by the same unreachability mechanism as is used by the rest of the heap.

Garbage Collector Modes

Although the CLR will tune some aspects of the GC's behavior at runtime (e.g., by dynamically adjusting the thresholds that trigger collections for each generation), it also offers a configurable choice between various modes designed to suit different kinds of applications. These fall into two broad categories—workstation and server, and then in each of these you can either use background or nonconcurrent collections. Background collection is on by default, but the default top-level mode depends on the project type: for console applications and applications using a GUI framework such as WPF, the GC runs in workstation mode, but ASP.NET Core web applications change this to server mode, as do older ASP.NET web applications. If you don't want the defaults, the way you configure server mode depends on which form of .NET you are targeting. For .NET Core, you can control the GC mode explicitly by defining a property in your `.csproj` file, as Example 7-6 shows. This can go anywhere inside the root `Project` element.

Example 7-6. Enabling server GC in a .NET Core application project file

```
<PropertyGroup>
  <ServerGarbageCollection>true</ServerGarbageCollection>
</PropertyGroup>
```

> Project file properties are not available to applications at runtime, so this `ServerGarbageCollection` works by making the build system add a setting to the `YourApplication.runtimeconfig.json` file that it generates for your application. This contains a config `Properties` section, which can contain one or more *CLR host configuration knobs*. Enabling server GC in the project file sets the `System.GC.Server` knob to true in this configuration file. All GC settings are also controlled through configuration knobs, as are some other CLR behaviors, such as the JIT compiler mode.

For applications running on the .NET Framework, you use an application configuration file to change GC settings. These are XML files, and they are essentially the predecessor of *.runtimeconfig.json* files. (.NET Core moved to JSON to avoid needing to load an XML parser on application startup.) Web applications built for the .NET Framework (i.e., not .NET Core) usually have one called *web.config*, although since web applications written using ASP.NET will run with server GC by default, you won't need to add this particular setting to a *web.config* file. Outside of the ASP.NET web framework, the configuration file is normally called *App.config*, and many Visual Studio project templates provide this file automatically. Example 7-7 shows a configuration file that enables server GC mode for an application running on the .NET Framework. The relevant lines are in bold.

Example 7-7. Legacy server GC configuration (for .NET Framework)

```
<?xml version="1.0" ?>
<configuration>
  <startup>
      <supportedRuntime version="v4.0" sku=".NETFramework,Version=v4.8" />
  </startup>
  <runtime>
    <gcServer enabled="true" />
  </runtime>
</configuration>
```

The workstation modes are designed, predictably enough, for the workloads that client-side code typically has to deal with, in which the process is usually working on either a single task or a small number of tasks at any one time. Workstation mode offers two variations: nonconcurrent and background.

In background mode (the default) the GC minimizes the amount of time for which it suspends threads during a garbage collection. There are certain phases of the GC in which the CLR has to suspend execution to ensure consistency. For collections from the ephemeral generations, threads will be suspended for the majority of the operation. This is usually fine because these collections normally run very quickly—they take a similar amount of time as a page fault that didn't cause any disk activity. (These nonblocking page faults happen fairly often and are fast enough that a lot of developers seem to be unaware that they even occur.) Full collections are the problem, and it's these that the background mode handles differently. Not all of the work done in a collection really needs to bring everything to a halt, and background mode exploits this, enabling full (generation 2) collections to proceed on a background thread without forcing other threads to block until that collection completes. This can enable machines with multiple processor cores (most machines, these days) to perform full GC collections on one core while other cores continue with productive work. It is especially useful in applications with a UI, because it reduces the likelihood of an application becoming unresponsive due to GCs.

The nonconcurrent mode is designed to optimize throughput on a single processor with a single core. It can be more efficient, because background GC uses slightly more memory and more CPU cycles for any particular workload than nonconcurrent GC in exchange for the lower latency. For some workloads, you may find your code runs faster if you disable it by setting the `ConcurrentGarbageCollection` property to `false` in your project file (or, if you're running on .NET Framework, add `<gcConcurrent enabled="false" />` inside the `<runtime>` element of your configuration file). For most client-side code, the greatest concern is to avoid delays that are long enough to be visible to users. Users are more sensitive to unresponsiveness than they are to suboptimal average CPU utilization, so for interactive applications, using a bit more memory and CPU cycles in exchange for improved perceived performance is usually a good trade-off.

Server mode is significantly different than workstation mode. It is available only when you have multiple hardware threads; e.g., a multicore CPU or multiple physical CPUs. (If you have enabled server GC but your code ends up running on a single-core machine,[5] it falls back to using the workstation GC.) Its availability has nothing to do with which OS you're running, by the way—for example, server mode is available on nonserver and server editions of Windows alike if you have suitable hardware, and workstation mode is always available. In server mode, each processor gets its own section of the heap, so when a thread is working on its own problem independently of the rest of the process, it can allocate heap blocks with minimal contention. In server mode, the CLR creates several threads dedicated to garbage collection work, one for each logical CPU in the machine. These run with higher priority than normal threads, so when garbage collections do occur, all available CPU cores go to work on their own heaps, which can provide better throughput with large heaps than workstation mode.

 Objects created by one thread can still be accessed by others—logically, the heap is still a unified service. Server mode is just an implementation strategy optimized for workloads where all the threads work on their own jobs mostly in isolation. Be aware that it works best if the jobs all have similar heap allocation patterns.

Some problems can arise with server mode. It works best when only one process on the machine uses this mode, because it is set up to try to use all CPU cores simultaneously during collections. It also tends to use considerably more memory than workstation mode. If a single server hosts multiple .NET processes that all do this,

---

5 Rare though single-core CPUs are these days, it's still common to run in virtual machines that present only one core to the code they host. This is often the case if your application runs on a cloud-hosted service using a consumption-based tariff, for example.

contention for resources could reduce efficiency. Another issue with server GC is that it favors throughput over response time. In particular, collections happen less frequently, because this tends to increase the throughput benefits that multi-CPU collections can offer, but it also means that each individual collection takes longer.

As with workstation GC, the server GC uses background collection by default. In some cases you may find you can improve throughput by disabling it, but be wary of the problems this can cause. The duration of a full collection in nonconcurrent server mode can cause serious delays in responsiveness on a website, for example, especially if the heap is large. You can mitigate this in a couple of ways. You can request notifications shortly before the collection occurs (using the System.GC class's RegisterFor FullGCNotification, WaitForFullGCApproach, and WaitForFullGCComplete methods), and if you have a server farm, a server that's running a full GC may be able to ask the load balancer to avoid passing it requests until the GC completes. The simpler alternative is to leave background collection enabled. Since background collections allow application threads to continue to run and even to perform generation 0 and 1 collections while the full collection proceeds in the background, it significantly improves the application's response time during collections, while still delivering the throughput benefits of server mode.

Temporarily Suspending Garbage Collections

It is possible to ask .NET to disallow garbage collection while a particular section of code runs. This is useful if you are performing time-sensitive work. Windows, macOS, and Linux are not real-time operating systems, so there are never any guarantees, but temporarily ruling out garbage collections at critical moments can nonetheless be useful for reducing the chances of things going slowly at the worst possible moment. Be aware that this mechanism works by bringing forward any GC work that might otherwise have happened in the relevant section of code, so this can cause GC-related delays to happen earlier than they otherwise would have. It only guarantees that once your designated region of code starts to run, there will be no further GCs if you meet certain requirements—in effect, it gets necessary delays out of the way before the time-sensitive work begins.

The GC class offers a TryStartNoGCRegion method, which you call to indicate that you want to begin some work that needs to be free from GC-related interruption. You must pass in a value indicating how much memory you will need during this work, and it will attempt to ensure that at least that much memory is available before proceeding (performing a GC to free up that space if necessary). If the method indicates success, then as long as you do not consume more memory than requested, your code will not be interrupted by the GC. You should call EndNoGCRegion once you have finished the time-critical work, enabling the GC to return to its normal operation. If, before it calls EndNoGCRegion, your code uses more memory than you requested, the CLR may have to perform a GC, but it will only do so if it absolutely cannot avoid it until you call EndNoGCRegion.

Although the single-argument form of TryStartNoGCRegion will perform a full GC if necessary to meet your request, some overloads take a bool, enabling you to tell it that if a full blocking GC will be required to free up the necessary space, you'd prefer to abort. There are also overloads in which you can specify your memory requirements on the ordinary heap and the large object heap separately.

Accidentally Defeating Compaction

Heap compaction is an important feature of the CLR's GC, because it has a strong positive impact on performance. Certain operations can prevent compaction, and that's something you'll want to minimize, because fragmentation can increase memory use and reduce performance significantly.

To be able to compact the heap, the CLR needs to be able to move heap blocks around. Normally, it can do this because it knows all of the places in which your application refers to heap blocks, and it can adjust all the references when it relocates a block. But what if you're calling an OS API that works directly with the memory you provide? For example, if you read data from a file or a network socket, how will that interact with garbage collection?

If you use system calls that read or write data using devices such as the hard drive or network interface, these normally work directly with your application's memory. If you read data from the disk, the OS may instruct the disk controller to put the bytes directly into the memory your application passed to the API. The OS will perform the necessary calculations to translate the virtual address into a physical address. (With virtual memory, the value your application puts in a pointer is only indirectly related to the actual address in your computer's RAM.) The OS will lock the pages into place for the duration of the I/O request to ensure that the physical address remains valid. It will then supply the disk system with that address. This enables the disk controller to copy data from the disk directly into memory, without needing further involvement from the CPU. This is very efficient, but runs into problems when it encounters a compacting heap. What if the block of memory is a byte[] array on the heap? Suppose a GC occurs between us asking to read the data and the disk being able to supply the data. (The chances are fairly high; a mechanical disk with spinning platters can take 10 ms or more to start supplying data, which is an age in CPU terms.) If the GC decided to relocate our byte[] array to compact the heap, the physical memory address that the OS gave the disk controller would be out of date, so when the controller started putting data into memory, it would be writing to the wrong place.

There are three ways the CLR could deal with this. One would be to make the GC wait—heap relocations could be suspended while I/O operations are in progress. But that's a nonstarter; a busy server can run for days without ever entering a state in which no I/O operations are in progress. In fact, the server doesn't even need to be busy. It might allocate several byte[] arrays to hold the next few incoming network requests, and would typically try to avoid getting into a state where it didn't have at least one such buffer available. The OS would have pointers to all of these and may well have supplied the network card with the corresponding physical address so that it can get to work the moment data starts to arrive. So even an idle server has certain buffers that cannot be relocated.

An alternative would be for the CLR to provide a separate nonmoving heap for these sorts of operations. Perhaps we could allocate a fixed block of memory for an I/O operation, and then copy the results into the byte[] array on the GC heap once the I/O has finished. But that's also not a brilliant solution. Copying data is expensive—the more copies you make of incoming or outgoing data, the slower your server will run, so you really want network and disk hardware to copy the data directly to or from its natural location. And if this hypothetical fixed heap were more than an implementation detail of the CLR, if it were available for application code to use directly to minimize copying, that might open the door to all the memory management bugs that GC is supposed to banish.

So the CLR uses a third approach: it selectively prevents heap block relocations. The GC is free to run while I/O operations are in progress, but certain heap blocks can be *pinned*. Pinning a block sets a flag that tells the GC that the block cannot currently be moved. So, if the GC encounters such a block, it will simply leave it where it is, but will attempt to relocate everything around it.

There are three ways C# code normally causes heap blocks to be pinned. You can do so explicitly using the fixed keyword. This allows you to obtain a raw pointer to a storage location, such as a field or an array element, and the compiler will generate code that ensures that for as long as a fixed pointer is in scope, the heap block to which it refers will be pinned. A more common way to pin a block is through interop (i.e., calls into unmanaged code, such as a method on a COM component, or an OS API). If you make an interop call to an API that requires a pointer to something, the CLR will detect when that points to a heap block, and it will automatically pin the block. (By default, the CLR will unpin it automatically when the method returns. If you're calling an asynchronous API, you can use the GCHandle class mentioned earlier to pin a heap block until you explicitly unpin it.)

The third and most common way to pin heap blocks is also the least direct: many class library APIs call unmanaged code on your behalf and will pin the arrays you pass in as a result. For example, the class library defines a Stream class that represents a stream of bytes. There are several implementations of this abstract class. Some streams work entirely in memory, but some wrap I/O mechanisms, providing access to files or to the data being sent or received through a network socket. The abstract Stream base class defines methods for reading and writing data via byte[] arrays, and the I/O-based stream implementations will often pin the heap blocks containing those arrays for as long as necessary.

If you are writing an application that does a lot of pinning (e.g., a lot of network I/O), you may need to think carefully about how you allocate the arrays that get pinned. Pinning does the most harm for recently allocated objects, because these live in the area of the heap where most compaction activity occurs. Pinning recently allocated blocks tends to cause the ephemeral section of the heap to fragment. Memory that would normally have been recovered almost instantly must now wait for blocks to become unpinned, so by the time the collector can get to those blocks, a lot more other blocks will have been allocated after them, meaning that a lot more work is required to recover the memory.

If pinning is causing your application problems, there will be a few common symptoms. The percentage of CPU time spent in the GC will be relatively high—anything over 10% is considered to be bad. But that alone does not necessarily implicate pinning—it could be the result of middle-aged objects causing too many full collections. So you can monitor the number of pinned blocks on the heap[6] to see if these are the specific culprit. If it looks like excessive pinning is causing you pain, there are two ways to avoid this. One is to design your application so that you only ever pin blocks that live on the large object heap. Remember, by default the LOH is not compacted, so pinning does not impose any cost—the GC wasn't going to move the block in any case. The challenging part of this is that it forces you to do all of your I/O with arrays that are at least 85,000 bytes long. That's not necessarily a problem, because most I/O APIs can be told to work with a subsection of the array. So, if you actually wanted to work with, say, 4,096 byte blocks, you could create one array large enough to hold at least 21 of those blocks. You'd need to write some code to keep track of which slots in the array were in use, but if it fixes a performance problem, it may be worth the effort. The Span<T> and MemoryPool<T> types discussed in Chapter 18 can make it easier to work with arrays in this way. (They also make it much easier than it used to be to work with memory that does not live on the GC heap. So you could sidestep pinning entirely, although you'd be taking on the responsibility for managing the relevant memory.)

---

6 With .NET Core, you can use a free Microsoft tool called *PerfView*. With .NET Framework, you use instead the Performance Monitor tool built into Windows. These can report numerous useful statistics for garbage collection and other CLR activities, including the percentage of CPU time spent in the GC, the number of pinned objects, and the number of generation 0, 1, and 2 collections. Alternatively, the free *BenchMarkDotNet* tool has a memory diagnosis feature.

If you choose to mitigate pinning by attempting to use the LOH, you need to remember that it is an implementation detail. Future versions of .NET could conceivably remove the LOH entirely. So you'd need to revisit this aspect of your design for each new release of .NET.

The other way to minimize the impact of pinning is to try to ensure that pinning mostly happens only to objects in generation 2. If you allocate a pool of buffers and reuse them for the duration of the application, this will mean that you're pinning blocks that the GC is fairly unlikely to want to move, keeping the ephemeral generations free to be compacted at any time. The earlier you allocate the buffers, the better, because the older an object is, the less likely the GC is to want to move it.

Forcing Garbage Collections

The System.GC class provides a Collect method that allows you to force a garbage collection to occur. You can pass a number indicating the generation you would like to collect, and the overload that takes no arguments performs a full collection. You will rarely have good reason to call GC.Collect. I'm mentioning it here because it comes up a lot on the web, which could easily make it seem more useful than it is.

Forcing a GC can cause problems. The GC monitors its own performance and tunes its behavior in response to your application's allocation patterns. But to do this, it needs to allow enough time between collections to get an accurate picture of how well its current settings are working. If you force collections to occur too often, it will not be able to tune itself, and the outcome will be twofold: the GC will run more often than necessary, and when it does run, its behavior will be suboptimal. Both problems are likely to increase the amount of CPU time spent in the GC.

So when would you force a collection? If you happen to know that your application has just finished some work and is about to go idle, it might be worth considering forcing a collection. Garbage collections are usually triggered by activity, so if you know that your application is about to go to sleep—perhaps it's a service that has just finished running a batch job, and will not do any more work for another few hours— you know that it won't be allocating new objects and will therefore not trigger the GC automatically. So forcing a GC would provide an opportunity to return memory to the OS before the application goes to sleep. That said, if this is your scenario, it might be worth looking at mechanisms that would enable your process to exit entirely— there are various ways in which jobs or services that are only required from time to time can be unloaded completely when they are inactive. But if that technique is inapplicable for some reason—perhaps your process has high startup costs or needs to stay running to receive incoming network requests—a forced full collection might be the next best option.

It's worth being aware that there is one way that a GC can be triggered without your application needing to do anything. When the system is running low on memory, Windows broadcasts a message to all running processes. The CLR handles this message, and forces a GC when it occurs. So even if your application does not proactively attempt to return memory, memory might be reclaimed eventually if something else in the system needs it.

Destructors and Finalization

The CLR works hard on our behalf to find out when our objects are no longer in use. It's possible to get it to notify you of this—instead of simply removing unreachable objects, the CLR can first tell an object that it is about to be removed. The CLR calls this finalization, but C# presents it through a special syntax: to exploit finalization, you must write a destructor.

 If your background is in C++, do not be fooled by the name, or the similar syntax. As you will see, a C# destructor is different than a C++ destructor in some important ways.

Example 7-8 shows a destructor. This code compiles into an override of a method called Finalize, which as Chapter 6 mentioned, is a special method defined by the object base class. Finalizers are required always to call the base implementation of Finalize that they override. C# generates that call for us to prevent us from violating the rule, which is why it doesn't let us simply write a Finalize method directly. You cannot write code that invokes a finalizer—they are called by the CLR, so we do not specify an accessibility level for the destructor.

Example 7-8. Class with destructor

```
public class LetMeKnowMineEnd
{
    ~LetMeKnowMineEnd()
    {
        Console.WriteLine("Goodbye, cruel world");
    }
}
```

The CLR does not guarantee to run finalizers on any particular schedule. First of all, it needs to detect that the object has become unreachable, which won't happen until the GC runs. If your program is idle, that might not happen for a long time; the GC runs only when your program is doing something, or when system-wide memory pressure causes the GC to spring into life. It's entirely possible that minutes, hours, or even days could pass between your object becoming unreachable and the CLR noticing that it has become unreachable.

Even when the CLR does detect unreachability, it still doesn't guarantee to call the finalizer straightaway. Finalizers run on a dedicated thread. Because current versions of the CLR have only one finalization thread (regardless of which GC mode you choose), a slow finalizer will cause other finalizers to wait.

In most cases, the CLR doesn't even guarantee to run finalizers at all. When a process exits, if the finalization thread hasn't already managed to run all extant finalizers, it will exit without waiting for them all to finish.

In summary, finalizers can be delayed indefinitely if your program is either idle or busy, and are not guaranteed to run. But it gets worse—you can't actually do much that is useful in a finalizer.

You might think that a finalizer would be a good place to ensure that certain work is properly completed. For example, if your object writes data to a file, but buffers that data so as to be able to write a small number of large chunks rather than writing in tiny dribs and drabs (because large writes are often more efficient), you might think that finalization is the obvious place to ensure that data in your buffers has been safely flushed out to disk. But think again.

During finalization, an object cannot trust the other objects it has references to. If your object's destructor runs, your object must have become unreachable. This means it's highly likely that any other objects yours refers to have also become unreachable. The CLR is likely to discover the unreachability of groups of related objects simultaneously—if your object created three or four objects to help it do its job, the whole lot will become unreachable at the same time. The CLR makes no guarantees about the order in which it runs finalizers. This means it's entirely possible that by the time your destructor runs, all the objects you were using have already been finalized. So, if they also perform any last-minute cleanup, it's too late to use them. For example, the FileStream class, which derives from Stream and provides access to a file, closes its file handle in its destructor. Thus, if you were hoping to flush your data out to the FileStream, it's too late—the file stream may well already be closed.

 To be fair, things are marginally less bad than I've made them sound so far. Although the CLR does not guarantee to run most finalizers, it will usually run them in practice. The absence of guarantees matters only in relatively extreme situations. Even so, this doesn't mitigate the fact that you cannot, in general, rely on other objects in your destructor.

Since destructors seem to be of remarkably little use—that is, you can have no idea if or when they will run, and you can't use other objects inside a destructor—then what use are they?

The main reason finalization exists at all is to make it possible to write .NET types that are wrappers for the sorts of entities that are traditionally represented by handles —things like files and sockets. These are created and managed outside of the CLR— files and sockets require the OS kernel to allocate resources; libraries may also provide handle-based APIs, and they will typically allocate memory on their own private heaps to store information about whatever the handle represents. The CLR cannot see these activities—all it sees is a .NET object with a field containing an integer, and it has no idea that the integer is a handle for some resource outside of the CLR. So it doesn't know that it's important that the handle be closed when the object falls out of use. This is where finalizers come in: they are a place to put code that tells something external to the CLR that the entity represented by the handle is no longer in use. The inability to use other objects is not a problem in this scenario.

 If you are writing code that wraps a handle, you should normally use one of the built-in classes that derive from SafeHandle or, if absolutely necessary, derive your own. This base class extends the basic finalization mechanism with some handle-oriented helpers, and when running on the .NET Framework it also uses a mechanism that can, in certain circumstances, guarantee that the finalizer will run. Furthermore, it gets special handling from the interop layer to avoid premature freeing of resources.

There are some other uses for finalization, although the unpredictability and unreliability already discussed mean there are limits to what it can do for you. Some classes contain a finalizer that does nothing other than check that the object was not abandoned in a state where it had unfinished work. For example, if you had written a class that buffers data before writing it to a file as described previously, you would need to define some method that callers should use when they are done with your object (perhaps called Flush or Close), and you could write a finalizer that checks to see if the object was put into a safe state before being abandoned, raising an error if not. This would provide a way to discover when programs have forgotten to clean things up correctly. (.NET's Task Parallel Library, which I'll describe in Chapter 16, uses this technique. When an asynchronous operation throws an exception, it uses a finalizer to discover when the program that launched it fails to get around to detecting that exception.)

If you write a finalizer, you should disable it when your object is in a state where it no longer requires finalization, because finalization has its costs. If you offer a Close or Flush method, finalization is unnecessary once these have been called, so you should

---

call the `System.GC` class's `SuppressFinalize` method to let the GC know that your object no longer needs to be finalized. If your object's state subsequently changes, you can call the `ReRegisterForFinalize` method to reenable it.

The greatest cost of finalization is that it guarantees that your object will survive at least into the first generation and possibly beyond. Remember, all objects that survive from generation 0 make it into generation 1. If your object has a finalizer, and you have not disabled it by calling `SuppressFinalize`, the CLR cannot get rid of your object until it has run its finalizer. And since finalizers run asynchronously on a separate thread, the object has to remain alive even though it has been found to be unreachable. So the object is not yet collectable, even though it is unreachable. It therefore lives on into generation 1. It will usually be finalized shortly afterward, meaning that the object will then become a waste of space until a generation 1 collection occurs. Those happen rather less frequently than generation 0 collections. If your object had already made it into generation 1 before becoming unreachable, a finalizer increases the chances of getting into generation 2 just before it is about to fall out of use. A finalized object therefore makes inefficient use of memory, which is a reason to avoid finalization, and a reason to disable it whenever possible in objects that do sometimes require it.

 Even though `SuppressFinalize` can save you from the most egregious costs of finalization, an object that uses this technique still has higher overheads than an object with no finalizer at all. The CLR does some extra work when constructing finalizable objects to keep track of those which have not yet been finalized. (Calling `SuppressFinalize` just takes your object back out of this tracking list.) So, although suppressing finalization is much better than letting it occur, it's better still if you don't ask for it in the first place.

A slightly weird upshot of finalization is that an object that the GC discovered was unreachable can make itself reachable again. It's possible to write a destructor that stores the `this` reference in a root reference, or perhaps in a collection that is reachable via a root reference. Nothing stops you from doing this, and the object will continue to work (although its finalizer will not run a second time if the object becomes unreachable again), but it's an odd thing to do. This is referred to as *resurrection*, and just because you can do it doesn't mean you should. It is best avoided.

I hope that by now, I have convinced you that destructors do not provide a general-purpose mechanism for shutting down objects cleanly. They are mostly useful only for dealing with handles for things that live outside of the CLR's control and it's best to avoid relying on them. If you need timely, reliable cleanup of resources, there's a better mechanism.

IDisposable

The .NET class library defines an interface called IDisposable. The CLR does not treat this interface as being in any way special, but C# has some built-in support for it. IDisposable is a simple abstraction; as Example 7-9 shows, it defines just one member, the Dispose method.

Example 7-9. The IDisposable interface

```
public interface IDisposable
{
    void Dispose();
}
```

The idea behind IDisposable is simple. If your code creates an object that implements this interface, you should call Dispose once you've finished using that object (with the occasional exception—see "Optional Disposal" on page 339). This then provides the object with an opportunity to free up resources it may have allocated. If the object being disposed of was using resources represented by handles, it will typically close those handles immediately rather than waiting for finalization to kick in (and it will suppress finalization at the same time). If the object was using services on some remote machine in a stateful way—perhaps holding a connection open to a server to be able to make requests—it would immediately let the remote system know that it no longer requires the services, in whatever way is necessary (for example, by closing the connection).

 There is a persistent myth that calling Dispose causes the GC to do something. You may read on the web that Dispose finalizes the object, or even that it causes the object to be garbage collected. This is nonsense. The CLR does not handle IDisposable or Dispose differently than any other interface or method.

IDisposable is important because it's possible for an object to consume very little memory and yet tie up some expensive resources. For example, consider an object that represents a connection to a database. Such an object might not need many fields —it could even have just a single field containing a handle representing the connection. From the CLR's point of view, this is a pretty cheap object, and we could allocate hundreds of them without triggering a garbage collection. But in the database server, things would look different—it might need to allocate a considerable amount of memory for each incoming connection. Connections might even be strictly limited by licensing terms. (This illustrates that "resource" is a fairly broad concept—it means pretty much anything that you might run out of.)

Relying on GC to notice when database connection objects are no longer in use is likely to be a bad strategy. The CLR will know that we've allocated, say, 50 of the things, but if that consumes only a few hundred bytes in total, it will see no reason to run the GC. And yet our application may be about to grind to a halt—if we have only 50 connection licenses for the database, the next attempt to create a connection will fail. And even if there's no licensing limitation, we could still be making highly inefficient use of database resources by opening far more connections than we need.

It's imperative that we close connection objects as soon as we can, without waiting for the GC to tell us which ones are out of use. This is where IDisposable comes in. It's not just for database connections, of course. It's critically important for any object that is a front for something that lives outside the CLR, such as a file or a network connection. Even for resources that aren't especially constrained, IDisposable provides a way to tell objects when we're finished with them, so that they can shut down cleanly, solving the problem described earlier for objects that perform internal buffering.

 If a resource is expensive to create, you may want to reuse it. This is often the case with database connections, so the usual practice is to maintain a pool of connections. Instead of closing a connection when you're finished with it, you return it to the pool, making it available for reuse. (Most of .NET's data access providers can do this for you.) The IDisposable model is still useful here. When you ask a resource pool for a resource, it usually provides a wrapper around the real resource, and when you dispose that wrapper, it returns the resource to the pool instead of freeing it. So calling Dispose is really just a way of saying, "I'm done with this object," and it's up to the IDisposable implementation to decide what to do next with the resource it represents.

Implementations of IDisposable are required to tolerate multiple calls to Dispose. Although this means consumers can call Dispose multiple times without harm, they should not attempt to use an object after it has been disposed. In fact, the class library defines a special exception that objects can throw if you misuse them in this way: ObjectDisposedException. (I will discuss exceptions in Chapter 8.)

You're free to call Dispose directly, of course, but C# also supports IDisposable in three ways: foreach loops, using statements, and using declarations. A using statement is a way to ensure that you reliably dispose an object that implements IDisposable once you're done with it. Example 7-10 shows how to use it.

Example 7-10. A using statement

```
using (StreamReader reader = File.OpenText(@"C:\temp\File.txt"))
{
    Console.WriteLine(reader.ReadToEnd());
}
```

This is equivalent to the code in Example 7-11. The `try` and `finally` keywords are part of C#'s exception handling system, which I'll discuss in detail in Chapter 8. In this case, they're being used to ensure that the call to `Dispose` inside the `finally` block executes even if something goes wrong in the code inside the `try` block. This also ensures that `Dispose` gets called if you execute a `return` statement in the middle of the block. (It even works if you use a `goto` statement to jump out of it.)

Example 7-11. How using statements expand

```
{
    StreamReader reader = File.OpenText(@"C:\temp\File.txt");
    try
    {
        Console.WriteLine(reader.ReadToEnd());
    }
    finally
    {
        if (reader != null)
        {
            ((IDisposable) reader).Dispose();
        }
    }
}
```

If the `using` statement's declaration's variable type is a value type, C# will not generate the code that checks for `null`, and will just invoke `Dispose` directly. (The same is true for a `using` declaration.)

C# 8.0 adds a simpler alternative, a `using` declaration, shown in Example 7-12. The difference is that we don't need to provide a block. A `using` declaration disposes its variable when the variable goes out of scope. It still generates `try` and `finally` blocks, so in cases where a `using` statement's block happens to finish at the end of some other block (e.g., it finishes at the end of a method), you can change to a `using` declaration with no change of behavior. This reduces the number of nested blocks, which can make your code easier to read. (On the other hand, with an ordinary `using` block it may be easier to see exactly when the object is no longer used. So each style has its pros and cons.)

Example 7-12. A using declaration

```
using StreamReader reader = File.OpenText(@"C:\temp\File.txt");
Console.WriteLine(reader.ReadToEnd());
```

If you need to use multiple disposable resources within the same scope, you can nest them, but it might be easier to read if you stack multiple `using` statements in front of a single block. Example 7-13 uses this to copy the contents of one file to another.

Example 7-13. Stacking using statements

```
using (Stream source = File.OpenRead(@"C:\temp\File.txt"))
using (Stream copy = File.Create(@"C:\temp\Copy.txt"))
{
    source.CopyTo(copy);
}
```

Stacking `using` statements is not a special syntax; it's just an upshot of the fact that a `using` statement is always followed by single embedded statement, which will be executed before `Dispose` gets called. Normally, that statement is a block, but in Example 7-13, the first `using` statement's embedded statement is the second `using` statement. If you use `using` declarations instead, stacking is unnecessary because these don't have an associated embedded statement.

A `foreach` loop generates code that will use `IDisposable` if the enumerator implements it. Example 7-14 shows a `foreach` loop that uses just such an enumerator.

Example 7-14. A foreach loop

```
foreach (string file in Directory.EnumerateFiles(@"C:\temp"))
{
    Console.WriteLine(file);
}
```

The `Directory` class's `EnumerateFiles` method returns an `IEnumerable<string>`. As you saw in Chapter 5, this has a `GetEnumerator` method that returns an `IEnumerator<string>`, an interface that inherits from `IDisposable`. Consequently, the C# compiler will produce code equivalent to Example 7-15.

Example 7-15. How foreach loops expand

```
{
    IEnumerator<string> e =
        Directory.EnumerateFiles(@"C:\temp").GetEnumerator();
    try
    {
        while (e.MoveNext())
```

```
        {
            string file = e.Current;
            Console.WriteLine(file);
        }
    }
    finally
    {
        if (e != null)
        {
            ((IDisposable) e).Dispose();
        }
    }
}
```

There are a few variations the compiler can produce, depending on the collection's enumerator type. If it's a value type that implements IDisposable, the compiler won't generate the check for null in the finally block (just as in a using statement). If the static type of the enumerator does not implement IDisposable, the outcome depends on whether the type is open for inheritance. If it is sealed, or if it is a value type, the compiler will not generate code that attempts to call Dispose at all. If it is not sealed, the compiler generates code in the finally block that tests at runtime whether the enumerator implements IDisposable, calling Dispose if it does, and doing nothing otherwise.

The IDisposable interface is easiest to consume when you obtain a resource and finish using it in the same method, because you can write a using statement (or where applicable, a foreach loop) to ensure that you call Dispose. But sometimes, you will write a class that creates a disposable object and puts a reference to it in a field, because it will need to use that object over a longer timescale. For example, you might write a logging class, and if a logger object writes data to a file, it might hold on to a StreamWriter object. C# provides no automatic help here, so it's up to you to ensure that any contained objects get disposed. You would write your own implementation of IDisposable that disposes the other objects. As Example 7-16 shows, this is not rocket science. Note that this example sets _file to null, so it will not attempt to dispose the file twice. This is not strictly necessary, because the StreamWriter will tolerate multiple calls to Dispose. But it does give the Logger object an easy way to know that it is in a disposed state, so if we were to add some real methods, we could check _file and throw an ObjectDisposedException if it is null.

Example 7-16. Disposing a contained instance

```
public sealed class Logger : IDisposable
{
    private StreamWriter _file;

    public Logger(string filePath)
```

```
    {
        _file = File.CreateText(filePath);
    }

    public void Dispose()
    {
        if (_file != null)
        {
            _file.Dispose();
            _file = null;
        }
    }
    // A real class would go on to do something with the StreamWriter, of course
}
```

This example dodges an important problem. The class is sealed, which avoids the issue of how to cope with inheritance. If you write an unsealed class that implements IDisposable, you should provide a way for a derived class to add its own disposal logic. The most straightforward solution would be to make Dispose virtual so that a derived class can override it, performing its own cleanup in addition to calling your base implementation. However, there is a marginally more complicated pattern that you will see from time to time in .NET.

Some objects implement IDisposable and also have a finalizer. Since the introduction of SafeHandle and related classes, it's relatively unusual for a class to need to provide both (unless it derives from SafeHandle). Only wrappers for handles normally need finalization, and classes that use handles now typically defer to a SafeHandle to provide that, rather than implementing their own finalizers. However, there are exceptions, and some library types implement a pattern designed to support both finalization and IDisposable, allowing you to provide custom behaviors for both in derived classes. For example, the Stream base class works this way.

This pattern is called the *Dispose Pattern*, but do not take that to mean that you should normally use this when implementing IDisposable. On the contrary, it is extremely unusual to need this pattern. Even back when it was invented, few classes needed it, and now that we have SafeHandle, it is almost never necessary. (SafeHandle was introduced in .NET 2.0, so it has been a very long time since this pattern was broadly useful.) Unfortunately, some people misunderstood the narrow utility of this pattern, so you will find a certain amount of well-intentioned but utterly wrong advice telling you that you should use this for all IDisposable implementations. Ignore it. The pattern's main relevance today is that you sometimes encounter it in old types such as Stream.

The pattern is to define a protected overload of Dispose that takes a single bool argument. The base class calls this from its public Dispose method and also its destructor, passing in true or false, respectively. That way, you have to override only one method, the protected Dispose. It can contain logic common to both finalization and disposal, such as closing handles, but you can also perform any disposal-specific or finalization-specific logic because the argument tells you which sort of cleanup is being performed. Example 7-17 shows how this might look.

Example 7-17. Custom finalization and disposal logic

```
public class MyFunkyStream : Stream
{
    // For illustration purposes only. Usually better to avoid this whole
    // pattern and to use some type derived from SafeHandle instead.
    private IntPtr _myCustomLibraryHandle;
    private Logger _log;

    protected override void Dispose(bool disposing)
    {
        base.Dispose(disposing);

        if (_myCustomLibraryHandle != IntPtr.Zero)
        {
            MyCustomLibraryInteropWrapper.Close(_myCustomLibraryHandle);
            _myCustomLibraryHandle = IntPtr.Zero;
        }
        if (disposing)
        {
            if (_log != null)
            {
                _log.Dispose();
                _log = null;
            }
        }
    }

    // ... overloads of Stream's abstract methods would go here
}
```

This hypothetical example is a custom implementation of the Stream abstraction that uses some external non-.NET library that provides handle-based access to resources. We prefer to close the handle when the public Dispose method is called, but if that hasn't happened by the time our finalizer runs, we want to close the handle then. So the code checks to see if the handle is still open and closes it if necessary, and it does this whether the call to the Dispose(bool) overload happened as a result of the object being explicitly disposed or being finalized—we need to ensure that the handle is closed in either case. However, this class also appears to use an instance of the Logger class from Example 7-16. Because that's an ordinary object, we shouldn't attempt to use it during finalization, so we attempt to dispose it only if our object is being disposed. If we are being finalized, then although `Logger` itself is not finalizable, it uses a `FileStream`, which is finalizable; and it's quite possible that the `FileStream` finalizer will already have run by the time our `MyFunkyStream` class's finalizer runs, so it would be a bad idea to call methods on the `Logger`.

When a base class provides this virtual protected form of `Dispose`, it should call `GC.SuppressFinalization` in its public `Dispose`. The `Stream` base class does this. More generally, if you find yourself writing a class that offers both `Dispose` and a finalizer, then whether or not you choose to support inheritance with this pattern, you should in any case suppress finalization when `Dispose` is called.

Optional Disposal

Although you should call `Dispose` at some point on most objects that implement `IDisposable`, there are a few exceptions. For example, the Reactive Extensions for .NET (described in Chapter 11) provide `IDisposable` objects that represent subscriptions to streams of events. You can call `Dispose` to unsubscribe, but some event sources come to a natural end, automatically shutting down any subscriptions. If that happens, you are not required to call `Dispose`. Also, the `Task` type, which is used extensively in conjunction with the asynchronous programming techniques described in Chapter 17, implements `IDisposable` but does not need to be disposed unless you cause it to allocate a `WaitHandle`, something which will not occur in normal usage. The way `Task` is generally used makes it particularly awkward to find a good time to call `Dispose` on it, so it's fortunate that it's not normally necessary.

The `HttpClient` class is another exception to the normal rules, but in a different way. We rarely call `Dispose` on instances of this type, but in this case it's because we are encouraged to reuse instances. If you construct, use, and dispose an `HttpClient` each time you need one, you will defeat its ability to reuse existing connections when making multiple requests to the same server. This can cause two problems. First, opening an HTTP connection can sometimes take longer than sending the request and receiving the response, so preventing `HttpClient` from reusing connections to send multiple requests over time can cause significant performance problems. Connection reuse only works if you reuse the `HttpClient`.[7] Second, the TCP protocol (which underpins HTTP) has characteristics that mean the OS cannot always instantly reclaim all the resources associated with a connection: it may need to keep the connection's TCP

---

7 Strictly speaking, it's the underlying `MessageHandler` that needs to be reused. If you obtain an `HttpClient` from an `IHttpClientFactory`, it is harmless to dispose it because the factory holds on to the handler and reuses it across `HttpClient` instances.

port reserved for a considerable time (maybe a few minutes) after you've told the OS to close the connection, and it's possible to run out of ports, preventing all further communication.

Such exceptions are unusual. It is only safe to omit calls to Dispose when the documentation for the class you're using explicitly states that it is not required.

Boxing

While I'm discussing garbage collection and object lifetime, there's one more topic I should talk about in this chapter: *boxing*. Boxing is the process that enables a variable of type object to refer to a value type. An object variable is capable only of holding a reference to something on the heap, so how can it refer to an int? What happens when the code in Example 7-18 runs?

Example 7-18. Using an int as an object

```
class Program
{
    static void Show(object o)
    {
        Console.WriteLine(o.ToString());
    }

    static void Main(string[] args)
    {
        int num = 42;
        Show(num);
    }
}
```

The Show method expects an object, and I'm passing it num, which is a local variable of the value type int. In these circumstances, C# generates a box, which is essentially a reference type wrapper for a value. The CLR can automatically provide a box for any value type, although if it didn't, you could write your own class that does something similar. Example 7-19 shows a hand-built box.

Example 7-19. Not actually how a box works

```
// Not a real box, but similar in effect.
public class Box<T>
    where T : struct
{
    public readonly T Value;
    public Box(T v)
    {
        Value = v;
```

```
    }

    public override string ToString() => Value.ToString();
    public override bool Equals(object obj) => Value.Equals(obj);
    public override int GetHashCode() => Value.GetHashCode();
}
```

This is a fairly ordinary class that contains a single instance of a value type as its only field. If you invoke the standard members of object on the box, this class's overrides make it look as though you invoked them directly on the field itself. So, if I passed new Box<int>(num) as the argument to Show in Example 7-18, Show would receive a reference to that box. When Show called ToString, the box would call the int field's ToString, so you'd expect the program to display 42.

We don't need to write Example 7-19, because the CLR will build the box for us. It will create an object on the heap that contains a copy of the boxed value, and forwards the standard object methods to the boxed value. And it does some things that we can't. If you ask a boxed int its type by calling GetType, it will return the same Type object as you'd get if you called GetType directly on an int variable—I can't do that with my custom Box<T>, because GetType is not virtual. Also, getting back the underlying value is easier than it would be with a hand-built box, because unboxing is an intrinsic CLR feature.

If you have a reference of type object, and you cast it to int, the CLR checks to see if the reference does indeed refer to a boxed int; if it does, the CLR returns a copy of the boxed value. (If not, it throws an InvalidCastException.) So, inside the Show method of Example 7-18, I could write (int) o to get back a copy of the original value, whereas if I were using the class in Example 7-19, I'd need the more convoluted ((Box<int>) o).Value.

I can also use pattern matching to extract a boxed value. Example 7-20 uses a type pattern to detect whether the variable o contains a reference to a boxed int, and if it does, it extracts that into the local variable i. As we saw in Chapter 2, when you use a pattern with the is operator like this, the resulting expression evaluates to true if the pattern matches, and false if it does not. So the body of this if statement runs only if there was an int value there to be unboxed.

Example 7-20. Unboxing a value with a type pattern

```
if (o is int i)
{
    Console.WriteLine(i * 2);
}
```

Boxes are automatically available for all structs,[8] not just the built-in value types. If the struct implements any interfaces, the box will provide all the same interfaces. (That's another trick that Example 7-19 cannot perform.)

Some implicit conversions cause boxing. You can see this in Example 7-18. I have passed an expression of type int where object was required, without needing an explicit cast. Implicit conversions also exist between a value and any of the interfaces that value's type implements. For example, you can assign a value of type int into a variable of type IComparable<int> (or pass it as a method argument of that type) without needing a cast. This causes a box to be created, because variables of any interface type are like variables of type object, in that they can hold only a reference to an item on the garbage-collected heap.

 Implicit boxing conversions are not implicit reference conversions. This means that they do not come into play with covariance or contravariance. For example, IEnumerable<int> is not compatible with IEnumerable<object> despite the existence of an implicit conversion from int to object, because that is not an implicit reference conversion.

Implicit boxing can occasionally cause problems for either of two reasons. First, it makes it easy to generate extra work for the GC. The CLR does not attempt to cache boxes, so if you write a loop that executes 100,000 times, and that loop contains an expression that uses an implicit boxing conversion, you'll end up generating 100,000 boxes, which the GC will eventually have to clean up just like anything else on the heap. Second, each box operation (and each unbox) copies the value, which might not provide the semantics you were expecting. Example 7-21 illustrates some potentially surprising behavior.

Example 7-21. Illustrating the pitfalls of mutable structs

```
public struct DisposableValue : IDisposable
{
    private bool _disposedYet;

    public void Dispose()
    {
        if (!_disposedYet)
        {
            Console.WriteLine("Disposing for first time");
            _disposedYet = true;
        }
```

---

8 Except for ref struct types, because those invariably live on the stack.

```
        else
        {
            Console.WriteLine("Was already disposed");
        }
    }
}

class Program
{
    static void CallDispose(IDisposable o)
    {
        o.Dispose();
    }

    static void Main(string[] args)
    {
        var dv = new DisposableValue();
        Console.WriteLine("Passing value variable:");
        CallDispose(dv);
        CallDispose(dv);
        CallDispose(dv);

        IDisposable id = dv;
        Console.WriteLine("Passing interface variable:");
        CallDispose(id);
        CallDispose(id);
        CallDispose(id);

        Console.WriteLine("Calling Dispose directly on value variable:");
        dv.Dispose();
        dv.Dispose();
        dv.Dispose();

        Console.WriteLine("Passing value variable:");
        CallDispose(dv);
        CallDispose(dv);
        CallDispose(dv);
    }
}
```

The DisposableValue struct implements the IDisposable interface we saw earlier. It keeps track of whether it has been disposed already. The program contains a CallDispose method that calls Dispose on any IDisposable instance. The program declares a single variable of type DisposableValue and passes this to CallDispose three times. Here's the output from that part of the program:

```
Passing value variable:
Disposing for first time
Disposing for first time
Disposing for first time
```

On all three occasions, the struct seems to think this is the first time we've called Dispose on it. That's because each call to CallDispose created a new box—we are not really passing the dv variable, we are passing a newly boxed copy each time, so the CallDispose method is working on a different instance of the struct each time. This is consistent with how value types normally work—even when they're not boxed, when you pass them as arguments, you end up passing a copy (unless you use the ref or in keywords).

The next part of the program ends up generating just a single box—it assigns the value into another local variable of type IDisposable. This uses the same implicit conversion as we did when passing the variable directly as an argument, so this creates yet another box, but it does so only once. We then pass the same reference to this particular box three times over, which explains why the output from this phase of the program looks different:

```
Passing interface variable:
Disposing for first time
Was already disposed
Was already disposed
```

These three calls to CallDispose all use the same box, which contains an instance of our struct, and so after the first call, it remembers that it has been disposed already. Next, our program calls Dispose directly on the local variable, producing this output:

```
Calling Dispose directly on value variable:
Disposing for first time
Was already disposed
Was already disposed
```

No boxing at all is involved here, so we are modifying the state of the local variable. Someone who only glanced at the code might not have expected this output—we have already passed the dv variable to a method that called Dispose on its argument, so it might be surprising to see that it thinks it hasn't been disposed the first time around. But once you understand that CallDispose requires a reference and therefore cannot use a value directly, it's clear that every call to Dispose before this point has operated on some boxed copy, and not the local variable.

Finally, we make three more calls passing the dv directly to CallDispose again. This is exactly what we did at the start of the code, so these calls generate yet more boxed copies. But this time, we are copying a value that's already in the state of having been disposed, so we see different output:

```
Passing value variable:
Was already disposed
Was already disposed
Was already disposed
```

The behavior is all straightforward when you understand what's going on, but it requires you to be mindful that you're dealing with a value type, and to understand when boxing causes implicit copying. This is one of the reasons Microsoft discourages developers from writing value types that can change their state—if a value cannot change, then a boxed value of that type also cannot change. It matters less whether you're dealing with the original or a boxed copy, so there's less scope for confusion, although it is still useful to understand when boxing will occur to avoid performance penalties.

Boxing used to be a much more common occurrence in early versions of .NET. Before generics arrived in .NET 2.0, collection classes all worked in terms of `object`, so if you wanted a resizable list of integers, you'd end up with a box for each `int` in the list. Generic collection classes do not cause boxing—a `List<int>` is able to store unboxed values directly.

Boxing Nullable<T>

Chapter 3 described the `Nullable<T>` type, a wrapper that adds null value support to any value type. Remember, C# has special syntax for this, in which you can just put a question mark on the end of a value type name, so we'd normally write `int?` instead of `Nullable<int>`. The CLR has special support for `Nullable<T>` when it comes to boxing.

`Nullable<T>` itself is a value type, so if you attempt to get a reference to it, the compiler will generate code that attempts to box it, as it would with any other value type. However, at runtime, the CLR will not produce a box containing a copy of the `Nullable<T>` itself. Instead, it checks to see if the value is in a null state (i.e., its `HasValue` property returns `false`), and if so, it just returns `null`. Otherwise, it boxes the contained value. For example, if a `Nullable<int>` has a value, boxing it will produce a box of type `int`. This will be indistinguishable from the box you'd get if you had started with an ordinary `int` value. (One upshot of this is that the pattern matching shown in Example 7-20 works whether the type of variable originally boxed was an `int` or an `int?`. You use `int` in the type pattern in either case.)

You can unbox a boxed `int` into variables of either type `int?` or `int`. So all three unboxing operations in Example 7-22 will succeed. They would also succeed if the first line were modified to initialize the `boxed` variable from a `Nullable<int>` that was not in the null state. (If you were to initialize `boxed` from a `Nullable<int>` in the null state, that would have the same effect as initializing it to `null`, in which case the final line of this example would throw a `NullReferenceException`.)

Example 7-22. Unboxing an int to nullable and nonnullable variables

```
object boxed = 42;
int? nv = boxed as int?;
int? nv2 = (int?) boxed;
int v = (int) boxed;
```

This is a runtime feature, and not simply the compiler being clever. The IL box instruction, which is what C# generates when it wants to box a value, detects `Nulla ble<T>` values; the `unbox` and `unbox.any` IL instructions are able to produce a `Nulla ble<T>` value from either a `null` or a reference to a boxed value of the underlying type. So, if you wrote your own wrapper type that looked like `Nullable<T>`, it would not behave in the same way; if you assigned a value of your type into an `object`, it would box your whole wrapper just like any other value. It's only because the CLR knows about `Nullable<T>` that it behaves differently.

Summary

In this chapter, I described the heap that the runtime provides. I showed the strategy that the CLR uses to determine which heap objects can still be reached by your code, and the generation-based mechanism it uses to reclaim the memory occupied by objects that are no longer in use. The GC is not clairvoyant, so if your program keeps an object reachable, the GC has to assume that you might use that object in the future. This means you will sometimes need to be careful to make sure you don't cause memory leaks by accidentally keeping hold of objects for too long. We looked at the finalization mechanism, and its various limitations and performance issues, and we also looked at `IDisposable`, which is the preferred system for cleaning up nonmemory resources. Finally, we saw how value types can act like reference types thanks to boxing.

In the next chapter, I will show how C# presents the error-handling mechanisms of the CLR.

CHAPTER 8

Exceptions

Some operations can fail. If your program is reading data from a file stored on an external drive, someone might disconnect the drive. Your application might try to construct an array only to discover that the system does not have enough free memory. Intermittent wireless network connectivity can cause network requests to fail. One widely used way for a program to discover these sorts of failures is for each API to return a value indicating whether the operation succeeded. This requires developers to be vigilant if all errors are to be detected, because programs must check the return value of every operation. This is certainly a viable strategy, but it can obscure the code; the logical sequence of work to be performed when nothing goes wrong can get buried by all of the error checking, making the code harder to maintain. C# supports another popular error-handling mechanism that can mitigate this problem: *exceptions*.

When an API reports failure with an exception, this disrupts the normal flow of execution, leaping straight to the nearest suitable error-handling code. This enables a degree of separation between error-handling logic and the code that tries to perform the task at hand. This can make code easier to read and maintain, although it does have the downside of making it harder to see all the possible ways in which the code may execute.

Exceptions can also report problems with operations where a return code might not be practical. For example, the runtime can detect and report problems for basic operations, even something as simple as using a reference. Reference type variables can contain null, and if you try to invoke a method on a null reference, it will fail. The runtime reports this with an exception.

Most errors in .NET are represented as exceptions. However, some APIs offer you a choice between return codes and exceptions. For example, the int type has a Parse method that takes a string and attempts to interpret its contents as a number, and if you pass it some nonnumeric text (e.g., "Hello"), it will indicate failure by throwing a `FormatException`. If you don't like that, you can call `TryParse` instead, which does exactly the same job, but if the input is nonnumeric, it returns `false` instead of throwing an exception. (Since the method's return value has the job of reporting success or failure, the method provides the integer result via an `out` parameter.) Numeric parsing is not the only operation to use this pattern, in which a pair of methods (`Parse` and `TryParse`, in this case) provides a choice between exceptions and return values. As you saw in Chapter 5, dictionaries offer a similar choice. The indexer throws an exception if you use a key that's not in the dictionary, but you can also look up values with `TryGetValue`, which returns `false` on failure, just like `TryParse`. Although this pattern crops up in a few places, for the majority of APIs, exceptions are the only choice.

If you are designing an API that could fail, how should it report failure? Should you use exceptions, a return value, or both? Microsoft's class library design guidelines contain instructions that seem unequivocal:

> Do not return error codes. Exceptions are the primary means of reporting errors in frameworks.
>
> —.NET Framework Design Guidelines

But how does that square with the existence of `int.TryParse`? The guidelines have a section on performance considerations for exceptions that says this:

> Consider the `TryParse` pattern for members that may throw exceptions in common scenarios to avoid performance problems related to exceptions.
>
> —.NET Framework Design Guidelines

Failing to parse a number is not necessarily an error. For example, you might want your application to allow the month to be specified numerically or as text. So there are certainly common scenarios in which the operation might fail, but the guideline has another criterion: it suggests using it for "extremely performance-sensitive APIs," so you should offer the `TryParse` approach only when the operation is fast compared to the time taken to throw and handle an exception.

Exceptions can typically be thrown and handled in a fraction of a millisecond, so they're not desperately slow—not nearly as slow as reading data over a network connection, for example—but they're not blindingly fast either. I find that on my computer, a single thread can parse five-digit numeric strings at a rate of roughly 65 million strings per second on .NET Core 3.0, and it's capable of rejecting nonnumeric strings at a similar speed if I use `TryParse`. The `Parse` method handles numeric strings just as fast, but it's roughly 1,000 times slower at rejecting nonnumeric strings than `TryParse`, thanks to the cost of exceptions. Of course, converting strings to integers is a pretty fast operation, so this makes exceptions look particularly bad, but that's why this pattern is most common on operations that are naturally fast.

Exceptions can be especially slow when debugging. This is partly because the debugger has to decide whether to break in, but it's particularly pronounced with the first unhandled exception your program hits. This can give the impression that exceptions are considerably more expensive than they really are. The numbers in the preceding paragraph are based on observed runtime behavior without debugging overheads. That said, those numbers slightly understate the costs, because handling an exception tends to cause the CLR to run bits of code and access data structures it would not otherwise need to use, which can have the effect of pushing useful data out of the CPU's cache. This can cause code to run slower for a short while after the exception has been handled, until the nonexceptional code and data can make their way back into the cache. The simplicity of the test reduces this effect.

Most APIs do not offer a TryXxx form, and will report all failures as exceptions, even in cases where failure might be common. For example, the file APIs do not provide a way to open an existing file for reading without throwing an exception if the file is missing. (You can use a different API to test whether the file is there first, but that's no guarantee of success. It's always possible for some other process to delete the file between your asking whether it's there and attempting to open it.) Since filesystem operations are inherently slow, the TryXxx pattern would not offer a worthwhile performance boost here even though it might make logical sense.

Exception Sources

Class library APIs are not the only source of exceptions. They can be thrown in any of the following scenarios:

- Your own code detects a problem.
- Your program uses a class library API, which detects a problem.
- The runtime detects the failure of an operation (e.g., arithmetic overflow in a checked context, or an attempt to use a null reference, or an attempt to allocate an object for which there is not enough memory).
- The runtime detects a situation outside of your control that affects your code (e.g., the runtime tries to allocate memory for some internal purpose and finds that there is not enough free memory).

Although these all use the same exception-handling mechanisms, the places in which the exceptions emerge are different. When your own code throws an exception (which I'll show you how to do later), you'll know what conditions cause it to happen, but when do these other scenarios produce exceptions? I'll describe where to expect each sort of exception in the following sections.

Exceptions from APIs

With an API call, there are several kinds of problems that could result in exceptions. You may have provided arguments that make no sense, such as a null reference where a non-null one is required, or an empty string where the name of a file was expected. Or the arguments might look OK individually, but not collectively. For example, you could call an API that copies data into an array, asking it to copy more data than will fit. You could describe these as "that will never work"-style errors, and they are usually the result of mistakes in the code. (One developer who used to work on the C# compiler team refers to these as *boneheaded* exceptions.)

A different class of problems arises when the arguments all look plausible, but the operation turns out not to be possible given the current state of the world. For example, you might ask to open a particular file, but the file may not be present; or perhaps it exists, but some other program already has it open and has demanded exclusive access to the file. Yet another variation is that things may start well, but conditions can change, so perhaps you opened a file successfully and have been reading data for a while, but then the file becomes inaccessible. As suggested earlier, someone may have unplugged a disk, or the drive could have failed due to overheating or age.

Software that communicates with external services over a network needs to take into account that an exception doesn't necessarily indicate that anything is really wrong—sometimes requests fail due to some temporary condition, and you may simply need to retry the operation. This is particularly common in cloud environments, where it's common for individual servers to come and go as part of the load balancing that cloud platforms typically offer—it is normal for a few operations to fail for no particular reason.

When using services via a library you should find out whether it already handles this for you. For example, the Azure Storage libraries perform retries automatically by default, and will only throw an exception if you disable this behavior, or if problems persist after several attempts. You shouldn't normally add your own exception handling and retry loops for this kind of error around libraries that do this for you.

Asynchronous programming adds yet another variation. In Chapters 16 and 17 , I'll show various asynchronous APIs—ones where work can progress after the method that started it has returned. Work that runs asynchronously can also fail asynchronously, in which case the library might have to wait until your code next calls into it before it can report the error.

Despite the variations, in all these cases the exception will come from some API that your code calls. (Even when asynchronous operations fail, exceptions emerge either when you try to collect the result of an operation, or when you explicitly ask whether an error has occurred.) Example 8-1 shows some code where exceptions of this kind could emerge.

Example 8-1. Getting an exception from a library call

```
static void Main(string[] args)
{
    using (var r = new StreamReader(@"C:\Temp\File.txt"))
    {
        while (!r.EndOfStream)
        {
            Console.WriteLine(r.ReadLine());
        }
    }
}
```

There's nothing categorically wrong with this program, so we won't get any exceptions complaining about arguments being self-evidently wrong. (In the unofficial terminology, it makes no boneheaded mistakes.) If your computer's *C:* drive has a *Temp* folder, and if that contains a *File.txt* file, and if the user running the program has permission to read that file, and if nothing else on the computer has already acquired exclusive access to the file, and if there are no problems—such as disk corruption—that could make any part of the file inaccessible, and if no new problems (such as the drive catching fire) develop while the program runs, this code will work just fine: it will show each line of text in the file. But that's a lot of *ifs*.

If there is no such file, the `StreamReader` constructor will not complete. Instead, it will throw an exception. This program makes no attempt to handle that, so the application would terminate. If you ran the program outside of Visual Studio's debugger, you would see the following output:

```
Unhandled Exception: System.IO.DirectoryNotFoundException: Could not find a part
 of the path 'C:\Temp\File.txt'.
   at System.IO.FileStream.ValidateFileHandle(SafeFileHandle fileHandle)
   at System.IO.FileStream.CreateFileOpenHandle(FileMode mode, FileShare share,
FileOptions options)
   at System.IO.FileStream..ctor(String path, FileMode mode, FileAccess access,
FileShare share, Int32 bufferSize, FileOptions options)
   at System.IO.StreamReader.ValidateArgsAndOpenPath(String path, Encoding encod
ing, Int32 bufferSize)
   at System.IO.StreamReader..ctor(String path)
   at Exceptional.Program.Main(String[] args) in c:\Examples\Ch08\Example1\Progr
am.cs:line 10
```

This tells us what error occurred, and shows the full call stack of the program at the point at which the problem happened. On Windows, the system-wide error handling will also step in, so depending on how your computer is configured, you might see its error reporting dialog and it may even report the crash to Microsoft's error-reporting service. If you run the same program in a debugger, it will tell you about the exception and will also highlight the line on which the error occurred, as Figure 8-1 shows.

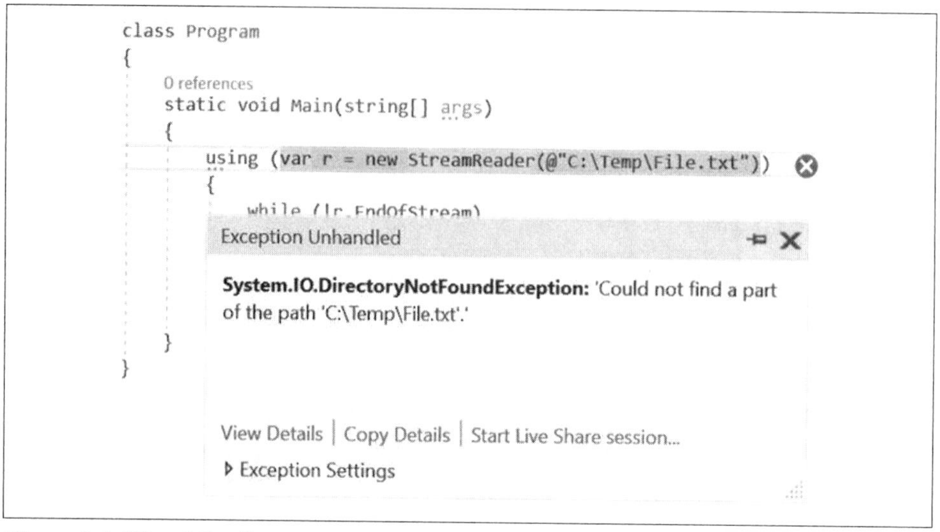

Figure 8-1. Visual Studio reporting an exception

What we're seeing here is the default behavior that occurs when a program does nothing to handle exceptions: if a debugger is attached, it will step in, and if not, the program just crashes. I'll show how to handle exceptions soon, but this illustrates that you cannot simply ignore them.

The call to the `StreamReader` constructor is not the only line that could throw an exception in Example 8-1, by the way. The code calls `ReadLine` multiple times, and any of those calls could fail. In general, any member access could result in an exception, even just reading a property, although class library designers usually try to minimize the extent to which properties throw exceptions. If you make an error of the "that will never work" (boneheaded) kind, then a property might throw an exception, but usually not for errors of the "this particular operation didn't work" kind. For example, the documentation states that the `EndOfStream` property used in Example 8-1 would throw an exception if you tried to read it after having called `Dispose` on the `StreamReader` object—an obvious coding error—but if there are problems reading the file, `StreamReader` will throw exceptions only from methods or the constructor.

Failures Detected by the Runtime

Another source of exceptions is when the CLR itself detects that some operation has failed. Example 8-2 shows a method in which this could happen. As with Example 8-1, there's nothing innately wrong with this code (other than not being very useful). It is perfectly possible to use this without causing problems. However, if someone passes in 0 as the second argument, the code will attempt an illegal operation.

Example 8-2. A potential runtime-detected failure

```
static int Divide(int x, int y)
{
    return x / y;
}
```

The CLR will detect when this division operation attempts to divide by zero and will throw a DivideByZeroException. This will have the same effect as an exception from an API call: if the program makes no attempt to handle the exception, it will crash, or the debugger will break in.

 Division by zero is not always illegal in C#. Floating-point types support special values representing positive and negative infinity, which is what you get when you divide a positive or negative value by zero; if you divide zero by itself, you get the special Not a Number value. None of the integer types support these special values, so integer division by zero is always an error.

The final source of exceptions I described earlier is also the detection of certain failures by the runtime, but they work a bit differently. They are not necessarily triggered directly by anything that your code did on the thread on which the exception occurred. These are sometimes referred to as *asynchronous exceptions,* and in theory they can be thrown at literally any point in your code, making it hard to ensure that you can deal with them correctly. However, these tend to be thrown only in fairly catastrophic circumstances, often when your program is about to be shut down, so you can't normally handle them in a useful way. For example, in .NET Core, StackOver flowException and OutOfMemoryException can in theory be thrown at any point (because the CLR may need to allocate memory for its own purposes even if your code didn't do anything that explicitly attempts this).

I've described the usual situations in which exceptions are thrown, and you've seen the default behavior, but what if you want your program to do something other than crash?

Handling Exceptions

When an exception is thrown, the CLR looks for code to handle the exception. The default exception-handling behavior comes into play only if there are no suitable handlers anywhere on the entire call stack. To provide a handler, we use C#'s try and catch keywords, as Example 8-3 shows.

Example 8-3. Handling an exception

```
try
{
    using (StreamReader r = new StreamReader(@"C:\Temp\File.txt"))
    {
        while (!r.EndOfStream)
        {
            Console.WriteLine(r.ReadLine());
        }
    }
}
catch (FileNotFoundException)
{
    Console.WriteLine("Couldn't find the file");
}
```

The block immediately following the try keyword is usually known as a *try block*, and if the program throws an exception while it's inside such a block, the CLR looks for matching *catch blocks*. Example 8-3 has just a single catch block, and in the parentheses following the catch keyword, you can see that this particular block is intended to handle exceptions of type FileNotFoundException.

You saw earlier that if there is no *C:\Temp\File.txt* file, the StreamReader constructor throws a FileNotFoundException. In Example 8-1, that caused our program to crash, but because Example 8-3 has a catch block for that exception, the CLR will run that catch block. At this point, it will consider the exception to have been handled, so the program does not crash. Our catch block is free to do whatever it wants, and in this case, my code just displays a message indicating that it couldn't find the file.

Exception handlers do not need to be in the method in which the exception originated. The CLR walks up the stack until it finds a suitable handler. If the failing Stream Reader constructor call were in some other method that was called from inside the try block in Example 8-3, our catch block would still run (unless that method provided its own handler for the same exception).

Exception Objects

Exceptions are objects, and their type derives from the Exception base class.[1] This defines properties providing information about the exception, and some derived types add properties specific to the problem they represent. Your catch block can get a reference to the exception if it needs information about what went wrong. Example 8-4 shows a modification to the catch block from Example 8-3. In the parentheses after the catch keyword, as well as specifying the exception type, we also provide an identifier (x) with which code in the catch block can refer to the exception object. This enables the code to read a property specific to the FileNotFoundExcep tion class: FileName.

Example 8-4. Using the exception in a catch block

```
try
{
    // ... same code as Example 8-3 ...
}
catch (FileNotFoundException x)
{
    Console.WriteLine($"File '{x.FileName}' is missing");
}
```

This will display the name of the file that couldn't be found. With this simple program, we already knew which file we were trying to open, but you could imagine this property being helpful in a more complex program that deals with multiple files.

The general-purpose members defined by the base Exception class include the Mes sage property, which returns a string containing a textual description of the problem. The default error handling for console applications displays this. The text Could not find file 'C:\Temp\File.txt' that we saw when first running Example 8-1 came from the Message property. This property is important when you're diagnosing unexpected exceptions.

---

[1] Strictly speaking, the CLR allows any type as an exception. However, C# can throw only Exception-derived types. Some languages let you throw other types, but it is strongly discouraged. C# can handle exceptions of any type, though only because the compiler automatically sets a RuntimeCompatibility attribute on every component it produces, asking the CLR to wrap exceptions not derived from Exception in a RuntimeWrappe dException.

The Message property is intended for human consumption, so many APIs localize these messages. It is therefore a bad idea to write code that attempts to interpret an exception by inspecting the Message property, because this may well fail when your code runs on a computer configured to run in a region where the main spoken language is different than yours. (And Microsoft doesn't treat exception message changes as breaking changes, so the text might change even within the same locale.) It is best to rely on the actual exception type, although as you'll see in Chapter 15 some exceptions such as IOException get used in ambiguous ways. So you sometimes need to inspect the HResult property which will be set to an error code from the OS in such cases.

Exception also defines an InnerException property. This is often null, but it comes into play when one operation fails as a result of some other failure. Sometimes, exceptions that occur deep inside a library would make little sense if they were allowed to propagate all the way up to the caller. For example, .NET provides a library for parsing XAML files. (XAML—Extensible Application Markup Language—is used by various .NET UI frameworks, including WPF.) XAML is extensible, so it's possible that your code (or perhaps some third-party code) will run as part of the process of loading a XAML file, and this extension code could fail—suppose a bug in your code causes an IndexOutOfRangeException to be thrown while trying to access an array element. It would be somewhat mystifying for that exception to emerge from a XAML API, so regardless of the underlying cause of the failure, the library throws a XamlParseException. This means that if you want to handle the failure to load a XAML file, you know exactly which exception to handle, but the underlying cause of the failure is not lost: when some other exception caused the failure, it will be in the InnerException.

All exceptions contain information about where the exception was thrown. The StackTrace property provides the call stack as a string. As you've already seen, the default exception handler for console applications displays that. There's also a Target Site property, which tells you which method was executing. It returns an instance of the reflection API's MethodBase class. See Chapter 13 for details on reflection.

Multiple catch Blocks

A try block can be followed by multiple catch blocks. If the first catch does not match the exception being thrown, the CLR will then look at the next one, then the next, and so on. Example 8-5 supplies handlers for both FileNotFoundException and IOException.

Example 8-5. Handling multiple exception types

```
try
{
    using (StreamReader r = new StreamReader(@"C:\Temp\File.txt"))
    {
        while (!r.EndOfStream)
        {
            Console.WriteLine(r.ReadLine());
        }
    }
}
catch (FileNotFoundException x)
{
    Console.WriteLine($"File '{x.FileName}' is missing");
}
catch (IOException x)
{
    Console.WriteLine($"IO error: '{x.Message}'");
}
```

An interesting feature of this example is that `FileNotFoundException` derives from `IOException`. I could remove the first `catch` block, and this would still handle the exception correctly (just with a less specific message), because the CLR considers a `catch` block to be a match if it handles the base type of the exception. So Example 8-5 has two viable handlers for a `FileNotFoundException`, and in these cases, C# requires the more specific one to come first. If I were to swap them over so that the `IOExcep tion` handler came first, I'd get this compiler error for the `FileNotFoundException` handler:

```
error CS0160: A previous catch clause already catches all exceptions of this or
of a super type ('IOException')
```

If you write a `catch` block for the `Exception` base type, it will catch all exceptions. In most cases, this is the wrong thing to do. Unless there is some specific and useful thing you can do with an exception, you should normally let it pass. Otherwise, you risk masking a problem. If you let the exception carry on, it's more likely to get to a place where it will be noticed, increasing the chances that you will fix the problem properly at some point. A catchall handler would be appropriate if you intend to wrap all exceptions in another exception and throw that, like the `XamlParseExcep tion` described earlier. A catchall exception handler might also make sense if it's at a point where the only place left for the exception to go is the default handling supplied by the system. (That might mean the `Main` method for a console application, but for multithreaded applications, it might mean the code at the top of a newly created thread's stack.) It might be appropriate in these locations to catch all exceptions and write the details to a logfile or some similar diagnostic mechanism. Even then, once you've logged it, you would probably want to rethrow the exception, as described later in this chapter, or even terminate the process with a nonzero exit code.

 For critically important services, you might be tempted to write code that swallows the exception so that your application can limp on. This is a bad idea. If an exception you did not anticipate occurs, your application's internal state may no longer be trustworthy, because your code might have been halfway through an operation when the failure occurred. If you cannot afford for the application to go offline, the best approach is to arrange for it to restart automatically after a failure. A Windows Service can be configured to do this automatically, for example.

Exception Filters

You can make a `catch` block conditional: if you provide an *exception filter* for your catch block, it will only catch exceptions when the filter condition is true. Example 8-6 shows how this can be useful. It uses the client API for Azure Table Storage, a no-SQL storage service offered as part of Microsoft's Azure cloud computing platform. This API's `CloudTable` class has an `Execute` method that will throw a `StorageException` if something goes wrong. The problem is that "something goes wrong" is very broad, and covers more than connectivity and authentication failures. You will also see this exception for situations such as an attempt to insert a row when another row with the same keys already exists. That is not necessarily an error—it can occur as part of normal usage in some optimistic concurrency models.

Example 8-6. Catch block with exception filter

```
public static bool InsertIfDoesNotExist(MyEntity item, CloudTable table)
{
    try
    {
        table.Execute(TableOperation.Insert(item));
        return true;
    }
    catch (StorageException x)
    when (x.RequestInformation.HttpStatusCode == 409)
    {
        return false;
    }
}
```

Example 8-6 looks for that specific failure case, and returns `false` instead of allowing the exception out. It does this with a `when` clause containing a filter, which must be an expression of type `bool`. If the `Execute` method throws a `StorageException` that does not match the filter condition, the exception will propagate as usual—it will be as though the catch block were not there.

An exception filter must be an expression that produces a bool. It can invoke external methods if necessary. Example 8-6 just fetches a couple of properties and performs a comparison, but you are free to invoke any method as part of the expression.[2] However, you should be careful to avoid doing anything in your filter that might cause another exception. If that happens, it will be lost.

Nested try Blocks

If an exception occurs in a try block that does not provide a suitable handler, the CLR will keep looking. It will walk up the stack if necessary, but you can have multiple sets of handlers in a single method by nesting one try/catch inside another try block, as Example 8-7 shows. ShowFirstLineLength nests a try/catch pair inside the try block of another try/catch pair. Nesting can also be done across methods—the Main method will catch any NullReferenceException that emerges from the Show FirstLineLength method (which will be thrown if the file is completely empty—the call to ReadLine will return null in that case).

Example 8-7. Nested exception handling

```
static void Main(string[] args)
{
    try
    {
        ShowFirstLineLength(@"C:\Temp\File.txt");
    }
    catch (NullReferenceException)
    {
        Console.WriteLine("NullReferenceException");
    }
}

static void ShowFirstLineLength(string fileName)
{
    try
    {
        using (var r = new StreamReader(fileName))
        {
            try
            {
                Console.WriteLine(r.ReadLine().Length);
            }
```

---

2 Exception filters cannot use the await keyword, which is discussed in Chapter 17.

```
        catch (IOException x)
        {
            Console.WriteLine("Error while reading file: {0}",
                x.Message);
        }
    }
}
catch (FileNotFoundException x)
{
    Console.WriteLine("Couldn't find the file '{0}'", x.FileName);
}
}
```

I nested the `IOException` handler here to make it apply to one particular part of the work: it handles only errors that occur while reading the file after it has been opened successfully. It might sometimes be useful to respond to that scenario differently than for an error that prevented you from opening the file in the first place.

The cross-method handling here is somewhat contrived. The `NullReferenceExcep tion` could be avoided by testing the return value of `ReadLine` for `null`. However, the underlying CLR mechanism this illustrates is extremely important. A particular `try` block can define `catch` blocks just for those exceptions it knows how to handle, allowing others escape up to higher levels.

Letting exceptions carry on up the stack is often the right thing to do. Unless there is something useful your method can do in response to discovering an error, it's going to need to let its caller know there's a problem, so unless you want to wrap the exception in a different kind of exception, you may as well let it through.

 If you're familiar with Java, you may be wondering if C# has anything equivalent to checked exceptions. It does not. Methods do not formally declare the exceptions they throw, so there's no way the compiler can tell you if you have failed either to handle them or declare that your method might, in turn, throw them.

You can also nest a `try` block inside a `catch` block. This is important if there are ways in which your error handler itself can fail. For example, if your exception handler logs information about a failure to disk, that could fail if there's a problem with the disk.

Some `try` blocks never catch anything. It's illegal to write a `try` block that isn't followed directly by something, but that something doesn't have to be a `catch` block: it can be a *finally block*.

finally Blocks

A `finally` block contains code that always runs once its associated `try` block has finished. It runs whether execution left the `try` block simply by reaching the end, returning from the middle, or throwing an exception. The `finally` block will run even if you use a `goto` statement to jump right out of the block. Example 8-8 shows a `finally` block in use.

Example 8-8. A finally block

```
using Microsoft.Office.Interop.PowerPoint;


...

[STAThread]
static void Main(string[] args)
{
    var pptApp = new Application();
    Presentation pres = pptApp.Presentations.Open(args[0]);
    try
    {
        ProcessSlides(pres);
    }
    finally
    {
        pres.Close();
    }
}
```

This is an excerpt from a utility I wrote to process the contents of a Microsoft Office PowerPoint file. This just shows the outermost code; I've omitted the actual detailed processing code, because it's not relevant here (although if you're curious, the full version in the downloadable examples for this book exports animated slides as video clips). I'm showing it because it uses `finally`. This example uses COM interop to control the PowerPoint application. This example closes the file once it has finished, and the reason I put that code in a `finally` block is that I don't want the program to leave things open if something goes wrong partway through. This is important because of the way COM automation works. It's not like opening a file, where the OS automatically closes everything when the process terminates. If this program exits suddenly, PowerPoint will not close whatever had been opened—it just assumes that you meant to leave things open. (You might do this deliberately when creating a new document that the user will then edit.) I don't want that, and closing the file in a `finally` block is a reliable way to avoid it.

Normally, you'd write a `using` statement for this sort of thing, but PowerPoint's COM-based automation API doesn't support .NET's `IDisposable` interface. In fact, as we saw in the previous chapter, the `using` statement works in terms of `finally` blocks under the covers, as does `foreach`, so you're relying on the exception-handling system's `finally` mechanism even when you write `using` statements and `foreach` loops.

 `finally` blocks run correctly when your exception blocks are nested. If some method throws an exception that is handled by a method that's, say, five levels above it in the call stack, and if some of the methods in between were in the middle of `using` statements, `foreach` loops, or `try` blocks with associated `finally` blocks, all of these intermediate `finally` blocks (whether explicit or generated implicitly by the compiler) will execute before the handler runs.

Handling exceptions is only half of the story, of course. Your code may well detect problems, and exceptions may be an appropriate mechanism for reporting them.

Throwing Exceptions

Throwing an exception is very straightforward. You simply construct an exception object of the appropriate type, and then use the `throw` keyword. Example 8-9 does this when it is passed a `null` argument.

Example 8-9. Throwing an exception

```
public static int CountCommas(string text)
{
    if (text == null)
    {
        throw new ArgumentNullException(nameof(text));
    }
    return text.Count(ch => ch == ',');
}
```

The CLR does all of the work for us. It captures the information required for the exception to be able to report its location through properties like `StackTrace` and `TargetSite`. (It doesn't calculate their final values, because these are relatively expensive to produce. It just makes sure that it has the information it needs to be able to produce them if asked.) It then hunts for a suitable `try`/`catch` block, and if any `finally` blocks need to be run, it'll execute those.

Example 8-9 illustrates a common technique used when throwing exceptions that report a problem with a method argument. Exceptions such as `ArgumentNullException`, `ArgumentOutOfRangeException`, and their base class `ArgumentException` can all report the name of the offending argument. (This is optional because sometimes you need to report inconsistency across multiple arguments, in which case there isn't a single argument to be named.) It's a good idea to use C#'s nameof operator. You can use this with any expression that refers to a named item such as an argument, a variable, a property, or a method. It compiles into a string containing the item's name.

I could have simply used the string literal "text" here instead, but the advantages of nameof are that it can avoid silly mistakes (if I type txt instead of text, the compiler will tell me that there's no such symbol), and it can help avoid problems caused when renaming a symbol. If I were to rename the text argument in Example 8-9, I could easily forget to change a string literal to match. But by using nameof(text), I'll get an error if I change the name of the argument to, say, input, without also changing nameof(text)—the compiler will report that there is no identifier called text. If I ask Visual Studio to rename the argument, it will automatically update all the places in the code that use the symbol, so it will replace the exception's constructor argument with nameof(input) for me.

 Many exception types provide a constructor overload that lets you set the Message text. A more specialized message may make problems easier to diagnose, but there's one thing to be careful of. Exception messages often find their way into diagnostic logs, and may also be sent automatically in emails by monitoring systems. You should therefore be careful about what information you put in these messages. This is particularly important if your software will be used in countries with data protection laws—putting information in an exception message that refers in any way to a specific user can sometimes contravene those laws.

Rethrowing Exceptions

Sometimes it is useful to write a catch block that performs some work in response to an error, but allows the error to continue once that work is complete. There's an obvious but wrong way to do this, illustrated in Example 8-10.

Example 8-10. How not to rethrow an exception

```
try
{
    DoSomething();
}
catch (IOException x)
{
    LogIOError(x);
    // This next line is BAD!
    throw x;  // Do not do this
}
```

This will compile without errors, and it will even appear to work, but it has a serious problem: it loses the context in which the exception was originally thrown. The CLR treats this as a brand-new exception (even though you're reusing the exception object) and will reset the location information: the `StackTrace` and `TargetSite` will report that the error originated inside your `catch` block. This could make it hard to diagnose the problem, because you won't be able to see where it was originally thrown. Example 8-11 shows how you can avoid this problem.

Example 8-11. Rethrowing without loss of context

```
try
{
    DoSomething();
}
catch (IOException x)
{
    LogIOError(x);
    throw;
}
```

The only difference between this and Example 8-10 (aside from removing the warning comments) is that I'm using the `throw` keyword without specifying which object to use as the exception. You're allowed to do this only inside a `catch` block, and it rethrows whichever exception the `catch` block was in the process of handling. This means that the `Exception` properties that report the location from which the exception was thrown will still refer to the original throw location, not the rethrow.

 On .NET Framework (i.e., if you're not using .NET Core) Example 8-11 does not completely fix the problem. Although the point at which the exception was thrown (which happens somewhere inside the `DoSomething` method in this example) will be preserved, the part of the stack trace showing where the method in Example 8-11 had reached will not. Instead of reporting that the method had reached the line that calls to `DoSomething`, it will indicate that it was on the line containing the `throw`. The slightly strange effect of this is that the stack trace will make it look as though the `DoSomething` method was called by the `throw` keyword. .NET Core doesn't have this problem.

There is another context-related issue to be aware of when handling exceptions that you might need to rethrow that arises from how the CLR supplies information to

Windows Error Reporting[3] (WER), the component that leaps into action when an application crashes on Windows. Depending on how your machine is configured, WER might show a crash dialog that can offer options including restarting the application, reporting the crash to Microsoft, debugging the application, or just terminating it. In addition to all that, when a Windows application crashes, WER captures several pieces of information to identify the crash location. For .NET applications, this includes the name, version, and timestamp of the component that failed, and the exception type that was thrown. Furthermore, it identifies not just the method, but also the offset into that method's IL from which the exception was thrown. These pieces of information are sometimes referred to as the *bucket* values. If the application crashes twice with the same values, those two crashes go into the same bucket, meaning that they are considered to be in some sense the same crash.

Crash bucket values are not exposed as public properties of exceptions, but you can see them in the Windows event log for any exception that reached the CLR's default handler. In the Windows Event Viewer application, these log entries show up in the Application section under Windows Logs. The Source and Event ID columns for these entries will contain WER and 1001, respectively. WER reports various kinds of crashes, so if you open a WER log entry, it will contain an Event Name value. For .NET crashes, this will be CLR20r3. The assembly name and version are easy enough to spot, as is the exception type. The method is more obscure: it's on the line labeled P7, but it's just a number based on the method's *metadata token*; to find out what method that refers to, the ILDASM tool supplied with Visual Studio has a command-line option to report the metadata tokens for all your methods.

Retrieving this information from the Windows Event Log is all very well for code running on computers you control (or you might prefer to use more direct ways to monitor such applications, using systems such as Microsoft's Application Insights to collect telemetry, in which case WER is not very interesting). Where WER becomes more important is for applications that may run on other computers outside of your control, e.g., applications with a UI that run entirely locally, or console applications. Computers can be configured to upload crash reports to an error reporting service, and usually, just the bucket values get sent, although the services can request additional data if the end user consents. Bucket analysis can be useful when deciding how to prioritize bug fixes: it makes sense to start with the largest bucket, because that's the crash your users are seeing most often. (Or, at least, it's the one seen most often by users who have not disabled crash reporting. I always enable this on my computers, because I want the bugs I encounter in the programs I use to be fixed first.)

---

3 Some people refer to WER by the name of an older Windows crash reporting mechanism: Dr. Watson.

The way to get access to accumulated crash bucket data depends on the kind of application you're writing. For a line-of-business application that runs only inside your enterprise, you will probably want to run an error reporting server of your own, but if the application runs outside of your administrative control, you can use Microsoft's own crash servers. There's a certificate-based process for verifying that you are entitled to the data, but once you've jumped through the relevant hoops, Microsoft will show you all reported crashes for your applications, sorted by bucket size.

Certain exception-handling tactics can defeat the crash bucket system. If you write common error-handling code that gets involved with all exceptions, there's a risk that WER will think that your application only ever crashes inside that common handler, which would mean that crashes of all kinds would go into the same bucket. This is not inevitable, but to avoid it, you need to understand how your exception-handling code affects WER crash bucket data.

If an exception rises to the top of the stack without being handled, WER will get an accurate picture of exactly where the crash happened, but things may go wrong if you catch an exception before eventually allowing it (or some other exception) to continue up the stack. A bit surprisingly, .NET will successfully preserve the location for WER even if you use the bad approach shown in Example 8-10. (It's only from .NET perspective's inside that application that this loses the exception context—Stack Trace will show the rethrow location. So WER does not necessarily report the same crash location as .NET code will see in the exception object.) It's a similar story when you wrap an exception as the InnerException of a new one: .NET will use that inner exception's location for the crash bucket values.

This means that it's relatively easy to preserve the WER bucket. The only ways to lose the original context are either to handle the exception completely (i.e., not to crash) or to write a catch block that handles the exception and then throws a new one without passing the original one in as an InnerException.

Although Example 8-11 preserves the original context, this approach has a limitation: you can rethrow the exception only from inside the block in which you caught it. With asynchronous programming becoming more prevalent, it is increasingly common for exceptions to occur on some random worker thread. We need a reliable way to capture the full context of an exception, and to be able to rethrow it with that full context some arbitrary amount of time later, possibly from a different thread.

The ExceptionDispatchInfo class solves these problems. If you call its static Capture method from a catch block, passing in the current exception, it captures the full context, including the information required by WER. The Capture method returns an instance of ExceptionDispatchInfo. When you're ready to rethrow the exception, you can call this object's `Throw` method, and the CLR will rethrow the exception with the original context fully intact. Unlike the mechanism shown in Example 8-11, you don't need to be inside a `catch` block when you rethrow. You don't even need to be on the thread from which the exception was originally thrown.

 If you use the `async` and `await` keywords described in Chapter 17, they use `ExceptionDispatchInfo` so you can ensure that exception context is preserved correctly.

Failing Fast

Some situations call for drastic action. If you detect that your application is in a hopelessly corrupt state, throwing an exception may not be sufficient, because there's always the chance that something may handle it and then attempt to continue. This risks corrupting persistent state—perhaps the invalid in-memory state could lead to your program writing bad data into a database. It may be better to bail out immediately before you do any lasting damage.

The `Environment` class provides a `FailFast` method. If you call this, the CLR will then terminate your application. (If you're running on Windows, it will also write a message to the Windows event log and provide details to WER.) You can pass a string to be included in the event log entry, and you can also pass an exception, in which case on Windows the exception's details will also be written to the log, including the WER bucket values for the point at which the exception was thrown.

Exception Types

When your code detects a problem and throws an exception, you need to choose which type of exception to throw. You can define your own exception types, but the .NET class library defines a large number of exception types, so in a lot of situations, you can just pick an existing type. There are hundreds of exception types, so a full list would be inappropriate here; if you want to see the complete set, the online documentation for the `Exception` class lists the derived types. However, there are certain ones that it's important to know about.

The class library defines an `ArgumentException` class, which is the base of several exceptions that indicate when a method has been called with bad arguments. Example 8-9 used `ArgumentNullException`, and there's also `ArgumentOutOfRangeException`. The base `ArgumentException` defines a `ParamName` property, which contains the name of the parameter that was supplied with a bad argument. This is important for multiargument methods, because the caller will need to know which one was wrong. All these exception types have constructors that let you specify the parameter name, and you can see one of these in use in Example 8-9. The base `ArgumentExcep tion` is a concrete class, so if the argument is wrong in a way that is not covered by one of the derived types, you can just throw the base exception, providing a textual description of the problem.

Besides the general-purpose types just described, some APIs define more specialized derived argument exceptions. For example, the `System.Globalization` namespace defines an exception type called `CultureNotFoundException` that derives from `Argu mentException`. You can do something similar, and there are two reasons you might want to. If there is additional information you can supply about why the argument is invalid, you will need a custom exception type so you can attach that information to the exception. (`CultureNotFoundException` provides three properties describing aspects of the culture information for which it was searching.) Alternatively, it might be that a particular form of argument error could be handled specially by a caller. Often, an argument exception simply indicates a programming error, but in situations where it might indicate an environment or configuration problem (e.g., not having the right language packs installed), developers might want to handle that specific issue differently. Using the base `ArgumentException` would be unhelpful in that case, because it would be hard to distinguish between the particular failure they want to handle and any other problem with the arguments.

Some methods may want to perform work that could produce multiple errors. Perhaps you're running some sort of batch job, and if some individual tasks in the batch fail, you'd like to abort those but carry on with the rest, reporting all the failures at the end. For these scenarios, it's worth knowing about `AggregateException`. This extends the `InnerException` concept of the base `Exception`, adding an `InnerExcep tions` property that returns a collection of exceptions.

 If you nest work that can produce an `AggregateException` (e.g., if you run a batch within a batch), you can end up with some of your inner exceptions also being of type `AggregateException`. This exception offers a `Flatten` method; this recursively walks through any such nested exceptions and produces a single flat list with all the nesting removed, returning an `AggregateException` with that list as its `InnerExceptions`.

Another commonly used type is `InvalidOperationException`. You would throw this if someone tries to do something with your object that it cannot support in its current state. For example, suppose you have written a class that represents a request that can be sent to a server. You might design this in such a way that each instance can be used only once, so if the request has already been sent, trying to modify the request further would be a mistake, and this would be an appropriate exception to throw. Another important example is if your type implements `IDisposable`, and someone tries to use an instance after it has been disposed. That's a sufficiently common case that there's a specialized type derived from `InvalidOperationException` called `ObjectDisposedException`.

You should be aware of the distinction between `NotImplementedException` and the similar-sounding but semantically different `NotSupportedException`. The latter should be thrown when an interface demands it. For example, the `IList<T>` interface defines methods for modifying collections, but does not require collections to be modifiable—instead, it says that read-only collections should throw `NotSupportedEx ception` from members that would modify the collection. An implementation of `IList<T>` can throw this and still be considered to be complete, whereas `NotImplemen tedException` means something is missing. You will most often see this in code generated by Visual Studio. The IDE can create stub methods if you ask it to generate an interface implementation or provide an event handler. It generates this code to save you from having to type in the full method declaration, but it's still your job to implement the body of the method, so Visual Studio will often supply a method that throws this exception so that you do not accidentally leave an empty method in place.

You would normally want to remove all code that throws `NotImplementedException` before shipping, replacing it with appropriate implementations. However, there is a situation in which you might want to throw it. Suppose you've written a library containing an abstract base class, and your customers write classes that derive from this. When you release new versions of the library, you can add new methods to that base class. Now imagine that you want to add a new library feature for which it would seem to make sense to add a new abstract method to your base class. That would be a breaking change—existing code that successfully derives from the old version of the class would no longer work. You can avoid this problem by providing a virtual method instead of an abstract method, but what if there's no useful default implementation that you can provide? In that case, you might write a base implementation that throws a `NotImplementedException`. Code built against the old version of the library will not try to use the new feature, so it would never attempt to invoke the method. But if a customer tried to use the new library feature without overriding the relevant method in their class, they would then get this exception. In other words, this provides a way to enforce a requirement of the form: you must override this method if and only if you want to use the feature it represents. (You could use the same approach when adding new members to an interface if you use C# 8.0's newly added support for default interface implementations.)

There are, of course, other, more specialized exceptions in the framework, and you should always try to find an exception that matches the problem you wish to report. However, you will sometimes need to report an error for which the .NET class library does not supply a suitable exception. In this case, you will need to write your own exception class.

Custom Exceptions

The minimum requirement for a custom exception type is that it should derive from `Exception` (either directly or indirectly). However, there are some design guidelines. The first thing to consider is the immediate base class: if you look at the built-in exception types, you'll notice that many of them derive only indirectly from `Exception`, through either `ApplicationException` or `SystemException`. You should avoid both of these. They were originally introduced with the intention of distinguishing between exceptions produced by applications and ones produced by .NET. However, this did not prove to be a useful distinction. Some exceptions could be thrown by both in different scenarios, and in any case, it was not normally useful to write a handler that caught all application exceptions but not all system ones, or vice versa. The class library design guidelines now tell you to avoid these two base types.

Custom exception classes normally derive directly from `Exception`, unless they represent a specialized form of some existing exception. For example, we already saw that `ObjectDisposedException` is a special case of `InvalidOperationException`, and the class library defines several more specialized derivatives of that same base class, such as `ProtocolViolationException` for networking code. If the problem you wish your code to report is clearly an example of some existing exception type, but it still seems useful to define a more specialized type, then you should derive from that existing type.

Although the `Exception` base class has a parameterless constructor, you should not normally use it. Exceptions should provide a useful textual description of the error, so your custom exception's constructors should all call one of the `Exception` constructors that take a string. You can either hardcode the message string[4] in your derived class, or define a constructor that accepts a message, passing it on to the base class; it's common for exception types to provide both, although that might be a waste of effort if your code uses only one of the constructors. It depends on whether your exception might be thrown by other code, or just yours.

It's also common to provide a constructor that accepts another exception, which will become the `InnerException` property value. Again, if you're writing an exception entirely for your own code's use, there's not much point in adding this constructor until you need it, but if your exception is part of a reusable library, this is a common feature. Example 8-12 shows a hypothetical example that offers various constructors, along with an enumeration type that is used by the property the exception adds.

---

4 You could also consider looking up a localized string with the facilities in the `System.Resources` namespace instead of hardcoding it. The exceptions in the .NET class library all do this. It's not mandatory, because not all programs run in multiple regions, and even for those that do, exception messages will not necessarily be shown to end users.

Example 8-12. A custom exception

```
public class DeviceNotReadyException : InvalidOperationException
{
    public DeviceNotReadyException(DeviceStatus status)
        : this("Device status must be Ready", status)
    {
    }

    public DeviceNotReadyException(string message, DeviceStatus status)
        : base(message)
    {
        Status = status;
    }

    public DeviceNotReadyException(string message, DeviceStatus status,
                                   Exception innerException)
        : base(message, innerException)
    {
        Status = status;
    }

    public DeviceStatus Status { get; }
}

public enum DeviceStatus
{
    Disconnected,
    Initializing,
    Failed,
    Ready
}
```

The justification for a custom exception here is that this particular error has something more to tell us besides the fact that something was not in a suitable state. It provides information about the object's state at the moment at which the operation failed.

The .NET Framework Design Guidelines used to recommend that exceptions be serializable. Historically, this was to enable them to cross between *appdomains*. An appdomain is an isolated execution context; however, they are now deprecated because they are not supported in .NET Core. That said, there are still some application types in which serialization of exceptions is interesting, most notably microservice-based architectures such as those running on Akka.NET (see *https://github.com/akkadot net/akka.net*) or Microsoft Service Fabric, in which a single application runs across multiple processes, often spread across many different machines. By making an exception serializable, you make it possible for the exception to cross process boundaries—the original exception object cannot be used directly across the boundary, but serialization enables a copy of the exception to be built in the target process.

So although serialization is no longer recommended for all exception types, it is useful for exceptions that may be used in these kinds of multiprocess environments. Most exception types in .NET Core continue to support serialization for this reason. If you don't need to support this, your exceptions don't have to be made serializable, but since it's fairly common to do so, I'll describe the changes you would need to make. First, you would need to add the [Serializable] attribute in front of the class declaration. Then, you'd need to override a method defined by Exception that handles serialization. Finally, you must provide a special constructor to be used when deserializing your type. Example 8-13 shows the members you would need to add to make the custom exception in Example 8-12 support serialization. The GetObject Data method simply stores the current value of the exception's Status property in a name/value container supplied during serialization. It retrieves this value in the constructor that gets called during deserialization.

Example 8-13. Adding serialization support

```
public override void GetObjectData(SerializationInfo info,
                                   StreamingContext context)
{
    base.GetObjectData(info, context);
    info.AddValue("Status", Status);
}

protected DeviceNotReadyException(SerializationInfo info,
                                  StreamingContext context)
    : base(info, context)
{
    Status = (DeviceStatus) info.GetValue("Status", typeof(DeviceStatus));
}
```

Unhandled Exceptions

Earlier, you saw the default behavior that a console application exhibits when your application throws an exception that it does not handle. It displays the exception's type, message, and stack trace and then terminates the process. This happens whether the exception went unhandled on the main thread or a thread you created explicitly, or even a thread pool thread that the CLR created for you.

Be aware that there have been a couple of changes to unhandled exception behavior over the years which still have some relevance because you can optionally re-enable the old behavior. Before .NET 2.0, threads created for you by the CLR would swallow exceptions without reporting them or crashing. You may occasionally encounter old applications that still rely on this: if the application has a .NET Framework-style configuration file (the XML kind, which I showed in Chapter 7 to configure the GC) that contains a legacyUnhandledExceptionPolicy element with an enabled="1" attribute, the old .NET v1 behavior returns, meaning that unhandled exceptions can vanish silently. .NET 4.5 moved in the opposite direction for one feature. If you use the Task class (described in Chapter 16) to run concurrent work instead of using threads or the thread pool directly, any unhandled exceptions inside tasks would once have terminated the process, but as of .NET 4.5, they no longer do by default. You can revert to the old behavior through the configuration file. (See Chapter 16 for details.)

The CLR provides a way to discover when unhandled exceptions reach the top of the stack. The AppDomain class provides an UnhandledException event, which the CLR raises when this happens on any thread.[5] I'll be describing events in Chapter 9, but jumping ahead a little, Example 8-14 shows how to handle this event. It also throws an unhandled exception to try the handler out.

Example 8-14. Unhandled exception notifications

```
static void Main(string[] args)
{
    AppDomain.CurrentDomain.UnhandledException += OnUnhandledException;

    // Crash deliberately to illustrate the UnhandledException event
    throw new InvalidOperationException();
}

private static void OnUnhandledException(object sender,
    UnhandledExceptionEventArgs e)
{
    Console.WriteLine($"An exception went unhandled: {e.ExceptionObject}");
}
```

When the handler is notified, it's too late to stop the exception—the CLR will terminate the process shortly after calling your handler. The main reason this event exists is to provide a place to put logging code so that you can record some information about the failure for diagnostic purposes. In principle, you could also attempt to store any unsaved data to facilitate recovery if the program restarts, but you should be careful: if your unhandled exception handler gets called, then by definition your program is in a suspect state, so whatever data you save may be invalid.

Some application frameworks provide their own ways to deal with unhandled exceptions. For example, UI frameworks (e.g., Windows Forms or WPF) for desktop applications for Windows do this, partly because the default behavior of writing details to

---

5 Although .NET Core does not support the creation of new appdomains, it does still provide the AppDomain class, because it exposes certain important features, such as this event. It will provide a single instance via AppDomain.CurrentDomain.

the console is not very useful for applications that don't show a console window. These applications need to run a message loop to respond to user input and system messages. It inspects each message and may decide to call one or more methods in your code, in which case it wraps each call in a `try` block so that it can catch any exceptions your code may throw. The frameworks may show error information in a window instead. And web frameworks, such as ASP.NET Core, need a different mechanism: at a minimum, they should generate a response that indicates a server-side error in the way recommended by the HTTP specification.

This means that the `UnhandledException` event that Example 8-14 uses may not be raised when an unhandled exception escapes from your code, because it may be caught by a framework. If you are using an application framework, you should check to see if it provides its own mechanism for dealing with unhandled exceptions. For example, ASP.NET Core applications can supply a callback to a method called `UseEx ceptionHandler`. WPF has its own `Application` class, and its `DispatcherUnhandle dException` event is the one to use. Likewise, Windows Forms provides an `Application` class with a `ThreadException` member.

Even when you're using these frameworks, their unhandled exception mechanisms deal only with exceptions that occur on threads the frameworks control. If you create a new thread and throw an unhandled exception on that, it would show up in the `AppDomain` class's `UnhandledException` event, because frameworks don't control the whole CLR.

Summary

In .NET, errors are usually reported with exceptions, apart from in certain scenarios where failure is expected to be common and the cost of exceptions is likely to be high compared to the cost of the work at hand. Exceptions allow error-handling code to be separate from code that does work. They also make it hard to ignore errors—unexpected errors will propagate up the stack and eventually cause the program to terminate and produce an error report. `catch` blocks allow us to handle those exceptions that we can anticipate. (You can also use them to catch all exceptions indiscriminately, but that's usually a bad idea—if you don't know why a particular exception occurred, you cannot know for certain how to recover from it safely.) `finally` blocks provide a way to perform cleanup safely regardless of whether code executes successfully or encounters exceptions. The .NET class library defines numerous useful exception types, but if necessary, we can write our own.

In the chapters so far, we've looked at the basic elements of code, classes and other custom types, collections, and error handling. There's one last feature of the C# type system to look at: a special kind of object called a *delegate*.

CHAPTER 9

Delegates, Lambdas, and Events

The most common way to use an API is to invoke the methods and properties its classes provide, but sometimes, things need to work in reverse—the API may need to call your code. In Chapter 5, I showed the search features offered by arrays and lists. To use these, I wrote a method that returned `true` when its argument met my criteria, and the relevant APIs called my method for each item they inspected. Not all callbacks are immediate. Asynchronous APIs can call a method in our code when long-running work completes. In a client-side application, I want my code to run when the user interacts with certain visual elements in particular ways, such as clicking a button.

Interfaces and virtual methods can enable callbacks. In Chapter 4, I showed the `IComparer<T>` interface, which defines a single `CompareTo` method. This is called by methods like `Array.Sort` when we want a customized sort ordering. You could imagine a UI framework that defined an `IClickHandler` interface with a `Click` method, and perhaps also `DoubleClick`. The framework could require us to implement this interface if we want to be notified of button clicks.

In fact, none of .NET's UI frameworks use the interface-based approach, because it gets cumbersome when you need multiple kinds of callback. Single- and double-clicks are the tip of the iceberg for user interactions—in WPF applications, each UI element can provide over 100 kinds of notifications. Most of the time, you need to handle only one or two events from any particular element, so an interface with 100 methods to implement would be annoying.

Splitting notifications across multiple interfaces could mitigate this inconvenience. Also, C# 8.0's support for default interface implementations could help, because it would make it possible to provide default, empty implementations for all callbacks, meaning we'd need to override only the ones we were interested in. (If you need to target runtimes older than .NET Core 3.0, the first to support this feature, you could supply a base class with virtual methods instead.) But even with these improvements, there's a serious drawback with this object-oriented approach. Imagine a UI with four buttons. In a hypothetical UI framework that used the approach I've just described, if you wanted different Click handler methods for each button, you'd need four distinct implementations of the IClickHandler interface. A single class can implement any particular interface only once, so you'd need to write four classes. That seems very cumbersome when all we really want to do is tell a button to call a particular method when clicked.

C# provides a much simpler solution in the form of a *delegate*, which is a reference to a method. If you want a library to call your code back for any reason, you will normally just pass a delegate referring to the method you'd like it to call. I showed an example of that in Chapter 5, which I've reproduced in Example 9-1. This finds the index of the first nonzero element in an int[] array.

Example 9-1. Searching an array using a delegate

```
public static int GetIndexOfFirstNonEmptyBin(int[] bins) =>
    Array.FindIndex(bins, IsGreaterThanZero);

private static bool IsGreaterThanZero(int value) => value > 0;
```

At first glance, this seems very simple: the second parameter to Array.FindIndex requires a method that it can call to ask whether a particular element is a match, so I passed my IsGreaterThanZero method as an argument. But what does it really mean to pass a method, and how does this fit in with .NET's type system, the CTS?

Delegate Types

Example 9-2 shows the declaration of the FindIndex method used in Example 9-1. The first parameter is the array to be searched, but it's the second one we're interested in—that's where I passed a method.

Example 9-2. Method with a delegate parameter

```
public static int FindIndex<T>(
    T[] array,
    Predicate<T> match)
```

The method's second argument's type is Predicate<T>, where T is the array element type, and since Example 9-1 uses an int[], that will be a Predicate<int>. (In case you don't have a background in either formal logic or computer science, this type uses the word *predicate* in the sense of a function that determines whether something is true or false. For example, you could have a predicate that tells you whether a number is even. Predicates are often used in this kind of filtering operation.) Example 9-3 shows how this type is defined. This is the whole of the definition, not an excerpt; if you wanted to write a type that was equivalent to Predicate<T>, that's all you'd need to write.

Example 9-3. The Predicate<T> delegate type

```
public delegate bool Predicate<in T>(T obj);
```

Breaking Example 9-3 down, we begin as usual with type definitions, with the accessibility, and we can use all the same keywords we could for other types, such as `pub lic` or `internal`. (Like any type, delegate types can optionally be nested inside some other type, so you can also use `private` or `protected`.) Next is the `delegate` keyword, which just tells the C# compiler that we're defining a delegate type. The rest of the definition looks, not coincidentally, just like a method declaration. We have a return type of `bool`. You put the delegate type name where you'd normally see the method name. The angle brackets indicate that this is a generic type with a single type argument `T`, and the `in` keyword indicates that `T` is contravariant. (Chapter 6 described contravariance.) Finally, the method signature has a single parameter of that type.

Delegates are special types in .NET, and they work quite differently than classes or structs. The compiler generates a superficially normal-looking class definition with various members that we'll look at in more detail later, but the members are all empty —C# produces no IL for any of them. The CLR provides the implementation at runtime.

Instances of delegate types are usually just called delegates, and they refer to methods. A method is compatible with (i.e., can be referred to by an instance of) a particular delegate type if its signature matches. The `IsGreaterThanZero` method in Example 9-1 takes an `int` and returns a `bool`, so it is compatible with `Predi cate<int>`. The match does not have to be precise. If implicit reference conversions are available for parameter types, you can use a more general method. (This has nothing to do with `T` being contravariant. Variance makes certain implicit reference conversions available between delegate types instantiated from the same unbound generic delegate with different type arguments. Here we're discussing the range of method signatures acceptable for a single delegate type.) For example, a method with a return type of `bool`, and a single parameter of type `object`, would be compatible with `Predicate<object>`, but because such a method can accept `string` arguments, it would also be compatible with `Predicate<string>`. (It would not be compatible with `Predicate<int>`, because there's no implicit reference conversion from `int` to `object`. There's an implicit conversion, but it's a boxing conversion, not a reference conversion.)

Creating a Delegate

You can use the new keyword to create a delegate. Where you'd normally pass constructor arguments, you can supply the name of a compatible method. Example 9-4 constructs a Predicate<int>, so it needs a method with a bool return type that takes an int, and as we've just seen, the IsGreaterThanZero method in Example 9-1 fits the bill. (You could write this code only where IsGreaterThanZero is in scope—that is, inside the same class.)

Example 9-4. Constructing a delegate

```
var p = new Predicate<int>(IsGreaterThanZero);
```

In practice, we rarely use new for delegates. It's necessary only in cases where the compiler cannot infer the delegate type. Expressions that refer to methods are unusual in that they have no innate type—the expression IsGreaterThanZero is compatible with Predicate<int>, but there are other compatible delegate types. You could define your own nongeneric delegate type that takes an int and returns a bool. Later in this chapter, I'll show the Func family of delegate types; you could store a reference to IsGreaterThanZero in a Func<int, bool> delegate. So IsGreaterThan Zero does not have a type of its own, which is why the compiler needs to know which particular delegate type we want. Example 9-4 assigns the delegate into a variable declared with var, which tells the compiler nothing about what type to use, and that is why I've had to tell it explicitly with the constructor syntax.

In cases where the compiler knows what type is required, it can implicitly convert the method name to the target delegate type. Example 9-5 declares the variable with an explicit type, so the compiler knows a Predicate<int> is required. This compiles to the same code as Example 9-4. Example 9-1 relies on the same mechanism—the compiler knows that the second argument to FindIndex is Predicate<T>, and because we supply a first argument of type int[], it deduces that T is int, so it knows the second argument's full type is Predicate<int>. Having worked that out, it uses the same built-in implicit conversion rules to construct the delegate as Example 9-5.

Example 9-5. Implicit delegate construction

```
Predicate<int> p = IsGreaterThanZero;
```

When code refers to a method by name like this, the name is technically called a *method group*, because multiple overloads may exist for a single name. The compiler narrows this down by looking for the best possible match, in a similar way to how it chooses an overload when you invoke a method. As with method invocation, it is

---

possible that there will be either no matches or multiple equally good matches, and in these cases the compiler will produce an error.

Method groups can take several forms. In the examples shown so far, I have used an unqualified method name, which works only when the method in question is in scope. If you want to refer to a static method defined in some other class, you would need to qualify it with the class name, as Example 9-6 shows.

Example 9-6. Delegates to methods in another class

```
internal class Program
{
    static void Main(string[] args)
    {
        Predicate<int> p1 = Tests.IsGreaterThanZero;
        Predicate<int> p2 = Tests.IsLessThanZero;
    }
}

internal class Tests
{
    public static bool IsGreaterThanZero(int value) => value > 0;

    public static bool IsLessThanZero(int value) => value < 0;
}
```

Delegates don't have to refer to static methods. They can refer to an instance method. There are a couple of ways you can make that happen. One is simply to refer to an instance method by name from a context in which that method is in scope. The GetIsGreaterThanPredicate method in Example 9-7 returns a delegate that refers to IsGreaterThan. Both are instance methods, so they can be used only with an object reference, but GetIsGreaterThanPredicate has an implicit this reference, and the compiler automatically provides that to the delegate that it implicitly creates.

Example 9-7. Implicit instance delegate

```
public class ThresholdComparer
{
    public int Threshold { get; set; }

    public bool IsGreaterThan(int value) => value > Threshold;

    public Predicate<int> GetIsGreaterThanPredicate() => IsGreaterThan;
}
```

Alternatively, you can be explicit about which instance you want. Example 9-8 creates three instances of the `ThresholdComparer` class from Example 9-7, and then creates three delegates referring to the `IsGreaterThan` method, one for each instance.

Example 9-8. Explicit instance delegate

```
var zeroThreshold = new ThresholdComparer { Threshold = 0 };
var tenThreshold = new ThresholdComparer { Threshold = 10 };
var hundredThreshold = new ThresholdComparer { Threshold = 100 };

Predicate<int> greaterThanZero = zeroThreshold.IsGreaterThan;
Predicate<int> greaterThanTen = tenThreshold.IsGreaterThan;
Predicate<int> greaterThanOneHundred = hundredThreshold.IsGreaterThan;
```

You don't have to limit yourself to simple expressions of the form *variable Name.MethodName*. You can take any expression that evaluates to an object reference, and then just append *.MethodName*; if the object has one or more methods called *Meth odName*, that will be a valid method group.

I've shown only single-argument delegates so far, but you can define delegate types with any number of arguments. For example, the class library defines `Comparison<T>`, which compares two items, and therefore takes two arguments (both of type `T`).

C# will not let you create a delegate that refers to an instance method without specifying either implicitly or explicitly which instance you mean, and it will always initialize the delegate with that instance.

When you pass a delegate to some other code, that code does not need to know whether the delegate's target is a static or an instance method. And for instance methods, the code that uses the delegate does not supply the instance. Delegates that refer to instance methods always know which instance they refer to, as well as which method.

There's another way to create a delegate that can be useful if you do not necessarily know which method or object you will use until runtime: you can use the reflection API (which I will explain in detail in Chapter 13). First, you obtain a `MethodInfo`, an object representing a particular method. Then you call its `CreateDelegate` method, passing the delegate type and, where required, the target object. (If you're creating a delegate referring to a static method, there is no target object, so there's an overload that takes only the delegate type.) This will create a delegate referring to whichever method the `MethodInfo` instance identifies. Example 9-9 uses this technique. It obtains a Type object (also part of the reflection API; it's a way to refer to a particular type) representing the ThresholdComparer class. Next, it asks it for a MethodInfo representing the IsGreaterThan method. On this, it calls the overload of CreateDele gate that takes the delegate type and the target instance.

Example 9-9. CreateDelegate

```
MethodInfo m = typeof(ThresholdComparer).GetMethod("IsGreaterThan");
var greaterThanZero = (Predicate<int>) m.CreateDelegate(
    typeof(Predicate<int>), zeroThreshold);
```

There is another way to perform the same job: the Delegate type has a static Create Delegate method, which avoids the need to obtain the MethodInfo. You pass it two type objects—the delegate type and the type defining the target method—and also the method name. If you already have a MethodInfo to hand, you may as well use that, but if all you have is the name, this alternative is more convenient.

So a delegate identifies a specific function, and if that's an instance function, the delegate also contains an object reference. But some delegates do more.

Multicast Delegates

If you look at any delegate type with a reverse-engineering tool such as ILDASM,[1] you'll see that whether it's a type supplied by the .NET class library or one you've defined yourself, it derives from a base type called MulticastDelegate. As the name suggests, this means delegates can refer to more than one method. This is mostly of interest in notification scenarios where you may need to invoke multiple methods when some event occurs. However, all delegates support this whether you need it or not.

Even delegates with non-void return types derive from MulticastDelegate. That doesn't usually make much sense. For example, code that requires a Predicate<T> will normally inspect the return value. Array.FindIndex uses it to find out whether an element matches our search criteria. If a single delegate refers to multiple methods, what's FindIndex supposed to do with multiple return values? As it happens, it will execute all the methods, but will ignore the return values of all except the final method that runs. (As you'll see in the next section, that's the default behavior you get if you don't provide special handling for multicast delegates.)

The multicast feature is available through the Delegate class's static Combine method. This takes any two delegates and returns a single delegate. When the resulting

---

1 ILDASM ships with Visual Studio. At the time of writing Microsoft doesn't provide a cross-platform version, but open source alternatives are available.

pass[<span class="keep-together">delegate</span>] is invoked, it is as though you invoked the two original delegates one after the other. This works even when the delegates you pass to `Combine` already refer to multiple methods—you can chain together ever larger multicast delegates. If the same method is referred to in both arguments, the resulting combined delegate will invoke it twice.

 Delegate combination always produces a new delegate. The `Com` `bine` method does not modify either of the delegates you pass it.

In fact, we rarely call `Delegate.Combine` explicitly, because C# has built-in support for combining delegates. You can use the + or += operators. Example 9-10 shows both, combining the three delegates from Example 9-8 into a single multicast delegate. The two resulting delegates are equivalent—this just shows two ways of writing the same thing. Both cases compile into a couple of calls to `Delegate.Combine`.

Example 9-10. Combining delegates

```
Predicate<int> megaPredicate1 =
    greaterThanZero + greaterThanTen + greaterThanOneHundred;

Predicate<int> megaPredicate2 = greaterThanZero;
megaPredicate2 += greaterThanTen;
megaPredicate2 += greaterThanOneHundred;
```

You can also use the - or -= operators, which produce a new delegate that is a copy of the first operand, but with its last reference to the method referred to by the second operand removed. As you might guess, this turns into a call to `Delegate.Remove`.

Delegate removal behaves in a potentially surprising way if the delegate you remove refers to multiple methods. Subtraction of a multicast delegate succeeds only if the delegate from which you are subtracting contains all of the methods in the delegate being subtracted *sequentially and in the same order*. (The operation is effectively looking for one exact match for its input, rather than removing each of the items contained by its input.) Given the delegates in Example 9-10, subtracting (greaterThanTen + greaterThanOneHundred) from megaPredicate1 would work, but subtracting (greaterThanZero + greaterThanOneHundred) would not. Although megaPredicate1 contains references to the same two methods and in the same order, the sequence is not the same, because megaPredicate1 has an additional delegate in the middle. So it can sometimes be simpler to avoid removing multicast delegates—removing handlers one at a time avoids these problems.

Invoking a Delegate

So far, I've shown how to create a delegate, but what if you're writing your own API that needs to call back into a method supplied by your caller? First, you would need to pick a delegate type. You could use one supplied by the class library or, if necessary, you can define your own. You can use this delegate type for a method parameter or a property. Example 9-11 shows what to do when you want to call the method (or methods) the delegate refers to.

Example 9-11. Invoking a delegate

```
public static void CallMeRightBack(Predicate<int> userCallback)
{
    bool result = userCallback(42);
    Console.WriteLine(result);
}
```

As this not terribly realistic example shows, you can use an argument of delegate type as though it were a function. This also works for local variables, fields, and properties. In fact, any expression that produces a delegate can be followed by an argument list in parentheses. The compiler will generate code that invokes the delegate. If the delegate has a non-void return type, the invocation expression's value will be whatever the underlying method returns (or, in the case of a delegate referring to multiple methods, whatever the final method returns).

Although delegates are special types with runtime-generated code, there is ultimately nothing magical about invoking them. The call happens on the same thread, and exceptions propagate through methods that were invoked via a delegate in exactly the same way as they would if the method were invoked directly. Invoking a delegate with a single target method works as though your code had called the target method in the conventional way. Invoking a multicast delegate is just like calling each of its target methods in turn.

If you want to get all the return values from a multicast delegate, you can take control of the invocation process. Example 9-12 retrieves an *invocation list* for a delegate, which is an array containing a single-method delegate for each of the methods to which the original multicast delegate refers. If the original delegate contained only a single method, this list will contain just that one delegate, but if the multicast feature is being exploited, this provides a way to invoke each in turn. This enables the example to look at what each individual predicate says.

 Example 9-12 relies on a trick with foreach. The GetInvocation List method returns an array of type Delegate[]. The foreach loop nonetheless specifies an iteration variable type of Predi cate<int>. This causes the compiler to generate a loop that casts each item to that type as it retrieves it from the collection. You should only do this if you're sure the items are of that type, because it will throw an exception at runtime if you're wrong.

Example 9-12. Invoking each delegate individually

```
public static void TestForMajority(Predicate<int> userCallbacks)
{
    int trueCount = 0;
    int falseCount = 0;
    foreach (Predicate<int> p in userCallbacks.GetInvocationList())
    {
        bool result = p(42);
        if (result)
        {
            trueCount += 1;
        }
        else
        {
            falseCount += 1;
        }
    }
    if (trueCount > falseCount)
    {
        Console.WriteLine("The majority returned true");
    }
    else if (falseCount > trueCount)
    {
        Console.WriteLine("The majority returned false");
    }
    else
    {
```

```
        Console.WriteLine("It's a tie");
    }
}
```

There is one more way to invoke a delegate that is occasionally useful. The base Dele
gate class provides a DynamicInvoke method. You can call this on a delegate of any
type without needing to know at compile time exactly what arguments are required.
It takes a params array of type object[], so you can pass any number of arguments.
It will verify the number and type of arguments at runtime. This can enable certain
late binding scenarios, although the intrinsic dynamic features (discussed in Chapter 2) added in C# 4.0 are more comprehensive. However, the dynamic keyword is
slightly more heavyweight due to its extra flexiblity, so if DynamicInvoke does precisely what you need, it is the better choice.

Common Delegate Types

The .NET class library provides several useful delegate types, and you will often be
able to use these instead of needing to define your own. For example, it defines a set
of generic delegates named Action with varying numbers of type parameters. These
all follow a common pattern: for each type parameter, there's a single method parameter of that type. Example 9-13 shows the first four, including the zero-argument
form.

Example 9-13. The first few Action delegates

```
public delegate void Action();
public delegate void Action<in T1>(T1 arg1);
public delegate void Action<in T1, in T2 >(T1 arg1, T2 arg2);
public delegate void Action<in T1, in T2, in T3>(T1 arg1, T2 arg2, T3 arg3);
```

Although this is clearly an open-ended concept—you could imagine delegates of this
form with any number of arguments—the CTS does not provide a way to define this
sort of type as a pattern, so the class library has to define each form as a separate type.
Consequently, there is no 200-argument form of Action. The upper limit is 16 arguments.

The obvious limitation with Action is that these types have a void return type, so
they cannot refer to methods that return values. But there's a similar family of delegate types, Func, that allows any return type. Example 9-14 shows the first few delegates in this family, and as you can see, they're pretty similar to Action. They just get
an additional final type parameter, TResult, which specifies the return type. As with
Action<T>, you can go up to 16 arguments.

Example 9-14. The first few Func delegates

```
public delegate TResult Func<out TResult>();
public delegate TResult Func<in T1, out TResult>(T1 arg1);
public delegate TResult Func<in T1, in T2, out TResult>(T1 arg1, T2 arg2);
public delegate TResult Func<in T1, in T2, in T3, out TResult>(
    T1 arg1, T2 arg2, T3 arg3);
```

These two families of delegates would appear to have most requirements covered. Unless you're writing monster methods with more than 16 arguments, when would you ever need anything else? Why does the class library define a separate `Predi cate<T>` when it could just use `Func<T, bool>` instead? In some cases, the answer is history: many delegate types have been around since before these general-purposes types were added. But that's not the only reason—new delegate types continue to be added even now. The main reason is that sometimes it's useful to define a specialized delegate type to indicate particular semantics. Also, if you need a delegate that can work with `ref` or `out` arguments, you'll have to write a matching delegate type.

If you have a `Func<T, bool>`, all you know is that you've got a method that takes a `T` and returns a `bool`. But with a `Predicate<T>`, there's an implied meaning: it makes a decision about that `T` instance, and returns `true` or `false` accordingly; not all methods that take a single argument and return a `bool` necessarily fit that pattern. By providing a `Predicate<T>`, you're not just saying that you have a method with a particular signature, you're saying you have a method that serves a particular purpose. For example, `HashSet<T>` (described in Chapter 5) has an `Add` method that takes a single argument and returns a `bool`, so it matches the signature of `Predi cate<T>` but not the semantics. `Add`'s main job is to perform an action with side effects, returning some information about what it did, whereas predicates just tell you something about a value or object. (As it happens, `Predicate<T>` was introduced before `Func<T, bool>`, so history is part of the reason some APIs use it. However, semantics still matter—there are some newer APIs for which `Func<T, bool>` was an option that nonetheless opted for `Predicate<T>`.)

Since C# 7 introduced `ref struct` types, there has been another reason to define a custom delegate type: you cannot use a `ref struct` as a generic type argument. (Chapter 18 discusses these types.) So if you try to instantiate the generic `Action<T>` type with `Span<int>`, which is a `ref struct` type, by writing `Action<Span<int>>`, you will get a compiler error. The reason for this is that `ref struct` types can only be used in certain scenarios (they must always live on the stack), and there's no way to determine whether any particular generic type or method uses its type arguments only in the ways that are allowed. (You could imagine a new kind of type argument constraint that expressed this, but at the time of writing this, no such constraint exists.) So if you want a delegate type that can refer to a method that takes a `ref struct` argument, it needs to be a dedicated, nongeneric delegate.

The .NET class library defines many delegate types, most of them even more specialized than `Predicate<T>`. For example, the `System.IO` namespace and its descendants define several that relate to specific events, such as `SerialPinChangedEventHandler`, which is used only when you're working with old-fashioned serial ports such as the once-ubiquitous RS232 interface.

Type Compatibility

Delegate types do not derive from one another. Any delegate type you define in C# will derive directly from `MulticastDelegate`, as do all of the delegate types in the class library. However, the type system supports certain implicit reference conversions for generic delegate types through covariance and contravariance. The rules are very similar to those for interfaces. As the `in` keyword in Example 9-3 showed, the type argument `T` in `Predicate<T>` is contravariant, which means that if an implicit reference conversion exists between two types, A and B, an implicit reference conversion also exists between the types `Predicate<B>` and `Predicate<A>`. Example 9-15 shows an implicit conversion that this enables.

Example 9-15. Delegate covariance

```
public static bool IsLongString(object o)
{
    return o is string s && s.Length > 20;
}

static void Main(string[] args)
{
    Predicate<object> po = IsLongString;
    Predicate<string> ps = po;
    Console.WriteLine(ps("Too short"));
}
```

The `Main` method first creates a `Predicate<object>` referring to the `IsLongString` method. Any target method for this predicate type is capable of inspecting any `object` of any kind; thus, it's clearly able to meet the needs of code that requires a predicate capable of inspecting strings, so it makes sense that the implicit conversion to `Predicate<string>` should succeed—which it does, thanks to contravariance. Covariance also works in the same way as it does with interfaces, so it would typically be associated with a delegate's return type. (We denote covariant type parameters with the `out` keyword.) All of the built-in `Func` delegate types have a covariant type argument representing the function's return type called `TResult`. The type parameters for the function's parameters are all contravariant, as are all of the type arguments for the `Action` delegate types.

The variance-based delegate conversions are implicit reference conversions. This means that when you convert the reference, the result still refers to the same delegate instance. (All implicit reference conversions have this characteristic, but not all implicit conversions work this way. Implicit numeric conversions create a new instance of the target type; implicit boxing conversions create a new box on the heap.) So in Example 9-15, po and ps refer to the same delegate on the heap. This is subtly different from assigning IsLongString into both variables—that would create two delegates of different types.

You might also expect delegates that look the same to be compatible. For example, a Predicate<int> can refer to any method that a Func<int, bool> can use, and vice versa, so you might expect an implicit conversion to exist between these two types. You might be further encouraged by the "Delegate compatibility" section in the C# specification, which says that delegates with identical parameter lists and return types are compatible. (In fact, it goes further, saying that certain differences are allowed. For example, I mentioned earlier that argument types may be different as long as certain implicit reference conversions are available.) However, if you try the code in Example 9-16, it won't work.

Example 9-16. Illegal delegate conversion

```
Predicate<string> pred = IsLongString;
Func<string, bool> f = pred;  // Will fail with compiler error
```

An explicit cast doesn't work either—adding one avoids the compiler error, but you'll just get a runtime error instead. The CTS considers these to be incompatible types, so a variable declared with one delegate type cannot hold a reference to a different delegate type even if their method signatures are compatible (except for when the two delegate types in question are based on the same generic delegate type, and are compatible thanks to covariance or contravariance). This is not the scenario for which C#'s delegate compatibility rules are designed—they are mainly used to determine whether a particular method can be the target for a particular delegate type.

The lack of type compatibility between "compatible" delegate types may seem odd, but structurally identical delegate types don't necessarily have the same semantics, as we've already seen with Predicate<T> and Func<T,bool>. If you find yourself needing to perform this sort of conversion, it may be a sign that something is not quite right in your code's design.[2]

---

2 Alternatively, you may just be one of nature's dynamic language enthusiasts, with an allergy to expressing semantics through static types. If that's the case, C# may not be the language for you.

That said, it is possible to create a new delegate that refers to the same method as the original if the new type is compatible with the old type. It's always best to stop and ask why you find yourself needing to do that, but it's occasionally necessary, and at first glance, it seems simple. Example 9-17 shows one way to do it. However, as the remainder of this section shows, it's a bit more complex than it looks, and this is not actually the most efficient solution (which is another reason you might want to see if you can modify the design to avoid needing to do this in the first place).

Example 9-17. A delegate referring to another delegate

```
Predicate<string> pred = IsLongString;
var pred2 = new Func<string, bool>(pred); // Less efficient than
                                          // a direct reference
```

The problem with Example 9-17 is that it adds an unnecessary level of indirection. The second delegate does not refer to the same method as the first one, it actually refers to the first delegate—so instead of a delegate that's a reference to IsLong String, the pred2 variable ends up referring to a delegate that is a reference to a delegate that is a reference to IsLongString. This is because the compiler treats Example 9-17 as though you had written the code in Example 9-18. (All delegate types have an Invoke method. It is implemented by the CLR, and it does the work necessary to invoke all of the methods to which the delegate refers.)

Example 9-18. A delegate explicitly referring to another delegate

```
Predicate<string> pred = IsLongString;
var pred2 = new Func<string, bool>(pred.Invoke);
```

In either Example 9-17 or 9-18, when you invoke the second delegate through the pred2 variable, it will in turn invoke the delegate referred to by pred, which will end up invoking the IsLongString method. The right method gets called, just not as directly as we might like. If you know that the delegate refers to a single method (i.e., you're not using the multicast capability), Example 9-19 produces a more direct result.

Example 9-19. New delegate for the current target

```
Predicate<string> pred = IsLongString;
var pred2 = (Func<string, bool>) pred.Method.CreateDelegate(
    typeof(Func<string, bool>), pred.Target);
```

This retrieves the MethodInfo representing the target method from the pred delegate and passes it the required delegate type and the pred delegate's target to create a new Func<string, bool> delegate. The result is a new delegate that refers directly to the same `IsLongString` method as `pred`. (The `Target` will be `null` because this is a static method, but I'm still passing it to `CreateDelegate`, because I want to show code that works for both static and instance methods.) If you need to deal with multicast delegates, Example 9-19 won't work, because it presumes that there's only one target method. You would need to call `CreateDelegate` in a similar way for each item in the invocation list. This isn't a scenario that comes up very often, but for completeness, Example 9-20 shows how it's done.

Example 9-20. Converting a multicast delegate

```
public static TResult DuplicateDelegateAs<TResult>(MulticastDelegate source)
    where TResult : Delegate
{
    Delegate result = null;
    foreach (Delegate sourceItem in source.GetInvocationList())
    {
        var copy = sourceItem.Method.CreateDelegate(
            typeof(TResult), sourceItem.Target);
        result = Delegate.Combine(result, copy);
    }

    return (TResult) (object) result;
}
```

In Example 9-20, the argument for the `TResult` type parameter has to be a delegate, so I have specified a corresponding constraint for this type parameter. Note that C# did not allow a constraint of this kind to be expressed until C# 7.3, so if you encounter code that seems like it should specify a constraint of this kind, but which does not, that may be why.

These last few examples have depended upon various members of delegate types: `Target`, `Method`, and `Invoke`. The first two come from the `Delegate` class, which is the base class of `MulticastDelegate`, from which all delegate types derive. The `Target` property's type is `object`. It will be `null` if the delegate refers to a static method; otherwise, it will refer to the instance on which the method will be invoked. The `Method` property returns a `MethodInfo` identifying the target method. The third member, `Invoke`, is generated by the compiler. This is one of a few standard members that the C# compiler produces when you define a delegate type.

Behind the Syntax

Although it takes just a single line of code to define a delegate type (as Example 9-3 showed), the compiler turns this into a type that defines three methods and a constructor. Of course, the type also inherits members from its base classes. All delegates derive from `MulticastDelegate`, although all of the interesting instance members come from its base class, `Delegate`. (`Delegate` inherits from `object`, so delegates all have the ubiquitous `object` methods too.) Even `GetInvocationList`, clearly a multicast-oriented feature, is defined by the `Delegate` base class.

 The split between `Delegate` and `MulticastDelegate` is the meaningless and arbitrary result of a historical accident. The original plan was to support both multicast and unicast delegates, but toward the end of the prerelease period for .NET 1.0 this distinction was dropped, and now all delegate types support multicast instances. This happened sufficiently late in the day that Microsoft felt it was too risky to merge the two base types into one, so the split remained even though it serves no purpose.

I've already shown all of the public instance members that `Delegate` defines. `Dynami cInvoke`, `GetInvocationList`, `Target`, and `Method`.) Example 9-21 shows the signatures of the compiler-generated constructor and methods for a delegate type. The details vary from one type to the next; these are the generated members in the `Predi cate<T>` type.

Example 9-21. The members of a delegate type

```
public Predicate(object target, IntPtr method);

public bool Invoke(T obj);

public IAsyncResult BeginInvoke(T obj, AsyncCallback callback, object state);
public bool EndInvoke(IAsyncResult result);
```

Any delegate type you define will have four similar members, and none of them will have bodies. The compiler generates the declarations, but the implementation is supplied automatically by the CLR at runtime.

The constructor takes the target object, which is `null` for static methods, and an `IntPtr` identifying the method.[3] Notice that this is not the `MethodInfo` returned by the `Method` property. Instead, this is a *function token*, an opaque binary identifier for the target method. The CLR can provide binary metadata tokens for all members and types, but there's no C# syntax for working with them, so we don't normally see them. When you construct a new instance of a delegate type, the compiler automati-

---

3 `IntPtr` is a value type typically used for opaque handle values. You also sometimes see it in interop scenarios —on the rare occasions that you see a raw handle from an OS API in .NET, it may be represented as an `IntPtr`, although in many cases is has been superseded by `SafeHandle`.

cally generates IL that fetches the function token. The reason delegates use tokens internally is that they can be more efficient than working with reflection API types such as `MethodInfo`.

The `Invoke` method is the one that calls the delegate's target method (or methods). You can use this explicitly from C#, as Example 9-22 shows. It is almost identical to Example 9-11, the only difference being that the delegate variable is followed by `.Invoke`. This generates exactly the same code as Example 9-11, so whether you write `Invoke`, or just use the syntax that treats delegate identifiers as though they were method names, is a matter of style. As a former C++ developer, I've always felt at home with the Example 9-11 syntax, because it's similar to using function pointers in that language, but there's an argument that writing `Invoke` explicitly makes it easier to see that the code is using a delegate.

Example 9-22. Using Invoke explicitly

```
public static void CallMeRightBack(Predicate<int> userCallback)
{
    bool result = userCallback.Invoke(42);
    Console.WriteLine(result);
}
```

One benefit of this explicit form is that you can use the null-conditional operator to handle the case where the delegate variable is null. Example 9-23 uses this to attempt invocation only when a non-null argument is supplied.

Example 9-23. Using Invoke with the null-conditional operator

```
public static void CallMeMaybe(Action<int> userCallback)
{
    userCallback?.Invoke(42);
}
```

The `Invoke` method is the home for a delegate type's method signature. When you define a delegate type, this is where the return type and parameter list you specify end up. When the compiler needs to check whether a particular method is compatible with a delegate type (e.g., when you create a new delegate of that type), the compiler compares the `Invoke` method with the method you've supplied.

As Example 9-21 shows, all delegate types also have `BeginInvoke` and `EndInvoke` methods. These are deprecated, and do not work on .NET Core. (They throw a `Plat formNotSupportedException`.) They still work on .NET Framework, but they are obsolete. They provide a way of invoking methods asynchronously via the thread pool known as *asynchronous delegate invocation*. Although this was once a popular way to perform asynchronous work, with early versions of .NET, it had fallen out of widespread use some time before being deprecated, for three reasons. First, .NET 4.0 introduced the Task Parallel Library (TPL), which provides a more flexible and powerful abstraction for the services of the thread pool. (See Chapter 16 for details.) Second, these methods implement an older pattern known as the Asynchronous Programming Model (also described in Chapter 16), which does not fit directly with the new asynchronous language features of C# (described in Chapter 17). Finally, the largest benefit of asynchronous delegate invocation was that it provided an easy way to pass a set of values from one thread to another—you could just pass whatever you needed as the arguments for the delegate. However, C# 2.0 introduced a much better way to solve the problem: anonymous functions.

Anonymous Functions

C# lets you create delegates without needing to define a separate method explicitly. You can write a special kind of expression whose value is a method. You could think of them as *method expressions* or *function expressions*, but the official name is *anonymous functions*. Expressions can be passed directly as arguments, or assigned directly into variables, so the methods these expressions produce don't have names. (At least, not in C#. The runtime requires all methods to have names, so C# generates hidden names for these things, but from a C# language perspective, they are anonymous.)

For simple methods, the ability to write them inline as expressions can remove a lot of clutter. And as we'll see in "Captured Variables" on page 396, the compiler exploits the fact that delegates are more than just a reference to a method to provide anonymous functions with access to any variables that were in scope in the containing method at the point at which the anonymous function appears.

For historical reasons, C# provides two ways to define an anonymous function. The older way involves the `delegate` keyword, and is shown in Example 9-24. This form is known as an *anonymous method*.[4] I've put each argument for `FindIndex` on a separate line to make the anonymous functions (the second argument) stand out, but C# does not require this.

Example 9-24. Anonymous method syntax

```
public static int GetIndexOfFirstNonEmptyBin(int[] bins)
{
    return Array.FindIndex(
```

---

4 Unhelpfully, there are two similar terms that somewhat arbitrarily mean almost but not quite the same thing. The C# documentation uses the term *anonymous function* as the general term for either kind of method expression. *Anonymous method* would be a better name for this because not all of these things are strictly functions—they can have a void return, but by the time Microsoft needed a general term for these things, that name was already taken.

```
    bins,
    delegate (int value) { return value > 0; }
    );
}
```

In some ways, this resembles the normal syntax for defining methods. The parameter list appears in parentheses and is followed by a block containing the body of the method (which can contain as much code as you like, by the way, and is free to contain nested blocks, local variables, loops, and anything else you can put in a normal method). But instead of a method name, we just have the keyword `delegate`. The compiler infers the return type. In this case, the `FindIndex` method's signature declares the second argument to be a `Predicate<T>`, which tells the compiler that the return type has to be `bool`.

In fact, the compiler knows more. I've passed `FindIndex` an `int[]` array, so the compiler knows that the type argument `T` is `int`, so we need a `Predicate<int>`. This means that in Example 9-24, I had to supply information—the type of the delegate's argument—that the compiler already knew. C# 3.0 introduced a more compact anonymous function syntax that takes better advantage of what the compiler can deduce, shown in Example 9-25.

Example 9-25. Lambda syntax

```
public static int GetIndexOfFirstNonEmptyBin(int[] bins)
{
    return Array.FindIndex(
        bins,
        value => value > 0
    );
}
```

This form of anonymous function is called a *lambda expression*, and it is named after a branch of mathematics that is the foundation of a function-based model for computation. There is no particular significance to the choice of the Greek letter lambda (λ). It was the accidental result of the limitations of 1930s printing technology. The inventor of lambda calculus, Alonzo Church, originally wanted a different notation, but when he published his first paper on the subject, the typesetting machine operator decided to print λ instead, because that was the closest approximation to Church's notation that the machine could produce. Despite these inauspicious origins, this arbitrarily chosen term has become ubiquitous. LISP, an early and influential programming language, used the name *lambda* for expressions that are functions, and since then, many languages have followed suit, including C#.

Example 9-25 is exactly equivalent to Example 9-24; I've just been able to leave various things out. The => token unambiguously marks this out as being a lambda, so the compiler does not need that cumbersome and ugly `delegate` keyword just to recognize this as an anonymous function. The compiler knows from the surrounding context that the method has to take an `int`, so there's no need to specify the parameter's type; I just provided the parameter's name: `value`. For simple methods that consist of just a single expression, the lambda syntax lets you omit the block and the `return` statement. This all makes for very compact lambdas, but in some cases, you might not want to omit quite so much, so as Example 9-26 shows, there are various optional features. Every lambda in that example is equivalent.

Example 9-26. Lambda variations

```
Predicate<int> p1 = value => value > 0;
Predicate<int> p2 = (value) => value > 0;
Predicate<int> p3 = (int value) => value > 0;
Predicate<int> p4 = value => { return value > 0; };
Predicate<int> p5 = (value) => { return value > 0; };
Predicate<int> p6 = (int value) => { return value > 0; };
```

The first variation is that you can put parentheses around the parameter. This is optional with a single parameter, but it is mandatory for multiparameter lambdas. You can also be explicit about the parameters' types (in which case you will also need parentheses, even if there's only one parameter). And, if you like, you can use a block instead of a single expression, at which point you also have to use the `return` keyword if the lambda returns a value. The normal reason for using a block would be if you wanted to write multiple statements inside the method.

You may be wondering why there are quite so many different forms—why not have just one syntax and be done with it? Although the final line of Example 9-26 shows the most general form, it's also a lot more cluttered than the first line. Since one of the goals of lambdas is to provide a more concise alternative to anonymous methods, C# supports these shorter forms where they can be used without ambiguity.

You can also write a lambda that takes no arguments. As Example 9-27 shows, we just put an empty pair of parentheses in front of the => token. (And, as this example also shows, lambdas that use the greater than or equals operator, >=, can look a bit odd due to the meaningless similarity between the => and >= tokens.)

Example 9-27. A zero-argument lambda

```
Func<bool> isAfternoon = () => DateTime.Now.Hour >= 12;
```

The flexible and compact syntax means that lambdas have all but displaced the older anonymous method syntax. However, the older syntax offers one advantage: it allows you to omit the argument list entirely. In some situations where you provide a callback, you need to know only that whatever you were waiting for has now happened.

This is particularly common when using the standard event pattern described later in this chapter, because that requires event handlers to accept arguments even in situations where they serve no purpose. For example, when a button is clicked, there's not much else to say beyond the fact that it was clicked, and yet all of the button types in .NET's various UI frameworks pass two arguments to the event handler. Example 9-28 successfully ignores this by using an anonymous method that omits the parameter list.

Example 9-28. Ignoring arguments in an anonymous method

```
EventHandler clickHandler = delegate { Debug.WriteLine("Clicked!"); };
```

EventHandler is a delegate type that requires its target methods to take two arguments, of type object and EventArgs. If our handler needed access to either, we could, of course, add a parameter list, but the anonymous method syntax lets us leave it out if we want. You cannot do this with a lambda.

Captured Variables

While anonymous functions often take up much less space in your source code than a full, normal method, they're not just about conciseness. The C# compiler uses a delegate's ability to refer not just to a method, but also to some additional context to provide an extremely useful feature: it can make variables from the containing method available to the anonymous function. Example 9-29 shows a method that returns a Predicate<int>. It creates this with a lambda that uses an argument from the containing method.

Example 9-29. Using a variable from the containing method

```
public static Predicate<int> IsGreaterThan(int threshold)
{
    return value => value > threshold;
}
```

This provides the same functionality as the ThresholdComparer class from Example 9-7, but it now achieves it in a single, simple method, rather than requiring us to write an entire class. We can make this even more compact by using an expression-bodied method, as Example 9-30 shows.

Example 9-30. Using a variable from the containing method

```
public static Predicate<int> IsGreaterThan(int threshold) =>
    value => value > threshold;
```

In fact, the code is almost deceptively simple, so it's worth looking closely at what it does. The IsGreaterThan method returns a delegate instance. That delegate's target method performs a simple comparison—it evaluates the value > threshold expression and returns the result. The value variable in that expression is just the delegate's argument—the int passed by whichever code invokes the Predicate<int> that IsGreaterThan returns. The second line of Example 9-31 invokes that code, passing in 200 as the argument for value.

Example 9-31. Where value comes from

```
Predicate<int> greaterThanTen = IsGreaterThan(10);
bool result = greaterThanTen(200);
```

The threshold variable in the expression is trickier. This is not an argument to the anonymous function. It's the argument of IsGreaterThan, and Example 9-31 passes a value of 10 as the threshold argument. However, IsGreaterThan has to return before we can invoke the delegate it returns. Since the method for which that thres hold variable was an argument has already returned, you might think that the variable would no longer be available by the time we invoke the delegate. In fact, it's fine, because the compiler does some work on our behalf. If an anonymous function uses arguments of, or local variables that were declared by the containing method, the compiler generates a class to hold those variables so that they can outlive the method that created them. The compiler generates code in the containing method to create an instance of this class. (Remember, each invocation of a block gets its own set of local variables, so if any locals get pushed into an object to extend their lifetime, a new object will be required for each invocation.) This is one of the reasons why the popular myth that says local variables of value type always live on the stack is not true —in this case, the compiler copies the incoming threshold argument's value to a field of an object on the heap, and code that uses the threshold variable ends up using that field instead. Example 9-32 shows the generated code that the compiler produces for the anonymous function in Example 9-29.

Example 9-32. Code generated for an anonymous function

```
[CompilerGenerated]
private sealed class <>c__DisplayClass1_0
{
    public int threshold;

    public bool <IsGreaterThan>b__0(int value)
    {
        return (value > this.threshold);
    }
}
```

The class and method names all begin with characters that are illegal in C# identifiers, to ensure that this compiler-generated code cannot clash with anything we write —this is technically an *unspeakable name*. (The exact names are not fixed, by the way —you may find they are slightly different if you try this.) This generated code bears a striking resemblance to the ThresholdComparer class from Example 9-7, which is unsurprising, because the goal is the same: the delegate needs some method that it can refer to, and that method's behavior depends on a value that is not fixed. Anonymous functions are not a feature of the runtime's type system, so the compiler has to generate a class to provide this kind of behavior on top of the CLR's basic delegate functionality.

 Local functions (described in Chapter 3) can also access the local variables of their containing methods. Normally, this doesn't change those variables' lifetimes, because the local function is inaccessible outside of its containing method. However, if you create a delegate that refers to a local function, this means it might be invoked after the containing method returns, so the compiler will then perform the same trick that it does for anonymous functions, enabling variables to live on after the outer method returns.

Once you know that this is what's really happening when you write an anonymous function, it follows naturally that the inner method is able not just to read the variable, but also to modify it. This variable is just a field in an object that two methods— the anonymous function and the containing method—have access to. Example 9-33 uses this to maintain a count that is updated from an anonymous function.

Example 9-33. Modifying a captured variable

```
static void Calculate(int[] nums)
{
    int zeroCount = 0;
    int[] nonZeroNums = Array.FindAll(
        nums,
        v =>
        {
            if (v == 0)
            {
                zeroCount += 1;
                return false;
            }
            else
            {
                return true;
            }
        });
    Console.WriteLine($"Number of zero entries: {zeroCount}");
```

```
    Console.WriteLine($"First non-zero entry: {nonZeroNums[0]}");
}
```

Everything in scope for the containing method is also in scope for anonymous functions. If the containing method is an instance method, this includes any instance members of the type, so your anonymous function could access fields, properties, and methods. (The compiler supports this by adding a field to the generated class to hold a copy of the this reference.) The compiler puts only what it needs to in generated classes of the kind shown in Example 9-32, and if you don't use variables or instance members from the containing scope, it might not even have to generate a class at all, and may be able just to add a static method to your existing type.

The FindAll method in the preceding examples does not hold on to the delegate after it returns—any callbacks will happen while FindAll runs. Not everything works that way, though. Some APIs perform asynchronous work and will call you back at some point in the future, by which time the containing method may have returned. This means that any variables captured by the anonymous function will live longer than the containing method. In general, this is fine, because all of the captured variables live in an object on the heap, so it's not as though the anonymous function is relying on a stack frame that is no longer present. The one thing you need to be careful of, though, is explicitly releasing resources before callbacks have finished. Example 9-34 shows an easy mistake to make. This uses an asynchronous, callback-based API to download the resource at a particular URL via HTTP. (This calls the ContinueWith method on the Task<Stream> returned by HttpClient.GetStreamAsync, passing a delegate that will be invoked once the HTTP response comes back. This method is part of the Task Parallel Library described in Chapter 16.)

Example 9-34. Premature disposal

```
HttpClient http = GetHttpClient();
using (FileStream file = File.OpenWrite(@"c:\temp\page.txt"))
{
    http.GetStreamAsync("https://endjin.com/")
        .ContinueWith((Task<Stream> t) => t.Result.CopyToAsync(file));
} // Will probably dispose StreamWriter before callback runs
```

The using statement in this example will dispose the FileStream as soon as execution reaches the point at which the file variable goes out of scope in the outer method. The problem is that this file variable is also used in an anonymous function, which will in all likelihood run after the thread executing that outer method has left that using statement's block. The compiler has no understanding of when the inner block will run—it doesn't know whether that's a synchronous callback like Array.FindAll uses, or an asynchronous one. So it cannot do anything special here —it just calls Dispose at the end of the block, as that's what our code told it to do.

The asynchronous language features discussed in Chapter 17 can help avoid this sort of problem. When you use those to consume APIs that present this kind of Task-based pattern, the compiler can then know exactly how long things remain in scope. This enables the compiler to generate continuation callbacks for you, and as part of this, it can arrange for the using statement to call Dispose at the correct moment.

In performance-critical code, you may need to bear the costs of anonymous functions in mind. If the anonymous function uses variables from the outer scope, then in addition to the delegate object that you create to refer to the anonymous function, you may be creating an additional one: an instance of the generated class to hold shared local variables. The compiler will reuse these variable holders when it can—if one method contains two anonymous functions, they may be able to share an object, for example. Even with this sort of optimization, you're still creating additional objects, increasing the pressure on the garbage collector. (And in some cases you can end up creating this object even if you never hit the code path that creates the delegate.) It's not particularly expensive—these are typically small objects—but if you're up against a particularly oppressive performance problem, you might be able to eke out some small improvements by writing things in a more long-winded fashion in order to reduce the number of object allocations.

Local functions do not always incur this same overhead. When a local function uses its outer method's variables, it does not extend their lifetime. The compiler therefore doesn't need to create an object on the heap to hold the shared variables. It still creates a type to hold all the shared variables, but it defines this as a struct that it passes by reference as a hidden in argument, avoiding the need for a heap block. (If you create a delegate that refers to a local function, it can no longer use this optimization, and it reverts to the same strategy as it uses for anonymous functions, putting shared variables in an object on the heap.)

More subtly, using local variables from an outer scope in an anonymous function will extend the liveness of those variables, which may mean the GC will take longer to detect when objects those variables refer to are no longer in use. As you may recall from Chapter 7, the CLR analyzes your code to work out when variables are in use, so that it can free objects without waiting for the variables that refer to them to go out of scope. This enables the memory used by some objects to be reclaimed significantly earlier, particularly in methods that take a long time to complete. But liveness analysis applies only to conventional local variables. It cannot be applied for variables that are used in an anonymous function, because the compiler transforms those variables into fields. (From the CLR's perspective, they are not local variables at all.) Since C#

typically puts all of these transformed variables for a particular scope into a single object, you will find that none of the objects these variables refer to can be reclaimed until the method completes and the object containing the variables becomes unreachable itself. This can mean that in some cases there may be a measurable benefit to setting a local variable to null when you're done with it, enabling that particular object's memory to be reclaimed at the next GC. (Normally, that would be bad advice, and even with anonymous functions it might not have a useful effect in practice. You should only do this if performance testing demonstrates a clear advantage. But it's worth investigating in cases where you're seeing GC-related performance problems, and you make heavy use of long-running anonymous functions.)

Variable capture can also occasionally lead to bugs, particularly due to a subtle scope-related issue with for loops. (This used to afflict foreach loops too, but Microsoft changed how foreach behaved in C# 5.0, having decided that the original behavior was unlikely to be something that any developer actually wanted.) Example 9-35 runs into this problem.

Example 9-35. Problematic variable capture in a for loop

```
public static void Caught()
{
    var greaterThanN = new Predicate<int>[10];
    for (int i = 0; i < greaterThanN.Length; ++i)
    {
        greaterThanN[i] = value => value > i; // Bad use of i
    }

    Console.WriteLine(greaterThanN[5](20));
    Console.WriteLine(greaterThanN[5](6));
}
```

This example initializes an array of Predicate<int> delegates, where each delegate tests whether the value is greater than some number. (You wouldn't have to use arrays to see the problem I'm about to describe, by the way. Your loop might instead pass the delegates it creates into one of the mechanisms described in Chapter 16 that enable parallel processing by running the code on multiple threads. But arrays make it easier to show the problem.) Specifically, it compares the value with i, the loop counter that decides where in the array each delegate goes, so you might expect the element at index 5 to refer to a method that compares its argument with 5. If that were so, this code would show True twice. In fact, it displays True and then False. It turns out that Example 9-35 produces an array of delegates where every single element compares its argument with 10.

This usually surprises people when they encounter it. With hindsight, it's easy enough to see why this happens when you know how the C# compiler enables an anonymous function to use variables from its containing scope. The for loop declares the i variable, and because it is used not only by the containing Caught method, but also by each delegate the loop creates, the compiler will generate a class similar to the one in Example 9-32, and the variable will live in a field of that class. Since the variable comes into scope when the loop starts, and remains in scope for the duration of the loop, the compiler will create one instance of that generated class, and it will be shared by all of the delegates. So, as the loop increments i, this modifies the behavior of all of the delegates, because they all use that same i variable.

Fundamentally, the problem is that there's only one i variable here. You can fix the code by introducing a new variable inside the loop. Example 9-36 copies the value of i into another local variable, current, which does not come into scope until an iteration is under way, and goes out of scope at the end of each iteration. So, although there is only one i variable, which lasts for as long as the loop runs, we get what is effectively a new current variable each time around the loop. Because each delegate gets its own distinct current variable, this modification means that each delegate in the array compares its argument with a different value—the value that the loop counter had for that particular iteration.

Example 9-36. Modifying a loop to capture the current value

```
for (int i = 0; i < greaterThanN.Length; ++i)
{
    int current = i;
    greaterThanN[i] = value => value > current;
}
```

The compiler still generates a class similar to the one in Example 9-32 to hold the current variable that's shared by the inline and containing methods, but this time, it will create a new instance of that class each time around the loop in order to give each anonymous function a different instance of that variable. (This happens automatically when you use a foreach loop because its scoping rules are a little different: its iteration variable's scope is per iteration, meaning that it's logically a different instance of the variable each time around the loop, so there's no need to add an extra variable inside the loop as we had to with for.)

You may be wondering what would happen if you wrote an anonymous function that used variables at multiple scopes. Example 9-37 declares a variable called offset before the loop, and the lambda uses both that and a variable whose scope lasts for only one iteration.

Example 9-37. Capturing variables at different scopes

```
int offset = 10;
for (int i = 0; i < greaterThanN.Length; ++i)
{
    int current = i;
    greaterThanN[i] = value => value > (current + offset);
}
```

In that case, the compiler would generate two classes, one to hold any per-iteration shared variables (current, in this example) and one to hold those whose scope spans the whole loop (offset, in this case). Each delegate's target object would be the object containing inner scope variables, and that would contain a reference to the outer scope.

Figure 9-1 shows roughly how this would work, although it has been simplified to show just the first five items. The greaterThanN variable contains a reference to an array. Each array element contains a reference to a delegate. Each delegate refers to the same method, but each one has a different target object, which is how each delegate can capture a different instance of the current variable. Each of these target objects refers to a single object containing the offset variable captured from the scope outside of the loop.

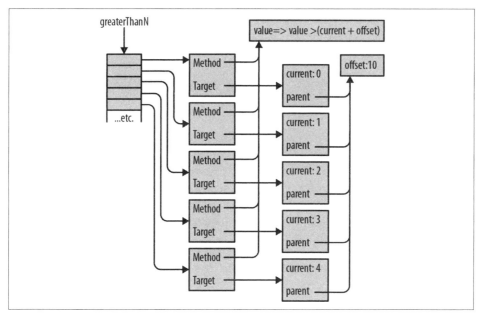

Figure 9-1. Delegates and captured scopes

Lambdas and Expression Trees

Lambdas have an additional trick up their sleeves beyond providing delegates. Some lambdas produce a data structure that represents code. This occurs when you use the lambda syntax in a context that requires an `Expression<T>`, where T is a delegate type. `Expression<T>` itself is not a delegate type; it is a special type in the .NET class library (in the `System.Linq.Expressions` namespace) that triggers this alternative handling of lambdas in the compiler. Example 9-38 uses this type.

Example 9-38. A lambda expression

```
Expression<Func<int, bool>> greaterThanZero = value => value > 0;
```

This example looks similar to some of the lambdas and delegates I've shown already in this chapter, but the compiler handles this very differently. It will not generate a method—there will be no compiled IL representing the lambda's body. Instead, the compiler will produce code similar to that in Example 9-39.

Example 9-39. What the compiler does with a lambda expression

```
ParameterExpression valueParam = Expression.Parameter(typeof(int), "value");
ConstantExpression constantZero = Expression.Constant(0);
BinaryExpression comparison = Expression.GreaterThan(valueParam, constantZero);
Expression<Func<int, bool>> greaterThanZero =
    Expression.Lambda<Func<int, bool>>(comparison, valueParam);
```

This code calls various factory functions provided by the `Expression` class to produce an object for each subexpression in the lambda. This starts with the simple operands —the `value` parameter and the constant value 0. These are fed into an object representing the "greater than" comparison expression, which in turn becomes the body of an object representing the whole lambda expression.

The ability to produce an object model for an expression makes it possible to write an API where the behavior is controlled by the structure and content of an expression. For example, some data access APIs can take an expression similar to the ones produced by Examples 9-38 and 9-39 and use it to generate part of a database query. I'll be talking about C#'s integrated query features in Chapter 10, but Example 9-40 gives a flavor of how a lambda expression can be used as the basis of a query.

Example 9-40. Expressions and database queries

```
var expensiveProducts = dbContext.Products.Where(p => p.ListPrice > 3000);
```

This example happens to use a Microsoft library called the Entity Framework, but various other data access technologies support the same approach. In this example, the `Where` method takes an argument of type `Expression<Func<Product,bool>>`.[5] `Product` is a class that corresponds to an entity in the database, but the important part here is the use of `Expression<T>`. That means that the compiler will generate code that creates a tree of objects whose structure corresponds to that lambda expression. The `Where` method processes this expression tree, generating a SQL query that includes this clause: `WHERE [Extent1].[ListPrice] > cast(3000 as deci mal(18))`. So, although I wrote my query as a C# expression, the work required to find matching objects will all happen on my database server.

Lambda expressions were added to C# to enable this sort of query handling as part of the set of features known collectively as *LINQ* (which is the subject of Chapter 10). However, as with most LINQ-related features, it's possible to use them for other things. For example, a popular .NET library used in automated testing called Moq (*https://github.com/moq*) exploits this. It creates fake implementations of interfaces for test purposes, and it uses lambda expressions to provide a simple API for configuring how those fakes should behave. Example 9-41 uses Moq's `Mock<T>` class to create a fake implementation of .NET's `IEqualityComparer<string>` interface. The code calls the `Setup` method, which takes an expression indicating a specific invocation we'd like to define special handling for—in this case if the fake's implementation of `IEqualityComparer<string>.Equals` is called with the arguments of `"Color"` and `"Colour"`, we'd like it to return `true`.

Example 9-41. Use of lambda expressions by the Moq library

```
var fakeComparer = new Mock<IEqualityComparer<string>>();
fakeComparer
    .Setup(c => c.Equals("Color", "Colour"))
    .Returns(true);
```

If that argument to `Setup` were just a delegate, there would be no way for Moq to inspect it. But because it's an expression tree, Moq is able to delve into it and find out what we've asked for.

 Unfortunately, expression trees are an area of C# that have lagged behind the rest of the language. They were introduced in C# 3.0, and various language features added since then, such as support for tuples and asynchronous expressions, cannot be used in an expression tree because the object model has no way to represent them.

---

5 You may be surprised to see `Func<Product,bool>` here and not `Predicate<Product>`. The `Where` method is part of a .NET feature called LINQ that makes extensive use of delegates. To avoid defining huge numbers of new delegate types, LINQ uses `Func` types, and for consistency across the API, it prefers `Func` even when other standard types would fit.

Events

Sometimes it is useful for objects to be able to provide notifications of when interesting things have happened—in a client-side UI framework, you will want to know when the user clicks on one of your application's buttons, for example. Delegates provide the basic callback mechanism required for notifications, but there are many ways you could go about using them. Should the delegate be passed as a method argument, a constructor argument, or perhaps as a property? How should you support unsubscribing from notifications? The CTS formalizes the answers to these questions through a special kind of class member called an *event*, and C# has syntax for working with events. Example 9-42 shows a class with one event member.

Example 9-42. A class with an event

```
public class Eventful
{
    public event Action<string> Announcement;

    public void Announce(string message)
    {
        Announcement?.Invoke(message);
    }
}
```

As with all members, you can start with an accessibility specifier, and it will default to private if you leave that off. Next, the event keyword singles this out as an event. Then there's the event's type, which can be any delegate type. I've used Action<string>, although as you'll soon see, this is an unorthodox choice. Finally, we put the member name, so this example defines an event called Announcement.

To handle an event, you must provide a delegate of the right type, and you must use the += syntax to attach that delegate as the handler. Example 9-43 uses a lambda, but you can use any expression that produces, or is implicitly convertible to, a delegate of the type the event requires.

Example 9-43. Handling events

```
var source = new Eventful();
source.Announcement += m => Console.WriteLine("Announcement: " + m);
```

Example 9-42 also shows how to *raise* an event—that is, how to invoke all the handlers that have been attached to the event. Its Announce uses the same syntax we would use if Announcement were a field containing a delegate that we wanted to invoke. In fact, as far as the code inside the class is concerned, that's exactly what an event looks like—it appears to be a field. I've chosen to use the delegate's Invoke

---

member explicitly here instead of writing Announcement(message) (despite saying earlier that I usually prefer the latter approach) because this lets me use the null-conditional operator (?.). This causes the compiler to generate code that only invokes the delegate if it is not null. Otherwise I would have had to write an if statement verifying that the field is not null before invoking it.

So why do we need a special member type if this looks just like a field? Well, it looks like a field only from inside the defining class. Code outside of the class cannot raise the event, so the code shown in Example 9-44 will not compile.

Example 9-44. How not to raise an event

```
var source = new Eventful();
source.Announcement("Will this work?"); // No, this will not even compile
```

From the outside, the only things you can do to an event are to attach a handler using += and to remove one using -=. The syntax for adding and removing event handlers is unusual in that it's the only case in C# in which you get to use += and -= without the corresponding standalone + or - operators being available. The actions performed by += and -= on events both turn out to be method calls in disguise. Just as properties are really pairs of methods with a special syntax, so are events. They are similar in concept to the code shown in Example 9-45. (In fact, the real code includes some moderately complex lock-free, thread-safe code. I've not shown this because the multithreading obscures the basic intent.) This won't have quite the same effect, because the event keyword adds metadata to the type identifying the methods as being an event, so this is just for illustration.

Example 9-45. The approximate effect of declaring an event

```
private Action<string> Announcement;

// Not the actual code.
// The real code is more complex, to tolerate concurrent calls.
public void add_Announcement(Action<string> handler)
{
    Announcement += handler;
}
public void remove_Announcement(Action<string> handler)
{
    Announcement -= handler;
}
```

Just as with properties, events exist mainly to offer a convenient, distinctive syntax, and to make it easier for tools to know how to present the features that classes offer. Events are particularly important for UI elements. In most UI frameworks, the objects representing interactive elements can often raise a wide range of events, corresponding to various forms of input such as keyboard, mouse, or touch. There are also often events relating to behavior specific to a particular control, such as selecting a new item in a list. Because the CTS defines a standard idiom by which elements can expose events, visual UI designers, such as the ones built into Visual Studio, can display the available events and offer to generate handlers for you.

Standard Event Delegate Pattern

The event in Example 9-42 is unusual in that it uses the `Action<T>` delegate type. This is perfectly legal, but in practice, you will rarely see that, because almost all events use delegate types that conform to a particular pattern. This pattern requires the delegate's method signature to have two arguments. The first argument's type is `object`, and the second's type is either `EventArgs` or some type derived from `EventArgs`. Example 9-46 shows the `EventHandler` delegate type in the `System` namespace, which is the simplest and most widely used example of this pattern.

Example 9-46. The EventHandler delegate type

```
public delegate void EventHandler(object sender, EventArgs e);
```

The first argument is usually called `sender`, because the event source passes a reference to itself for this argument. This means that if you attach a single delegate to multiple event sources, that handler can always know which source raised any particular notification.

The second argument provides a place to put information specific to the event. For example, WPF UI elements define various events for handling mouse input that use more specialized delegate types, such as `MouseButtonEventHandler`, with signatures that specify a corresponding specialized event argument that offers details about the event. For example, `MouseButtonEventArgs` defines a `GetPosition` method that tells you where the mouse was when the button was clicked, and it defines various other properties offering further detail, including `ClickCount` and `Timestamp`.

Whatever the specialized type of the second argument may be, it will always derive from the base `EventArgs` type. That base type is not very interesting—it does not add members beyond the standard ones provided by `object`. However, it does make it possible to write a general-purpose method that can be attached to any event that uses this pattern. The rules for delegate compatibility mean that even if the delegate type specifies a second argument of type `MouseButtonEventArgs`, a method whose second argument is of type `EventArgs` is an acceptable target. This can occasionally be useful for code generation or other infrastructure scenarios. However, the main benefit of the standard event pattern is simply one of familiarity—experienced C# developers generally expect events to work this way.

Custom Add and Remove Methods

Sometimes, you might not want to use the default event implementation generated by the C# compiler. For example, a class may define a large number of events, most of which will not be used on the majority of instances. UI frameworks often have this characteristic. A WPF UI can have thousands of elements, every one of which offers over 100 events, but you normally attach handlers only to a few of these elements, and even with these, you handle only a fraction of the events on offer. It is inefficient for every element to dedicate a field to every available event in this case.

Using the default field-based implementation for large numbers of rarely used events could add hundreds of bytes to the footprint of each element in a UI, which can have a discernible effect on performance. (In WPF, this could add up to a few hundred thousand bytes. That might not sound like much given modern computers' memory capacities, but it can put your code in a place where it is no longer able to make efficient use of the CPU's cache, causing a nosedive in application responsiveness. Even if the cache is several megabytes in size, the fastest parts of the cache are usually much smaller, and wasting a few hundred kilobytes in a critical data structure can make a world of difference to performance.)

Another reason you might want to eschew the default compiler-generated event implementation is that you may want more sophisticated semantics when raising events. For example, WPF supports *event bubbling*: if a UI element does not handle certain events, they will be offered to the parent element, then the parent's parent, and so on up the tree until a handler is found or it reaches the top. Although it would be possible to implement this sort of scheme with the standard event implementation C# supplies, much more efficient strategies are possible when event handlers are relatively sparse.

To support these scenarios, C# lets you provide your own add and remove methods for an event. It will look just like a normal event from the outside—anyone using your class will use the same += and -= syntax to add and remove handlers—and it won't be possible to tell that it provides a custom implementation. Example 9-47 shows a class with two events, and it uses a single dictionary, shared across all instances of the class, to keep track of which events have been handled on which objects. The approach is extensible to larger numbers of events—the dictionary uses pairs of objects as the key, so each entry represents a particular (source, event) pair. (This is not production-quality code by the way. It's not safe for multithreaded use and it will also leak memory when a `ScarceEventSource` instance that still has event handlers attached falls out of use. This example just illustrates how custom event handlers look; it's not a fully engineered solution.)

Example 9-47. Custom add and remove for sparse events

```
public class ScarceEventSource
{
    // One dictionary shared by all instances of this class,
    // tracking all handlers for all events.
    // Beware of memory leaks - this code is for illustration only.
    private static readonly
      Dictionary<(ScarceEventSource, object), EventHandler> _eventHandlers
        = new Dictionary<(ScarceEventSource, object), EventHandler>();

    // Objects used as keys to identify particular events in the dictionary.
    private static readonly object EventOneId = new object();
    private static readonly object EventTwoId = new object();


    public event EventHandler EventOne
    {
        add
        {
            AddEvent(EventOneId, value);
        }
        remove
        {
            RemoveEvent(EventOneId, value);
        }
    }

    public event EventHandler EventTwo
    {
        add
        {
            AddEvent(EventTwoId, value);
        }
        remove
        {
            RemoveEvent(EventTwoId, value);
        }
    }

    public void RaiseBoth()
    {
        RaiseEvent(EventOneId, EventArgs.Empty);
        RaiseEvent(EventTwoId, EventArgs.Empty);
    }

    private (ScarceEventSource, object) MakeKey(object eventId) => (this, eventId);

    private void AddEvent(object eventId, EventHandler handler)
    {
        var key = MakeKey(eventId);
        eventHandlers.TryGetValue(key, out EventHandler entry);
```

```
        entry += handler;
        _eventHandlers[key] = entry;
    }

    private void RemoveEvent(object eventId, EventHandler handler)
    {
        var key = MakeKey(eventId);
        EventHandler entry = _eventHandlers[key];
        entry -= handler;
        if (entry == null)
        {
            _eventHandlers.Remove(key);
        }
        else
        {
            _eventHandlers[key] = entry;
        }
    }

    private void RaiseEvent(object eventId, EventArgs e)
    {
        var key = MakeKey(eventId);
        if (_eventHandlers.TryGetValue(key, out EventHandler handler))
        {
            handler(this, e);
        }
    }
}
}
```

The syntax for custom events is reminiscent of the full property syntax: we add a block after the member declaration that contains the two members, although they are called add and remove instead of get and set. (Unlike with properties, you must always supply both methods.) This disables the generation of the field that would normally hold the event, meaning that the ScarceEventSource class has no instance fields at all—instances of this type are as small as it's possible for an object to be.

The price for this small memory footprint is a considerable increase in complexity; I've written about 16 times as many lines of code as I would have needed with compiler-generated events, and we'd need even more to fix the shortcomings described earlier. Moreover, this technique provides an improvement only if the events really are not handled most of the time—if I attached handlers to both events for every instance of this class, the dictionary-based storage would consume more memory than simply having a field for each event in each instance of the class. So you should consider this sort of custom event handling only if you either need nonstandard event-raising behavior, or if you are very sure that you really will be saving memory, and that the savings are worthwhile.

Events and the Garbage Collector

As far as the GC is concerned, delegates are normal objects like any other. If the GC discovers that a delegate instance is reachable, then it will inspect the `Target` property, and whichever object that refers to will also be considered reachable, along with whatever objects that object in turn refers to. Although there is nothing remarkable about this, there are situations in which leaving event handlers attached can cause objects to hang around in memory when you might have expected them to be collected by the GC.

There's nothing intrinsic to delegates and events that makes them unusually likely to defeat the GC. If you do get an event-related memory leak, it will have the same structure as any other .NET memory leak: starting from a root reference, there will be some chain of references that keeps an object reachable even after you've finished using it. The only reason events get special blame for memory leaks is that they are often used in ways that can cause problems.

For example, suppose your application maintains some object model representing its state, and that your UI code is in a separate layer that makes use of that underlying model, adapting the information it contains for presentation on screen. This sort of layering is usually advisable—it's a bad idea to intermingle code that deals with user interactions and code that implements the application's logic. But a problem can arise if the underlying model advertises changes in state that the UI needs to reflect. If these changes are advertised through events, your UI code will typically attach handlers to those events.

Now imagine that someone closes one of your application's windows. You would hope that the objects representing that window's UI would all be detected as unreachable the next time the GC runs. The UI framework is likely to have attempted to make that possible. For example, WPF ensures that each instance of its `Window` class is reachable for as long as the corresponding window is open, but once the window has been closed, it stops holding references to the window, to enable all of the UI objects for that window to be collected.

However, if you handle an event from your main application's model with a method in a `Window`-derived class, and if you do not explicitly remove that handler when the window is closed, you will have a problem. As long as your application is still running, something somewhere will presumably be keeping your application's underlying model reachable. This means that the target objects of any delegates held by your application model (e.g., delegates that were added as event handlers) will continue to be reachable, preventing the GC from freeing them. So, if a `Window`-derived object for the now-closed window is still handling events from your application model, that window—and all of the UI elements it contains—will still be reachable and will not be garbage collected.

There's a persistent myth that this sort of event-based memory leak has something to do with circular references. In fact, GC copes perfectly well with circular references. It's true that there are often circular references in these scenarios, but they're not the issue. The problem is caused by accidentally keeping objects reachable after you no longer need them. Doing that will cause problems regardless of whether circular references are present.

You can deal with this by ensuring that if your UI layer ever attaches handlers to objects that will stay alive for a long time, you remove those handlers when the relevant UI element is no longer in use. Alternatively, you could use weak references to ensure that if your event source is the only thing holding a reference to the target, it doesn't keep it alive. WPF can help you with this—it provides a `WeakEventManager` class that allows you to handle an event in such a way that the handling object is able to be garbage collected without needing to unsubscribe from the event. WPF uses this technique itself when databinding the UI to a data source that provides property change notification events.

Although event-related leaks often arise in UIs, they can occur anywhere. As long as an event source remains reachable, all of its attached handlers will also remain reachable.

Events Versus Delegates

Some APIs provide notifications through events, while others just use delegates directly. How should you decide which approach to use? In some cases, the decision may be made for you because you want to support some particular idiom. For example, if you want your API to support the new asynchronous features in C#, you will need to implement the pattern described in Chapter 17, which uses delegates, but not events, for completion callbacks. Events, on the other hand, provide a clear way to subscribe and unsubscribe, which will make them a better choice in some situations. Convention is another consideration: if you are writing a UI element, events will most likely be appropriate, because that's the predominant idiom.

In cases where constraints or conventions do not provide an answer, you need to think about how the callback will be used. If there will be multiple subscribers for a notification, an event could be the best choice. This is not absolutely necessary, because any delegate is capable of multicast behavior, but by convention, this behavior is usually offered through events. If users of your class will need to remove the handler at some point, events are also likely to be a good choice. That being said, the `IObservable` interface also supports unsubscription, and might be a better choice if you need more advanced functionality. This interface is part of the Reactive Extensions for .NET, and is described in Chapter 11.

You would typically pass a delegate as an argument to a method or constructor if it only makes sense to have a single target method. For example, if the delegate type has a non-void return value that the API depends on (such as the `bool` returned by the predicate passed to `Array.FindAll`), it makes no sense to have multiple targets or zero targets. An event is the wrong idiom here, because its subscription-oriented model considers it perfectly normal to attach either no handlers or multiple handlers.

Occasionally, it might make sense to have either zero handlers or one handler, but never more than one. For example, take WPF's `CollectionView` class, which can sort, group, and filter data from a collection. You configure filtering by providing a `Predicate<object>`. This is not passed as a constructor argument, because filtering is optional, so instead, the class defines a `Filter` property. An event would be inappropriate here, partly because `Predicate<object>` does not fit the usual event delegate pattern, but mainly because the class needs an unambiguous answer of yes or no, so it does not want to support multiple targets. (The fact that all delegate types support multicast means that it's still possible to supply multiple targets, of course. But the decision to use a property rather than an event signals the fact that it's not useful to attempt to provide multiple callbacks here.)

Delegates Versus Interfaces

Back at the start of this chapter, I argued that delegates offer a less cumbersome mechanism for callbacks and notifications than interfaces. So why do some APIs require callers to implement an interface to enable callbacks? Why do we have `IComparer<T>` and not a delegate? Actually, we have both—there's a delegate type called `Comparison<T>`, which is supported as an alternative by many of the APIs that accept an `IComparer<T>`. Arrays and `List<T>` have overloads of their `Sort` methods that take either.

There are some situations in which the object-oriented approach may be preferable to using delegates. An object that implements `IComparer<T>` could provide properties to adjust the way the comparison works (e.g., the ability to select between various sorting criteria). You may want to collect and summarize information across multiple callbacks, and although you can do that through captured variables, it may be easier to get the information back out again at the end if it's available through properties of an object.

This is really a decision for whoever is writing the code that is being called back, and not for the developer writing the code that makes the call. Delegates ultimately are more flexible, because they allow the consumer of the API to decide how to structure their code, whereas an interface imposes constraints. However, if an interface happens to align with the abstractions you want, delegates can seem like an irritating extra detail. This is why some APIs present both options, such as the sorting APIs that accept either an IComparer<T> or a Comparison<T>.

One situation in which interfaces might be preferable to delegates is if you need to provide multiple related callbacks. The Reactive Extensions for .NET define an abstraction for notifications that include the ability to know when you've reached the end of a sequence of events or when there has been an error, so in that model, subscribers implement an interface with three methods—OnNext, OnCompleted, and OnError. It makes sense to use an interface, because all three methods are typically required for a complete subscription.

Summary

Delegates are objects that provide a reference to a method, which can be either a static or an instance method. With instance methods, the delegate also holds a reference to the target object, so the code that invokes the delegate does not need to supply a target. Delegates can also refer to multiple methods, although that complicates matters if the delegate's return type is not void. While delegate types get special handling from the CLR, they are still just reference types, meaning that a reference to a delegate can be passed as an argument, returned from a method, and stored in a field, variable, or property. A delegate type defines a signature for the target method. This is represented through the type's Invoke method, but C# can hide this, offering a syntax in which you can invoke a delegate expression directly without explicitly referring to Invoke. You can construct a delegate that refers to any method with a compatible signature. You can also get C# to do more of the work for you—if you write an anonymous function, C# will supply a suitable declaration for you, and can also do work behind the scenes to make variables in the containing method available to the inner one. Delegates are the basis of events, which provide a formalized publish/subscribe model for notifications.

One C# feature that makes particularly extensive use of delegates is LINQ, which is the subject of the next chapter.

CHAPTER 10

LINQ

Language Integrated Query (LINQ) is a powerful collection of C# language features for working with sets of information. It is useful in any application that needs to work with multiple pieces of data (i.e., almost any application). Although one of its original goals was to provide straightforward access to relational databases, LINQ is applicable to many kinds of information. For example, it can also be used with in-memory object models, HTTP-based information services, JSON, and XML documents.

LINQ is not a single feature. It relies on several language elements that work together. The most conspicuous LINQ-related language feature is the *query expression*, a form of expression that loosely resembles a database query but which can be used to perform queries against any supported source, including plain old objects. As you'll see, query expressions rely heavily on some other language features such as lambdas, extension methods, and expression object models.

Language support is only half the story. LINQ needs class libraries to implement a set of querying primitives called *LINQ operators*. Each different kind of data requires its own implementation, and a set of operators for any particular type of information is referred to as a *LINQ provider*. (These can also be used from Visual Basic and F#, by the way, because those languages support LINQ too.) Microsoft supplies several providers, some built into the .NET class library and some available as separate NuGet packages. There is a provider for the Entity Framework for example, an object/relational mapping system for working with databases. They offer a LINQ provider for their Cosmos DB cloud database (a feature of Microsoft Azure). And the Reactive Extensions for .NET (Rx) described in Chapter 11 provide LINQ support for live streams of data. In short, LINQ is a widely supported idiom in .NET, and it's extensible, so you will also find open source and other third-party providers.

Most of the examples in this chapter use LINQ to Objects. This is partly because it avoids cluttering the examples with extraneous details such as database or service connections, but there's a more important reason. LINQ's introduction in 2007 significantly changed the way I write C#, and that's entirely because of LINQ to Objects. Although LINQ's query syntax makes it look like it's primarily a data access technology, I have found it to be far more valuable than that. Having LINQ's services available on any collection of objects makes it useful in every part of your code.

Query Expressions

The most visible feature of LINQ is the query expression syntax. It's not the most important—as we'll see later, it's entirely possible to use LINQ productively without ever writing a query expression. However, it's a very natural syntax for many kinds of queries.

At first glance, a query expression loosely resembles a database query, but the syntax works with any LINQ provider. Example 10-1 shows a query expression that uses LINQ to Objects to search for certain `CultureInfo` objects. (A `CultureInfo` object provides a set of culture-specific information, such as the symbol used for the local currency, what language is spoken, and so on. Some systems call this a *locale*.) This particular query looks at the character that denotes what would, in English, be called the decimal point. Many countries actually use a comma instead of a period, and in those countries, 100,000 would mean the number 100 written out to three decimal places; in English-speaking cultures, we would normally write this as 100.000. The query expression searches all the cultures known to the system and returns those that use a comma as the decimal separator.

Example 10-1. A LINQ query expression

```
IEnumerable<CultureInfo> commaCultures =
    from culture in CultureInfo.GetCultures(CultureTypes.AllCultures)
    where culture.NumberFormat.NumberDecimalSeparator == ","
    select culture;

foreach (CultureInfo culture in commaCultures)
{
    Console.WriteLine(culture.Name);
}
```

The `foreach` loop in this example shows the results of the query. On my system, this lists the name of 389 cultures, indicating that slightly under half of the 841 available cultures use a comma, not a decimal point. Of course, I could easily have achieved this without using LINQ. Example 10-2 will produce the same results.

Example 10-2. The non-LINQ equivalent

```
CultureInfo[] allCultures = CultureInfo.GetCultures(CultureTypes.AllCultures);
foreach (CultureInfo culture in allCultures)
{
    if (culture.NumberFormat.NumberDecimalSeparator == ",")
    {
        Console.WriteLine(culture.Name);
    }
}
```

Both examples have eight nonblank lines of code, although if you ignore lines that contain only braces, Example 10-2 contains just four, two fewer than Example 10-1. Then again, if we count statements, the LINQ example has just three, compared to four in the loop-based example. So it's difficult to argue convincingly that either approach is simpler than the other.

However, Example 10-1 has a significant advantage: the code that decides which items to choose is well separated from the code that decides what to do with those items. Example 10-2 intermingles these two concerns: the code that picks the objects is half outside and half inside the loop.

Another difference is that Example 10-1 has a more declarative style: it focuses on what we want, not how to get it. The query expression describes the items we'd like, without mandating that this be achieved in any particular way. For this very simple example, that doesn't matter much, but for more complex examples, and particularly when using a LINQ provider for database access, it can be very useful to allow the provider a free hand in deciding exactly how to perform the query. Example 10-2's approach of iterating over everything in a foreach loop and picking the item it wants would be a bad idea if we were talking to a database—you generally want to let the server do this sort of filtering work.

The query in Example 10-1 has three parts. All query expressions are required to begin with a from clause, which specifies the source of the query. In this case, the source is an array of type CultureInfo[], returned by the CultureInfo class's GetCul tures method. As well as defining the source for the query, the from clause contains a name, which here is culture. This is called the *range variable*, and we can use it in the rest of the query to represent a single item from the source. Clauses can run many times—the where clause in Example 10-1 runs once for every item in the collection, so the range variable will have a different value each time. This is reminiscent of the iteration variable in a foreach loop. In fact, the overall structure of the from clause is similar—we have the variable that will represent an item from a collection, then the in keyword, then the source for which that variable will represent individual items. Just as a foreach loop's iteration variable is in scope only inside the loop, the range variable culture is meaningful only inside this query expression.

Although analogies with foreach can be helpful for understanding the intent of LINQ queries, you shouldn't take this too literally. For example, not all providers directly execute the expressions in a query. Some LINQ providers convert query expressions into database queries, in which case the C# code in the various expressions inside the query does not run in any conventional sense. So, although it is true to say that the range variable represents a single value from the source, it's not always true to say that that clauses will execute once for every item they process, with the range value taking that item's value. It happens to be true for Example 10-1 because it uses LINQ to Objects, but it's not so for all providers.

The second part of the query in Example 10-1 is a where clause. This clause is optional, or if you want, you can have several in one query. A where clause filters the results, and the one in this example states that I want only the CultureInfo objects with a NumberFormat that indicates that the decimal separator is a comma.

The final part of the query is a select clause, and all query expressions end with either one of these or a group clause. This determines the final output of the query. This example indicates that we want each CultureInfo object that was not filtered out by the query. The foreach loop in Example 10-1 that shows the results of the query uses only the Name property, so I could have written a query that extracted only that. As Example 10-3 shows, if I do this, I also need to change the loop, because the resulting query now produces strings instead of CultureInfo objects.

Example 10-3. Extracting just one property in a query

```
IEnumerable<string> commaCultures =
    from culture in CultureInfo.GetCultures(CultureTypes.AllCultures)
    where culture.NumberFormat.NumberDecimalSeparator == ","
    select culture.Name;

foreach (string cultureName in commaCultures)
{
    Console.WriteLine(cultureName);
}
```

This raises a question: in general, what type do query expressions have? In Example 10-1, commaCultures is an IEnumerable<CultureInfo>; in Example 10-3, it's an IEnumerable<string>. The output item type is determined by the final clause of the query—the select or, in some cases, the group clause. However, not all query expressions result in an IEnumerable<T>. It depends on which LINQ provider you use—I've ended up with IEnumerable<T> because I'm using LINQ to Objects.

It's very common to use the var keyword when declaring variables that hold LINQ queries. This is necessary if a select clause produces instances of an anonymous type, because there is no way to write the name of the resulting query's type. Even if anonymous types are not involved, var is still widely used, and there are two reasons. One is just a matter of consistency: some people feel that because you have to use var for some LINQ queries, you should use it for all of them. Another argument is that LINQ query types often have verbose and ugly names, and var results in less cluttered code. This can be a particularly pressing concern in the strictly limiting confines of a book's layout, so in many examples in this chapter I have departed from my usual preference for explicit types, and have used var to make things fit.

How did C# know that I wanted to use LINQ to Objects? It's because I used an array as the source in the from clause. More generally, LINQ to Objects will be used when you specify any IEnumerable<T> as the source, unless a more specialized provider is available. However, this doesn't really explain how C# discovers the existence of providers in the first place, and how it chooses between them. To understand that, you need to know what the compiler does with a query expression.

How Query Expressions Expand

The compiler converts all query expressions into one or more method calls. Once it has done that, the LINQ provider is selected through exactly the same mechanisms that C# uses for any other method call. The compiler does not have any built-in concept of what constitutes a LINQ provider. It just relies on convention. Example 10-4 shows what the compiler does with the query expression in Example 10-3.

Example 10-4. The effect of a query expression

```
IEnumerable<string> commaCultures =
    CultureInfo.GetCultures(CultureTypes.AllCultures)
    .Where(culture => culture.NumberFormat.NumberDecimalSeparator == ",")
    .Select(culture => culture.Name);
```

The Where and Select methods are examples of LINQ operators. A LINQ operator is nothing more than a method that conforms to one of the standard patterns. I'll describe these patterns later, in "Standard LINQ Operators" on page 432.

The code in Example 10-4 is all one statement, and I'm chaining method calls together—I call the Where method on the return value of GetCultures, and I call the Select method on the return value of Where. The formatting looks a little peculiar, but it's too long to go on one line; and, even though it's not terribly elegant, I prefer to put the . at the start of the line when splitting chained calls across multiple lines, because it makes it much easier to see that each new line continues from where the last one left off. Leaving the period at the end of the preceding line looks neater, but also makes it much easier to misread the code.

The compiler has turned the `where` and `select` clauses' expressions into lambdas. Notice that the range variable ends up as a parameter in each lambda. This is one example of why you should not take the analogy between query expressions and `foreach` loops too literally. Unlike a `foreach` iteration variable, the range variable does not exist as a single conventional variable. In the query, it is just an identifier that represents an item from the source, and in expanding the query into method calls, C# may end up creating multiple real variables for a single range variable, like it has with the arguments for the two separate lambdas here.

All query expressions boil down to this sort of thing—chained method calls with lambdas. (This is why we don't strictly need the query expression syntax—you could write any query using method calls instead.) Some are more complex than others. The expression in Example 10-1 ends up with a simpler structure despite looking almost identical to Example 10-3. Example 10-5 shows how it expands. It turns out that when a query's `select` clause just passes the range variable straight through, the compiler interprets that as meaning that we want to pass the results of the preceding clause straight through without further processing, so it doesn't add a call to `Select`. (There is one exception to this: if you write a query expression that contains nothing but a `from` and a `select` clause, it will generate a call to `Select` even if the `select` clause is trivial.)

Example 10-5. How trivial select clauses expand

```
IEnumerable<CultureInfo> commaCultures =
    CultureInfo.GetCultures(CultureTypes.AllCultures)
    .Where(culture => culture.NumberFormat.NumberDecimalSeparator == ",");
```

The compiler has to work harder if you introduce multiple variables within the query's scope. You can do this with a `let` clause. Example 10-6 performs the same job as Example 10-3, but I've introduced a new variable called `numFormat` to refer to the number format. This makes my `where` clause shorter and easier to read, and in a more complex query that needed to refer to that format object multiple times, this technique could remove a lot of clutter.

Example 10-6. Query with a let clause

```
IEnumerable<string> commaCultures =
    from culture in CultureInfo.GetCultures(CultureTypes.AllCultures)
    let numFormat = culture.NumberFormat
    where numFormat.NumberDecimalSeparator == ","
    select culture.Name;
```

When you write a query that introduces additional variables like this, the compiler automatically generates a hidden class with a field for each of the variables so that it can make them all available at every stage. To get the same effect with ordinary method calls, we'd need to do something similar, and an easy way to do that is to introduce an anonymous type to contain them, as Example 10-7 shows.

Example 10-7. How multivariable query expressions expand (approximately)

```
IEnumerable<string> commaCultures =
    CultureInfo.GetCultures(CultureTypes.AllCultures)
    .Select(culture => new { culture, numFormat = culture.NumberFormat })
    .Where(vars => vars.numFormat.NumberDecimalSeparator == ",")
    .Select(vars => vars.culture.Name);
```

No matter how simple or complex they are, query expressions are simply a specialized syntax for method calls. This suggests how we might go about writing a custom source for a query expression.

Supporting Query Expressions

Because the C# compiler just converts the various clauses of a query expression into method calls, we can write a type that participates in these expressions by defining some suitable methods. To illustrate that the C# compiler really doesn't care what these methods do, Example 10-8 shows a class that makes absolutely no sense but nonetheless keeps C# happy when used from a query expression. The compiler just mechanically converts a query expression into a series of method calls, so if suitable-looking methods exist, the code will compile successfully.

Example 10-8. Nonsensical Where and Select

```
public class SillyLinqProvider
{
    public SillyLinqProvider Where(Func<string, int> pred)
    {
        Console.WriteLine("Where invoked");
        return this;
    }

    public string Select<T>(Func<DateTime, T> map)
    {
        Console.WriteLine($"Select invoked, with type argument {typeof(T)}");
        return "This operator makes no sense";
    }
}
```

I can use an instance of this class as the source of a query expression. That's crazy because this class does not in any way represent a collection of data, but the compiler doesn't care. It just needs certain methods to be present, so if I write the code in Example 10-9, the compiler will be perfectly happy even though the code doesn't make any sense.

Example 10-9. A meaningless query

```
var q = from x in new SillyLinqProvider()
        where int.Parse(x)
        select x.Hour;
```

The compiler converts this into method calls in exactly the same way that it did with the more sensible query in Example 10-1. Example 10-10 shows the result. If you're paying close attention, you'll have noticed that my range variable actually changes type partway through—my `Where` method requires a delegate that takes a string, so in that first lambda, x is of type `string`. But my `Select` method requires its delegate to take a `DateTime`, so that's the type of x in that lambda. (And it's all ultimately irrelevant, because my `Where` and `Select` methods don't even use these lambdas.) Again, this is nonsense, but it shows how mechanically the C# compiler converts queries to method calls.

Example 10-10. How the compiler transforms the meaningless query

```
var q = new SillyLinqProvider().Where(x => int.Parse(x)).Select(x => x.Hour);
```

Obviously, it's not useful to write code that makes no sense. The reason I'm showing you this is to demonstrate that the query expression syntax knows nothing about semantics—the compiler has no particular expectation of what any of the methods it invokes will do. All that it requires is that they accept lambdas as arguments, and return something other than `void`.

Clearly, the real work is happening elsewhere. It's the LINQ providers themselves that make things happen. So now I'll outline what we would need to write to make the queries I showed in the first couple of examples work if LINQ to Objects didn't exist.

You've seen how LINQ queries are transformed into code such as that shown in Example 10-4, but this isn't the whole story. The `where` clause becomes a call to the `Where` method, but we're calling it on an array of type `CultureInfo[]`, a type that does not in fact have a `Where` method. This works only because LINQ to Objects defines an appropriate extension method. As I showed in Chapter 3, it's possible to add new methods to existing types, and LINQ to Objects does that for `IEnumerable<T>`. (Since most collections implement `IEnumerable<T>`, this means LINQ to Objects can be used on almost any kind of collection.) To use these extension methods, you need a `using` directive for the `System.Linq` namespace. (The extension methods are all defined by a static class in that namespace called `Enumerable`, by the way.) If attempt to use LINQ without that directive, the compiler would produce this error for the query expression for Example 10-1 or Example 10-3:

```
error CS1935: Could not find an implementation of the query pattern for source
type 'System.Globalization.CultureInfo[]'.  'Where' not found.  Are you missing
a reference to 'System.Core.dll' or a using directive for 'System.Linq'?
```

In general, that error message's suggestion would be helpful,[1] but in this case, I want to write my own LINQ implementation. Example 10-11 does this, and I've shown the whole source file because extension methods are sensitive to the use of namespaces and `using` directives. The contents of the `Main` method should look familiar—this is the code from Example 10-3, but this time, instead of using the LINQ to Objects provider, it will use the extension methods from my `CustomLinqProvider` class. (Normally, you make extension methods available with a `using` directive, but because `CustomLinqProvider` is in the same namespace as the `Program` class, all of its extension methods are automatically available to `Main`.)

 Although Example 10-11 behaves as intended, you should not take this as an example of how a LINQ provider normally executes its queries. This does illustrate how LINQ providers put themselves in the picture, but as I'll show later, there are some issues with how this code goes on to perform the query. Also, it's rather minimalistic—there's more to LINQ than `Where` and `Select`, and most real providers offer slightly more than just these two operators.

Example 10-11. A custom LINQ provider for CultureInfo[]

```csharp
using System;
using System.Globalization;

namespace CustomLinqExample
{
    public static class CustomLinqProvider
    {
        public static CultureInfo[] Where(this CultureInfo[] cultures,
                                           Predicate<CultureInfo> filter)
        {
            return Array.FindAll(cultures, filter);
        }

        public static T[] Select<T>(this CultureInfo[] cultures,
```

---

[1] Well, the using directive suggestion is helpful. The `System.Core.dll` suggestion is only correct on .NET Framework, since the relevant code lives in `System.Linq.dll` on .NET Core, which is in any case included in the references you get by default in .NET Core applications.

```
                    Func<CultureInfo, T> map)
{
    var result = new T[cultures.Length];
    for (int i = 0; i < cultures.Length; ++i)
    {
        result[i] = map(cultures[i]);
    }
    return result;
}
}

class Program
{
    static void Main(string[] args)
    {
        var commaCultures =
          from culture in CultureInfo.GetCultures(CultureTypes.AllCultures)
          where culture.NumberFormat.NumberDecimalSeparator == ","
          select culture.Name;

        foreach (string cultureName in commaCultures)
        {
            Console.WriteLine(cultureName);
        }
    }
}
}
```

As you're now well aware, the query expression in Main will first call Where on the source, and will then call Select on whatever Where returns. As before, the source is the return value of GetCultures, which is an array of type CultureInfo[]. That's the type for which CustomLinqProvider defines extension methods, so this will invoke CustomLinqProvider.Where. That uses the Array class's FindAll method to find all of the elements in the source array that match the predicate. The Where method passes its own argument straight through to FindAll as the predicate, and as you know, when the C# compiler calls Where, it passes a lambda based on the expression in the LINQ query's where clause. That predicate will match the cultures that use a comma as their decimal separator, so the Where clause returns an array of type CultureInfo[] that contains only those cultures.

Next, the code that the compiler created for the query will call Select on the CultureInfo[] array returned by Where. Arrays don't have a Select method, so the extension method in CustomLinqProvider will be used. My Select method is generic, so the compiler will need to work out what the type argument should be, and it can infer this from the expression in the select clause.

First, the compiler transforms it into a lambda: culture => culture.Name. Because this becomes the second argument for Select, the compiler knows that we require a

Func<CultureInfo, T>, so it knows that the culture parameter must be of type CultureInfo. This enables it to infer that T must be string, because the lambda returns culture.Name, and that Name property's type is string. So the compiler knows that it is invoking CustomLinqProvider.Select<string>. (The deduction I just described is not specific to query expressions here, by the way. The type inference takes place after the query has been transformed into method calls. The compiler would have gone through exactly the same process if we had started with the code in Example 10-4.)

The Select method will now produce an array of type string[] (because T is string here). It populates that array by iterating through the elements in the incoming CultureInfo[], passing each CultureInfo as the argument to the lambda that extracts the Name property. So we end up with an array of strings, containing the name of each culture that uses a comma as its decimal separator.

That's a slightly more realistic example than my SillyLinqProvider, because this does now provide the expected behavior. However, although the query produces the same strings as it did when using the real LINQ to Objects provider, the mechanism by which it does so is somewhat different. My CustomLinqProvider performed each operation immediately—the Where and Select methods both returned fully populated arrays. LINQ to Objects does something quite different. In fact, so do most LINQ providers.

Deferred Evaluation

If LINQ to Objects worked in the same way as my custom provider in Example 10-11, it would not cope well with Example 10-12. This has a Fibonacci method that returns a never-ending sequence—it will keep providing numbers from the Fibonacci series for as long as the code keeps asking for them. I have used the IEnumerable<BigInteger> returned by this method as the source for a query expression. Since we have a using directive for System.Linq in place near the start, I'm back to using LINQ to Objects here.

Example 10-12. Query with an infinite source sequence

```
using System;
using System.Collections.Generic;
using System.Linq;
using System.Numerics;

class Program
{
    static IEnumerable<BigInteger> Fibonacci()
    {
        BigInteger n1 = 1;
        BigInteger n2 = 1;
```

```
            yield return n1;
            while (true)
            {
                yield return n2;
                BigInteger t = n1 + n2;
                n1 = n2;
                n2 = t;
            }
        }

        static void Main(string[] args)
        {
            var evenFib = from n in Fibonacci()
                          where n % 2 == 0
                          select n;

            foreach (BigInteger n in evenFib)
            {
                Console.WriteLine(n);
            }
        }
    }
}
```

This will use the Where extension method that LINQ to Objects provides for IEnumer
able<T>. If that worked the same way as my CustomLinqExtension class's Where
method for CultureInfo[], this program would never make it as far as displaying a
single number. My Where method did not return until it had filtered the whole of its
input and produced a fully populated array as its output. If the LINQ to Objects
Where method tried that with my infinite Fibonacci enumerator, it would never
finish.

In fact, Example 10-12 works perfectly—it produces a steady stream of output consisting of the Fibonacci numbers that are divisible by 2. This means it can't be
attempting to perform all of the filtering when we call Where. Instead, its Where
method returns an IEnumerable<T> that filters items on demand. It won't try to fetch
anything from the input sequence until something asks for a value, at which point it
will start retrieving one value after another from the source until the filter delegate
says that a match has been found. It then returns that and doesn't try to retrieve anything more from the source until it is asked for the next item. Example 10-13 shows
how you could implement this behavior by taking advantage of C#'s yield return
feature.

Example 10-13. A custom deferred Where operator

```
public static class CustomDeferredLinqProvider
{
    public static IEnumerable<T> Where<T>(this IEnumerable<T> src,
                                          Func<T, bool> filter)
```

```
    {
        foreach (T item in src)
        {
            if (filter(item))
            {
                yield return item;
            }
        }
    }
}
```

The real LINQ to Objects implementation of Where is somewhat more complex. It detects certain special cases, such as arrays and lists, and it handles them in a way that is slightly more efficient than the general-purpose implementation that it falls back to for other types. However, the principle is the same for Where and all of the other operators: these methods do not perform the specified work. Instead, they return objects that will perform the work on demand. It's only when you attempt to retrieve the results of a query that anything really happens. This is called *deferred evaluation.*

Deferred evaluation has the benefit of not doing work until you need it, and it makes it possible to work with infinite sequences. However, it also has disadvantages. You may need to be careful to avoid evaluating queries multiple times. Example 10-14 makes this mistake, causing it to do much more work than necessary. This loops through several different numbers, and writes out each one using the currency format of each culture that uses a comma as a decimal separator.

 If you run this on Windows, you may find that most of the lines this code displays will contain ? characters, indicating that the console cannot display the most of the currency symbols. In fact, it can —it just needs permission. By default, the Windows console uses an 8-bit code page for backward-compatibility reasons. If you run the command chcp 65001 from a Command Prompt, it will switch that console window into a UTF-8 code page, enabling it to show any Unicode characters supported by your chosen console font. You might want to configure the console to use either Consolas or Lucida Console to take best advantage of that.

Example 10-14. Accidental reevaluation of a deferred query

```
var commaCultures =
    from culture in CultureInfo.GetCultures(CultureTypes.AllCultures)
    where culture.NumberFormat.NumberDecimalSeparator == ","
    select culture;

object[] numbers = { 1, 100, 100.2, 10000.2 };

foreach (object number in numbers)
```

```
{
    foreach (CultureInfo culture in commaCultures)
    {
        Console.WriteLine(string.Format(culture, "{0}: {1:c}",
                          culture.Name, number));
    }
}
```

The problem with this code is that even though the `commaCultures` variable is initialized outside of the number loop, we iterate through it for each number. And because LINQ to Objects uses deferred evaluation, that means that the actual work of running the query is redone every time around the outer loop. So, instead of evaluating that `where` clause once for each culture (841 times on my system), it ends up running four times for each culture (3,364 times) because the whole query is evaluated once for each of the four items in the `numbers` array. It's not a disaster—the code still works correctly. But if you do this in a program that runs on a heavily loaded server, it will harm your throughput.

If you know you will need to iterate through the results of a query multiple times, consider using either the `ToList` or `ToArray` extension methods provided by LINQ to Objects. These immediately evaluate the whole query once, producing an `IList<T>` or a `T[]` array, respectively (so you shouldn't use these methods on infinite sequences, obviously). You can then iterate through that as many times as you like without incurring any further costs (beyond the minimal cost inherent in reading array or list elements). But in cases where you iterate through a query only once, it is usually better not to use these methods, as they'll consume more memory than necessary.

LINQ, Generics, and IQueryable<T>

Most LINQ providers use generic types. Nothing enforces this, but it is very common. LINQ to Objects uses `IEnumerable<T>`. Several of the database providers use a type called `IQueryable<T>`. More broadly, the pattern is to have some generic type *Source*<T>, where *Source* represents some source of items, and T is the type of an individual item. A source type with LINQ support makes operator methods available on *Source*<T> for any T, and those operators also typically return *Source*<TResult>, where TResult may or may not be different than T.

`IQueryable<T>` is interesting because it is designed to be used by multiple providers. This interface, its base `IQueryable`, and the related `IQueryProvider` are shown in Example 10-15.

Example 10-15. IQueryable and IQueryable<T>

```
public interface IQueryable : IEnumerable
{
    Type ElementType { get; }
    Expression Expression { get; }
    IQueryProvider Provider { get; }
}

public interface IQueryable<out T> : IEnumerable<T>, IQueryable
{
}

public interface IQueryProvider
{
    IQueryable CreateQuery(Expression expression);
    IQueryable<TElement> CreateQuery<TElement>(Expression expression);
    object Execute(Expression expression);
    TResult Execute<TResult>(Expression expression);
}
```

The most obvious feature of IQueryable<T> is that it adds no members to its bases. That's because it's designed to be used entirely via extension methods. The Sys tem.Linq namespace defines all of the standard LINQ operators for IQueryable<T> as extension methods provided by the Queryable class. However, all of these simply defer to the Provider property defined by the IQueryable base. So, unlike LINQ to Objects, where the extension methods on IEnumerable<T> define the behavior, an IQueryable<T> implementation is able to decide how to handle queries because it gets to supply the IQueryProvider that does the real work.

However, all IQueryable<T>-based LINQ providers have one thing in common: they interpret the lambdas as expression objects, not delegates. Example 10-16 shows the declaration of the Where extension methods defined for IEnumerable<T> and IQuerya ble<T>. Compare the predicate parameters.

Example 10-16. Enumerable versus Queryable

```
public static class Enumerable
{
    public static IEnumerable<TSource> Where<TSource>(
        this IEnumerable<TSource> source,
        Func<TSource, bool> predicate)
    ...
}

public static class Queryable
{
    public static IQueryable<TSource> Where<TSource>(
        this IQueryable<TSource> source,
```

```
    Expression<Func<TSource, bool>> predicate)
    ...
}
```

The Where extension for IEnumerable<T> (LINQ to Objects) takes a Func<TSource, bool>, and as you saw in Chapter 9, this is a delegate type. But the Where extension method for IQueryable<T> (used by numerous LINQ providers) takes Expression<Func<TSource, bool>>, and as you also saw in Chapter 9, this causes the compiler to build an object model of the expression and pass that as the argument.

A LINQ provider typically uses IQueryable<T> if it wants these expression trees. And that's usually because it's going to inspect your query and convert it into something else, such as a SQL query.

There are some other common generic types that crop up in LINQ. Some LINQ features guarantee to produce items in a certain order, and some do not. More subtly, a handful of operators produce items in an order that depends upon the order of their input. This can be reflected in the types for which the operators are defined and the types they return. LINQ to Objects defines IOrderedEnumerable<T> to represent ordered data, and there's a corresponding IOrderedQueryable<T> type for IQueryable<T>-based providers. (Providers that use their own types tend to do something similar—Parallel LINQ (see Chapter 16) defines an OrderedParallelQuery<T>, for example.) These interfaces derive from their unordered counterparts, such as IEnumerable<T> and IQueryable<T>, so all the usual operators are available, but they make it possible to define operators or other methods that need to take the existing order of their input into account. For example, in "Ordering" on page 443, I will show a LINQ operator called ThenBy, which is available only on sources that are already ordered.

When looking at LINQ to Objects, this ordered/unordered distinction may seem unnecessary, because IEnumerable<T> always produces items in some sort of order. But some providers do not necessarily do things in any particular order, perhaps because they parallelize query execution, or because they get a database to execute the query for them, and databases reserve the right to meddle with the order in certain cases if it enables them to work more efficiently.

Standard LINQ Operators

In this section, I will describe the standard operators that LINQ providers can supply. Where applicable, I will also describe the query expression equivalent, although many operators do not have a corresponding query expression form. Some LINQ features are available only through explicit method invocation. This is even true with certain operators that can be used in query expressions, because most operators are overloaded, and query expressions can't use some of the more advanced overloads.

LINQ operators are not operators in the usual C# sense—they are not symbols such as + or &&. LINQ has its own terminology, and for this chapter, an operator is a query capability offered by a LINQ provider. In C#, it looks like a method.

All of these operators have something in common: they have all been designed to support composition. This means that you can combine them in almost any way you like, making it possible to build complex queries out of simple elements. To enable this, operators not only take some type representing a set of items (e.g., an `IEnumerable<T>`) as their input, but most of them also return something representing a set of items. As already mentioned, the item type is not always the same—an operator might take some `IEnumerable<T>` as input, and produce `IEnumerable<TResult>` as output, where `TResult` does not have to be the same as `T`. Even so, you can still chain the things together in any number of ways. Part of the reason this works is that LINQ operators are like mathematical functions in that they do not modify their inputs; rather, they produce a new result that is based on their operands. (Functional programming languages typically have the same characteristic.) This means that not only are you free to plug operators together in arbitrary combinations without fear of side effects, but you are also free to use the same source as the input to multiple queries, because no LINQ query will ever modify its input. Each operator returns a new query based on its input.

Nothing enforces this functional style. As you saw with my `SillyLinqProvider`, the compiler doesn't care what a method representing a LINQ operator does. However, the convention is that operators are functional, in order to support composition. The built-in LINQ providers all work this way.

Not all providers offer complete support for all operators. The main providers Microsoft supplies—such as LINQ to Objects or the LINQ support in Entity Framework and Rx—are as comprehensive as they can be, but there are some situations in which certain operators will not make sense.

To demonstrate the operators in action, I need some source data. Many of the examples in the following sections will use the code in Example 10-17.

Example 10-17. Sample input data for LINQ queries

```
public class Course
{
    public string Title { get; set; }

    public string Category { get; set; }

    public int Number { get; set; }
```

```csharp
    public DateTime PublicationDate { get; set; }

    public TimeSpan Duration { get; set; }

    public static readonly Course[] Catalog =
    {
        new Course
        {
            Title = "Elements of Geometry",
            Category = "MAT", Number = 101, Duration = TimeSpan.FromHours(3),
            PublicationDate = new DateTime(2009, 5, 20)
        },
        new Course
        {
            Title = "Squaring the Circle",
            Category = "MAT", Number = 102, Duration = TimeSpan.FromHours(7),
            PublicationDate = new DateTime(2009, 4, 1)
        },
        new Course
        {
            Title = "Recreational Organ Transplantation",
            Category = "BIO", Number = 305, Duration = TimeSpan.FromHours(4),
            PublicationDate = new DateTime(2002, 7, 19)
        },
        new Course
        {
            Title = "Hyperbolic Geometry",
            Category = "MAT", Number = 207, Duration = TimeSpan.FromHours(5),
            PublicationDate = new DateTime(2007, 10, 5)
        },
        new Course
        {
            Title = "Oversimplified Data Structures for Demos",
            Category = "CSE", Number = 104, Duration = TimeSpan.FromHours(2),
            PublicationDate = new DateTime(2019, 9, 21)
        },
        new Course
        {
            Title = "Introduction to Human Anatomy and Physiology",
            Category = "BIO", Number = 201, Duration = TimeSpan.FromHours(12),
            PublicationDate = new DateTime(2001, 4, 11)
        },
    };
}
```

Filtering

One of the simplest operators is `Where`, which filters its input. You provide a predicate, which is a function that takes an individual item and returns a `bool`. `Where` returns an object representing the items from the input for which the predicate is true. (Conceptually, this is very similar to the `FindAll` method available on `List<T>` and array types, but using deferred execution.)

As you've already seen, query expressions represent this with a `where` clause. However, there's an overload of the `Where` operator that provides an additional feature not accessible from a query expression. You can write a filter lambda that takes two arguments: an item from the input and an index representing that item's position in the source. Example 10-18 uses this form to remove every second number from the input, and it also removes courses shorter than three hours.

Example 10-18. Where operator with index

```
IEnumerable<Course> q = Course.Catalog.Where(
    (course, index) => (index % 2 == 0) && course.Duration.TotalHours >= 3);
```

Indexed filtering is meaningful only for ordered data. It always works with LINQ to Objects, because that uses `IEnumerable<T>`, which produces items one after another, but not all LINQ providers process items in sequence. For example, with the Entity Framework, the LINQ queries you write in C# will be handled on the database. Unless a query explicitly requests some particular order, a database is usually free to process items in whatever order it sees fit, possibly in parallel. In some cases, a database may have optimization strategies that enable it to produce the results a query requires using a process that bears little resemblance to the original query. So it might not even be meaningful talk about, say, the 14th item handled by a `WHERE` clause. Consequently, if you were to write a query similar to Example 10-18 using the Entity Framework, executing the query would cause an exception, complaining that the indexed `Where` operator is not applicable. If you're wondering why the overload is even present if the provider doesn't support it, it's because the Entity Framework uses `IQueryable<T>`, so all the standard operators are available at compile time; providers that choose to use `IQueryable<T>` can only report the nonavailability of operators at runtime.

LINQ providers that implement some or all of the query logic on the server side usually impose limitations on what you can do in the lambdas that make up a query. Conversely, LINQ to Objects runs queries in process so it lets you invoke any method from inside a filter lambda—if you want to call `Console.WriteLine` or read data from a file in your predicate, LINQ to Objects can't stop you. But only a very limited selection of methods is available in providers for databases. These providers need to be able to translate your lambdas into something the server can process, and they will reject expressions that attempt to invoke methods that have no server-side equivalent.

Even so, you might have expected the exception to emerge when you invoke `Where`, instead of when you try to execute the query (i.e., when you first try to retrieve one or more items). However, providers that convert LINQ queries into some other form, such as a SQL query, typically defer all validation until you execute the query. This is because some operators may be valid only in certain scenarios, meaning that the provider may not know whether any particular operator will work until you've finished building the whole query. It would be inconsistent if errors caused by nonviable queries sometimes emerged while building the query and sometimes when executing it, so even in cases where a provider could determine earlier that a particular operator will fail, it will usually wait until you execute the query to tell you.

The `Where` operator's filter lambda must take an argument of the item type (the `T` in `IEnumerable<T>`, for example), and it must return a `bool`. You may remember from Chapter 9 that the class library defines a suitable delegate type called `Predicate<T>`, but I also mentioned in that chapter that LINQ avoids this, and we can now see why. The indexed version of the `Where` operator cannot use `Predicate<T>`, because there's an additional argument, so that overload uses `Func<T, int, bool>`. There's nothing stopping the unindexed form of `Where` from using `Predicate<T>`, but LINQ providers tend to use `Func` across the board to ensure that that operators with similar meanings have similar-looking signatures. Most providers therefore use `Func<T, bool>` instead, to be consistent with the indexed version. (C# doesn't care which you use— query expressions still work if the provider uses `Predicate<T>`, as my custom `Where` operator in Example 10-11 shows, but none of Microsoft's providers do this.)

LINQ defines another filtering operator: `OfType<T>`. This is useful if your source contains a mixture of different item types—perhaps the source is an `IEnumerable<object>` and you'd like to filter this down to only the items of type `string`. Example 10-19 shows how the `OfType<T>` operator can do this.

Example 10-19. The OfType<T> operator

```
static void ShowAllStrings(IEnumerable<object> src)
{
    foreach (string s in src.OfType<string>())
    {
        Console.WriteLine(s);
    }
}
```

Both `Where` and `OfType<T>` will produce empty sequences if none of the objects in the source meet the requirements. This is not considered to be an error—empty sequences are quite normal in LINQ. Many operators can produce them as output, and most operators can cope with them as input.

Select

When writing a query, we may want to extract only certain pieces of data from the source items. The `select` clause at the end of most queries lets us supply a lambda that will be used to produce the final output items, and there are a couple of reasons we might want to make our `select` clause do more than simply passing each item straight through. We might want to pick just one specific piece of information from each item, or we might want to transform it into something else entirely.

You've seen several `select` clauses already, and I showed in Example 10-3 that the compiler turns them into a call to `Select`. However, as with many LINQ operators, the version accessible through a query expression is not the only option. There's one other overload, which provides not just the input item from which to generate the output item, but also the index of that item. Example 10-20 uses this to generate a numbered list of course titles.

Example 10-20. Select operator with index

```
IEnumerable<string> nonIntro = Course.Catalog.Select((course, index) =>
    $"Course {index}: {course.Title}");
```

Be aware that the zero-based index passed into the lambda will be based on what comes into the `Select` operator, and will not necessarily represent the item's original position in the underlying data source. This might not produce the results you were hoping for in code such as Example 10-21.

Example 10-21. Indexed Select downstream of Where operator

```
IEnumerable<string> nonIntro = Course.Catalog
    .Where(c => c.Number >= 200)
    .Select((course, index) => $"Course {index}: {course.Title}");
```

This code will select the courses found at indexes 2, 3, and 5, respectively, in the `Course.Catalog` array, because those are the courses whose `Number` property satisfies the `Where` expression. However, this query will number the three courses as 0, 1, and 2, because the `Select` operator sees only the items the `Where` clause let through. As far as it is concerned, there are only three items, because the `Select` clause never had access to the original source. If you wanted the indexes relative to the original collection, you'd need to extract those upstream of the `Where` clause, as Example 10-22 shows.

Example 10-22. Indexed Select upstream of Where operator

```
IEnumerable<string> nonIntro = Course.Catalog
    .Select((course, index) => new { course, index })
    .Where(vars => vars.course.Number >= 200)
    .Select(vars => $"Course {vars.index}: {vars.course.Title}");
```

You may be wondering why I've used an anonymous type here and not a tuple. I could replace `new { course, index }` with just `(course, index)`, and the code would work equally well. However, in general, tuples will not always work in LINQ. The lightweight tuple syntax was introduced in C# 7.0, so they weren't around when expression trees were added back in C# 3.0. The expression object model has not been updated to support this language feature, so if you try to use a tuple with an `IQueryable<T>`-based LINQ provider, you will get compiler error CS8143, telling you that `An expression tree may not contain a tuple literal`. So I tend to use anonymous types in this chapter because they work with query-based providers. But if you're using a purely local LINQ provider (e.g., Rx, or LINQ to Objects) feel free to use tuples.

The indexed `Select` operator is similar to the indexed `Where` operator. So, as you would probably expect, not all LINQ providers support it in all scenarios.

Data shaping and anonymous types

If you are using a LINQ provider to access a database, the `Select` operator can offer an opportunity to reduce the quantity of data you fetch, which could reduce the load on the server. When you use a data access technology such as the Entity Framework to execute a query that returns a set of objects representing persistent entities, there's a trade-off between doing too much work up front and having to do lots of extra deferred work. Should those frameworks fully populate all of the object properties that correspond to columns in various database tables? Should they also load related objects? In general, it's more efficient not to fetch data you're not going to use, and data that is not fetched up front can always be loaded later on demand. However, if you try to be too frugal in your initial request, you may ultimately end up making a lot of extra requests to fill in the gaps, which could outweigh any benefit from avoiding unnecessary work.

When it comes to related entities, the Entity Framework allows you to configure which related entities should be prefetched and which should be loaded on demand, but for any particular entity that gets fetched, all properties relating to columns are typically fully populated. This means queries that request whole entities end up fetching all the columns for any row that they touch.

If you needed to use only one or two columns, this is relatively expensive. Example 10-23 uses this somewhat inefficient approach. It shows a fairly typical Entity Framework query.

Example 10-23. Fetching more data than is needed

```
var pq = from product in dbCtx.Product
         where product.ListPrice > 3000
         select product;
foreach (var prod in pq)
{
    Console.WriteLine($"{prod.Name} ({prod.Size}): {prod.ListPrice}");
}
```

This LINQ provider translates the `where` clause into an efficient SQL equivalent. However, the SQL `SELECT` clause retrieves all the columns from the table. Compare that with Example 10-24. This modifies only one part of the query: the LINQ `select` clause now returns an instance of an anonymous type that contains only those properties we require. (The loop that follows the query can remain the same. It uses `var` for its iteration variable, which will work fine with the anonymous type, which provides the three properties that loop requires.)

Example 10-24. A select clause with an anonymous type

```
var pq = from product in dbCtx.Product
         where (product.ListPrice > 3000)
         select new { product.Name, product.ListPrice, product.Size };
```

The code produces exactly the same results, but it generates a much more compact SQL query that requests only the `Name`, `ListPrice`, and `Size` columns. If you're using a table with many columns, this will produce a significantly smaller response because it's no longer dominated by data we don't need, reducing the load on the network connection to the database server, and also resulting in faster processing because the data will take less time to arrive. This technique is called *data shaping*.

This approach will not always be an improvement. For one thing, it means you are working directly with data in the database instead of using entity objects. This might mean working at a lower level of abstraction than would be possible if you use the entity types, which might increase development costs. Also, in some environments, database administrators do not allow ad hoc queries, forcing you to use stored procedures, in which case you won't have the flexibility to use this technique.

Projecting the results of a query into an anonymous type is not limited to database queries, by the way. You are free to do this with any LINQ provider, such as LINQ to Objects. It can sometimes be a useful way to get structured information out of a query without needing to define a class specially. (As I mentioned in Chapter 3, anonymous types can be used outside of LINQ, but this is one of the main scenarios for which they were designed. Grouping by composite keys is another, as I'll describe in "Grouping" on page 459.)

Projection and mapping

The `Select` operator is sometimes referred to as *projection*, and it is the same operation that many languages call *map*, which provides a slightly different way to think about the `Select` operator. So far, I've presented `Select` as a way to choose what comes out of a query, but you can also look at it as a way to apply a transformation to every item in the source. Example 10-25 uses `Select` to produce modified versions of a list of numbers. It variously doubles the numbers, squares them, and turns them into strings.

Example 10-25. Using Select to transform numbers

```
int[] numbers = { 0, 1, 2, 3, 4, 5 };

IEnumerable<int> doubled = numbers.Select(x => 2 * x);
IEnumerable<int> squared = numbers.Select(x => x * x);
IEnumerable<string> numberText = numbers.Select(x => x.ToString());
```

SelectMany

The `SelectMany` LINQ operator is used in query expressions that have multiple `from` clauses. It's called `SelectMany` because, instead of selecting a single output item for each input item, you provide it with a lambda that produces a whole collection for each input item. The resulting query produces all of the objects from all of these collections, as though each of the collections your lambda returns were merged into one. (This won't remove duplicates. Sequences can contain duplicates in LINQ. You can remove them with the `Distinct` operator described in "Set Operations" on page 457.) There are a couple of ways of thinking about this operator. One is that it provides a means of flattening two levels of hierarchy—a collection of collections—into a single level. Another way to look at it is as a Cartesian product—that is, a way to produce every possible combination from some input sets.

Example 10-26 shows how to use this operator in a query expression. This code highlights the Cartesian-product-like behavior. It shows every combination of the letters A, B, and C with a single digit from 1 to 5—that is, A1, B1, C1, A2, B2, C2, etc. (If you're wondering about the apparent incompatibility of the two input sequences, the `select` clause of this query relies on the fact that if you use the + operator to add a string and some other type, C# generates code that calls `ToString` on the nonstring operand for you.)

Example 10-26. Using SelectMany from a query expression

```
int[] numbers = { 1, 2, 3, 4, 5 };
string[] letters = { "A", "B", "C" };

IEnumerable<string> combined = from number in numbers
                               from letter in letters
                               select letter + number;
foreach (string s in combined)
{
    Console.WriteLine(s);
}
```

Example 10-27 shows how to invoke the operator directly. This is equivalent to the query expression in Example 10-26.

Example 10-27. SelectMany operator

```
IEnumerable<string> combined = numbers.SelectMany(
        number => letters,
        (number, letter) => letter + number);
```

Example 10-26 uses two fixed collections—the second `from` clause returns the same `letters` collection every time. However, you can make the expression in the second `from` clause return a value based on the current item from the first `from` clause. You can see in Example 10-27 that the first lambda passed to `SelectMany` (which actually corresponds to the second `from` clause's final expression) receives the current item from the first collection through its `number` argument, so you can use that to choose a different collection for each item from the first collection. I can use this to exploit `SelectMany`'s flattening behavior.

I've copied a jagged array from Example 5-16 in Chapter 5 into Example 10-28, which then processes it with a query containing two `from` clauses. Note that the expression in the second `from` clause is now `row`, the range variable of the first `from` clause.

Example 10-28. Flattening a jagged array

```
int[][] arrays =
{
    new[] { 1, 2 },
    new[] { 1, 2, 3, 4, 5, 6 },
    new[] { 1, 2, 4 },
    new[] { 1 },
    new[] { 1, 2, 3, 4, 5 }
};

IEnumerable<int> flattened = from row in arrays
```

```
                    from number in row
                    select number;
```

The first `from` clause asks to iterate over each item in the top-level array. Each of these items is also an array, and the second `from` clause asks to iterate over each of these nested arrays. This nested array's type is `int[]`, so the range variable of the second `from` clause, `number`, represents an `int` from that nested array. The `select` clause just returns each of these `int` values.

The resulting sequence provides every number in the arrays in turn. It has flattened the jagged array into a simple linear sequence of numbers. This behavior is conceptually similar to writing a nested pair of loops, one iterating over the outer `int[][]` array, and an inner loop iterating over the contents of each individual `int[]` array.

The compiler uses the same overload of `SelectMany` for Example 10-28 as it does for Example 10-27, but there's an alternative in this case. The final `select` clause is simpler in Example 10-28—it just passes on items from the second collection unmodified, which means the simpler overload shown in Example 10-29 does the job equally well. With this overload, we just provide a single lambda, which chooses the collection that `SelectMany` will expand for each of the items in the input collection.

Example 10-29. SelectMany without item projection

```
var flattened = arrays.SelectMany(row => row);
```

That's a somewhat terse bit of code, so in case it's not clear quite how that could end up flattening the array, Example 10-30 shows how you might implement `SelectMany` for `IEnumerable<T>` if you had to write it yourself.

Example 10-30. One implementation of SelectMany

```
static IEnumerable<T2> MySelectMany<T, T2>(
            this IEnumerable<T> src, Func<T, IEnumerable<T2>> getInner)
{
    foreach (T itemFromOuterCollection in src)
    {
        IEnumerable<T2> innerCollection = getInner(itemFromOuterCollection);
        foreach (T2 itemFromInnerCollection in innerCollection)
        {
            yield return itemFromInnerCollection;
        }
    }
}
```

Why does the compiler not use the simpler option shown in Example 10-29? The C# language specification defines how query expressions are translated into method calls, and it mentions only the overload shown in Example 10-26. Perhaps the reason the specification doesn't mention the simpler overload is to reduce the demands C# makes of types that want to support this double-from query form—you'd need to write only one method to enable this syntax for your own types. However, .NET's various LINQ providers are more generous, providing this simpler overload for the benefit of developers who choose to use the operators directly. In fact, some providers define two more overloads: there are versions of both the SelectMany forms we've seen so far that also pass an item index to the first lambda. (The usual caveats about indexed operators apply, of course.)

Although Example 10-30 gives a reasonable idea of what LINQ to Objects does in SelectMany, it's not the exact implementation. There are optimizations for special cases. Moreover, other providers may use very different strategies. Databases often have built-in support for Cartesian products, so some providers may implement SelectMany in terms of that.

Ordering

In general, LINQ queries do not guarantee to produce items in any particular order unless you explicitly define the order you require. You can do this in a query expression with an orderby clause. As Example 10-31 shows, you specify the expression by which you'd like the items to be ordered, and a direction—so this will produce a collection of courses ordered by ascending publication date. As it happens, ascending is the default, so you can leave off that qualifier without changing the meaning. As you've probably guessed, you can specify descending to reverse the order.

Example 10-31. Query expression with orderby clause

```
var q = from course in Course.Catalog
        orderby course.PublicationDate ascending
        select course;
```

The compiler transforms the orderby clause in Example 10-31 into a call to the OrderBy method, and it would use OrderByDescending if you had specified a descending sort order. With source types that make a distinction between ordered and unordered collections, these operators return the ordered type (for example, IOrderedEnumerable<T> for LINQ to Objects, and IOrderedQueryable<T> for IQueryable<T>-based providers).

With LINQ to Objects, these operators have to retrieve every element from their input before they can produce any output elements. An ascending `OrderBy` can determine which item to return first only once it has found the lowest item, and it won't know for certain which is the lowest until it has seen all of them. It still uses deferred evaluation—it won't do anything until you ask it for the first item. But as soon as you do ask it for something, it has to do all the work at once. Some providers will have additional knowledge about the data that can enable more efficient strategies. (For example, a database may be able to use an index to return values in the order required.)

LINQ to Objects' `OrderBy` and `OrderByDescending` operators each have two overloads, only one of which is available from a query expression. If you invoke the methods directly, you can supply an additional parameter of type `IComparer<TKey>`, where `TKey` is the type of the expression by which the items are being sorted. This is likely to be important if you sort based on a `string` property, because there are several different orderings for text, and you may need to choose one based on your application's locale, or you may want to specify a culture-invariant ordering to ensure consistency across all environments.

The expression that determines the order in Example 10-31 is very simple—it just retrieves the `PublicationDate` property from the source item. You can write more complex expressions if you want to. If you're using a provider that translates a LINQ query into something else, there may be limitations. If the query runs on the database, you may be able to refer to other tables—the provider might be able to convert an expression such as `product.ProductCategory.Name` into a suitable join. However, you will not be able to run any old code in that expression, because it must be something that the database can execute. But LINQ to Objects just invokes the expression once for each object, so you really can put in there whatever code you like.

You may want to sort by multiple criteria. You should *not* do this by writing multiple `orderby` clauses. Example 10-32 makes this mistake.

Example 10-32. How not to apply multiple ordering criteria

```
var q = from course in Course.Catalog
        orderby course.PublicationDate ascending
        orderby course.Duration descending // BAD! Could discard previous order
        select course;
```

This code orders the items by publication date and then by duration, but does so as two separate and unrelated steps. The second `orderby` clause guarantees only that the results will be in the order specified in that clause, and does not guarantee to preserve anything about the order in which the elements originated. If what you actually wanted was for the items to be in order of publication date, and for any items with the same publication date to be ordered by descending duration, you would need to write the query in Example 10-33.

Example 10-33. Multiple ordering criteria in a query expression

```
var q = from course in Course.Catalog
        orderby course.PublicationDate ascending, course.Duration descending
        select course;
```

LINQ defines separate operators for this multilevel ordering: `ThenBy` and `ThenByDescending`. Example 10-34 shows how to achieve the same effect as the query expression in Example 10-33 by invoking the LINQ operators directly. For LINQ providers whose types make a distinction between ordered and unordered collections, these two operators will be available only on the ordered form, such as `IOrderedQueryable<T>` or `IOrderedEnumerable<T>`. If you were to try to invoke `ThenBy` directly on `Course.Catalog`, the compiler would report an error.

Example 10-34. Multiple ordering criteria with LINQ operators

```
var q = Course.Catalog
    .OrderBy(course => course.PublicationDate)
    .ThenByDescending(course => course.Duration);
```

You will find that some LINQ operators preserve some aspects of ordering even if you do not ask them to. For example, LINQ to Objects will typically produce items in the same order in which they appeared in the input unless you write a query that causes it to change the order. But this is simply an artifact of how LINQ to Objects works, and you should not rely on it in general. In fact, even when you are using that particular LINQ provider, you should check with the documentation to see whether the order you're getting is guaranteed, or just an accident of implementation. In most cases, if you care about the order, you should write a query that makes that explicit.

Containment Tests

LINQ defines various standard operators for discovering things about what the collection contains. Some providers may be able to implement these operators without needing to inspect every item. (For example, a database-based provider might use a `WHERE` clause, and the database could be able to use an index to evaluate that without needing to look at every element.) However, there are no restrictions—you can use these operators however you like, and it's up to the provider to discover whether it can exploit a shortcut.

Unlike most LINQ operators, in the majority of providers these return neither a collection nor an item from their input. They generally just return true or false, or in some cases, a count. Rx is a notable exception: its implementations of these operators wrap the bool or int in a single-element IObservable<T> that produces the result. It does this to preserve the reactive nature of processing in Rx.

The simplest operator is Contains. You pass an item, and some providers (including LINQ to Objects) provide an overload that also takes an IEqualityComparer<T> so that you can customize how the operator determines whether an item in the source is the same as the specified item. Contains returns true if the source contains the specified item, and false if it does not. (If you use the single-argument version with a collection that implements ICollection<T> (which includes all IList<T> implementations) LINQ to Objects will detect that, and its implementation of Contains just defers to the collection. If you use a non-ICollection<T> collection, or you provide a custom equality comparer, it will have to examine every item in the collection.)

If, instead of looking for a particular value, you want to know whether a collection contains any values that satisfy some particular criteria, you can use the Any operator. This takes a predicate, and it returns true if the predicate is true for at least one item in the source. If you want to know how many items match some criteria, you can use the Count operator. This also takes a predicate, and instead of returning a bool, it returns an int. If you are working with very large collections, the range of int may be insufficient, in which case you can use the LongCount operator, which returns a 64-bit count. (This is likely to be overkill for most LINQ to Objects applications, but it could matter when the collection lives in a database.)

The Any, Count, and LongCount operators have overloads that do not take any arguments. For Any, this tells you whether the source contains at least one element, and for Count and LongCount, these overloads tell you how many elements the source contains.

Be wary of code such as if (q.Count() > 0). Calculating the exact count may require the entire source query (q in this case) to be evaluated, and in any case, it is likely to require more work than simply answering the question, *is this empty?* If q refers to a LINQ query, writing if (q.Any()) is likely to be more efficient. (That said, outside of LINQ this is not the case for list-like collections, where retrieving an element count is cheap and may actually be more efficient than the Any operator.)

A close relative to the `Any` operator is the `All` operator. This one is not overloaded—it takes a predicate, and it returns `true` if and only if the source contains no items that do not match the predicate. I used an awkward double negative in the preceding sentence for a reason: `All` returns `true` when applied to an empty sequence, because an empty sequence certainly doesn't contain any elements that fail to match the predicate for the simple reason that it doesn't contain any elements at all.

This may seems like a curiously pig-headed form of logic. It's reminiscent of the child who, when asked, "Have you eaten your vegetables?" unhelpfully replies, "I ate all the vegetables I put on my plate," neglecting to mention that he didn't put any vegetables on his plate in the first place. It's not technically untrue, but it fails to provide the information the parent was looking for. Nonetheless, the operators work this way for a reason: they correspond to some standard mathematical logical operators. `Any` is the *existential quantifier*, usually written as a backward E ($\exists$) and pronounced "there exists," and `All` is the *universal quantifier*, usually written as an upside-down A ($\forall$) and pronounced "for all." Mathematicians long ago agreed on a convention for statements that apply the universal quantifier to an empty set. For example, defining $\mathbb{V}$ as the set of all vegetables, I can assert that $\forall\{v : (v \in \mathbb{V}) \wedge \text{putOnPlateByMe}(v)\}$ eatenByMe(v), or, in English, "for each vegetable that I put on my plate, it is true to say that I ate that vegetable." This statement is deemed to be true if the set of vegetables I put on my plate is empty. (Perhaps mathematicians don't like vegetables either.) Rather pleasingly, the proper term for such a statement is a *vacuous truth*.

Asynchronous Immediate Evaluation

Although most LINQ operators defer execution, as you've now seen there are some exceptions. With most LINQ providers, the `Contains`, `Any` and `All` operators do not produce a wrapped result. (E.g., in LINQ to Objects, these return a `bool`, not an `IEnumerable<bool>`.) This sometimes means that these operators need to do some slow work. For example, the Entity Framework's LINQ provider will need to send a query off to the database and wait for the response before being able to return the `bool` result. The same goes for `ToArray` and `ToList`, which produce fully-populated collections, instead of an `IEnumerable<T>` or `IQueryable<T>` that have the potential to produce results in the future.

As Chapter 16 describes, it is common for slow operations like these to implement the Task-based Asynchronous Pattern (TAP), enabling us to use the `await` keyword described in Chapter 17. Some LINQ providers therefore choose to offer asynchronous versions of these operators. For example, Entity Framework offers `SingleAsync`, `ContainsAsync`, `AnyAsync`, `AllAsync`, `ToArrayAsync`, and `ToListAsync`, and equivalents for the other operators we'll see that perform immediate evaluation.

Specific Items and Subranges

It can be useful to write a query that produces just a single item. Perhaps you're looking for the first object in a list that meets certain criteria, or maybe you want to fetch information in a database identified by a particular key. LINQ defines several operators that can do this, and some related ones for working with a subrange of the items a query might return.

Use the `Single` operator when you have a query that you believe should produce exactly one result. Example 10-35 shows just such a query—it looks up a course by its category and number, and in my sample data, this uniquely identifies a course.

Example 10-35. Applying the Single operator to a query

```
var q = from course in Course.Catalog
        where course.Category == "MAT" && course.Number == 101
        select course;

Course geometry = q.Single();
```

Because LINQ queries are built by chaining operators together, we can take the query built by the query expression and add on another operator—the `Single` operator, in this case. While most operators would return an object representing another query (an `IEnumerable<T>` here, since we're using LINQ to Objects) `Single` is different. Like `ToArray` and `ToList`, the `Single` operator evaluates the query immediately, but it then returns the one and only object that the query produced. If the query fails to produce exactly one object—perhaps it produces no items, or two—this will throw an `InvalidOperationException`. (Since this is another of the operators that produces an operator immediately, some providers offer `SingleAsync` as described in the sidebar "Asynchronous Immediate Evaluation" on page 447.)

There's an overload of the `Single` operator that takes a predicate. As Example 10-36 shows, this allows us to express the same logic as the whole of Example 10-35 more compactly. (As with the `Where` operator, all the predicate-based operators in this section use `Func<T, bool>`, not `Predicate<T>`.)

Example 10-36. Single operator with predicate

```
Course geometry = Course.Catalog.Single(
    course => course.Category == "MAT" && course.Number == 101);
```

The `Single` operator is unforgiving: if your query does not return exactly one item, it will throw an exception. There's a slightly more flexible variant called `SingleOrDefault`, which allows a query to return either one item or no items. If the query returns nothing, this method returns the default value for the item type (i.e., `null` if it's a reference type, 0 if it's a numeric type, and `false` if the type is `bool`). Multiple matches still cause an exception. As with `Single`, there are two overloads: one with no arguments for use on a source that you believe contains no more than one object, and one that takes a predicate lambda.

LINQ defines two related operators, `First` and `FirstOrDefault`, each of which offer overloads taking no arguments or a predicate. For sequences containing zero or one matching items, these behave in exactly the same way as `Single` and `SingleOrDefault`: they return the item if there is one; if there isn't, `First` will throw an exception, while `FirstOrDefault` will return `null` or an equivalent value. However, these operators respond differently when there are multiple results—instead of throwing an exception, they just pick the first result and return that, discarding the rest. This might be useful if you want to find the most expensive item in a list—you could order a query by descending price and then pick the first result. Example 10-37 uses a similar technique to pick the longest course from my sample data.

Example 10-37. Using First to select the longest course

```
var q = from course in Course.Catalog
        orderby course.Duration descending
        select course;
Course longest = q.First();
```

If you have a query that doesn't guarantee any particular order for its results, these operators will pick one item arbitrarily.

Do not use `First` or `FirstOrDefault` unless you expect there to be multiple matches and you want to process only one of them. Some developers use these when they expect only a single match. The operators will work, of course, but the `Single` and `SingleOrDefault` operators more accurately express your expectations. They will let you know when your expectations were misplaced by throwing an exception when there are multiple matches. If your code embodies incorrect assumptions, it's usually best to know about it instead of plowing on regardless.

The existence of `First` and `FirstOrDefault` raises an obvious question: can I pick the last item? The answer is yes, there are also `Last` and `LastOrDefault` operators, and again, each offers two overloads—one taking no arguments, and one taking a predicate.

The next obvious question is: what if I want a particular element that's neither the first nor the last? Your wish is, in this particular instance, LINQ's command, because it offers `ElementAt` and `ElementAtOrDefault` operators, both of which take just an

index. (There are no overloads.) This provides a way to access elements of any IEnu
merable<T> by index, but be careful: if you ask for the 10,000th element, these operators may need to request and discard the first 9,999 elements to get there. As it
happens, LINQ to Objects detects when the source object implements IList<T>, in
which case it uses the indexer to retrieve the element directly instead of going the
slow way around. But not all IEnumerable<T> implementations support random
access, so these operators can be very slow. In particular, even if your source implements IList<T>, once you've applied one or more LINQ operators to it, the output of
those operators will typically not support indexing. So it would be particularly disastrous to use ElementAt in a loop of the kind shown in Example 10-38.

Example 10-38. How not to use ElementAt

```
var mathsCourses = Course.Catalog.Where(c => c.Category == "MAT");
for (int i = 0; i < mathsCourses.Count(); ++i)
{
    // Never do this!
    Course c = mathsCourses.ElementAt(i);
    Console.WriteLine(c.Title);
}
```

Even though Course.Catalog is an array, I've filtered its contents with the Where
operator, which returns a query of type IEnumerable<Course> that does not implement IList<Course>. The first iteration won't be too bad—I'll be passing ElementAt
an index of 0, so it just returns the first match, and with my sample data, the very first
item Where inspects will match. But the second time around the loop, we're calling
ElementAt again. The query that mathsCourses refers to does not keep track of where
we got to in the previous loop—it's an IEnumerable<T>, not an IEnumerator<T>—so
this will start again. ElementAt will ask that query for the first item, which it will
promptly discard, and then it will ask for the next item, and that becomes the return
value. So the Where query has now been executed twice—the first time, ElementAt
asked it for only one item, and then the second time it asked it for two, so it has processed the first course twice now. The third time around the loop (which happens to
be the final time), we do it all again, but this time, ElementAt will discard the first two
matches and will return the third, so now it has looked at the first course three times,
the second one twice, and the third and fourth courses once. (The third course in my
sample data is not in the MAT category, so the Where query will skip over this when
asked for the third item.) So, to retrieve three items, I've evaluated the Where query
three times, causing it to evaluate my filter lambda seven times.

In fact, it's worse than that, because the for loop will also invoke that Count method
each time, and with a nonindexable source such as the one returned by Where, Count
has to evaluate the entire sequence—the only way the Where operator can tell you

how many items match is to look at all of them. So this code fully evaluates the query returned by Where three times in addition to the three partial evaluations performed by ElementAt. We get away with it here because the collection is small, but if I had an array with 1,000 elements, all of which turned out to match the filter, we'd be fully evaluating the Where query 1,000 times, and performing partial evaluations another 1,000 times. Each full evaluation calls the filter predicate 1,000 times, and the partial evaluations here will do so on average 500 times, so the code would end up executing the filter 1,500,000 times. Iterating through the Where query with the foreach loop would evaluate the query just once, executing the filter expression 1,000 times, and would produce the same results.

So be careful with both Count and ElementAt. If you use them in a loop that iterates over the collection on which you invoke them, the resulting code will have $O(n^2)$ complexity.

All of the operators I've just described return a single item from the source. There are two more operators that also get selective about which items to use but can return multiple items: Skip and Take. Both of these take a single int argument. As the name suggests, Skip discards the specified number of elements and then returns everything else from its source. Take returns the specified number of elements from the start of the sequence and then discards the rest (so it is similar to TOP in SQL). TakeLast does the same except it works at the end, e.g. you could use it to get the final 5 items from the source.

There are predicate-driven equivalents, SkipWhile and TakeWhile. SkipWhile will discard items from the sequence until it finds one that matches the predicate, at which point it will return that and every item that follows for the rest of the sequence (whether or not the remaining items match the predicate). Conversely, TakeWhile returns items until it encounters the first item that does not match the predicate, at which point it discards that and the remainder of the sequence.

Although Skip, Take, SkipWhile, and TakeWhile are all clearly order-sensitive, they are not restricted to just the ordered types, such as IOrderedEnumerable<T>. They are also defined for IEnumerable<T>, which is reasonable, because even though there may be no particular order guaranteed, an IEnumerable<T> always produces elements in some order. (The only way you can extract items from an IEnumerable<T> is one after another, so there will always be an order, even if it's meaningless. It might not be the same every time you enumerate the items, but for any single evaluation, the items must come out in some order.) Moreover, IOrderedEnumerable<T> is not widely implemented outside of LINQ, so it's quite common to have non-LINQ-aware objects that produce items in a known order but which implement only IEnumerable<T>. These operators are useful in these scenarios, so the restriction is relaxed. Slightly more surprisingly, IQueryable<T> also supports these operations, but that's consistent with the fact that many databases support TOP (roughly equivalent to Take) even on unordered queries. As always, individual providers may choose not to support individual operations, so in scenarios where there's no reasonable interpretation of these operators, they will just throw an exception.

Aggregation

The Sum and Average operators add together the values of all the source items. Sum returns the total, and Average returns the total divided by the number of items. LINQ providers that support these typically make them available for collections of items of these numeric types: decimal, double, float, int, and long. There are also overloads that work with any item type in conjunction with a lambda that takes an item and returns one of those numeric types. That allows us to write code such as Example 10-39, which works with a collection of Course objects and calculates the average of a particular value extracted from the object: the course length in hours.

Example 10-39. Average operator with projection

```
Console.WriteLine("Average course length in hours: {0}",
    Course.Catalog.Average(course => course.Duration.TotalHours));
```

LINQ also defines Min and Max operators. You can apply these to any type of sequence, although it is not guaranteed to succeed—the particular provider you're using may report an error if it doesn't know how to compare the types you've used. For example, LINQ to Objects requires the objects in the sequence to implement IComparable.

Min and Max both have overloads that accept a lambda that gets the value to use from the source item. Example 10-40 uses this to find the date on which the most recent course was published.

Example 10-40. Max with projection

```
DateTime m = mathsCourses.Max(c => c.PublicationDate);
```

Notice that this does not return the course with the most recent publication date; it returns that course's publication date. If you want to select the object for which a particular property has the maximum value, you could use the OrderByDescending operator followed by First, although that might be somewhat inefficient, since it may do more work than necessary—you're asking it to sort the entire input.

LINQ to Objects defines specialized overloads of Min and Max for sequences that return the same numeric types that Sum and Average deal with (i.e., decimal, double, float, int, and long). It also defines similar specializations for the form that takes a lambda. These overloads exist to improve performance by avoiding boxing. The general-purpose form relies on `IComparable` and getting an interface type reference to a value always involves boxing that value. For large collections, boxing every single value would put considerable extra pressure on the garbage collector.

 Microsoft provides a NuGet package called `System.Interactive`[2] that provides various extra LINQ-style operators. It includes `MaxBy`, which is a more direct (and likely more efficient) way to achieve the same result. And if you want even more LINQ, there's the non-Microsoft MoreLINQ project.

LINQ defines an operator called `Aggregate`, which generalizes the pattern that `Min`, `Max`, `Sum`, and `Average` all use, which is to produce a single result with a process that involves taking every source item into consideration. It's possible to implement all four of these operators in terms of `Aggregate`. Example 10-41 uses the `Sum` operator to calculate the total duration of all courses, and then shows how to use the `Aggregate` operator to perform the exact same calculation.

Example 10-41. Sum and equivalent with Aggregate

```
double t1 = Course.Catalog.Sum(course => course.Duration.TotalHours);
double t2 = Course.Catalog.Aggregate(
    0.0, (hours, course) => hours + course.Duration.TotalHours);
```

Aggregation works by building up a value that represents what we know about all the items inspected so far, referred to as the *accumulator*. The type we use depends on the knowledge we want to accumulate. Here, I'm just adding all the numbers together, so I'll use a `double` (because the `TimeSpan` type's `TotalHours` property is also a `double`).

Initially we have no knowledge, because we haven't looked at any items yet. We need to provide an accumulator value to represent this starting point, so the `Aggregate` operator's first argument is the *seed*, an initial value for the accumulator. In Example 10-41, the accumulator is just a running total, so the seed is `0.0`.

The second argument is a lambda that describes how to update the accumulator to incorporate information for a single item. Since my goal here is simply to calculate the total time, I just add the duration of the current course to the running total.

---

2 This name requires some explanation. It's part of the Reactive Extensions project described in Chapter 11. The `System.Reactive` package defines standard LINQ operators for an interface called `IObservable<T>`, but it also adds a load of useful non-standard operators. `System.Interactive` provides all of those extra operators for `IEnumerable<T>`, and its name is meant as a sort of mirror image of `System.Reactive`.

Once `Aggregate` has looked at every item, this particular overload returns the accumulator directly. It will be the total number of hours across all courses in this case. The accumulator doesn't have to use addition. We can implement `Max`, using the same process, but a different accumulation strategy. Instead of maintaining a running total, the value representing everything we know so far about the data is simply the highest value seen yet. Example 10-42 shows the rough equivalent of Example 10-40. (It's not exactly the same, because Example 10-42 makes no attempt to detect an empty source. `Max` will throw an exception if this source is empty, but this will just return the date 0/0/0000.)

Example 10-42. Implementing Max with Aggregate

```
DateTime m = mathsCourses.Aggregate(
    new DateTime(),
    (date, c) => date > c.PublicationDate ? date : c.PublicationDate);
```

This illustrates that `Aggregate` does not impose any single meaning for the value that accumulates knowledge—the way you use it depends on what you're doing. Some operations require an accumulator with a bit more structure. Example 10-43 calculates the average course duration with `Aggregate`.

Example 10-43. Implementing Average with Aggregate

```
double average = Course.Catalog.Aggregate(
    new { TotalHours = 0.0, Count = 0 },
    (totals, course) => new
    {
        TotalHours = totals.TotalHours + course.Duration.TotalHours,
        Count = totals.Count + 1
    },
    totals => totals.Count >= 0
        ? totals.TotalHours / totals.Count
        : throw new InvalidOperationException("Sequence was empty"));
```

The average duration requires us to know two things: the total duration, and the number of items. So, in this example, my accumulator uses a type that can contain two values, one to hold the total and one to hold the item count. I've used an anonymous type because as already mentioned, that is sometimes the only option in LINQ and I want to show the most general case. However, it's worth mentioning that in this particular case, a tuple might be better. It will work because this is LINQ to objects, and since lightweight tuples are value types whereas anonymous types are reference types, a tuple would reduce the number of objects being allocated.

Example 10-43 relies on the fact that when two separate methods in the same component create instances of two structurally identical anonymous types, the compiler generates a single type that is used for both. The seed produces an instance of an anonymous type consisting of a `double` called `TotalHours` and an `int` called `Count`. The accumulation lambda also returns an instance of an anonymous type with the same member names and types in the same order. The C# compiler deems that these will be the same type, which is important, because `Aggregate` requires the lambda to accept and also return an instance of the accumulator type.

Example 10-43 uses a different overload than the earlier example. It takes an extra lambda, which is used to extract the return value from the accumulator—the accumulator builds up the information I need to produce the result, but the accumulator itself is not the result in this example.

Of course, if all you want to do is calculate the sum, maximum, or average values, you wouldn't use `Aggregate`—you'd use the specialized operators designed to do those jobs. Not only are they simpler, but they're often more efficient. (For example, a LINQ provider for a database might be able to generate a query that uses the database's built-in features to calculate the minimum or maximum value.) I just wanted to show the flexibility, using examples that are easily understood. But now that I've done that, Example 10-44 shows a particularly concise example of `Aggregate` that doesn't correspond to any other built-in operator. This takes a collection of rectangles, and returns the bounding box that contains all of those rectangles.

Example 10-44. Aggregating bounding boxes

```
public static Rect GetBounds(IEnumerable<Rect> rects) =>
    rects.Aggregate(Rect.Union);
```

The `Rect` structure in this example is from the `System.Windows` namespace. This is part of WPF, and it's a very simple data structure that just contains four numbers—X, Y, Width, and Height—so you can use it in non-WPF applications if you like.[3] Example 10-44 uses the `Rect` type's static `Union` method, which takes two `Rect` arguments, and returns a single `Rect` that is the bounding box of the two inputs (i.e., the smallest rectangle that contains both of the input rectangles).

---

3 If you do so, be careful not to confuse it with another WPF type, `Rectangle`. That's an altogether more complex beast that supports animation, styling, layout, user input, data binding, and various other WPF features. Do not attempt to use `Rectangle` outside of a WPF application.

I'm using the simplest overload of Aggregate here. It does the same thing as the one I used in Example 10-41, but it doesn't require me to supply a seed—it just uses the first item in the list. Example 10-45 is equivalent to Example 10-44, but makes the steps more explicit. I've provided the first Rect in the sequence as an explicit seed value, using Skip to aggregate over everything except that first element. I've also written a lambda to invoke the method, instead of passing the method itself. If you're using this sort of lambda that just passes its arguments straight on to an existing method with LINQ to Objects, you can just pass the method name instead, and it will call the target method directly rather than going through your lambda. (You can't do that with expression-based providers, because they require a lambda.)

Using the method directly is more succinct and marginally more efficient, but it also makes for slightly obscure code, which is why I've spelled it out in Example 10-45.

Example 10-45. More verbose and less obscure bounding box aggregation

```
public static Rect GetBounds(IEnumerable<Rect> rects)
{
    IEnumerable<Rect> theRest = rects.Skip(1);
    return theRest.Aggregate(rects.First(), (r1, r2) => Rect.Union(r1, r2));
}
```

These two examples work the same way. They start with the first rectangle as the seed. For the next item in the list, Aggregate will call Rect.Union, passing in the seed and the second rectangle. The result—the bounding box of the first two rectangles—becomes the new accumulator value. And that then gets passed to Union along with the third rectangle, and so on. Example 10-46 shows what the effect of this Aggregate operation would be if performed on a collection of four Rect values. (I've represented the four values here as r1, r2, r3, and r4. To pass them to Aggregate, they'd need to be inside a collection such as an array.)

Example 10-46. The effect of Aggregate

```
Rect bounds = Rect.Union(Rect.Union(Rect.Union(r1, r2), r3), r4);
```

As I mentioned earlier, Aggregate is LINQ's name for an operation sometimes called *reduce*. You also sometimes see it called *fold*. LINQ went with the name Aggregate for the same reason it calls its projection operator Select instead of map (the more common name in functional programming languages): LINQ's terminology is more influenced by SQL than it is by functional programming languages.

Set Operations

LINQ defines three operators that use some common set operations to combine two sources. `Intersect` produces a result that contains only those items that were in both of the input sources. `Except` includes only those items from the first input source that were not in the second. The output of `Union`[4] contains items that were in either (or both) of the input sources.

Although LINQ defines these set operations, most LINQ source types do not correspond directly to the abstraction of a set. With a mathematical set, any particular item either belongs to a set or it does not, with no innate concept of order, or of the number of times a particular item appears in a set. `IEnumerable<T>` is not like that—it's a sequence of items, so it's possible to have duplicates, and the same is true of `IQueryable<T>`. This is not necessarily a problem, because some collections will happen never to get into a situation where they contain duplicates, and in some cases, the presence of duplicates won't cause a problem. However, it can sometimes be useful to take a collection that contains duplicates and remove them. For this, LINQ defines the `Distinct` operator, which removes duplicates. Example 10-47 contains a query that extracts the category names from all the courses, and then feeds that into the `Distinct` operator to ensure that each unique category name appears just once.

Example 10-47. Removing duplicates with Distinct

```
var categories = Course.Catalog.Select(c => c.Category).Distinct();
```

All of these set operators are available in two forms, because you can optionally pass any of them an `IEqualityComparer<T>`. This allows you to customize how the operators decide whether two items are the same thing.

Whole-Sequence, Order-Preserving Operations

LINQ defines certain operators whose output includes every item from the source, and that preserve or reverse the order. Not all collections necessarily have an order, so these operators will not always be supported. However, LINQ to Objects supports all of them. The simplest is `Reverse`, which reverses the order of the elements.

The `Concat` operator combines two sequences. It returns a sequence that produces all of the elements from the first sequence (in whatever order that sequence returns them), followed by all of the elements from the second sequence (again, preserving the order). In cases where you need to add just a single element to the end of the first sequence, you can use `Append` instead. There is also `Prepend` which adds a single item

---

4 This is unrelated to the `Rect.Union` method used in the preceding example.

at the start. The `Repeat` operator effectively concatenates the specified number of copies of the source.

The `DefaultIfEmpty` operator returns all of the elements from its source. However, if the source is empty, it returns a single element that has the default, zero-like value of the element type.

The `Zip` operator also combines two sequences, but instead of returning one after the other, it works with pairs of elements. So the first item it returns will be based on both the first item from the first sequence and the first item from the second sequence. The second item in the zipped sequence will be based on the second items from each of the sequences, and so on. The name `Zip` is meant to bring to mind how a zipper in an article of clothing brings two things together in perfect alignment. (It's not an exact analogy. When a zipper brings together the two parts, the teeth from the two halves interlock in an alternating fashion. But the `Zip` operator does not interleave its inputs like a physical zipper's teeth. It brings items from the two sources together in pairs.)

Since `Zip` works with pairs of items, you need to tell it how you'd like them combined. It takes a lambda with two arguments, and it will pass item pairs from the two sources as those arguments, and produce whatever your lambda returns as output items. Example 10-48 uses a selector that combines each pair of items using string concatenation.

.NET Core adds an overload of `Zip` that does not require the lambda. It just returns a sequence of tuples.

Example 10-48. Combining lists with Zip

```
string[] firstNames = { "Carmel", "Ed", "Arthur", "Arthur" };
string[] lastNames = { "Eve", "Freeman", "Dent", "Pewty" };
IEnumerable<string> fullNames = firstNames.Zip(lastNames,
    (first, last) => first + " " + last);
foreach (string name in fullNames)
{
    Console.WriteLine(name);
}
```

The two lists that this example zips together contain first names and last names, respectively. The output looks like this:

```
Carmel Eve
Ed Freeman
```

```
Arthur Dent
Arthur Pewty
```

If the input sources contain different numbers of items, Zip will stop once it reaches the end of the shorter collection, and will not attempt to retrieve any further items from the longer collection. It does not treat mismatched lengths as an error.

The SequenceEqual operator bears a resemblance to Zip in that it works on two sequences, and acts on pairs of items found at the same position in the two sequences. But, instead of passing them to a lambda to be combined, SequenceEqual just compares each pair. If this comparison process finds that the two sources contain the same number of items, and that for every pair, the two items are equal, then it returns true. If the sources are of different lengths, or if even just one pair of items is not equal, it returns false. SequenceEqual has two overloads, one that accepts just the list with which to compare the source, and another that also takes an IEqualityCom parer<T> to customize what you mean by equal.

Grouping

Sometimes you will want to process all items that have something in common as a group. Example 10-49 uses a query to group courses by category, writing out a title for each category before listing all the courses in that category.

Example 10-49. Grouping query expression

```
var subjectGroups = from course in Course.Catalog
                    group course by course.Category;

foreach (var group in subjectGroups)
{
    Console.WriteLine("Category: " + group.Key);
    Console.WriteLine();

    foreach (var course in group)
    {
        Console.WriteLine(course.Title);
    }
    Console.WriteLine();
}
```

A group clause takes an expression that determines group membership—in this case, any courses whose Category properties return the same value will be deemed to be in the same group. A group clause produces a collection in which each item implements a type representing a group. Since I am using LINQ to Objects, and I am grouping by category string, the type of the subjectGroup variable in Example 10-49 will be IEnu merable<IGrouping<string, Course>>. This particular example produces three group objects, depicted in Figure 10-1.

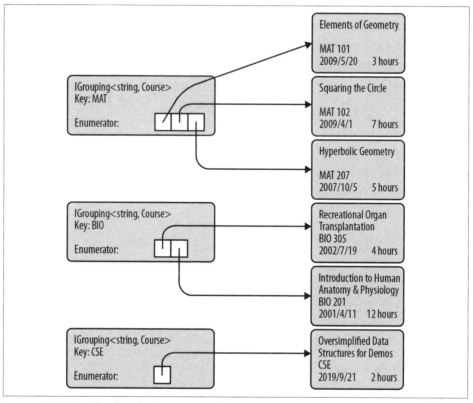

Figure 10-1. Result of evaluating a grouping query

Each of the IGrouping<string, Course> items has a Key property, and because the query groups items by the course's Category property, each key contains a string value from that property. There are three different category names in the sample data in Example 10-17: MAT, BIO, and CSE, so these are the Key values for the three groups.

The IGrouping<TKey, TItem> interface derives from IEnumerable<TItem>, so each group object can be enumerated to find the items it contains. So in Example 10-49, the outer foreach loop iterates over the three groups returned by the query, and then the inner foreach loop iterates over the Course objects in each of the groups.

The query expression turns into the code in Example 10-50.

Example 10-50. Expanding a simple grouping query

```
var subjectGroups = Course.Catalog.GroupBy(course => course.Category);
```

Query expressions offer some variations on the theme of grouping. With a slight modification to the original query, we can arrange for the items in each group to be something other than the original `Course` objects. In Example 10-51, I've changed the expression immediately after the `group` keyword from just `course` to `course.Title`.

Example 10-51. Group query with item projection

```
var subjectGroups = from course in Course.Catalog
                    group course.Title by course.Category;
```

This still has the same grouping expression, `course.Category`, so this produces three groups as before, but now it's of type `IGrouping<string, string>`. If you were to iterate over the contents of one of the groups, you'd find each group offers a sequence of strings, containing the course names. As Example 10-52 shows, the compiler expands this query into a different overload of the `GroupBy` operator.

Example 10-52. Expanding a group query with an item projection

```
var subjectGroups = Course.Catalog
    .GroupBy(course => course.Category, course => course.Title);
```

Query expressions are required to have either a `select` or a `group` as their final clause. However, if a query contains a `group` clause, that doesn't have to be the last clause. In Example 10-51, I modified how the query represents each item within a group (i.e., the boxes on the right of Figure 10-1), but I'm also free to customize the objects representing each group (the items on the left). By default, I get the `IGroup ing<TKey, TItem>` objects (or the LINQ provider in question's equivalent), but I can change this. Example 10-53 uses the optional `into` keyword in its `group` clause. This introduces a new range variable, which iterates over the group objects, which I can go on to use in the rest of the query. I could follow this with other clause types, such as `orderby` or `where`, but in this case, I've chosen to use a `select` clause.

Example 10-53. Group query with group projection

```
var subjectGroups =
    from course in Course.Catalog
    group course by course.Category into category
    select $"Category '{category.Key}' contains {category.Count()} courses";
```

The result of this query is an `IEnumerable<string>`, and if you display all the strings it produces, you get this:

```
Category 'MAT' contains 3 courses
Category 'BIO' contains 2 courses
Category 'CSE' contains 1 courses
```

As Example 10-54 shows, this expands into a call to the same `GroupBy` overload that Example 10-50 uses, and then uses the ordinary `Select` operator for the final clause.

Example 10-54. Expanded group query with group projection

```
IEnumerable<string> subjectGroups = Course.Catalog
    .GroupBy(course => course.Category)
    .Select(category =>
        $"Category '{category.Key}' contains {category.Count()} courses");
```

LINQ to Objects defines some more overloads for the `GroupBy` operator that are not accessible from the query syntax. Example 10-55 shows an overload that provides a slightly more direct equivalent to Example 10-53.

Example 10-55. GroupBy with key and group projections

```
IEnumerable<string> subjectGroups = Course.Catalog.GroupBy(
    course => course.Category,
    (category, courses) =>
        $"Category '{category}' contains {courses.Count()} courses");
```

This overload takes two lambdas. The first is the expression by which items are grouped. The second is used to produce each group object. Unlike the previous examples, this does not use the `IGrouping<TKey, TItem>` interface. Instead, the final lambda receives the key as one argument, and then a collection of the items in the group as the second. This is exactly the same information that `IGrouping<TKey, TItem>` encapsulates, but because this form of the operator can pass these as separate arguments, it removes the need for objects to represent the groups.

There's yet another version of this operator shown in Example 10-56. It combines the functionality of all the other flavors.

Example 10-56. GroupBy operator with key, item, and group projections

```
IEnumerable<string> subjectGroups = Course.Catalog.GroupBy(
    course => course.Category,
    course => course.Title,
    (category, titles) =>
        $"Category '{category}' contains {titles.Count()} courses: " +
            string.Join(", ", titles));
```

This overload takes three lambdas. The first is the expression by which items are grouped. The second determines how individual items in a group are represented—this time I've chosen to extract the course title. The third lambda is used to produce each group object, and as with Example 10-55, this final lambda is passed the key as one argument, and its other argument gets the group items, as transformed by the second lambda. So, rather than the original `Course` items, this second argument will be an `IEnumerable<string>` containing the course titles, because that's what the second lambda in this example requested. The result of this `GroupBy` operator is once again a collection of strings, but now it looks like this:

```
Category 'MAT' contains 3 courses: Elements of Geometry, Squaring the Circle, Hy
perbolic Geometry
Category 'BIO' contains 2 courses: Recreational Organ Transplantation, Introduct
ion to Human Anatomy and Physiology
Category 'CSE' contains 1 courses: Oversimplified Data Structures for Demos
```

I've shown four versions of the `GroupBy` operator. All four take a lambda that selects the key to use for grouping, and the simplest overload takes nothing else. The others let you control the representation of individual items in the group, or the representation of each group, or both. There are four more versions of this operator. They offer all the same services as the four I've shown already, but also take an `IEqualityCom parer<T>`, which lets you customize the logic that decides whether two keys are considered to be the same for grouping purposes.

Sometimes it is useful to group by more than one value. For example, suppose you want to group courses by both category and publication year. You could chain the operators, grouping first by category, and then by year within the category (or vice versa). But you might not want this level of nesting—instead of groups of groups, you might want to group courses under each unique combination of `Category` and publication year. The way to do this is simply to put both values into the key, and you can do that by using an anonymous type, as Example 10-57 shows.

Example 10-57. Composite group key

```
var bySubjectAndYear =
    from course in Course.Catalog
    group course by new { course.Category, course.PublicationDate.Year };
foreach (var group in bySubjectAndYear)
{
    Console.WriteLine($"{group.Key.Category} ({group.Key.Year})");
    foreach (var course in group)
    {
        Console.WriteLine(course.Title);
    }
}
```

This takes advantage of the fact that anonymous types implement `Equals` and `GetHashCode` for us. It works for all forms of the `GroupBy` operator. With LINQ providers that don't treat their lambdas as expressions (e.g., LINQ to Objects) you could use a tuple instead, which would be slightly more succinct, while having the same effect.

There is one other operator that groups its outputs, called GroupJoin, but it does so as part of a join operation, and we'll look at the simpler joins first.

Joins

LINQ defines a Join operator that enables a query over one source to use related data from some other source, much as a database query can join information from one table with data in another table. Suppose our application stored a list of which students had signed up for which courses. If you stored that information in a file, you wouldn't want to copy the full details for either the course or the student out into every line—you'd want just enough information to identify a student and a particular course. In my example data, courses are uniquely identified by the combination of the category and the number. So, to record who's signed up for what, we'd need records containing three pieces of information: the course category, the course number, and something to identify the student. The class in Example 10-58 shows how we might represent such a record in memory.

Example 10-58. Class associating a student with a course

```
public class CourseChoice
{
    public int StudentId { get; set; }

    public string Category { get; set; }

    public int Number { get; set; }
}
```

Once our application has loaded this information into memory, we may want access to the Course objects, rather than just the information identifying the course. We can get this with a join clause, as shown in Example 10-59 (which also supplies some additional sample data using the CourseChoice class, so that the query has something to work with).

Example 10-59. Query with join clause

```
CourseChoice[] choices =
{
    new CourseChoice { StudentId = 1, Category = "MAT", Number = 101 },
    new CourseChoice { StudentId = 1, Category = "MAT", Number = 102 },
    new CourseChoice { StudentId = 1, Category = "MAT", Number = 207 },
    new CourseChoice { StudentId = 2, Category = "MAT", Number = 101 },
    new CourseChoice { StudentId = 2, Category = "BIO", Number = 201 },
};

var studentsAndCourses = from choice in choices
```

```
        join course in Course.Catalog
          on new { choice.Category, choice.Number }
          equals new { course.Category, course.Number }
        select new { choice.StudentId, Course = course };

foreach (var item in studentsAndCourses)
{
    Console.WriteLine(
        $"Student {item.StudentId} will attend {item.Course.Title}");
}
```

This displays one line for each entry in the choices array. It shows the title for each course, because even though that was not available in the input collection, the join clause located the relevant item in the course catalog. Example 10-60 shows how the compiler translates the query in Example 10-59.

Example 10-60. Using the Join operator directly

```
var studentsAndCourses = choices.Join(
    Course.Catalog,
    choice => new { choice.Category, choice.Number },
    course => new { course.Category, course.Number },
    (choice, course) => new { choice.StudentId, Course = course });
```

The Join operator's job is to find an item in the second sequence that corresponds to the item in the first. This correspondence is determined by the first two lambdas; items from the two sources will be considered to correspond to one another if the values returned by these two lambdas are equal. This example uses an anonymous type, and depends on the fact that two structurally identical anonymously typed instances in the same assembly share the same type. In other words, those two lambdas both produce objects with the same type. The compiler generates an Equals method for any anonymous type that compares each member in turn, so the effect of this code is that two rows are considered to correspond if their Category and Number properties are equal. (Once again, with IQueryable<T>-based providers we have to use anonymous types, not tuples, because these lambdas will be turned into expression trees. But since this example uses a non-expression-based provider, LINQ to Objects, you could simplify this code slightly by using tuples instead.)

I've set up this example so that there can be only one match, but what would happen if the course category and number did not uniquely identify a course for some reason? If there are multiple matches for any single input row, the Join operator will produce one output item for each match, so in that case, we'd get more output items than there were entries in the choices array. Conversely, if an item in the first source has no corresponding item in the second collection, Join will not produce any output for the item—it effectively ignores that input item.

LINQ offers an alternative join type that handles input rows with either zero or multiple corresponding rows differently than the `Join` operator. Example 10-61 shows the modified query expression. (The difference is the addition of `into courses` on the end of the `join` clause, and the final `select` clause refers to that instead of the `course` range variable.) This produces output in a different form, so I've also modified the code that writes out the results.

Example 10-61. A grouped join

```
var studentsAndCourses =
    from choice in choices
    join course in Course.Catalog
      on new { choice.Category, choice.Number }
      equals new { course.Category, course.Number }
      into courses
    select new { choice.StudentId, Courses = courses };

foreach (var item in studentsAndCourses)
{
    Console.WriteLine($"Student {item.StudentId} will attend " +
        string.Join(",", item.Courses.Select(course => course.Title)));
}
```

As Example 10-62 shows, this causes the compiler to generate a call to the `GroupJoin` operator instead of `Join`.

Example 10-62. GroupJoin operator

```
var studentsAndCourses = choices.GroupJoin(
    Course.Catalog,
    choice => new { choice.Category, choice.Number },
    course => new { course.Category, course.Number },
    (choice, courses) => new { choice.StudentId, Courses = courses });
```

This form of join produces one result for each item in the input collection by invoking the final lambda. Its first argument is the input item, and its second argument will be a collection of all the corresponding objects from the second collection. (Compare this with `Join`, which invokes its final lambda once for each match, passing the corresponding items one at a time.) This provides a way to represent an input item that has no corresponding items in the second collection: the operator can just pass an empty collection.

Both `Join` and `GroupJoin` also have overloads that accept an `IEqualityComparer<T>` so that you can define a custom meaning for equality for the values returned by the first two lambdas.

Conversion

Sometimes you will need to convert a query of one type to some other type. For example, you might have ended up with a collection where the type argument specifies some base type (e.g., object), but you have good reason to believe that the collection actually contains items of some more specific type (e.g., Course). When dealing with individual objects, you can just use the C# cast syntax to convert the reference to the type you believe you're dealing with. Unfortunately, this doesn't work for types such as IEnumerable<T> or IQueryable<T>.

Although covariance means that an IEnumerable<Course> is implicitly convertible to an IEnumerable<object>, you cannot convert in the other direction even with an explicit downcast. If you have a reference of type IEnumerable<object>, attempting to cast that to IEnumerable<Course> will succeed only if the object implements IEnumerable<Course>. It's quite possible to end up with a sequence that consists entirely of Course objects but does not implement IEnumerable<Course>. Example 10-63 creates just such a sequence, and it will throw an exception when it tries to cast to IEnumerable<Course>.

Example 10-63. How not to cast a sequence

```
IEnumerable<object> sequence = Course.Catalog.Select(c => (object) c);
var courseSequence = (IEnumerable<Course>) sequence; // InvalidCastException
```

This is a contrived example, of course. I forced the creation of an IEnumerable<object> by casting the Select lambda's return type to object. However, it's easy enough to end up in this situation for real, in only slightly more complex circumstances. Fortunately, there's an easy solution. You can use the Cast<T> operator, shown in Example 10-64.

Example 10-64. How to cast a sequence

```
var courseSequence = sequence.Cast<Course>();
```

This returns a query that produces every item in its source in order, but it casts each item to the specified target type as it does so. This means that although the initial Cast<T> might succeed, it's possible that you'll get an InvalidCastException some point later when you try to extract values from the sequence. After all, in general, the only way the Cast<T> operator can verify that the sequence you've given it really does only ever produce values of type T is to extract all those values and attempt to cast them. It can't evaluate the whole sequence up front because you might have supplied an infinite sequence. If the first billion items your sequence produces will be of the right type, but after that you return one of an incompatible type, the only way Cast<T> can discover this is to try casting items one at a time.

LINQ to Objects defines an AsEnumerable<T> operator. This just returns the source without modification—it does nothing. Its purpose is to force the use of LINQ to Objects even if you are dealing with something that might have been handled by a different LINQ provider. For example, suppose you have something that implements IQueryable<T>. That interface derives from IEnumerable<T>, but the extension methods that work with IQueryable<T> will take precedence over the LINQ to Objects ones. If your intention is to execute a particular query on a database, and then use further client-side processing of the results with LINQ to Objects, you can use AsEnumerable<T> to draw a line that says, "this is where we move things to the client side."

 Cast<T> and OfType<T> look similar, and developers sometimes use one when they should have used the other (usually because they didn't know both existed). OfType<T> does almost the same thing as Cast<T>, but it silently filters out any items of the wrong type instead of throwing an exception. If you expect and want to ignore items of the wrong type, use OfType<T>. If you do not expect items of the wrong type to be present at all, use Cast<T>, because if you turn out to be wrong, it will let you know by throwing an exception, reducing the risk of allowing a potential bug to remain hidden.

Conversely, there's also AsQueryable<T>. This is designed to be used in scenarios where you have a variable of static type IEnumerable<T> that you believe might contain a reference to an object that also implements IQueryable<T>, and you want to ensure that any queries you create use that instead of LINQ to Objects. If you use this operator on a source that does not in fact implement IQueryable<T>, it returns a wrapper that implements IQueryable<T> but uses LINQ to Objects under the covers.

Yet another operator for selecting a different flavor of LINQ is AsParallel. This returns a ParallelQuery<T>, which lets you build queries to be executed by Parallel LINQ, a LINQ provider that can execute certain operations in parallel to improve performance when multiple CPU cores are available.

There are some operators that convert the query to other types, and also have the effect of executing the query immediately rather than building a new query chained off the back of the previous one. ToArray, ToList, and ToHashSet return an array, list, or hash set respectively, containing the complete results of executing the input query. ToDictionary and ToLookup do the same, but rather than producing a straightforward list of the items, they both produce results that support associative lookup. ToDictionary returns an IDictionary<TKey, TValue>, so it is intended for scenarios where a key corresponds to exactly one value. ToLookup is designed for scenarios where a key may be associated with multiple values, so it returns a different type, ILookup<TKey, TValue>.

I did not mention this interface in Chapter 5 because it is specific to LINQ. It is essentially the same as the dictionary interface, except the indexer returns an IEnumerable<TValue> instead of a single TValue.

While the array and list conversions take no arguments, the dictionary and lookup conversions need to be told what value to use as the key for each source item. You tell them by passing a lambda, as Example 10-65 shows. This uses the course's Category property as the key.

Example 10-65. Creating a lookup

```
ILookup<string, Course> categoryLookup =
    Course.Catalog.ToLookup(course => course.Category);
foreach (Course c in categoryLookup["MAT"])
{
    Console.WriteLine(c.Title);
}
```

The ToDictionary operator offers an overload that takes the same argument but returns a dictionary instead of a lookup. It would throw an exception if you called it in the same way that I called ToLookup in Example 10-65, because multiple course objects share categories, so they would map to the same key. ToDictionary requires each object to have a unique key. To produce a dictionary from the course catalog, you'd either need to group the data by category first and have each dictionary entry refer to an entire group, or you'd need a lambda that returned a composite key based on both the course category and number, because that combination is unique to a course.

Both operators also offer an overload that takes a pair of lambdas—one that extracts the key, and a second that chooses what to use as the corresponding value (you are not obliged to use the source item as the value). Finally, there are overloads that also take an IEqualityComparer<T>.

You've now seen all of the standard LINQ operators, but since that has taken quite a few pages, you may find it useful to have a concise summary. Table 10-1 lists the operators and describes briefly what each is for.

Table 10-1. Summary of LINQ operators

Operator	Purpose
Aggregate	Combines all items through a user-supplied function to produce a single result.
All	Returns true if the predicate supplied is false for no items.
Any	Returns true if predicate supplied is true for at least one item.
Append	Returns a sequence with all the items from its input sequence with one item added to the end.
AsEnumerable	Returns the sequence as an IEnumerable<T>. (Useful for forcing use of LINQ to Objects.)
AsParallel	Returns a ParallelQuery<T> for parallel query execution.
AsQueryable	Ensures use of IQueryable<T> handling where available.
Average	Calculates the arithmetic mean of the items.
Cast	Casts each item in the sequence to the specified type.
Concat	Forms a sequence by concatenating two sequences.
Contains	Returns true if the specified item is in the sequence.
Count, LongCount	Return the number of items in the sequence.
DefaultIfEmpty	Produces the source sequence's elements, unless there are none, in which case it produces a single element with the default value for the element type.
Distinct	Removes duplicate values.
ElementAt	Returns the element at the specified position (throwing an exception if out of range).
ElementAtOrDefault	Returns the element at the specified position (producing the element type's default value if out of range).
Except	Filters out items that are in the other collection provided.
First	Returns the first item, throwing an exception if there are no items.
FirstOrDefault	Returns the first item, or the element type's default value if there are no items.
GroupBy	Gathers items into groups.
GroupJoin	Groups items in another sequence by how they relate to items in the input sequence.
Intersect	Filters out items that are not in the other collection provided.
Join	Produces an item for each matching pair of items from the two input sequences.
Last	Returns the final item, throwing an exception if there are no items.
LastOrDefault	Returns the final item, or the element type's default value if there are no items.
Max	Returns the highest value.
Min	Returns the lowest value.
OfType	Filters out items that are not of the specified type.
OrderBy	Produces items in an ascending order.
OrderByDescending	Produces items in a descending order.
Prepend	Returns a sequence starting with a specified single item, followed by all the items from its input sequence.
Reverse	Produces items in the opposite order than the input.
Select	Projects each item through a function.

Operator	Purpose
SelectMany	Combines multiple collections into one.
SequenceEqual	Returns true only if all items are equal to those in the other sequence provided.
Single	Returns the only item, throwing an exception if there are no items or more than one item.
SingleOrDefault	Returns the only item, or the element type's default value if there are no items; throws an exception if there is more than one item.
Skip	Filters out the specified number of items from the start.
SkipWhile	Filters out items from the start for as long as the items match a predicate.
Sum	Returns the result of adding all the items together.
Take	Produces the specified number of items, discarding the rest.
TakeLast	Produces the specified number of items from the end of the input (discarding all items before that).
TakeWhile	Produces items as long as they match a predicate, discarding the rest of the sequence as soon as one fails to match.
ToArray	Returns an array containing all of the items.
ToDictionary	Returns a dictionary containing all of the items.
ToHashSet	Returns a HashSet<T> containing all of the items.
ToList	Returns a List<T> containing all of the items.
ToLookup	Returns a multivalue associative lookup containing all of the items.
Union	Produces all items that are in either or both of the inputs.
Where	Filters out items that do not match the predicate provided.
Zip	Combines pairs of items from two inputs.

Sequence Generation

The Enumerable class defines the extension methods for IEnumerable<T> that constitute LINQ to Objects. It also offers a few additional (nonextension) static methods that can be used to create new sequences. Enumerable.Range takes two int arguments, and returns an IEnumerable<int> that produces a sequentially increasing series of numbers, starting from the value of the first argument and containing as many numbers as the second argument. For example, Enumerable.Range(15, 10) produces a sequence containing the numbers 15 to 24 (inclusive).

Enumerable.Repeat<T> takes a value of type T and a count. It returns a sequence that will produce that value the specified number of times.

Enumerable.Empty<T> returns an IEnumerable<T> that contains no elements. This may not sound very useful, because there's a much less verbose alternative. You could write new T[0], which creates an array that contains no elements. (Arrays of type T implement IEnumerable<T>.) However, the advantage of Enumerable.Empty<T> is that for any given T, it returns the same instance every time. This means that if for any reason you end up needing an empty sequence repeatedly in a loop that executes many iterations, `Enumerable.Empty<T>` is more efficient, because it puts less pressure on the garbage collector.

Other LINQ Implementations

Most of the examples I've shown in this chapter have used LINQ to Objects, except for a handful that have referred to the Entity Framework. In this final section, I will provide a quick description of some other LINQ-based technologies. This is not a comprehensive list, because anyone can write a LINQ provider.

Entity Framework

The database examples I have shown have used the LINQ provider that is part of the Entity Framework (EF). The EF is a data access technology that shipped as part of the .NET Framework, but which has now been moved into a separate NuGet package, `Microsoft.EntityFrameworkCore`. (Older versions are still built into .NET Framework, but not .NET Core. In any case, if you wish to use the latest version, you must use the NuGet package.) EF can map between a database and an object layer. It supports multiple database vendors.

The EF relies on `IQueryable<T>`. For each persistent entity type in a data model, the EF can provide an object that implements `IQueryable<T>` and that can be used as the starting point for building queries to retrieve entities of that type and of related types. Since `IQueryable<T>` is not unique to the EF, you will be using the standard set of extension methods provided by the `Queryable` class in the `System.Linq` namespace, but that mechanism is designed to allow each provider to plug in its own behavior.

Because `IQueryable<T>` defines the LINQ operators as methods that accept `Expression<T>` arguments and not plain delegate types, any expressions you write in either query expressions or as lambda arguments to the underlying operator methods will turn into compiler-generated code that creates a tree of objects representing the structure of the expression. The EF relies on this to be able to generate database queries that fetch the data you require. This means that you are obliged to use lambdas; unlike with LINQ to Objects, you cannot use anonymous methods or delegates with an EF query.

Because `IQueryable<T>` derives from `IEnumerable<T>`, it's possible to use LINQ to Objects operators on any EF source. You can do this explicitly with the `AsEnumerable<T>` operator, but it could also happen accidentally if you used an overload that's supported by LINQ to Objects and not `IQueryable<T>`. For example, if you attempt to use a delegate instead of a lambda as, say, the predicate for the `Where` operator, this will fall back to LINQ to Objects. The upshot here is that EF will end up downloading the entire contents of the table and then evaluating the `Where` operator on the client side. This is unlikely to be a good idea.

Parallel LINQ (PLINQ)

Parallel LINQ is similar to LINQ to Objects in that it is based on objects and delegates rather than expression trees and query translation. But when you start asking for results from a query, it will use multithreaded evaluation where possible, using the thread pool to try to use the available CPU resources efficiently. Chapter 16 will show multithreading in action.

LINQ to XML

LINQ to XML is not a LINQ provider. I'm mentioning it here because its name makes it sound like one. It's really an API for creating and parsing XML documents. It's called *LINQ to XML* because it was designed to make it easy to execute LINQ queries against XML documents, but it achieves this by presenting XML documents through a .NET object model. The .NET class library provides two separate APIs that do this: as well as LINQ to XML, it also offers the XML Document Object Model (DOM). The DOM is based on a platform-independent standard, and thus, it's not a brilliant match for .NET idioms, and feels unnecessarily quirky compared with most of the class library. LINQ to XML was designed purely for .NET, so it integrates better with normal C# techniques. This includes working well with LINQ, which it does by providing methods that extract features from the document in terms of `IEnumerable<T>`. This enables it to defer to LINQ to Objects to define and execute the queries.

Reactive Extensions

The Reactive Extensions for .NET (or Rx, as they're often abbreviated) are the subject of the next chapter, so I won't say too much about them here, but they are a good illustration of how LINQ operators can work on a variety of types. Rx inverts the model shown in this chapter where we ask a query for items once we're good and ready. So, instead of writing a `foreach` loop that iterates over a query, or calling one of the operators that evaluates the query such as `ToArray` or `SingleOrDefault`, an Rx source calls us when it's ready to supply data.

Despite this inversion, there is a LINQ provider for Rx that supports most of the standard LINQ operators.

Tx (LINQ to Logs and Traces)

One of the less known LINQ providers is Tx, which supports running LINQ queries directly on log files and Event Tracing for Windows (ETW) files. This is an open source project available at *https://github.com/Microsoft/Tx* written by Microsoft.

Summary

In this chapter, I showed the query syntax that supports some of the most commonly used LINQ features. This lets us write queries in C# that resemble database queries but can query any LINQ provider, including LINQ to Objects, which lets us run queries against our object models. I showed the standard LINQ operators for querying, all of which are available with LINQ to Objects, and most of which are available with database providers. I also provided a quick roundup of some of the common LINQ providers for .NET applications.

The last provider I mentioned was Rx. But before we look at Rx's LINQ provider, the next chapter will begin by looking at how Rx itself works.

CHAPTER 11

Reactive Extensions

The Reactive Extensions for .NET, or Rx, are designed for working with asynchronous and event-based sources of information. Rx provides services that help you orchestrate and synchronize the way your code reacts to data from these kinds of sources. We already saw how to define and subscribe to events in Chapter 9, but Rx offers much more than these basic features. It provides an abstraction for event sources that has a steeper learning curve than events, but it comes with a powerful set of operators that makes it far easier to combine and manage multiple streams of events than is possible with the free-for-all that delegates and .NET events provide.

Rx's fundamental abstraction, `IObservable<T>`, represents a sequence of items, and its operators are defined as extension methods for this interface. This might sound a lot like LINQ to Objects, and there are similarities—not only does `IObservable<T>` have a lot in common with `IEnumerable<T>`, but Rx also supports almost all of the standard LINQ operators. If you are familiar with LINQ to Objects, you will also feel at home with Rx. The difference is that in Rx, sequences are less passive. Unlike `IEnumerable<T>`, Rx sources do not wait to be asked for their items, nor can the consumer of an Rx source demand to be given the next item. Instead, Rx uses a *push* model in which the source notifies its recipients when items are available.

For example, if you're writing an application that deals with live financial information, such as stock market price data, `IObservable<T>` is a much more natural model than `IEnumerable<T>`. Because Rx implements standard LINQ operators, you can write queries against a live source—you could narrow down the stream of events with a `where` clause, or group them by stock symbol. Rx goes beyond standard LINQ, adding its own operators that take into account the temporal nature of a live event source. For example, you could write a query that provides data only for stocks that are changing price more frequently than some minimum rate.

Rx's push-oriented approach makes it a better match than IEnumerable<T> for event-like sources. But why not just use events, or even plain delegates? Rx addresses four shortcomings of those alternatives. First, it defines a standard way for sources to report errors. Second, it is able to deliver items in a well-defined order, even in multithreaded scenarios involving numerous sources. Third, Rx provides a clear way to signal when there are no more items. Fourth, because a traditional event is represented by a special kind of member, not a normal object, there are significant limits on what you can do with an event—you can't pass an event as an argument to a method, for example. Rx makes an event source a first-class entity, because it's just an object. This means you can pass an event source as an argument, store it in a field, or offer it in a property—all things you can't do with an ordinary .NET event. You can pass a delegate as an argument, of course, but that's not the same thing—delegates handle events, but they do not represent them. There's no way to write a method that subscribes to some .NET event that you pass as an argument, because you can't pass the actual event itself. Rx fixes this by representing event sources as objects, instead of a special distinctive feature of the type system that doesn't work like anything else.

These are all features you get for free back in the world of IEnumerable<T>, of course. A collection can simply throw an exception when its contents are being enumerated, but with callbacks, it's less obvious when and where to deliver exceptions. IEnumerable<T> makes consumers retrieve items one at a time, so the ordering is unambiguous, but with plain events and delegates, nothing enforces that. And IEnumerable<T> tells consumers when the end of the collection has been reached, but with a simple callback, it's not necessarily clear when you've had the last call. IObservable<T> handles all of these eventualities, bringing the things we can take for granted with IEnumerable<T> into the world of events.

By providing a coherent abstraction that addresses these problems, Rx is able to bring all of the benefits of LINQ to event-driven scenarios. Rx does not replace events; I wouldn't have dedicated one-fifth of Chapter 9 to them if it did. In fact, Rx can integrate with events. It can bridge between its own abstractions and several others, not just ordinary events, but also IEnumerable<T> and various asynchronous programming models. Far from deprecating events, Rx raises their capabilities to a new level. It's considerably harder to get your head around Rx than events, but it offers much more power once you do.

Two interfaces form the heart of Rx. Sources that present items through this model implement IObservable<T>. Subscribers are required to supply an object that implements IObserver<T>. These two interfaces are built into .NET. The other parts of Rx are in the System.Reactive NuGet package.

Fundamental Interfaces

The two most important types in Rx are the IObservable<T> and IObserver<T> interfaces. They are important enough to be in the System namespace. Example 11-1 shows their definitions.

Example 11-1. IObservable<T> and IObserver<T>

```
public interface IObservable<out T>
{
    IDisposable Subscribe(IObserver<T> observer);
}

public interface IObserver<in T>
{
    void OnCompleted();
    void OnError(Exception error);
    void OnNext(T value);
}
```

The fundamental abstraction in Rx, IObservable<T>, is implemented by event sources. Instead of using the event keyword, it models events as a sequence of items. An IObservable<T> provides items to subscribers as and when it's ready to.

As you can see, the type argument for IObservable<T> is covariant, meaning if you have a type Base that is the base type of another type Derived, then just as you can pass a Derived to any method expecting a Base, you can pass an IObservable<Derived> to anything expecting an IObservable<Base>. It makes sense intuitively to see the out keyword here, because like IEnumerable<T>, this is a source of information—items come out of it. Conversely, items go into a subscriber's IObserver<T> implementation, so that has the in keyword, which denotes contravariance—you can pass an IObserver<Base> to anything expecting an IObserver<Derived>. (I described variance in Chapter 6.)

We can subscribe to a source by passing an implementation of IObserver<T> to the Subscribe method. The source will invoke OnNext when it wants to report events, and it can call OnCompleted to indicate that there will be no further activity. If the source wants to report an error, it can call OnError. Both OnCompleted and OnError indicate the end of the stream—an observable should not call any further methods on the observer after that.

You will not necessarily get an exception immediately if you break these rules. In some cases you will—if you use the NuGet System.Reactive library to help implement and consume these interfaces, there are certain circumstances in which it can detect this kind of mistake. But in general it is the responsibility of code calling these methods to stick to the rules.

There's a visual convention for representing Rx activity. It's sometimes called a *marble diagram*, because it consists mainly of small circles that look a bit like marbles. Figure 11-1 uses this convention to represent two sequences of events. The horizontal lines represent subscriptions to sources, with the vertical bar on the left indicating the start of the subscription, and the horizontal position indicating when something occurred (with elapsed time increasing from left to right). The circles indicate calls to OnNext, i.e., events being reported by the source). An arrow on the righthand end indicates that the subscription was still active by the end of the time the diagram represents. A vertical bar on the right indicates the end of the subscription—either due to a call to OnError or OnCompleted, or because the subscriber unsubscribed.

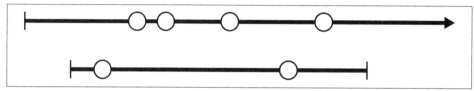

Figure 11-1. Simple marble diagram

When you call Subscribe on an observable, it returns an object that implements IDisposable, which provides a way to unsubscribe. If you call Dispose, the observable will not deliver any more notifications to your observer. This can be more convenient than the mechanism for unsubscribing from an event; to unsubscribe from an event, you must pass in an equivalent delegate to the one you used for subscription. If you're using anonymous methods, that can be surprisingly awkward, because often the only way to do that is to keep hold of a reference to the original delegate. With Rx, any subscription to a source is represented as an IDisposable, making it easier to handle in a uniform way. In fact, you often do not need to unsubscribe anyway—this is necessary only if you want to stop receiving notifications before the source completes (making this an example of something that is relatively unusual in .NET: optional disposability).

IObserver<T>

As you'll see, in practice we often don't call a source's Subscribe method directly, nor do we usually need to implement IObserver<T> ourselves. Instead, it's common to use one of the delegate-based extension methods that Rx provides, and that attaches an Rx-supplied implementation. However, those extension methods are not part of Rx's fundamental types, so for now I'll show what you'd need to write if these interfaces are all you've got. Example 11-2 shows a simple but complete observer.

Example 11-2. Simple IObserver<T> implementation

```
class MySubscriber<T> : IObserver<T>
{
    public void OnNext(T value) => Console.WriteLine("Received: " + value);
    public void OnCompleted() => Console.WriteLine("Complete");
    public void OnError(Exception ex) => Console.WriteLine("Error: " + ex);
}
```

Rx sources (i.e., implementations of IObservable<T>) are required to make certain guarantees about how they call an observer's methods. As I already mentioned, the calls happen in a certain order: OnNext is called for each item that the source provides, but once either OnCompleted or OnError is called, the observer knows that there will be no further calls to any of the three methods. Either of those methods signals the end of the sequence.

Also, calls are not allowed to overlap—when an observable source calls one of our observer's methods, it must wait for that method to return before calling again. A multithreaded observable must take care to coordinate its calls, and even in a single-threaded world, the possibility of recursion can make it can necessary for sources to detect and prevent re-entrant calls.

This makes life simple for the observer. Because Rx provides events as a sequence, my code doesn't need to deal with the possibility of concurrent calls. It's up to the source to call methods in the correct order. So, although IObservable<T> may look like the simpler interface, having just one method, it's the more demanding one to implement. As you'll see later, it's usually easiest to let the Rx libraries implement this for you, but it's still important to know how observable sources work, so I'll implement it by hand to begin with.

IObservable<T>

Rx makes a distinction between *hot* and *cold* observable sources. A hot observable produces each value as and when something of interest happens, and if no subscribers are attached at that moment, that value will be lost. A hot observable typically represents something live, such as mouse input, keypresses, or data reported by a sensor, which is why the values it produces are independent of how many subscribers, if any, are attached. Hot sources typically have broadcast-like behavior—they send each item to all of their subscribers. These can be the more complex kind of source to implement, so I'll discuss cold sources first.

Implementing cold sources

Whereas hot sources report items as and when they want to, cold observables work differently. They start pushing values when an observer subscribes, and they provide values to each subscriber separately, rather than broadcasting. This means that a subscriber won't miss anything by being too late, because the source starts providing items when you subscribe. Example 11-3 shows a very simple cold source.

Example 11-3. A simple cold observable source

```
public class SimpleColdSource : IObservable<string>
{
    public IDisposable Subscribe(IObserver<string> observer)
    {
        observer.OnNext("Hello,");
        observer.OnNext("world!");
        observer.OnCompleted();
        return NullDisposable.Instance;
    }

    private class NullDisposable : IDisposable
    {
        public readonly static NullDisposable Instance = new NullDisposable();
        public void Dispose() { }
    }
}
```

The moment an observer subscribes, this source will provide two values, the strings "Hello," and "world!", and will then indicate the end of the sequence by calling OnCompleted. It does all that inside Subscribe, so this doesn't really look like a subscription—the sequence is already over by the time Subscribe returns, so there's nothing meaningful to do to support unsubscription. That's why this returns a trivial implementation of IDisposable. (I've chosen an extremely simple example so I can show the basics. Real sources will be more complex.)

To show this in action, we need to create an instance of SimpleColdSource, and also an instance of my observer class from Example 11-2, and use that to subscribe to the source, as Example 11-4 does.

Example 11-4. Attaching an observer to an observable

```
var source = new SimpleColdSource();
var sub = new MySubscriber<string>();
source.Subscribe(sub);
```

Predictably, this produces the following output:

```
Received: Hello,
Received: world!
Complete
```

In general, a cold observer will have access to some underlying source of information, which it can push to a subscriber on demand. In Example 11-3, that "source" was just two hardcoded values. Example 11-5 shows a slightly more interesting cold observable, which reads the lines out of a file and provides them to a subscriber.

Example 11-5. A cold observable representing a file's contents

```
public class FilePusher : IObservable<string>
{
    private readonly string _path;
    public FilePusher(string path)
    {
        _path = path;
    }

    public IDisposable Subscribe(IObserver<string> observer)
    {
        using (var sr = new StreamReader(_path))
        {
            while (!sr.EndOfStream)
            {
                observer.OnNext(sr.ReadLine());
            }
        }
        observer.OnCompleted();
        return NullDisposable.Instance;
    }

    private class NullDisposable : IDisposable
    {
        public static NullDisposable Instance = new NullDisposable();
        public void Dispose() { }
    }
}
```

As before, this does not represent a live source of events, and it leaps into action only when something subscribes, but it's a little more interesting than Example 11-3. This calls into the observer as and when it retrieves each line from a file, so although the point at which it starts doing its work is determined by the subscriber, this source is in control of the rate at which it provides values. Just like Example 11-3, this delivers all the items to the observer on the caller's thread inside the call to Subscribe, but it would be a relatively small conceptual leap from Example 11-5 to one in which the code reading from the file either ran on a separate thread or used asynchronous techniques (such as those described in Chapter 17), thus enabling Subscribe to return before the work is complete (at which point you'd need to write a more interesting

IDisposable implementation to enable callers to unsubscribe). This would still be a cold source, because it represents some underlying set of data that it can enumerate from the start for the benefit of each individual subscriber.

Example 11-5 is not quite complete—it fails to handle errors that occur while reading from the file. We need to catch these and call the observer's OnError method. Unfortunately, it's not quite as simple as wrapping the whole loop in a try block, because that would also catch exceptions that emerged from the observer's OnNext method. If that throws an exception, we should allow it to carry on up the stack—we should handle only exceptions that emerge from the places we expect in our code. Unfortunately, this rather complicates the code. Example 11-6 puts all the code that uses FileStream inside a try block, but will allow any exceptions thrown by the observer to propagate up the stack, because it's not up to us to handle those.

Example 11-6. Handling filesystem errors but not observer errors

```
public IDisposable Subscribe(IObserver<string> observer)
{
    StreamReader sr = null;
    string line = null;
    bool failed = false;

    try
    {
        while (true)
        {
            try
            {
                if (sr == null)
                {
                    sr = new StreamReader(_path);
                }
                if (sr.EndOfStream)
                {
                    break;
                }
                line = sr.ReadLine();
            }
            catch (IOException x)
            {
                observer.OnError(x);
                failed = true;
                break;
            }

            observer.OnNext(line);
        }
    }
    finally
```

```
{
    if (sr != null)
    {
        sr.Dispose();
    }
}
if (!failed)
{
    observer.OnCompleted();
}
return NullDisposable.Instance;
}
```

If I/O exceptions occur while reading from the file, this reports them to the observer's OnError method—so this source uses all three of the IObserver<T> methods.

Implementing hot sources

Hot sources notify all current subscribers of values as they become available. This means that any hot observable must keep track of which observers are currently subscribed. Subscription and notification are separated out with hot sources in a way that they usually aren't with cold ones.

Example 11-7 is an observable source that reports a single item for each keypress, and it's a particularly simple source as hot ones go. It's single-threaded, so it doesn't need to do anything special to avoid overlapping calls. It doesn't report errors, so it never needs to call observers' OnError methods. And it never stops, so it doesn't need to call OnCompleted either. Even so, it's quite involved. (Things will get much simpler once I introduce the Rx library support—this example is relatively complex because for now, I'm sticking with just the two fundamental interfaces.)

Example 11-7. IObservable<T> for monitoring keypresses

```
public class KeyWatcher : IObservable<char>
{
    private readonly List<Subscription> _subscriptions = new List<Subscription>();

    public IDisposable Subscribe(IObserver<char> observer)
    {
        var sub = new Subscription(this, observer);
        _subscriptions.Add(sub);
        return sub;
    }

    public void Run()
    {
        while (true)
        {
            // Passing true here stops the console from showing the character
```

```
        char c = Console.ReadKey(true).KeyChar;
        // Iterate over snapshot to handle the case where the observer
        // unsubscribes from inside its OnNext method.
        foreach (Subscription sub in _subscriptions.ToArray())
        {
            sub.Observer.OnNext(c);
        }
    }
}

private void RemoveSubscription(Subscription sub)
{
    _subscriptions.Remove(sub);
}

private class Subscription : IDisposable
{
    private KeyWatcher _parent;
    public Subscription(KeyWatcher parent, IObserver<char> observer)
    {
        _parent = parent;
        Observer = observer;
    }

    public IObserver<char> Observer { get; }

    public void Dispose()
    {
        if (_parent != null)
        {
            _parent.RemoveSubscription(this);
            _parent = null;
        }
    }
}
}
}
```

This defines a nested class called Subscription to keep track of each observer that subscribes, and this also provides the implementation of IDisposable that our Sub scribe method is required to return. The observable creates a new instance of this nested class and adds it to a list of current subscribers during Subscribe, and then if Dispose is called, it removes itself from that list.

As a general rule in .NET, you should Dispose any IDisposable resources allocated on your behalf when you've finished using them. However, in Rx, it is common not to dispose objects representing subscriptions, so if you implement such an object, you should not count on it being disposed. It's typically unnecessary, because Rx can clean up for you. Unlike with ordinary .NET events or delegates, observables can unambiguously come to an end, at which point any resources allocated to subscribers can be freed. (Some run indefinitely, but in that case, subscriptions usually remain active for the life of the program.) Admittedly, the examples I've shown so far don't clean up automatically, because I've provided my own implementations that are simple enough not to need to, but the Rx libraries do if you use their source and subscriber implementations. The only time you'd normally dispose of a subscription in Rx is if you want to unsubscribe before the source completes.

 Subscribers are not obliged to ensure that the object returned by Subscribe remains reachable. You can simply ignore it if you don't need the ability to unsubscribe early, and it won't matter if the garbage collector frees the object, because none of the IDisposable implementations that Rx supplies to represent subscriptions have finalizers. (And although you don't normally implement these yourself—I'm doing so here only to illustrate how it works—if you did decide to write your own, take the same approach: do not implement a finalizer on a class that represents a subscription.)

The KeyWatcher class in Example 11-7 has a Run method. That's not a standard Rx feature, it's just a loop that sits and waits for keyboard input—this observable won't actually produce any notifications unless something calls that method. Each time this loop receives a key, it calls the OnNext method on every currently subscribed observer. Notice that I'm building a copy of the subscriber list (by calling ToArray— that's a simple way to get a List<T> to duplicate its contents), because there's every possibility that a subscriber might choose to unsubscribe in the middle of a call to OnNext, meaning that if I passed the subscriber list directly to foreach, I would get an exception. This is because lists don't allow items to be added and removed if you're in the middle of iterating through them.

 This example only guards against re-entrant calls on the same thread; handling multithreaded unsubscription would be altogether more complex. In fact, even building a copy is not sufficiently paranoid. I should really be checking that each observer in my snapshot is still currently subscribed before calling its OnNext, because it's possible that one observer might choose to unsubscribe some other observer. This also makes no attempt to deal with unsubscription from another thread. Later on, I'll replace all of this with a much more robust implementation from the Rx library.

In use, this hot source is very similar to my cold sources. We need to create an instance of the KeyWatcher, and also another instance of my observer class (with a type argument of char this time, because this source produces characters instead of strings). Because this source does not generate items until its monitoring loop runs, I need to call Run to kick it off, as Example 11-8 does.

Example 11-8. Attaching an observer to an observable

```
var source = new KeyWatcher();
var sub = new MySubscriber<char>();
source.Subscribe(sub);
source.Run();
```

Running that code, the application will wait for keyboard input, and if you press, say, the *m* key, the observer (Example 11-2) will display the message `Received: m`. (And since my source never ends, the `Run` method will never return.)

You might need to deal with a mixture of hot and cold observables. Also, some cold sources have some hot characteristics. For example, you could imagine a source that represented alert messages, and it might make sense to implement that in such a way that it stored alerts, to make sure you didn't miss anything that happens in between creating the source and attaching a subscriber. So it would be a cold source—any new subscriber would get all the events so far—but once a subscriber has caught up, the ongoing behavior would look more like a hot source, because any new events would be broadcast to all current subscribers. As you'll see, the Rx libraries provide various ways to mix and adapt between the two types of sources.

While it's useful to see what observers and observables need to do, it's more productive to let Rx take care of the grunt work, so now I'll show how you would write sources and subscribers if you were using the `System.Reactive` NuGet library instead of just the two fundamental interfaces.

Publishing and Subscribing with Delegates

If you use the `System.Reactive` NuGet package, you do not need to implement either `IObservable<T>` or `IObserver<T>` directly. The library provides several implementations. Some of these are adapters, bridging between other representations of asynchronously generated sequences. Some wrap existing observable streams. But the helpers aren't just for adapting existing things. They can also help if you want to write code that originates new items or that acts as the final destination for items. The simplest of these helpers provide delegate-based APIs for creating and consuming observable streams.

Creating an Observable Source with Delegates

As you have seen in some of the preceding examples, although `IObservable<T>` is a simple interface, sources that implement it may have to do a fair amount of work to track subscribers. And we've not even seen the whole story yet. As you'll see in "Schedulers" on page 517, a source often needs to take extra measures to ensure that it integrates well with Rx's threading mechanisms. Fortunately, the Rx libraries can do some of that work for us. Example 11-9 shows how to use the `Observable` class's static `Create` method to implement a cold source. (Each call to `GetFilePusher` will create a new source, so this is effectively a factory method.)

Example 11-9. Delegate-based observable source

```
public static IObservable<string> GetFilePusher(string path)
{
    return Observable.Create<string>(observer =>
        {
            using (var sr = new StreamReader(path))
            {
                while (!sr.EndOfStream)
                {
                    observer.OnNext(sr.ReadLine());
                }
            }
            observer.OnCompleted();
            return () => { };
        });
}
```

This serves the same purpose as Example 11-5—it provides an observable source that supplies each line in a file in turn to subscribers. (As with Example 11-5, I've left out error handling for clarity. In practice, you'd need to report errors in the same way as Example 11-6.) The heart of the code is the same, but I've been able to write just a single method instead of a whole class, because Rx is now providing the `IObserva ble<T>` implementation. Each time an observer subscribes to that observable, Rx calls the callback I passed to `Create`. So all I have to do is write the code that provides the items. As well as not needing the outer class implementing `IObservable<T>`, I've also been able to omit the nested class that implements `IDisposable`—the `Create` method allows us to return an `Action` delegate instead of an object, and it will invoke that if the subscriber chooses to unsubscribe. Since my method doesn't return until after it has finished producing items, there's nothing useful I can do, so I've just returned an empty method.

So I've written rather less code than in Example 11-5, but as well as simplifying my implementation, `Observable.Create` does two more slightly subtle things for us that are not immediately apparent from the code.

First, if a subscriber unsubscribes early, this code will now correctly stop sending it items, even though I've written no code to handle that. When an observer subscribes to a source of this kind, Rx does not pass the `IObserver<T>` directly to our callback. The `observer` argument in the nested method in Example 11-9 refers to an Rx-supplied wrapper. If the underlying observer unsubscribes, that wrapper automatically stops forwarding notifications. My loop will carry on running through the file even after the subscriber stops listening, which is wasteful, but at least the subscriber doesn't get items after it has asked me to stop. (You may be wondering how the subscriber even gets a chance to unsubscribe, given that my code doesn't return until it has finished. But in multithreaded scenarios, it's possible to get the IDisposable provided by Rx's wrapper representing the subscription before my code returns.)

You can use Rx in conjunction with the C# asynchronous language features (specifically, the async and await keywords) to implement a version of Example 11-9 that not only handles unsubscription more efficiently, but also reads from the file asynchronously, meaning subscription does not need to block. This is significantly more efficient, and yet the code is almost identical. I won't be introducing the asynchronous language features until Chapter 17, so this might not make complete sense yet, but if you're curious, Example 11-10 shows how it looks. The modified lines are in bold. (Again, this is the version without error handling. Asynchronous methods can handle exceptions in much the same way as synchronous ones, so you could manage errors with the same approach as Example 11-6.)

Example 11-10. An asynchronous source

```
public static IObservable<string> GetFilePusher(string path)
{
    return Observable.Create<string>(async (observer, cancel) =>
    {
        using (var sr = new StreamReader(path))
        {
            while (!sr.EndOfStream && !cancel.IsCancellationRequested)
            {
                observer.OnNext(await sr.ReadLineAsync());
            }
        }
        observer.OnCompleted();
        return () => { };
    });
}
```

The second thing Observable.Create does for us under the covers is that in certain circumstances, it will use Rx's scheduler system to call our code via a work queue instead of invoking it directly. This avoids possible deadlocks in cases where you've chained multiple observables together. I will be describing schedulers later in this chapter.

This technique is good for cold sources such as Example 11-9. Hot sources work differently, broadcasting live events to all subscribers, and Observable.Create does not cater for them directly because it invokes the delegate you pass once for each subscriber. However, the Rx libraries can still help.

Rx provides a Publish extension method for any IObservable<T>, defined by the Observable class in the System.Reactive.Linq namespace. This method is designed to wrap a source whose subscription method (i.e., the delegate you pass to `Observa ble.Create`) supports being run only once, but to which you want to attach multiple subscribers—it handles the multicast logic for you. Strictly speaking, a source that supports only a single subscription is degenerate, but as long as you hide it behind `Publish`, it doesn't matter, and you can use this as a way to implement a hot source. Example 11-11 shows how to create a source that provides the same functionality as the `KeyWatcher` in Example 11-7. I've also hooked up two subscribers, just to illustrate the point that this supports multiple subscribers.

Example 11-11. Delegate-based hot source

```
IObservable<char> singularHotSource = Observable.Create(
    (Func<IObserver<char>, IDisposable>) (obs =>
    {
        while (true)
        {
            obs.OnNext(Console.ReadKey(true).KeyChar);
        }
    }));

IConnectableObservable<char> keySource = singularHotSource.Publish();

keySource.Subscribe(new MySubscriber<char>());
keySource.Subscribe(new MySubscriber<char>());
```

The `Publish` method does not call `Subscribe` on the source immediately. Nor does it do so when you first attach a subscriber to the source it returns. So, by the time all of the code in Example 11-11 has run, the loop that reads the keypresses will not yet be executing. I have to tell the published source when I want it to start. Notice that `Pub lish` returns an `IConnectableObservable<T>`. This derives from `IObservable<T>` and adds a single extra method, `Connect`. This interface represents a source that doesn't start until it's told to, and it's designed to let you hook up all the subscribers you need before you set it running. Calling `Connect` on the source returned by `Pub lish` causes it to subscribe to my original source, which will invoke the subscription callback I passed to `Observable.Create`, running my loop. This causes the `Connect` method to have the same effect as calling `Run` on my original Example 11-7.

 `Connect` returns an `IDisposable`. This provides a way to disconnect at some later point—that is, to unsubscribe from the underlying source. (If you don't call this, the connectable observable returned by `Publish` will remain subscribed to your source even if you `Dispose` each of the individual downstream subscriptions.)

The combination of the delegate-based `Observable.Create` and the multicasting offered by `Publish` has enabled me to throw away everything in Example 11-7 except for the loop that actually generates items, and even that has become simpler. Being able to remove about 80% of the code isn't the whole story, either. This will work better—`Publish` lets Rx handle my subscribers, which will deal correctly with the awkward situations in which subscribers unsubscribe while being notified.

Of course, the Rx libraries don't just help with implementing sources. They can simplify subscribers too.

Subscribing to an Observable Source with Delegates

Just as you don't have to implement `IObservable<T>`, it's also not necessary to provide an implementation of `IObserver<T>`. You won't always care about all three methods—the `KeyWatcher` observable in Example 11-7 never even calls the `OnComple ted` or `OnError` methods, because it runs indefinitely and has no error detection. Even when you do need to provide all three methods, you won't necessarily want to write a whole separate type to provide them. So the Rx libraries provide extension methods to simplify subscription, defined by the `ObservableExtensions` class in the `System` namespace. Most C# source files include a `using System;` directive, so the extensions it offers will usually be available as long as your project has a reference to the `System.Reactive` NuGet package. There are several overloads for the `Subscribe` method available for any `IObservable<T>`. Example 11-12 uses one of them.

Example 11-12. Subscribing without implementing IObserver<T>

```
var source = new KeyWatcher();
source.Subscribe(value => Console.WriteLine("Received: " + value));
source.Run();
```

This example has the same effect as Example 11-8. However, by using this approach, we no longer need most of the code in Example 11-2. With this `Subscribe` extension method, Rx provides the `IObserver<T>` implementation for us, and we provide methods only for the notifications we want.

The `Subscribe` overload used by Example 11-12 takes an `Action<T>`, where `T` is the item type of the `IObservable<T>`, which in this case is `char`. My source doesn't provide error notifications, nor does it use `OnCompleted` to indicate the end of the items, but plenty of sources do, so there are three overloads of `Subscribe` to handle that. One takes an extra delegate of type `Action<Exception>` to handle errors. Another takes a second delegate of type `Action` (i.e., one that takes no arguments) to handle the completion notification. The third overload takes three delegates—the same per-item callback that they all take, and then an exception handler and a completion handler.

If you do not provide an exception handler when using delegate-based subscription, but the source calls OnError, the IObserver<T> Rx supplies throws the exception to keep the error from going unnoticed. Example 11-5 calls OnError in the catch block where it handles I/O exceptions, and if you subscribed using the technique in Example 11-12, you'd find that the call to OnError throws the IOException right back out again—the same exception is then thrown twice in a row, once by the StreamReader, and then again by the Rx-supplied IObserver<T> implementation. Since we'd already be in the catch block in Example 11-5 by this time (and not the try block), this second throw would cause the exception to emerge from the Subscribe method, either to be handled farther up the stack, or crashing the application.

There's one more overload of the Subscribe extension method that takes no arguments. This subscribes to a source and then does nothing with the items it receives. (It will throw any errors back to the source, just like the other overloads that don't take an error callback.) This would be useful if you have a source that does something important as a side effect of subscription, although it's probably best to avoid designs where that's necessary.

Sequence Builders

Rx defines several methods that create new sequences from scratch, without requiring either custom types or callbacks. These are designed for certain simple scenarios such as single-element sequences, empty sequences, or particular patterns. These are all static methods defined by the Observable class.

Empty

The Observable.Empty<T> method is similar to the Enumerable.Empty<T> method from LINQ to Objects that I showed in Chapter 10: it produces an empty sequence. (The difference, of course, is that it implements IObservable<T>, not IEnumerable<T>.) As with the LINQ to Objects method, this is useful when you're working with APIs that demand an observable source, and you have no items to provide.

Any observer that subscribes to an Observable.Empty<T> sequence will have its OnCompleted method called immediately.

Never

The Observable.Never<T> method produces a sequence that never does anything—it produces no items, and unlike an empty sequence, it never even completes. (The Rx team considered calling this Infinite<T> to emphasize the fact that as well as never producing anything, it also never ends.) There is no counterpart in LINQ to Objects. If you wanted to write an IEnumerable<T> equivalent of Never, it would be one that blocked indefinitely when you first tried to retrieve an item. In the pull-based world of LINQ to Objects, this would not be at all useful—it would cause the calling thread to freeze for the lifetime of the process. But in Rx's reactive world, sources don't block threads just because they are in a state where they're not currently producing items, so Never is a less disastrous idea. It can be helpful with some of the operators I'll show later that can use an IObservable<T> to represent duration. Never can represent an activity you want to run indefinitely.

Return

The Observable.Return<T> method takes a single argument, and returns an observable sequence that immediately produces that one value and then completes. This is a cold source—you can subscribe to it any number of times, and each subscriber will receive the same value. There is no exact equivalent in LINQ to Objects, although the Rx team provides a library called the Interactive Extensions for .NET (or Ix for short, available in the System.Interactive NuGet package) that provides IEnumerable<T> versions of this and several of the other operators described in this chapter that are in Rx but not LINQ to Objects.

Throw

The Observable.Throw<T> method takes a single argument of type Exception, and returns an observable sequence that passes that exception to OnError immediately for any subscriber. Like Return, this is also a cold source that can be subscribed to any number of times, and it will do the same thing to each subscriber.

Range

The Observable.Range method generates a sequence of numbers. Like the Enumerable.Range method, it takes a starting number and a count. This is a cold source that will produce the entire range for each subscriber.

Repeat

The Observable.Repeat<T> method takes an input and produces a sequence that repeatedly produces that input over and over again. The input can be a single value, but it can also be another observable sequence, in which case it will forward items until that input completes, and will then resubscribe to produce the whole sequence repeatedly. (That means that this will only genuinely repeat the data if you pass it a cold observable.)

If you pass no other arguments, the resulting sequence will produce values indefinitely—the only way to stop it is to unsubscribe. You can also pass a count, saying how many times you would like the input to repeat.

Generate

The `Observable.Generate<TState, TResult>` method can produce more complex sequences than the other methods I've just described. You provide `Generate` with an object or value representing the generator's initial state. This can be any type you like —it's one of the method's generic type arguments. You must also supply three functions: one that inspects the current state to decide whether the sequence is complete yet, one that advances the state in preparation for producing the next item, and one that determines the value to produce for the current state. Example 11-13 uses this to create a source that produces random numbers until the sum total of all the numbers produced exceeds 10,000.

Example 11-13. Generating items

```
IObservable<int> src = Observable.Generate(
    (Current: 0, Total: 0, Random: new Random()),
    state => state.Total <= 10000,
    state =>
    {
        int value = state.Random.Next(1000);
        return (value, state.Total + value, state.Random);
    },
    state => state.Current);
```

This always produces 0 as the first item, illustrating that it calls the function that determines the current value (the final lambda in Example 11-13) before making the first call to the function that iterates the state.

You could achieve the same effect as this example by using `Observable.Create` and a loop. However, `Generate` inverts the flow of control: instead of your code sitting in a loop telling Rx when to produce the next item, Rx asks your functions for the next item. This gives Rx more flexibility over scheduling of the work. For example, it enables `Generate` to offer overloads that bring timing into the picture. Example 11-14 produces items in a similar way but passes an extra function as the final argument that tells Rx to delay the delivery of each item by a random amount.

Example 11-14. Generating timed items

```
IObservable<int> src = Observable.Generate(
    (Current: 0, Total: 0, Random: new Random()),
    state => state.Total < 10000,
    state =>
```

```
{
    int value = state.Random.Next(1000);
    return (value, state.Total + value, state.Random);
},
state => state.Current,
state => TimeSpan.FromMilliseconds(state.Random.Next(1000)));
```

For this to work, Rx needs to be able to schedule work to happen at some point in the future. I'll explain how this works in "Schedulers" on page 517.

LINQ Queries

One of the greatest benefits of using Rx is that it has a LINQ implementation, enabling you to write queries to process asynchronous streams of items such as events. Example 11-15 illustrates this. It begins by producing an observable source representing MouseMove events from a UI element. I'll talk about this technique in more detail in "Adaptation" on page 524, but for now it's enough to know that Rx can wrap any .NET event as an observable source. Each event produces an item that provides two properties containing the values normally passed to event handlers as arguments (i.e., the sender and the event arguments).

Example 11-15. Filtering items with a LINQ query

```
IObservable<EventPattern<MouseEventArgs>> mouseMoves =
    Observable.FromEventPattern<MouseEventArgs>(
        background, nameof(background.MouseMove));

IObservable<Point> dragPositions =
    from move in mouseMoves
    where Mouse.Captured == background
    select move.EventArgs.GetPosition(background);

dragPositions.Subscribe(point => { line.Points.Add(point); });
```

The where clause in the LINQ query filters the events so that we process only those events that were raised while a specific UI element (background) has captured the mouse. This particular example is based on WPF, but in general, Windows desktop applications that want to support dragging *capture* the mouse when the mouse button is pressed, and *release* it afterward. This ensures that the capturing element receives mouse move events for as long as the drag is in progress, even if the mouse moves over other UI elements. Typically, UI elements receive mouse move events when the mouse is over them even if they have not captured the mouse. So I need that where clause in Example 11-15 to ignore those events, leaving only mouse movements that occur while a drag is in progress. So, for the code in Example 11-15 to work, you'd need to attach event handlers such as those in Example 11-16 to the relevant element's MouseDown and MouseUp events.

Example 11-16. Capturing the mouse

```
private void OnBackgroundMouseDown(object sender, MouseButtonEventArgs e)
{
    background.CaptureMouse();
}

private void OnBackgroundMouseUp(object sender, MouseButtonEventArgs e)
{
    if (Mouse.Captured == background)
    {
        background.ReleaseMouseCapture();
    }
}
```

The select clause in Example 11-15 works in Rx just like it does in LINQ to Objects, or with any other LINQ provider. It allows us to extract information from the source items to use as the output. In this case, mouseMoves is an observable sequence of Even tPattern<MouseEventArgs> objects, but what I really want is an observable sequence of mouse locations. So the select clause in Example 11-15 asks for the position relative to a particular UI element.

The upshot of this query is that dragPositions refers to an observable sequence of Point values, which will report each change of mouse position that occurs while a particular UI element in my application has captured the mouse. This is a hot source, because it represents something that's happening live: mouse input. The LINQ filtering and projection operators do not change the nature of the source, so if you apply them to a hot source, the resulting query will also be hot, and if the source is cold, the filtered result will be too.

 Operators do not detect the hotness of the source. The Where and Select operators just pass this aspect straight through. Each time you subscribe to the final query produced by the Select operator, it will subscribe to its input. In this case, the input was the observable returned by the Where operator, which will in turn subscribe to the source produced by adapting the mouse move events. If you subscribe a second time, you'll get a second chain of subscriptions. The hot event source will broadcast every event to both chains, so each item will go through the filtering and projection process twice. So be aware that attaching multiple subscribers to a complex query of a hot source will work but may incur unnecessary expense. If you need to do this, it may be better to call to Publish on the query, which as you've seen, can make a single subscription to its input and then multicast each item to all its subscribers.

The final line of Example 11-15 subscribes to the filtered and projected source, and adds each Point value it produces to the Points collection of another UI element called line. That's a Polyline element, not shown here,[1] and the upshot of this is that you can scrawl on the application's window with the mouse. (If you've been doing Windows development for long enough, you may remember the Scribble examples—the effect here is much the same.)

Rx provides most of the standard query operators described in Chapter 10.[2] Most of these work in Rx exactly as they do with other LINQ implementations. However, some work in ways that may seem slightly surprising at first glance, as I will describe in the next few sections.

Grouping Operators

The standard grouping operator, GroupBy, produces a sequence of sequences. With LINQ to Objects, it returns IEnumerable<IGrouping<TKey, TSource>>, and as you saw in Chapter 10, IGrouping<TKey, TSource> itself derives from IEnumerable<TSource>. The GroupJoin is similar in concept: although it returns a plain IEnumerable<T>, that T is the result of a projection function that is passed a sequence as input. So, in either case, you get what is logically a sequence of sequences.

In the world of Rx, grouping produces an observable sequence of observable sequences. This is perfectly consistent, but can seem a little surprising because Rx introduces a temporal aspect: the observable source that represents all the groups produces a new item (a new observable source) at the instant it discovers each new group. Example 11-17 illustrates this by watching for changes in the filesystem and then forming them into groups based on the folder in which they occurred. For each group, we get an IGroupedObservable<TKey, TSource>, which is the Rx equivalent of IGrouping<TKey, TSource>.

Example 11-17. Grouping events

```
string path = Environment.GetFolderPath(Environment.SpecialFolder.MyDocuments);
var w = new FileSystemWatcher(path);
IObservable<EventPattern<FileSystemEventArgs>> changes =
    Observable.FromEventPattern<FileSystemEventHandler, FileSystemEventArgs>(
        h => w.Changed += h, h => w.Changed -= h);
w.IncludeSubdirectories = true;
w.EnableRaisingEvents = true;
```

---

[1] You can download the full WPF example to which this snippet belongs as part of the examples for this book.

[2] It is missing the OrderBy and ThenBy operators, because these make little sense in a push-based world. They cannot produce any items until they have seen all of their input items.

```
IObservable<IGroupedObservable<string, string>> folders =
    from change in changes
    group Path.GetFileName(change.EventArgs.FullPath)
        by Path.GetDirectoryName(change.EventArgs.FullPath);

folders.Subscribe(f =>
{
    Console.WriteLine("New folder ({0})", f.Key);
    f.Subscribe(file =>
        Console.WriteLine("File changed in folder {0}, {1}", f.Key, file));
});
```

The lambda that subscribes to the grouping source, `folders`, subscribes to each group that the source produces. The number of folders from which events could occur is endless, as new ones could be added while the program is running. So the `folders` observable will produce a new observable source each time it detects a change in a folder it hasn't seen before, as Figure 11-2 shows.

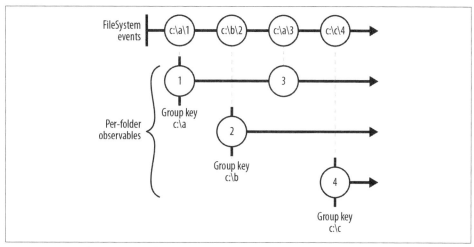

Figure 11-2. Splitting an IObservable<T> into groups

Notice that the production of a new group doesn't mean that any previous groups are now complete, which is different than how grouping works in LINQ to Objects. When you run a grouping query on an `IEnumerable<T>`, as it produces each group you can enumerate the contents entirely before moving on to the next one. But you can't do that with Rx, because each group is represented as an observable, and observables aren't finished until they tell you they're complete—instead, each group subscription remains active. In Example 11-17, it's entirely possible that a folder for which a group had already started will be dormant for a long time while activity occurs in other folders, only for it to start up again later. And more generally, Rx's grouping operators have to be prepared for that to happen with any source.

Join Operators

Rx provides the standard `Join` and `GroupJoin` operators. However, they work a bit differently than how LINQ to Objects or most database LINQ providers handle joins. In those worlds, items from two input sets are typically joined based on having some value in common. In a database, a very common example when joining two tables would be to connect rows where a foreign key column in a row from one table has the same value as a primary key column in a row from the other table. However, Rx does not base joins on values. Instead, items are joined if they are contemporaneous —if their durations overlap, then they are joined.

But hang on a minute. What exactly is an item's duration? Rx deals in instantaneous events; producing an item, reporting an error, and finishing a stream are all things that happen at a particular moment. So the join operators use a convention: for each source item, you can provide a function that returns an `IObservable<T>`. The duration for that source item starts when the item is produced and finishes when the corresponding `IObservable<T>` first reacts (i.e., it either completes or generates an item or an error). Figure 11-3 illustrates this idea. At the top is an observable source, beneath which is a series of sources that define each item's duration. At the bottom, I've shown the duration that the per-item observables establish for their source items.

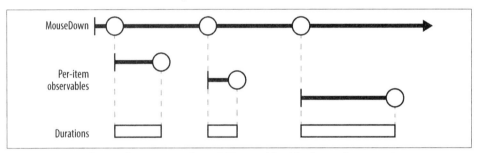

Figure 11-3. Defining duration with an IObservable<T> for each source item

Although you can use a different `IObservable<T>` for each source item, as Figure 11-3 shows, you don't have to—it's valid to use the same source every time. For example, if you apply the group operator to an `IObservable<T>` representing a stream of `MouseDown` events, and you then use another `IObservable<T>` representing a stream of `MouseUp` events to define the duration of each item, this would cause Rx to consider each `MouseDown` event's "duration" to last until the next `MouseUp` event. Figure 11-4 depicts this arrangement, and you can see that the effective duration of each `MouseDown` event, shown at the bottom, is delineated by a pair of `MouseDown` and `MouseUp` events.

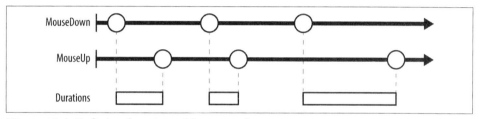

Figure 11-4. Defining duration with a pair of event streams

A source can even define its own duration. For example, if you provide an observable source representing MouseDown events, you might want each item's duration to end when the next item begins. This would mean that the items had contiguous durations —after the first item arrives, there is always exactly one current item, and it is the last one that occurred. Figure 11-5 illustrates this.

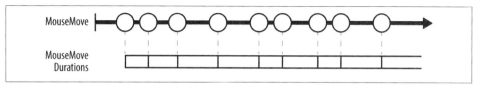

Figure 11-5. Adjacent item duration

Item durations are allowed to overlap. If you wanted to, you could supply a duration-defining IObservable<T> that indicated that an input item's duration finishes some time after the next item begins.

Now that we know how Rx decides what constitutes an item's duration for the purposes of a join, how does it use that information? Remember, join operators combine two inputs. (The duration-defining sources do not count as an input. They provide additional information about one of the inputs.) Rx considers a pair of items from the two input streams to be related if their durations overlap. The way it presents related items in the output depends on whether you use the Join or the GroupJoin operator. The Join operator's output is a stream containing one item for each pair of related items. (You provide a projection function that will be passed each pair, and it's up to you what to do with them. This function gets to decide the output item type for the joined stream.) Figure 11-6 shows two input streams, both based on events and their corresponding durations. These are similar to the sources in Figure 11-4 and Figure 11-5, but I've added letters and numbers to make it easier to refer to each of the items in these streams. At the bottom of the diagram is the observable the Join operator would produce for these two streams.

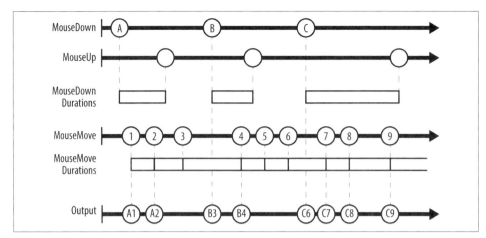

Figure 11-6. Join operator

As you can see, any place where the durations of two items from the input streams overlap, we get an output item combining the two inputs. If the overlapping items started at different times (which will normally be the case), the output item is produced whenever the later of the two inputs started. The MouseDown event A starts before the MouseMove event 1, so the resulting output, A1, occurs where the overlap begins (i.e., when MouseMove event 1 occurs). But event 3 occurs before event B, so the joined output B3 occurs when B starts.

Event 5's duration does not overlap with any MouseDown items' durations, so we do not see any items for that in the output stream. Conversely, it would be possible for a MouseMove event to appear in multiple output items (just like each MouseDown event does). If there had been no 3 event, event 2 would have a duration that started inside A and finished inside B, so as well as the A2 shown in Figure 11-6, there would be a B2 event at the same time as B starts.

Example 11-18 shows code that performs the join illustrated in Figure 11-6, using a query expression. As you saw in Chapter 10, the compiler turns query expressions into a series of method calls, and Example 11-19 shows the method-based equivalent of the query in Example 11-18.

Example 11-18. Query expression with join

```
IObservable<EventPattern<MouseEventArgs>> downs =
    Observable.FromEventPattern<MouseEventArgs>(
        background, nameof(background.MouseDown));
IObservable<EventPattern<MouseEventArgs>> ups =
    Observable.FromEventPattern<MouseEventArgs>(
        background, nameof(background.MouseUp));
IObservable<EventPattern<MouseEventArgs>> allMoves =
```

```
Observable.FromEventPattern<MouseEventArgs>(
    background, nameof(background.MouseMove));

IObservable<Point> dragPositions =
    from down in downs
    join move in allMoves
      on ups equals allMoves
    select move.EventArgs.GetPosition(background);
```

Example 11-19. Join in code

```
IObservable<Point> dragPositions = downs.Join(
    allMoves,
    down => ups,
    move => allMoves,
    (down, move) => move.EventArgs.GetPosition(background));
```

We can use the dragPositions observable source produced by either of these examples to replace the one in Example 11-15. We no longer need to filter based on whether the background element has captured the mouse, because Rx is now providing us only move events whose duration overlaps with the duration of a mouse down event. Any moves that happen in between mouse presses will either be ignored or, if they are the last move to occur before a mouse down, we'll receive that position at the moment the mouse button is pressed.

GroupJoin combines items in a similar way, but instead of producing a single observable output, it produces an observable of observables. For the present example, that would mean that its output would produce a new observable source for each Mouse Down input. This would consist of all the pairs containing that input, and it would have the same duration as that input. Figure 11-7 shows this operator in action with the same input events as Figure 11-6. I've put vertical bars on the ends of the output sequences to clarify when they will call their observers' OnComplete methods. The start and finish of these observables align exactly with the duration of the corresponding input, so they often finish some time after producing their final output item.

In general, with LINQ, the GroupJoin operator is able to produce empty groups, so unlike the Join operator, there will be one output for each item from the first input even if there are no corresponding items from the other stream. The Rx GroupJoin works the same way, adding in a temporal aspect. Each output group starts at the same moment the corresponding input event happens (MouseDown, in this example) and ends when that event is deemed to have finished (at the next MouseUp here); if there were no moves in that time, that observable will generate no items. Since move event durations are contiguous here, that could happen only before receiving the first move. But in joins where the second input's items have noncontiguous durations, empty groups are more likely.

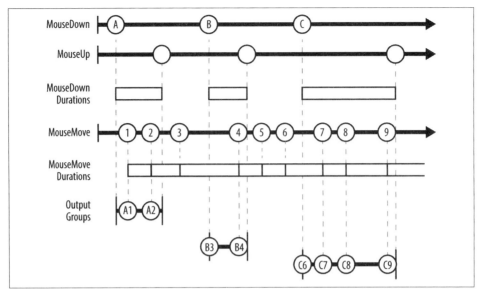

Figure 11-7. GroupJoin operator

In the context of my example application that allows the user to scribble in a window with the mouse, this grouped output is useful, because it presents each individual drag as a separate object. This means I could create a new line for each drag, rather than adding points onto the same increasingly long line. With the code in Example 11-15, each new drag operation will draw a line from wherever the previous drag finished to the new location, making it impossible to draw separate shapes. But grouped output makes separation easy. Example 11-20 subscribes to the grouped output, and for each new group (which represents a new drag operation), it creates a new Polyline to render the scribble and then subscribes to the items in the group to populate that individual line.

Example 11-20. Adding a new line for each drag operation

```
var dragPointSets = from mouseDown in downs
                    join move in allMoves
                      on ups equals allMoves into m
                    select m.Select(e => e.EventArgs.GetPosition(background));

dragPointSets.Subscribe(dragPoints =>
{
    var currentLine = new Polyline { Stroke = Brushes.Black, StrokeThickness = 2 };
    background.Children.Add(currentLine);

    dragPoints.Subscribe(point =>
    {
        currentLine.Points.Add(point);
```

```
    });
});
```

Just to be clear, all of this works in real time even with a join operator—these are all hot sources. The `IObservable<IObservable<Point>>` returned by `GroupJoin` in Example 11-20 will produce a new group the instant the mouse button is pressed. The `IObservable<Point>` from that group will produce a new `Point` immediately for each `MouseMove` event. The upshot is that the user sees the line appear and grow instantly when dragging the mouse.

SelectMany Operator

As you saw in Chapter 10, the `SelectMany` operator effectively flattens a collection of collections into a single one. This operator gets used when a query expression has multiple `from` clauses, and with LINQ to Objects, its operation is similar to having nested `foreach` loops. With Rx, it still has this flattening effect—it lets you take an observable source where each item it produces is also an observable source (or can be used to generate one), and the result of the `SelectMany` operator will be a single observable sequence that contains all of the items from all of the child sources. However, as with grouping, the effect is rather less orderly than in LINQ to Objects. The push-driven nature of Rx, with its potential for asynchronous operation, makes it possible for all of the observable sources involved to be pushing new items at once, including the original source that is used as a source of nested sources. (The operator still ensures that only one event will be delivered at a time—when it calls on `OnNext`, it waits for that to return before making another call. The potential for chaos only goes as far as mixing up the order in which events are delivered.)

When you use LINQ to Objects to iterate through a jagged array, everything happens in a straightforward order. It will retrieve the first nested array and then iterate through all the elements in that array before moving to the next nested array and iterating through that, and so on. But this orderly flattening occurs only because with `IEnumerable<T>`, the consumer of items is in control of when to retrieve which items. With Rx, subscribers receive items when sources provide them.

Despite the free-for-all, the behavior is straightforward enough: the output stream produced by `SelectMany` just provides items as and when the sources provide them.

Aggregation and Other Single-Value Operators

Several of the standard LINQ operators reduce an entire sequence of values to a single value. These include the aggregation operators, such as `Min`, `Sum`, and `Aggregate`; the quantifiers `Any` and `All`; and the `Count` operator. It also includes selective operators, such as `ElementAt`. These are available in Rx, but unlike most LINQ implementations, the Rx implementations do not return plain single values. They all return an IObservable<T>, just like operators that produce sequences as outputs.

 The First, Last, FirstOrDefault, LastOrDefault, Single, and SingleOrDefault operators should all work the same way, but for historical reasons, they do not. Introduced in v1 of Rx, they returned single values that were not wrapped in an IObserva ble<T>, which meant they would block until the source provided what they needed. This doesn't fit well with a push-based model and risks introducing deadlock, so these are now deprecated, and there are new asynchronous versions that work the same way as the other single-value operators in Rx. These all just append Async to the original operators' names (e.g., FirstAsync, LastAsync, etc.).

Each of these operators still produces a single value, but they all present that value as an observable source. The reason is that unlike LINQ to Objects, Rx cannot enumerate its input to calculate the aggregate value or to find the value being selected. The source is in control, so the Rx versions of these operators have to wait for the source to provide its values—like all operators, the single-value operators have to be reactive, not proactive. Operators that need to see every value, such as Average, cannot produce their result until the source says it has finished. Even an operator that doesn't need to wait until the very end of the input, such as FirstAsync or ElementAt, still cannot do anything until the source decides to provide the value the operator is waiting for. As soon as a single-value operator is able to provide a value, it does so and then completes.

The ToArray, ToList, ToDictionary, and ToLookup operators work in a similar way. Although these all produce the entire contents of the source, they do so as a single output object, which is wrapped as a single-item observable source.

If you really want to sit and wait for the value of any of these items, you can use the Wait operator, a nonstandard operator specific to Rx available on any IObserva ble<T>. This blocking operator waits for the source to complete and then returns the final element, so the "sit and wait" behavior of the deprecated First, Last, etc., operators is still available, it's just no longer the default. Alternatively, you can use C#'s asynchronous language features—you can give the await keyword an observable source. Logically, it does the same thing as Wait, but it does so with an efficient nonblocking asynchronous wait of the kind described in Chapter 17.

Concat Operator

Rx's Concat operator shares the same concept as other LINQ implementations: it combines two input sequences to produce a sequence that will produce every item in its first input, followed by every item in its second input. (In fact, Rx goes further than some LINQ providers, and can accept a collection of inputs and will concatenate them all.) This is useful only if the first stream eventually completes—that's true in LINQ to Objects too, of course, but infinite sources are more common in Rx. Also, be aware that this operator does not subscribe to the second stream until the first has finished. This is because cold streams typically start producing items when you subscribe, and the `Concat` operator does not want to have to buffer the second source's items while it waits for the first to complete. This means that `Concat` may produce nondeterministic results when used with hot sources. (If you want an observable source that contains all the items from two hot sources, use `Merge`, which I'll describe shortly.)

Rx is not satisfied with merely providing standard LINQ operators. It defines many more of its own operators.

Rx Query Operators

One of Rx's main goals is to simplify working with multiple potentially independent observable sources that produce items asynchronously. Rx's designers sometimes refer to "orchestration and synchronization," meaning that your system may have many things going on at once, but that you need to achieve some kind of coherency in how your application reacts to events. Many of Rx's operators are designed with this goal in mind.

Not everything in this section is driven by the unique requirements of Rx. A few of Rx's nonstandard operators (e.g., `Scan`) would make perfect sense in other LINQ providers. And versions of many of these are available for `IEnumerable<T>` in the Interactive Extensions for .NET (Ix) which, as mentioned earlier, are to be found in the `System.Interactive` NuGet package.

Rx has such a large repertoire of operators that to do them all justice would roughly quadruple the size of this chapter, which is already on the long side. Since this is not a book about Rx, and because some of the operators are very specialized, I will just pick some of the most useful. I recommend browsing through the Rx documentation (or the source, at *https://github.com/dotnet/reactive*) to discover the full and remarkably comprehensive set of operators it provides.

Merge

The `Merge` operator combines all of the elements from two or more observable sequences into a single observable sequence. I can use this to fix a problem that occurs in Examples 11-15, 11-18, and 11-20. These all process mouse input, and if you've done much Windows UI programming, you know that you will not necessarily get a mouse move notification corresponding to the points at which the mouse button was pressed and released. The notifications for these button events include mouse location information, so Windows sees no need to send a separate mouse move message providing these locations, because it would just be sending you the same information twice. This is perfectly logical, and also rather annoying.[3] These start and end locations are not in the observable source that represents mouse positions in those examples. I can fix that by merging in the positions from all three events. Example 11-21 shows how to fix Example 11-15.

Example 11-21. Merging observables

```
IObservable<EventPattern<MouseEventArgs>> downs =
    Observable.FromEventPattern<MouseEventArgs>(
        background, nameof(background.MouseDown));
IObservable<EventPattern<MouseEventArgs>> ups =
    Observable.FromEventPattern<MouseEventArgs>(
        background, nameof(background.MouseUp));
IObservable<EventPattern<MouseEventArgs>> allMoves =
    Observable.FromEventPattern<MouseEventArgs>(
        background, nameof(background.MouseMove));

IObservable<EventPattern<MouseEventArgs>> dragMoves =
    from move in allMoves
    where Mouse.Captured == background
    select move;

IObservable<EventPattern<MouseEventArgs>> allDragPositionEvents =
    Observable.Merge(downs, ups, dragMoves);

IObservable<Point> dragPositions =
    from move in allDragPositionEvents
    select move.EventArgs.GetPosition(background);
```

I've created three observables to represent the three relevant events: MouseDown, MouseUp, and MouseMove. Since all three of these need to share the same projection (the select clause), but only one needs to filter events, I've restructured things a bit. Only mouse moves need filtering, so I've written a separate query for that. I've then used the Observable.Merge method to combine all three event streams into one.

---

3 Like some developers.

Merge is available both as an extension method and a nonextension static method. If you use the extension methods available on a single observable, the only Merge overloads available combine it with a single other source (optionally specifying a scheduler). In this case, I had three sources, which is why I used the nonextension method form. However, if you have an expression that is either an enumerable of observable sources, or an observable source of observable sources, you'll find that there are also Merge extension methods for these. So I could have written new[] { downs, ups, dragMoves }.Merge().

My allDragPositionEvents variable refers to a single observable stream that will report all the mouse moves I need. Finally, I run this through a projection to extract the mouse position for each item. Again, the result is a hot stream. As before, it will produce a position any time the mouse moves while the background element has captured the mouse, but it will also produce a position each time either the MouseDown or MouseUp event occurs. I could subscribe to this with the same call shown in the final line of Example 11-15 to keep my UI up to date, and this time, I wouldn't be missing the start and end positions.

In the example I've just shown, the sources are all endless, but that will not always be the case. What should a merged observable do when one of its inputs stops? If one stops due to an error, that error will be passed on by the merged observable, at which point it will be complete—an observable is not allowed to continue producing items after reporting an error. However, although an input can unilaterally terminate the output with an error, if inputs complete normally, the merged observable doesn't complete until all of its inputs are complete.

Windowing Operators

Rx defines two operators, Buffer and Window, that both produce an observable output where each item is based on multiple adjacent items from the source. (The name Window has nothing to do with UIs, by the way.) Figure 11-8 shows three ways in which you could use the Buffer operator. I've numbered the circles representing items in the input, and below this are blobs representing the items that will emerge from the observable source produced by Buffer, with lines and numbers indicating which input items are associated with each output item. Window works in a very similar way, as you'll see shortly.

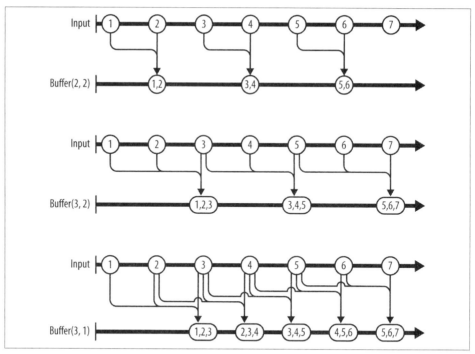

Figure 11-8. Sliding windows with the Buffer operator

In the first case, I've passed arguments of (2, 2), indicating that I want each output item to correspond to two input items, and that I want to start a new buffer on every second input item. That may sound like two different ways of saying the same thing until you look at the second example in Figure 11-8, in which arguments of (3, 2) indicate that each output item corresponds to three items from the input, but I still want the buffers to begin on every other input. This means that each *window*—the set of items from the input used to build an output item—overlaps with its neighbors. This will happen whenever the second argument, the *skip*, is smaller than the window. The first output item's window contains the first, second, and third input. The second output's window contains the third, fourth, and fifth, so the third item appears in both.

The final example in the figure shows a window size of three, but this time I've asked for a skip size of one—so in this case, the window moves along by only one input item at a time, but it incorporates three items from the source each time. I could also specify a skip that is larger than the window, in which case the input items that fell between windows would simply be ignored.

The Buffer and Window operators tend to introduce a lag. In the second and third cases, the window size of three means that the input observable needs to produce its third value before the whole window can be provided for the output item. With

Buffer, this always means a delay of the size of the window, but as you'll see, with the Window operator, each window can get under way before it is full.

The difference between the Buffer and Window operators is the way in which they present the windowed items. Buffer is the most straightforward. It provides an IObservable<IList<T>>, where T is the input item type. In other words, if you subscribe to the output of Buffer, for each window produced, your subscriber will be passed a list containing all the items in the window. Example 11-22 uses this to produce a smoothed-out version of the mouse locations from Example 11-15.

Example 11-22. Smoothing input with Buffer

```
IObservable<Point> smoothed = from points in dragPositions.Buffer(5, 2)
                              let x = points.Average(p => p.X)
                              let y = points.Average(p => p.Y)
                              select new Point(x, y);
```

The first line of this query states that I want to see groups of five consecutive mouse locations, and I want one group for every other input. The rest of the query calculates the average mouse position within the window and produces that as the output item. Figure 11-9 shows the effect. The top line is the result of using the raw mouse positions. The line immediately beneath it uses the smoothed points generated by Example 11-22 from the same input. As you can see, the top line is rather ragged, but the bottom line has smoothed out a lot of the lumps.

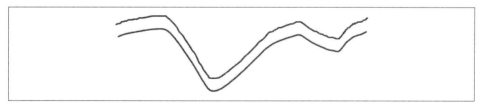

Figure 11-9. Smoothing in action

Example 11-22 uses a mixture of LINQ to Objects and Rx's LINQ implementation. The query expression itself uses Rx, but the range variable, points, is of type IList<Point> (because Buffer returns an IObservable<IList<Point>> in this example). So the nested queries that invoke the Average operator on points will get the LINQ to Objects implementation.

If the Buffer operator's input is hot, it will produce a hot observable as a result. So you could subscribe to the observable in the smoothed variable in Example 11-22 with similar code to the final line of Example 11-15, and it would show the smoothed line in real time as you drag the mouse. As discussed, there will be a slight lag, of course—the code specifies a skip of two, so it will update the screen only for every other mouse event. Averaging over the last five points will also tend to increase the gap between the mouse pointer and the end of the line. With these parameters, the discrepancy is small enough not to be too distracting, but with more aggressive smoothing, it could get annoying.

The `Window` operator is very similar to the `Buffer` operator, but instead of presenting each window as an `IList<T>`, it provides an `IObservable<T>`. If you used `Window` on `dragPositions` in Example 11-22, the result would be `IObservable<IObserva ble<Point>>`. Figure 11-10 shows how the `Window` operator would work in the last of the scenarios illustrated in Figure 11-8, and as you can see, it can start each window sooner. It doesn't have to wait until all of the items in the window are available; instead of providing a fully populated list containing the window, each output item is an `IObservable<T>` that will produce the window's items as and when they become available. Each observable produced by `Window` completes immediately after supplying the final item (i.e., at the same instant at which `Buffer` would have provided the whole window). So, if your processing depends on having the whole window, `Window` can't get it to you any faster, because it's ultimately governed by the rate at which input items arrive, but it will start to provide values earlier.

One potentially surprising feature of the observables produced by `Window` in this example is their start times. Whereas they end immediately after producing their final item, they do not start immediately before producing their first. The observable representing the very first window starts right away—you will receive that observable as soon as you subscribe to the observable of observables the operator returns. So the first window will be available immediately, even if the `Window` operator's input hasn't done anything yet. Then each new window starts as soon as all the input items it needs to skip have been received. In this example, I'm using a skip count of one, so the second window starts after the input has produced one item, the third after two have been produced, and so on.

As you'll see later in this section, and also in "Timed Operations" on page 530, `Window` and `Buffer` support some other ways to define when each window starts and stops. The general pattern is that as soon as the `Window` operator gets to a point where a new item from the source would go into a new window, the operator creates that window, anticipating the window's first item rather than waiting for it.

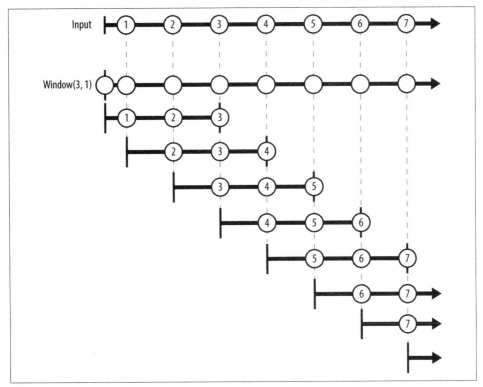

Figure 11-10. Window operator

If the input completes, all currently open windows will also complete. This means that it's possible to see empty windows. (In fact, with a skip size of one, you're guaranteed to get one empty window if the source completes.) In Figure 11-10, one window right at the bottom has started but has not yet produced any items. If the input were to complete without producing any more items, the three observable sources still in progress would also complete, including that final one that hasn't yet produced anything.

Because Window delivers items into windows as soon as the source provides them, it might enable you to get started with processing sooner than you can with Buffer, perhaps improving overall responsiveness. The downside of Window is that it tends to be more complex—your subscribers will start receiving output values before all the items for the corresponding input window are available. Whereas Buffer provides you with a list that you can inspect at your leisure, with Window, you'll need to continue working in Rx's world of sequences that produce items only when they're good and ready. To perform the same smoothing as Example 11-22 with Window requires the code in Example 11-23.

Example 11-23. Smoothing with Window

```
IObservable<Point> smoothed =
    from points in dragPositions.Window(5, 2)
    from totals in points.Aggregate(
      new { X = 0.0, Y = 0.0, Count = 0 },
      (acc, point) => new
          { X = acc.X + point.X, Y = acc.Y + point.Y, Count = acc.Count + 1 })
    where totals.Count > 0
    select new Point(totals.X / totals.Count, totals.Y / totals.Count);
```

This is a little more complicated because I've been unable to use the `Average` operator, due to the need to cope with the possibility of empty windows. (Strictly speaking, that doesn't matter in the case where I have one `Polyline` that keeps getting longer and longer. But if I group the points by drag operation, as Example 11-20 does, each individual observable source of points will complete at the end of the drag, forcing me to handle any empty windows.) The `Average` operator produces an error if you provide it with an empty sequence, so I've used the `Aggregate` operator instead, which lets me add a `where` clause to filter out empty windows instead of crashing. But that's not the only aspect that is more complex.

As I mentioned earlier, all of Rx's aggregation operators—`Aggregate`, `Min`, `Max`, and so on—work differently than with most LINQ providers. LINQ requires these operators to reduce the stream down to a single value, so they normally return a single value. For example, if I were to call the LINQ to Objects version of `Aggregate` with the arguments shown in Example 11-23, it would return a single value of the anonymous type I'm using for my accumulator. But in Rx, the return type is `IObservable<T>` (where `T` is that accumulator type in this case). It still produces a single value, but it presents that value through an observable source. Unlike LINQ to Objects, which can enumerate its input to calculate, say, an average, the Rx operator has to wait for the source to provide its values, so it can't produce an aggregate of those values until the source says it has finished.

Because the `Aggregate` operator returns an `IObservable<T>`, I've had to use a second `from` clause. This passes that source to the `SelectMany` operator, which extracts all values and makes them appear in the final stream—in this case, there is just one value (per window), so `SelectMany` is effectively unwrapping the averaged point from its single-item stream.

The code in Example 11-23 is a little more complex than Example 11-22, and I think it's considerably harder to understand how it works. Worse, it doesn't even offer any benefit. The `Aggregate` operator will begin its work as soon as inputs become available, but the code cannot produce the final result—the average—until it has seen every point in the window. If I'm going to have to wait until the end of the window before I can update the UI, I may as well stick with `Buffer`. So, in this particular case,

Window was a lot more work for no benefit. However, if the work being done on the items in the window was less trivial, or if the volumes of data involved were so large that you didn't want to buffer the entire window before starting to process it, the extra complexity could be worth the benefit of being able to start the aggregation process without having to wait for the whole input window to become available.

Demarcating windows with observables

The Window and Buffer operators provide some other ways of defining when windows should start and finish. Just as the join operators can specify duration with an observable, you can supply a function that returns a duration-defining observable for each window. Example 11-24 uses this to break keyboard input into words. The key Source variable in this example is the one from Example 11-11. It's an observable sequence that produces an item for each keypress.

Example 11-24. Breaking text into words with windows

```
IObservable<IObservable<char>> wordWindows = keySource.Window(
    () => keySource.FirstAsync(char.IsWhiteSpace));

IObservable<string> words = from wordWindow in wordWindows
                            from chars in wordWindow.ToArray()
                            select new string(chars).Trim();

words.Subscribe(word => Console.WriteLine("Word: " + word));
```

The Window operator will immediately create a new window in this example, and it will also invoke the lambda I've supplied to find out when that window should end. It will keep it open until the observable source my lambda returns either produces a value or completes. When that happens, Window will immediately open the next window, invoking my lambda again to get another observable to determine the length of the second window, and so on. The lambda here produces the next whitespace character from the keyboard, so the window will close on the next space. In other words, this breaks the input sequence into a series of windows where each window contains zero or more nonwhitespace characters followed by one whitespace character.

The observable sequence the Window operator returns presents each window as an IObservable<char>. The second statement in Example 11-24 is a query that converts each window to a string. (This will produce empty strings if the input contains multiple adjacent whitespace characters. That's consistent with the behavior of the string type's Split method, which performs the pull-oriented equivalent of this partitioning. If you don't like it, you can always filter out the blanks with a where clause.)

Because Example 11-24 uses Window, it will start making characters for each word available as soon as the user types them. But because my query calls ToArray on the window, it will end up waiting until the window completes before producing any-thing. This means Buffer would be equally effective. It would also be simpler. As Example 11-25 shows, I don't need a second from clause to collect the completed window if I use Buffer, because it provides me with windows only once they are complete.

Example 11-25. Word breaking with Buffer

```
IObservable<IList<char>> wordWindows = keySource.Buffer(
    () => keySource.FirstAsync(char.IsWhiteSpace));

IObservable<string> words = from wordWindow in wordWindows
                            select new string(wordWindow.ToArray()).Trim();
```

The Scan Operator

The Scan operator is very similar to the standard Aggregate operator, with one dif-ference. Instead of producing a single result after its source completes, it produces a sequence containing each accumulator value in turn. To illustrate this, I will first introduce a class that will act as a very simple model for a stock trade. This class, shown in Example 11-26, also defines a static method that provides a randomly gen-erated stream of trades for test purposes.

Example 11-26. Simple stock trade with test stream

```
public class Trade
{
    public string StockName { get; set; }
    public decimal UnitPrice { get; set; }
    public int Number { get; set; }

    public static IObservable<Trade> TestStream()
    {
        return Observable.Create<Trade>(obs =>
            {
                string[] names = { "MSFT", "GOOGL", "AAPL" };
                var r = new Random(0);
                for (int i = 0; i < 100; ++i)
                {
                    var t = new Trade
                    {
                        StockName = names[r.Next(names.Length)],
                        UnitPrice = r.Next(1, 100),
                        Number = r.Next(10, 1000)
                    };
                    obs.OnNext(t);
                }
                obs.OnCompleted();
```

```
        return default(IDisposable);
    });
}
}
```

Example 11-27 shows the normal `Aggregate` operator being used to calculate the total number of stocks traded, by adding up the `Number` property of every trade. (You'd normally just use the `Sum` operator, of course, but I'm showing this for comparison with `Scan`.)

Example 11-27. Summing with Aggregate

```
IObservable<Trade> trades = Trade.TestStream();

IObservable<long> tradeVolume = trades.Aggregate(
    0L, (total, trade) => total + trade.Number);
tradeVolume.Subscribe(Console.WriteLine);
```

This displays a single number, because the observable produced by `Aggregate` provides only a single value. Example 11-28 shows almost exactly the same code, but using `Scan` instead.

Example 11-28. Running total with Scan

```
IObservable<Trade> trades = Trade.TestStream();

IObservable<long> tradeVolume = trades.Scan(
    0L, (total, trade) => total + trade.Number);
tradeVolume.Subscribe(Console.WriteLine);
```

Instead of producing a single output value, this produces one output item for each input, which is the running total for all items the source has produced so far. `Scan` is particularly useful if you need aggregation-like behavior in an endless stream, such as one based on an event source. `Aggregate` is no use in that scenario because it will not produce anything if its input never completes.

The Amb Operator

Rx defines an operator with the somewhat cryptic name of `Amb`. (See the next sidebar, "Why Amb?") This takes any number of observable sequences and waits to see which one does something first. (The documentation talks about which of the inputs "reacts" first. This means that it calls any of the three `IObserver<T>` methods.) Whichever input jumps into action first effectively becomes the `Amb` operator's output —it forwards everything the chosen stream does, immediately unsubscribing from the other streams. (If any of them manage to produce elements after the first stream does, but before the operator has had time to unsubscribe, those elements will be ignored.)

Why Amb?

The Amb operator's name is short for *ambiguous*. This seems like a violation of Microsoft's own class library design guidelines, which forbid abbreviations unless the shortened form is more widely used than the full name and likely to be understood even by nonexperts. This operator's name is well established—it was introduced in 1963 in a paper by John McCarthy (inventor of the LISP programming language). However, it's not all that widely used, so the name fails the test of being instantly understandable by nonexperts.

However, the expanded name isn't really any more transparent. If you're not already familiar with the operator, the name Ambiguous wouldn't be much more help in trying to guess what it does than just Amb. If you are familiar with it, you will already know that it's called Amb. So there is no obvious downside to using the abbreviation, and there's a benefit for people who already know it.

Another reason the Rx team used this name was to pay homage to John McCarthy, whose work was profoundly influential for computing in general, and for the LINQ and Rx projects in particular. (Many of the features discussed in this chapter and Chapter 10 are directly influenced by McCarthy's work.)

You might use this operator to optimize a system's response time by sending a request to multiple machines in a server pool, and using the result from whichever responds first. (There are dangers with this technique, of course, not least of which is that it could increase the overall load on your system so much that the effect is to slow everything down, not speed anything up. However, there are some scenarios in which careful application of this technique can be successful.)

DistinctUntilChanged

The final operator I'm going to describe in this section is very simple, but rather useful. The DistinctUntilChanged operator removes adjacent duplicates. Suppose you have an observable source that produces items on a regular basis, but tends to produce the same value multiple times in a row. You might need to take action only when a different value emerges. DistinctUntilChanged is for exactly this scenario—when its input produces an item, it will be passed on only if it was different from the previous item (or if it was the first item).

I've not yet shown all of the Rx operators I want to introduce. However, the remaining ones, which I'll discuss in "Timed Operations" on page 530, are all time sensitive. And before I can show those, I need to describe how Rx handles timing.

Schedulers

Rx performs certain work through *schedulers*. A scheduler is an object that provides three services. The first is to decide when to execute a particular piece of work. For example, when an observer subscribes to a cold source, should the source's items be delivered to the subscriber immediately, or should that work be deferred? The second service is to run work in a particular context. A scheduler might decide always to execute work on a particular thread, for example. The third job is to keep track of time. Some Rx operations are time dependent; to ensure predictable behavior and to enable testing, schedulers provide a virtualized model for time, so Rx code does not have to depend on the current time of day reported by .NET's `DateTimeOffset` class.

The scheduler's first two roles are sometimes interdependent. For example, Rx supplies a few schedulers for use in UI applications. There's a `CoreDispatcherScheduler` for Windows Store apps,[4] `DispatcherScheduler` for WPF applications, `Control Scheduler` for Windows Forms programs, and a more generic one called `Synchroni zationContextScheduler`, which will work in all .NET UI frameworks, albeit with slightly less control over the details than the framework-specific ones. All of these have a common characteristic: they ensure that work executes in a suitable context for accessing UI objects, which typically means running the work on a particular thread. If code that schedules work is running on some other thread, the scheduler may have no choice but to defer the work, because it will not be able to run it until the UI framework is ready. This might mean waiting for a particular thread to finish whatever it is doing. In this case, running the work in the right context necessarily also has an impact on when the work is executed.

This isn't always the case, though. Rx provides two schedulers that use the current thread. One of them, `ImmediateScheduler`, is extremely simple: it runs work the instant it is scheduled. When you give this scheduler some work, it won't return until the work is complete. The other, `CurrentThreadScheduler`, maintains a work queue, which gives it some flexibility with ordering. For example, if some work is scheduled in the middle of executing some other piece of work, it can allow the work item in progress to finish before starting on the next. If no work items are queued or in progress, `CurrentThreadScheduler` runs work immediately, just like `ImmediateSchedu ler`. When a work item it has invoked completes, the `CurrentThreadScheduler` inspects the queue and will invoke the next item if it's not empty. So it attempts to complete all work items as quickly as possible, but unlike `ImmediateScheduler`, it will not start to process a new work item before the previous one has finished.

---

4 This name (which is now a bit anachronistic) comes from the fact that for a while, Windows Store apps were the only supported environment for using .NET Core. However, this `CoreDispatcherScheduler` is not available in any other .NET Core-based framework.

Specifying Schedulers

Rx operations often do not go through schedulers. Many observable sources invoke their subscribers' methods directly. Sources that can generate a large number of items in quick succession are typically an exception. For example, the `Range` and `Repeat` methods for creating sequences use a scheduler to govern the rate at which they provide items to new subscribers. You can pass in an explicit scheduler, or let them pick a default one. You can also get a scheduler involved explicitly even when using sources that don't accept one as an argument.

ObserveOn

A common way to specify a scheduler is with one of the `ObserveOn` extension methods defined by various static classes in the `System.Reactive.Linq` namespace.[5] This is useful if you want to handle events in a specific context (such as the UI thread) even though they may originate from somewhere else.

You can invoke `ObserveOn` on any `IObservable<T>`, passing in an `IScheduler`, and it returns another `IObservable<T>`. If you subscribe to the observable that returns, your observer's `OnNext`, `OnCompleted`, and `OnError` methods will all be invoked through the scheduler you specified. Example 11-29 uses this to ensure that it's safe to update the UI in the item handler callback.

Example 11-29. ObserveOn

```
IObservable<Trade> trades = GetTradeStream();
IObservable<Trade> tradesInUiContext =
    trades.ObserveOn(DispatcherScheduler.Current);
tradesInUiContext.Subscribe(t =>
{
    tradeInfoTextBox.AppendText(
        $"{t.StockName}: {t.Number} at {t.UnitPrice}\r\n");
});
```

In this example, I used the `DispatcherScheduler` class's static `Current` property, which returns a scheduler that executes work via the current thread's `Dispatcher`. (`Dispatcher` is the class that manages the UI message loop in WPF applications.) There's an alternative `ObserveOn` overload I could have used here. The `DispatcherOb` servable class defines some extension methods providing WPF-specific overloads,

---

5 The overloads are spread across multiple classes because some of these extension methods are technology specific. WPF gets `ObserveOn` overloads that work directly with its `Dispatcher` class instead of `IScheduler`, for example.

enabling me to call ObserveOn passing just a Dispatcher object. I could use this in the codebehind for a UI element with code such as that in Example 11-30.

Example 11-30. WPF-specific ObserveOn overload

```
IObservable<Trade> tradesInUiContext = trades.ObserveOn(this.Dispatcher);
```

The advantage of this overload is that I don't need to be on the UI thread at the point at which I call ObserveOn. The Current property used in Example 11-29 works only if you are on the thread for the dispatcher you require. If I'm already on that thread, there's an even simpler way to set this up. I can use the ObserveOnDispatcher extension method, which obtains a DispatcherScheduler for the current thread's dispatcher, as shown in Example 11-31.

Example 11-31. Observing on the current dispatcher

```
IObservable<Trade> tradesInUiContext = trades.ObserveOnDispatcher();
```

SubscribeOn

Most of the various ObserveOn extension methods have corresponding SubscribeOn methods. (There's also SubscribeOnDispatcher, the counterpart of ObserveOnDis patcher.) Instead of arranging for each call to an observer's methods to be made through the scheduler, SubscribeOn performs the call to the source observable's Sub scribe method through the scheduler. And if you unsubscribe by calling Dispose, that will also be delivered through the scheduler. This can be important for cold sources, because many perform significant work in their Subscribe method, some even delivering all of their items immediately.

> In general, there's no guarantee of any correspondence between the context in which you subscribe to a source and the context in which the items it produces will be delivered to a subscriber. Some sources will notify you from their subscription context, but many won't. If you need to receive notifications in a particular context, then unless the source provides some way to specify a scheduler, use ObserveOn.

Passing schedulers explicitly

Some operations accept a scheduler as an argument. You will tend to find this in operations that can generate many items. The Observable.Range method that generates a sequence of numbers optionally takes a scheduler as a final argument to control the context from which these numbers are generated. This also applies to the APIs for adapting other sources, such as IEnumerable<T> to observable sources, as described in "Adaptation" on page 524.

Another scenario in which you can usually provide a scheduler is when using an observable that combines inputs. Earlier, you saw how the Merge operator combines the output of multiple sequences. You can provide a scheduler to tell the operator to subscribe to the sources from a specific context.

Finally, timed operations all depend on a scheduler. I will show some of these in "Timed Operations" on page 530.

Built-in Schedulers

I've already described the four UI-oriented schedulers, DispatcherScheduler (for WPF), CoreDispatcherScheduler (for Windows Store apps), ControlScheduler (for Windows Forms), and SynchronizationContextScheduler, and also the two schedulers for running work on the current thread, CurrentThreadScheduler and ImmediateScheduler. But there are some others worth being aware of.

EventLoopScheduler runs all work items on a specific thread. It can create a new thread for you, or you can provide it with a callback method that it will invoke when it wants you to create the thread. You might use this in a UI application to process incoming data. It lets you move work off the UI thread to keep the application responsive, but ensures that all processing happens on a single thread, which can simplify concurrency issues.

NewThreadScheduler creates a new thread for each top-level work item it processes. (If that work item spawns further work items, those will run on the same thread, rather than creating new ones.) This is appropriate only if you need to do a lot of work for each item, because threads have relatively high startup and teardown costs in Windows. You are normally better off using a thread pool if you need concurrent processing of work items.

TaskPoolScheduler uses the Task Parallel Library's (TPL) thread pool. The TPL, described in Chapter 16, provides an efficient pool of threads that can reuse a single thread for multiple work items, amortizing the startup costs of creating the thread.

ThreadPoolScheduler uses the CLR's thread pool to run work. This is similar in concept to the TPL thread pool, but it's a somewhat older piece of technology. (The TPL was introduced in .NET 4.0, but the CLR threadpool has existed since v1.0.) This is a bit less efficient in certain scenarios. Rx introduced this scheduler because early versions of Rx supported old versions of .NET that didn't have the TPL. It retains it for backward-compatibility reasons.

HistoricalScheduler is useful when you want to test time-sensitive code without needing to execute your tests in real time. All schedulers will provide a time-keeping service, but the `HistoricalScheduler` lets you decide the exact rate at which you want the scheduler to behave as though time is elapsing. So, if you need to test what happens if you wait 30 seconds, you can just tell the `HistoricalScheduler` to act as though 30 seconds have passed, without having to actually wait.

Subjects

Rx defines various *subjects*, classes that implement both `IObserver<T>` and `IObservable<T>`. These can sometimes be useful if you need Rx to provide a robust implementation of either of these interfaces, but the usual `Observable.Create` or `Subscribe` methods are not convenient. For example, perhaps you need to provide an observable source, and there are several different places in your code from which you want to provide values for that source to produce. This is awkard to fit into the `Create` method's subscription callback model, and can be easier to handle with a subject. Some of the subject types provide additional behavior, but I'll start with the simplest, `Subject<T>`.

Subject<T>

The `Subject<T>` class's `IObserver<T>` implementation just relays calls to all observers that have subscribed using its `IObservable<T>` interface. So, if you subscribe one or more observables to a `Subject<T>` and then call `OnNext`, the subject will call `OnNext` on each of its subscribers. It's the same for the other methods, `OnCompleted` and `OnError`. This multicast relay is very similar to the facility provided by the `Publish` operator[6] I used in Example 11-11, so this provides an alternative way for me to remove all of the code for tracking subscribers from my `KeyWatcher` source, resulting in the code shown in Example 11-32. This is much simpler than the original in Example 11-7, although not quite as simple as the delegate-based version in Example 11-11.

Example 11-32. Implementing IObservable<T> with a Subject<T>

```
public class KeyWatcher : IObservable<char>
{
    private readonly Subject<char> _subject = new Subject<char>();

    public IDisposable Subscribe(IObserver<char> observer)
    {
        return _subject.Subscribe(observer);
    }
```

---

6 In fact, `Publish` uses `Subject<T>` internally in the current version of Rx.

```
    public void Run()
    {
        while (true)
        {
            _subject.OnNext(Console.ReadKey(true).KeyChar);
        }
    }
}
```

This defers to a Subject<char> in its Subscribe method, so everything that tries to subscribe to this KeyWatcher will end up being subscribed to that subject instead. My loop can then just call the subject's OnNext method, and it'll take care of broadcasting that to all the subscribers.

In fact, I can simplify things further by exposing the observable as a separate property, rather than making my entire type observable, as Example 11-33 shows. Not only does this make the code slightly simpler, but it also means my KeyWatcher could now provide multiple sources if it wanted to.

Example 11-33. Providing an IObservable<T> as a property

```
public class KeyWatcher
{
    private readonly Subject<char> _subject = new Subject<char>();

    public IObservable<char> Keys => _subject;

    public void Run()
    {
        while (true)
        {
            _subject.OnNext(Console.ReadKey(true).KeyChar);
        }
    }
}
```

This is still not quite as simple as the combination of Observable.Create and the Publish operator that I used in Example 11-11, but it does offer two advantages. First, it's now easier to see when the loop that generates keypress notifications runs. I was in control of that in Example 11-11, but for anyone not totally familiar with how Publish works, it would not be obvious how this was being achieved. I find Example 11-33 a little less cryptic. Second, if I wanted to, I could use this subject from anywhere inside my KeyWatcher class, whereas in Example 11-11, the only place from which I could easily provide an item was inside the callback function invoked by Observable.Create. As it happens, in this example I don't need this flexibility, but in scenarios where you do, a Subject<T> is likely to be a better choice than the callback approach.

BehaviorSubject<T>

BehaviorSubject<T> looks almost exactly like a Subject<T> except for one thing: when any observer first subscribes, it is guaranteed to receive a value straightaway as long you have not completed the subject by calling OnComplete. (If you have already completed the subject, it'll just call OnComplete immediately on any further subscribers.) It remembers the last item it passed on, and hands that out to new subscribers. When you construct a BehaviorSubject<T>, you have to provide an initial value that it will provide to new subscribers until the first call to OnNext.

One way to think of this subject is as Rx's version of a variable. It's something that has a value that you can retrieve at any time, and its value can also change over time. But being reactive, you subscribe to it to retrieve its value, and your observer will be notified of any further changes until you unsubscribe.

This subject has a mix of hot and cold characteristics. It will instantly provide a value to any subscriber, making it seem like a cold source, but once that's happened, it then broadcasts new values to all subscribers, more like a hot source does. There's another subject with a similar mix, but that takes the cold side a bit further.

ReplaySubject<T>

ReplaySubject<T> can record every value it receives from whichever source you subscribe it to. (Or, if you invoke its methods directly, it remembers every value you provide through OnNext.) Each new subscriber to this subject will receive every item that the ReplaySubject<T> has seen so far. So this is much more like an ordinary cold subject—instead of just getting the most recent value as you would from a Behavior Subject<T>, you get a complete set of items. However, once the ReplaySubject<T> has provided a particular subscriber with all of the items it has recorded, it then transitions into more hot-like behavior for that subscriber, because it will continue to provide new incoming items.

So, in the long run, every subscriber to a ReplaySubject<T> will by default see every item that the ReplaySubject<T> receives from its source, regardless of how early or late that subscriber subscribed to the subject.

In its default configuration, a ReplaySubject<T> will consume ever more memory for as long as it is subscribed to a source. There's no way to tell it that it will have no more new subscribers, and that it's now OK for it to discard old items that it has already distributed to all of its existing subscribers. You should therefore not leave it subscribed indefinitely to an endless source. However, you can limit the amount that a ReplaySubject<T> buffers. It offers various constructor overloads, some of which let you specify either an upper limit on the number of items to replay, or an upper limit on the time for which it will hold onto items. Obviously, if you do this, new subscribers can no longer depend on getting all of the items previously received.

AsyncSubject<T>

`AsyncSubject<T>` remembers just one value from its source, but unlike `BehaviorSub ject<T>`, which remembers the most recent value, `AsyncSubject<T>` waits for its source to complete. It will then produce the final item as its output. If the source completes without providing any values, the `AsyncSubject<T>` will do the same to its subscribers.

If you subscribe to an `AsyncSubject<T>` before its source has completed, the `Asyn cSubject<T>` will do nothing with your observer until the source completes. But once the source has completed, the `AsyncSubject<T>` acts as a cold source that provides a single value, unless the source completed without providing a value, in which case this subject will complete all new subscribers immediately.

Adaptation

Interesting and powerful though Rx is, it would not be much use if it existed in a vacuum. If you are working with asynchronous notifications, it's possible that they will be supplied by an API that does not support Rx. Although `IObservable<T>` and `IOb server<T>` have been around for a long time (since .NET 4.0, which was released in 2010), not every API that could support these interfaces does. Also, because Rx's fundamental abstraction is a sequence of items, there's a good chance that at some point you might need to convert between Rx's push-oriented `IObservable<T>`, and the pull-oriented equivalents, `IEnumerable<T>` and `IAsyncEnumerable<T>`. Rx provides ways to adapt all these kinds of sources into `IObservable<T>`, and in some cases, it can adapt in either direction.

IEnumerable<T> and IAsyncEnumerable<T>

Any `IEnumerable<T>` can easily be brought into the world of Rx thanks to the `ToOb servable` extension methods. These are defined by the `Observable` static class in the `System.Reactive.Linq` namespace. Example 11-34 shows the simplest form, which takes no arguments.

Example 11-34. Converting an IEnumerable<T> to an IObservable<T>

```
public static void ShowAll(IEnumerable<string> source)
{
    IObservable<string> observableSource = source.ToObservable();
    observableSource.Subscribe(Console.WriteLine);
}
```

The ToObservable method itself does nothing with the input—it just returns a wrapper that implements IObservable<T>. This wrapper is a cold source, and each time you subscribe an observer to it, only then does it iterate through the input, passing each item to the observer's OnNext method, and calling OnCompleted at the end. If the source throws an exception, this adapter will call OnError. Example 11-35 shows how ToObservable might work if it weren't for the fact that it needs to use a scheduler.

Example 11-35. How ToObservable might look without scheduler support

```
public static IObservable<T> MyToObservable<T>(this IEnumerable<T> input)
{
    return Observable.Create((IObserver<T> observer) =>
        {
            bool inObserver = false;
            try
            {
                foreach (T item in input)
                {
                    inObserver = true;
                    observer.OnNext(item);
                    inObserver = false;
                }
                inObserver = true;
                observer.OnCompleted();
            }
            catch (Exception x)
            {
                if (inObserver)
                {
                    throw;
                }
                observer.OnError(x);
            }
            return () => { };
        });
}
```

This is not how it really works, because Example 11-35 cannot use a scheduler. (A full implementation would have been much harder to read, defeating the purpose of the example, which was to show the basic idea behind ToObservable.) The real method uses a scheduler to manage the iteration process, enabling subscription to occur asynchronously if required. It also supports stopping the work if the observer's subscription is cancelled early. There's an overload that takes a single argument of type IScheduler, which lets you tell it to use a particular scheduler; if you don't provide one, it'll use CurrentThreadScheduler.

When it comes to going in the other direction—that is, when you have an IObservable<T>, but you would like to treat it as an IEnumerable<T>—you can call the

ToEnumerable extension methods, also provided by the Observable class. Example 11-36 wraps an IObservable<string> as an IEnumerable<string> so that it can iterate over the items in the source using an ordinary foreach loop.

Example 11-36. Using an IObservable<T> as an IEnumerable<T>

```
public static void ShowAll(IObservable<string> source)
{
    foreach (string s in source.ToEnumerable())
    {
        Console.WriteLine(s);
    }
}
```

The wrapper subscribes to the source on your behalf. If the source provides items faster than you can iterate over them, the wrapper will store the items in a queue so you can retrieve them at your leisure. If the source does not provide items as fast as you can retrieve them, the wrapper will just wait until items become available.

.NET Core 3.0 and .NET Standard 2.1 add the IAsyncEnumerable<T> interface, which provides the same model as IEnumerable<T> but in a way that enables efficient asynchronous operation using the techniques discussed in Chapter 17. Rx offers a ToOb servable extension method for this, and also a ToAsyncEnumerable method extension method for IObservable<T>. These both come from the AsyncEnumerable class, and to use that you' will need a reference to a separate NuGet package called System.Linq.Async.

.NET Events

Rx can wrap a .NET event as an IObservable<T> using the Observable class's static FromEventPattern method. Earlier in Example 11-17 I used a FileSystemWatcher, a class from the System.IO namespace that raises various events when files are added, deleted, renamed, or otherwise modified in a particular folder. Example 11-37 reproduces the first part of that example, which I glossed over last time. This code uses the Observable.FromEventPattern static method to produce an observable source representing the watcher's Created event. (If you want to handle a static event, you can pass a Type object as the first argument instead. Chapter 13 describes the Type class.)

Example 11-37. Wrapping an event in an IObservable<T>

```
string path = Environment.GetFolderPath(Environment.SpecialFolder.MyPictures);
var watcher = new FileSystemWatcher(path);
watcher.EnableRaisingEvents = true;

IObservable<EventPattern<FileSystemEventArgs>> changes =
```

```
Observable.FromEventPattern<FileSystemEventArgs>(
    watcher, nameof(watcher.Created));
changes.Subscribe(evt => Console.WriteLine(evt.EventArgs.FullPath));
```

On the face of it, this seems significantly more complicated than just subscribing to the event in the normal way shown in Chapter 9, and with no obvious advantage. And in this particular example, that would have been better. However, one obvious benefit of using Rx is that if you were writing a UI application, you could use ObserveOn with a suitable scheduler to ensure that your handler was always invoked on the right thread, regardless of which thread raised the event. Of course, another benefit—and the usual reason for doing this—is that you can use any of Rx's query operators to process the events. (That's why the original Example 11-17 did this.)

The element type of the observable source that Example 11-37 produces is EventPattern<FileSystemEventArgs>. The generic EventPattern<T> is a type defined by Rx specifically for representing the raising of an event, where the event's delegate type conforms to the standard pattern described in Chapter 9 (i.e., it takes two arguments, the first being of type object, representing the object that raised the event, and the second being some type derived from EventArgs, containing information about the event). EventPattern<T> has two properties, Sender and EventArgs, corresponding to the two arguments that an event handler would receive. In effect, this is an object that represents what would normally be a method call to an event handler.

A surprising feature of Example 11-37 is that the second argument to FromEventPattern is a string containing the name of the event. Rx resolves this to the real event member at runtime. This is less than ideal for a couple of reasons. First, it means that if you type the name in wrong, the compiler won't notice (although using the nameof operator mitigates this). Second, it means the compiler can't help you with types—if you handle a .NET event directly with a lambda, the compiler can infer the argument types from the event definition, but here, because we're passing the event name as a string, the compiler doesn't know which event I'm using (or even that I'm using an event at all), so I've had to specify the generic type argument for the method explicitly. And again, if I get that wrong, the compiler won't know—it'll be checked at runtime instead.

This string-based approach arises from a shortcoming of events: you can't pass an event as an argument. In fact, events are very limited members. You can't do anything with an event from outside of the class that defines it other than adding or removing handlers. This is one of the ways in which Rx improves on events—once you're in the world of Rx, event sources and subscribers are both represented as objects (implementing IObservable<T> and IObserver<T>, respectively), making it straightforward to pass them into methods as arguments. But that doesn't help us at the point where we're dealing with an event that's not yet in Rx's world.

Rx does provide an overload that doesn't require you to use a string—you can pass in delegates that add and remove the handlers for Rx, as Example 11-38 shows.

Example 11-38. Delegate-based event wrapping

```
IObservable<EventPattern<FileSystemEventArgs>> changes =
    Observable.FromEventPattern<FileSystemEventHandler, FileSystemEventArgs>(
    h => watcher.Created += h, h => watcher.Created -= h);
```

This is somewhat more verbose, because it requires a generic type argument specifying the handler delegate type as well as the event argument type. The string-based version discovers the handler type for itself at runtime, but because the normal reason for using the approach in Example 11-38 is to get compile-time type checking, the compiler needs to know what types you're using, and the lambdas in that example don't provide quite enough information for the compiler to infer all the type arguments automatically.

As well as wrapping an event as an observable source, it's possible to go in the other direction. Rx defines an operator for IObservable<EventPattern<T>> called ToEvent Pattern<T>. (Note that this is not available for any old observable source—it has to be an observable sequence of EventPattern<T>.) If you call this, it returns an object that implements IEventPatternSource<T>. This defines a single event called OnNext, of type EventHandler<T>, which allows you to hook up an event handler in the ordinary .NET way to an observable source.

The Universal Windows Platform (UWP, which provides Windows Store applications with the common API used by both .NET and C++ apps) has its own variation on the event pattern based around a type called TypedEventHandler. The Sys tem.Reactive.Linq namespace defines a WindowsObservable class with methods for mapping between these and Rx. (This is only available when you target UWP—Rx's NuGet packages provide separate versions of the DLLs for various target platforms, so that it can offer platform-specific features like these.) It defines FromEventPattern and ToEventPattern methods that provide the same services as the versions I've already shown, but for UWP events instead of ordinary .NET events.

Asynchronous APIs

.NET supports various asynchronous patterns, which I'll be describing in detail in Chapter 16 and Chapter 17. The first to be introduced in .NET was the Asynchronous Programming Model (APM). However, this pattern is not supported directly by the new C# asynchronous language features, so most .NET APIs now use the TPL, and for older APIs the TPL offers adapters that can provide a task-based wrapper for an APM-based API. Rx can represent any TPL task as an observable source.

The basic model for all of .NET's asynchronous patterns is that you start some work that will eventually complete, optionally producing a result. So it may seem odd to translate this into Rx, where the fundamental abstraction is a sequence of items, not a single result. In fact, one useful way to understand the difference between Rx and the TPL is that IObservable<T> is analogous to IEnumerable<T>, while Task<T> is analogous to a property of type T. Whereas with IEnumerable<T> and properties, the caller decides when to fetch information from the source, with IObservable<T> and Task<T>, the source provides the information when it's ready. The choice of which party decides when to provide information is separate from the question of whether the information is singular or a sequence of items. So a mapping between singular asynchronous APIs and IObservable<T> seems a little mismatched. But then we can cross similar boundaries in the nonasynchronous world—as you saw in Chapter 10, LINQ defines various standard operators that produce a single item from a sequence, such as First or Last. Rx supports those operators, but it additionally supports going in the other direction: bringing singular asynchronous sources into a stream-like world. The upshot is an IObservable<T> source that produces just a single item (or reports an error if the operation fails). The analogy in the nonasynchronous world would be taking a single value and wrapping it in an array so that you can pass it to an API that requires an IEnumerable<T>.

Example 11-39 uses this facility to produce an IObservable<string> that will either produce a single value containing the text downloaded from a particular URL, or report a failure should the download fail.

Example 11-39. Wrapping a Task<T> as an IObservable<T>

```
public static IObservable<string> GetWebPageAsObservable(
    Uri pageUrl, IHttpClientFactory cf)
{
    HttpClient web = cf.CreateClient();
    Task<string> getPageTask = web.GetStringAsync(pageUrl);
    return getPageTask.ToObservable();
}
```

The ToObservable method used in this example is an extension method defined for Task by Rx. For this to be available, you'll need the System.Reactive.Threading.Tasks namespace to be in scope.

One potentially unsatisfactory feature of Example 11-39 is that it will attempt the download only once, no matter how many observers subscribe to the source. Depending on your requirements, that might be fine, but in some scenarios, it might make sense to attempt to download a fresh copy every time. If you want that, a better approach would be to use the Observable.FromAsync method, because you pass that a lambda that it invokes each time a new observer subscribes. Your lambda returns a task that will then be wrapped as an observable source. Example 11-40 uses this to start a new download for each subscriber.

Example 11-40. Creating a new task for each subscriber

```
public static IObservable<string> GetWebPageAsObservable(
    Uri pageUrl, IHttpClientFactory cf)
{
    return Observable.FromAsync(() =>
        {
            HttpClient web = cf.CreateClient();
            return web.GetStringAsync(pageUrl);
        });
}
```

This might be suboptimal if you have many subscribers. On the other hand, it's more efficient when nothing attempts to subscribe at all. Example 11-39 starts the asynchronous work immediately without even waiting for any subscribers. That may be a good thing—if the stream will definitely have subscribers, kicking off slow work without waiting for the first subscriber will reduce your overall latency. However, if you are writing a class in a library that presents multiple observable sources, which might not all be used, deferring work until the first subscription might be better.

The Windows Runtime defines some asynchronous patterns of its own through the `IAsyncOperation` and `IAsyncOperationWithProgress` interfaces. The `System.Reactive.Windows.Foundation` namespace defines extension methods for mapping between these and Rx. It defines `ToObservable` extension methods for these types, and also `ToAsyncOperation` and `ToAsyncOperationWithProgress` extension methods for `IObservable<T>`.

Timed Operations

Because Rx can work with live streams of information, you may need to handle items in a time-sensitive way. For example, the rate at which items arrive might be important, or you may wish to group items based on when they were provided. In this final section, I'll describe some of the time-based operators that Rx offers.

Interval

The `Observable.Interval` method returns a sequence that regularly produces values at the interval specified by an argument of type `TimeSpan`. Example 11-41 creates and subscribes to a source that will produce one value every second.

Example 11-41. Regular items with Interval

```
IObservable<long> src = Observable.Interval(TimeSpan.FromSeconds(1));
src.Subscribe(i => Console.WriteLine($"Event {i} at {DateTime.Now:T}"));
```

The items produced by `Interval` are of type `long`. It produces values of zero, one, two, etc.

`Interval` handles each subscriber independently (i.e., it is a cold source). To demonstrate this, add the code in Example 11-42 after that in Example 11-41 to wait for a short while and then create a second subscription.

Example 11-42. Two subscribers for one Interval source

```
Thread.Sleep(2500);
src.Subscribe(i => Console.WriteLine(
    $"Event {i} at {DateTime.Now:T} (2nd subscriber)"));
```

The second subscriber subscribes two and a half seconds after the first one, so this will produce the following output:

```
Event 0 at 09:46:58
Event 1 at 09:46:59
Event 2 at 09:47:00
Event 0 at 09:47:00 (2nd subscriber)
Event 3 at 09:47:01
Event 1 at 09:47:01 (2nd subscriber)
Event 4 at 09:47:02
Event 2 at 09:47:02 (2nd subscriber)
Event 5 at 09:47:03
Event 3 at 09:47:03 (2nd subscriber)
```

You can see that the second subscriber's values start from zero, and that's because it gets its own sequence. If you want a single set of these timed items to feed into multiple subscribers, you can use the `Publish` operator described earlier.

You could use an `Interval` source in conjunction with a group join as a way to break items into chunks based on when they arrive. (This is not the only way—there are overloads of `Buffer` and `Window` that can do the same.) Example 11-43 combines a timer with an observable sequence representing the words the user types. (That second sequence is in the `words` variable, which comes from Example 11-25.)

Example 11-43. Calculating words per minute

```
IObservable<long> ticks = Observable.Interval(TimeSpan.FromSeconds(6));
IObservable<int> wordGroupCounts = from tick in ticks
                                   join word in words
                                     on ticks equals words into wordsInTick
                                   from count in wordsInTick.Count()
```

```
                           select count * 10;

wordGroupCounts.Subscribe(c => Console.WriteLine($"Words per minute: {c}"));
```

Having grouped the words into boundaries based on events from the Interval source, this query goes on to count the number of items in each group. Since the groups are evenly spaced in time, this can be used to calculate the approximate rate at which the user is typing words. I'm forming a group once every 6 seconds, so we can multiply the number of words in the group by 10 to estimate the words per minute.

The results are not entirely accurate, because Rx will join two items if their durations overlap. That will cause words to be counted multiple times here. The final word at the end of one interval will also be the first word at the start of the next interval. In this case, the measurements are pretty approximate, so I'm not too worried, but you would need to bear in mind how overlaps affect this sort of operation if you wanted more precise results. Window or Buffer may offer a better solution.

Timer

The Observable.Timer method can create a sequence that produces exactly one item. It waits for the duration specified with a TimeSpan argument before producing that item. It looks very similar to Observable.Interval, because not only does it take the same argument, but it even returns a sequence of the same type: IObservable<long>. So I can subscribe to this kind of source in almost exactly the same way as with an interval sequence, as Example 11-44 shows.

Example 11-44. Single item with Timer

```
IObservable<long> src = Observable.Timer(TimeSpan.FromSeconds(1));
src.Subscribe(i => Console.WriteLine($"Event {i} at {DateTime.Now:T}"));
```

The effect is the same as an Interval that stops after producing its first item, so you will always get a value of zero. There are also overloads that accept an extra TimeSpan, which will repeatedly produce the value just like Interval. In fact, Interval uses Timer internally—it's just a wrapper offering a simpler API.

Timestamp

In the preceding two sections, I used DateTime.Now when writing out messages to indicate when the sources produced items. One potential problem with this is that it tells us the time at which our handler processed the message, which will not always be an accurate reflection of when the message was received. For example, if you have used ObserveOn to ensure that your handler always runs on the UI thread, there may be a significant delay in between the item being produced and your code getting to handle it, because the UI thread may be busy doing other things. You can mitigate this with the Timestamp operator, available on any IObservable<T>. Example 11-45 uses this as an alternative way to show the time at which an Interval produces its items.

Example 11-45. Timestamped items

```
IObservable<Timestamped<long>> src =
    Observable.Interval(TimeSpan.FromSeconds(1)).Timestamp();
src.Subscribe(i => Console.WriteLine(
    $"Event {i.Value} at {i.Timestamp.ToLocalTime():T}"));
```

If the source observable's item type is some type T, this operator will produce an observable of Timestamped<T> items. This defines a Value property, containing the original value from the source observable, and a Timestamp property, indicating when the value went through the Timestamp operator.

> The Timestamp property is a DateTimeOffset, and it picks a time zone offset of zero (i.e., it is in UTC). This provides a stable basis for timing by removing any possibility of moving in or out of daylight saving time while your program runs. However, if you want to show the timestamp to an end user, you may want to adjust it, which is why Example 11-45 calls ToLocalTime on it.

You should apply this operator directly to the observable you want to timestamp, rather than leaving it later on in the chain. Writing src.ObserveOn(sched).Time stamp() would defeat the purpose, because you would be timing the items after they had been dispatched by the scheduler passed to ObserveOn. You would want to write src.Timestamp().ObserveOn(sched) to ensure that you acquire a timestamp before feeding the items into a processing chain that might introduce delay.

TimeInterval

Whereas Timestamp records the current time at which items are produced, its relative counterpart TimeInterval records the time between successive items. Example 11-46 uses this on an observable sequence produced by Observable.Interval, so we'd expect the items to be reasonably evenly spaced.

Example 11-46. Measuring the gaps

```
IObservable<long> ticks = Observable.Interval(TimeSpan.FromSeconds(0.75));
IObservable<TimeInterval<long>> timed = ticks.TimeInterval();
timed.Subscribe(x => Console.WriteLine(
    $"Event {x.Value} took {x.Interval.TotalSeconds:F3}"));
```

While the `Timestamped<T>` items produced by the `Timestamp` operator provide a `Time stamp` property, the `TimeInterval<T>` items produced by the `TimeInterval` operator define an `Interval` property. This is a `TimeSpan` instead of a `DateTimeOffset`. I've chosen to show the number of seconds between each item to three decimal places. Here's some of what I see when I run it on my computer:

```
Event 0 took 0.760
Event 1 took 0.757
Event 2 took 0.743
Event 3 took 0.751
Event 4 took 0.749
Event 5 took 0.750
```

This shows intervals that are as much as 10 ms away from what I asked for, but that's fairly typical. Windows is not a real-time operating system.

Throttle

The `Throttle` operator lets you limit the rate at which you process items. You pass a `TimeSpan` that specifies the minimum time interval you want between any two items. If the underlying source produces items faster than this, `Throttle` will just discard them. If the source is slower than the specified rate, `Throttle` just passes everything straight through.

Surprisingly (or at least, I found this surprising), once the source exceeds the specified rate, `Throttle` drops *everything* until the rate drops back down below the specified level. So, if you specify a rate of 10 items a second, and the source produces 100 per second, it won't simply return every 10th item—it'll return nothing until the source slows down.

Sample

The `Sample` operator produces items from its input at the interval specified by its `TimeSpan` argument, regardless of the rate at which the input observable is generating items. If the underlying source produces items faster than the chosen rate, `Sample` drops items to limit the rate. However, if the source is running slower, the `Sample` operator will just repeat the last value to ensure a constant supply of notifications.

Timeout

The `Timeout` operator passes everything through from its source observable unless the source leaves too large a gap between either the subscription time and the first item, or between two subsequent calls to the observer. You specify the minimum acceptable gap with a `TimeSpan` argument. If no activity occurs within that time, the `Timeout` operator completes by reporting a `TimeoutException` to `OnError`.

Windowing Operators

I described the `Buffer` and `Window` operators earlier, but I didn't show their time-based overloads. As well as being able to specify a window size and skip count, or to mark window boundaries with an ancillary observable source, you can also specify time-based windows.

If you pass just a `TimeSpan`, both operators will break the input into adjacent windows at the specified interval. This provides a considerably simpler way to estimate the words per minute than Example 11-43. Example 11-47 shows how to achieve the same effect with the `Buffer` operator using a timed window.

Example 11-47. Timed windows with Buffer

```
IObservable<int> wordGroupCounts =
    from wordGroup in words.Buffer(TimeSpan.FromSeconds(6))
    select wordGroup.Count * 10;
wordGroupCounts.Subscribe(c => Console.WriteLine("Words per minute: " + c));
```

There are also overloads accepting both a `TimeSpan` and an `int`, enabling you to close the current window (thus starting the next window) either when the specified interval elapses or when the number of items exceeds a threshold. In addition, there are overloads accepting two `TimeSpan` arguments. These support the time-based equivalent of the combination of a window size and a skip count. The first `TimeSpan` argument specifies the window duration, while the second specifies the interval at which to start new windows. This means the windows do not need to be strictly adjacent—you can have gaps between them, or they can overlap. Example 11-48 uses this to provide more frequent estimates of the word rate while still using a six-second window.

Example 11-48. Overlapping timed windows

```
IObservable<int> wordGroupCounts =
    from wordGroup in words.Buffer(TimeSpan.FromSeconds(6),
                                   TimeSpan.FromSeconds(1))
    select wordGroup.Count * 10;
```

Unlike the join-based chunking I showed in Example 11-43, `Window` and `Buffer` do not double-count items because they are not based on a concept of overlapping durations. They treat item arrivals as instantaneous events, which are either inside or outside of any given window. So the examples I've just shown will provide a slightly more accurate measure of rate.

Delay

The `Delay` operator allows you to time-shift an observable source. You can pass a `TimeSpan`, in which case the operator will delay everything by the specified amount, or you can pass a `DateTimeOffset`, indicating a specific time at which you would like it to start replaying its input. Alternatively, you can pass an observable, and whenever that observable first produces something or completes, the `Delay` operator will start producing the values it has stored.

Regardless of how the time-shift duration is determined, in all cases the `Delay` operator attempts to maintain the same spacing between inputs. So, if the underlying source produces an item immediately, then another item after three seconds, and then a third item after a minute, the observable produced by `Delay` will produce items separated by the same time intervals.

Obviously, if your source starts producing items at a ferocious rate—two million items in a second, perhaps—there's a limit to the fidelity with which `Delay` can reproduce the exact timing of the items, but it will do its best. The limits on accuracy are not fixed. They will be determined by the nature of the scheduler you're using, and the available CPU capacity on the machine. For example, if you use one of the UI-based schedulers, it will be limited by the availability of the UI thread, and the rate at which that can dispatch work. (As with all time-based operators, `Delay` will pick a default scheduler for you, but it provides overloads that let you pass one.)

DelaySubscription

The `DelaySubscription` operator offers a similar set of overloads to the `Delay` operator, but the way it tries to effect a delay is different. When you subscribe to an observable source produced by `Delay`, it will immediately subscribe to the underlying source and start buffering items, forwarding each item only when the required delay has elapsed. The strategy employed by `DelaySubscription` is simply to delay the subscription to the underlying source and then forward each item immediately.

For cold sources, `DelaySubscription` will typically do what you need, because delaying the start of work for a cold source will typically time-shift the entire process. But for a hot source, `DelaySubscription` will cause you to miss any events that occurred during the delay, and after that, you'll start getting events with no time shift.

The `Delay` operator is more dependable—by time-shifting each item individually, it works for both hot and cold sources. However, it has to do more work—it needs to buffer everything it receives for the delay duration. For busy sources or long delays, this could consume a lot of memory. And the attempt to reproduce the original timings with a time shift is considerably more complicated than just passing items straight on. So, in scenarios where it is viable, `DelaySubscription` is more efficient.

Summary

As you've now seen, the Reactive Extensions for .NET provide a lot of functionality. The concept underpinning Rx is a well-defined abstraction for sequences of items where the source decides when to provide each item, and a related abstraction representing a subscriber to such a sequence. By representing both concepts as objects, event sources and subscribers both become first-class entities, meaning you can pass them as arguments, store them in fields, and generally do anything with them that you can do with any other data type in .NET. While you can do all of that with a delegate too, .NET events are not first class. Moreover, Rx provides a clearly defined mechanism for notifying a subscriber of errors, something that neither delegates nor events handle well. As well as defining a first-class representation for event sources, Rx defines a comprehensive LINQ implementation, which is why Rx is sometimes described as LINQ to Events. In fact, it goes well beyond the set of standard LINQ operators, adding numerous operators that exploit and help to manage the live and potentially time-sensitive world that event-driven systems occupy. Rx also provides various services for bridging between its basic abstractions and those of other worlds, including standard .NET events, `IEnumerable<T>`, and various asynchronous models.

CHAPTER 12

Assemblies

So far in this book, I've used the term *component* to describe either a library or an executable. It's now time to look more closely at exactly what that means. In .NET the proper term for a software component is an *assembly*, and it is typically a *.dll* or *.exe* file. Occasionally, an assembly will be split into multiple files, but even then it is an indivisible unit of deployment—you must either make the whole assembly available to the runtime, or not deploy it at all. Assemblies are an important aspect of the type system, because each type is identified not just by its name and namespace, but also by its containing assembly. Assemblies provide a kind of encapsulation that operates at a larger scale than individual types, thanks to the `internal` accessibility specifier, which works at the assembly level.

The runtime provides an *assembly loader*, which automatically finds and loads the assemblies a program needs. To ensure that the loader can find the right components, assemblies have structured names that include version information, and they can optionally contain a globally unique element to prevent ambiguity.

In Visual Studio, most of the C# project types in the "Create a new project" dialog produce a single assembly as their main output. They will often put additional files in the output folder too, such as copies of any assemblies that your project relies on that are not built into the .NET runtime, and other files needed by your application. (For example, a website project will typically need to produce CSS and script files in addition to server-side code.) But there will usually be a particular assembly that is the build target of your project, containing all of the types your project defines along with the code those types contain.

Anatomy of an Assembly

Assemblies use the Win32 Portable Executable (PE) file format, the same format that executables (EXEs) and dynamic link libraries (DLLs) have always used in modern versions of Windows.[1] It is "portable" in the sense that the same basic file format is used across different CPU architectures. Non-.NET PE files are generally architecture-specific, but .NET assemblies often aren't. Even if you're running .NET Core on Linux or macOS, it'll still use this Windows-based format—assemblies built for .NET Core or .NET Standard can usually run on all supported operating systems, so we use the same file format everywhere.

The C# compiler produces an assembly as its output, with an extension of either *.dll* or *.exe*. Tools that understand the PE file format will recognize a .NET assembly as a valid, but rather dull, PE file. The CLR essentially uses PE files as containers for a .NET-specific data format, so to classic Win32 tools, a C# DLL will not appear to export any APIs. Remember that C# compiles to a binary intermediate language (IL), which is not directly executable. The normal Windows mechanisms for loading and running the code in an executable or DLL won't work with IL, because that can run only with the help of the CLR. Similarly, .NET defines its own format for encoding metadata, and does not use the PE format's native capability for exporting entry points or importing the services of other DLLs.

 The Ahead-of-Time (AoT) compilation tools in .NET Core can add native executable code to your assemblies later in the build process, but with *Ready to Run* assemblies (as the output of .NET Core's AoT tools are called), even the embedded native code is loaded and executed under the control of the CLR, and is directly accessible only to managed code.

With .NET Core 3.0 or later, you won't build .NET assemblies with an extension of *.exe*. Even project types that produce directly runnable outputs (such as console or WPF applications) produce a *.dll* as their primary output. They also generate an executable file too, but it's not a .NET assembly. It's just a bootstrapper that starts the runtime and then loads and executes your application's main assembly. By default, the type of bootstrapper you get depends on what OS you build on—for example, if you build on Windows you'll get a Windows *.exe* bootstrapper, whereas on Linux it will be an executable in the ELF format.[2] (If you target the .NET Framework, it is different. Since that supports only Windows, it doesn't need different bootstrappers for

---

1 I'm using *modern* in a very broad sense here—Windows NT introduced PE support in 1993.

2 With suitable build settings you can produce bootstrappers for all supported targets regardless of which OS you build on.

different operating systems, so these projects produce a .NET assembly with an extension of *.exe* that incorporates the bootstrapper.)

.NET Metadata

As well as containing the compiled IL, an assembly contains *metadata*, which provides a full description of all of the types it defines, whether public or private. The CLR needs to have complete knowledge of all the types your code uses to be able to make sense of the IL and turn it into running code—the binary format for IL frequently refers to the containing assembly's metadata and is meaningless without it. The reflection API, which is the subject of Chapter 13, makes the information in this metadata available to your code.

Resources

You can embed binary resources in a DLL alongside the code and metadata. Client-side applications might do this with bitmaps, for example. To embed a file, you can add it to a project, select it in Solution Explorer, and then use the Properties panel to set its Build Action to Embedded Resource. This compiles a copy of the entire file into the component. To extract the resource at runtime, you use the `Assembly` class's `GetManifestResourceStream` method, which is part of the reflection API described in Chapter 13. However, in practice, you wouldn't normally use this facility directly—most applications use embedded resources through a localizable mechanism that I'll describe later in this chapter.

So, in summary, an assembly contains a comprehensive set of metadata describing all the types it defines; it holds all of the IL for those types' methods, and it can optionally embed any number of binary streams. This is typically all packaged up into a single PE file. However, that is not always the whole story.

Multifile Assemblies

.NET Framework allowed an assembly to span multiple files. You could split the code and metadata across multiple *modules*, and it was also possible for some binary streams that are logically embedded in an assembly to be put in separate files. This feature was rarely used, and .NET Core does not support it. However, it's necessary to know about it because some of its consequences persist. In particular, parts of the design of the Reflection API (Chapter 13) make no sense unless you know about this feature.

With a multifile assembly, there's always one master file that represents the assembly. This will be a PE file, and it contains a particular element of the metadata called the *assembly manifest*. This is not to be confused with the Win32-style manifest that most executables contain. The assembly manifest is just a description of what's in the assembly, including a list of any external modules or other external files; in a multi-module assembly, the manifest describes which types are defined in which files. When writing code that uses the types in an assembly directly, you generally didn't need to care whether it was split across multiple modules, because the loader would inspect the manifest and automatically load whichever modules were needed. Multiple modules were typically only an issue for code that inspected the structure of a component using reflection.

Other PE Features

Although C# does not use the classic Win32 mechanisms for representing code or exporting APIs in EXEs and DLLs, there are still a couple of old-school features of the PE format that assemblies can use.

Win32-style resources

.NET defines its own mechanism for embedding binary resources, and a localization API built on top of that, so for the most part it makes no use of the PE file format's intrinsic support for embedding resources. There's nothing stopping you from putting classic Win32-style resources into a .NET component—the C# compiler offers various command-line switches that do this. However, there's no .NET API for accessing these resources at runtime from within your application, which is why you'd normally use .NET's own resource system. But there are some exceptions.

Windows expects to find certain resources in executables. For example, it defines a way to embed version information as an unmanaged resource. C# assemblies normally do this, but you don't need to define a version resource explicitly. The compiler can generate one for you, as I show in "Version" on page 558. This ensures that if an end user looks at your assembly's properties in Windows File Explorer, they will be able to see the version number. (By convention, .NET assemblies typically contain this Win32-style version information whether they target just Windows, or can run on any platform.)

Windows *.exe* files typically contain two additional Win32 resources. You may want to define a custom icon for your application to control how it appears on the task bar or in Windows File Explorer. This requires you to embed the icon in the Win32 way, because File Explorer doesn't know how to extract .NET resources. Also, if you're writing a classic Windows desktop application or console application (whether written with .NET or not), it should supply an application manifest. Without this, Windows will presume that your application was written before 2006[3] and will modify or disable certain features for backward compatibility. The manifest also needs to be

---

3 This was the year Windows Vista shipped. Application manifests existed before then, but this was the first version of Windows to treat their absence as signifying legacy code.

---

present if you are writing a desktop application and you want it to pass certain Microsoft certification requirements. This kind of manifest has to be embedded as a Win32 resource. Again, the Application tab in the project properties pages has special support for embedding an icon and a manifest, and if you create a desktop application, Visual Studio configures your project to provide a suitable manifest by default.

Remember that with .NET Core, the main assembly is a *.dll*, even for Windows desktop applications, and the build process produces a separate *.exe* that launches the .NET runtime and then loads that assembly. As far as Windows is concerned, this bootstrapper is your application, so when you target .NET Core, the icon and manifest resources will end up in this bootstrapping assembly. But if you target the .NET Framework, there will be no separate bootstrapper, so these resources end up in the main assembly.

Console versus GUI

Windows makes a distinction between console applications and Windows applications. To be precise, the PE format requires an *.exe* file to specify a *subsystem*, and back in the old days of Windows NT, this enabled the use of multiple operating system *personalities*—early versions included a POSIX subsystem, for example. (Subsystems briefly made a reappearance in 2017 with the Linux Subsystem for Windows, which enables Linux executable files to run directly on Windows 10. But in 2019 Microsoft switched Linux support from the subsystem feature to a specialized lightweight utility virtual machine to improve compatibility.) So these days, PE files target one of just three subsystems, and one of those is for kernel-mode device drivers. The two user-mode options used today select between Windows graphical user interface (GUI) and Windows console applications. The principal difference is that Windows will show a console window when running the latter (or if you run it from a command prompt, it will just use the existing console window), but a Windows GUI application does not get a console window.

You can select between these subsystems in the project's Application property page using the "Output type" drop-down list. This offers Windows Application and Console Application. (It also offers Class Library, which builds a DLL, but since the subsystem is determined when a process launches, it makes no difference whether a DLL targets the Windows Console or Windows GUI subsystem. The Class Library setting always targets the former.) If you target the .NET Framework, this subsystem setting applies to the *.exe* file that is built as your application's main assembly, and with newer versions of .NET, it will apply to the bootstrapper *.exe*. (As it happens, it will also apply to the main assembly *.dll* that the bootstrapper loads, but this has no effect because the subsystem is determined by the *.exe* for which the process is launched.)

Type Identity

As a C# developer, your first point of contact with assemblies will usually be the fact that they form part of a type's identity. When you write a class, it will end up in an assembly. When you use a type from the .NET class library or from some other library, your project will need a reference to the assembly that contains the type before you can use it.

This is not always obvious when using system types. The build system automatically adds references to various .NET class library assemblies, so most of the time, you will not need to add a reference before you can use a .NET class library type, and since you do not normally refer to a type's assembly explicitly in the source code, it's not immediately obvious that the assembly is a mandatory part of what it takes to pin-point a type. But despite not being explicit in the code, the assembly has to be part of a type's identity, because there's nothing stopping you or anyone else from defining new types that have the same name as existing types. For example, you could define a class called `System.String` in your project. This is a bad idea, and the compiler will warn you that this introduces ambiguity, but it won't stop you. And even though your class will have the exact same fully qualified name as the built-in string type, the compiler and the runtime can still distinguish between these types.

Whenever you use a type, either explicitly by name (e.g., in a variable or parameter declaration) or implicitly through an expression, the C# compiler knows exactly what type you're referring to, meaning it knows which assembly defined the type. So it is able to distinguish between the `System.String` intrinsic to .NET, and a `System.String` unhelpfully defined in your own component. The C# scoping rules mean that an explicit reference to `System.String` identifies the one that you defined in your own project, because local types effectively hide ones of the same name in external assemblies. If you use the `string` keyword, that always refers to the built-in type. You'll also be using the built-in type when you use a string literal, or if you call an API that returns a string. Example 12-1 illustrates this—it defines its own `System.String`, and then uses a generic method that displays the type and assembly name for the static type of whatever argument you pass it. (This uses the Reflection API, which is described in Chapter 13.)

Example 12-1. What type is a piece of string?

```
using System;

// Never do this!
namespace System
{
    public class String
    {
    }
```

```
}

class Program
{
    static void Main(string[] args)
    {
        System.String s = null;
        ShowStaticTypeNameAndAssembly(s);
        string s2 = null;
        ShowStaticTypeNameAndAssembly(s2);
        ShowStaticTypeNameAndAssembly("String literal");
        ShowStaticTypeNameAndAssembly(Environment.OSVersion.VersionString);
    }

    static void ShowStaticTypeNameAndAssembly<T>(T item)
    {
        Type t = typeof(T);
        Console.WriteLine(
            $"Type: {t.FullName}. Assembly {t.Assembly.FullName}.");
    }
}
```

The Main method in this example tries each of the ways of working with strings I just described, and it writes out the following:

```
Type: System.String. Assembly MyApp, Version=1.0.0.0, Culture=neutral,
    PublicKeyToken=null.
Type: System.String. Assembly System.Private.CoreLib, Version=4.0.0.0,
    Culture=neutral, PublicKeyToken=7cec85d7bea7798e.
Type: System.String. Assembly System.Private.CoreLib, Version=4.0.0.0,
    Culture=neutral, PublicKeyToken=7cec85d7bea7798e.
Type: System.String. Assembly System.Private.CoreLib, Version=4.0.0.0,
    Culture=neutral, PublicKeyToken=7cec85d7bea7798e.
```

The explicit use of System.String ended up with my type, and the rest all used the system-defined string type. This demonstrates that the C# compiler can cope with multiple types with the same name. This also shows that IL is able to make that distinction. IL's binary format ensures that every reference to a type identifies the containing assembly. But just because you can create and use multiple identically named types doesn't mean you should. Because you do not usually name the containing assembly explicitly in C#, it's a particularly bad idea to introduce pointless collisions by defining, say, your own System.String class. (As it happens, in a pinch you can resolve this sort of collision if you really need to—see the sidebar "Extern Aliases" on page 546 for details—but it's better to avoid it.)

By the way, if you run Example 12-1 on .NET Framework, you'll see mscorlib in place of System.Private.CoreLib. .NET Core changed which assemblies many class library types live in. You might be wondering how this can work with .NET Standard, which enables you to write a single DLL that can run on both .NET Framework and .NET Core. How could a .NET Standard component correctly identify a type that lives in different assemblies on different targets? The answer is that .NET has a *type forwarding* feature in which references to types in one assembly can be redirected to some other assembly at runtime. (A type forwarder is just an assembly-level attribute that describes where the real type definition can be found. Attributes are the subject of Chapter 14.) .NET Standard components reference neither `mscorlib` nor `System.Private.CoreLib`—they are built as though class library types are defined in an assembly called `netstandard`. Each .NET runtime supplies a `netstandard` implementation that forwards to the appropriate types at runtime. In fact, even code built directly for .NET Core often ends up using type forwarding. If you inspect the compiled output you'll find that it expects most .NET class library types to be defined in an assembly called `System.Runtime`, and it's only through type forwarding that these end up using types in `System.Private.CoreLib`.

Extern Aliases

When multiple types with the same name are in scope, C# normally uses the one from the nearest scope, which is why a locally defined `System.String` can hide the built-in type of the same name. It's unwise to introduce this sort of name clash in the first place, but occasionally you can end up with this problem when external libraries that you depend on have made bad naming decisions. If that's where you are, C# offers a mechanism that lets you specify the assembly you want. You can define an *extern alias*.

In Chapter 1, I showed type aliases defined with the `using` keyword that make it easier to refer to types that have the same simple name but different namespaces. An extern alias makes it possible to distinguish between types with the same fully qualified name in different assemblies.

To define an extern alias, expand the Dependencies list in Solution Explorer, and then expand either the Projects or Assemblies section and select a reference. (You can't use this technique for references obtained via NuGet.) You can then set the alias for that reference in the Properties panel. If you define an alias of `A1` for one assembly and `A2` for another, you can then declare that you want to use these aliases by putting the following at the top of a C# file:

```
extern alias A1;
extern alias A2;
```

With these in place, you can qualify type names with `A1::` or `A2::` followed by the fully qualified name. This tells the compiler that you want to use types defined by the assembly (or assemblies) associated with that alias, even if some other type of the same name would otherwise have been in scope.

If it's a bad idea to have multiple types with the same name, why does .NET make it possible in the first place? In fact, supporting name collisions was not the goal, it's just a side effect of the fact that .NET makes the assembly part of the type. The assembly needs to be part of the type definition so that the CLR can know which assembly to load for you at runtime when you first use some feature of that type.

Loading Assemblies

You may have been alarmed earlier when I said that the build system automatically adds references to all the .NET class library components available on your target framework. Perhaps you wondered how you might go about removing some of these in the name of efficiency. As far as runtime overhead is concerned, you do not need to worry. The C# compiler effectively ignores any references to built-in assemblies that your project never uses, so there's no danger of loading DLLs that you don't need. (It is, however, worth removing references to unused components that are *not* built in to avoid copying unneeded DLLs when you deploy the app—there's no sense in making deployments larger than they need to be. But unused references to DLLs that are already installed as part of .NET cost you nothing.)

Even if C# didn't strip out unused references at compile time, there would still be no risk of unnecessary loading of unused DLLs. The CLR does not attempt to load assemblies until your application first needs them. Most applications do not exercise every possible code path each time they execute, so it's fairly common for significant portions of the code in your application not to run. Your program may even finish its work having left entire classes unused—perhaps classes that get involved only when an unusual error condition arises. If the only place you use a particular assembly is inside a method of such a class, that assembly won't get loaded.

The CLR has some discretion for deciding exactly what it means to "use" a particular assembly. If a method contains any code that refers to a particular type (e.g., it declares a variable of that type or it contains expressions that use the type implicitly), then the CLR may consider that type to be used when that method first runs even if you don't get to the part that really uses it. Consider Example 12-2.

Example 12-2. Type loading and conditional execution

```
static IComparer<string> GetComparer(bool useStandardOrdering)
{
    if (useStandardOrdering)
    {
        return StringComparer.CurrentCulture;
    }
    else
    {
        return new MyCustomComparer();
```

```
    }
}
```

Depending on its argument, this function either returns an object provided by the .NET class library's `StringComparer`, or constructs a new object of type `MyCustom Comparer`. The `StringComparer` type is defined in the same assembly as core types such as `int` and `string`, so that will have been loaded when our program started. But suppose the other type, `MyCustomComparer`, was defined in a separate assembly from my application, called *ComparerLib*. Obviously, if this `GetComparer` method is called with an argument of `false`, the CLR will need to load *ComparerLib* if it hasn't already. But what's slightly more surprising is that it will probably load *ComparerLib* the first time this method is called even if the argument is `true`. To be able to JIT compile this `GetComparer` method, the CLR will need access to the `MyCustomCom parer` type definition—for one thing it will need to check that the type really has a zero-argument constructor. (Obviously Example 12-2 wouldn't compile in that case, but it's possible that code was compiled against a different version of *ComparerLib* than is present at runtime.) The JIT compiler's operation is an implementation detail, so it's not fully documented and could change from one version to the next, but it seems to operate one method at a time. So simply invoking this method is likely to be enough to trigger the loading of the *ComparerLib* assembly.

This raises the question of how .NET finds assemblies. If assemblies can be loaded implicitly as a result of running a method, we don't necessarily have a chance to tell the runtime where to find them. So .NET has a mechanism for this.

Assembly Resolution

When the runtime needs to load an assembly, it goes through a process called *assembly resolution*. In some cases you will tell .NET to load a particular assembly (e.g., when you first run an application), but the majority are loaded implicitly. The exact mechanism depends on a couple of factors: whether you target .NET Core or the older .NET Framework, and, if the former, whether your application is *self-contained*.

.NET Core supports two deployment options for applications: *self-contained* and *framework-dependent*. When you publish a self-contained application, it includes a complete copy of .NET Core—the whole of the CLR and all the built-in assemblies. Example 12-3 shows the command line for building an application this way—if you run this from the folder containing a *.csproj* file, it will compile the project and then produce a *publish* folder containing your compiled code and a complete copy of a suitable version of .NET Core. (The version will depend on your project's configured target framework. Generally, your project file will specify a major and minor version, e.g., `netcoreapp3.0`, and then the SDK will copy the latest patch version that is installed on your machine. The available versions will be determined by what versions of the .NET Core SDK you have installed.) The `-r` switch indicates the platform to build for: the CLR for Linux is necessarily somewhat different from the one for Windows, and the macOS one is different again. And for Windows and Linux, there are versions for Intel architecture CPUs (both 32-bit and 64-bit) and also ARM. The build system needs to know which one to copy. Example 12-3 selects the runtime for Windows running on 64-bit Intel architecture CPUs.

Example 12-3. Publishing a self-contained application

```
dotnet publish -c Release -r win-x64 --self-contained true
```

When you build this way, assembly resolution is pretty straightforward because everything—your application's own assemblies, any external libraries you depend on, all of the system assemblies built into .NET, and the CLR itself—ends up in one folder. (At the time of writing, that amounts to about 66 MB for a simple *Hello world* console application for this target architecture on .NET Core 3.0.)

There are two main advantages to self-contained deployment. First, there is no need to install .NET on target machines—the application can just run directly because it contains its own copy of .NET. Second, you know exactly what version of .NET and which versions of all DLLs you are running against. Microsoft goes to great lengths to ensure backward compatibility with new releases, but breaking changes can sometimes occur, and a self-contained deployment can be one way out if you find that your application stops working after an update to .NET Core. With self-contained deployment, unless the application directs the CLR to look elsewhere everything will load from the application folder, including all assemblies built into .NET.

But what if you don't want to put an entire copy of .NET Core into your build output? The default build behavior for applications is to create a framework-dependent executable. (There's a variation on this called *framework-dependent deployment*, which is almost the same thing, except it omits the bootstrapper executable. To run a framework-dependent deployment, you will need to use the dotnet command-line tool to launch the runtime, which will then run your application. Prior to v3.0, .NET Core defaulted to framework-dependent deployment. This has the advantage of being completely platform independent; the bootstrapper in a framework-dependent executable deployment is always OS specific. But it is less convenient—you can't run the build output without the dotnet tool.) In this case, your code relies on a suitable version of .NET Core already being installed on the machine. The build output will contain your own application assembly, and may contain assemblies your application depends on, but it will not contain any of the libraries built into .NET.

Framework-dependent applications necessarily use a more complex resolution mechanism than self-contained ones. When such an application starts up it will first determine exactly which version of .NET Core to run. This won't necessarily be the version your application was built against, and there are various options to configure exactly which is chosen. By default, if the same *Major.Minor* version is available, that will be used. E.g., if a framework-dependent application built for .NET Core 2.2 runs on a machine with .NET Core versions 2.1.12, 2.2.6, and 3.0.0 installed, it will run on 2.2.6. In cases where such a match isn't available, but a major version number match is, it will typically roll forward to that; e.g., if the app targets 2.1, and the machine has only 2.2.6, it will run on 2.2.6. It is also possible to run on a higher major version number than the app was built against (e.g., build for 2.1 but run on 3.0) but only by explicitly requesting this through configuration.

The chosen runtime version selects not just the CLR, but also the assemblies making up the parts of the class library built into .NET. You can typically find all the installed runtime versions in the *C:\Program Files\dotnet\shared\Microsoft.NETCore.App* folder on Windows, or */usr/share/dotnet/shared/Microsoft.NETCore.app* on Linux, with version-based subfolders such as *3.0.0*. (You should not rely on these paths—the files may move in future versions of .NET.) The assembly resolution process will look in this version-specific folder, and this is how framework-dependent applications get to use built-in .NET assemblies.

If you poke around these folders, you may notice other folders under *shared*, such as *Microsoft.AspNetCore.App*. It turns out that this mechanism is not just for the .NET class library files built into .NET—it is also possible to install the assemblies for whole frameworks. .NET Core applications declare that they are using a particular application framework. (The build tools automatically produce a file with a *.runtimeconfig.json* in your build output declaring the framework you are using. Console apps specify `Microsoft.NETCore.App`, whereas a web application will specify `Microsoft.AspNetCore.App`.) This enables applications that target specific Microsoft frameworks not to have to include a complete copy of all of the framework's DLLs even though that framework is not part of .NET Core itself.

If you install the plain .NET Core runtime, you will get just *Microsoft.NETCore.App*, and none of the application frameworks. So applications that target frameworks such as ASP.NET Core or WPF will be unable to run if they are built in the default way, because that presumes that those frameworks will be preinstalled on target machines, and the assembly resolution process will fail to find framework-specific components. The .NET Core SDK installs these additional framework components, so you won't see this problem on your development machine, but you might see it when deploying at runtime. You can tell the build tools to include the framework's components, but this is not normally necessary. If you run your application on a public cloud service such as Azure, these generally preinstall relevant framework components, so in practice you will usually only run into this situation if you are configuring a server yourself, or when deploying desktop applications. For those cases, Microsoft offers installers for the .NET Core runtime that also include the components for web or desktop frameworks.

The *shared* folder in the *dotnet* installation folder is not one you should modify yourself. It is intended only for Microsoft's own frameworks. However, it is possible to install additional system-wide components if you want, because .NET Core also supports something called the *runtime package store*. This is an additional directory structured in much the same way as the *shared* folder just described. You can build a suitable directory layout with the `dotnet store` command, and if you set the `DOT NET_SHARED_STORE` environment variable, the CLR will look in there during assembly resolution. This enables you to play the same trick as is possible with Microsoft's frameworks: you can build applications that depend on a set of components without needing to include them in your build output, as long as you've arranged for those components to be preinstalled on the target machine.

Aside from looking in these two locations for common frameworks, the CLR will also look in the application's own directory during assembly resolution, just as it would for a self-contained application. Also, the CLR has some mechanisms for enabling updates to be applied. For example, on Windows, it is possible for Microsoft to push out critical updates to .NET Core components via Windows Update.

But broadly speaking, the basic process of assembly resolution for framework-dependent applications is that implicit assembly loading occurs either from your application directory, or from a shared set of components installed on the machine. (This is also true for applications running on the older .NET Framework, although the mechanisms are a bit different. It has something called the *Global Assembly Cache* (GAC), which effectively combines the functionality provided by both of the shared stores in .NET Core. It is less flexible, because the store location is fixed; .NET Core's use of an environment variable opens up the possibility of different shared stores for different applications.)

Explicit Loading

Although the CLR will load assemblies automatically, you can also load them explicitly. For example, if you are creating an application that supports plugins, during development you will not know exactly what components you will load at runtime. The whole point of a plugin system is that it's extensible, so you'd probably want to load all the DLLs in a particular folder. (You would need to use reflection to discover and make use of the types in those DLLs, as Chapter 13 describes.)

In some scenarios, dynamic loading is restricted. For example, apps built for Windows 10 using the UWP installed from Microsoft's store can only run code from the components that ship as part of the application. This is because Microsoft runs various tests on these store apps designed to avoid security and stability problems, for which they need access to all of your app's code. The ability to download and run external code would defeat these checks.

If you know the full path of an assembly, loading it is very straightforward: you call the `Assembly` class's static `LoadFrom` method, passing the path of the file. The path can be relative to the current directory, or it can be absolute. This static method returns an instance of the `Assembly` class, which is part of the Reflection API. It provides ways of discovering and using the types defined by the assembly.

Occasionally, you might want to load a component explicitly (e.g., to use it via reflection) without wanting to specify the path. For example, you might want to load a particular assembly from the .NET class library. You should never hardcode the location for a system component—they tend to move from one version of .NET to the next. If your project has a reference to the relevant assembly and you know the name of a type it defines, you can write `typeof(TheType).Assembly`. But if that's not an option, you should use the `Assembly.Load` method, passing the name of the assembly.

`Assembly.Load` uses exactly the same mechanism as implicitly triggered loading. So you can refer to either a component that you've installed alongside your application, or a system component. In either case, you should specify a full name, which must contain name and version information, e.g., `ComparerLib, Version=1.0.0.0, Culture=neutral, PublicKeyToken=null`.

The .NET Framework version of the CLR remembers which assemblies were loaded with `LoadFrom`. If an assembly loaded in this way triggers the implicit loading of further assemblies, the CLR will search the location from which that assembly was loaded. This means that if your application keeps plugins in a separate folder that the CLR would not normally look in, those plugins could install other components that they depend on in that same plugin folder. The CLR will then find them without needing further calls to `LoadFrom`, even though it would not normally have looked in that folder for an implicitly triggered load. However, .NET Core does not support this behavior. It provides a different mechanism to support plugin scenarios.

Isolation and Plugins with AssemblyLoadContext

.NET Core introduced a type called `AssemblyLoadContext`. It enables a degree of isolation between groups of assemblies within a single application.[4] This solves a problem that can arise in applications that support a plugin model.

If a plugin depends on some component that the hosting application also uses, but each wants a different version, this can cause problems if you use the simple mechanisms described in the preceding section. Typically, the .NET runtime *unifies* these references, loading just a single version. In any cases where the types in that shared

---

4 This is not available in .NET Framework, and is also not in any current version of .NET Standard at the time of writing. Isolation was typically managed with *appdomains* on .NET Framework, an older mechanism that is not supported in .NET Core.

component are part of the plugin interface, this is exactly what you need: if an application requires plugins to implement some interface that relies on types from, say, the Newtonsoft.Json library, it's important that the application and the plugins all agree on which version of that library is in use.

But unification can cause problems with components used as implementation details, and not as part of the API between the application and its plugins. If the host application uses, say, v2.2 of Microsoft.Extensions.Logging internally, and a plugin uses v3.0 of the same component, there's no particular need to unify this to a single version choice at runtime—there would be no harm in the application and plugin each using the version they require. Unification could cause problems: forcing the plugin to use v2.2 would cause exceptions at runtime if it attempted to use features only present in v3.0. Forcing the application to use v3.0 could also cause problems because major version number changes often imply that a breaking change was introduced.

To avoid these kinds of problems, you can introduce custom assembly load contexts. You can write a class that derives from AssemblyLoadContext, and for each of these that you instantiate, the .NET runtime creates a corresponding load context which supports loading of different versions of assemblies than may already have been loaded by the application. You can define the exact policy you require by overloading the Load method, as Example 12-4 shows.

Example 12-4. A custom AssemblyLoadContext for plugins

```
using System;
using System.Collections.Generic;
using System.Reflection;
using System.Runtime.Loader;

namespace HostApp
{
    public class PlugInLoadContext : AssemblyLoadContext
    {
        private readonly AssemblyDependencyResolver _resolver;
        private readonly ICollection<string> _plugInApiAssemblyNames;

        public PlugInLoadContext(
            string pluginPath,
            ICollection<string> plugInApiAssemblies)
        {
            _resolver = new AssemblyDependencyResolver(pluginPath);
            _plugInApiAssemblyNames = plugInApiAssemblies;
        }

        protected override Assembly Load(AssemblyName assemblyName)
        {
            if (!_plugInApiAssemblyNames.Contains(assemblyName.Name))
            {
```

```
            string assemblyPath = _resolver.ResolveAssemblyToPath(assemblyName);
            if (assemblyPath != null)
            {
                return LoadFromAssemblyPath(assemblyPath);
            }
        }

        return AssemblyLoadContext.Default.LoadFromAssemblyName(
            assemblyName);
    }
}
}
```

This takes the location of the plugin DLL, along with a list of the names of any special assemblies where the plugin must use the same version as the host application. (This would include interfaces defining types used in your plugin interface. You don't need to include assemblies that are included as part of .NET itself—these are always unified, even if you use custom load contexts.) The runtime will call this class's Load method each time an assembly is loaded in this context. This code checks to see whether the assembly being loaded is one of the special ones that must be common to plugins and the host application. If not, this looks in the plugin's folder to see if the plugin has supplied its own version of that assembly. In cases where it will not use an assembly from the plugin folder (either because the plugin hasn't supplied this particular assembly, or because it is one of the special ones), this context defers to Assembly LoadContext.Default, meaning that the application host and plugin use the same assemblies in these cases. Example 12-5 shows this in use.

Example 12-5. Using the plugin load context

```
Assembly[] plugInApiAssemblies =
{
    typeof(IPlugIn).Assembly,
    typeof(JsonReader).Assembly
};
var plugInAssemblyNames = new HashSet<string>(
    plugInApiAssemblies.Select(a => a.GetName().Name));

var ctx = new PlugInLoadContext(plugInDllPath, plugInAssemblyNames);
Assembly plugInAssembly = ctx.LoadFromAssemblyPath(plugInDllPath);
```

This builds a list of assemblies that the plugin and application must share, and passes their names into the plugin context, along with a path to the plugin DLL. Any DLLs that the plugin depends on and which are copied into the same folder as the plugin will be loaded, unless they are in that list, in which case the plugin will use the same assembly as the host application itself.

Assembly Names

Assembly names are structured. They always include a *simple name*, which is the name by which you would normally refer to the DLL, such as *MyLibrary* or *System.Runtime*. This is usually the same as the filename but without the extension. It doesn't technically have to be,[5] but the assembly resolution mechanism assumes that it is. Assembly names always include a version number. There are also some optional components, including the *public key token*, a string of hexadecimal digits, which is required if you want a unique name.

Strong Names

If an assembly's name includes a public key token, it is said to be a *strong name*. Microsoft advises that any .NET component that is published for shared use (e.g., made available via NuGet) should have a strong name. Since the purpose of strong naming is to make the assembly name unique, you may be wondering why .NET does not simply use a Globally Unique Identifier (GUID). The answer is that historically, strong names also did another job: they were designed to provide some degree of assurance that the assembly has not been tampered with. Early versions of .NET checked strongly named assemblies for tampering at runtime, but these checks were removed because they imposed a considerable runtime overhead, often for little or no benefit. Microsoft's documentation now explicitly advises against treating strong names as a security feature. However, in order to understand and use strong names, you need to know how they were originally meant to work.

As the terminology suggests, an assembly name's public key token has a connection with cryptography. It is the hexadecimal representation of a 64-bit hash of a public key. Strongly named assemblies are required to contain a copy of the full public key from which the hash was generated. The assembly file format also provides space for a digital signature, generated with the corresponding private key.

Asymmetric Encryption

If you're not familiar with asymmetric encryption, this is not the place for a thorough introduction, but here's a very rough summary. Strong names use an encryption algorithm called RSA, which works with a pair of keys: the public key and the private key. Messages encrypted with the public key can be decrypted only with the private key, and vice versa. .NET exploits this to form a digital signature for an assembly: to sign an assembly you calculate a hash of its contents, and then encrypt that hash with the private key. This signature is then copied into the assembly, and its validity can be

---

5 If you use Assembly.LoadFrom, the CLR does not care whether the filename matches the simple name.

verified by anyone with access to the public key—they can calculate the hash of the assembly's contents themselves, and they can decrypt your signature with the public key, and if the results are different, the signature is invalid, implying either that it was not produced by the owner of the private key, or that the file has been modified since the signature was generated, so the file is suspect. The mathematics of encryption are such that it is thought to be essentially impossible to create a valid-looking signature unless you have access to the private key, and it's also essentially impossible to modify the assembly without modifying the hash. And in cryptography, "essentially impossible" means "theoretically possible, but too computationally expensive to be practical, unless some major unexpected breakthrough in number theory or perhaps quantum computing emerges, rendering most current cryptosystems useless."

The uniqueness of a strong name relies on the fact that key generation systems use cryptographically secure random-number generators, and the chances of two people generating two key pairs with the same public key token are vanishingly small. The assurance that the assembly has not been tampered with comes from the fact that a strongly named assembly must be signed, and only someone in possession of the private key can generate a valid signature. Any attempt to modify the assembly after signing it will invalidate the signature.

The signature associated with a strong name is independent of Authenticode, a longer-established code signing mechanism in Windows. These serve different purposes. Authenticode provides traceability, because the public key is wrapped in a certificate that tells you something about where the code came from. With a strong name's public key token, all you get is a number, so unless you happen to know who owns that token, it tells you nothing. Authenticode lets you ask, "Where did this component come from?" A public key token lets you say, "This is the component I want." It's common for a single .NET component to use both mechanisms.

If an assembly's private key becomes public knowledge, anyone can generate valid-looking assemblies with the corresponding key token. Some open source projects deliberately publish both keys, so that anyone can build the components from source. This completely abandons any security the key token could offer, but that's fine because Microsoft now recommends that we should not treat strong names as a security feature. The practice of publishing your strong naming private key recognizes that it is useful to have a unique name, even without a guarantee of authenticity. .NET Core takes this one step further, by making it possible for components to have a strong name without needing to use a private key at all. In keeping with Microsoft's adoption of open source development, this means you can now build and use your own versions of Microsoft-authored components that have the same strong name, even though Microsoft has not published its private key. See the next sidebar, "Strong Name Keys and Public Signing", for information on how to work with keys.

Strong Name Keys and Public Signing

There are three popular approaches for working with strong names. The simplest is to use the real names throughout the development process, and to copy the public and private keys to all developers' machines so that they can sign the assemblies every time they build. This approach is viable only if you don't need to keep the private key secret, because it's easy for developers to compromise the secrecy of the private key either accidentally or deliberately. Since strong names no longer offer security, there's nothing wrong with this. However, some organizations nonetheless attempt to keep their private keys secret as a matter of policy, so you may encounter other ways of working.

Another approach is to use a completely different set of keys during development, switching to the real name only for designated release builds. This avoids the need for all developers to have a copy of the real private key, but it can cause confusion, because developers may end up with two sets of components on their machines, one with development names, and one with real names.

The third approach is to use the real names across the board, but instead of signing every build, just filling the part of the file reserved for the signature with 0 values. .NET Core calls this *Public Signing*, and it's more of a convention than a feature: it works because the .NET Core CLR never checks the signatures of strongly named assemblies. (.NET Framework does still check signatures in certain cases. For example, to install an assembly in the GAC, it must have a strong name with a valid signature. It has a slightly more complex mechanism called *Delay Signing*, which makes you jump through a few more hoops, but the effect is the same: developers can compile assemblies that have the real strong names without then needing to generate signatures.)

You can generate a key file for a strong name from the Signing tab of a project's properties in Visual Studio. Alternatively, you can use a command-line utility called *sn* (short for *strong name*), which can do things Visual Studio cannot, such as adding a signature to an assembly that was originally built with delay signing, or configuring the locally installed .NET Framework to ignore the absence of a valid signature for specific delay-signed assemblies.

Microsoft uses the same token on most of the assemblies in the .NET class library. (Many groups at Microsoft produce .NET components, so this token is common only to the components that are part of .NET, not for Microsoft as a whole.) Here's the full name of *mscorlib*, a system assembly that offers definitions of various core types such as System.String:

```
mscorlib, Version=4.0.0.0, Culture=neutral, PublicKeyToken=b77a5c561934e089
```

By the way, that's the right name even for the latest versions of .NET at the time of writing. It reports 4.0.0.0 even though .NET Framework is now on v4.8, and .NET Core on 3.0. (In .NET Core, *mscorlib* contains nothing but type forwarders, because the relevant types have moved, mostly to *System.Private.CoreLib*, but the version number is the same.) Assembly version numbers have technical significance, so Microsoft does not always update the version number in the names of library components in step with the marketing version numbers—the versions don't necessarily even match on the major number. The .NET 3.5 version of *mscorlib* had a version number of 2.0.0.0, for example.

While the public key token is an optional part of an assembly's name, the version is mandatory.

Version

All assembly names include a four-part version number. When an assembly name is represented as a string (e.g., when you pass one as an argument to Assembly.Load), the version consists of four decimal integers separated by dots (e.g., 4.0.0.0). The binary format that IL uses for assembly names and references limits the range of these numbers—each part must fit in a 16-bit unsigned integer (a ushort), and the highest allowable value in a version part is actually one less than the maximum value that would fit, making the highest legal version number 65534.65534.65534.65534.

Each of the four parts has a name. From left to right, they are the *major version*, the *minor version*, the *build*, and the *revision*. However, there's no particular significance to any of these. Some developers use certain conventions, but nothing checks or enforces them. A common convention is that any change in the public API requires a change to either the major or minor version number, and a change likely to break existing code should involve a change of the major number. (Marketing is another popular reason for a major version change.) If an update is not intended to make any visible changes to behavior (except, perhaps, fixing a bug), changing the build number is sufficient. The revision number could be used to distinguish between two components that you believe were built against the same source, but not at the same time. Alternatively, some people relate the version numbers to branches in source control, so a change in just the revision number might indicate a patch applied to a version that has long since stopped getting major updates. However, you're free to make up your own meanings. As far as the CLR is concerned, there's really only one interesting thing you can do with a version number, which is to compare it with some other version number—either they match or one is higher than the other.

NuGet packages also have version numbers, and these do not need to be connected in any way to assembly versions. Many package authors make them similar by convention, but this is not universal. NuGet *does* treat the components of a package version number as having particular significance: it has adopted the widely used *semantic versioning* rules. This uses versions with three parts, named major, minor, and patch.

Version numbers in .NET class library assembly names ignore all the conventions I have just described. Most of the components had the same version number (2.0.0.0) across four major updates. With .NET 4.0, everything changed to 4.0.0.0, which is still in use with the latest version of .NET Framework (4.8), at the time of writing. .NET Core 3.0 also uses 4 as the major version of most of its class library components.

You typically specify the version number by adding a `<Version>` element inside a `<PropertyGroup>` of your *.csproj* file. (Visual Studio also offers a UI for this: if you open the Properties page for the project, its Package tab lets you configure various naming-related settings. The "Package version" field sets the version.) The build system uses this in two ways: it sets the version number on the assembly, but also, if you generate a NuGet package for your project, by default it will also use this same version number for the package, and since NuGet versions numbers have three parts, you normally specify just three numbers here, and the fourth part of the assembly version will default to zero. (If you want to specify all four digits, consult the documentation for how to set the assembly and NuGet versions separately.)

The build system tells the compiler which version number to use for the assembly name via an assembly-level attribute. I'll describe attributes in more detail in Chapter 14, but this one's pretty straightforward. If you want to find it, the build system typically generates a file called *ProjectName*`.AssemblyInfo.cs` in a subfolder of your project's *obj* folder. This contains various attributes describing details about the assembly, including an `AssemblyVersion` attribute, such as the one shown in Example 12-6.

Example 12-6. Specifying an assembly's version

```
[assembly: System.Reflection.AssemblyVersion("1.0.0.0")]
```

The C# compiler provides special handling for this attribute—it does not apply it blindly as it would most attributes. It parses the version number and embeds it in the way required by .NET's metadata format. It also checks that the string conforms to the expected format and that the numbers are in the allowed range.

By the way, the version that forms part of an assembly's name is distinct from the one stored using the standard Win32 mechanism for embedding versions. Most .NET files contain both kinds. By default, the build system will use the `<Version>` setting for both, but it's common for the file version to change more frequently. For example, although many of the files in the current .NET class library have an assembly name version number of `4.0.0.0`, if you look at the Windows-style file version information, you'll usually see something different. This was particularly important with .NET Framework in which only a single instance of any major version can be installed at once—if a machine has .NET Framework 4.7.2 installed and you install .NET Framework 4.8, that will replace version 4.7.2. (.NET Core doesn't do this—you can install any number of versions side by side on a single computer.) This in-place updating combined with Microsoft's tendency to keep assembly versions the same across releases could make it hard to work out exactly what is installed, at which point the file version becomes important. On a computer with .NET Framework 4.0 sp1 installed, its version of *mscorlib.dll* has a Win32 version number of `4.0.30319.239`, but if you've installed .NET 4.8, this changes to `4.8.4018.0`. (As service packs and other updates are released, the last part will keep climbing.)

By default, the build system will use the `<Version>` for both the assembly and Windows file versions, but if you want to set the file version separately, you can add a `<FileVersion>` to your project file. (Visual Studio's project properties Package page also lets you set this.) Under the covers, this works with another attribute that gets special handling from the compiler, `AssemblyFileVersion`. It causes the compiler to embed a Win32 version resource in the file, so this is the version number users see if they right-click on your assembly in Windows Explorer and show the file properties.

This file version is usually a more appropriate place to put a version number that identifies the build provenance than the version that goes into the assembly name. The latter is really a declaration of the supported API version, and any updates that are designed to be fully backward compatible should probably leave it unaltered, and should change only the file version.

Version numbers and assembly loading

Since version numbers are part of an assembly's name (and therefore its identity), they are also, ultimately, part of a type's identity. The `System.String` in *mscorlib* version `2.0.0.0` is not the same thing as the type of the same name in *mscorlib* version `4.0.0.0`.

The handling of assembly version numbers changed with .NET Core. In .NET Framework, when you load a strongly named assembly by name (either implicitly by using types it defines, or explicitly with `Assembly.Load`), the CLR requires the version number to be an exact match.[6] .NET Core relaxes this, so if the version on disk has a version number equal to or higher than the version requested, it will use it. There are two factors behind this change. The first is that the .NET development ecosystem has come to rely on NuGet (which didn't even exist for most of the first decade of .NET's existence), meaning that it has become increasingly common to depend on fairly large numbers of external components. Second, the rate of change has increased—in the early days we would often need to wait for years between new releases of .NET components. (Security patches and other bug fixes might turn up more often, but new functionality would tend to emerge slowly, and typically in big chunks, as part of a whole wave of updates to the runtime, frameworks, and development tools.) But today, it can be rare to go for as long as a month without the version of some component somewhere changing. .NET Framework's strict versioning policy now looks unhelpful. (In fact, there are parts of the build system dedicated to digging through your NuGet dependencies, working out the specific versions of each component you're using, and automatically generating a configuration file with a vast number of version substitution rules telling the CLR to use those versions no matter which version any single assembly says it wants. So even if you target the .NET Framework, the build system will, by default, effectively disable strict versioning.)

Another change is that .NET Framework only takes assembly versions into account for strongly named assemblies. .NET Core checks that the version number of the assembly on disk is equal to or greater than the required version regardless of whether the target assembly is strongly named.

Culture

So far we've seen that assembly names include a simple name, a version number, and optionally a public key token. They also have a *culture* component. (A culture represents a language and a set of conventions, such as currency, spelling variations, and date formats.) This is not optional, although the most common value for this is the default: `neutral`, indicating that the assembly contains no culture-specific code or data. The culture is usually set to something else only on assemblies that contain culture-specific resources. The culture of an assembly's name is designed to support localization of resources such as images and strings. To show how, I'll need to explain the localization mechanism that uses it.

All assemblies can contain embedded binary streams. (You can put text in these streams, of course. You just have to pick a suitable encoding.) The `Assembly` class in the reflection API provides a way to work directly with these, but it's more common to use the `ResourceManager` class in the `System.Resources` namespace. This is far

---

6 It's possible to configure the CLR to substitute a specific different version, but even then, the loaded assembly has to have the exact version specified by the configuration.

more convenient than working with the raw binary streams, because the Resource Manager defines a container format that allows a single stream to hold any number of strings, images, sound files, and other binary items, and Visual Studio has a built-in editor for working with this container format. The reason I'm mentioning all of this in the middle of a section that's ostensibly about assembly names is that ResourceManager also provides localization support, and the assembly name's culture is part of that mechanism. To demonstrate how this works, I'll walk you through a quick example.

The easiest way to use the ResourceManager is to add a resource file in the *.resx* format to your project. (This is not the format used at runtime. It's an XML format that gets compiled into the binary format required by ResourceManager. It's easier to work with text than binary in most source control systems.) To add one of these from the Add New Item dialog, select the Visual C#→General category and then choose Resources File. I'll call mine *MyResources.resx*. Visual Studio will show its resource editor, which opens in string editing mode, as Figure 12-1 shows. As you can see, I've defined a single string with a name of ColString and a value of Color.

Figure 12-1. Resource file editor in string mode

I can retrieve this value at runtime. The build system generates a wrapper class for each *.resx* file you add, with a static property for each resource you define. This makes it very easy to look up a string resource, as Example 12-7 shows.

Example 12-7. Retrieving a resource with the wrapper class

```
string colText = MyResources.ColString;
```

The wrapper class hides the details, which is usually convenient, but in this case, the details are the whole reason I'm demonstrating a resource file, so I've shown how to use the ResourceManager directly in Example 12-8. I've included the entire source for the file, because namespaces are significant here—Visual Studio prepends your project's default namespace to the embedded resource stream name, so I've had to ask for ResourceExample.MyResources instead of just MyResources. (If I had put the resources in a folder in Solution Explorer, Visual Studio would also include the name of that folder in the resource stream name.)

Example 12-8. Retrieving a resource at runtime

```
using System;
using System.Resources;

namespace ResourceExample
{
    class Program
    {
        static void Main(string[] args)
        {
            var rm = new ResourceManager(
                "ResourceExample.MyResources", typeof(Program).Assembly);
            string colText = rm.GetString("ColString");
            Console.WriteLine("And now in " + colText);
        }
    }
}
```

So far, this is just a rather long-winded way of getting hold of the string "Color". However, now that we've got a ResourceManager involved, I can define some localized resources. Being British, I have strong opinions on the correct way to spell the word *color*. They are not consistent with O'Reilly's editorial policy, and in any case I'm happy to adapt my work for my predominantly American readership. But a program can do better—it should be able to provide different spellings for different audiences. (And taking it a step further, it should be able to change the language entirely for countries in which some form of English is not the predominant language.) In fact, my program already contains all the code it needs to support localized spellings of the word *color*. I just need to provide it with the alternative text.

I can do this by adding a second resource file with a carefully chosen name: *MyResources.en-GB.resx*. That's almost the same as the original but with an extra *.en-GB* before the *.resx* extension. That is short for English-Great Britain, and it is the standardized (albeit politically tone-deaf) name of the culture for my home. (The name for the culture that denotes English-speaking parts of the US is *en-US*.) Having added such a file to my project, I can add a string entry with the same name as before, ColString, but this time with the correct (where I'm sitting[7]) value of Colour. If you run the application on a machine configured with a British locale, it will use the British spelling. The odds are that your machine is not configured for this locale, so if you want to try this, you can add the code in Example 12-9 at the very start of the Main method in Example 12-8 to force .NET to use the British culture when looking up resources.

---

7 England.

Example 12-9. Forcing a nondefault culture

```
Thread.CurrentThread.CurrentUICulture =
    new System.Globalization.CultureInfo("en-GB");
```

How does this relate to assemblies? Well, if you look at the compiled output, you'll see that, as well as the usual executable file and related debug files, Visual Studio has created a subdirectory called *en-GB*, which contains an assembly file called *ResourceExample.resources.dll*. (*ResourceExample* is the name of my project. If you created a project called *SomethingElse*, you'd see *SomethingElse.resources.dll*.) That assembly's name will look like this:

```
ResourceExample.resources, Version=1.0.0.0, Culture=en-GB, PublicKeyToken=null
```

The version number and public key token will match those for the main project—in my example, I've left the default version number, and I've not given my assembly a strong name. But notice the `Culture`. Instead of the usual `neutral` value, I've got `en-GB`, the same culture string I specified in the filename for the second resource file I added. If you add more resource files with other culture names, you'll get a folder containing a culture-specific assembly for each culture you specify. These are called *satellite resource assemblies*.

When you first ask a `ResourceManager` for a resource, it will look for a satellite resource assembly with the same culture as the thread's current UI culture. So it would attempt to load an assembly using the name shown a couple of paragraphs ago. If it doesn't find that, it tries a more generic culture name—if it fails to find `en-GB` resources, it will look for a culture called just `en`, denoting the English language without specifying any particular region. Only if it finds neither (or if it finds matching assemblies, but they do not contain the resource being looked up) does it fall back to the neutral resource built into the main assembly.

The CLR's assembly loader looks in different places when a nonneutral culture is specified. It looks in a subdirectory named for the culture. That's why Visual Studio placed my satellite resource assembly in an *en-GB* folder.

The search for culture-specific resources incurs some runtime costs. These are not large, but if you're writing an application that will never be localized, you might want to avoid paying the price for a feature you're not using. You might still want to use the `ResourceManager`, however—it's a more convenient way to embed resources than using assembly manifest resource streams directly. The way to avoid the costs is to tell .NET that the resources built directly into your main assembly are the right ones for a particular culture. You can do this with the assembly-level attribute shown in Example 12-10.

Example 12-10. Specifying the culture for built-in resources

```
[assembly: NeutralResourcesLanguage("en-US")]
```

When an application with that attribute runs on a machine in the usual US locale, the `ResourceManager` will not attempt to search for resources. It will just go straight for the ones compiled into your main assembly.

Protection

In Chapter 3, I described some of the accessibility specifiers you can apply to types and their members, such as `private` or `public`. In Chapter 6, I showed some of the additional mechanisms available when you use inheritance. It's worth quickly revisiting these features, because assemblies play a part.

Also in Chapter 3, I introduced the `internal` keyword, and said that classes and methods with this accessibility are available only within the same *component*, a slightly vague term that I chose because I had not yet introduced assemblies. Now that it's clear what an assembly is, it's safe for me to say that a more precise description of the `internal` keyword is that it indicates that a member or type should be accessible only to code in the same assembly.[8] Likewise, `protected internal` members are available to code in derived types, and also to code defined in the same assembly, and the similar but more restrictive `protected private` protection level makes members available only to code that is in a derived type that is defined in the same assembly.

Summary

An assembly is a deployable unit, almost always a single file, typically with a *.dll* or *.exe* extension. It is a container for types and code. A type belongs to exactly one assembly, and that assembly forms part of the type's identity—the .NET runtime can distinguish between two types with the same name in the same namespace if they are defined in different assemblies. Assemblies have a composite name consisting of a simple textual name, a four-part version number, a culture string, and optionally a public key token. Assemblies with a public key token are called strongly named assemblies, giving them a globally unique name. Assemblies can either be deployed alongside the application that uses them, or stored in a machine-wide repository. (In .NET Framework, that repository was the Global Assembly Cache, and assemblies must be strongly named to use this. .NET Core provides shared copies of built-in

---

8 Internal items are also available to *friend assemblies*, meaning any assemblies referred to with an `InternalsVi sibleTo` attribute, as described in Chapter 14.

assemblies, and depending on how you install it, it may also have shared copies of frameworks such as ASP.NET Core and WPF. And you can optionally set up a separate runtime package store containing other shared assemblies to avoid having to include them in application folders.)

The runtime can load assemblies automatically on demand, which typically happens the first time you run a method that contains some code that depends on a type defined in the relevant assembly. You can also load assemblies explicitly if you need to.

As I mentioned earlier, every assembly contains comprehensive metadata describing the types it contains. In the next chapter, I'll show how you can get access to this metadata at runtime.

CHAPTER 13

Reflection

The CLR knows a great deal about the types our programs define and use. It requires all assemblies to provide detailed metadata, describing each member of every type, including private implementation details. It relies on this information to perform critical functions, such as JIT compilation and garbage collection. However, it does not keep this knowledge to itself. The *reflection* API grants access to this detailed type information, so your code can discover everything that the runtime can see. Moreover, you can use reflection to make things happen. For example, a reflection object representing a method not only describes the method's name and signature, but it also lets you invoke the method. And you can go further still and generate code at runtime.

Reflection is particularly useful in extensible frameworks, because they can use it to adapt their behavior at runtime based on the structure of your code. For example, Visual Studio's Properties panel uses reflection to discover what public properties a component offers, so if you write a component that can appear on a design surface, such as a UI element, you do not need to do anything special to make its properties available for editing—Visual Studio will find them automatically.

Many reflection-based frameworks that can automatically discover what they need to know also allow components to enrich that information explicitly. For example, although you don't need to do anything special to support editing in the Properties panel, you can customize the categorization, description, and editing mechanisms if you want to. This is normally achieved with *attributes*, which are the topic of Chapter 14.

Reflection Types

The reflection API defines various classes in the System.Reflection namespace. These classes have a structural relationship that mirrors the way that assemblies and the type system work. For example, a type's containing assembly is part of its identity, so the reflection class that represents a type (Type[1]) has an Assembly property that returns its containing Assembly object. And you can navigate this relationship in both directions—you can discover all of the types in an assembly from the Assembly class's DefinedTypes property. An application that can be extended by loading plugin DLLs would typically use this to find the types each plugin provides. Figure 13-1 shows the reflection types that correspond to .NET types, their members, and the components that contain them. The arrows represent containment relationships. (As with assemblies and types, these are all navigable in both directions.)

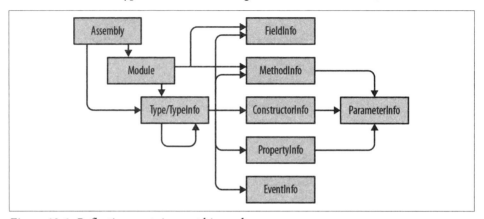

Figure 13-1. Reflection containment hierarchy

Figure 13-2 illustrates the inheritance hierarchy for these types. This shows a couple of extra abstract types, MemberInfo and MethodBase, which are shared by various reflection classes that have a certain amount in common. For example, constructors and methods both have parameter lists, and the mechanism for inspecting these is provided by their shared base class, MethodBase. All members of types have certain common features, such as accessibility, so anything that is (or can be) a member of a type is represented in reflection by an object that derives from MemberInfo.

---

1 For reasons of history discussed later, a subset of this functionality is in a derived type called TypeInfo. But the base Type class is the one you most often encounter.

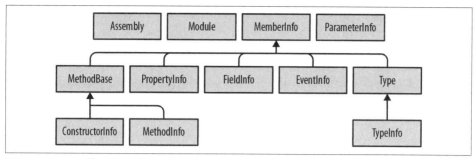

Figure 13-2. Reflection inheritance hierarchy

Assembly

The Assembly class represents, predictably enough, a single assembly. If you're writing a plugin system, or some other sort of framework that needs to load user-supplied DLLs and use them (such as a unit test runner), the Assembly type will be your starting point. As Chapter 12 showed, the static Assembly.Load method takes an assembly name and returns the object for that assembly. (That method will load the assembly if necessary, but if it has already been loaded, it just returns a reference to the relevant Assembly object.) But there are some other ways to get hold of objects of this kind.

The Assembly class defines three context-sensitive static methods that each return an Assembly. The GetEntryAssembly method returns the object representing the EXE file containing your program's Main method. The GetExecutingAssembly method returns the assembly that contains the method from which you called it. GetCallingAssembly walks up the stack by one level, and returns the assembly containing the code that called the method that called GetCallingAssembly.

> The JIT compiler's optimizations can sometimes produce surprising results with GetExecutingAssembly and GetCallingAssembly. Method inlining and tail call optimizations can both cause these methods to return the assembly for methods that are one stack frame farther back than you would expect. You can prevent inlining optimizations by annotating a method with the MethodImplAttribute, passing the NoInlining flag from the MethodImplOptions enumeration. (Attributes are described in Chapter 14.) There's no way to disable tail call optimizations explicitly, but those will be applied only when a particular method call is the last thing a method does before returning.

GetCallingAssembly can sometimes be useful in diagnostic logging, because it provides information about the code that called your method. The GetExecutingAssembly method is less useful: you presumably already know which assembly the code will be in because you're the developer writing it. It may still be useful to get hold of the `Assembly` object for the component you're writing, but there are other ways. The `Type` object described in the next section provides an `Assembly` property. Example 13-1 uses that to get the `Assembly` via the containing class. Empirically, this seems to be faster, which is not entirely surprising because it's doing less work—both techniques need to retrieve reflection objects, but one of them also has to inspect the stack.

Example 13-1. Obtaining your own Assembly via a Type

```
class Program
{
    static void Main(string[] args)
    {
        Assembly me = typeof(Program).Assembly;
        Console.WriteLine(me.FullName);
    }
}
```

If you want to use an assembly from a specific place on disk, you can use the `Load File` method described in Chapter 12. Alternatively, you can use another of the `Assembly` class's static methods, `ReflectionOnlyLoadFrom`. This loads the assembly in such a way that you can inspect its type information, but no code in the assembly will execute, nor will any assemblies it depends on be loaded automatically. This is an appropriate way to load an assembly if you're writing a tool that displays or otherwise processes information about a component but does not want to run its code. There are a few reasons it can be important to avoid loading an assembly in the usual way with such a tool. Loading an assembly and inspecting its types can sometimes trigger the execution of code (such as static constructors) in that assembly. Also, if you load for reflection purposes only, the processor architecture is not significant, so you could load a 32-bit-only DLL into a 64-bit process, or you could inspect an ARM-only assembly in an x86 process.

Having obtained an `Assembly` from any of the aforementioned mechanisms, you can discover various things about it. The `FullName` property provides the display name, for example. Or you can call `GetName`, which returns an `AssemblyName` object, providing easy programmatic access to all of the components of the assembly's name.

You can retrieve a list of all of the other assemblies on which a particular `Assembly` depends by calling `GetReferencedAssemblies`. If you call this on an assembly you've written, it will not necessarily return all of the assemblies you can see in the Dependencies node in Visual Studio's Solution Explorer, because the C# compiler strips out unused references.

Assemblies contain types, so you can find `Type` objects representing those types by calling an `Assembly` object's `GetType` method, passing in the name of the type you require, including its namespace. This will return `null` if the type is not found, unless you call one of the overloads that additionally accept a `bool`—with these, passing `true` produces an exception if the type is not found. There's also an overload that takes two `bool` arguments, the second of which lets you pass `true` to request a case-insensitive search. All of these methods will return either `public` or `internal` types. You can also request a nested type, by specifying the name of the containing type, then a + symbol, then the nested type name. Example 13-2 gets the `Type` object for a type called `Inside` nested inside a type called `ContainingType` in the `MyLib` namespace. This works even if the nested type is private.

Example 13-2. Getting a nested type from an assembly

```
Type nt = someAssembly.GetType("MyLib.ContainingType+Inside");
```

The `Assembly` class also provides a `DefinedTypes` property that returns a collection containing a `TypeInfo` object for every type (top-level or nested) the assembly defines, and also `ExportedTypes`, which returns only public types, and it returns `Type` objects and not full `TypeInfo` objects. (The distinction between `TypeInfo` and `Type` is described in "Type and TypeInfo" on page 577.) That will also include any `public` nested types. It will not include `protected` types nested inside `public` types, which is perhaps a bit surprising because such types are accessible from outside the assembly (albeit only to classes that derive from the containing type).

Besides returning types, `Assembly` can also create new instances of them with the `CreateInstance` method. If you pass just the fully qualified name of the type as a string, this will create an instance if the type is public and has a no-arguments constructor. There's an overload that lets you work with nonpublic types and types with constructors that require arguments; however, it is rather more complex to use, because it also takes arguments that specify whether you want a case-insensitive match for the type name, along with a `CultureInfo` object that defines the rules to use for case-insensitive comparisons—different countries have different ideas about how such comparisons work. It also has arguments for controlling more advanced scenarios. However, you can pass `null` for most of these, as Example 13-3 shows.

Example 13-3. Dynamic construction

```
object o = asm.CreateInstance(
    "MyApp.WithConstructor",
    false,
    BindingFlags.Public | BindingFlags.Instance,
    null,
    new object[] { "Constructor argument" },
```

```
null,
null);
```

This creates an instance of a type called `WithConstructor` in the `MyApp` namespace in the assembly to which `asm` refers. The `false` argument indicates that we want an exact match on the name, not a case-insensitive comparison. The `BindingFlags` indicate that we are looking for a public instance constructor. (See the following sidebar, "BindingFlags".) The first `null` argument is where you could pass a `Binder` object, which allows you to customize the behavior when the arguments you have supplied do not exactly match the types of the required arguments. By leaving this out, I'm indicating that I expect the ones I've supplied to match exactly. (I'll get an exception if they don't.) The `object[]` argument contains the list of arguments I'd like to pass to the constructor—a single string, in this case. The penultimate `null` is where I'd pass a culture if I were using either case-insensitive comparisons or automatic conversions between numeric types and strings, but since I'm doing neither, I can leave it out. And the final argument once supported scenarios that have now been deprecated, so it should always be `null`.

BindingFlags

Many of the reflection APIs take an argument of the `BindingFlags` enumeration type to determine which members to return. For example, you can specify `Binding Flags.Public` to indicate that you want only public members or types, or `Binding Flags.NonPublic` to indicate that you want only items that are not public, or you can combine both flags to indicate that you'd like either.

Be aware that it's possible to specify combinations that will return nothing. When working with members, you must include either `BindingFlags.Instance`, `Binding Flags.Static`, or both, for example, because all type members are one or the other (likewise for `BindingFlags.Public` and `BindingFlags.NonPublic`).

Often, methods that can accept `BindingFlags` offer an overload that does not. This typically defaults to specifying public members, both instance and static (i.e., `Binding Flags.Public | BindingFlags.Static | BindingFlags.Instance`).

`BindingFlags` defines numerous options, but not all are applicable in every scenario. For example, it defines a `FlattenHierarchy` value, which is used for reflection APIs that return type members: if this flag is present, members defined by the base class will be considered, as well as those defined by the class specified. This option is not applicable to `Assembly.CreateInstance` because you cannot use a base class constructor directly to construct a derived type.

If the assembly comprises multiple files, you can get a complete list of these with the `GetFiles` method, which returns an array of `FileStream` objects, the type .NET uses to represent files. If you pass `true`, this will include any resource streams stored as separate files external to the main assembly. Otherwise, it will just provide one stream per module. Alternatively, you could call `GetModules`, which also returns an array representing the modules making up the assembly, but instead of returning `File Stream` objects, it returns `Module` objects.

Module

The `Module` class represents one of the modules that make up an assembly. The majority of assemblies are single-module (and on .NET Core, they always are), so you do not often need to use this type. It is important if you generate code at runtime, because you need to tell .NET in which module to place the code you generate, so even in the usual single-module scenarios, you need to be explicit about the module involved. But when you are not generating new components at runtime, you can often ignore the `Module` class completely—you can normally do everything you need with the other types in the reflection API. (.NET's APIs for generating code at runtime are beyond the scope of this book.)

If you do need a `Module` object for some reason, you can retrieve modules from their containing `Assembly` object's `Modules` property. Alternatively, you can use any of the API types described in the following sections that derive from `MemberInfo`. (Figure 13-2 shows which types do so.) This defines a `Module` property that returns the `Module` in which the relevant member is defined.

The `Module` class provides an `Assembly` property, which returns a reference to the module's containing assembly. The `Name` property returns the filename for this module, and `FullyQualifiedName` provides the filename, including the full path.

As with the `Assembly` class, `Module` defines a `GetType` method. In a single-module assembly, this will be indistinguishable from the same method on the `Assembly` class, but if you have split your assembly's code across multiple modules, these methods will provide access only to the types defined in the module to which you have a reference.

More surprisingly, the `Module` class also defines `GetField`, `GetFields`, `GetMethod`, and `GetMethods` properties. These provide access to globally scoped methods and fields. You never see these in C#, because the language requires all fields and methods to be defined within a type, but the CLR allows globally scoped methods and fields, and so the reflection API has to be able to present them. (C++/CLI can create global fields.)

MemberInfo

Like all the classes I'm describing in this section, MemberInfo is abstract. However, unlike the rest, it does not correspond to one particular feature of the type system. It is a shared base class providing common functionality for all of the types that represent items that can be members of other types. So this is the base class of Construc torInfo, MethodInfo, FieldInfo, PropertyInfo, EventInfo, and Type, because all of those can be members of other types. In fact, in C#, all except Type are *required* to be members of some other type (although, as you just saw in the preceding section, some languages allow methods and fields to be scoped to a module instead of a type).

MemberInfo defines common properties required by all type members. There's a Name property, of course, and also a DeclaringType, which refers to the Type object for the item's containing type; this returns null for nonnested types and module-scoped methods and fields. MemberInfo also defines a Module property that refers to the containing module, regardless of whether the item in question is module-scoped or a member of a type.

As well as DeclaringType, MemberInfo defines a ReflectedType, which indicates the type from which the MemberInfo was retrieved. These will often be the same, but can be different when inheritance is involved. Example 13-4 shows the distinction.

Example 13-4. DeclaringType versus ReflectedType

```
class Base
{
    public void Foo()
    {
    }
}

class Derived : Base
{
}

class Program
{
    static void Main(string[] args)
    {
        MemberInfo bf = typeof(Base).GetMethod("Foo");
        MemberInfo df = typeof(Derived).GetMethod("Foo");

        Console.WriteLine("Base    Declaring: {0}, Reflected: {1}",
                        bf.DeclaringType, bf.ReflectedType);
        Console.WriteLine("Derived Declaring: {0}, Reflected: {1}",
                        df.DeclaringType, df.ReflectedType);
    }
}
```

This gets the `MethodInfo` for the `Base.Foo` and `Derived.Foo` methods. (`MethodInfo` derives from `MemberInfo`.) These are just different ways of describing the same method—`Derived` does not define its own `Foo`, and simply inherits the one defined by `Base`. The program produces this output:

```
Base    Declaring: Base, Reflected: Base
Derived Declaring: Base, Reflected: Derived
```

When retrieving the information for `Foo` via the `Base` class's `Type` object, the `DeclaringType` and `ReflectedType` are, unsurprisingly, both `Base`. However, when we retrieve the `Foo` method's information via the `Derived` type, the `DeclaringType` tells us that the method is defined by `Base`, while the `ReflectedType` tells us that we obtained this method via the `Derived` type.

Because a `MemberInfo` remembers which type you retrieved it from, comparing two `MemberInfo` objects is not a reliable way to detect whether they refer to the same thing. Comparing `bf` and `df` in Example 13-4 with either the `==` operator or their `Equals` method would return `false` despite the fact that they both refer to `Base.Foo`. In one sense, it's logical—these are different objects and their properties are not all identical, so clearly they are not equal. But if you had been unaware of the `ReflectedType` property, you might not have expected this behavior.

Slightly surprisingly, `MemberInfo` does not provide any information about the visibility of the member it describes. This may seem odd, because in C#, all of the constructs that correspond to the types that derive from `MemberInfo` (such as constructors, methods, or properties) can be prefixed with `public`, `private`, etc. The reflection API does make this information available, but not through the `MemberInfo` base class. This is because the CLR handles visibility for certain member types a little differently from how C# presents it. From the CLR's perspective, properties and events do not have an accessibility of their own. Instead, their accessibility is managed at the level of the individual methods. This enables a property's `get` and `set` to have different accessibility levels, and likewise for an event's accessors. Of course, we can control property accessor accessibility independently in C# if we want to. Where C# misleads us is that it lets us specify a single accessibility level for the entire property. But this is just shorthand for setting both accessors to the same level. The confusing part is that it lets us specify the accessibility for the property and then a different accessibility for one of the members, as Example 13-5 does.

Example 13-5. Property accessor accessibility

```
public int Count
{
    get;
    private set;
}
```

This is a bit misleading because, despite how it looks, that `public` accessibility does not apply to the whole property. This property-level accessibility simply tells the compiler what to use for accessors that don't specify their own accessibility level. The first version of C# required both property accessors to have the same accessibility so it made sense to state it for the whole property. (It still has an equivalent restriction for events.) But this was an arbitrary restriction—the CLR has always allowed each accessor to have a different accessibility. C# now supports this, but because of the history, the syntax for exploiting this is misleadingly asymmetric. From the CLR's point of view, Example 13-5 just says to make the `get` `public` and the `set` `private`. Example 13-6 would be a better representation of what's really going on.

Example 13-6. How the CLR sees property accessibility

```
// Won't compile, but arguably should
int Count
{
    public get;
    private set;
}
```

But we can't write it that way, because C# demands that the accessibility for the more visible of the two accessors be stated at the property level. This makes the syntax simpler when both properties have the same accessibility, but it makes things a bit weird when they're different. Moreover, the syntax in Example 13-5 (i.e., the syntax the compiler actually supports) makes it look like we should be able to specify accessibility in three places: the property and both of the accessors. The CLR does not support that, so the compiler will produce an error if you try to specify accessibility for both of the accessors in a property or an event. So there is no accessibility for the property or event itself. (Imagine if there were—what would it even mean if a property had `public` accessibility but its `get` were `internal` and its `set` were `private`?) Consequently, not everything that derives from `MemberInfo` has a particular accessibility, so the reflection API provides properties representing accessibility farther down in the class hierarchy.

Type and TypeInfo

The `Type` class represents a particular type. It is more widely used than any of the other classes in this chapter, which is why it alone lives in the `System` namespace while the rest are defined in `System.Reflection`. It's the easiest to get hold of because C# has an operator designed for just this job: `typeof`. I've shown this in a few examples already, but Example 13-7 shows it in isolation. As you can see, you can use either a built-in name, such as `string`, or an ordinary type name, such as `IDisposa ble`. You could also include the namespace, but that's not necessary when the type's namespace is in scope.

Example 13-7. Getting a Type with typeof

```
Type stringType = typeof(string);
Type disposableType = typeof(IDisposable);
```

Also, as I mentioned in Chapter 6, the `System.Object` type (or `object`, as we usually write it in C#) provides a `GetType` instance method that takes no arguments. You can call this on any reference type variable to retrieve the type of the object that variable refers to. This will not necessarily be the same type as the variable itself, because the variable may refer to an instance of a derived type. You can also call this method on any value type variable, and because value types do not support inheritance, it will always return the type object for the variable's static type.

So all you need is an object, a value, or a type identifier (such as `string`), and it is trivial to get a `Type` object. And, there are many other places `Type` objects can come from.

In addition to `Type` we also have `TypeInfo`. This was introduced in early versions of .NET Core with the intention of enabling `Type` to serve purely as a lightweight identifier, and for `TypeInfo` to be the mechanism by which you reflect against a type. This was a departure from how `Type` had always worked in the .NET Framework, where it performs both roles. This dual role was arguably a mistake because if you only need an identifier, `Type` is unnecessarily heavyweight. .NET Core was originally envisaged as having a separate existence from the .NET Framework with no need for strict compatibility, so it seemed to provide an opportunity to fix historical design problems. However, once Microsoft took the decision that .NET Core would be the basis of all future versions of .NET, it became necessary to bring it back into line with how the .NET Framework had always worked. However, by this time, the .NET Framework had also introduced `TypeInfo`, and for a while, new type-level reflection features were added to that instead of `Type` to minimize incompatibilities with .NET Core 1. .NET Core 2.0 realigned with the .NET Framework, but this meant that the split of functionality between `Type` and `TypeInfo` is now just an upshot of what was added when. `TypeInfo` contains members added during the brief period between its introduction, and the decision to revert to the old way. In cases where you have a `Type` but you need to use a feature specific to `TypeInfo`, you can get this from a type by calling `GetTypeInfo`.

As you've already seen, you can retrieve `Type` objects from an `Assembly`, either by name or as a comprehensive list. The reflection types that derive from `MemberInfo` also provide a reference to their containing type through `DeclaringType`. (`Type` derives from `MemberInfo`, so it also offers this property, which is relevant when dealing with nested types.)

You can also call the `Type` class's own static `GetType` method. If you pass just a namespace-qualified string, it will search for the named type in a system assembly called *mscorlib*, and also in the assembly from which you called the method. However, you can pass an *assembly-qualified name*, which combines an assembly name and a type name. A name of this form starts with the namespace-qualified type name, followed by a comma and the assembly name. For example, this is the assembly-qualified name of the `System.String` class in .NET 4.8 (split across two lines to fit in this book):

```
System.String, mscorlib, Version=4.0.0.0, Culture=neutral,
   PublicKeyToken=b77a5c561934e089
```

You can discover a type's assembly-qualified name through the `Type.AssemblyQuali fiedName` property. Be aware that this won't always match what you asked for. If you pass the preceding type name into `Type.GetType` on .NET Core, it will work, but if you then ask the returned `Type` for its `AssemblyQualifiedName`, it will return this instead:

```
System.String, System.Private.CoreLib, Version=4.0.0.0, Culture=neutral,
   PublicKeyToken=7cec85d7bea7798e
```

The only reason it works when you pass either the first string or just `System.String` is because *mscorlib* still exists for backward compatibility purposes. I described this in the preceding chapter, but to summarize, in .NET Framework, the *mscorlib* assembly contains the core types of the class library, but in .NET Core, the code has moved elsewhere. *mscorlib* still exists, but it contains only type forwarding entries indicating which assembly each class now lives in. For example, it forwards `System.String` to its new home, which, at the time of this writing, is the `System.Private.CoreLib` assembly.

There is a corresponding `ReflectionOnlyGetType` method that works in a similar way but will load assemblies in the reflection-only context, just like the `Assembly` class's `ReflectionOnlyLoadFrom` method described earlier.

As well as the standard MemberInfo properties, such as Module and Name, the Type and TypeInfo classes add various properties of their own. The inherited Name property contains the unqualified name, so Type adds a Namespace property. All types are scoped to an assembly, so Type defines an Assembly property. (You could, of course, get there via Module.Assembly, but it's more convenient to use the Assembly property.) It also defines a BaseType property, although that will be null for some types (e.g., nonderived interfaces, and the type object for the System.Object class).

Since Type can represent all sorts of types, there are properties you can use to determine exactly what you've got: IsArray, IsClass, IsEnum, IsInterface, IsPointer, and IsValueType. (You can also get Type objects for non-.NET types in interop scenarios, so there's also an IsCOMObject property.) If it represents a class, there are some properties that tell you more about what kind of class you've got: IsAbstract, IsSealed, and IsNested. That last one is applicable to value types as well as classes.

Type also defines numerous properties providing information about the type's visibility. For nonnested types, IsPublic tells you whether it's public or internal, but things are more complex for nested types. IsNestedAssembly indicates an internal nested type, while IsNestedPublic and IsNestedPrivate indicate public and private nested types. Instead of the usual C-family "protected" terminology, the CLR uses the term "family," so we have IsNestedFamily for protected, IsNestedFamORAssem for protected internal, and IsNestedFamANDAssem for protected private.

The TypeInfo class also provides methods to discover related reflection objects. (The properties in this paragraph are all defined on TypeInfo not Type. As previously discussed, this is just an accident of when they were defined.) Most of these come in two forms: one where you know the name of the thing you're looking for, and one where you want a complete list of all the items of the specified kind. For example, we have DeclaredConstructors, DeclaredEvents, DeclaredFields, DeclaredMethods, DeclaredNestedTypes, and DeclaredProperties, and their counterparts, GetDeclaredConstructor, GetDeclaredEvent, GetDeclaredField, GetDeclaredMethod, GetDeclaredNestedType, and GetDeclaredProperty.

The Type class lets you discover type compatibility relationships. You can ask whether one type derives from another type by calling the type's IsSubclassOf method. Inheritance is not the only reason one type may be compatible with a reference of a different type—a variable whose type is an interface can refer to an instance of any type that implements that interface, regardless of its base class. The Type class therefore offers a more general method called IsAssignableFrom, which Example 13-8 uses.

Example 13-8. Testing type compatibility

```
Type stringType = typeof(string);
Type objectType = typeof(object);
Console.WriteLine(stringType.IsAssignableFrom(objectType));
Console.WriteLine(objectType.IsAssignableFrom(stringType));
```

This shows `False` and then `True`, because you cannot take a reference to an instance of type `object` and assign it into a variable of type `string`, but you can take a reference to an instance of type `string` and assign it into a variable of type `object`.

As well as telling you things about a type and its relationships to other types, the `Type` class provides the ability to use a type's members at runtime. It defines an `InvokeMem ber` method, the exact meaning of which depends on what kind member you invoke —it could mean calling a method, or getting or setting a property or field, for example. Since some member types support multiple kinds of invocation (e.g., both get and set), you need to specify which particular operation you want. Example 13-9 uses `InvokeMember` to invoke a method identified by its name (the `member` string argument) on an instance of a type, also identified by name, that it instantiates dynamically. This illustrates how reflection can be used to work with types and members whose identities are not known until runtime.

Example 13-9. Invoking a method with InvokeMember

```
public static object CreateAndInvokeMethod(
  string typeName, string member, params object[] args)
{
    Type t = Type.GetType(typeName);
    object instance = Activator.CreateInstance(t);
    return t.InvokeMember(
      member,
      BindingFlags.Instance | BindingFlags.Public | BindingFlags.InvokeMethod,
      null,
      instance,
      args);
}
```

This example first creates an instance of the specified type—this uses a slightly different approach to dynamic creation than the one I showed earlier with `Assembly.Crea teInstance`. Here I'm using `Type.GetType` to look up the type, and then I'm using a class I've not mentioned before, `Activator`. This class's job is to create new instances of objects whose type you have determined at runtime. Its functionality overlaps somewhat with `Assembly.CreateInstance`, but in this case, it's the most convenient way to get from a `Type` to a new instance of that type. Then I've used the `Type` object's `InvokeMember` to invoke the specified method. As with Example 13-3, I've had to specify binding flags to indicate what kind of member I'm looking for and also what to do with it—here I'm looking to call a method (as opposed to, say, setting a property value). The `null` argument is, as with Example 13-3, a place where I would have specified a `Binder` if I had wanted to support automatic coercion of the method argument types.

Generic types

.NET's support for generics complicates the role of the `Type` class. As well as representing an ordinary nongeneric type, a `Type` can represent a particular instance of a generic type (e.g., `List<int>`), but also an unbound generic type (e.g., `List<>`, although that's an illegal type identifier in all but one very specific scenario). Example 13-10 shows how to obtain both kinds of `Type` objects.

Example 13-10. Type objects for generic types

```
Type bound = typeof(List<int>);
Type unbound = typeof(List<>);
```

The `typeof` operator is the only place in which you can use an unbound generic type identifier in C#—in all other contexts, it would be an error not to supply type arguments. By the way, if the type takes multiple type arguments, you must provide commas—for example, `typeof(Dictionary<,>)`. This is necessary to avoid ambiguity when there are multiple generic types with the same names, distinguished only by the number of type parameters they require (also known as the *arity*)—for example, `typeof(Func<,>)` versus `typeof(Func<,,,>)`. You cannot specify a partially bound generic type. For example, `typeof(Dictionary<string,>)` would fail to compile.

You can tell when a `Type` object refers to a generic type—the `IsGenericType` property will return `true` for both bound and unbound from Example 13-10. You can also determine whether or not the type arguments have been supplied by using the `IsGenericTypeDefinition` property, which would return `false` and `true` for the `Type` objects corresponding to bound and unbound, respectively. If you have a bound generic type and you'd like to get the unbound type from which it was constructed, you use the `GetGenericTypeDefinition` method—calling that on bound would return the same type object that unbound refers to.

Given a `Type` object whose `IsGenericTypeDefinition` property returns `true`, you can construct a new bound version of that type by calling `MakeGenericType`, passing an array of `Type` objects, one for each type argument.

If you have a generic type, you can retrieve its type arguments from the `GenericTypeArguments` property. Perhaps surprisingly, this even works for unbound types, although it behaves differently than with a bound type. If you get `GenericTypeArguments` from bound from Example 13-10, it will return an array containing a single

Type object, which will be the same one you would get from typeof(int). If you get unbound.GenericTypeArguments, you will also get an array containing a single Type, but this time, it will be a Type object that does not represent a specific type—its IsGe nericParameter property will be true, indicating that this represents a placeholder. Its name in this case will be T. In general, the name will correspond to whatever placeholder name the generic type chooses. For example, with typeof(Dictio nary<,>), you'll get two Type objects called TKey and TValue, respectively. You will encounter similar generic argument placeholder types if you use the reflection API to look up members of generic types. For example, if you retrieve the MethodInfo for the Add method of the unbound List<> type, you'll find that it takes a single argu-ment of a type named T, which returns true from its IsGenericParameter property.

When a Type object represents an unbound generic parameter, you can find out whether the parameter is covariant or contravariant (or neither) through its Generi cParameterAttributes method.

MethodBase, ConstructorInfo, and MethodInfo

Constructors and methods have a great deal in common. The same accessibility options are available for both kinds of members, they both have argument lists, and they can both contain code. Consequently, the MethodInfo and ConstructorInfo reflection types share a base class, MethodBase, which defines properties and methods for handling these common aspects.

To obtain a MethodInfo or ConstructorInfo, besides using the Type class properties I mentioned earlier, you can also call the MethodBase class's static GetCurrentMethod method. This inspects the calling code to see if it's a constructor or a normal method, and returns either a MethodInfo or ConstructorInfo accordingly.

As well as the members it inherits from MemberInfo, MethodBase defines properties specifying the member's accessibility. These are similar in concept to those I described earlier for types, but the names are marginally different, because unlike Type, MethodBase does not define accessibility properties that make a distinction between nested and nonnested members. So with MethodBase, we find IsPublic, IsPrivate, IsAssembly, IsFamily, IsFamilyOrAssembly, and IsFamilyAndAssembly for public, private, internal, protected, protected internal, and protected private, respectively.

In addition to accessibility-related properties, MethodBase defines properties that tell you about aspects of the method, such as IsStatic, IsAbstract, IsVirtual, IsFinal, and IsConstructor.

There are also properties for dealing with generic methods. IsGenericMethod and IsGenericMethodDefinition are the method-level equivalents of the type-level

IsGenericType and IsGenericTypeDefinition properties. As with Type, there's a GetGenericMethodDefinition method to get from a bound generic method to an unbound one, and a MakeGenericMethod to produce a bound generic method from an unbound one. You can retrieve type arguments by calling GetGenericArguments, and as with generic types, this will return specific types when called on a bound method, and will return placeholder types when used with an unbound method.

You can inspect the implementation of the method by calling GetMethodBody. This returns a MethodBody object that provides access to the IL (as an array of bytes), and also to the local variable definitions used by the method.

The MethodInfo class derives from MethodBase and represents only methods (and not constructors). It adds a ReturnType property that provides a Type object indicating the method's return type. (There's a special system type, System.Void, whose Type object is used here when a method returns nothing.)

The ConstructorInfo class does not add any properties beyond those it inherits from MethodBase. It does define two read-only static fields, though: ConstructorName and TypeConstructorName. These contain the strings ".ctor" and ".cctor", respectively, which are the values you will find in the Name property for ConstructorInfo objects for instance and static constructors. As far as the CLR is concerned, these are the real names—although in C# constructors appear to have the same name as their containing type, that's true only in your C# source files, and not at runtime.

You can invoke the method or constructor represented by a MethodInfo or Constructor Info by calling the Invoke method. This does the same thing as Type.InvokeMember—Example 13-9 used that to call a method. However, because Invoke is specialized for working with just methods and constructors, it's rather simpler to use. With a ConstructorInfo, you need to pass only an array of arguments. With Method Info, you also pass the object on which you want to invoke the method, or null if you want to invoke a static method. Example 13-11 performs the same job as Example 13-9, but using MethodInfo.

Example 13-11. Invoking a method

```
public static object CreateAndInvokeMethod(
   string typeName, string member, params object[] args)
{
    Type t = Type.GetType(typeName);
    object instance = Activator.CreateInstance(t);
    MethodInfo m = t.GetMethod(member);
    return m.Invoke(instance, args);
}
```

For either methods or constructors, you can call GetParameters, which returns an array of ParameterInfo objects representing the method's parameters.

ParameterInfo

The ParameterInfo class represents parameters for methods or constructors. Its ParameterType and Name properties provide the basic information you'd see from looking at the method signature. It also defines a Member property that refers back to the method or constructor to which the parameter belongs. The HasDefaultValue property will tell you whether the parameter is optional, and if it is, DefaultValue provides the value to be used when the argument is omitted.

If you are working with members defined by unbound generic types, or with an unbound generic method, be aware that the ParameterType of a ParameterInfo could refer to a generic type argument, and not a real type. This is also true of any Type objects returned by the reflection objects described in the next three sections.

FieldInfo

FieldInfo represents a field in a type. You typically obtain it from a Type object with GetField or GetFields, or if you're using code written in a language that supports global fields, you can retrieve those from the containing Module.

FieldInfo defines a set of properties representing accessibility. These look just like the ones defined by MethodBase. Additionally, there's FieldType, representing the type a field can contain. (As always, if the member belongs to an unbound generic type, this might refer to a type argument rather than a specific type.) There are also some properties providing further information about the field, including IsStatic, IsInitOnly, and IsLiteral. These correspond to static, readonly, and const in C#, respectively. (Fields representing values in enumeration types will also return true from IsLiteral.)

FieldInfo defines GetValue and SetValue methods that let you read and write the value of the field. These take an argument specifying the instance to use, or null if the field is static. As with the MethodBase class's Invoke, these do not do anything you couldn't do with the Type class's InvokeMember, but these methods are typically more convenient.

PropertyInfo

The PropertyInfo type represents a property. You can obtain these from the containing Type object's GetProperty or GetProperties methods. As I mentioned earlier, PropertyInfo does not define any properties for accessibility, because the accessibility is determined at the level of the individual get and set methods. You can retrieve those with the GetGetMethod and GetSetMethod methods, which both return MethodInfo objects.

Much like with FieldInfo, the PropertyInfo class defines GetValue and SetValue methods for reading and writing the value. Properties are allowed to take arguments —C# indexers are properties with arguments, for example. So there are overloads of GetValue and SetValue that take arrays of arguments. Also, there is a GetIndexParameters method that returns an array of ParameterInfo objects, representing the arguments required to use the property. The property's type is available through the PropertyType property.

EventInfo

Events are represented by EventInfo objects, which are returned by the Type class's GetEvent and GetEvents methods. Like PropertyInfo, this does not have any accessibility properties, because the event's add and remove methods each define their own accessibility. You can retrieve those methods with GetAddMethod and GetRemoveMethod, which both return a MethodInfo. EventInfo defines an EventHandlerType, which returns the type of delegate that event handlers are required to supply.

You can attach and remove handlers by calling the AddEventHandler and RemoveEventHandler methods. As with all other dynamic invocation, these just offer a more convenient alternative to the Type class's InvokeMember method.

Reflection Contexts

.NET has a feature called *reflection contexts*. These enable reflection to provide a virtualized view of the type system. By writing a custom reflection context, you can modify how types appear—you can cause a type to look like it has extra properties, or you can add to the set of attributes that members and parameters appear to offer. (Chapter 14 will describe attributes.)

Reflection contexts did not work in .NET Core prior to version 3.0. It is possible to compile code that uses them thanks to the existence of a `System.Reflection.Context` NuGet package, which might lead you to expect them to work. However, this initially existed to aid porting code from .NET Framework to .NET Core and .NET Standard. It made it possible to write .NET Standard libraries that used custom reflection contexts, and if you used these libraries on the .NET Framework, everything would be fine. If you used these libraries on .NET Core in a way that didn't hit any code path that tried to use custom reflection contexts, everything would also be fine. It was only if you tried to use a feature that relied on custom reflection contexts while running on .NET Core that problems arose: it would throw a `PlatformNotSupportedException`. But with .NET Core 3.0, and v4.6 or later of the `System.Reflec tion.Context` NuGet package, everything will work because .NET Core 3.0 added the necessary capabilities to the CLR.

Reflection contexts are useful because they make it possible to write reflection-driven frameworks that enable individual types to customize how they are handled, but without forcing every type that participates into providing explicit support. Prior to the introduction of custom reflection contexts in .NET 4.5, this was handled with various ad hoc systems. Take the Properties panel in Visual Studio, for example. This can automatically display every public property defined by any .NET object that ends up on a design surface (e.g., any UI component you write). It's great to have automatic editing support even for components that do not provide any explicit handling for that, but components should have the opportunity to customize how they behave at design time.

Because the Properties panel predates .NET 4.5, it uses one of the ad hoc solutions: the `TypeDescriptor` class. This is a wrapper on top of reflection, which allows any class to augment its design-time behavior by implementing `ICustomTypeDescriptor`, enabling a class to customize the set of properties it offers for editing, and also to control how they are presented, even offering custom editing UIs. This is flexible, but has the downside of coupling the design-time code with the runtime code—components that use this model cannot easily be shipped without also supplying the design-time code. So Visual Studio introduced its own virtualization mechanisms for separating the two.

To avoid having each framework define its own virtualization system, custom reflection contexts add virtualization directly into the reflection API. If you want to write code that can consume type information provided by reflection but can also support design-time augmentation or modification of that information, it's no longer necessary to use some sort of wrapper layer. You can use the usual reflection types described earlier in this chapter, but it's now possible to ask reflection to give you different implementations of these types, providing different virtualized views.

You do this by writing a custom reflection context that describes how you want to modify the view that reflection provides. Example 13-12 shows a particularly boring type followed by a custom reflection context that makes that type look like it has a property.

Example 13-12. A simple type, enhanced by a reflection context

```
class NotVeryInteresting
{
}

class MyReflectionContext : CustomReflectionContext
{
    protected override IEnumerable<PropertyInfo> AddProperties(Type type)
    {
        if (type == typeof(NotVeryInteresting))
        {
            var fakeProp = CreateProperty(
                MapType(typeof(string).GetTypeInfo()),
                "FakeProperty",
                o => "FakeValue",
                (o, v) => Console.WriteLine($"Setting value: {v}"));

            return new[] { fakeProp };
        }
        else
        {
            return base.AddProperties(type);
        }
    }
}
```

Code that uses the reflection API directly will see the NotVeryInteresting type directly as it is, with no properties. However, we can map that type through MyReflectionContext, as Example 13-13 shows.

Example 13-13. Using a custom reflection context

```
var ctx = new MyReflectionContext();
TypeInfo mappedType = ctx.MapType(typeof(NotVeryInteresting).GetTypeInfo());

foreach (PropertyInfo prop in mappedType.DeclaredProperties)
{
    Console.WriteLine($"{prop.Name} ({prop.PropertyType.Name})");
}
```

The `mappedType` variable holds a reference to the resulting mapped type. It still looks like an ordinary reflection `TypeInfo` object, and we can iterate through its properties in the usual way with `DeclaredProperties`, but because we've mapped the type through my custom reflection context, we see the modified version of the type. This code's output will show that the type appears to define one property called `FakeProperty`, of type `string`.

Summary

The reflection API makes it possible to write code whose behavior is based on the structure of the types it works with. This might involve deciding which values to present in a UI grid based on the properties an object offers, or it might mean modifying the behavior of a framework based on what members a particular type chooses to define. For example, parts of the ASP.NET Core web framework will detect whether your code is using synchronous or asynchronous programming techniques and adapt appropriately. These techniques require the ability to inspect code at runtime, which is what reflection enables. All of the information in an assembly required by the type system is available to our code. Furthermore, you can present this through a virtualized view by writing a custom reflection context, making it possible to customize the behavior of reflection-driven code.

CHAPTER 14

Attributes

In .NET, you can annotate components, types, and their members with *attributes*. An attribute's purpose is to control or modify the behavior of a framework, a tool, the compiler, or the CLR. For example, in Chapter 1, I showed a class annotated with the [TestClass] attribute. This told a unit testing framework that the annotated class contains some tests to be run as part of a test suite.

Attributes are passive containers of information that do nothing on their own. To draw an analogy with the physical world, if you print out a shipping label containing destination and tracking information and attach it to a package, that label will not in itself cause the package to make its way to a destination. Such a label is useful only once the package is in the hands of a shipping company. When the company picks up your parcel, it'll expect to find the label, and will use it to work out how to route your package. So the label is important, but ultimately, its only job is to provide information that some system requires. .NET attributes work the same way—they have an effect only if something goes looking for them. Some attributes are handled by the CLR or the compiler, but these are in the minority. The majority of attributes are consumed by frameworks, libraries, tools (such as a unit test runner), or your own code.

Applying Attributes

To avoid having to introduce an extra set of concepts into the type system, .NET models attributes as instances of .NET types. To be used as an attribute, a type must derive from the System.Attribute class, but it can otherwise be entirely ordinary. To apply an attribute, you put the type's name in square brackets, and this usually goes directly before the attribute's target. Example 14-1 shows some attributes from Microsoft's test framework. I've applied one to the class to indicate that this contains tests I'd like to run, and I've also applied attributes to individual methods, telling the test framework which ones represent tests and which contain initialization code to be run before each test.

Example 14-1. Attributes in a unit test class

```csharp
using Microsoft.VisualStudio.TestTools.UnitTesting;

namespace ImageManagement.Tests
{
    [TestClass]
    public class WhenPropertiesRetrieved
    {
        private ImageMetadataReader _reader;

        [TestInitialize]
        public void Initialize()
        {
            _reader = new ImageMetadataReader(TestFiles.GetImage());
        }

        [TestMethod]
        public void ReportsCameraMaker()
        {
            Assert.AreEqual(_reader.CameraManufacturer, "Fabrikam");
        }

        [TestMethod]
        public void ReportsCameraModel()
        {
            Assert.AreEqual(_reader.CameraModel, "Fabrikam F450D");
        }
    }
}
```

If you look at the documentation for most attributes, you'll find that their real name ends with `Attribute`. If there's no class with the name you specify in the brackets, the C# compiler tries appending `Attribute`, so the `[TestClass]` attribute in Example 14-1 refers to the `TestClassAttribute` class. If you really want to, you can spell the class name out in full—for example, `[TestClassAttribute]`—but it's more common to use the shorter version.

If you want to apply multiple attributes, you have two options. You can either provide multiple sets of brackets, or put multiple attributes inside a single pair of brackets, separated by commas.

Some attribute types can take constructor arguments. For example, Microsoft's test framework includes a `TestCategoryAttribute`. When running tests, you can choose to execute only those in a certain category. This attribute requires you to pass the category name as a constructor argument, because there would be no point in applying this attribute without specifying the name. As Example 14-2 shows, the syntax for specifying an attribute's constructor arguments is unsurprising.

Example 14-2. Attribute with constructor argument

```
[TestCategory("Property Handling")]
[TestMethod]
public void ReportsCameraMaker()
{
    ...
```

You can also specify property or field values. Some attributes have features that can be controlled only through properties or fields, and not constructor arguments. (If an attribute has lots of optional settings, it's usually easier to present these as properties or fields, instead of defining a constructor overload for every conceivable combination of settings.) The syntax for this is to write one or more *PropertyOrField Name=Value* entries after the constructor arguments (or instead of them, if there are no constructor arguments). Example 14-3 shows another attribute used in unit testing, `ExpectedExceptionAttribute`, which allows you to specify that when your test runs, you expect it to throw a particular exception. The exception type is mandatory, so we pass that as a constructor argument, but this attribute also allows you to state whether the test runner should accept exceptions of a type derived from the one specified. (By default, it will accept only an exact match.) This is controlled with the `AllowDerivedTypes` property.

Example 14-3. Specifying optional attribute settings with properties

```
[ExpectedException(typeof(ArgumentException), AllowDerivedTypes = true)]
[TestMethod]
public void ThrowsWhenNameMalformed()
{
    ...
```

Applying an attribute will not cause it to be constructed. All you are doing when you apply an attribute is providing instructions on how the attribute should be created and initialized if something should ask to see it. (There is a common misconception that method attributes are instantiated when the method runs. Not so.) When the compiler builds the metadata for an assembly, it includes information about which attributes have been applied to which items, including a list of constructor arguments and property values, and the CLR will dig that information out and use it only if something asks for it. For example, when you tell Visual Studio to run your unit tests, it will load your test assembly, and then for each public type, it asks the CLR for any test-related attributes. That's the point at which the attributes get constructed. If you were simply to load the assembly by, say, adding a reference to it from another project and then using some of the types it contains, the attributes would never come into existence—they would remain as nothing more than a set of building instructions frozen into your assembly's metadata.

Attribute Targets

Attributes can be applied to numerous different kinds of targets. You can put attributes on any of the features of the type system represented in the reflection API that I showed in Chapter 13. Specifically, you can apply attributes to assemblies, modules, types, methods, method parameters, constructors, fields, properties, events, and generic type parameters. In addition, you can supply attributes that target a method's return value.

For most of these, you denote the target simply by putting the attribute in front of it. But that's not an option for assemblies or modules, because there is no single feature that represents those in your source code—everything in your project goes into the assembly it produces, and modules are likewise an aggregate (typically constituting the whole assembly, as I described in Chapter 12). So for these, we have to state the target explicitly at the start of the attribute. You will often see assembly-level attributes like the one shown in Example 14-4 in a *GlobalSuppressions.cs* file. Visual Studio sometimes makes suggestions for modifying your code, and if you choose to suppress these, it does so with assembly-level attributes.

Example 14-4. Assembly-level attributes

```
[assembly: System.Diagnostics.CodeAnalysis.SuppressMessage(
    "StyleCop.CSharp.NamingRules",
    "SA1313:Parameter names should begin with lower-case letter",
    Justification = "Triple underscore acceptable for unused lambda parameter",
    Scope = "member",
    Target = "~M:Idg.Examples.SomeMethod")]
```

You can put assembly-level attributes in any file. The sole restriction is that they must appear before any namespace or type definitions. The only things that should come before assembly-level attributes are whichever using directives you need, comments, and whitespace (all of which are optional).

Module-level attributes follow the same pattern, although they are much less common, not least because multimodule assemblies are pretty rare, and are not supported in .NET Core. Example 14-5 shows how to configure the debuggability of a particular module, should you want one module in a multimodule assembly to be easily debuggable but the rest to be JIT-compiled with full optimizations. (This is a contrived scenario so that I can show the syntax. In practice, you're unlikely ever to want to do this.) I'll talk about the `DebuggableAttribute` later, in "JIT compilation" on page 603.

Example 14-5. Module-level attribute

```
using System.Diagnostics;

[module: Debuggable(DebuggableAttribute.DebuggingModes.DisableOptimizations)]
```

Methods' return values can be annotated, and this also requires qualification, because return value attributes go in front of the method, the same place as attributes that apply to the method itself. (Attributes for parameters do not need qualification, because these appear inside the parentheses with the arguments.) Example 14-6 shows a method with attributes applied to both the method and the return type. (The attributes in this example are part of the interop services that enable .NET code to call external code, such as OS APIs. This example imports a function from a Win32 DLL, enabling you to use it from C#. There are several different representations for Boolean values in unmanaged code, so I've annotated the return type here with a `Mar shalAsAttribute` to say which particular one the CLR should expect.)

Example 14-6. Method and return value attributes

```
[DllImport("User32.dll")]
[return: MarshalAs(UnmanagedType.Bool)]
static extern bool IsWindowVisible(HandleRef hWnd);
```

Another kind of target that needs qualification is a compiler-generated field. You get these with properties in which you do not supply code for the getter or setter, and `event` members without explicit `add` and `remove` implementations. The attributes in Example 14-7 apply to the fields that hold the property's value and the delegate for the event; without the `field:` qualifiers, attributes in those positions would apply to the property or event itself.

Example 14-7. Attribute for compiler-generated property and event fields

```
[field: NonSerialized]
public int DynamicId { get; set; }

[field: NonSerialized]
public event EventHandler Frazzled;
```

Compiler-Handled Attributes

The C# compiler recognizes certain attribute types and handles them in special ways. For example, assembly names and versions are set via attributes, and also some related information about your assembly. As Chapter 12 described, in modern .NET projects, the build process generates a hidden source file containing these for you. If you're curious, it usually ends up in the *obj\Debug* or *obj\Release* folder of your project, and it will be named something like *YourProject.AssemblyInfo.cs*. Example 14-8 shows a typical example.

Example 14-8. A typical generated file with assembly-level attributes

```
//------------------------------------------------------------------------------
// <auto-generated>
//     This code was generated by a tool.
//     Runtime Version:4.0.30319.42000
//
//     Changes to this file may cause incorrect behavior and will be lost if
//     the code is regenerated.
// </auto-generated>
//------------------------------------------------------------------------------

using System;
using System.Reflection;

[assembly: System.Reflection.AssemblyCompanyAttribute("MyCompany")]
[assembly: System.Reflection.AssemblyConfigurationAttribute("Debug")]
[assembly: System.Reflection.AssemblyFileVersionAttribute("1.0.0.0")]
[assembly: System.Reflection.AssemblyInformationalVersionAttribute("1.0.0")]
[assembly: System.Reflection.AssemblyProductAttribute("MyApp")]
[assembly: System.Reflection.AssemblyTitleAttribute("MyApp")]
[assembly: System.Reflection.AssemblyVersionAttribute("1.0.0.0")]

// Generated by the MSBuild WriteCodeFragment class.
```

In projects created before .NET Core came along, the build process didn't generate this file automatically, so instead most projects included a *AssemblyInfo.cs* file (although by default Visual Studio hid it inside the project's Properties node in Solution Explorer).

Even though you only control these attributes indirectly, it's useful to understand them since they affect the compiler output.

Names and versions

As you saw in Chapter 12, assemblies have a compound name. The simple name, which is typically the same as the filename but without the *.exe* or *.dll* extension, is configured as part of the project settings. The name also includes a version number, and this is controlled with an attribute, as Example 14-9 shows.

Example 14-9. Version attributes

```
[assembly: AssemblyVersion("1.0.0.0")]
[assembly: AssemblyFileVersion("1.0.0.0")]
```

As you may recall from Chapter 12, the first of these sets the version part of the assembly's name. The second has nothing to do with .NET—the compiler uses this to generate a Win32-style version resource. This is the version number end users will see if they select your assembly in Windows Explorer and open the Properties window.

The culture is also part of the assembly name. This will often be set automatically if you're using the satellite resource assembly mechanisms described in Chapter 12. You can set it explicitly with the `AssemblyCulture` attribute, but for nonresource assemblies, the culture should usually not be set. (The only culture-related assembly-level attribute you will normally specify explicitly is the `NeutralResourcesLangua geAttribute`, which I showed in Chapter 12.)

Strongly named assemblies have an additional component in their name: the public key token. The easiest way to set up a strong name is with the Signing tab of your project's properties. However, you can also manage strong naming from the source code, because the compiler recognizes some special attributes for this. `AssemblyKeyFi leAttribute` takes the name of a file that contains a key. Alternatively, you can install a key in the computer's key store (which is part of the Windows cryptography system). If you want to do that, you can use the `AssemblyKeyNameAttribute` instead. The presence of either of these attributes causes the compiler to embed the public key in the assembly, and include a hash of that key as the public key token of the strong name. If the key file includes the private key, the compiler will sign your assembly too. If it does not, it will fail to compile, unless you also enable either delay signing or public signing. You can enable delay signing by applying the `AssemblyDelaySignAt tribute` with a constructor argument of `true`. Alternatively you can add either `<DelaySign>true</DelaySign>` or `<PublicSign>true</PublicSign>` to your *.csproj* file.

 Although the key-related attributes trigger special handling from the compiler, it still embeds them in the metadata as normal attributes. So, if you use the `AssemblyKeyFileAttribute`, the path to your key file will be visible in the final compiled output. This is not necessarily a problem, but you might prefer not to advertise these sorts of details, so it may be better to use the project-level configuration for strong names than the attribute-based approach.

Description and related resources

The version resource produced by the `AssemblyFileVersion` attribute is not the only information that the C# compiler can embed in Win32-style resources. There are several other attributes providing copyright information and other descriptive text. Example 14-10 shows a typical selection.

Example 14-10. Typical assembly description attributes

```
[assembly: AssemblyTitle("ExamplePlugin")]
[assembly: AssemblyDescription("An example plug-in DLL")]
[assembly: AssemblyConfiguration("Retail")]
[assembly: AssemblyCompany("Endjin Ltd.")]
[assembly: AssemblyProduct("ExamplePlugin")]
[assembly: AssemblyCopyright("Copyright © 2019 Endjin Ltd.")]
[assembly: AssemblyTrademark("")]
```

As with the file version, these are all visible in the Details tab of the Properties window that Windows Explorer can show for the file. And as with all of these attributes, you can also cause them to be generated by editing the project file, either directly, or using Visual Studio's project properties page.

Caller information attributes

There are some compiler-handled attributes designed for scenarios where your methods need information about the context from which they were invoked. This is useful for certain diagnostic logging scenarios, and it is also helpful when implementing a particular interface commonly used in UI code.

Example 14-11 illustrates how you can use these attributes in logging code. If you annotate method parameters with one of these three new attributes, the compiler provides some special handling when callers omit the arguments. It will pass in either the name of the member (method or property) that calls the attributed method, the filename containing the code that called the method, or the line number from which the call was made.

 These attributes are allowed only for optional parameters. The only way to make an argument optional is to provide a default value with that argument. C# will always substitute a different value when these attributes are present, so the default you specify will not be used if you invoke the method from C# (or Visual Basic, which also supports these attributes). Nonetheless, you must provide a default because without one, the parameter is not optional, so we normally use empty strings, null, or the number 0.

Example 14-11. Applying caller info attributes to method parameters

```
public static void Log(
    string message,
    [CallerMemberName] string callingMethod = "",
    [CallerFilePath] string callingFile = "",
    [CallerLineNumber] int callingLineNumber = 0)
{
    Console.WriteLine("Message {0}, called from {1} in file '{2}', line {3}",
```

```
        message, callingMethod, callingFile, callingLineNumber);
}
```

If you supply all arguments when invoking this method, nothing unusual happens. But if you omit any of the optional arguments, C# will generate code that provides information about the site from which the method was invoked. The default values for the three optional arguments in Example 14-11 will be the name of the method or property that called this Log method, the full path of the source code containing the code that made the call, and the line number from which Log was called.

The CallerMemberName attribute has a superficial resemblance to the nameof operator, which we saw in Chapter 8. Both cause the compiler to create a string containing the name of some feature of the code, but they work quite differently. With nameof, you always know exactly what string you'll get, because it's determined by the expression you supply. (E.g., nameof(message) inside Log in Example 14-11 will always evaluate to "message".) But CallerMemberName changes the way the compiler invokes the method to which they apply—callingMethod has that attribute, and its value is not fixed. It will depend on where this method is called from.

> You can discover the calling method another way: the StackTrace and StackFrame class in the System.Diagnostics namespace can report information about methods above you in the call stack. However, these have a considerably higher runtime expense—the caller information attributes calculate the values at compile time, making the runtime overhead very low. (Likewise with nameof.) Also, StackFrame can determine the filename and line number only if debug symbols are available.

Although diagnostic logging is the obvious application for this, I also mentioned a certain scenario that most .NET UI developers will be familiar with. The .NET class library defines an interface called INotifyPropertyChanged. As Example 14-12 shows, this is a very simple interface with just one member, an event called Property Changed.

Example 14-12. INotifyPropertyChanged

```
public interface INotifyPropertyChanged
{
    event PropertyChangedEventHandler PropertyChanged;
}
```

Types that implement this interface raise the PropertyChanged event every time one of their properties changes. The PropertyChangedEventArgument provides a string containing the name of the property that just changed. These change notifications are useful in UIs, because they enable an object to be used with data binding technologies (such as those provided by .NET's WPF UI framework) that can automatically update the UI any time a property changes. Data binding can help you to achieve a clean separation between the code that deals directly with UI types and code that contains the logic that decides how the application should respond to user input.

Implementing `INotifyPropertyChanged` can be both tedious and error-prone. Because the `PropertyChanged` event indicates which property changed as a string, it is very easy to mistype the property name, or to accidentally use the wrong name if you copy and paste the implementation from one property to another. Also, if you rename a property, it's easy to forget to change the text used for the event, meaning that code that was previously correct will now provide the wrong name when raising the `PropertyChanged` event. The `nameof` operator helps avoid mistyping, and helps with renames, but can't always detect cut-and-paste errors. (It won't notice if you fail to update the name when pasting code between properties of the same class, for example.)

Caller information attributes can help make implementing this interface much less error-prone. Example 14-13 shows a base class that implements `INotifyProperty Changed`, supplying a helper for raising change notifications in a way that exploits one of these attributes. (It also uses the null-conditional `?.` operator to ensure that it only invokes the event's delegate if it is non-null. By the way, when you use the operator this way, C# generates code that only evaluates the delegate's `Invoke` method's arguments if it is non-null. So not only does it skip the call to `Invoke` when the delegate is null, it will also avoid constructing the `PropertyChangedEventArgs` that would have been passed as an argument.) This code also detects whether the value really has changed, only raising the event when that's the case, and its return value indicates whether it changed, in case callers might find that useful.

Example 14-13. A reusable INotifyPropertyChanged implementation

```
public class NotifyPropertyChanged : INotifyPropertyChanged
{
    public event PropertyChangedEventHandler PropertyChanged;

    protected bool SetProperty<T>(
        ref T field,
        T value,
        [CallerMemberName] string propertyName = null)
    {
        if (!Equals(field, value))
        {
            return false;
        }

        field = value;
```

```
        PropertyChanged?.Invoke(this, new PropertyChangedEventArgs(propertyName));
        return true;
    }
}
```

The presence of the [CallerMemberName] attribute means that a class deriving from this type does not need to specify the property name if it calls SetProperty from inside a property setter, as Example 14-14 shows.

Example 14-14. Raising a property changed event

```
public class MyViewModel : NotifyPropertyChanged
{
    private string _name;

    public string Name
    {
        get => _name;
        set => SetProperty(ref _name, value);
    }
}
```

Even with the new attribute, implementing INotifyPropertyChanged is clearly more effort than an automatic property, where you just write { get; set; } and let the compiler do the work for you. But it's only a little more complex than an explicit implementation of a trivial field-backed property, and it's simpler than would be possible without [CallerMemberName], because I've been able to omit the property name when asking the base class to raise the event. More importantly, it's less error prone: I can now be confident that the right name will be used every time, even if I rename the property at some point in the future.

CLR-Handled Attributes

Some attributes get special treatment at runtime from the CLR. There is no official comprehensive list of such attributes, so in the next few sections, I will just describe some of the most widely used examples.

InternalsVisibleToAttribute

You can apply the InternalsVisibleToAttribute to an assembly to declare that any internal types or members it defines should be visible to one or more other assemblies. A popular use for this is to enable unit testing of internal types. As Example 14-15 shows, you just pass the name of the assembly as a constructor argument.

Strong naming complicates matters. Strongly named assemblies cannot make their internals visible to assemblies that are not strongly named, and vice versa. When a strongly named assembly makes its internals visible to another strongly named assembly, it must specify not just the simple name, but also the public key of the assembly to which it is granting access. And this is not just the public key token I described in Chapter 12—it is the hexadecimal for the entire public key, which will be several hundred digits. You can discover an assembly's full public key with the .NET SDK's *sn.exe* utility, using the `-Tp` switch followed by the assembly's path.

Example 14-15. InternalsVisibleToAttribute

```
[assembly:InternalsVisibleTo("ImageManagement.Tests")]
[assembly:InternalsVisibleTo("ImageServices.Tests")]
```

This shows that you can make the types visible to multiple assemblies by applying the attribute multiple times, with a different assembly name each time.

The CLR is responsible for enforcing accessibility rules. Normally, if you try to use an internal class from another assembly, you'll get an error at runtime. (C# won't even let you compile such code, but it's possible to trick the compiler. Or you could write directly in IL. The IL assembler, *ILASM*, does what you tell it and imposes far fewer restrictions than C#. Once you get past the compile-time restrictions, then you'll hit the runtime ones.) But when this attribute is present, the CLR relaxes its rules for the assemblies you list. The compiler also understands this attribute and lets code that tries to use externally defined internal types compile as long as the external library names your assembly in an `InternalsVisibleToAttribute`.

This attribute provides a better solution to the problem I encountered with the first example in Chapter 1—I wanted to exercise the program entry point from a test, but by default, the containing `Program` class is internal. I fixed this by making that and the `Main` method `public`, but if I had used an `InternalsVisibleTo` attribute instead, I could have left the class as `internal`. I would still have had to make `Main` more visible—it's `private` by default, and I would have needed to make it at least `internal`, but that's still an improvement on making it `public`.

Besides being useful in unit test scenarios, this attribute can also be helpful if you want to split code across multiple assemblies. If you have written a large class library, you might not want to put it into one massive DLL. If it has several areas that your customers might want to use in isolation, it could make sense to split it up so that they can deploy just the parts that they need. However, although you may be able to partition your library's public-facing API, the implementation might not be as easy to divide, particularly if your codebase performs a lot of reuse. You might have many classes that are not designed for public consumption but that you use throughout your code.

If it weren't for the `InternalsVisibleToAttribute`, it would be awkward to reuse shared implementation details across assemblies. Either each assembly would need to contain its own copy of the relevant classes, or you'd need to make them public types in some common assembly. The problem with that second technique is that making types public effectively invites people to use them. Your documentation might state that the types are for the internal use of your framework and should not be used, but that won't stop some people.

Fortunately, you don't have to make them `public`. Any types that are just implementation details can remain `internal`, and you can make them available to all of your assemblies with the `InternalsVisibleToAttribute`, while keeping them inaccessible to everyone else.

Serialization attributes

The CLR can *serialize* certain objects, meaning that it can write all of the values in the object's fields into a binary stream. It can *deserialize* this stream back into a new object some time later, possibly in a different process or even on a different computer. When serialization encounters fields containing references it automatically serializes other objects that yours refer to. It detects circular references to avoid entering an infinite loop. This feature has a curious status: Microsoft discourages its use, did not initially include it in .NET Core, and had been intending to deprecate it. However, it got a partial reprieve in .NET Core 2.1. You are still mostly discouraged from using it, and many of the .NET class library types that support serialization in .NET Framework do not in .NET Core. However, in some cases you have to use it: for example, if you want to enable exceptions to be serialized across process boundaries, this is the mechanism that enables that. Serialization is of particular interest in this chapter because its attributes are somewhat unusual.

Not all objects are serializable. For example, consider an object that represents a network connection. What would it mean if you were to serialize this, copy the resulting binary stream to a different computer, and then deserialize it? Would you expect to get an object that was also connected to the same endpoint as the original object? For many network protocols, this cannot possibly work. (Take TCP, the wildly popular protocol that underpins HTTP and numerous other forms of communication. The addresses of the two communicating computers form an integral part of a TCP connection, so if you move to a different machine, then by definition, you need a new connection.)

In practice, because the OS provides the networking stack, an object representing a connection will probably have a numeric field containing some opaque OS-supplied handle for the connection that won't work in another process. Even within a single machine there are issues. In Windows, handle values are usually scoped to one process. (There are ways to share handles in certain situations, but there's no completely general mechanism for doing so. Apart from anything else, it's very common for one particular numeric handle value to mean different things in different processes, so even if you want to share a handle in your process with another process, that other process may already be using that same handle value to refer to something else. So, although two different processes might be able to get handles for the same underlying thing, the actual numeric values of those handles will often be different.) Deserializing objects that contain handles without special handling will at best cause errors, but could well cause more subtle problems. And even if you're happy to customize the process, serialization is not meaningful for many handle types.

So serialization is necessarily an opt-in feature—only the author of a type will know whether making a field-by-field copy of an object (which is effectively what serialization does) will have a useful result. You can opt in by applying the `SerializableAttribute` to your class. Unlike most attributes, this one gets special handling in .NET's metadata format—it just ends up setting a flag in part of the class's definition. See the next sidebar, "Attributes or Custom Attributes?" for some related details.

Attributes or Custom Attributes?

You will sometimes come across the term *custom attribute*. The C# specification does not define a meaning for this term, but the CLI specification does. It defines a custom attribute as any attribute that does not have special intrinsic handling in the metadata format, and when you see the text `CustomAttribute` in a .NET API, that's usually the definition that applies. The vast majority of attributes you'll use fit into this category, including most attributes defined by the .NET class library. Even some of the CLR-handled attributes, such as `InternalsVisibleToAttribute`, are custom attributes by this definition. Attributes with intrinsic support in the file format, such as `SerializableAttribute`, are exceptional.

In a few places, the documentation uses the term in a slightly different way: sometimes *custom attribute* is used to mean an attribute type that didn't ship as part of .NET. In other words, the distinction appears to be whether you wrote the attribute type or Microsoft did. Conversely, at one point, some documentation used a broader definition, presenting `StructLayoutAttribute` as an example of a custom attribute. That attribute is part of the CLR's interop services (which make it possible to call native code, such as OS APIs), and like `SerializeableAttribute`, it's one of the very few intrinsic attribute types—the .NET metadata format has native handling for certain interop features. Microsoft has in recent years improved the documentation, and now tends to use *custom attribute* in the CLI sense, and uses the term *pseudo-attribute* for the kind with intrinsic metadata support. However, you may still come across content that doesn't use these names.

Part of the reason for the vagueness and inconsistency is that in most situations, there's no real technical need to draw a distinction. If you're writing a tool that works directly with the binary format for metadata, obviously you'll need to know which attributes are supported directly by the format, but most code can ignore those details; in C#, it's the same syntax either way, and the compiler and runtime will handle the difference for you. There are several serialization mechanisms in .NET, and only one of them gets intrinsic metadata support, but that doesn't make a significant difference in the way you use them. And there's no technical difference between one of your classes that derives from `Attribute` and a similar class that happens to ship as part of the .NET class library.

By applying the `SerializableAttribute`, you're giving .NET's serialization system permission to dig directly into your class's fields and write their values to a stream. You're also giving it permission to bypass the usual constructors when reconstituting an instance of your type from a serialized stream. (In fact, you can provide a special constructor for serialization purposes, as I showed in Chapter 8, but if you don't provide that particular form of constructor, serialization will bring instances of your type into existence without invoking any constructor. This is one of the reasons that serialization is a CLR feature rather than a library feature.) You can opt individual fields out of serialization by applying the `NonSerializedAttribute`.

By the way, there are several mechanisms in the .NET class libraries that perform a similar job to CLR serialization. In fact, the number of options is somewhat bewildering, with `XmlSerializer`, `DataContractSerializer`, `NetDataContractSerializer`, and `DataContractJsonSerializer` offering various serialization formats and philosophies. I'll discuss the most widely used ones in Chapter 15, but for now, these systems are relevant only because they define numerous attributes. However, since these other forms of serialization are all just library features rather than intrinsic runtime services, their attributes don't get any special treatment from the CLR.

JIT compilation

There are a few attributes that influence how the JIT compiler generates code. You can apply the `MethodImplAttribute` to a method, passing values from the `MethodImplOptions` enumeration. Its `NoInlining` value ensures that whenever your method is called by another method, it will be a full method call. Without this, the JIT compiler will sometimes just copy a method's code directly into the calling code.

In general, you'll want to leave inlining enabled. The JIT compiler inlines only small methods, and it's particularly important for tiny methods, such as property accessors. For simple field-based properties, invoking accessors with a normal function call often requires more code than inlining, so this optimization can produce code that's smaller, as well as faster. (Even if the code is no smaller, it may still be faster, because function calls can be surprisingly expensive. Modern CPUs tend to handle long sequential streams of instructions more efficiently than code that leaps around from one location to another.) However, inlining is an optimization with observable side effects—an inlined method does not get its own stack frame. Earlier, I mentioned some diagnostic APIs you can use to inspect the stack, and inlining will change the number of reported stack frames. If you just want to ask the question, "Which method is calling me?" the caller info attributes described earlier provide a more efficient way to discover this, and will not be defeated by inlining, but if you have code that inspects the stack for any reason, it can sometimes be confused by inlining. So, just occasionally, it's useful to disable it.

Conversely, you can specify `AggressiveInlining`, which encourages the JIT compiler to inline things it might otherwise leave as normal method calls. If you have identified a particular method as being highly performance sensitive, it might be worth trying this setting to see if it makes any difference, although be aware that it could make code either slower or faster—it will depend on the circumstances. Conversely, you can disable all optimizations with the `NoOptimization` option (although the documentation implies that this is more for the benefit of the CLR team at Microsoft than for consumers, because it is for "debugging possible code generation problems").

Another attribute that has an impact on optimization is the `DebuggableAttribute`. The C# compiler automatically applies this to your assembly in Debug builds. The attribute tells the CLR to be less aggressive about certain optimizations, particularly ones that affect variable lifetime, and ones that change the order in which code executes. Normally, the compiler is free to change such things as long as the final result of the code is the same, but this can cause confusion if you break into the middle of an optimized method with the debugger. This attribute ensures that variable values and the flow of execution are easy to follow in that scenario.

STAThread and MTAThread

Applications that run only on Windows and which present a UI (e.g., anything using .NET's WPF or Windows Forms frameworks) typically have the [`STAThread`] attribute on their `Main` method (although you won't always see it, because the entry point is often generated by the build system for these kinds of applications). This is an instruction to the CLR's COM interop layer, but it has broader implications: you need this attribute on `Main` if you want your main thread to host UI elements.

Various Windows UI features rely on COM under the covers. The clipboard uses it, for example, as do certain kinds of controls. COM has several threading models, and only one of them is compatible with UI threads. One of the main reasons for this is that UI elements have thread affinity, so COM needs to ensure that it does certain work on the right thread. Also, if a UI thread doesn't regularly check for messages and handle them, deadlock can ensue. If you don't tell COM that a particular thread is a UI thread, it will omit these checks, and you will encounter problems.

 Even if you're not writing UI code, some interop scenarios need the [STAThread] attribute, because certain COM components are incapable of working without it. However, UI work is the most common reason for seeing it.

Since COM is managed for you by the CLR, the CLR needs to know that it should tell COM that a particular thread needs to be handled as a UI thread. When you create a new thread explicitly using the techniques shown in Chapter 16, you can configure its COM threading mode, but the main thread is a special case—the CLR creates it for you when your application starts, and by the time your code runs, it's too late to configure the thread. Placing the [STAThread] attribute on the Main method tells the CLR that your main thread should be initialized for UI-compatible COM behavior.

STA is short for *single-threaded apartment*. Threads that participate in COM always belong to either an STA or a *multithreaded apartment* (MTA). There are other kinds of apartments, but threads have only temporary membership of those; when a thread starts using COM, it must pick either STA or MTA mode. So there is, unsurprisingly, also an [MTAThread] attribute.

Interop

The CLR's interop services define numerous attributes. Most of them are handled directly by the CLR, because interop is an intrinsic feature of the runtime. Since the attributes make sense only in the context of the mechanisms they support, and because there are so many, I will not describe them in full here, but Example 14-16 illustrates the kinds of things they can do.

Example 14-16. Interop attributes

```
[DllImport("advapi32.dll", CharSet = CharSet.Unicode, SetLastError = true,
        EntryPoint = "LookupPrivilegeValueW")]
internal static extern bool LookupPrivilegeValue(
    [MarshalAs(UnmanagedType.LPTStr)] string lpSystemName,
    [MarshalAs(UnmanagedType.LPTStr)] string lpName,
    out LUID lpLuid);
```

This uses two interop attributes that we saw earlier in Example 14-6, but in a somewhat more complex way. This calls into a function exposed by *advapi32.dll*, part of the Win32 API. The first argument to the DllImport attribute tells us that, but unlike the earlier example, this goes on to provide the interop layer with additional information. This API deals with strings, so interop needs to know which particular character representation is in use. This particular API uses a common Win32 idiom: it returns a Boolean value to indicate success or failure, but it also uses the Windows SetLastError API to provide more information in the failure case. The attribute's SetLastError property tells the interop layer to retrieve that immediately after calling this API so that .NET code can inspect it if necessary. The EntryPoint property deals with the fact that Win32 APIs taking strings sometimes come in two forms, working with either 8-bit or 16-bit characters (Windows 95 only supported 8-bit text, to conserve memory), and that we want to call the *Wide* form (hence the W suffix). It then uses MarshalAs on the two string arguments to tell the interop layer which of the many different string representations available in unmanaged code this particular API expects.

Defining and Consuming Attributes

The vast majority of attributes you will come across are not intrinsic to the runtime or compiler. They are defined by class libraries and have an effect only if you are using the relevant libraries or frameworks. You are free to do exactly the same in your own code—you can define your own attribute types. Because attributes don't do anything on their own—they don't even get instantiated unless something asks to see them—it is normally useful to define an attribute type only if you're writing some sort of framework, particularly one that is driven by reflection.

For example, unit test frameworks often discover the test classes you write via reflection, and enable you to control the test runner's behavior with attributes. Another example is how Visual Studio uses reflection to discover the properties of editable objects on design surfaces (such as UI controls), and it will look for certain attributes that enable you to customize the editing behavior. Another application of attributes is how you can configure exceptions to rules applied by Visual Studio's static code analysis tools by annotating your code with attributes. In all these cases, some tool or framework examines your code and decides what to do based on what it finds. This is the kind of scenario in which attributes are a good fit.

For example, attributes could be useful if you write an application that end users could extend. You might support loading of external assemblies that augment your application's behavior—this is often known as a *plugin* model. It might be useful to define an attribute that allows a plugin to provide descriptive information about itself. It's not strictly necessary to use attributes—you would probably define at least one interface that all plugins are required to implement, and you could have members in that interface for retrieving the necessary information. However, one advantage of using attributes is that you would not need to create an instance of the plugin just to retrieve the description information. That would enable you to show the plugin's details to the user before loading it, which might be important if constructing the plugin could have side effects that the user might not want.

Attribute Types

Example 14-17 shows how an attribute containing information about a plugin might look.

Example 14-17. An attribute type

```
[AttributeUsage(AttributeTargets.Class)]
public class PluginInformationAttribute : Attribute
{
    public PluginInformationAttribute(string name, string author)
    {
        Name = name;
        Author = author;
    }

    public string Name { get; }

    public string Author { get; }

    public string Description { get; set; }
}
```

To act as an attribute, a type must derive from the `Attribute` base class. Although `Attribute` defines various static methods for discovering and retrieving attributes, it does not provide very much of interest for instances. We do not derive from it to get any particular functionality; we do so because the compiler will not let you use a type as an attribute unless it derives from `Attribute`.

Notice that my type's name ends in the word `Attribute`. This is not an absolute requirement, but it is an extremely widely used convention. As you saw earlier, it's even built into the compiler, which automatically adds the `Attribute` suffix if you leave it out when applying an attribute. So there's usually no reason not to follow this convention.

 As you've seen, sometimes when we apply an attribute, we need to state its target. For example, when an attribute appears before a method, its target is the method, unless you qualify it with the `return:` prefix. You might have hoped that you'd be able to leave out these prefixes when using attributes that can target only certain members. For example, if an attribute can be applied only to an assembly, do you really need the `assembly:` qualifier? However, C# doesn't let you leave it off. It uses the `AttributeUsageAttribute` only to verify that an attribute has not been misapplied.

I've annotated my attribute type with an attribute. Most attribute types are annotated with the `AttributeUsageAttribute`, indicating the targets to which the attribute can usefully be applied. The C# compiler will enforce this. Since my attribute in Example 14-17 states that it may be applied only to classes, the compiler will generate an error if anyone attempts to apply it to anything else.

The attribute defines only one constructor, so any code that uses it will have to pass the arguments that the constructor requires, as Example 14-18 does.

Example 14-18. Applying an attribute

```
[PluginInformation("Reporting", "Endjin Ltd.")]
public class ReportingPlugin
{
    ...
}
```

Attribute classes are free to define multiple constructor overloads to support different sets of information. They can also define properties as a way to support optional pieces of information. My attribute defines a `Description` property, which is not required because the constructor does not demand a value for it, but which I can set using the syntax I described earlier in this chapter. Example 14-19 shows how that looks for my attribute.

Example 14-19. Providing an optional property value for an attribute

```
[PluginInformation("Reporting", "Endjin Ltd.",
    Description = "Automated report generation")]
public class ReportingPlugin
{
    ...
}
```

So far, nothing I've shown will cause an instance of my `PluginInformationAttri`
`bute` type to be created. These annotations are simply instructions for how the attribute should be initialized if anything asks to see it. So, if this attribute is to be useful, I need to write some code that will look for it.

Retrieving Attributes

You can discover whether a particular kind of attribute has been applied using the reflection API, which can also instantiate the attribute for you. In Chapter 13, I showed all of the reflection types representing the various targets to which attributes can be applied—types such as `MethodInfo`, `Type`, and `PropertyInfo`. These all implement an interface called ICustomAttributeProvider, which is shown in Example 14-20.

Example 14-20. ICustomAttributeProvider

```
public interface ICustomAttributeProvider
{
    object[] GetCustomAttributes(bool inherit);
    object[] GetCustomAttributes(Type attributeType, bool inherit);
    bool IsDefined(Type attributeType, bool inherit);
}
```

The IsDefined method simply tells you whether a particular attribute type is present —it does not instantiate it. The two GetCustomAttributes overloads create attributes and return them. (This is the point at which attributes are constructed, and also when any properties the annotations specify are set.) The first overload returns all attributes applied to the target, while the second lets you request only those attributes of a particular type.

All of these methods take a bool argument that lets you specify whether you want only attributes that were applied directly to the target you're inspecting, or also attributes defined by the base type or types.

This interface was introduced in .NET 1.0, so it does not use generics, meaning you need to cast the objects that come back. Fortunately the CustomAttributeExtensions static class defines several extension methods. Instead of defining them for the ICustomAttributeProvider interface, it extends the reflection classes that offer attributes. For example, if you have a variable of type Type, you could call GetCustomAttribute<PluginInformationAttribute>() on it, which would construct and return the plugin information attribute, or null if the attribute is not present. Example 14-21 uses this to show all of the plugin information from all the DLLs in a particular folder.

Example 14-21. Showing plugin information

```
static void ShowPluginInformation(string pluginFolder)
{
    var dir = new DirectoryInfo(pluginFolder);
    foreach (var file in dir.GetFiles("*.dll"))
    {
        Assembly pluginAssembly = Assembly.LoadFrom(file.FullName);
        var plugins =
            from type in pluginAssembly.ExportedTypes
            let info = type.GetCustomAttribute<PluginInformationAttribute>()
            where info != null
            select new { type, info };
```

```
    foreach (var plugin in plugins)
    {
        Console.WriteLine($"Plugin type: {plugin.type.Name}");
        Console.WriteLine(
            $"Name: {plugin.info.Name}, written by {plugin.info.Author}");
        Console.WriteLine($"Description: {plugin.info.Description}");
    }
  }
}
```

There's one potential problem with this. I said that one benefit of attributes is that they can be retrieved without instantiating their target types. That's true here—I'm not constructing any of the plugins in Example 14-21. However, I am loading the plugin assemblies, and a possible side effect of enumerating the plugins would be to run static constructors in the plugin DLLs. So, although I'm not deliberately running any code in those DLLs, I can't guarantee that no code from those DLLs will run. If my goal is to present a list of plugins to the user, and to load and run only the ones explicitly selected, I've failed, because I've given plugin code a chance to run. However, we can fix this.

Reflection-only load

You do not need to load an assembly fully in order to retrieve attribute information. As I discussed in Chapter 13, you can load an assembly for reflection purposes only. This prevents any of the code in the assembly from running, but enables you to inspect the types it contains. However, this presents a challenge for attributes. The usual way to inspect an attribute's properties is to instantiate it by calling `GetCusto mAttributes` or a related extension method. Since that involves constructing the attribute—which means running some code—it is not supported for assemblies loaded for reflection (not even if the attribute type in question were defined in a different assembly that has been fully loaded in the normal way). If I modified Example 14-21 to load the assembly with `ReflectionOnlyLoadFrom`, the call to `Get CustomAttribute<PluginInformationAttribute>` would throw an exception.

When loading for reflection only, you have to use the `GetCustomAttributesData` method. Instead of instantiating the attribute for you, this returns the information stored in the metadata—the instructions for creating the attribute. Example 14-22 shows a version of the relevant code from Example 14-21 modified to work this way.

Example 14-22. Retrieving attributes with the reflection-only context

```
Assembly pluginAssembly = Assembly.ReflectionOnlyLoadFrom(file.FullName);
var plugins =
    from type in pluginAssembly.ExportedTypes
    let info = type.GetCustomAttributesData().SingleOrDefault(
        attrData => attrData.AttributeType.FullName == pluginAttributeType.FullName)
```

```
    where info != null
    let description = info.NamedArguments
                        .SingleOrDefault(a => a.MemberName == "Description")
    select new
    {
        type,
        Name = (string) info.ConstructorArguments[0].Value,
        Author = (string) info.ConstructorArguments[1].Value,
        Description =
            description == null ? null : description.TypedValue.Value
    };

foreach (var plugin in plugins)
{
    Console.WriteLine($"Plugin type: {plugin.type.Name}");
    Console.WriteLine($"Name: {plugin.Name}, written by {plugin.Author}");
    Console.WriteLine($"Description: {plugin.Description}");
}
```

The code is rather more cumbersome because we don't get back an instance of the attribute. GetCustomAttributesData returns a collection of CustomAttributeData objects. Example 14-22 uses LINQ's SingleOrDefault operator to find the entry for the PluginInformationAttribute, and if that's present, the info variable in the query will end up holding a reference to the relevant CustomAttributeData object. The code then picks through the constructor arguments and property values using the ConstructorArguments and NamedArguments properties, enabling it to retrieve the three descriptive text values embedded in the attribute.

As this demonstrates, the reflection-only context adds complexity, so you should use it only if you need the benefits it offers. One benefit is the fact that it won't run any of the assemblies you load. It can also load assemblies that might be rejected if they were loaded normally (e.g., because they target a specific processor architecture that doesn't match your process). But if you don't need the reflection-only option, accessing the attributes directly, as Example 14-21 does, is more convenient.

Summary

Attributes provide a way to embed custom data into an assembly's metadata. You can apply attributes to a type, any member of a type, a parameter, a return value, or even a whole assembly or one of its modules. A handful of attributes get special handling from the CLR, and a few control compiler features, but most have no intrinsic behavior, acting merely as passive information containers. Attributes do not even get instantiated unless something asks to see them. All of this makes attributes most useful in systems with reflection-driven behavior—if you already have one of the reflection API objects such as ParameterInfo or Type, you can ask it directly for attributes. You therefore most often see attributes used in frameworks that inspect your code with reflection, such as unit test frameworks, serialization frameworks, data-driven UI elements like Visual Studio's Properties panel, or plugin frameworks. If you are using a framework of this kind, you will typically be able to configure its behavior by annotating your code with the attributes the framework recognizes. If you are writing this sort of framework, then it may make sense to define your own attribute types.

CHAPTER 15

Files and Streams

Most of the techniques I've shown so far in this book revolve around the information that lives in objects and variables. This kind of state is stored in a particular process's memory, but to be useful, a program must interact with a broader world. This might happen through UI frameworks, but there's one particular abstraction that can be used for many kinds of interactions with the outside world: a *stream*.

Streams are so widely used in computing that you will no doubt already be familiar with them, and a .NET stream is much the same as in most other programming systems: it is simply a sequence of bytes. That makes a stream a useful abstraction for many commonly encountered features such as a file on disk, or the body of an HTTP response. A console application uses streams to represent its input and output. If you run such a program interactively, the text that the user types at the keyboard becomes the program's input stream, and anything the program writes to its output stream appears on screen. A program doesn't necessarily know what kind of input or output it has, though—you can redirect these streams with console programs. For example, the input stream might actually provide the contents of a file on disk, or it could even be the output from some other program.

Not all I/O APIs are stream-based. For example, in addition to the input stream, the `Console` class provides a `ReadKey` method that gives information about exactly which key was pressed, which works only if the input comes from the keyboard. So, although you can write programs that do not care whether their input comes interactively or from a file, some programs are pickier.

The stream APIs present you with raw byte data. However, it is possible to work at a different level. For example, there are text-oriented APIs that can wrap underlying streams, so you can work with characters or strings instead of raw bytes. There are also various *serialization* mechanisms that enable you to convert .NET objects into a stream representation, which you can turn back into objects later, making it possible to save an object's state persistently or to send that state over the network. I'll show these higher-level APIs later, but first, let's look at the stream abstraction itself.

The Stream Class

The `Stream` class is defined in the `System.IO` namespace. It is an abstract base class, with concrete derived types such as `FileStream` or `GZipStream` representing particular kinds of streams. Example 15-1 shows the `Stream` class's three most important members. It has several other members, but these are at the heart of the abstraction. (As you'll see later, there are also asynchronous versions of `Read` and `Write`. .NET Core 3.0 and .NET Standard also add overloads that take one of the *span* types described in Chapter 18 in place of an array. Everything I say in this section about these methods also applies to the asynchronous and span-based forms.)

Example 15-1. The most important members of Stream

```
public abstract int Read(byte[] buffer, int offset, int count);
public abstract void Write(byte[] buffer, int offset, int count);
public abstract long Position { get; set; }
```

Some streams are read-only. For example, when the input stream for a console application represents the keyboard or the output of some other program, there's no meaningful way for the program to write to that stream. (And for consistency, even if you use input redirection to run a console application with a file as its input, the input stream will be read-only.) Some streams are write-only, such as the output stream of a console application. If you call `Read` on a write-only stream or `Write` on a read-only one, these methods throw a `NotSupportedException`.

 The `Stream` class defines various `bool` properties that describe a stream's capabilities, so you don't have to wait until you get an exception. You can check the `CanRead` or `CanWrite` properties.

Both `Read` and `Write` take a `byte[]` array as their first argument, and these methods copy data into or out of that array, respectively. The `offset` and `count` arguments that follow indicate the array element at which to start, and the number of bytes to read or write; you do not have to use the whole array. Notice that there are no arguments to specify the offset within the stream at which to read or write. This is managed by the `Position` property—this starts at zero, but each time you read or write, the position advances by the number of bytes processed.

Notice that the Read method returns an int. This tells you how many bytes were read from the stream—the method does not guarantee to provide the amount of data you requested. One obvious reason for this is that you could reach the end of the stream, so even though you may have asked to read 100 bytes into your array, there may have been only 30 bytes of data left between the current Position and the end of the stream. However, that's not the only reason you might get less than you asked for, and this often catches people out, so for the benefit of people skim-reading this chapter, I'll put this in a scary warning.

> If you ask for more than one byte at a time, a Stream is always free to return less data than you requested from Read for any reason. You should never presume that a call to Read returned as much data as it could, even if you have good reason to know that the amount you asked for will be available.

The reason Read is slightly tricky is that some streams are live, representing a source of information that produces data gradually as the program runs. For example, if a console application is running interactively, its input stream can provide data only as fast as the user types; a stream representing data being received over a network connection can provide data only as fast as it arrives. If you call Read and you ask for more data than is currently available, a stream might wait until it has as much as you've asked for, but it doesn't have to—it may return whatever data it has immediately. (The only situation in which it is obliged to wait before returning is if it currently has no data at all, but is not yet at the end of the stream. It has to return at least one byte, because a 0 return value indicates the end of the stream.) If you want to ensure that you read a specific number of bytes, you'll have to check whether Read returned fewer bytes than you wanted, and if necessary, keep calling it until you have what you need. Example 15-2 shows how to do this.

Example 15-2. Reading a specific number of bytes

```
static int ReadAll(Stream s, byte[] buffer, int offset, int length)
{
    if ((offset + length) > buffer.Length)
    {
        throw new ArgumentException("Buffer too small to hold requested data");
    }

    int bytesReadSoFar = 0;
    while (bytesReadSoFar < length)
    {
        int bytes = s.Read(
            buffer, offset + bytesReadSoFar, length - bytesReadSoFar);
        if (bytes == 0)
        {
```

```
        break;
    }
    bytesReadSoFar += bytes;
    }
}

    return bytesReadSoFar;
}
```

Notice that this code checks for a 0 return value from Read to detect the end of the stream. Without that, it would loop forever if it reached the end of the stream before reading as much data as has been asked for. That means that if we do reach the end of the stream, this method will have to provide less data than the caller requested, so this may seem like it hasn't really solved the problem. However, it does rule out the situation where you get less than you asked for despite not reaching the end of the stream. (Of course, you could change the method so that it throws an exception if it reaches the end of the stream before providing the specified number of bytes. That way, if the method returns at all, it is guaranteed to return exactly as many bytes as have been requested.)

Stream offers a simpler way to read. The ReadByte method returns a single byte, unless you hit the end of the stream, at which point it returns a value of –1. (Its return type is int, enabling it to return any possible value for byte as well as negative values.) This avoids the problem of being handed back only some of the data you requested, because if you get anything back at all, you always get exactly one byte. However, it's not especially convenient or efficient if you want to read larger chunks of data.

The Write method doesn't have any of these issues. If it succeeds, it always accepts all of the data you provide. Of course, it might fail—it could throw an exception before it manages to write all of the data because of an error (e.g., running out of space on disk or losing a network connection).

Position and Seeking

tion property")))Streams automatically update their current position each time you read or write. As you can see in Example 15-1, the Position property can be set, so you can attempt to move directly to a particular position. This is not guaranteed to work because it's not always possible to support it. For example, a Stream that represents data being received over a TCP network connection could produce data indefinitely—as long as the connection remains open and the other end keeps sending data, the stream will continue to honor calls to Read. A connection could remain open for many days, and might receive terabytes of data in that time. If such a stream let you set its Position property, enabling your code to go back and reread data received earlier, the stream would have to find somewhere to store every single byte it received just in case the code using the stream wants to see it again. Since that might involve storing more data than you have space for on disk, this is clearly not practical, so some streams will throw `NotSupportedException` when you try to set the `Position` property. (There's a `CanSeek` property you can use to discover whether a particular stream supports changing the position, so just like with read-only and write-only streams, you don't have to wait until you get an exception to find out whether it will work.)

As well as the `Position` property, `Stream` also defines a `Seek` method, whose signature is shown in Example 15-3. This lets you specify the position you require relative to the stream's current position. (This also throws `NotSupportedException` on streams that don't support seeking.)

Example 15-3. The Seek method

```
public abstract long Seek(long offset, SeekOrigin origin);
```

If you pass `SeekOrigin.Current` as the second argument, it will set the position by adding the first argument to the current position. You can pass a negative `offset` if you want to move backward. You can also pass `SeekOrigin.End` to set the position to be some specified number of bytes from the end of the stream. Passing `SeekOrigin.Begin` has the same logical effect as just setting `Position`—it sets the position relative to the start of the stream.[1]

Flushing

As with many stream APIs on other programming systems, writing data to a `Stream` does not necessarily cause the data to reach its destination immediately. When a call to `Write` returns, all you know is that it has copied your data somewhere; but that might be a buffer in memory, not the final target. For example, if you write a single byte to a stream representing a file on disk, the stream object will typically defer writing that to the disk until it has enough bytes to make it worth the effort. Disks are block-based devices, meaning that writes happen in fixed-size chunks, typically several kilobytes in size, so it generally makes sense to wait until there's enough data to fill a block before writing anything out.

This buffering is usually a good thing—it improves write performance while enabling you to ignore the details of how the disk works. However, a downside is that if you write data only occasionally (e.g., when writing error messages to a logfile), you could

---

1 Although `Seek` is logically equivalent to setting the `Position`, some streams handle these subtly differently, although not for any discernible reason. The class library's `BufferedStream` discards all previously read data when you set `Position` directly, whereas the `Seek` method checks to see whether the new position is within data it has already loaded.

easily end up with long delays between the program writing data to a stream, and that data reaching the disk. This could be perplexing for someone trying to diagnose a problem by looking at the logfiles of a program that's currently running. And more insidiously, if your program crashes, anything in a stream's buffers that has not yet made it to disk will probably be lost.

The Stream class therefore offers a Flush method. This lets you tell the stream that you want it to do whatever work is required to ensure that any buffered data is written to its target, even if that means making suboptimal use of the buffer.

 When using a FileStream, the Flush method does not necessarily guarantee that the data being flushed has made it to disk yet. It merely makes the stream pass the data to the OS. Before you call Flush, the OS hasn't even seen the data, so if you were to terminate the process suddenly, the data would be lost. After Flush has returned, the OS has everything your code has written, so the process could be terminated without loss of data. However, the OS may perform additional buffering of its own, so if the power fails before the OS gets around to writing everything to disk, the data will still be lost. If you need to guarantee that data has been written persistently (rather than merely ensuring that you've handed it to the OS), you will also need to use either the WriteThrough flag, described in "FileStream Class" on page 633, or call the Flush overload that takes a bool, passing true to force flushing to disk.

A stream automatically flushes its contents when you call Dispose. You need to use Flush only when you want to keep a stream open after writing out buffered data. It is particularly important if there will be extended periods during which the stream is open but inactive. (If the stream represents a network connection, and if your application depends on prompt data delivery—this would be the case in an online chat application or game, for example—you would call Flush even if you expect only fairly brief periods of inactivity.)

Copying

Copying all of the data from one stream to another is occasionally useful. It wouldn't be hard to write a loop to do this, but you don't have to, because the Stream class's CopyTo method (or the equivalent CopyToAsync) does it for you. There's not much to say about it. The main reason I'm mentioning it is that it's not uncommon for developers to write their own version of this method because they didn't know the functionality was built into Stream.

Length

Some streams are able to report their length through the predictably named `Length` property. As with `Position`, this property's type is `long`—`Stream` uses 64-bit numbers because streams often need to be larger than 2 GB, which would be the upper limit if sizes and positions were represented with `int`.

`Stream` also defines a `SetLength` method that lets you define the length of a stream (where supported). You might think about using this when writing a large quantity of data to a file, to ensure that there is enough space to contain all the data you wish to write—better to get an `IOException` before you start than wasting time on a doomed operation and potentially causing system-wide problems by using up all of the free space. However, many filesystems support sparse files, letting you create files far larger than the available free space, so in practice you might not see any error until you start writing nonzero data. Even so, if you specify a length that is longer than the filesystem supports, `SetLength` will throw an `ArgumentException`.

Not all streams support length operations. The `Stream` class documentation says that the `Length` property is available only on streams that support `CanSeek`. This is because streams that support seeking are typically ones where the whole content of the stream is known and accessible up front. Seeking is unavailable on streams where the content is produced at runtime (e.g., input streams representing user input, or streams representing data received over the network), and in those cases the length is also very often not known in advance. As for `SetLength`, the documentation states that this is supported only on streams that support both writing and seeking. (As with all members representing optional features, `Length` and `SetLength` will throw a `NotSupportedException` if you try to use these members on streams that do not support them.)

Disposal

Some streams represent resources external to the .NET runtime. For example, `File Stream` provides stream access to the contents of a file, so it needs to obtain a file handle from the OS. It's important to close handles when you're done with them; otherwise you might prevent other applications from being able to use the file. Consequently, the `Stream` class implements the `IDisposable` interface (described in Chapter 7) so that it can know when to do that. And, as I mentioned earlier, buffering streams such as `FileStream` flush their buffers when you call `Dispose`, before closing handles.

Not all stream types depend on `Dispose` being called: `MemoryStream` works entirely in memory, so the GC would be able to take care of it. But in general, if you caused a stream to be created, you should call `Dispose` when you no longer need it.

There are some situations in which you will be provided with a stream, but it is not your job to dispose it. For example, ASP.NET Core can provide streams to represent data in HTTP requests and responses. It creates these for you and then disposes them after you've used them, so you should not call Dispose on them.

Confusingly, the Stream class also has a Close method. This is an accident of history. The first public beta release of .NET 1.0 did not define IDisposable, and C# did not have using statements—the keyword was only for using directives, which bring namespaces into scope. The Stream class needed some way of knowing when to clean up its resources, and since there was not yet a standard way to do this, it invented its own idiom. It defined a Close method, which was consistent with the terminology used in many stream-based APIs in other programming systems. IDisposable was added before the final release of .NET 1.0, and the Stream class added support for this, but it left the Close method in place; removing it would have disrupted a lot of early adopters who had been using the betas. But Close is redundant, and the documentation actively advises against using it. It says you should call Dispose instead (through a using statement if that is convenient). There's no harm in calling Close—there's no practical difference between that and Dispose—but Dispose is the more common idiom, and is therefore preferred.

Asynchronous Operation

The Stream class offers asynchronous versions of Read and Write. Be aware that there are two forms. Stream first appeared in .NET 1.0, so it supported what was then the standard asynchronous mechanism, the Asynchronous Programming Model (APM, described in Chapter 16) through the BeginRead, EndRead, BeginWrite, and End Write methods. This model is now deprecated, having been superseded by the newer Task-based Asynchronous Pattern (or TAP, also described in Chapter 16). Stream supports this through its ReadAsync and WriteAsync methods. There are two more operations that did not originally have any kind of asynchronous form that now have TAP versions: FlushAsync and CopyToAsync. (These support only TAP, because APM was already deprecated by the time Microsoft added these methods.)

Avoid the old APM-based Begin/End forms of Read and Write. They weren't present at all in early versions of .NET Core, nor in .NET Standard prior to 2.0. They reappeared to make it easier to migrate existing code from .NET Framework to .NET Core, so they are supported only for legacy scenarios.

Some stream types implement asynchronous operations using very efficient techniques that correspond directly to the asynchronous capabilities of the underlying OS.

(FileStream does this, as do the various streams .NET can provide to represent content from network connections.) You may come across libraries with custom stream types that do not do this, but even then, the asynchronous methods will be available, because the base Stream class can fall back to using multithreaded techniques instead.

One thing you need to be careful of when using asynchronous reads and writes is that a stream only has a single Position property. Reads and writes depend on the current Position and also update it when they are done, so in general you must avoid starting a new operation before one already in progress is complete. (If you wish to perform multiple concurrent read or write operations from a particular file, you can either create multiple stream objects for that file, or you can open the file in asynchronous mode. FileStream has special handling for asynchronous files. Operations use the value Position has at the start of the operation, and once an asynchronous read or write has started, you are allowed to change Position and start another operation without waiting for all the previous ones to complete. But this only applies to FileStream, and only when the file was opened in asynchronous mode.)

.NET Core 3.0 and .NET Standard 2.1 have added IAsyncDisposable, an asynchronous form of Dispose. The Stream class implements this, because disposal often involves flushing, which is a potentially slow operation.

Concrete Stream Types

The Stream class is abstract, so to use a stream, you'll need a concrete derived type. In some situations, this will be provided for you—the ASP.NET Core web framework supplies stream objects representing HTTP request and response bodies, for example, and the client-side HttpClient class will do something similar. But sometimes you'll need to create a stream object yourself. This section describes a few of the more commonly used types that derive from Stream.

The FileStream class represents a file on the filesystem. I will describe this in "Files and Directories" on page 632.

MemoryStream lets you create a stream on top of a byte[] array. You can either take an existing byte[] and wrap it in a MemoryStream, or you can create a MemoryStream and then populate it with data by calling Write (or the asynchronous equivalent). You can retrieve the populated byte[] once you're done by calling either ToArray or GetBuffer. (ToArray allocates a new array, with the size based on the number of bytes actually written. GetBuffer is more efficient because it returns the underlying array MemoryStream is using, but unless the writes happened to fill it completely, the array returned will contain more bytes than were written.) This class is useful when you are working with APIs that require a stream and you don't have one for some reason. For example, most of the serialization APIs described later in this chapter work with streams, but you might end up wanting to use that in conjunction with some other API that works in terms of byte[]. MemoryStream lets you bridge between those two representations.

Both Windows and Unix define an interprocess communication (IPC) mechanism enabling you to connect two processes through a stream. Windows calls these *named pipes*. Unix also has a mechanism with that name but it is completely different; it does however offer a mechanism similar to Windows named pipes: *domain sockets*. Although the precise details of Windows named pipes and Unix domain sockets differ, the various classes derived from PipeStream provide a common abstraction for both in .NET.

BufferedStream derives from Stream, but also takes a Stream in its constructor. It adds a layer of buffering, which is useful if you want to perform small reads or writes on a stream that is designed to work best with larger operations. (You don't need to use this with FileStream because that has its own built-in buffering mechanism.)

There are various stream types that transform the contents of other streams in some way. For example, DeflateStream, GZipStream, and BrotliStream implement three widely used compression algorithms. You can wrap these around other streams to compress the data written to the underlying stream, or to decompress the data read from it. (These just provide the lowest-level compression service. If you want to work with the popular ZIP format for packages of compressed files, use the ZipArchive class.) There's also a class called CryptoStream, which can encrypt or decrypt the contents of other streams using any of the wide variety of encryption mechanisms supported in .NET.

One Type, Many Behaviors

As you've now seen, the abstract base class Stream gets used in a wide range of scenarios. It is arguably an abstraction that has been stretched a little too thin. The presence of properties such as CanSeek that tell you whether the particular Stream you have can be used in a certain way is arguably a symptom of an underlying problem, an example of something known as a *code smell*. .NET streams did not invent this particular one-size-fits-all approach—it was popularized by Unix and the C programming language's standard library a long time ago. The problem is that when writing code that deals with a Stream, you might not know what sort of thing you are dealing with.

There are many different ways to use a Stream, but three usage styles come up a lot:

- Sequential access of a sequence of bytes
- Random access, with a presumption of efficient caching
- Access to some underlying capability of a device or system

As you know, not all `Stream` implementations support all three models—if `CanSeek` returns `false`, that rules out the middle option. But what is less obvious is that even when these properties indicate that a capability is available, not all streams support all usage models equally efficiently.

For example, I worked on a project that used a library for accessing files in a cloud-hosted storage service that was able to represent those files with `Stream` objects. This looks convenient because you can pass those to any API that works with a `Stream`. However, it was designed very much for the third style of use above: every single call to `Read` (or `ReadAsync`) would cause the library to make an HTTP request to the storage service. We had initially hoped to use this with another library that knew how to parse Parquet files (a binary tabular data storage format widely used in high-volume data processing). However, it turned out that the library was expecting a stream that supported the second type of access: it jumped back and forth through the file, making large numbers of fairly small reads. It worked perfectly well with the `FileStream` type I'll be describing later, because that supports the first two modes of use well. (For the second style, it relies on the OS to do the caching.) But it would have been a performance disaster to plug a `Stream` from the storage service library directly into the Parquet parsing library.

It's not always obvious when you have a mismatch of this kind. In this example, the properties reporting capabilities such as `CanSeek` gave no clue that there would be a problem. And applications that use Parquet files often use some sort of remote storage service, rather than the local filesystem, so there was no obvious reason to think that this library would presume that any `Stream` would offer local filesystem-like caching. It did technically work when we tried it: the storage library `Stream` worked hard to do everything asked of it, and the code worked correctly...eventually. So whenever you use a `Stream`, it's important to make sure you have fully understood what access patterns it will be subjected to, and how efficiently it supports those patterns.

In some cases you might be able to bridge the gap. The `BufferedStream` class can often take a `Stream` designed only for the third usage style above and adapt it for the first style of usage. However, there's nothing in the .NET class library that can add support for the second style of usage to a `Stream` that doesn't already innately support it. (This is typically only available either with streams that represent something already fully in memory, or which wrap some local API that does the caching for you, such as the OS filesystem APIs.) In these cases you will either need to rethink your design (e.g., make a local copy of the stream), change the way that the `Stream` is consumed, or write some sort of custom caching adapter. (In the end, we wrote an adapter that augmented the capabilities of `BufferedStream` with just enough random access caching to solve the performance problems.)

Text-Oriented Types

The `Stream` class is byte oriented, but it's common to work with files that contain text. If you want to process text stored in a file (or received over the network), it is cumbersome to use a byte-based API, because this forces you to deal explicitly with all of the variations that can occur. For example, there are multiple conventions for how to represent the end of a line—Windows typically uses two bytes with values of 13 and 10, as do many internet standards such as HTTP, but Unix-like systems often use just a single byte with the value 10.

There are also multiple character encodings in popular use. Some files use one byte per character, some use two, and some use a variable-length encoding. There are many different single-byte encodings too, so if you encounter a byte value of, say, 163 in a text file, you cannot know what that means unless you know which encoding is in use.

In a file using the single-byte Windows-1252 encoding, the value 163 represents a pound sign: £.[2] But if the file is encoded with ISO/IEC 8859-5 (designed for regions that use Cyrillic alphabets), the exact same code represents the Cyrillic capital letter DJE: Ђ. And if the file uses the UTF-8 encoding, that character would only be allowed as part of a multibyte sequence representing a single character.

Awareness of these issues is, of course, an essential part of any developer's skill set, but that doesn't mean you should have to handle every little detail any time you encounter text. So .NET defines specialized abstractions for working with text.

TextReader and TextWriter

The abstract `TextReader` and `TextWriter` classes present data as a sequence of `char` values. Logically speaking, these classes are similar to a stream, but each element in the sequence is a `char` instead of a `byte`. However, there are some differences in the details. For one thing, there are separate abstractions for reading and writing. `Stream` combines these, because it's common to want read/write access to a single entity, particularly if the stream represents a file on disk. For byte/oriented random access this makes sense, but it's a problematic abstraction for text.

Variable-length encodings make it tricky to support random write access (i.e., the ability to change values at any point in the sequence). Consider what it would mean to take a 1 GB UTF-8 text file whose first character is a $ and replace that first character with a £. In UTF-8, the $ character takes only one byte, but £ requires two, so

---

2 You might have thought that the pound sign was #, but if, like me, you're British, that's just not on. It would be like someone insisting on referring to @ as a dollar sign. Unicode's canonical name for # is *number sign*, and it also allows my preferred option, *hash*, as well as *octothorpe*, *crosshatch*, and, regrettably, *pound sign*.

changing that first character would require an extra byte to be inserted at the start of the file. This would mean moving the remaining file contents—almost 1 GB of data—along by one byte.

Even read-only random access is relatively expensive. Finding the millionth character in a UTF-8 file requires you to read the first 999,999 characters, because without doing that, you have no way of knowing what mix of single-byte and multibyte characters there is. The millionth character might start at the millionth byte, but it could also start some 4 million bytes in, or anywhere in between. Since supporting random access with variable-length text encodings is expensive, particularly for writeable data, these text-based types don't offer it. Without random access, there's no real benefit in merging readers and writers into one type. Also, separating reader and writer types removes the need to check the CanWrite property—you know that you can write because you've got a TextWriter.

TextReader offers several ways to read data. The simplest is the zero-argument overload of Read, which returns an int. This will return −1 if you've reached the end of the input, and will otherwise return a character value. (You'll need to cast it to a char once you've verified that it's nonnegative.) Alternatively, there are two methods that look similar to the Stream class's Read method, as Example 15-4 shows.

Example 15-4. TextReader chunk reading methods

```
public virtual int Read(char[] buffer, int index, int count) { ... }
public virtual int ReadBlock(char[] buffer, int index, int count) { ... }
```

Just like Stream.Read, these take an array, as well as an index into that array and a count, and will attempt to read the number of values specified. The most obvious difference from Stream is that these use char instead of byte. But what's the difference between Read and ReadBlock? Well, ReadBlock solves the same problem that I had to solve manually for Stream in Example 15-2: whereas Read may return fewer characters than you asked for, ReadBlock will not return until either as many characters as you asked for are available or it reaches the end of the content.

One of the challenges of handling text input is dealing with the various conventions for line endings, and TextReader can insulate you from that. Its ReadLine method reads an entire line of input and returns it as a string. This string will not include the end-of-line character or characters.

TextReader does not presume one particular end-of-line convention. It accepts either a carriage return (character value 13, which we write as \r in string literals) or a line feed (10, or \n). And if both characters appear adjacently, the character pair is treated as being a single end of line, despite being two characters. This processing happens only when you use either ReadLine or ReadLineA sync. If you work directly at the character level by using Read or ReadBlock, you will see the end-of-line characters exactly as they are.

TextReader also offers ReadToEnd, which reads the input in its entirety and returns it as a single string. And finally, there's Peek, which does the same thing as the single-argument Read method, except it does not change the state of the reader. It lets you look at the next character without consuming it, so the next time you call either Peek or Read, it will return the same character again.

As for TextWriter, it offers two overloaded methods for writing: Write and Write Line. Each of these offers overloads for all of the built-in value types (bool, int, float, etc.). Functionally, the class could have got away with a single overload that takes an object, because that can just call ToString on its argument, but these specialized overloads make it possible to avoid boxing the argument. TextWriter also offers a Flush method for much the same reason that Stream does.

By default, a TextWriter will use the default end of line sequence for the OS you are running on. On Windows this is the \r\n sequence (13, then 10). On Linux you will just get a single \n at each line end. You can change this by setting the writer's New Line property.

Both these abstract classes implement IDisposable because some of the concrete-derived text reader and writer types are wrappers around either unmanaged resources or other disposable resources.

As with Stream, these classes offer asynchronous versions of their methods. Unlike with Stream, this was a fairly recent addition, so they support only the task-based pattern described in Chapter 16, which can be consumed with the await keyword described in Chapter 17.

Concrete Reader and Writer Types

As with Stream, various APIs in .NET will present you with TextReader and Text Writer objects. For example, the Console class defines In and Out properties that provide textual access to the process's input and output streams. You've not seen these before, but we have been using them implicitly—the Console.WriteLine method overloads are all just wrappers that call Out.WriteLine for you. Likewise, the

Console class's Read and ReadLine methods simply forward to In.Read and In.Read Line. There's also Error, another TextWriter for writing to the standard error output stream. However, there are some concrete classes that derive from TextReader or TextWriter that you might want to instantiate directly.

StreamReader and StreamWriter

Perhaps the most useful concrete text reader and writer types are StreamReader and StreamWriter, which wrap a Stream object. You can pass a Stream as a constructor argument, or you can just pass a string containing the path of a file, in which case they will automatically construct a FileStream for you and then wrap that. Example 15-5 uses this technique to write some text to a file.

Example 15-5. Writing text to a file with StreamWriter

```
using (var fw = new StreamWriter(@"c:\temp\out.txt"))
{
    fw.WriteLine($"Writing to a file at {DateTime.Now}");
}
```

There are various constructor overloads offering more fine-grained control. When passing a string in order to use a file with a StreamWriter (as opposed to some Stream you have already obtained), you can optionally pass a bool indicating whether to start from scratch or to append to an existing file if one exists. (A true value enables appending.) If you do not pass this argument, appending is not used, and writing will begin from the start. You can also specify an encoding. By default, StreamWriter will use UTF-8 with no byte order mark (BOM), but you can pass any type derived from the Encoding class, which is described in "Encoding" on page 628.

StreamReader is similar—you can construct it by passing either a Stream or a string containing the path of a file, and you can optionally specify an encoding. However, if you don't specify an encoding, the behavior is subtly different from StreamWriter. Whereas StreamWriter just defaults to UTF-8, StreamReader will attempt to detect the encoding from the stream's content. It looks at the first few bytes, and will look for certain features that are typically a good sign that a particular encoding is in use. If the encoded text begins with a Unicode BOM, this makes it possible to determine with high confidence what the encoding is.

StringReader and StringWriter

The StringReader and StringWriter classes serve a similar purpose to MemoryStream: they are useful when you are working with an API that requires either a TextReader or TextWriter, but you want to work entirely in memory. Whereas MemoryStream presents a Stream API on top of a byte[] array, StringReader wraps a string as a `TextReader`, while `StringWriter` presents a `TextWriter` API on top of a `StringBuilder`.

One of the APIs .NET offers for working with XML, `XmlReader`, requires either a `Stream` or a `TextReader`. Suppose you have XML content in a `string`. If you pass a `string` when creating a new `XmlReader`, it will interpret that as a URI from which to fetch the content, rather than the content itself. The constructor for `StringReader` that takes a string just wraps that string as the content of the reader, and we can pass that to the `XmlReader.Create` overload that requires a `TextReader`, as Example 15-6 shows. (The line that does this is in bold—the code that follows just uses the `XmlReader` to read the content to show that it works as expected.)

Example 15-6. Wrapping a string in a StringReader

```
string xmlContent =
    "<message><text>Hello</text><recipient>world</recipient></message>";
var xmlReader = XmlReader.Create(new StringReader(xmlContent));
while (xmlReader.Read())
{
    if (xmlReader.NodeType == XmlNodeType.Text)
    {
        Console.WriteLine(xmlReader.Value);
    }
}
```

As for `StringWriter`, well, you already saw that in Chapter 1. As you may recall, the very first example in this book is a unit test that verifies that the program under test produces the expected output (the inevitable "Hello, world!" message). The relevant lines are reproduced in Example 15-7.

Example 15-7. Capturing console output in a StringWriter

```
var w = new System.IO.StringWriter();
Console.SetOut(w);
```

Just as Example 15-6 used an API that expects a `TextReader`, Example 15-7 uses one that requires a `TextWriter`. I want to capture everything written to that writer (i.e., all calls to `Console.Write` and `Console.WriteLine`) in memory so my test can look at it. The call to `SetOut` lets us provide the `StringWriter` that is used for console output.

Encoding

As I mentioned earlier, if you're using the `StreamReader` or `StreamWriter`, these need to know which character encoding the underlying stream uses to be able to convert correctly between the bytes in the stream and .NET's char or `string` types. To manage this, the System.Text namespace defines an abstract Encoding class, with various encoding-specific public concrete-derived types, including: ASCIIEncoding, UTF7Encoding, UTF8Encoding, UTF32Encoding, and UnicodeEncoding.

Most of those type names are self-explanatory, because they are named after the standard character encodings they represent, such as ASCII or UTF-8. The one that requires a little more explanation is UnicodeEncoding—after all, UTF-7, UTF-8, and UTF-32 are all Unicode encodings, so what's this other one for? When Windows introduced support for Unicode back in the first version of Windows NT, it adopted a slightly unfortunate convention: in documentation and various API names, the term *Unicode* was used to refer to a 2-byte little-endian[3] character encoding, which is just one of many possible encoding schemes, all of which could correctly be described as being "Unicode" of one form or another.

The UnicodeEncoding class is named to be consistent with this historical convention, although even then it's still a bit confusing. The encoding referred to as "Unicode" in Win32 APIs is effectively UTF-16LE, but the UnicodeEncoding class is also capable of supporting the big-endian UTF-16BE.

The base Encoding class defines static properties that return instances of all the encoding types I've mentioned, so if you need an object representing a particular encoding, you would normally just write Encoding.ASCII or Encoding.UTF8, etc., instead of constructing a new object. There are two properties of type UnicodeEncod ing: the Unicode property returns one configured for UTF-16LE, and BigEndianUni code returns one for UTF-16BE.

For the various Unicode encodings, these properties will return encoding objects that will tell StreamWriter to generate a BOM at the start of the output. The main purpose of the BOM is to enable software that reads encoded text to detect automatically whether the encoding is big- or little-endian. (You can also use it to recognize UTF-8, because that encodes the BOM differently than other encodings.) If you know that you will be using an endian-specific encoding (e.g., UTF-16LE), the BOM is unnecessary, because you already know the order, but the Unicode specification defines adaptable formats in which the encoded bytes can advertise the order in use by starting with a BOM, a character with Unicode code point U+FEFF. The 16-bit version of this encoding is just called UTF-16, and you can tell whether any particular set of UTF-16-encoded bytes is big- or little-endian by seeing whether it begins with 0xFE, 0xFF or 0xFF, 0xFE.

---

3 Just in case you've not come across the term, in *little-endian* representations, multibyte values start with the lower-order bytes, so the value 0x1234 in 16-bit little-endian would be 0x34, 0x12, whereas the big-endian version would be 0x12, 0x34. Little-endian looks reversed, but it's the native format for Intel's processors.

Although Unicode defines encoding schemes that allow the endianness to be detected, it is not possible to create an Encoding object that works that way—it will always have a specific endianness. So, although an Encoding specifies whether a BOM should be written when writing data, this does not influence the behavior when reading data—it will always presume the endianness specified when the Encoding was constructed. This means that the Encoding.UTF32 property is arguably misnamed—it always interprets data as little-endian even though the Unicode specification allows UTF-32 to use either big- or little-endian. Encoding.UTF32 is really UTF-32LE.

As mentioned earlier, if you do not specify an encoding when creating a Stream Writer, it defaults to UTF-8 with no BOM, which is different from Encoding.UTF8— that will generate a BOM. And recall that StreamReader is more interesting: if you do not specify an encoding, it will attempt to detect the encoding. So .NET is able to handle automatic detection of byte ordering as required by the Unicode specification for UTF-16 and UTF-32, it is just that the way to do it is *not* to specify any particular encoding when constructing a StreamReader. It will look for a BOM, and if it finds one present, it will use a suitable Unicode encoding; otherwise, it presumes UTF-8 encoding.

UTF-8 is a popular encoding. If your main language is English, it's a particularly convenient representation, because if you happen to use only the characters available in ASCII, each character will occupy a single byte, and the encoded text will have the exact same byte values as it would with ASCII encoding. But unlike ASCII, you're not limited to a 7-bit character set. All Unicode code points are available; you just have to use multibyte representations for anything outside of the ASCII range. However, although it's very widely used, UTF-8 is not the only popular 8-bit encoding.

Code page encodings

Windows, like DOS before it, has long supported 8-bit encodings that extend ASCII. ASCII is a 7-bit encoding, meaning that with 8-bit bytes you have 128 "spare" values to use for other characters. This is nowhere near enough to cover every character for every locale, but within a particular country, it's often enough to get by (although not always—many far Eastern countries need more than 8 bits per character). But each country tends to want a different set of non-ASCII characters, depending on which accented characters are popular in that locale, and whether a non-Roman alphabet is required. So various *code pages* exist for different locales. For example, code page 1253 uses values in the range 193–254 to define characters from the Greek alphabet (filling the remaining non-ASCII values with useful characters such as non-US currency symbols). Code page 1255 defines Hebrew characters instead, while 1256 defines Arabic characters in the upper range (and there is some common ground for these particular code pages, such as using 128 for the euro symbol, €, and 163 for the pound sign, £).

One of the most commonly encountered code pages is 1252, because that's Windows' default for English-speaking locales. This does not define a non-Roman alphabet; instead it uses the upper character range for useful symbols, and for various accented versions of the Roman alphabet that enable a wide range of Western European languages to be adequately represented.

You can create an encoding for a code page by calling the `Encoding.GetEncoding` method, passing in the code page number. (The concrete type of the object you get back is often not one of those I listed earlier. This method may return nonpublic types that derive from `Encoding`.) Example 15-8 uses this to write text containing a pound sign to a file using code page 1252.

Example 15-8. Writing with the Windows 1252 code page

```
using (var sw = new StreamWriter("Text.txt", false,
                                 Encoding.GetEncoding(1252)))
{
    sw.Write("£100");
}
```

This will encode the £ symbol as a single byte with the value 163. With the default UTF-8 encoding, it would have been encoded as two bytes, with values of 194 and 163, respectively.

Using encodings directly

`TextReader` and `TextWriter` are not the only way to use encodings. Objects representing encodings (such as `Encoding.UTF8`) define various members. The `GetBytes` method converts a `string` directly to a `byte[]` array, for example, and the `GetString` method converts back again.

You can also discover how much data these conversions will produce. `GetByteCount` tells you how large an array `GetBytes` would produce for a given string, while `GetCharCount` tells you how many characters decoding a particular array would generate. You can also find an upper limit for how much space will be required without knowing the exact text with `GetMaxByteCount`. Instead of a `string`, this takes a number, which it interprets as a string length; since .NET strings use UTF-16, this means that this API answers the question "If I have this many UTF-16 code units, what's the largest number of code units that might be required to represent the same text in the target encoding?" This can produce a significant overestimate for variable-length encodings. For example, with UTF-8 `GetMaxByteCount` multiplies the length of the input string by three[4] and adds an extra 3 bytes to deal with an edge case that can occur with surrogate characters. It produces a correct description of the worst possible case, but text containing any characters that don't require 3 bytes in UTF-8 (i.e., any text in English or any other languages that use the Latin alphabet, and also any text using Greek, Cyrillic, Hebrew, or Arabic writing systems, for example) will require significantly less space than `GetMaxByteCount` predicts.

Some encodings can provide a *preamble*, a distinctive sequence of bytes that, if found at the start of some encoded text, indicate that you are likely to be looking at something using that encoding. This can be useful if you are trying to detect which encoding is in use when you don't already know. The various Unicode encodings all return their encoding of the BOM as the preamble, which you can retrieve with the `Get Preamble` method.

The `Encoding` class defines instance properties offering information about the encoding. `EncodingName` returns a human-readable name for the encoding, but there are two more names available. The `WebName` property returns the standard name for the encoding registered with the Internet Assigned Numbers Authority (IANA), which manages standard names and numbers for things on the internet such as MIME types. Some protocols, such as HTTP, sometimes put encoding names into headers, and this is the text you should use in that situation. The other two names, `BodyName` and `HeaderName`, are somewhat more obscure, and are used only for internet email—there are different conventions for how certain encodings are represented in the body and headers of email.

Files and Directories

The abstractions I've shown so far in this chapter are very general purpose in nature —you can write code that uses a `Stream` without needing to have any idea where the bytes it contains come from or are going to, and likewise, `TextReader` and `Text Writer` do not demand any particular origin or destination for their data. This is useful because it makes it possible to write code that can be applied in a variety of scenarios. For example, the stream-based `GZipStream` can compress or decompress data from a file, over a network connection, or from any other stream. However, there are occasions where you know you will be dealing with files and want access to file-specific features. This section describes the classes for working with files and the filesystem.

---

4 Some Unicode characters can take up to 4 bytes in UTF-8, so multiplying by three might seem like it could underestimate. However, all such characters require two bytes in UTF-16. Any single char in .NET will never require more than 3 bytes in UTF-8.

FileStream Class

The FileStream class derives from Stream and represents a file from the filesystem. I've used it a few times in passing already. It adds relatively few members to those provided by the base class. The Lock and Unlock methods provide a way of acquiring exclusive access to specific byte ranges when using a single file from multiple processes. The Name property tells you the filename.

FileStream offers a great deal of control in its constructors—disregarding the ones marked with the [Obsolete] attribute,[5] there are no fewer than nine constructor overloads. The ways of creating a FileStream fall into two groups: ones where you already have an OS file handle, and ones where you don't. If you already have a handle from somewhere, you are required to tell the FileStream whether that handle offers read, write, or read/write access to the file, which you do by passing a value from the FileAccess enumeration. The other overloads optionally let you indicate the buffer size you'd like to use when reading or writing, and a flag indicating whether the handle was opened for overlapped I/O, a Win32 mechanism for supporting asynchronous operation. (The constructors that don't take that flag assume that you did not request overlapped I/O when creating the file handle.)

It is more common to use the other constructors, in which the FileStream uses OS APIs to create the file handle on your behalf. You can provide varying levels of detail on how you'd like this done. At a minimum, you must specify the file's path, and a value from the FileMode enumeration. Table 15-1 shows the values this enumeration defines and describes what the FileStream constructor will do for each value in situations where the named file already exists, and where it does not.

Table 15-1. FileMode enumeration

Value	Behavior if file exists	Behavior if file does not exist
CreateNew	Throws IOException	Creates new file
Create	Replaces existing file	Creates new file
Open	Opens existing file	Throws FileNotFoundException
OpenOrCreate	Opens existing file	Creates new file
Truncate	Replaces existing file	Throws FileNotFoundException
Append	Opens existing file, setting Position to end of file	Creates new file

---

5 Four overloads became obsolete when .NET 2.0 introduced a new way of representing OS handles. The overloads that accept an IntPtr were deprecated at that point, and new ones taking a SafeFileHandle replaced them.

You can optionally specify a FileAccess too. If you do not, the FileStream will use FileAccess.ReadWrite unless you've chosen a FileMode of Append. Files opened in append mode can only be written to, so FileStream chooses Write in that case. (If you pass an explicit FileAccess asking for anything other than Write when opening in Append mode, the constructor throws an ArgumentException.)

By the way, as I describe each additional constructor argument in this section, the relevant overload will take all of the previously described ones too (with the exception of the useAsync argument, which appears in just one constructor). As Example 15-9 shows, most of these constructors looks just like the one before it, with one additional argument.

Example 15-9. FileStream constructors taking a path

```
public FileStream(string path, FileMode mode)
public FileStream(string path, FileMode mode, FileAccess access)
public FileStream(string path, FileMode mode, FileAccess access,
                  FileShare share)
public FileStream(string path, FileMode mode, FileAccess access,
                  FileShare share, int bufferSize);
public FileStream(string path, FileMode mode, FileAccess access,
                  FileShare share, int bufferSize, bool useAsync);
public FileStream(string path, FileMode mode, FileAccess access,
                  FileShare share, int bufferSize, FileOptions options);
```

If you pass an argument of type FileShare, you can specify whether you want exclusive access to the file, or whether you are prepared to allow other processes (or other code in your process) to open the file simultaneously. By default, you get read sharing, meaning that multiple simultaneous readers are allowed, but if anything opens the file with write or read/write file access, no other handles may be open at the same time. More strangely, you can enable write sharing, in which any number of handles with write access may be active simultaneously, but no readers will be allowed until all other handles are released. There's a ReadWrite value, which allows simultaneous reading and writing. You can also pass Delete, indicating that you don't mind if someone else tries to delete the file while you have it open. Obviously, you'll get I/O exceptions if you try to use a file after it has been deleted, so you'd need to be prepared for that, but this can sometimes be worth the effort; otherwise, attempts to delete a file will be blocked while you have it open.

All parties must agree on sharing to be able to open multiple handles. If program A uses FileShare.ReadWrite to open a file, and program B then passes File Share.None while attempting to open the file for reading and writing, program B will get an exception because although A was ready to share, B was not, so B's requirements cannot be met. If program B had managed to open the file first, it would have succeeded, and A's request would have failed.

Unix has fewer comprehensive file-locking mechanisms than Windows, so these locking semantics will often be mapped to something simpler in those environments. Also, file locks are advisory in Unix, meaning processes can simply ignore them if they want to.

The next piece of information we can pass is the buffer size. This controls the size of block that the FileStream will use when reading from and writing to disk. It defaults to 4,096 bytes. In most scenarios, this value works just fine, but if you are processing very high volumes of data from disk, a large buffer size might provide better throughput. However, as with all performance matters, you should measure the effect of such a change to see if it is worthwhile—in some cases, you will not see any difference in data throughput, and will simply use a bit more memory than necessary.

The useAsync flag lets you determine whether the file handle is opened in a way that is optimized for large asynchronous reads and writes. (On Windows, this opens the file for *overlapped I/O*, a Win32 feature supporting asynchronous operations.) If you are reading data in relatively large chunks, and you use the stream's asynchronous APIs, you will typically get better performance by setting this flag. However, if you read data a few bytes at a time, this mode actually increases overhead. If the code accessing the file is particularly performance sensitive, it will be worth trying both settings to see which works better for your workload.

The next argument you can add is of type FileOptions. If you're paying close attention, you'll notice in Example 15-9 that each of the overloads we've looked at up to now adds one more argument, but with this one, the FileOptions argument *replaces* the bool useAsync argument. That's because one of the options you can specify with FileOptions is asynchronous access. FileOptions is a flags enumeration, so you can specify a combination of any of the flags it offers, which are described in Table 15-2.

Table 15-2. FileOptions flags

Flag	Meaning
WriteThrough	Disables OS write buffering so data goes straight to disk when you flush the stream.
Asynchronous	Specifies the use of asynchronous I/O.
RandomAccess	Hints to filesystem cache that you will be seeking, not reading or writing data in order.
SequentialScan	Hints to filesystem cache that you will be reading or writing data in order.
DeleteOnClose	Tells FileStream to delete the file when you call Dispose.
Encrypted	Encrypts the file so that its contents cannot be read by other users.

Be wary of the WriteThrough flag. Although it works as advertised, it might not have the desired effect, because some hard drives defer writes to improve performance. (Many hard drives have their own RAM, enabling them to receive data from the computer very quickly, and to report write operations as having completed before really storing the data.) The `WriteThrough` flag will ensure that when you dispose or flush the stream, all the data you've written will have been delivered to the drive, but the drive will not necessarily have written that data persistently, so you could still lose the data if the power fails. The exact behavior will depend on how you have told the OS to configure the drive.

While `FileStream` gives you control over the contents of the file, some operations you might wish to perform on files are either cumbersome or not supported at all with `FileStream`. For example, you can copy a file with this class, but it's not as straightforward as it could be, and `FileStream` does not offer any way to delete a file. So the .NET class library includes a separate class for these kinds of operations.

File Class

The static `File` class provides methods for performing various operations on files. The `Delete` method removes the named file from the filesystem. The `Move` method can either move or just rename a file. There are methods for retrieving information and attributes that the filesystem stores about each file, such as `GetCreationTime`, `GetLastAccessTime`, `GetLastWriteTime`,[6] and `GetAttributes`. (The last of those returns a `FileAttributes` value, which is a flags enumeration type telling you whether the file is read only, a hidden file, a system file, and so on.)

The `Encrypt` method overlaps with `FileStream` to some extent—as you saw earlier, you can request that a file be stored with encryption when you create it. However, `Encrypt` is able to work with a file that has already been created without encryption —it effectively encrypts it in situ. (This is only supported on Windows, and only on drives where the filesystem supports it. It will throw `PlatformNotSupportedExcep tion` on other operating systems, and `NotSupportedException` on Windows if encryption is not available for the specified file. This has the same effect as enabling encryption through a file's Properties window in Windows File Explorer.) You can also turn an encrypted file back into an unencrypted one by calling `Decrypt`.

---

6 These all return a `DateTime` that is relative to the computer's current time zone. Each of these methods has an equivalent that returns the time relative to time zone zero (e.g., `GetCreationTimeUtc`).

It is not necessary to call Decrypt before reading an encrypted file. When logged in under the same user account that encrypted a file, you can read its contents in the usual way—encrypted files look just like normal ones because Windows automatically decrypts the contents as you read from them. The purpose of this particular encryption mechanism is that if some other user manages to obtain access to the file (e.g., if it's on an external drive that gets stolen), the content will appear to be random junk. Decrypt removes this encryption, meaning that anyone who can access the file will be able to look at its contents.

The other methods provided by File all just offer slightly more convenient ways of doing things you could have done by hand with FileStream. The Copy method makes a copy of a file, and while you could do that with the CopyTo method on File Stream, Copy takes care of some awkward details. For example, it ensures that the target file carries over attributes such as whether it's read-only and whether encryption is enabled.

The Exists method lets you discover whether a file exists before you attempt to open it. You don't strictly need this, because FileStream will throw a FileNotFound exception if you attempt to open a nonexistent file, but Exists lets you avoid an exception. That might be useful if you expect to need to check for a file very frequently—exceptions are comparatively expensive. However, you should be wary of this method; just because Exists returns true, that's no guarantee that you won't get a FileNotFound exception. It's always possible that in between your checking for a file's existence and attempting to open it, another process might delete the file. Alternatively, the file might be on a network share, and you might lose network connectivity. So you should always be prepared for exceptions with file access, even if you've attempted to avoid provoking them.

File offers many helper methods to simplify the opening or creating of files. The Create method simply constructs a FileStream for you, passing in suitable File Mode, FileAccess, and FileShare values. Example 15-10 shows how to use it, and also shows what the equivalent code would look like without using the Create helper. The Create method provides overloads letting you specify the buffer size, FileOp tions, and FileSecurity, but these still provide the other arguments for you.

Example 15-10. File.Create versus new FileStream

```
using (FileStream fs = File.Create("foo.bar"))
{
    ...
}
```

```
// Equivalent code without using File class
using (var fs = new FileStream("foo.bar", FileMode.Create,
                                FileAccess.ReadWrite, FileShare.None))
{
    ...
}
```

The File class's OpenRead and OpenWrite methods provide similar decluttering for when you want to open an existing file for reading, or to open or create a file for writing. There's also an Open method that requires you to pass a FileMode. This is of more marginal utility—it's very similar to the FileStream constructor overload that also takes just a path and a mode, automatically supplying suitable other settings. The somewhat arbitrary difference is that while the FileStream constructor defaults to FileShare.Read, the File.Open method defaults to FileShare.None.

File also offers several text-oriented helpers. The simplest method, OpenText, opens a file for text reading, and is of limited value because it does exactly the same thing as the StreamReader constructor that takes a single string argument. The only reason to use this is if you happen to prefer how it makes your code look—if your code makes heavy use of the File helpers, you might choose to use this for idiomatic consistency.

Several of the methods exposed by File are text oriented. These enable us to improve on code of the kind shown in Example 15-11. This appends a line of text to a logfile.

Example 15-11. Appending to a file with StreamWriter

```
static void Log(string message)
{
    using (var sw = new StreamWriter(@"c:\temp\log.txt", true))
    {
        sw.WriteLine(message);
    }
}
```

One issue with this is that it's not all that easy to see at a glance how the Stream Writer is being opened—what does that true argument mean? As it happens, that tells the StreamWriter that we want it to create the underlying FileStream in append mode. Example 15-12 has the same effect—it uses File.AppendText, which just calls the exact same FileStream constructor for us. But while I was somewhat dismissive of File.OpenText earlier for offering similarly marginal value, I think File.Append Text did once provide a genuinely useful improvement in readability in a way that File.OpenText does not. It's much easier to see that Example 15-12 will append text to a file than it is with Example 15-11. However, since support for named arguments was added to C#, AppendText now looks less useful—we could just name the append argument in Example 15-11 for a similar improvement in readability.

Example 15-12. Creating an appending StreamWriter with File.AppendText

```
static void Log(string message)
{
    using (StreamWriter sw = File.AppendText(@"c:\temp\log.txt"))
    {
        sw.WriteLine(message);
    }
}
```

If you're only going to append some text to a file and immediately close it, there's an even easier way. As Example 15-13 shows, we can simplify things further with the AppendAllText helper.

Example 15-13. Appending a single string to a file

```
static void Log(string message)
{
    File.AppendAllText(@"c:\temp\log.txt", message);
}
```

Be careful, though. This does not do quite the same thing as Example 15-12. That example used WriteLine to append the text, but Example 15-13 is equivalent to using just Write. So, if you were to call the Log method in Example 15-13 multiple times, you'd end up with one long line in your output file, unless the strings you were using happened to contain end-of-line characters. If you want to work with lines, there's an AppendAllLines method that takes a collection of strings, and appends each as a new line to the end of a file. Example 15-14 uses this to append a full line with each call.

Example 15-14. Appending a single line to a file

```
static void Log(string message)
{
    File.AppendAllLines(@"c:\temp\log.txt", new[] { message });
}
```

Since AppendAllLines accepts an IEnumerable<string>, you can use it to append any number of lines. But it's perfectly happy to append just one if that's what you want. File also defines WriteAllText and WriteAllLines methods, which work in a very similar way, but if there is already a file at the specified path, these will replace it instead of appending to it.

There are also some related text-oriented methods for reading the contents of files. ReadAllText performs the equivalent of constructing a StreamReader and then calling its ReadToEnd method—it returns the entire content of the file as a single string. ReadAllBytes fetches the whole file into a byte[] array. ReadAllLines reads the whole file as a `string[]` array, with one element for each line in the file. `ReadLines` is superficially very similar. It provides access to the whole file as an `IEnumerable<string>` with one item for each line, but the difference is that it works lazily—unlike all the other methods I've described in this paragraph, it does not read the entire file into memory up front, so `ReadLines` would be a better choice for very large files. It not only consumes less memory, but it also enables your code to get started more quickly—you can begin to process data as soon as the first line can be read from disk, whereas none of the other methods return until they have read the whole file.

Directory Class

Just as `File` is a static class offering methods for performing operations with files, `Directory` is a static class offering methods for performing operations with directories. Some of the methods are very similar to those offered by `File`—there are methods to get and set the creation time, last access time, and last write time, for example, and we also get `Move`, `Exists`, and `Delete` methods. Unlike `File`, `Directory.Delete` has two overloads. One takes just a path, and works only if the directory is empty. The other takes a `bool` that, if `true`, will delete everything in the folder, recursively deleting any nested folders and the files they contain. Use that one carefully.

Of course, there are also directory-specific methods. `GetFiles` takes a directory path and returns a `string[]` array containing the full path of each file in that directory. There's an overload that lets you specify a pattern by which to filter the results, and a third overload that takes a pattern and also a flag that lets you request recursive searching of all subfolders. Example 15-15 uses that to find all files with a *.jpg* extension in my *Pictures* folder. (Unless you're also called Ian, you'd need to change that path to match your account name for this to work on your computer, obviously.) Then again, in a real application, you should get this path using the technique shown in "Known Folders" on page 644.

Example 15-15. Recursively searching for files of a particular type

```
foreach (string file in Directory.GetFiles(@"c:\users\ian\Pictures",
                                           "*.jpg",
                                           SearchOption.AllDirectories))
{
    Console.WriteLine(file);
}
```

There is a similar `GetDirectories` method, offering the same three overloads, which returns the directories inside the specified directory instead of returning files. And there's a `GetFileSystemEntries` method, again with the same three overloads, which returns both files and folders.

There are also methods called `EnumerateFiles`, `EnumerateDirectories`, and `EnumerateFileSystemEntries`, which do exactly the same thing as the three `GetXxx` methods, but they return `IEnumerable<string>`. This is a lazy enumeration, so you can start processing results immediately instead of waiting for all the results as one big array.

The `Directory` class offers methods relating to the process's current directory (i.e., the one used any time you call a file-based API without specifying the full path). `Get CurrentDirectory` returns the path, and `SetCurrentDirectory` sets it.

You can create new directories too. The `CreateDirectory` method takes a path and will attempt to create as many directories as are necessary to ensure that the path exists. So, if you pass *C:\new\dir\here*, and there is no *C:\new* directory, it will create three new directories: first it will create *C:\new*, then *C:\new\dir*, and then *C:\new\dir \here*. If the folder you ask for already exists, it doesn't treat that as an error, it just returns without doing anything.

The `GetDirectoryRoot` strips a directory path down to the drive name or other root, such as a network share name. For example, on Windows if you pass this *C:\temp \logs*, it will return *C:*; and if you pass *\\someserver\myshare\dir\test*, it will return *\\someserver\myshare*. This sort of string slicing, in which you split a path into its component parts, is a sufficiently common requirement that there's a class dedicated to various operations of this kind.

Path Class

The static `Path` class provides useful utilities for strings containing filenames. Some extract pieces from a file path, such as the containing folder name or the file extension. Some combine strings to produce new file paths. Most of these methods just perform specialized string processing and do not require the files or directories to which the paths refer to exist. However, there are a few that go beyond string manipulation. For example, `Path.GetFullPath` will take the current directory into account if you do not pass an absolute path as the argument. But only the methods that need to make use of real locations will do so.

The `Path.Combine` method deals with the fiddly issues around combining folder and filenames. If you have a folder name, *C:\temp*, and a filename, *log.txt*, passing both to `Path.Combine` returns *C:\temp\log.txt*. And it will also work if you pass *C:\temp* as the first argument, so one of the issues it deals with is working out whether it needs to supply an extra \ character. If the second path is absolute, it detects this and simply ignores the first path, so if you pass *C:\temp* and *C:\logs\log.txt*, the result will be *C: \logs\log.txt*. Although these may seem like trivial matters, it's surprisingly easy to get the file path combination wrong if you try to do it yourself by concatenating strings, so you should always avoid the temptation to do that and just use `Path.Combine`.

.NET Core has platform-specific behavior when it comes to paths. On Unix-like systems, only the / character is used as a directory separator, so the various methods in `Path` that expect paths to contain directories will treat only / as a separator on these systems. Windows uses a \ as a separator, although it is common for / to be tolerated as a substitute, and `Path` follows suit. So `Path.Combine("/x/y", "/z.txt")` will produce the same results on Windows and Linux, but `Path.Combine(@"\x\y", @"\z.txt")` will not. Also, on Windows, if a path begins with a drive letter, it is an absolute path, but Unix does not recognize drive letters. The examples in the preceding paragraph will produce strange-looking results on Linux or macOS because on those systems, all the paths will be treated as relative paths. If you remove the drive letters and replace \ with /, the results will be as you'd expect.

Given a file path, the `GetDirectoryName` method removes the filename part and just returns the directory. This method provides a good illustration of why you need to remember that most of the `Path` class's members do not look at the filesystem. If you didn't take that into account, you might expect that if you pass `GetDirectoryName` just the name of a folder (e.g., *C:\Program Files*), it would detect that this is a folder and return the same string, but in fact it will return just *C:*. The name *Program Files* is a perfectly good name for either a file or a directory, and since `GetDirectoryName` does not inspect the disk, and it expects to be passed a path that includes a filename, it will conclude in this case that it is a file. This method effectively looks for the final / or \ character and returns everything before that. (So, if you pass a folder name with a trailing \, such as *C:\Program Files*, it will return *C:\Program Files*. Then again, the whole point of this API is to remove the filename from a file's full path. If you already have a string with just a folder name, you should not call this API.)

The `GetFileName` method returns just the filename (including the extension, if any). Like `GetDirectoryName`, it also looks for the last directory separator character, but it returns the text that comes after it rather than before it. Again, it does not look at the filesystem—this works purely through string manipulation (although as with all of these operations, it takes into account the local system's rules for what counts as a directory separator, or an absolute path). `GetFileNameWithoutExtension` is similar, but if an extension is present (e.g., *.txt* or *.jpg*), it removes that from the end of the name. Conversely, `GetExtension` returns the extension and nothing else.

If you need to create temporary files to perform some work, `Path` provides three useful methods. `GetRandomFileName` uses a random-number generator to create a name you can use for either a random file or folder. The random number is cryptographically strong, which provides two useful properties: the name will be unique and hard to guess. (Certain kinds of attacks on a system's security can become possible if an attacker can predict the name or location of temporary files.) This method does not actually create anything on the filesystem—it just hands back a suitable name. `Get TempFileName`, on the other hand, will create a file in the location the OS provides for temporary files. This file will be empty, and the method returns you its path as a string. You can then open the file and modify it. (This does not guarantee to use cryptography to pick a truly random name, so you should not depend on this sort of file's location being unguessable. It will be unique, but that is all.) You should delete any file created by `GetTempFileName` once you have finished with it. Finally, `GetTemp Path` returns the path of the folder that `GetTempFileName` would use; this doesn't create anything, but you could use this in conjunction with a name returned by `GetRandomFileName` (combined with `Path.Combine`) to pick a location in which to create your own temporary file.

FileInfo, DirectoryInfo, and FileSystemInfo

Although the `File` and `Folder` classes provide you with access to information—such as a file's creation time, and whether it is a system file or a read-only file—those classes have an issue if you need access to multiple pieces of information. It's not very efficient to collect each bit of data with a separate call, because the information can be fetched from the underlying OS with fewer steps. And it can sometimes be easier to pass around a single object containing all the data you need instead of finding somewhere to put lots of separate items. So the `System.IO` namespace defines `FileInfo` and `DirectoryInfo` classes that contain the information about a file or directory. Since there's a certain amount of common ground, these types both derive from a base class, `FileSystemInfo`.

To construct instances of these classes, you pass the path of the file or folder you want, as Example 15-16 shows. By the way, if some time later you think the file may have been changed by some other program, and you want to update the information a `FileInfo` or `DirectoryInfo` returns, you can call `Refresh`, and it will reload information from the filesystem.

Example 15-16. Displaying information about a file with FileInfo

```
var fi = new FileInfo(@"c:\temp\log.txt");
Console.WriteLine(
    $"{fi.FullName} ({fi.Length} bytes) last modified on {fi.LastWriteTime}");
```

As well as providing properties corresponding to the various `File` and `Directory` methods that fetch information (`CreationTime`, `Attributes`, etc.), these information classes provide instance methods that correspond to many of the static methods of `File` and `Directory`. For example, if you have a `FileInfo`, it provides `Delete`, `Encrypt`, and `Decrypt`—methods that work just like their `File` namesakes, except you don't need to pass a path argument. There is also a counterpart of Move, although with a different name, MoveTo.

FileInfo also provides equivalents to the various helper methods for opening the file with a Stream or a FileStream, such as AppendText, OpenRead, and OpenText. Perhaps more surprisingly, Create and CreateText are also available. It turns out that you can construct a FileInfo for a file that does not exist yet, and then create it with these helpers. It doesn't attempt to populate any of the properties that describe the file until the first time you try to read them, so it will defer throwing a FileNotFoundException until that point, in case you were creating the FileInfo in order to create a new file.

As you'd expect, DirectoryInfo also offers instance methods that correspond to the various static helper methods defined by Directory.

Known Folders

Desktop applications sometimes need to use specific folders. For example, an application's settings will typically be stored in a certain folder under the user's profile. There's a separate folder for system-wide application settings. On Windows these are typically in the user's *AppData* folder and *C:\ProgramData*, respectively. Windows also defines standard places for pictures, videos, music, and documents, and there are also folders representing special shell features, such as the desktop and the user's "favorites."

Although these folders are often in much the same place from one system to another, you should never presume that they will be where you expect. (So you should never do what Example 15-15 does in real code.) Many of these folders have different names in localized versions of Windows. And even within a particular language, there's no guarantee that these folders will be in the usual place—it's possible to move some of them, and the locations have not remained fixed across different versions of Windows.

So, if you need access to a particular standard folder, you should use the Environment class's GetFolderPath method, as shown in Example 15-17. This takes a member from the nested Environment.SpecialFolder enum type, which defines values for all of the well-known folder types available in Windows.

Example 15-17. Discovering where to store settings

```
string appSettingsRoot =
    Environment.GetFolderPath(Environment.SpecialFolder.ApplicationData);
string myAppSettingsFolder =
    Path.Combine(appSettingsRoot, @"Endjin\FrobnicatorPro");
```

On non-Windows systems, `GetFolderPath` returns an empty string for most of these enumeration's entries, because there is no local equivalent. However, a few work, such as `MyDocuments`, `CommonAp plicationData`, and `UserProfile`.

The `ApplicationData` folder is in the roaming section of the user's profile. Information that does not need to be copied across all the machines a person uses (e.g., a cache that could be reconstructed if necessary) should go in the local section, which you can get with the `LocalApplicationData` enum entry.

Serialization

The `Stream`, `TextReader`, and `TextWriter` types provide the ability to read and write data in files, networks, or anything else stream-like that provides a suitable concrete class. But these abstractions support only byte or text data. Suppose you have an object with several properties of various types, including some numeric types and perhaps also references to other objects, some of which might be collections. What if you wanted to write all the information in that object out to a file or over a network connection, so that an object of the same type and with the same property values could be reconstituted at a later date, or on another computer at the other end of a connection?

You could do this with the abstractions shown in this chapter, but it would require a fair amount of work. You'd have to write code to read each property and write its value out to a `Stream` or `TextWriter`, and you'd need to convert the value to either binary or text. You'd also need to decide on your representation—would you just write values out in a fixed order, or would you come up with a scheme for writing name/value pairs, so that you're not stuck with an inflexible format if you need to add more properties later on? You'd also need to come up with ways to handle collections and references to other objects, and you'd need to decide what to do in the face of circular references—if two objects each refer to one another, naive code could end up getting stuck in an infinite loop.

.NET offers several solutions to this problem, each making varying trade-offs between the complexity of the scenarios they are able to support, how well they deal with versioning, and how suitable they are for interoperating with other platforms. These techniques all fall under the broad name of *serialization* (because they involve writing an object's state into some form that stores data sequentially—serially—such as a `Stream`). Many different mechanisms have been introduced over the years in .NET, so I won't cover all of them. I'll just present the ones that best represent particular approaches to the problem.

BinaryReader, BinaryWriter, and BinaryPrimitives

Although they are not strictly forms of serialization, no discussion of this area is complete without covering the `BinaryReader` and `BinaryWriter` classes, because they solve a fundamental problem that any attempt to serialize and deserialize objects must deal with: they can convert the CLR's intrinsic types to and from streams of bytes. `BinaryPrimitives` does the same thing, but it is able to work with `Span<byte>` and related types, which are discussed in Chapter 18.

`BinaryWriter` is a wrapper around a writable `Stream`. It provides a `Write` method that has overloads for all of the intrinsic types except for `object`. So it can take a value of any of the numeric types, or the `string`, `char`, or `bool` types, and it writes a binary representation of that value into a `Stream`. It can also write arrays of type `byte` or `char`.

`BinaryReader` is a wrapper around a readable `Stream`, and it provides various methods for reading data, each corresponding to the overloads of `Write` provided by `BinaryWriter`. For example, you have `ReadDouble`, `ReadInt32`, and `ReadString`.

To use these types, you would create a `BinaryWriter` when you want to serialize some data, and write out each value you wish to store. When you later want to deserialize that data, you'd wrap a `BinaryReader` around a stream containing the data written with the writer, and call the relevant read methods in the exact same order that you wrote the data out in the first place.

`BinaryPrimitives` works slightly differently. It is designed for code that needs to minimize the number of heap allocations, so it's not a wrapper type—it is a static class offering a wide range of methods, such as `ReadInt32LittleEndian` and `Write` `UInt16BigEndian`. These take `ReadOnlySpan<byte>` and `Span<byte>` arguments, respectively, because it is designed to work directly with data wherever it may lie in memory (not necessarily wrapped in a `Stream`). However, the basic principle is the same: it converts between byte sequences and primitive .NET types. (Also, string handling is rather more complex: there's no `ReadString` method because anything that returns a `string` will create a new string object on the heap, unless there's a fixed set of possible strings that you can preallocate and hand out again and again. See Chapter 18 for details.)

These classes only solve the problem of how to represent various .NET types in binary. You are still left with the task of working out how to represent whole objects, and what to do about more complex kinds of structures such as references between objects.

CLR Serialization

CLR serialization is, as the name suggests, a feature built into the runtime itself—it is not simply a library feature. It was not supported in .NET Core for the first few versions, but Microsoft eventually added it back in a somewhat reduced form to make it easier to migrate applications from the .NET Framework. They discourage its use, but it continues to be popular in certain scenarios. It is fairly widely used in microservice environments for sending exceptions and relatively straightforward data structures across service boundaries. .NET Core's limited support is aimed at these scenarios, so you cannot serialize just any old .NET object.

The most interesting aspect of CLR serialization is that it deals directly with object references. If you serialize, say, a List<SomeType> where multiple entries in the list refer to the same object, CLR serialization will detect this, storing just one copy of that object, and when deserializing, it will recreate that one-object-many-references structure. (Serialization systems based on the very widely used JSON format generally don't do this.)

Types are required to opt into CLR serialization. .NET defines a [Serializable] attribute that must be present before the CLR will serialize your type. But once you've added this, the CLR can take care of all of the details for you. Example 15-18 shows a type with this attribute that I'll use to illustrate serialization in action.

Example 15-18. A serializable type

```
using System;
using System.Collections.Generic;
using System.Linq;

[Serializable]
class Person
{
    public string Name { get; set; }

    public IList<Person> Friends { get; } = new List<Person>();

    public override string ToString() =>
        $"{Name} (friends: {string.Join(", ", Friends.Select(f => f.Name))})";
}
```

Serialization works directly with an object's fields. It uses reflection, which enables it to access all members, whether public or private. In this example class, there are two fields, both hidden and generated by the compiler, for the Friends and Name properties. (List<T> has the [Serializable] attribute, by the way. If it didn't, this example wouldn't work.) As Example 15-19 shows, we can use the BinaryFormatter type (which is in the System.Runtime.Serialization.Formatters.Binary namespace) to serialize an instance of this type to a stream.

Example 15-19. Serializing with the BinaryFormatter

```
var stream = new MemoryStream();
var serializer = new BinaryFormatter();
serializer.Serialize(stream, person);
```

As Example 15-20 shows, the BinaryFormatter type also performs deserialization.

Example 15-20. Deserializing with the BinaryFormatter

```
stream.Seek(0, SeekOrigin.Begin);
var serializer = new BinaryFormatter();
var personCopy = (Person) serializer.Deserialize(stream);
```

If the person variable in Example 15-19 referred to an object whose Friends property returns a collection that contains references to Person objects with Friends properties containing collections that in turn referred back to the same object as person, that would mean we had circular references. The BinaryFormatter correctly detects this, storing just one copy of each object in the stream, and when we deserialize, it would restore any such structure correctly.

So this is pretty powerful—by simply adding a single attribute, I can write out a complete graph of objects. There is a downside: if I change the implementation of any of the types being serialized, I will be in trouble if a new version of my code attempts to deserialize a stream produced by an old version. So this is not a good choice for writing out an application's settings to disk, because those are likely to evolve with each new version. As it happens, you can customize the way serialization works, which does make it possible to support versioning, but at that point, you're back to doing a lot of the work by hand. (It may actually be easier to use BinaryReader and Binary Writer.) Also, it's easy to introduce security problems with this style of serialization: someone who controls a stream that you deserialize essentially has complete control over all the fields of your objects.

Another issue with CLR serialization is that it produces binary streams in a .NET-specific format. If the only code that needs to deal with the stream is running .NET, then that's not a problem, but you might want to produce streams for a broader audience. However, there are other serialization mechanisms than CLR serialization, and these can produce streams that may be easier for other systems to consume.

JSON.NET

The most widely used serialization mechanism used on .NET is, surprisingly, not written by Microsoft, although several Microsoft frameworks make extensive use of it. The framework JSON.NET is an open source project written by James Newton-King, released under the MIT license. You can find it at *http://www.newtonsoft.com/ json* or via NuGet as `Newtonsoft.Json`. As the name suggests, it works with JSON, the JavaScript Object Notation, a wildly popular data interchange format. Its performance, relative ease of use, and comprehensive support of all flavors of .NET have made it the go-to library for JSON serialization.

 At one time, the ASP.NET Core web framework used JSON.NET internally. However, .NET Core 3.0 and .NET Standard 2.1 introduced a new Microsoft-produced JSON library, consisting of various types in the `System.Text.Json` namespace. These use the new memory-efficient techniques described in Chapter 18, making them somewhat less convenient to use, but also more efficient. ASP.NET Core has moved over to this library, partly for speed, but also partly to remove the dependency. (There are several different versions of JSON.NET, and dependency conflicts can arise if a framework depends on one particular version and you want to use a library that depends on a different version.)

JSON.NET supports three ways of working with JSON data. It defines `JsonReader` and `JsonWriter` interfaces, which are stream-like abstractions that present the contents of JSON data as a sequence of elements. These can be useful if you need to process JSON documents that are too large to load into memory as a single object, but more often you will use these types just as a means of getting data into and out of JSON.NET's other mechanisms. In practice, it is typically easier to use `JsonSerial izer` (often used indirectly through the simpler `JsonConvert` helper class). This converts between objects and entire streams of JSON. It requires you to define classes with a structure corresponding to the JSON. Finally, there is a more dynamic option called LINQ to JSON. As the name suggests, it supports LINQ queries over JSON data, but it's more than that: it is useful when you do not know at development time exactly what the structure of your JSON data will be.

JsonSerializer and JsonConvert

`JsonSerializer` offers an attribute-driven serialization model in which you define one or more classes reflecting the structure of the JSON data you need to deal with, and can then convert JSON data to and from that model. Often, you won't use the `JsonSerializer` type directly. Unless you need fine control over certain aspects of serialization, you would normally use the `JsonConvert` helper.

Example 15-21 shows a simple model suitable for use with JSON.NET. As you can see, I'm not required to use any particular base class, and there are no mandatory attributes.

Example 15-21. Simple JSON.NET model

```
public class SimpleData
{
    public int Id { get; set; }
    public IList<string> Names { get; set; }
    public NestedData Location { get; set; }
    public IDictionary<string, int> Map { get; set; }
}

public class NestedData
{
    public string LocationName { get; set; }
    public double Latitude { get; set; }
    public double Longitude { get; set; }
}
```

Example 15-22 creates an instance of this model, and then uses the `JsonConvert` class's `SerializeObject` method to serialize it to a string. (This uses `JsonSerializer` under the covers. For simple scenarios, it's easiest to use `JsonConvert`, because the flexibility offered by `JsonSerializer` makes things more complicated.)

Example 15-22. Serializing data with JsonConvert

```
var model = new SimpleData
{
    Id = 42,
    Names = new[] { "Bell", "Stacey", "her", "Jane" },
    Location = new NestedData
    {
        LocationName = "London",
        Latitude = 51.503209,
        Longitude = -0.119145
    },
    Map = new Dictionary<string, int>
    {
        { "Answer", 42 },
        { "FirstPrime", 2 }
    }
};

string json = JsonConvert.SerializeObject(model, Formatting.Indented);
Console.WriteLine(json);
```

The second argument to SerializeObject is optional. I've used it here to indent the JSON to make it easier to read. (By default, JSON.NET will use a more efficient layout with no unnecessary whitespace, but which is much harder to read.) The results look like this:

```
{
  "Id": 42,
  "Names": [
    "Bell",
    "Stacey",
    "her",
    "Jane"
  ],
  "Location": {
    "LocationName": "London",
    "Latitude": 51.503209,
    "Longitude": -0.119145
  },
  "Map": {
    "Answer": 42,
    "FirstPrime": 2
  }
}
```

As you can see, each object has become a JSON object, where the name/value pairs correspond to properties in my model. Numbers and strings are represented exactly as you would expect. The IList<string> has become a JSON array, and the IDic tionary<string, int> has become another JSON dictionary. I've used interfaces for these collections, but you can also use the concrete List<T> and Dictio nary<TKey,TValue> types. You can use ordinary arrays to represent lists if you prefer. I tend to use the interfaces, because it leaves you free to use whatever collection types you want. (E.g., Example 15-22 used a string array, but it could also have used List<string> without changing the model type.)

Converting serialized JSON back into the model is equally straightforward, as Example 15-23 shows.

Example 15-23. Deserializing data with JsonConvert

```
var deserialized = JsonConvert.DeserializeObject<SimpleData>(json);
```

Although a plain and simple model such as this will suffice, sometimes you may need to take control over some aspects of serialization, particularly if you are working with an externally defined JSON format. For example, some APIs use casing conventions that are different from .NET's—camelCasing is popular, but conflicts with the Pascal-Casing convention for .NET properties. You can resolve this by using the JsonProp erty attribute to specify the name to use in the JSON, as Example 15-24 shows.

Example 15-24. Controlling the JSON with JsonProperty attributes

```
public class NestedData
{
    [JsonProperty("locationName")]
    public string LocationName { get; set; }

    [JsonProperty("latitude")]
    public double Latitude { get; set; }

    [JsonProperty("longitude")]
    public double Longitude { get; set; }
}
```

JSON.NET will use the names specified in `JsonProperty` when serializing, and will look for those names when deserializing. Alternatively, you can tell JSON.NET that you want this casing convention for all properties by passing a suitably configured `JsonSerializerSettings` to `JsonConvert`, in which case you wouldn't need these attributes. You can control things in much more detail than this—you can define custom serialization mechanisms for data types, for example. (E.g., you might want to represent something as a `DateTimeOffset` in your C# code, but to have that become a string with a particular date time format in the JSON.) The full details can be found in the JSON.NET documentation.

LINQ to JSON

Whereas `JsonSerializer` requires you to define one or more types representing the structure of the JSON you want to work with, JSON.NET provides a set of types that take a more dynamic approach, which it calls LINQ to JSON. This parses JSON data into objects of type `JObject`, `JArray`, `JProperty`, and `JValue`, all of which derive from a `JToken` base class. Using these types is similar to working with JSON from JavaScript—you can just access the content directly without having to define classes (with the corresponding downside that certain kinds of mistakes that the compiler would detect with the `JsonSerializer` approach will only be discovered at runtime). Example 15-25 uses this technique to read some data from the same JSON that the last few examples have used.

Example 15-25. Reading JSON with JToken

```
var jo = (JObject) JToken.Parse(json);
Console.WriteLine(jo["Id"]);
foreach (JToken name in jo["Names"])
{
    Console.WriteLine(name);
}
foreach (JToken loc in jo["Location"])
{
```

```
    Console.WriteLine(loc);
}
```

As you can see, JObject provides an indexer with which you can retrieve properties of JSON objects. I've been able to use a foreach loop to iterate over the array of names. I can also do this for nested objects, such as the object in the Location property. Because this API has no idea what types to expect, everything is defined in terms of the base JToken type, with the concrete type being determined by what JSON.NET finds at runtime. So with the data we happen to have, that first foreach loop will find a series of JValue objects (one for each string in the array), while the second will find a series of JProperty objects (one for each property in the nested object).

In Example 15-25 I've cheated slightly by passing each JToken to Console.Write Line. Each concrete type derived from JToken implements ToString in a way that means this program will produce reasonably sensible output:

```
42
Bell
Stacey
her
Jane
"locationName": "London"
"latitude": 51.503209
"longitude": -0.119145
```

But what if you want to work with the data in code, rather than just showing it to the user? In that case you can work with arrays and nested objects by casting each JToken to the type you believe it to be (either because you've inspected the type at runtime, or just because you have reason to believe that the data will be in a particular format), and then with values, you can use the JToken class's Value<T> method to extract the data, specifying the type you think the value should have as the generic type argument, as Example 15-26 does.

Example 15-26. Working with data in LINQ to JSON

```
int id = jo["Id"].Value<int>();
var names = (JArray) jo["Names"];
string firstName = names[0].Value<string>();
```

Each line of this example could throw an exception at runtime. If the Id property is not present, or if it cannot be converted to an int, the first line will fail. If the Names property is not present, or it does not contain an array, the second line will fail. And if the array is empty, or its first element cannot be converted to a string (e.g., because it is a nested object) the final line will fail.

The upside is that you don't need to define any types to model the data, and it's also much easier to write code whose behavior is driven by the structure of the data, because this API is able to describe what it found. For example, you've already seen that using foreach on a JObject produces a sequence of JProperty objects. We can exploit this to write queries over JSON, which is where this API gets its name. Example 15-27 finds all of the JProperty elements in the data where the first letter of the property name is lowercase.

Example 15-27. Querying over JSON data

```
IEnumerable<JProperty> propsStartingWithLowerCase = jo.Descendants()
    .OfType<JProperty>()
    .Where(p => char.IsLower(p.Name[0]));
foreach (JProperty p in propsStartingWithLowerCase)
{
    Console.WriteLine(p);
}
```

The OfType and Where methods here both come from LINQ to Objects. JSON.NET does not supply its own implementation of the standard LINQ operators. It supports LINQ simply by presenting the structure of your JSON data through implementations of IEnumerable<T>, making it possible to use LINQ to Objects to perform queries. The only extra thing it does to help you is to provide methods such as Descendants, which recursively walks the entire structure of the JSON beneath the node on which you invoke it, returning every JToken in a single flattened collection.

Summary

The Stream class is an abstraction representing data as a sequence of bytes. A stream can support reading, writing, or both, and may support seeking to arbitrary offsets as well as straightforward sequential access. TextReader and TextWriter provide strictly sequential reading and writing of character data, abstracting away the character encoding. These types may sit on top of a file, a network connection, or memory, or you could implement your own versions of these abstract classes. The FileStream class also provides some other filesystem access features, but for full control, we also have the File and Directory classes. When bytes and strings aren't enough, .NET offers various serialization mechanisms that can automate the mapping between an object's state in memory and a representation that can be written out to disk or sent over the network or any other stream-like target; this representation can later be turned back into an object of the same type and with equivalent state.

CHAPTER 16

Multithreading

Multithreading enables an application to execute several pieces of code simultaneously. There are two common reasons for doing this. One is to exploit the computer's parallel processing capabilities—multicore CPUs are now more or less ubiquitous, and to realize their full performance potential, you'll need to provide the CPU with multiple streams of work to give all of the cores something useful to do. The other usual reason for writing multithreaded code is to prevent progress from grinding to a halt when you do something slow, such as reading from disk.

Multithreading is not the only way to solve that second problem—asynchronous techniques can be preferable. C# has features for supporting asynchronous work. Asynchronous execution doesn't necessarily mean multithreading, but the two are often related in practice, and I will be describing some of the asynchronous programming models in this chapter. However, this chapter focuses on the threading foundations. I will describe the language-level support for asynchronous code in Chapter 17.

Threads

All the operating systems that .NET can run on allow each process to contain multiple threads. Each thread has its own stack, and the OS presents the illusion that a thread gets a whole CPU *hardware thread* to itself. (See the next sidebar, "Processors, Cores, and Hardware Threads".) You can create far more OS threads than the number of hardware threads your computer provides, because the OS virtualizes the CPU, context switching from one thread to another. The computer I'm using as I write this has 16 hardware threads, which is a reasonably generous quantity, but some way short of the 8,893 threads currently active across the various processes running on the machine.

Processors, Cores, and Hardware Threads

A hardware thread is one piece of hardware capable of executing code. Back in the early 2000s, one processor chip gave you one hardware thread, and you got multiple hardware threads only in computers that had multiple, physically separate CPUs plugged into separate sockets on the motherboard. However, two inventions have made the relationship between hardware and threads more complex: multicore CPUs and hyperthreading.

With a multicore CPU, you effectively get multiple processors on a single piece of silicon. This means that opening up your computer and counting the number of processor chips doesn't necessarily tell you how many hardware threads you've got. But if you were to inspect the CPU's silicon with a suitable microscope, you'd see two or more distinct processors next to each other on the chip.

Hyperthreading, also known as simultaneous multithreading (SMT), complicates matters further. A hyperthreaded core is a single processor that has two sets of certain parts. (It could be more than two, but doubling seems most common.) So, although there might be only a single part of the core capable of performing, say, floating-point division, there will be two sets of registers. Each set of registers includes an instruction pointer (IP) register that keeps track of where execution has reached. Registers also contain the immediate working state of the code, so by having two sets, a single core can run code from two places at once—in other words, hyperthreading enables a single core to provide two hardware threads. Since only certain parts of the CPU are doubled up, two execution contexts have to share some resources—they can't both perform floating-point division operations simultaneously, because there's only one piece of hardware in the core to do that. However, if one of the hardware threads wants to do some division while another multiplies two numbers together, they will typically be able to do so in parallel, because those operations are performed by different areas of the core. Hyperthreading enables more parts of a single CPU core to be kept busy simultaneously. It doesn't give you quite the same throughput as two full cores (because if the two hardware threads both want to do the same kind of work at once, one of them will have to wait), but it can often provide better throughput from each core than would otherwise be possible.

In a hyperthreaded system, the total number of hardware threads available is the number of cores multiplied by the number of hyperthreaded execution units per core. For example, the Intel Core i9-9900K processor has 8 cores with two-way hyperthreading, giving a total of 16 hardware threads.

The CLR presents its own threading abstraction on top of OS threads. Normally, there will be a direct relationship—if you write a console application, a Windows desktop application, or a web application, each .NET Thread object corresponds directly to some particular underlying OS thread. However, this relationship is not guaranteed always to exist—the CLR was designed to make it possible for a .NET thread to hop between different OS threads. This happens only in an application that uses the CLR's unmanaged hosting APIs to customize the relationship between the CLR and its containing process. (SQL Server's CLR Integration feature does this, for example.) Most of the time, a CLR thread will, in practice, correspond to an OS thread, but library code should try not to depend on this; code that makes this assumption could break when used in an application that provides a custom CLR host.

I will get to the Thread class shortly, but before writing multithreaded code, you need to understand the ground rules for managing state[1] when using multiple threads.

Threads, Variables, and Shared State

Each CLR thread gets various thread-specific resources, such as the call stack (which holds method arguments and some local variables). Because each thread has its own stack, the local variables that end up there will be local to the thread. Each time you invoke a method, you get a new set of its local variables. Recursion relies on this, but it's also important in multithreaded code, because data that is accessible to multiple threads requires much more care, particularly if that data changes. Coordinating access to shared data is complex. I'll be describing some of the techniques for that in the section "Synchronization" on page 671, but it's better to avoid the problem entirely where possible, and the thread-local nature of the stack can be a great help.

For example, consider a web-based application. Busy sites have to handle requests from multiple users simultaneously, so you're likely to end up in a situation where a particular piece of code (e.g., the code for your site's home page) is being executed simultaneously on several different threads—ASP.NET Core uses multithreading to be able to serve the same logical page to multiple users. (Websites typically don't just serve up the exact same content, because pages are often tailored to particular users, so if 1,000 users ask to see the home page, it will run the code that generates that page 1,000 times.) ASP.NET Core provides you with various objects that your code will need to use, but most of these are specific to a particular request. So, if your code is able to work entirely with those objects and with local variables, each thread can operate completely independently. If you need shared state (such as objects that are visible to multiple threads, perhaps through a static field or property), life will get more difficult, but local variables are usually straightforward.

Why only "usually"? Things get more complex if you use lambdas or anonymous functions, because they make it possible to declare a variable in a containing method and then use that in an inner method. This variable is now available to two or more

---

1 I'm using the word *state* here broadly. I just mean information stored in variables and objects.

methods, and with multithreading, it's possible that these methods could execute concurrently. (As far as the CLR is concerned, it's not really a local variable anymore —it's a field in a compiler-generated class.) Sharing local variables across multiple methods removes the guarantee of complete locality, so you need to take the same sort of care with such variables as you would with more obviously shared items, like static properties and fields.

Another important point to remember in multithreaded environments is the distinction between a variable and the object it refers to. (This is an issue only with reference type variables.) Although a local variable is accessible only inside its declaring method, that variable may not be the only one that refers to a particular object. Sometimes it will be—if you create the object inside the method and never store it anywhere that would make it accessible to a wider audience, then you have nothing to worry about. The StringBuilder that Example 16-1 creates is only ever used within the method that creates it.

Example 16-1. Object visibility and methods

```
public static string FormatDictionary<TKey, TValue>(
    IDictionary<TKey, TValue> input)
{
    var sb = new StringBuilder();
    foreach (var item in input)
    {
        sb.AppendFormat("{0}: {1}", item.Key, item.Value);
        sb.AppendLine();
    }

    return sb.ToString();
}
```

This code does not need to worry about whether other threads might be trying to modify the StringBuilder. There are no nested methods here, so the sb variable is truly local, and that's the only thing that contains a reference to the StringBuilder. (This relies on the fact that the StringBuilder doesn't sneakily store copies of its this reference anywhere that other threads might be able to see.)

But what about the input argument? That's also local to the method, but the object it refers to is not: the code that calls FormatDictionary gets to decide what input refers to. Looking at Example 16-1 in isolation, it's not possible to say whether the dictionary object to which it refers is currently in use by other threads. The calling code could create a single dictionary and then create two threads, and have one modify the dictionary while the other calls this FormatDictionary method. This would cause a problem: most dictionary implementations do not support being modified on one thread at the same time as being used on some other thread. And even if you were working with a collection that was designed to cope with concurrent use, you're often not allowed to modify a collection while an enumeration of its contents is in progress (e.g., a `foreach` loop).

You might think that any collection designed to be used from multiple threads simultaneously (a *thread-safe* collection, you might say) should allow one thread to iterate over its contents while another modifies the contents. If it disallows this, then in what sense is it thread safe? In fact, the main difference between a thread-safe and a non-thread-safe collection in this scenario is predictability: whereas a thread-safe collection might throw an exception when it detects that this has happened, a non-thread-safe collection does not guarantee to do anything in particular. It might crash, or you might start getting perplexing results from the iteration such as a single entry appearing multiple times. It could do more or less anything because you're using it in an unsupported way. Sometimes, thread safety just means that failure happens in a well-defined and predictable manner.

As it happens, the various collections in the `System.Collection.Concurrent` namespace do in fact support changes while enumeration is in progress without throwing exceptions. However, for the most part they have a different API from the other collection classes specifically to support concurrency, so they are not always drop-in replacements.

There's nothing Example 16-1 can do to ensure that it uses its `input` argument safely in multithreaded environments, because it is at the mercy of its callers. Concurrency hazards need to be dealt with at a higher level. In fact, the term *thread safe* is potentially misleading, because it suggests something that is not, in general, possible. Inexperienced developers often fall into the trap of thinking that they are absolved of all responsibility for thinking about threading issues in their code by just making sure that all the objects they're using are thread safe. This usually doesn't work, because while individual thread-safe objects will maintain their own integrity, that's no guarantee that your application's state as a whole will be coherent.

To illustrate this, Example 16-2 uses the `ConcurrentDictionary<TKey, TValue>` class from the `System.Collections.Concurrent` namespace. Every operation this class defines is thread safe in the sense that each will leave the object in a consistent state, and will produce the expected result given the collection's state prior to the call. However, this example contrives to use it in a non-thread-safe fashion.

Example 16-2. Non-thread-safe use of a thread-safe collection

```
static string UseDictionary(ConcurrentDictionary<int, string> cd)
{
    cd[1] = "One";
    return cd[1];
}
```

This seems like it could not fail. (It also seems pointless; that's just to show how even a very simple piece of code can go wrong.) But if the dictionary instance is being used by multiple threads (which seems likely, given that we've chosen a type designed specifically for multithreaded use), it's entirely possible that in between setting a value for key 1 and trying to retrieve it, some other thread will have removed that entry. If I put this code into a program that repeatedly runs this method on several threads, but which also has several other threads busily removing the very same entry, I eventually see a `KeyNotFoundException`.

Concurrent systems need a top-down strategy to ensure system-wide consistency. (This is why database management systems often use transactions, which group sets of operations together as atomic units of work that either succeed completely, or have no effect at all. This atomic grouping is a critical part of how transactions help to ensure system-wide consistency of state.) Looking at Example 16-1, this means that it is the responsibility of code that calls `FormatDictionary` to ensure that the dictionary can be used freely for the duration of the method.

 Although calling code should guarantee that whatever objects it passes are safe to use for the duration of a method call, you cannot in general assume that it's OK to hold on to references to your arguments for future use. Anonymous functions and delegates make it easy to do this accidentally—if a nested method refers to its containing method's arguments, and if that nested method runs after the containing method returns, it may no longer be safe to assume that you're allowed to access the objects to which the arguments refer. If you need to do this, you will need to document the assumptions you're making about when you can use objects, and inspect any code that calls the method to make sure that these assumptions are valid.

Thread-local storage

Sometimes it can be useful to maintain thread-local state at a broader scope than a single method. Various parts of the .NET class library do this. For example, the `System.Transactions` namespace defines an API for using transactions with databases, message queues, and any other resource managers that support them. It provides an implicit model where you can start an *ambient transaction*, and any operations that support this will enlist in it without you needing to pass any explicit transaction-related arguments. (It also supports an explicit model, should you prefer that.) The `Transaction` class's static `Current` property returns the ambient transaction for the current thread, or it returns `null` if the thread currently has no ambient transaction in progress.

To support this sort of per-thread state, .NET offers the ThreadLocal<T> class. Example 16-3 uses this to provide a wrapper around a delegate that allows only a single call into the delegate to be in progress on any one thread at any time.

Example 16-3. Using ThreadLocal<T>

```
class Notifier
{
    private readonly ThreadLocal<bool> _isCallbackInProgress =
        new ThreadLocal<bool>();

    private readonly Action _callback;

    public Notifier(Action callback)
    {
        _callback = callback;
    }

    public void Notify()
    {
        if (_isCallbackInProgress.Value)
        {
            throw new InvalidOperationException(
                "Notification already in progress on this thread");
        }

        try
        {
            _isCallbackInProgress.Value = true;
            _callback();
        }
        finally
        {
            _isCallbackInProgress.Value = false;
        }
    }
}
```

If the method that Notify calls back attempts to make another call to Notify, this will block that attempt at recursion by throwing an exception. However, because it uses a ThreadLocal<bool> to track whether a call is in progress, this will allow simultaneous calls as long as each call happens on a separate thread.

You get and set the value that ThreadLocal<T> holds for the current thread through the Value property. The constructor is overloaded, and you can pass a Func<T> that will be called back each time a new thread first tries to retrieve the value to create a default initial value. (The initialization is lazy—the callback won't run every time a new thread starts. A ThreadLocal<T> invokes the callback only the first time a thread attempts to use the value.) There is no fixed limit to the number of `ThreadLocal<T>` objects you can create.

`ThreadLocal<T>` also provides some support for cross-thread communication. If you pass an argument of `true` to one of the constructor overloads that accepts a `bool`, the object will maintain a collection reporting the latest value stored for every thread, which is available through its `Values` property. It provides this service only if you ask for it when constructing the object, because it requires some additional housekeeping work. Also, if you use a reference type as the type argument, enabling tracking may mean that objects will be kept alive longer. Normally, any reference that a thread stores in a `ThreadLocal<T>` will cease to exist when the thread terminates, and if that reference was the only one keeping an object reachable, the GC will then be able to reclaim its memory. But if you enable tracking, all such references will remain reachable for as long as the `ThreadLocal<T>` instance itself is reachable, because `Values` reports values even for threads that have terminated.

There's one thing you need to be careful about with thread-local storage. If you create a new object for each thread, be aware that an application might create a large number of threads over its lifetime, especially if you use the thread pool (which is described in detail later). If the per-thread objects you create are expensive, this might cause problems. Furthermore, if there are any disposable per-thread resources, you will not necessarily know when a thread terminates; the thread pool regularly creates and destroys threads without telling you when it does so.

One last note of caution: be wary of thread-local storage (and any mechanism based on it) if you plan to use the asynchronous language features described in Chapter 17, because those make it possible for a single invocation of a method to use multiple different threads as it progresses. This would make it a bad idea for that sort of method to use ambient transactions, or anything else that relies on thread-local state. Many .NET features that you might think would use thread-local storage (e.g., the ASP.NET Core framework's static `HttpContext.Current` property, which returns an object relating to the HTTP request that the current thread is handling) turn out to associate information with something called the *execution context* instead. An execution context is more flexible, because it can hop across threads when required. I'll be describing it later.

For the issues I've just discussed to be relevant, we'll need to have multiple threads. There are four main ways to use multithreading. In one, the code runs in a framework that creates multiple threads on your behalf, such as ASP.NET Core. Another is to use certain kinds of callback-based APIs. A few common patterns for this are described in "Tasks" on page 694, and "Other Asynchronous Patterns" on page 707. But the two most direct ways to use threads are to create new threads explicitly, or to use the .NET thread pool.

The Thread Class

As I mentioned earlier, the Thread class (defined in the System.Threading namespace) represents a CLR thread. You can obtain a reference to the Thread object representing the thread that's executing your code with the Thread.CurrentThread property, but if you're looking to introduce some multithreading, you can simply construct a new Thread object.

A new thread needs to know what code it should run when it starts, so you must provide a delegate, and the thread will invoke the method the delegate refers to when it starts. The thread will run until that method returns normally, or allows an exception to propagate all the way to the top of the stack (or the thread is forcibly terminated through any of the OS mechanisms for killing threads or their containing processes). Example 16-4 creates three threads to download the contents of three web pages simultaneously.

Example 16-4. Creating threads

```
class Program
{
    private static void Main(string[] args)
    {
        var t1 = new Thread(MyThreadEntryPoint);
        var t2 = new Thread(MyThreadEntryPoint);
        var t3 = new Thread(MyThreadEntryPoint);

        t1.Start("https://endjin.com/");
        t2.Start("https://oreilly.com/");
        t3.Start("https://dotnet.microsoft.com/");
    }

    private static void MyThreadEntryPoint(object arg)
    {
        string url = (string) arg;

        using (var w = new WebClient())
        {
            Console.WriteLine($"Downloading {url}");
            string page = w.DownloadString(url);
            Console.WriteLine($"Downloaded {url}, length {page.Length}");
        }
    }
}
```

In most cases, HttpClient is preferred over the WebClient type shown in Example 16-4. I'm avoiding HttpClient for now because it only offers asynchronous methods, which we'll be getting to later.

The Thread constructor is overloaded, and accepts two delegate types. The ThreadStart delegate requires a method that takes no arguments and returns no value, but in Example 16-4, the MyThreadEntryPoint method takes a single object argument, which matches the other delegate type, ParameterizedThreadStart. This provides a way to pass an argument to each thread, which is useful if you're invoking the same method on several different threads, as this example does. The thread will not run until you call Start, and if you're using the ParameterizedThreadStart delegate type, you must call the overload that takes a single object argument. I'm using this to make each thread download from a different URL.

There are two more overloads of the Thread constructor, each adding an int argument after the delegate argument. This int specifies the size of stack for the thread. Current .NET implementations require stacks to be contiguous in memory, making it necessary to preallocate address space for the stack. If a thread exhausts this space, the CLR throws a StackOverflowException. (You normally see those only when a bug causes infinite recursion.) Without this argument, the CLR will use the default stack size for the process. (This varies by OS; on Windows it will usually be 1 MB. You can change it by setting the COMPlus_DefaultStackSize environment variable.) It's rare to need to change this, but not unheard of. If you have recursive code that produces very deep stacks, you might need to run it on a thread with a larger stack. Conversely, if you're creating huge numbers of threads, you might want to reduce the stack size to conserve resources, because the default of 1 MB is usually considerably more than is really required. However, it's usually not a great idea to create such a large number of threads. So, in most cases, you will create only a moderate number of threads, and just use the constructors that use the default stack size.

Notice that the Main method in Example 16-4 returns immediately after starting the three threads. Despite this, the application continues to run—it will run until all the threads finish. The CLR keeps the process alive until there are no *foreground threads* running, where a foreground thread is defined to be any thread that hasn't explicitly been designated as a background thread. If you want to prevent a particular thread from keeping the process running, set its IsBackground property to true. (This means that background threads may be terminated while they're in the middle of doing something, so you need to be careful about what kind of work you do on these threads.)

Creating threads directly is not the only option. The thread pool provides a commonly used alternative.

The Thread Pool

On most operating systems, it is relatively expensive to create and shut down threads. If you need to perform a fairly short piece of work (such as serving up a web page, or some similarly brief operation), it would be a bad idea to create a thread just for that job and to shut it down when the work completes. There are two serious problems with this strategy: first, you may end up expending more resources on the startup and shutdown costs than on useful work; second, if you keep creating new threads as more work comes in, the system may bog down under load—with heavy workloads, creating ever more threads will tend to reduce throughput. This is because, in addition to basic per-thread overheads such as the memory required for the stack, the OS needs to switch regularly between runnable threads to enable them all to make progress, and this switching has its own overheads.

To avoid these problems, .NET provides a thread pool. You can supply a delegate that the runtime will invoke on a thread from the pool. If necessary, it will create a new thread, but where possible, it will reuse one it created earlier, and it might make your work wait in a queue if all the threads created so far are busy. After your method runs, the CLR will not normally terminate the thread; instead, the thread will stay in the pool, waiting for other work items to amortize the cost of creating the thread over multiple work items. It will create new threads if necessary, but it tries to keep the thread count at a level that results in the number of runnable threads matching the hardware thread count, to minimize switching costs.

 The thread pool always creates background threads, so if the thread pool is in the middle of doing something when the last foreground thread in your process exits, the work will not complete, because all background threads will be terminated at that point. If you need to ensure that work being done on the thread pool completes, you must wait for that to happen before allowing all foreground threads to finish.

Launching thread pool work with Task

The usual way to use the thread pool is through the `Task` class. This is part of the Task Parallel Library (discussed in more detail in "Tasks" on page 694), but its basic usage is pretty straightforward, as Example 16-5 shows.

Example 16-5. Running code on the thread pool with a Task

```
Task.Run(() => MyThreadEntryPoint("https://oreilly.com/"));
```

This queues the lambda for execution on the thread pool (which, when it runs, just calls the `MyThreadEntryPoint` method from Example 16-4). If a thread is available, it will start to run straightaway, but if not, it will wait in a queue until a thread becomes available (either because some other work item in progress completes, or because the thread pool decides to add a new thread to the pool).

There are other ways to use the thread pool, the most obvious of which is through the ThreadPool class. Its QueueUserWorkItem method works in a similar way to StartNew —you pass it a delegate and it will queue the method for execution. This is a lower-level API—it does not provide any direct way to handle completion of the work, nor to chain operations together, so for most cases, the Task class is preferable.

Thread creation heuristics

.NET adjusts the number of threads based on the workload you present. The heuristics it uses are not documented and have changed across releases of .NET, so you should not depend on the exact behavior I'm about to describe; however, it is useful to know roughly what to expect.

If you give the thread pool only CPU-bound work, in which every method you ask it to execute spends its entire time performing computations, and never blocks waiting for I/O to complete, you might end up with one thread for each of the hardware threads in your system (although if the individual work items take long enough, the thread pool might decide to allocate more threads). For example, on the eight-core two-way hyperthreaded computer I'm using as I write this, queuing up a load of CPU-intensive work items initially causes the CLR to create 16 thread pool threads, and as long as the work items complete about once a second, the number of threads mostly stays at that level. (It occasionally goes over that because the runtime will try adding an extra thread from time to time to see what effect this has on throughput, and then it drops back down again.) But if the rate at which the program gets through items drops, the CLR gradually increases the thread count.

If thread pool threads get blocked (e.g., because they're waiting for data from disk, or for a response over the network from a server), the CLR increases the number of pool threads more quickly. Again, it starts off with one per hardware thread, but when slow work items consume very little processor time, it can add threads as frequently as twice a second.

In either case, the CLR will eventually stop adding threads. The exact default limit varies in 32-bit processes, depending on the exact version of .NET, although it's typically on the order of 1,000 threads. In 64-bit mode, the setting appears to default to 32,767. You can change this limit—the ThreadPool class has a SetMaxThreads method that lets you configure different limits for your process. You may run into other limitations that place a lower practical limit. For example, each thread has its own stack that has to occupy a contiguous range of virtual address space. By default, each thread gets 1 MB of the process's address space reserved for its stack, so by the time you have 1,000 threads, you'll be using 1 GB of address space for stacks alone.

Thirty-two-bit processes have only 4 GB of address space[2]—so you might not have space for the number of threads you request. In any case, 1,000 threads is usually more than is helpful, so if it gets that high, this may be a symptom of some underlying problem that you should investigate. So, if you call `SetMaxThreads`, it will normally be to specify a lower limit—you may find that with some workloads, constraining the number of threads improves throughput by reducing the level of contention for system resources.

`ThreadPool` also has a `SetMinThreads` method. This lets you ensure that the number of threads does not drop below a certain number. This can be useful in applications that work most efficiently with some minimum number of threads, and which want to be able to operate at maximum speed instantly, without waiting for the thread pool's heuristics to adjust the thread count.

I/O completion threads

On Windows, the thread pool contains two kinds of threads: worker threads and I/O completion threads. Worker threads are used for executing the delegates you queue up with the techniques for launching tasks I've shown so far (although, as I'll show later in "Schedulers" on page 702, you can select different threading strategies). The `ThreadPool` class also uses these threads with its `QueueUserWorkItem` method. I/O completion threads are used on Windows to invoke methods that you provide as callbacks for when an I/O operation (such as reading data from a file or a socket) that you initiated asynchronously eventually completes.

Internally, the Windows version of the CLR uses the I/O completion port mechanism that Windows provides for handling large numbers of concurrent asynchronous operations efficiently. The thread pool separates threads that service this completion port from the other worker threads. This reduces the chances of deadlocking the system when you hit the pool's maximum thread limit. If the CLR didn't keep I/O threads separate, it could get into a state where all the thread pool threads were busy waiting for I/O to complete, at which point the process would deadlock, because there would be no threads left to service the completion of the I/O operations that these other threads are waiting for. (On Unix, this mechanism does not exist, so any request to queue work on an I/O thread will just be directed to the worker thread pool.)

In practice, you can normally ignore the distinction between I/O threads and ordinary threads in the thread pool, because the CLR decides which to use. However, you will occasionally be confronted with the distinction. For example, if you decide for some reason to modify the thread pool size, you need to specify the upper limits for

---

2 On 32-bit versions of Windows, some of this is reserved for the system, meaning applications only get to use at most 3 GB of the address range.

normal and I/O completion threads separately—the `SetMaxThreads` method I mentioned in the preceding section takes two arguments.

Thread Affinity and SynchronizationContext

Some objects demand that you use them only from certain threads. This is particularly common with UI code—the WPF and Windows Forms UI frameworks require that UI objects be used from the thread on which they were created. This is called *thread affinity*, and although it is most often a UI concern, it can also crop up in interoperability scenarios—some COM objects have thread affinity.

Thread affinity can make life awkward if you want to write multithreaded code. Suppose you've carefully implemented a multithreaded algorithm that can exploit all of the hardware threads in an end user's computer, significantly improving performance when running on a multicore CPU compared to a single-threaded algorithm. Once the algorithm completes, you may want to present the results to the end user. The thread affinity of UI objects requires you to perform that final step on a particular thread, but your multithreaded code may well produce its final results on some other thread. (In fact, you will probably have avoided the UI thread entirely for the CPU-intensive work, to make sure that the UI remained responsive while the work was in progress.) If you try to update the UI from some random worker thread, the UI framework will throw an exception complaining that you've violated its thread affinity requirements. Somehow, you'll need to pass a message back to the UI thread so that it can display the results.

The .NET class library provides the `SynchronizationContext` class to help in these scenarios. Its `Current` static property returns an instance of the `SynchronizationContext` class that represents the context in which your code is currently running. For example, in a WPF application, if you retrieve this property while running on a UI thread, it will return an object associated with that thread. You can store the object that `Current` returns and use it from any thread, any time you need to perform further work on the UI thread. Example 16-6 does this so that it can perform some potentially slow work on a thread pool thread, and then update the UI back on the UI thread.

Example 16-6. Using the thread pool and then SynchronizationContext

```
private void findButton_Click(object sender, RoutedEventArgs e)
{
    SynchronizationContext uiContext = SynchronizationContext.Current;

    Task.Run(() =>
    {
        string pictures =
            Environment.GetFolderPath(Environment.SpecialFolder.MyPictures);
```

```
    var folder = new DirectoryInfo(pictures);
    FileInfo[] allFiles =
        folder.GetFiles("*.jpg", SearchOption.AllDirectories);
    FileInfo largest =
        allFiles.OrderByDescending(f => f.Length).FirstOrDefault();

    uiContext.Post(_ =>
    {
        long sizeMB = largest.Length / (1024 * 1024);
        outputTextBox.Text =
            $"Largest file ({sizeMB}MB) is {largest.FullName}";
    },
    null);
  });
}
```

This code handles a Click event for a button. (It happens to be a WPF application, but SynchronizationContext works in exactly the same way in other desktop UI frameworks, such as Windows Forms.) UI elements raise their events on the UI thread, so when the first line of the click handler retrieves the current Synchroniza tionContext, it will get the context for the UI thread. The code then runs some work on a thread pool thread via the Task class. The code looks at every picture in the user's *Pictures* folder, searching for the largest file, so this could take a while. It's a bad idea to perform slow work on a UI thread—UI elements that belong to that thread cannot respond to user input while the UI thread is busy doing something else. So pushing this into the thread pool is a good idea.

The problem with using the thread pool here is that once the work completes, we're on the wrong thread to update the UI. This code updates the Text property of a text box, and we'd get an exception if we tried that from a thread pool thread. So, when the work completes, it uses the SynchronizationContext object it retrieved earlier, and calls its Post method. That method accepts a delegate, and it will arrange to invoke that back on the UI thread. (Under the covers, it posts a custom message to the Windows message queue, and when the UI thread's main message processing loop picks up that message, it will invoke the delegate.)

 The Post method does not wait for the work to complete. There is a method that will wait, called Send, but I would recommend not using it. Making a worker thread block while it waits for the UI thread to do something can be risky, because if the UI thread is currently blocked waiting for the worker thread to do something, the application will deadlock. Post avoids this problem by enabling the worker thread to proceed concurrently with the UI thread.

Example 16-6 retrieves SynchronizationContext.Current while it's still on the UI thread, before it starts the thread pool work. This is important because this static property is context sensitive—it returns the context for the UI thread only while you're on the UI thread. (In fact, it's possible for each window to have its own UI thread in WPF, so it wouldn't be possible to have an API that returns *the* UI thread—there might be several.) If you read this property from a thread pool thread, the context object it returns will not post work to the UI thread.

The `SynchronizationContext` mechanism is extensible, so you can derive your own type from it if you want, and you can call its static `SetSynchronizationContext` method to make your context the current context for the thread. This can be useful in unit testing scenarios—it enables you to write tests to verify that objects interact with the `SynchronizationContext` correctly without needing to create a real UI.

ExecutionContext

The `SynchronizationContext` class has a cousin, `ExecutionContext`. This provides a similar service, allowing you to capture the current context, and then use it to run a delegate some time later in the same context, but it differs in two ways. First, it captures different things. Second, it uses a different approach for re-establishing the context. A `SynchronizationContext` will often run your work on some particular thread, whereas `ExecutionContext` will always use your thread, and it just makes sure that all of the contextual information it has captured is available on that thread. One way to think of the difference is that `SynchronizationContext` does the work in an existing context, whereas `ExecutionContext` brings the contextual information to you.

> Slightly confusingly, the implementation of `ExecutionContext` on .NET Framework captures the current `SynchonizationContext`, so there's a sense in which the `ExecutionContext` is a superset of the `SynchronizationContext`. However, `ExecutionContext` doesn't use the captured `SynchronizationContext` when it invokes your delegate. All it does is ensure that if code executed via an `ExecutionContext` reads the `SynchonizationContext.Current` property, it will get the `SynchronizationContext` property that was current at the point when the `ExecutionContext` was captured. This will not necessarily be the `SynchonizationContext` that the thread is currently running in! This design flaw was fixed in .NET Core.

You retrieve the current context by calling the `ExecutionContext.Capture` method. The execution context does not capture thread-local storage, but it does include any information in the current *logical call context*. You can access this through the `Call Context` class, which provides `LogicalSetData` and `LogicalGetData` methods to store and retrieve name/value pairs, or through the higher-level wrapper, `AsyncLocal<T>`. This information is usually associated with the current thread, but if you run code in a captured execution context, it will make information from the logical context available, even if that code runs on some other thread entirely.

.NET uses the `ExecutionContext` class internally whenever long-running work that starts on one thread later ends up continuing on a different thread (as happens with some of the asynchronous patterns described later in this chapter). You may want to use the execution context in a similar way if you write any code that accepts a callback that it will invoke later, perhaps from some other thread. To do this, you call `Capture` to grab the current context, which you can later pass to the `Run` method to invoke a delegate. Example 16-7 shows `ExecutionContext` at work.

Example 16-7. Using ExecutionContext

```
public class Defer
{
    private readonly Action _callback;
    private readonly ExecutionContext _context;

    public Defer(Action callback)
    {
        _callback = callback;
        _context = ExecutionContext.Capture();
    }

    public void Run()
    {
        ExecutionContext.Run(_context, (unusedStateArg) => _callback(), null);
    }
}
```

In .NET Framework, a single captured `ExecutionContext` cannot be used on multiple threads simultaneously. Sometimes you might need to invoke multiple different methods in a particular context, and in a multithreaded environment, you might not be able to guarantee that the previous method has returned before calling the next. For this scenario, `ExecutionContext` provides a `CreateCopy` method that generates a copy of the context, enabling you to make multiple simultaneous calls through equivalent contexts. In .NET Core, `ExecutionContext` became immutable, meaning this restriction no longer applies, and `CreateCopy` just returns its `this` reference.

Synchronization

Sometimes you will want to write multithreaded code in which multiple threads have access to the same state. For example, in Chapter 5, I suggested that a server could use a `Dictionary<TKey, TValue>` as part of a cache to avoid duplicating work when it receives multiple similar requests. While this sort of caching can offer significant performance benefits in some scenarios, it presents a challenge in a multithreaded environment. (And if you're working on server code with demanding performance requirements, you will most likely need more than one thread to handle requests.) The Thread Safety section of the documentation for the dictionary class says this:

> A `Dictionary<TKey, TValue>` can support multiple readers concurrently, as long as the collection is not modified. Even so, enumerating through a collection is intrinsically not a thread-safe procedure. In the rare case where an enumeration contends with write accesses, the collection must be locked during the entire enumeration. To allow the collection to be accessed by multiple threads for reading and writing, you must implement your own synchronization.

This is better than we might hope for—the vast majority of types in the .NET class library simply don't support multithreaded use of instances at all. Most types support multithreaded use at the class level, but individual instances must be used one thread at a time. `Dictionary<TKey, TValue>` is more generous: it explicitly supports multiple concurrent readers, which sounds good for our caching scenario. However, when modifying a collection, not only must we ensure that we do not try to change it from multiple threads simultaneously, but also we must not have any read operations in progress while we do so.

The other generic collection classes make similar guarantees (unlike most other classes in the library). For example, `List<T>`, `Queue<T>`, `Stack<T>`, `SortedDiction ary<TKey, TValue>`, `HashSet<T>`, and `SortedSet<T>` all support concurrent read-only use. (Again, if you modify any instance of these collections, you must make sure that no other threads are either modifying or reading from the same instance at the same time.) Of course, you should always check the documentation before attempting multithreaded use of any type.[3] Be aware that the generic collection interface types make no thread safety guarantees—although `List<T>` supports concurrent readers, not all implementations of `IList<T>` will. (For example, imagine an implementation that wraps something potentially slow, such as the contents of a file. It might make sense for this wrapper to cache data to make read operations faster. Reading an item from such a list could change its internal state, so reads could fail when performed simultaneously from multiple threads if the code did not take steps to protect itself.)

If you can arrange never to have to modify a data structure while it is in use from multithreaded code, the support for concurrent access offered by many of the collection classes may be all you need. But if some threads will need to modify shared state, you will need to coordinate access to that state. To enable this, .NET provides various synchronization mechanisms that you can use to ensure that your threads take it in

---

3 At the time of this writing, the documentation does not offer read-only thread safety guarantees for `Hash Set<T>` and `SortedSet<T>`. Nonetheless, I have been assured by Microsoft that these also support concurrent reads.

turns to access shared objects when necessary. In this section, I'll describe the most commonly used ones.

Monitors and the lock Keyword

The first option to consider for synchronizing multithreaded use of shared state is the `Monitor` class. This is popular because it is efficient, it offers a straightforward model, and C# provides direct language support, making it very easy to use. Example 16-8 shows a class that uses the `lock` keyword (which in turn uses the `Monitor` class) any time it either reads or modifies its internal state. This ensures that only one thread will be accessing that state at any one time.

Example 16-8. Protecting state with lock

```
public class SaleLog
{
    private readonly object _sync = new object();

    private decimal _total;

    private readonly List<string> _saleDetails = new List<string>();

    public decimal Total
    {
        get
        {
            lock (_sync)
            {
                return _total;
            }
        }
    }

    public void AddSale(string item, decimal price)
    {
        string details = $"{item} sold at {price}";
        lock (_sync)
        {
            _total += price;
            _saleDetails.Add(details);
        }
    }

    public string[] GetDetails(out decimal total)
    {
        lock (_sync)
        {
            total = _total;
            return _saleDetails.ToArray();
        }
```

```
        }
    }
}
```

To use the `lock` keyword, you provide a reference to an object, and a block of code. The C# compiler generates code that will cause the CLR to ensure that no more than one thread is inside a `lock` block for that object at any one time. Suppose you created a single instance of this `SaleLog` class, and on one thread you called the `AddSale` method, while on another thread you called `GetDetails` at the same time. Both threads will reach `lock` statements, passing in the same `_sync` field. Whichever thread happens to get there first will be allowed to run the block following the `lock`. The other thread will be made to wait—it won't be allowed to enter its `lock` block until the first thread leaves its `lock` block.

The `SaleLog` class only ever uses any of its fields from inside a `lock` block using the `_sync` argument. This ensures that all access to fields is serialized (in the concurrency sense—that is, threads get to access fields one at a time, rather than all piling in simultaneously). When the `GetDetails` method reads from both the `_total` and `_saleDetails` fields, it can be confident that it's getting a coherent view—the total will be consistent with the current contents of the list of sales details, because the code that modifies these two pieces of data does so within a single `lock` block. This means that updates will appear to be atomic from the point of view of any other `lock` block using `_sync`.

It may look excessive to use a `lock` block even for the `get` accessor that returns the total. However, `decimal` is a 128-bit value, so access to data of this type is not intrinsically atomic—without that `lock`, it would be possible for the returned value to be made up of a mixture of two or more values that `_total` had at different times. (For example, the bottom 64 bits might be from an older value than the top 64 bits.) This is often described as a *torn read*. The CLR guarantees atomic reads and writes only for data types whose size is no larger than 4 bytes, and also for references, even on a platform where they are larger than 4 bytes. (It guarantees this only for naturally aligned fields, but in C#, fields will always be aligned unless you have deliberately misaligned them for interop purposes.)

A subtle but important detail of Example 16-8 is that whenever it returns information about its internal state, it returns a copy. The `Total` property's type is `decimal`, which is a value type, and values are always returned as copies. But when it comes to the list of entries, the `GetDetails` method calls `ToArray`, which will build a new array containing a copy of the list's current contents. It would be a mistake to return the reference in `_saleDetails` directly, because that would enable code outside of the `SalesLog` class to access and modify the collection without using `lock`. We need to ensure that all access to that collection is synchronized, and we lose the ability to do that if our class hands out references to its internal state.

If you write code that performs some multithreaded work that eventually comes to a halt, it's OK to share references to the state after the work has stopped. But if multithreaded modifications to an object are ongoing, you need to ensure that all use of that object's state is protected.

The lock keyword accepts any object reference, so you might wonder why I've created an object specially—couldn't I have passed this instead? That would have worked, but the problem is that your this reference is not private—it's the same reference by which external code uses your object. Using a publicly visible feature of your object to synchronize access to private state is imprudent; some other code could decide that it's convenient to use a reference to your object as the argument to some completely unrelated lock blocks. In this case, it probably wouldn't cause a problem, but with more complex code, it could tie conceptually unrelated pieces of concurrent behavior together in a way that might cause performance problems or even deadlocks. Thus, it's usually better to code defensively, and use something that only your code has access to as the lock argument. Of course, I could have used the _saleDetails field because that refers to an object that only my class has access to. However, even if you code defensively, you should not assume that other developers will, so in general, it's safer to avoid using an instance of a class you didn't write as the argument for a lock, because you can never be certain that it isn't using its this reference for its own locking purposes.

The fact that you can use any object reference is a bit of an oddity in any case. Most of .NET's synchronization mechanisms use an instance of some distinct type as the point of reference for synchronization. (For example, if you want reader/writer locking semantics, you use an instance of the ReaderWriterLockSlim class, not just any old object.) The Monitor class (which is what lock uses) is an exception that dates back to an old requirement for a degree of compatibility with Java (which has a similar locking primitive). This is not relevant to modern .NET development, so this feature is now just a historical peculiarity. Using a distinct object whose only job is to act as a lock argument adds minimal overhead (compared to the costs of locking in the first place) and tends to make it easier to see how synchronization is being managed.

You cannot use a value type as an argument for lock—C# prevents this, and with good reason. The compiler performs an implicit conversion to object on the lock argument, which for reference types, doesn't require the CLR to do anything at runtime. But when you convert a value type to a reference of type object, a box needs to be created. That box would be the argument to lock, and that would be a problem, because you get a new box every time you convert a value to an object reference. So, each time you ran a lock, it would get a different object, meaning there would be no synchronization in practice. This is why the compiler prevents you from trying.

How the lock keyword expands

Each lock block turns into code that does three things: first, it calls Monitor.Enter, passing the argument you provided to lock. Then it attempts to run the code in the block. Finally, it will usually call Monitor.Exit once the block finishes. But it's not entirely straightforward, thanks to exceptions. The code will still call Monitor.Exit if the code you put in the block throws an exception, but it needs to handle the possibility that Monitor.Enter itself threw, which would mean that the code does not own the lock and should therefore not call Monitor.Exit. Example 16-9 shows what the compiler makes of the lock block in the GetDetails method in Example 16-8.

Example 16-9. How lock blocks expand

```
bool lockWasTaken = false;
var temp = _sync;
try
{
    Monitor.Enter(temp, ref lockWasTaken);
    {
        total = _total;
        return _saleDetails.ToArray();
    }
}
finally
{
    if (lockWasTaken)
    {
        Monitor.Exit(temp);
    }
}
```

Monitor.Enter is the API that does the work of discovering whether some other thread already has the lock, and if so, making the current thread wait. If this returns at all, it normally succeeds. (It might deadlock, in which case it will never return.) There is a small possibility of failure caused by an exception, e.g., due to running out of memory. That would be fairly unusual, but the generated code takes it into account nonetheless—this is the purpose of the slightly roundabout-looking code for the lockWasTaken variable. (In practice, the compiler will make that a hidden variable without an accessible name, by the way. I've named it to make it more readable here.) The Monitor.Enter method guarantees that acquisition of the lock will be atomic with updating the flag indicating whether the lock was taken, ensuring that the finally block will attempt to call Exit if and only if the lock was acquired.

Monitor.Exit tells the CLR that we no longer need exclusive access to whatever resources we're synchronizing access to, and if any other threads are waiting inside Monitor.Enter for the object in question, this will enable one of them to proceed. The compiler puts this inside a finally block to ensure that whether you exit from the block by running to the end, returning from the middle, or throwing an exception, the lock will be released.

The fact that the lock block calls Monitor.Exit on an exception is a double-edged sword. On the one hand, it reduces the chances of deadlock by ensuring that locks are released on failure. On the other hand, if an exception occurs while you're in the middle of modifying some shared state, the system may be in an inconsistent state; releasing locks will allow other threads access to that state, possibly causing further problems. In some situations, it might have been better to leave locks locked in the case of an exception—a deadlocked process might do less damage than one that plows on with corrupt state. A more robust strategy is to write code that guarantees consistency in the face of exceptions, either by rolling back any changes it has made if an exception prevents a complete set of updates, or by arranging to change state in an atomic way (e.g., by putting the new state into a whole new object, and substituting that for the previous one only once the updated object is fully initialized). But that's beyond what the compiler can automate for you.

Waiting and notification

The Monitor class can do more than just ensure that threads take it in turns. It provides a way for threads to sit and wait for a notification from some other thread. If a thread has acquired the monitor for a particular object, it can call Monitor.Wait, passing in that object. This has two effects: it releases the monitor and causes the thread to block. It will block until some other thread calls Monitor.Pulse or Pul seAll for the same object; a thread must have the monitor to be able to call either of these methods. (Wait, Pulse, and PulseAll all throw an exception if you call them while not holding the relevant monitor.)

If a thread calls Pulse, this enables one thread waiting in Wait to wake up. Calling PulseAll enables all of the threads waiting on that object's monitor to run. In either case, Monitor.Wait reacquires the monitor before returning, so even if you call PulseAll, the threads will wake up one at a time—a second thread cannot emerge from Wait until the first thread to do so relinquishes the monitor. In fact, no threads can return from Wait until the thread that called Pulse or PulseAll relinquishes the lock.

Example 16-10 uses Wait and Pulse to provide a wrapper around a Queue<T> that causes the thread that retrieves items from the queue to wait if the queue is empty. (This is for illustration only—if you want this sort of queue, you don't have to write your own. Use the built-in BlockingCollection<T>, or the types in System.Thread ing.Channels.)

Example 16-10. Wait and Pulse

```
public class MessageQueue<T>
{
    private readonly object _sync = new object();

    private readonly Queue<T> _queue = new Queue<T>();

    public void Post(T message)
    {
        lock (_sync)
        {
            bool wasEmpty = _queue.Count == 0;
            _queue.Enqueue(message);
            if (wasEmpty)
            {
                Monitor.Pulse(_sync);
            }
        }
    }

    public T Get()
    {
        lock (_sync)
        {
            while (_queue.Count == 0)
            {
                Monitor.Wait(_sync);
            }
            return _queue.Dequeue();
        }
    }
}
```

This example uses the monitor in two ways. It uses it through the lock keyword to ensure that only one thread at a time uses the Queue<T> that holds queued items. But it also uses waiting and notification to enable the thread that consumes items to block efficiently when the queue is empty, and for any thread that adds new items to the queue to wake up the blocked reader thread.

Timeouts

Whether you are waiting for a notification or just attempting to acquire the lock, it's possible to specify a timeout, indicating that if the operation doesn't succeed within the specified time, you would like to give up. For lock acquisition, you use a different method, TryEnter, but when waiting for notification, you just use a different overload. (There's no compiler support for this, so you won't be able to use the lock keyword.) In both cases, you can pass either an int representing the maximum time to wait, in milliseconds, or a TimeSpan value. Both return a bool indicating whether the operation succeeded.

You could use this to avoid deadlocking the process, but if your code does fail to acquire a lock within the timeout, this leaves you with the problem of deciding what to do about that. If your application is unable to acquire a lock it needs, then it can't just do whatever work it was going to do regardless. Termination of the process may be the only realistic option, because deadlock is usually a symptom of a bug, so if it occurs, your process may already be in a compromised state. That said, some developers take a less-than-rigorous approach to lock acquisition, and may regard deadlock as being normal. In this case, it might be viable to abort whatever operation you were trying, and to either retry the work later, or just log a failure, abandon this particular operation, and carry on with whatever else the process was doing. But that may be a risky strategy.

SpinLock

SpinLock presents a similar logical model to the Monitor class's Enter and Exit methods. (It does not support waiting and notification.) It is a value type, so in some circumstances, it can reduce the number of objects that need to be allocated to support locking—Monitor requires a heap-based object. However, it is also simpler: it only uses a single strategy for handling contention, whereas Monitor starts with the same strategy as SpinLock, then after a while it will switch to one with higher initial overhead, but that is more efficient if long waits are involved.

When you call either Enter method (Monitor or SpinLock), if the lock is available it will be acquired very quickly—the cost is typically a handful of CPU instructions. If the lock is already held by another thread, the CLR sits in a loop that polls the lock (i.e., it *spins*), waiting for it to be released. If the lock is only ever held for a very short length of time, this can be a very efficient strategy, because it avoids getting the OS involved, and is extremely fast in the case where the lock is available. Even when there is contention, spinning can be the most effective strategy on a multicore or multi-CPU system, because if the lock is only ever held for a very short duration (e.g., only for as long as it takes to add two decimals together), the thread will not have to spin for long before the lock becomes available again.

Where Monitor and SpinLock differ is that Monitor will eventually give up on spinning, falling back to using the OS scheduler. This will have a cost equivalent to executing many thousands (possibly even hundreds of thousands) of CPU instructions, which is why Monitor starts off using much the same approach as SpinLock. However, if the lock remains unavailable for long, spinning is inefficient—even spinning for just 1 ms will involve spinning millions of times on modern CPUs, at which point running thousands of instructions to be able to suspend the thread efficiently looks like a better bet. (Spinning is also problematic on single-core systems, because spinning relies on the thread holding the lock to be making progress.[4])

SpinLock doesn't have a fallback strategy. Unlike Monitor, it will spin until either it successfully acquires the lock, or the timeout (if you specified one) elapses. For this reason, the documentation recommends that you should not use a SpinLock if you do certain things while holding the lock, including doing anything else that might block (e.g., waiting for I/O to complete), or calling other code that might do the same. It also recommends against calling a method through a mechanism where you can't be certain which code will run (e.g., through an interface, a virtual method, or a delegate), or even allocating memory. If you're doing anything remotely nontrivial, it is better to stick with Monitor. However, access to a decimal is sufficiently simple that it might be suitable for protecting with a SpinLock, as Example 16-11 does.

Example 16-11. Protecting access to a decimal with SpinLock

```
public class DecimalTotal
{
    private decimal _total;

    private SpinLock _lock;

    public decimal Total
    {
        get
        {
            bool acquiredLock = false;
            try
            {
                _lock.Enter(ref acquiredLock);
                return _total;
            }
            finally
            {
```

---

4 On machines with just one hardware thread, when SpinLock enters its loop, it tells the OS scheduler that it wants to yield control of the CPU, so that other threads (hopefully including the one that currently has the lock) can make progress. SpinLock sometimes does this even on multicore systems to avoid some subtle problems that excessive spinning can cause.

```
            if (acquiredLock)
            {
                _lock.Exit();
            }
        }
    }
}

public void Add(decimal value)
{
    bool acquiredLock = false;
    try
    {
        _lock.Enter(ref acquiredLock);
        _total += value;
    }
    finally
    {
        if (acquiredLock)
        {
            _lock.Exit();
        }
    }
}
}
```

We have to write considerably more code than with lock due to the lack of compiler support. It might not be worth the effort—since Monitor spins to start with, it is likely to have similar performance, so the only benefit here is that we've avoided allocating an extra heap object to perform locking with (SpinLock is a struct, so it lives inside the DecimalTotal object's heap block). You should use a SpinLock only if you can demonstrate through profiling that under realistic workloads it performs better than a monitor.

Reader/Writer Locks

The ReaderWriterLockSlim class provides a different locking model than the one that Monitor and SpinLock present. With ReaderWriterLockSlim, when acquiring a lock, you specify whether you are a reader or a writer. The lock allows multiple threads to become readers simultaneously. However, when a thread asks to acquire the lock as a writer, the lock will temporarily block any further threads that try to read, and it waits for all threads that were already reading to release their locks before granting access to the thread that wants to write. Once the writer releases its lock, any threads that were waiting to read are allowed back in. This enables the writer thread to get exclusive access, but means that when no writing is occurring, readers can all proceed in parallel.

There is also a `ReaderWriterLock` class. You should not use this, because it has performance issues even when there is no contention for the lock, and it also makes suboptimal choices when both reader and writer threads are waiting to acquire the lock. The newer `ReaderWriterLockSlim` class has been around for a very long time (since .NET 3.5) and is recommended over the older class in all scenarios. The old class remains purely for backward compatibility.

This may sound like a good fit with many of the collection classes built into .NET. As I described earlier, they often support multiple concurrent reader threads, but require that modification be done exclusively by one thread at a time, and that no readers be active while modifications are made. However, you should not necessarily make this lock your first choice when you happen to have a mixture of readers and writers.

Despite the performance improvements that the "slim" lock made over its predecessor, it still takes longer to acquire this lock than it does to enter a monitor. If you plan to hold the lock only for a very short duration, it may be better just to use a monitor —the theoretical improvement offered by greater concurrency may be outweighed by the extra work required to acquire the lock in the first place. Even if you are holding the lock for a significant length of time, reader/writer locks offer benefits only if updates just happen occasionally. If you have a more or less constant stream of threads all wanting to modify the data, you are unlikely to see any performance improvement.

As with all performance-motivated choices, if you are considering using a `ReaderWriterLockSlim` instead of the simpler alternative of an ordinary monitor, you should measure performance under a realistic workload with both alternatives to see what impact, if any, the change has.

Event Objects

Windows' native API, Win32, has always offered a synchronization primitive called an *event*. From a .NET perspective, this name is a bit unfortunate, because it defines the term to mean something else entirely, as Chapter 9 discussed. In this section, when I refer to an event, I mean the synchronization primitive, unless I explicitly qualify it as a .NET event.

The `ManualResetEvent` class provides a mechanism where one thread can wait for a notification from another thread. This works differently than the `Monitor` class's `Wait` and `Pulse`. For one thing, you do not need to be in possession of a monitor or other lock to be able to wait for or signal an event. Second, the `Monitor` class's pulse methods only do anything if at least one other thread is blocked in `Monitor.Wait` for that object—if nothing was waiting, then it's as though the pulse never occurred. But a

ManualResetEvent remembers its state—once signaled, it won't return to its unsignaled state unless you manually reset it by calling Reset (hence the name). This makes it useful for scenarios where some thread A cannot proceed until some other thread B has done some work that will take an unpredictable amount of time to complete. Thread A might have to wait, but it's possible that thread B will have finished the work by the time A checks. Example 16-12 uses this technique to perform some overlapping work.

Example 16-12. Waiting for work to complete with ManualResetEvent

```
static void LogFailure(string message, string mailServer)
{
    var email = new SmtpClient(mailServer);

    using (var emailSent = new ManualResetEvent(false))
    {
        object sync = new object();
        bool tooLate = false; // Prevent call to Set after a timeout
        email.SendCompleted += (s, e) =>
            { lock(sync) { if (!tooLate) { emailSent.Set(); } } };
        email.SendAsync("logger@example.com", "sysadmin@example.com",
            "Failure Report", "An error occurred: " + message, null);

        LogPersistently(message);

        if (!emailSent.WaitOne(TimeSpan.FromMinutes(1)))
        {
            LogPersistently("Timeout sending email for error: " + message);
        }

        lock (sync)
        {
            tooLate = true;
        }
    }
}
```

This method sends an error report to a system administrator by email using the SmtpClient class from the System.Net.Mail namespace. It also calls an internal method (not shown here) called LogPersistently to record the failure in a local logging mechanism. Since these are both operations that could take some time, the code sends the email asynchronously—the SendAsync method returns immediately, and the class raises a .NET event once the email has been sent. This enables the code to get on with the call to LogPersistently while the email is being sent.

Having logged the message, the method waits for the email to go out before returning, which is where the ManualResetEvent comes in. By passing false to the constructor, I've put the event into an initial unsignaled state. But in the handler for the email `SendCompleted` .NET event, I call the synchronization event's `Set` method, which will put it into the signaled state. (In production code, I'd also check the .NET event handler's argument to see if there was an error, but I've omitted that here because it's not relevant to the point I'm illustrating.) Finally, I call `WaitOne`, which will block until the event is signaled. The `SmtpClient` might do its job so quickly that the email has already gone by the time my call to `LogPersistently` returns. But that's OK—in that case, `WaitOne` returns immediately, because the `ManualResetEvent` stays signaled once you call `Set`. So it doesn't matter which piece of work finishes first—the persistent logging or sending the email—in either case, `WaitOne` will let the thread continue when the email has been sent. (For the background on this method's curious name, see the next sidebar, "WaitHandle" on page 684.)

WaitHandle

In Windows implementations of .NET, `ManualResetEvent` is a wrapper around a Win32 event object. There are several other synchronization classes that are also wrappers around underlying OS synchronization primitives: `AutoResetEvent`, `Mutex`, and `Sempahore`. These all derive from a common base class, `WaitHandle`. (On non-Windows .NET implementations, the class library just implements equivalent behavior where directly equivalent OS primitives are not available.)

A `WaitHandle` can be in one of two states: signaled or not signaled. The exact meaning of this varies from one primitive to the next. A `ManualReset` event becomes signaled when you call `Set` (and it stays in the signaled state until explicitly unset). A `Mutex` is in the signaled state only if no thread currently possesses it. Despite the variations in interpretation, waiting for a `WaitHandle` will always block if it is not signaled, and will not block if it is signaled.

With Win32 synchronization objects, you can either wait for a single item to become signaled, or you can wait on multiple objects, either until any of them is signaled, or until all of them are. The `WaitHandle` class defines `WaitOne`, `WaitAny`, and `WaitAll` methods corresponding to these three ways of waiting. With primitives where a successful wait has the side effect of acquiring ownership (exclusively in the case of `Mutex`, or partially with `Semaphore`), there can be a problem with attempting to wait on multiple objects—if two threads both attempt to acquire the same objects but do so in a different order, deadlock will ensue if these attempts overlap. But `WaitAll` deals with that—the order in which you specify the items does not matter, because it acquires them atomically—it will not allow any of the waits to succeed until they can all succeed simultaneously. (Of course, if a single thread makes a second call to `WaitAll`, without first releasing all objects acquired in an earlier call, the door will still be open to deadlock. `WaitAll` helps only if you can acquire everything you need in a single step.)

WaitAll does not work on a thread that is using COM's STA mode because of a limitation in the underlying Windows API that it depends on. As I described in Chapter 14, if your program's entry point is annotated with [STAThread], it will be using this mode, as will any thread that hosts UI elements.

You can also use a WaitHandle in conjunction with the thread pool. The ThreadPool class has a RegisterWaitForSingleObject method that accepts any WaitHandle and invokes the callback you supply when the handle becomes signaled. As I'll discuss later, this can be a bad idea for certain kinds of WaitHandle-derived types, such as Mutex.

There's also an AutoResetEvent. As soon as a single thread has returned from waiting for such an event, it automatically reverts to the unsignaled state. Thus, calling Set on this event will allow at most one thread through. If you call Set once while no threads are waiting, the event will remain set, so unlike Monitor.Pulse, the notification will not be lost. However, the event does not maintain a count of the number of outstanding sets—if you call Set twice while no threads are waiting for the event, it will still allow only the first thread through, resetting immediately.

Both of these event types derive only indirectly from WaitHandle, through the EventWaitHandle base class. You can use this directly, and it lets you specify manual or automatic resetting with a constructor argument. But what's more interesting about EventWaitHandle is that it lets you work across process boundaries (on Windows only). The underlying Win32 event objects can be given names, and if you know the name of an event created by another process, you can open it by passing the name when constructing an EventWaitHandle. (If no event with the name you specify exists yet, your process will be the one that creates it.) No equivalent to named events exist on Unix, so you will get a PlatformNotSupportedException if you try to create one in those environments, although you are free to use these types as long as you don't attempt to specify a name.

There is also a ManualResetEventSlim class. However, unlike the nonslim reader/writer, ManualResetEvent has not been superseded by its slim successor because only the older type supports cross-process use. The ManualResetEventSlim class's main benefit is that if your code needs to wait only for a very short time, it can be more efficient because it will poll (much like a SpinLock) for a while. This saves it from having to use relatively expensive OS scheduler services. However, it will eventually give up and fall back to a more heavyweight mechanism. (Even in this case, it's marginally more efficient, because it doesn't need to support cross-process operation, so it uses a more lightweight mechanism.) There is no slim version of the automatic event, because automatic reset events are not all that widely used.

Barrier

In the preceding section, I showed how you can use an event to coordinate concurrent work, enabling one thread to wait until something else has happened before proceeding. The class library offers a class that can handle similar kinds of coordination, but with slightly different semantics. The `Barrier` class can handle multiple participants, and can also support multiple *phases*, meaning that threads can wait for one another several times as work progresses. `Barrier` is symmetric—whereas in Example 16-12, the event handler calls `Set` while another thread calls `WaitOne`, with a `Barrier`, all participants call the `SignalAndWait` method, which effectively combines the set and wait into one operation.

When a participant calls `SignalAndWait`, the method will block until all of the participants have called it, at which point they will all be unblocked and free to continue. The `Barrier` knows how many participants to expect, because you pass the count as a constructor argument.

Multiphase operation simply involves going around again. Once the final participant calls `SignalAndWait`, releasing the rest, if any thread calls `SignalAndWait` a second time, it will block just like before, until all the others call it a second time. The `CurrentPhaseNumber` tells you how many times this has occurred so far.

The symmetry makes `Barrier` a less suitable solution than `ManualResetEvent` in Example 16-12, because in that case, only one of the threads really needs to wait. There's no benefit in making the `SendComplete` event handler wait for the persistent log update to finish—only one of the participants cares when work is complete. `ManualResetEvent` supports only a single participant, but that's not necessarily a reason to use `Barrier`. If you want event-style asymmetry with multiple participants, there's another approach: countdowns.

CountdownEvent

The `CountdownEvent` class is similar to an event, but it allows you to specify that it must be signaled some particular number of times before it allows waiting threads through. The constructor takes an initial count argument, and you can increase the count at any time by calling `AddCount`. You call the `Signal` method to reduce the count; by default, it will reduce it by one, but there's an overload that lets you reduce it by a specified number.

The `Wait` method blocks until the count reaches zero. If you want to inspect the current count to see how far there is to go, you can read the `CurrentCount` property.

Semaphores

Another count-based system that is widely used in concurrent systems is known as a *semaphore*. Windows has native support for this, and .NET's Semaphore class was originally designed as a wrapper for it. Like the event wrappers, Semaphore derives from WaitHandle, and on non-Windows platforms, the behavior is emulated. Whereas a CountdownEvent lets through waiting threads only once the count gets to zero, a Semaphore starts blocking threads only when the count gets to zero. You could use this if you wanted to ensure that no more than a particular number of threads were performing certain work simultaneously.

Because Semaphore derives from WaitHandle, you call the WaitOne method to wait. This blocks only if the count is already zero. It decrements the count by one when it returns. You increment the count by calling Release. You specify the initial count as a constructor argument, and you must also supply a maximum count—if a call to Release attempts to set the count above the maximum, it will throw an exception.

As with events, Windows supports the cross-process use of semaphores, so you can optionally pass a semaphore name as a constructor argument. This will open an existing semaphore, or create a new one if a semaphore with the specified name does not yet exist.

There's also a SemaphoreSlim class. Like ManualResetEventSlim, this offers a performance benefit in scenarios where threads will not normally have to block for long. SemaphoreSlim offers two ways to decrement the count. Its Wait method works much like the Semaphore class's WaitOne, but it also offers WaitAsync, which returns a Task that completes once the count is nonzero (and it decrements the count as it completes the task). This means you do not need to block a thread while you wait for the semaphore to become available. Moreover, it means you can use the await keyword described in Chapter 17 to decrement a semaphore.

Mutex

Windows defines a *mutex* synchronization primitive for which .NET provides a wrapper class, Mutex. The name is short for "mutually exclusive," because only one thread at a time can be in possession of a mutex—if thread A owns the mutex, thread B cannot, and vice versa, for example. Of course, this is exactly what the lock keyword does for us through the Monitor class, but Mutex offers two advantages. It offers cross-process support: as with other cross-process synchronization primitives, you can pass in a name when you construct a mutex. (And unlike all the others, this type supports naming even on Unix-based platforms.) And with Mutex you can wait for multiple objects in a single operation.

The `ThreadPool.RegisterWaitForSingleObject` method does not work for a mutex, because Win32 requires mutex ownership to be tied to a particular thread, and the inner workings of the thread pool mean that `RegisterWaitForSingleObject` is unable to determine which thread pool thread handles the callback with the mutex.

You acquire a mutex by calling `WaitOne`, and if some other thread owns the mutex at the time, `WaitOne` will block until that thread calls `ReleaseMutex`. Once `WaitOne` returns successfully, you own the mutex. You must release the mutex from the same thread on which you acquired it.

There is no "slim" version of the `Mutex` class. We already have a low-overhead equivalent, because all .NET objects have the innate ability to provide lightweight mutual exclusion, thanks to `Monitor` and the `lock` keyword.

Interlocked

The `Interlocked` class is a little different from the other types I've described so far in this section. It supports concurrent access to shared data, but it is not a synchronization primitive. Instead, it defines static methods that provide atomic forms of various simple operations.

For example, it provides `Increment`, `Decrement`, and `Add` methods, with overloads supporting `int` and `long` values. (These are all similar—incrementing or decrementing are just addition by 1 or –1.) Addition involves reading a value from some storage location, calculating a modified value, and storing that back in the same storage location, and if you use normal C# operators to do this, things can go wrong if multiple threads try to modify the same location simultaneously. If the value is initially 0, and some thread reads that value and then another thread also reads the value, if both then add 1 and store the result back, they will both end up writing back 1—two threads attempted to increment the value, but it went up only by one. The `Interlocked` form of these operations prevents this sort of overlap.

`Interlocked` also offers various methods for swapping values. The `Exchange` method takes two arguments: a reference to a value and a value. This returns the value currently in the location referred to by the first argument, and also overwrites that location with the value supplied as a second argument, and it performs these two steps as a single atomic operation. There are overloads supporting `int`, `long`, `object`, `float`, `double`, and a type called `IntPtr`, which represents an unmanaged pointer. There is also a generic `Exchange<T>`, where `T` can be any reference type.

There is also support for conditional exchange, with the `CompareExchange` method. This takes three values—as with `Exchange`, it takes a reference to some variable you wish to modify, and the value you want to replace it with, but it also takes a third argument: the value you think is already in the storage location. If the value in the storage location does not match the expected value, this method will not change the storage location. (It still returns whatever value was in that storage location, whether it modifies it or not.) It's actually possible to implement the other `Interlocked` operations I've described in terms of this one. Example 16-13 uses it to implement an interlocked increment operation.

Example 16-13. Using CompareExchange

```
static int InterlockedIncrement(ref int target)
{
    int current, newValue;
    do
    {
        current = target;
        newValue = current + 1;
    }
    while (Interlocked.CompareExchange(ref target, newValue, current)
            != current);
    return newValue;
}
```

The pattern would be the same for other operations: read the current value, calculate the value with which to replace it, and then replace it only if the value doesn't appear to have changed in the meantime. If the value changes in between fetching the current value and replacing it, go around again. You need to be a little bit careful here—even if the `CompareExchange` succeeds, it's possible that other threads modified the value twice between your reading the value and updating it, with the second update putting things back how they were before the first. With addition and subtraction, that doesn't really matter, because it doesn't affect the outcome, but in general, you should not presume too much about what a successful update signifies. If you're in doubt, it's often better to stick with one of the more heavyweight synchronization mechanisms.

The simplest `Interlocked` operation is the `Read` method. This takes a `ref long`, and reads the value atomically with respect to any other operations on 64-bit values that you perform through `Interlocked`. This enables you to read 64-bit values safely—in general, the CLR does not guarantee that 64-bit reads will be atomic. (In a 64-bit process, they normally will be, but if you want atomicity on 32-bit architectures, you need to use `Interlocked.Read`.) There is no overload for 32-bit values, because reading and writing those is always atomic.

The operations supported by `Interlocked` correspond to the atomic operations that most CPUs can support more or less directly. (Some CPU architectures support all the operations innately, while others support only the compare and exchange, building everything else up out of that. But in any case, these operations are at most a few instructions.) This means they are reasonably efficient. They are considerably more costly than performing equivalent noninterlocked operations with ordinary code, because atomic CPU instructions need to coordinate across all CPU cores (and across all CPU chips in computers that have multiple physically separate CPUs installed) to guarantee atomicity. Nonetheless, they incur a fraction of the cost you pay when a lock statement ends up blocking the thread at the OS level.

These sorts of operations are sometimes described as *lock free*. This is not entirely accurate—the computer does acquire locks very briefly at a fairly low level in the hardware. Atomic read-modify-write operations effectively acquire an exclusive lock on the computer's memory for two bus cycles. However, no OS locks are acquired, the scheduler does not need to get involved, and the locks are held for an extremely short duration—often for just one machine code instruction. More significantly, the highly specialized and low-level form of locking used here does not permit holding onto one lock while waiting to acquire another—code can lock only one thing at a time. This means that this sort of operation will not deadlock. However, the simplicity that rules out deadlocks cuts both ways.

The downside of interlocked operations is that the atomicity applies only to extremely simple operations. It's very hard to build more complex logic in a way that works correctly in a multithreaded environment using just Interlocked. It's easier and considerably less risky to use the higher-level synchronization primitives, because those make it fairly easy to protect more complex operations rather than just individual calculations. You would typically use Interlocked only in extremely performance-sensitive work, and even then, you should measure carefully to verify that it's having the effect you hope—code such as Example 16-13 could in theory loop any number of times before eventually completing, so it could end up costing you more than you expect.

One of the biggest challenges with writing correct code when using low-level atomic operations is that you may encounter problems caused by the way CPU caches work. Work done by one thread may not become visible instantly to other threads, and in some cases, memory access may not necessarily occur in the order that your code specifies. Using higher-level synchronization primitives sidesteps these issues by enforcing certain ordering constraints, but if you decide instead to use Interlocked to build your own synchronization mechanisms, you will need to understand the memory model that .NET defines for when multiple threads access the same memory simultaneously, and you will typically need to use either the MemoryBarrier method defined by the Interlocked class or the various methods defined by the Volatile class to ensure correctness. This is beyond the scope of this book, and it's also a really good way to write code that looks like it works but turns out to go wrong under heavy load (i.e., when it probably matters most), so these sorts of techniques are rarely worth the cost. Stick with the other mechanisms I've discussed in this chapter unless you really have no alternative.

Lazy Initialization

When you need an object to be accessible from multiple threads, if it's possible for that object to be immutable (i.e., its fields never change after construction), you can often avoid the need for synchronization. It is always safe for multiple threads to read from the same location simultaneously—trouble sets in only if the data needs to change. However, there is one challenge: when and how do you initialize the shared object? One solution might be to store a reference to the object in a static field initialized from a static constructor or a field initializer—the CLR guarantees to run the static initialization for any class just once. However, this might cause the object to be created earlier than you want. If you perform too much work in static initialization, this can have an adverse effect on how long it takes your application to start running.

You might want to wait until the object is first needed before initializing it. This is called *lazy initialization*. This is not particularly hard to achieve—you can just check a field to see if it's null and initialize it if not, using lock to ensure that only one thread gets to construct the value. However, this is an area in which developers seem to have a remarkable appetite for showing how clever they are, with the potentially undesirable corollary of demonstrating that they're not as clever as they think they are. The lock keyword works fairly efficiently, but it's possible to do better by using Interlocked. However, the subtleties of memory access reordering on multiprocessor systems make it easy to write code that runs quickly, looks clever, and doesn't always work. To try to avert this recurring problem, .NET provides two classes to perform lazy initialization without using lock or other potentially expensive synchronization primitives. The easiest to use is Lazy<T>.

Lazy<T>

The Lazy<T> class provides a Value property of type T, and it will not create the instance that Value returns until the first time something reads the property. By default, Lazy<T> will use the no-arguments constructor for T, but you can provide a callback argument that lets you supply your own method for creating the instance.

Lazy<T> is able to handle race conditions for you. In fact, you can configure the exact level of multithreaded protection you require. Since lazy initialization can also be useful in single-threaded environments, you can disable multithreaded support entirely (by passing either false or LazyThreadSafetyMode.None as a constructor argument). But for multithreaded environments, you can choose between the other two modes in the LazyThreadSafetyMode enumeration. These determine what happens if multiple threads all try to read the Value property for the first time more or less simultaneously. PublicationOnly does not attempt to ensure that only one thread creates an object—it only applies any synchronization at the point at which a thread finishes creating an object. The first thread to complete construction or initialization gets to supply the object, and the ones produced by any other threads that had started initialization are all discarded. Once a value is available, all further attempts to read Value will just return that. If you choose ExecutionAndPublication, only a single thread will be allowed to attempt construction. That may seem less wasteful, but PublicationOnly offers a potential advantage: because it avoids holding any locks during initialization, you are less likely to introduce deadlock bugs if the initialization code itself attempts to acquire any locks. PublicationOnly also handles errors differently. If the first initialization attempt throws an exception, other threads that had begun a construction attempt are given a chance to complete, whereas with Executio nAndPublication, if the one and only attempt to initialize fails, the exception is retained and will be thrown each time any code reads Value.

LazyInitializer

The other class supporting lazy initialization is LazyInitializer. This is a static class, and you use it entirely through its static generic methods. It is marginally more complex to use than Lazy<T>, but it avoids the need to allocate an extra object in addition to the lazily allocated instance you require. Example 16-14 shows how to use it.

Example 16-14. Using LazyInitializer

```
public class Cache<T>
{
    private static Dictionary<string, T> _d;

    public static IDictionary<string, T> Dictionary =>
        LazyInitializer.EnsureInitialized(ref _d);
}
```

If the field is null, the EnsureInitialized method constructs an instance of the argument type—Dictionary<string, T>, in this case. Otherwise, it will return the value already in the field. There are some other overloads. You can pass a callback, much as you can to Lazy<T>. You can also pass a ref bool argument, which it will inspect to discover whether initialization has already occurred (and it sets this to true when it performs initialization).

A static field initializer would have given us the same once-and-once-only initialization, but might have ended up running far earlier in the process's lifetime. In a more complex class with multiple fields, static initialization might even cause unnecessary work, because it happens for the entire class, so you might end up constructing objects that don't get used. This could increase the amount of time it takes for an application to start up. LazyInitializer lets you initialize individual fields as and when they are first used, ensuring that you do only work that is needed.

Other Class Library Concurrency Support

The System.Collections.Concurrent namespace defines various collections that make more generous guarantees in the face of multithreading than the usual collections, meaning you may be able to use them without needing any other synchronization primitives. Take care, though—as always, even though individual operations may have well-defined behavior in a multithreaded world, that doesn't necessarily help you if the operation you need to perform involves multiple steps. You may still need coordination at a broader scope to guarantee consistency. But in some situations, the concurrent collections may be all you need.

Unlike the nonconcurrent collections, ConcurrentDictionary, ConcurrentBag, ConcurrentStack, and ConcurrentQueue all support modification of their contents even while enumeration (e.g., with a foreach loop) of those contents is in progress. The dictionary provides a live enumerator, in the sense that if values are added or removed while you're in the middle of enumerating, the enumerator might show you some of the added items and it might not show you the removed items. It makes no firm guarantees, not least because with multithreaded code, when two things happen on two different threads, it's not always entirely clear which happened first—the laws of relativity mean that it may depend on your point of view. This means that it's possible for an enumerator to seem to return an item after that item was removed from the dictionary. The bag, stack, and queue take a different approach: their enumerators all take a snapshot and iterate over that, so a foreach loop will see a set of contents that is consistent with what was in the collection at some point in the past, even though it may since have changed.

As I already mentioned in Chapter 5, the concurrent collections present APIs that are similar to their nonconcurrent counterparts, but with some additional members to support atomic addition and removal of items.

Another part of the class library that can help you deal with concurrency without needing to make explicit use of synchronization primitives is Rx (the subject of Chapter 11). It offers various operators that can combine multiple asynchronous streams together into a single stream. These manage concurrency issues for you— remember that any single observable will provide observers with items one at a time. Rx takes the necessary steps to ensure that it stays within these rules even when it combines inputs from numerous individual streams that are all producing items concurrently. It will never ask an observer to deal with more than one thing at a time.

The System.Threading.Channels NuGet package offers types that support producer/ consumer patterns, in which one or more threads generate data, while other threads consume that data. You can choose whether channels are buffered, enabling producers to get ahead of consumers, and if so, by how much. (The `BlockingCollection<T>` in `System.Collections.Concurrent` also offers this kind of service. However, it is less flexible, and it does not support the `await` keyword described in Chapter 17.)

Finally, in multithreaded scenarios it is worth considering the immutable collection classes, which I described in Chapter 5. These support concurrent access from any number of threads, and because they are immutable, the question of how to handle concurrent write access never arises. Obviously, immutability imposes considerable constraints but if you can find a way to work with these types (and remember, the built-in `string` type is immutable, so you already have some experience of working with immutable data), they can be very useful in some concurrent scenarios.

Tasks

Earlier in this chapter, I showed how to use the `Task` class to launch work in the thread pool. This class is more than just a wrapper for the thread pool. `Task` and the related types that form the Task Parallel Library (TPL) can handle a wider range of scenarios. Tasks are particularly important because C#'s asynchronous language features (which are the topic of Chapter 17) are able to work directly with task objects. A great many APIs in the .NET class library offer task-based asynchronous operation.

Although tasks are the preferred way to use the thread pool, they are not just about multithreading. The basic abstractions are more flexible than that.

The Task and Task<T> Classes

There are two classes at the heart of the TPL: `Task` and a class that derives from it, `Task<T>`. The `Task` base class represents some work that may take some time to complete. `Task<T>` extends this to represent work that produces a result (of type T) when it completes. (The nongeneric `Task` does not produce any result. It's the asynchronous equivalent of a `void` return type.) Notice that these are not concepts that necessarily involve threads.

Most I/O operations can take a while to complete, and in most cases, the .NET class library provides task-based APIs for them. Example 16-15 uses an asynchronous method to fetch the content of a web page as a string. Since it cannot return the string immediately—it might take a while to download the page—it returns a task instead.

Example 16-15. Task-based web download

```
var w = new HttpClient();
string url = "https://endjin.com/";
Task<string> webGetTask = w.GetStringAsync(url);
```

Most task-based APIs follow a naming convention in which they end in Async, and if there's a corresponding synchronous API, it will have the same name but without the Async suffix. For example, the Stream class in System.IO, which provides access to streams of bytes, has a Write method to write bytes to a stream, and that method is synchronous (i.e., it waits until it finishes its work before returning). It also offers a WriteAsync method. This does the same as Write, but because it's asynchronous, it returns without waiting for its work to complete. It returns a Task to represent the work; this convention called the *task-based asynchronous pattern* (TAP).

That GetStringAsync method does not wait for the download to complete, so it returns almost immediately. To perform the download, the computer has to send a message to the relevant server, and then it must wait for a response. Once the request is on its way, there's no work for the CPU to do until the response comes in, meaning that this operation does not need to involve a thread for the majority of the time that the request is in progress. So this method does not wrap some underlying synchronous version of the API in a call to Task.Run. In fact, HttpClient doesn't offer synchronous equivalents. And with classes that offer I/O APIs in both forms, such as Stream, the synchronous versions are often wrappers around a fundamentally asynchronous implementation: when you call a blocking API to perform I/O, it will typically perform an asynchronous operation under the covers, and then just block the calling thread until that work completes.

So, although the Task and Task<T> classes make it very easy to produce tasks that work by running methods on thread pool threads, they are also able to represent fundamentally asynchronous operations that do not require the use of a thread for most of their duration. Although it's not part of the official terminology, I describe this kind of operation as a *threadless task*, to distinguish it from tasks that run entirely on thread pool threads.

ValueTask and ValueTask<T>

Task and Task<T> are pretty flexible, and not just because they can represent both thread-based and threadless operations. As you'll see, they offer several mechanisms for discovering when the work they represent completes, including the ability to combine multiple tasks into one. Multiple threads can all wait on the same task simultaneously. You can write caching mechanisms that repeatedly hand out the same task, even long after the task completes. This is all very convenient, but it means that these task types also have some overheads. For more constrained cases, .NET defines less flexible ValueTask and ValueTask<T> types that are more efficient in certain circumstances.

The most important difference between these types and their ordinary counterparts is that `ValueTask` and `ValueTask<T>` are value types. This is significant in performance-sensitive code because it can reduce the number of objects that code allocates, reducing the amount of time an application spends performing garbage collection work. You might be thinking that the context switching costs typically involved with concurrent work are likely to be high enough that the cost of an object allocation will be the least of your concerns when dealing with asynchronous operations. And while this is often true, there's one very important scenario where the GC overhead of `Task<T>` can be problematic: operations that sometimes run slowly but usually don't.

It is very common for I/O APIs to perform buffering to reduce the number of calls into the OS. If you write a few bytes into a `Stream`, it will typically put those into a buffer, and wait until either you've written enough data to make it worth sending it to the OS, or you've explicitly called `Flush`. And it's also common for reads to be buffered—if you read a single byte from a file, the OS will typically have to read an entire sector from the disk (usually at least 4 KB), and that data usually gets saved somewhere in memory so that when you ask for the second byte, no more I/O needs to happen. The practical upshot is that if you write a loop that reads data from a file in relatively small chunks (e.g., one line of text at a time), the majority of read operations will complete straightaway because the data being read has already been fetched.

In these cases where the overwhelming majority of calls into asynchronous APIs complete immediately, the GC overheads of creating task objects can become significant. This is why .NET Core 2.0 introduced `ValueTask` and `ValueTask<T>`. (These are also available on older versions of .NET via the `System.Threading.Tasks.Exten sions` NuGet package, and they are part of .NET Standard 2.1.) These make it possible for potentially asynchronous operations to complete immediately without needing to allocate any objects. In cases where immediate completion is not possible, these types end up being wrappers for `Task` or `Task<T>` objects, at which point the overheads return, but in cases where only a small fraction of calls need to do that, these types can offer significant performance boosts, particularly in code that uses the low-allocation techniques described in Chapter 18.

`ValueTask` is rarely used, because asynchronous operations that produce no result can just return the `Task.CompletedTask` static property, which provides a reusable task that is already in the completed state, avoiding any GC overhead. But tasks that need to produce a result generally can't reuse existing tasks. (There are some exceptions: the .NET class library will often use cached precompleted tasks for `Task<bool>`, because there are only two possible outcomes. But for `Task<int>`, there's no practical way to maintain a list of precompleted tasks for every possible result.)

These value task types have some constraints. They are single use: unlike `Task` and `Task<T>`, you must not store these types in a dictionary or a `Lazy<T>` to provide a cached asynchronous value. It is an error to attempt to retrieve the Result of a Value Task<T> before it has completed. It is also an error to retreive the Result more than once. In general, you should use a ValueTask or ValueTask<T> with exactly one await operation (as described in Chapter 17) and then never use it again. (Alternatively, if necessary, you can escape these restrictions by calling its AsTask method to obtain a full Task, or Task<T> with all the corresponding overheads, at which point you should not do anything more with the value task.)

Because the value type tasks were introduced many years after the TPL first appeared, .NET class libraries often use Task<T> where you might expect to see a Val ueTask<T>. For example, the Stream class's ReadAsync methods are all prime candidates, but because most of those were defined long before ValueTask<T> existed, they mostly return Task<T>. The recently added overload that accepts a Memory<byte> instead of a byte[] does return a ValueTask<T>, though, and more generally, where APIs have been augmented to add support for the new memory-efficient techniques described in Chapter 18, these will usually return ValueTask<T>. And if you're in a performance-sensitive world where the GC overhead of a task is significant, you will likely want to be using those techniques in any case.

Task creation options

Instead of using Task.Run, you can get more control over certain aspects of a new thread-based task by creating it with the StartNew method of either Task.Factory or Task<T>.Factory, depending on whether your task needs to return a result. Some overloads of StartNew take an argument of the enum type TaskCreationOptions, which provides some control over how the TPL schedules the task.

The PreferFairness flag asks to opt out of the cache-friendly FIFO scheduling that the thread pool normally uses for tasks, and instead aims to run the task after any tasks that have already been scheduled (much like the legacy behavior you get if you use the ThreadPool class directly).

The LongRunning flag warns the TPL that the task may run for a long time. By default, the TPL's scheduler optimizes for relatively short work items—anything up to a few seconds. This flag indicates that the work might take longer than that, in which case the TPL may modify its scheduling. If there are too many long-running tasks, they might use up all the threads, and even though some of the queued work items might be for much shorter pieces of work, those will still take a long time to finish, because they'll have to wait in line behind the slow work before they can even start. But if the TPL knows which items are likely to run quickly and which are likely to be slower, it can prioritize them differently to avoid such problems.

The other TaskCreationOptions settings relate to parent/child task relationships and schedulers, which I'll describe later.

Task status

A task goes through a number of states in its lifetime, and you can use the `Task` class's `Status` property to discover where it has gotten to. This returns a value of the enum type `TaskStatus`. If a task completes successfully, the property will return the enumeration's `RanToCompletion` value. If the task fails, it will be `Faulted`. If you cancel a task using the technique shown in "Cancellation" on page 708, the status will then be `Canceled`.

There are several variations on a theme of "in progress," of which `Running` is the most obvious—it means that some thread is currently executing the task. A task representing I/O doesn't typically require a thread while it is in progress, so it never enters that state—it starts in the `WaitingForActivation` state and then typically transitions directly to one of the three final states (`RanToCompletion`, `Faulted`, or `Canceled`). A thread-based task can also be in this `WaitingForActivation` state, but only if something is preventing it from running, which would typically happen if you set it up to run only when some other task completes (which I'll show how to do shortly). A thread-based task may also be in the `WaitingToRun` state, which means that it's in a queue waiting for a thread pool thread to become available. It's possible to establish parent/child relationships between tasks, and a parent that has already finished but that created some child tasks that are not yet complete will be in the `WaitingForChildrenToComplete` state.

Finally, there's the `Created` state. You don't see this very often, because it represents a thread-based task that you have created but have not yet asked to run. You'll never see this with a task created using the task factory's `StartNew` method, or with `Task.Run`, but you will see this if you construct a new `Task` directly.

The level of detail in the `TaskStatus` property may not be very interesting most of the time, so the `Task` class defines various simpler `bool` properties. If you want to know only whether the task has no more work to do (and don't care whether it succeeded, failed, or was cancelled), there's the `IsCompleted` property. If you want to check for failure or cancellation, use `IsFaulted` or `IsCanceled`.

Retrieving the result

Suppose you've got a `Task<T>`, either from an API that provides one, or by creating a thread-based task that returns a value. If the task completes successfully, you are likely to want to retrieve its result. Predictably enough, you get this from the `Result` property. So the task created by Example 16-15 makes the web page content available in `webGetTask.Result`.

If you try to read the `Result` property before the task completes, it will block your thread until the result is available. (If you have a plain `Task`, which does not return a result, and you would like to wait for that to finish, you can just call Wait instead.) If the operation then fails, Result throws an exception (as does Wait), although that is not as straightforward as you might expect, as I will discuss in "Error Handling" on page 704.

 You should avoid using Result on an uncompleted task. In some scenarios, it risks deadlock. This is particularly common in desktop applications, because certain work needs to happen on particular threads, and if you block a thread by reading the Result of an incomplete task, you might prevent the task from completing. The task may have been depending indirectly on some other work to finish, and if that other work needs to be run on the same thread that you've just blocked, you've caused a deadlock. Even if you don't deadlock, blocking on Result can cause performance issues by hogging thread pool threads that might otherwise have been able to get on with useful work. And reading Result in an uncompleted ValueTask<T> is not permitted.

In most cases, it is far better to use C#'s asynchronous language features to retrieve the result. These are the subject of the next chapter, but as a preview, Example 16-16 shows how you could use this to get the result of the task that fetches a web page. (You'll need to apply the async keyword in front of the method declaration to be able to use the await keyword.)

Example 16-16. Getting a task's results with await

```
string pageContent = await webGetTask;
```

This may not look like an exciting improvement on simply writing webGet Task.Result, but as I'll show in Chapter 17, this code is not quite what it seems—the C# compiler restructures this statement into a callback-driven state machine that enables you to get the result without blocking the calling thread. (If the operation hasn't finished, the thread returns to the caller, and the remainder of the method runs some time later when the operation completes.)

If you're not using the asynchronous language features, how should you discover when a task has completed? Result or Wait let you just sit and wait for that to happen, blocking the thread, but that rather defeats the purpose of using an asynchronous API in the first place. You will normally want to be notified when the task completes, and you can do this with a *continuation*.

Continuations

Tasks provide various overloads of a method called `ContinueWith`. This creates a new thread-based task that will execute when the task on which you called `ContinueWith` finishes (whether it does so successfully or with failure or cancellation). Example 16-17 uses this on the task created in Example 16-15.

Example 16-17. A continuation

```
webGetTask.ContinueWith(t =>
{
    string webContent = t.Result;
    Console.WriteLine("Web page length: " + webContent.Length);
});
```

A continuation task is always a thread-based task (regardless of whether its antecedent task was thread-based, I/O-based, or something else). The task gets created as soon as you call `ContinueWith`, but does not become runnable until its antecedent task completes. (It starts out in the `WaitingForActivation` state.)

 A continuation is a task in its own right—`ContinueWith` returns either a `Task<T>` or `Task`, depending on whether the delegate you supply returns a result. You can set up a continuation for a continuation if you want to chain together a sequence of operations.

The method you provide for the continuation (such as the lambda in Example 16-17) receives the antecedent task as its argument, and I've used this to retrieve the result. I could also have used the `webGetTask` variable, which is in scope from the containing method, as it refers to the same task. However, by using the argument, the lambda in Example 16-17 doesn't use any variables from its containing method, which enables the compiler to produce slightly more efficient code—it doesn't need to create an object to hold shared variables, and it can reuse the delegate instance it creates because it doesn't have to create a context-specific one for each call. This means I could also easily separate this out into an ordinary noninline method, if I felt that would make the code easier to read.

You might be thinking that there's a possible problem in Example 16-17: what if the download completes extremely quickly, so that `webGetTask` has already completed before the code manages to attach the continuation? In fact, that doesn't matter—if you call `ContinueWith` on a task that has already completed, it will still run the continuation. It just schedules it immediately. You can attach as many continuations as you like. All the continuations you attach before the task completes will be scheduled for execution when it does complete. And any that you attach after the task has completed will be scheduled immediately.

By default, a continuation task will be scheduled for execution on the thread pool like any other task. However, there are some things you can do to change how it runs.

Continuation options

Some overloads of `ContinueWith` take an argument of the enum type `TaskContinua tionOptions`, which controls how (and whether) your task is scheduled. This includes all of the same options that are available with `TaskCreationOptions`, but adds some others specific to continuations.

You can specify that the continuation should run only in certain circumstances. For example, the `OnlyOnRanToCompletion` flag will ensure that the continuation runs only if the antecedent task succeeds. The `OnlyOnFaulted` and `OnlyOnCanceled` flags have obvious similar meanings. Alternatively, you can specify `NotOnRanToComple tion`, which means that the continuation will run only if the task either faults or is cancelled.

 You can create multiple continuations for a single task. So you could set up one to handle the success case, and another one to handle failures.

You can also specify `ExecuteSynchronously`. This indicates that the continuation should not be scheduled as a separate work item. Normally, when a task completes, any continuations for that task will be scheduled for execution and will have to wait until the normal thread pool mechanisms pick the work items out of the queue and execute them. (This won't take long if you use the default options—unless you specify `PreferFairness`, the LIFO operation the thread pool uses for tasks, which means that the most recently scheduled items run first.) However, if your completion does only the tiniest amount of work, the overhead of scheduling it as a completely separate item may be overkill. So `ExecuteSynchronously` lets you piggyback the completion task on the same thread pool work item that ran the antecedent—the TPL will run this kind of continuation immediately after the antecedent finishes before returning the thread to the pool. You should use this option only if the continuation will run quickly.

The `LazyCancellation` option handles a tricky situation that can occur if you make tasks cancellable (as described later in "Cancellation" on page 708), and you are using continuations. If you cancel a task, any continuations will, by default, become runnable instantly. If the task being cancelled was itself set up as a continuation for another task that hadn't yet finished, and if it has a continuation of its own, as Example 16-18 shows, this can have a mildly surprising effect.

Example 16-18. Cancellation and chained continuations

```
private static void ShowContinuations()
{
    Task op = Task.Run(DoSomething);
    var cs = new CancellationTokenSource();
    Task onDone = op.ContinueWith(
        _ => Console.WriteLine("Never runs"),
        cs.Token);
    Task andAnotherThing = onDone.ContinueWith(
        _ => Console.WriteLine("Continuation's continuation"));
    cs.Cancel();
}

static void DoSomething()
{
    Thread.Sleep(1000);
    Console.WriteLine("Initial task finishing");
}
```

This creates a task that will call DoSomething, followed by a cancellable continuation for that task (the Task in onDone), and then a final task that is a continuation for the first continuation (andAnotherThing). This code cancels almost immediately, which is almost certain to happen before the first task completes. The effect of this is that the final task runs before the first completes. The final andAnotherThing task becomes runnable when onDone completes, even if that completion was due to onDone being cancelled. Since there was a chain here—andAnotherThing is a continuation for onDone which is a continuation for op—it is a bit odd that andAnotherThing ends up running before op has finished. LazyCancellation changes the behavior so that the first continuation will not be deemed to have completed until its antecedent completes, meaning that the final continuation will run only after the first task has finished.

There's another mechanism for controlling how tasks execute: you can specify a scheduler.

Schedulers

All thread-based tasks are executed by a TaskScheduler. By default, you'll get the TPL-supplied scheduler that runs work items via the thread pool. However, there are other kinds of schedulers, and you can even write your own.

The most common reason for selecting a nondefault scheduler is to handle thread affinity requirements. The TaskScheduler class's static FromCurrentSynchroniza tionContext method returns a scheduler based on the current synchronization context for whichever thread you call the method from. This scheduler will execute all work via that synchronization context. So, if you call FromCurrentSynchronization

Context from a UI thread, the resulting scheduler can be used to run tasks that can safely update the UI. You would typically use this for a continuation—you can run some task-based asynchronous work, and then hook up a continuation that updates the UI when that work is complete. Example 16-19 shows this technique in use in the codebehind file for a window in a WPF application.

Example 16-19. Scheduling a continuation on the UI thread

```
public partial class MainWindow : Window
{
    public MainWindow()
    {
        InitializeComponent();
    }

    private static readonly HttpClient w = new HttpClient();
    private readonly TaskScheduler _uiScheduler =
        TaskScheduler.FromCurrentSynchronizationContext();

    private void FetchButtonClicked(object sender, RoutedEventArgs e)
    {
        string url = "https://endjin.com/";
        Task<string> webGetTask = w.GetStringAsync(url);

        webGetTask.ContinueWith(t =>
        {
            string webContent = t.Result;
            outputTextBox.Text = webContent;
        },
        _uiScheduler);

    }
}
```

This uses a field initializer to obtain the scheduler—the constructor for a UI element runs on the UI thread, so this will get a scheduler for the synchronization context for the UI thread. A click handler then downloads a web page using the HttpClient class's GetStringAsync. This runs asynchronously, so it won't block the UI thread, meaning that the application will remain responsive while the download is in progress. The method sets up a continuation for the task using an overload of Continue With that takes a TaskScheduler. This ensures that when the task that gets the content completes, the lambda passed to ContinueWith runs on the UI thread, so it's safe for it to access UI elements.

While this works perfectly well, the await keyword described in the next chapter provides a more straightforward solution to this particular problem.

The .NET class library provides three built-in kinds of schedulers. There's the default one that uses the thread pool, and the one I just showed that uses a synchronization context. The third is provided by a class called ConcurrentExclusiveSchedulerPair, and as the name suggests, this provides two schedulers, which it makes available through properties. The ConcurrentScheduler property returns a scheduler that will run tasks concurrently much like the default scheduler. The ExclusiveScheduler property returns a scheduler that can be used to run tasks one at a time, and it will temporarily suspend the other scheduler while it does so. (This is reminiscent of the reader/writer synchronization semantics I described earlier in the chapter—it allows exclusivity when required, but concurrency the rest of the time.)

Error Handling

A Task object indicates when its work has failed by entering the Faulted state. There will always be at least one exception associated with failure, but the TPL allows composite tasks—tasks that contain a number of subtasks. This makes it possible for multiple failures to occur, and the root task will report them all. Task defines an Exception property, and its type is AggregateException. You may recall from Chapter 8 that as well as inheriting the InnerException property from the base Exception type, AggregateException defines an InnerExceptions property that returns a collection of exceptions. This is where you will find the complete set of exceptions that caused the task to fault. (If the task was not a composite task, there will usually be just one.)

If you attempt to get the Result property or call Wait on a faulted task, it will throw the same AggregateException as it would return from the Exception property. A faulted task remembers whether you have used at least one of these members, and if you have not yet done so, it considers the exception to be *unobserved*. The TPL uses finalization to track faulted tasks with unobserved exceptions, and if you allow such a task to become unreachable, the TaskScheduler will raise its static UnobservedTaskException event. This gives you one last chance to do something about the exception, after which it will be lost.

Custom Threadless Tasks

Many I/O-based APIs return threadless tasks. You can do the same if you want. The TaskCompletionSource<T> class provides a way to create a Task<T> that does not have an associated method to run on the thread pool, and instead completes when you tell it to. There's no nongeneric TaskCompletionSource, but there doesn't need to be. Task<T> derives from Task, so you can just pick any type argument. By convention, most developers use TaskCompletionSource<object> when they don't need to provide a return value.

Suppose you're using a class that does not provide a task-based API, and you'd like to add a task-based wrapper. The SmtpClient class I used in Example 16-12 supports the older event-based asynchronous pattern, but not the task-based one. Example 16-20 uses that API in conjunction with TaskCompletionSource<object> to provide a task-based wrapper. (And, yes, there are two spellings of Canceled/Cancelled in there. The TPL consistently uses Canceled, but older APIs exhibit more variety.)

Example 16-20. Using TaskCompletionSource<T>

```
public static class SmtpAsyncExtensions
{
    public static Task SendTaskAsync(this SmtpClient mailClient, string from,
                                     string recipients, string subject, string body)
    {
        var tcs = new TaskCompletionSource<object>();

        void CompletionHandler(object s, AsyncCompletedEventArgs e)
        {
            mailClient.SendCompleted -= CompletionHandler;
            if (e.Cancelled)
            {
                tcs.SetCanceled();
            }
            else if (e.Error != null)
            {
                tcs.SetException(e.Error);
            }
            else
            {
                tcs.SetResult(null);
            }
        };

        mailClient.SendCompleted += CompletionHandler;
        mailClient.SendAsync(from, recipients, subject, body, null);

        return tcs.Task;
    }
}
```

The SmtpClient notifies us that the operation is complete by raising an event. The handler for this event first detaches itself (so that it doesn't run a second time if something uses that same `SmtpClient` for further work). Then it detects whether the operation succeeded, was cancelled, or failed, and calls the `SetResult`, `SetCanceled`, or `SetException` method, respectively, on the `TaskCompletionSource<object>`. This will cause the task to transition into the relevant state, and will also take care of running any continuations attached to that task. The completion source makes the threadless `Task` object it creates available through its `Task` property, which this method returns.

Parent/Child Relationships

If a thread-based task's method creates a new thread-based task, then by default, there will be no particular relationship between those tasks. However, one of the `Task CreationOptions` flags is `AttachedToParent`, and if you set this, the newly created task will be a child of the task currently executing. The significance of this is that the parent task won't report completion until all its children have completed. (Its own method also needs to complete, of course.) If any children fault, the parent task will fault, and it will include all the children's exceptions in its own `AggregateException`.

You can also specify the `AttachedToParent` flag for a continuation. Be aware that this does not make it a child of its antecedent task. It will be a child of whichever task was running when `ContinueWith` was called to create the continuation.

 Threadless tasks (e.g., most tasks representing I/O) often cannot be made children of another task. If you're creating one yourself through a `TaskCompletionSource<T>`, you can do it because that class has a constructor overload that accepts a `TaskCreationOp tions`. However, the majority of .NET APIs that return tasks do not provide a way to request that the task be a child.

Parent/child relationships are not the only way of creating a task whose outcome is based on multiple other items.

Composite Tasks

The `Task` class has static `WhenAll` and `WhenAny` methods. Each of these has overloads that accept either a collection of `Task` objects or a collection of `Task<T>` objects as the only argument. The `WhenAll` method returns either a `Task` or a `Task<T[]>` that completes only when all of the tasks provided in the argument have completed (and in the latter case, the composite task produces an array containing each of the individual tasks' results). The `WhenAny` method returns a `Task<Task>` or `Task<Task<T>>` that completes as soon as the first task completes, providing that task as the result.

As with a parent task, if any of the tasks that make up a task produced with WhenAll fail, the exceptions from all of the failed tasks will be available in the composite task's AggregateException. (WhenAny does not report errors. It completes as soon as the first task completes, and you must inspect that to discover if it failed.)

You can attach a continuation to these tasks, but there's a slightly more direct route. Instead of creating a composite task with WhenAll or WhenAny and then calling Con tinueWith on the result, you can just call the ContinueWhenAll or ContinueWhenAny method of a task factory. Again, these take a collection of Task or Task<T>, but they also take a method to invoke as the continuation.

Other Asynchronous Patterns

Although the TPL provides the preferred mechanism for exposing asynchronous APIs, .NET had been around for almost a decade before it was added, so you will come across older approaches. The longest established form is the Asynchronous Programming Model (APM). This was introduced in .NET 1.0, so it is widely implemented, but its use is now discouraged. With this pattern, methods come in pairs: one to start the work, and a second to collect the results when it is complete. Example 16-21 shows just such a pair from the Stream class in the System.IO namespace, and it also shows the corresponding synchronous method. (Code written today should use a task-based WriteAsync instead.)

Example 16-21. An APM pair and the corresponding synchronous method

```
public virtual IAsyncResult BeginWrite(byte[] buffer, int offset, int count,
    AsyncCallback callback, object state) ...
public virtual void EndWrite(IAsyncResult asyncResult) ...

public abstract void Write(byte[] buffer, int offset, int count) ...
```

Notice that the first three arguments of the BeginWrite method are identical to those of the Write method. In the APM, the Begin*Xxx* method takes all of the inputs (i.e., any normal arguments and any ref arguments, but not out arguments, should any be present). The End*Xxx* method provides any outputs, which means the return value, any ref arguments (because those can pass information either in or out), and any out arguments.

The Begin*Xxx* method also takes two additional arguments: a delegate of type AsyncCallback, which will be invoked when the operation completes, and an argument of type object that accepts any object you would like to associate with the operation (or null if you have no use for this). This method also returns an IAsyncResult, which represents the asynchronous operation.

When your completion callback gets invoked, you can call the End*Xxx* method, passing in the same IAsyncResult object returned by the Begin*Xxx* method, and this will provide the return value if there is one. If the operation failed, the End*Xxx* method will throw an exception.

You can wrap APIs that use the APM with a Task. The TaskFactory objects provided by Task and Task<T> provide FromAsync methods to which you can pass a pair of delegates for the Begin*Xxx* and End*Xxx* methods, and you also pass any arguments that the Begin*Xxx* method requires. This will return a Task or Task<T> that represents the operation.

Another common older pattern is the Event-based Asynchronous Pattern (EAP). You've seen an example in this chapter—it's what the SmtpClient uses. With this pattern, a class provides a method that starts the operation and a corresponding event that it raises when the operation completes. The method and event usually have related names, such as SendAsync and SendCompleted. An important feature of this pattern is that the method captures the synchronization context and uses that to raise the event, meaning that if you use an object that supports this pattern in UI code, it effectively presents a single-threaded asynchronous model. This makes it much easier to use than the APM, because you don't need to write any extra code to get back onto the UI thread when asynchronous work completes.

There's no automated mechanism for wrapping the EAP in a task, but as I showed in Example 16-20, it's not particularly hard to do.

There's one more common pattern used in asynchronous code: the *awaitable* pattern supported by the C# asynchronous language features (the async and await keywords). As I showed in Example 16-16, you can consume a TPL task directly with these features, but the language does not recognize Task directly, and it's possible to await things other than tasks. You can use the await keyword with anything that implements a particular pattern. I will show this in Chapter 17.

Cancellation

.NET defines a standard mechanism for cancelling slow operations. Cancellable operations take an argument of the type CancellationToken, and if you set this into a cancelled state, the operation will stop early if possible instead of running to completion.

The CancellationToken type itself does not offer any methods to initiate cancellation —the API is designed so that you can tell operations when you want them to be cancelled without giving them power to cancel whatever other operations you have associated with the same CancellationToken. The act of cancellation is managed through a separate object, CancellationTokenSource. As the name suggests, you can use this to get hold of any number of `CancellationToken` instances. If you call the `Cancella tionTokenSource` object's `Cancel` method, that sets all of the associated `Cancella tionToken` instances into a cancelled state.

Some of the synchronization mechanisms I described earlier can be passed a `Cancel lationToken`. (The ones that derive from `WaitHandle` cannot, because the underlying Windows primitives do not support .NET's cancellation model. `Monitor` also does not support cancellation, but many newer APIs do.) It's also common for task-based APIs to take a cancellation token, and the TPL itself also offers overloads of the `Start New` and `ContinueWith` methods that take them. If the task has already started to run, there's nothing the TPL can do to cancel it, but if you cancel a task before it begins to run, the TPL will take it out of the scheduled task queue for you. If you want to be able to cancel your task after it starts running, you'll need to write code in the body of your task that inspects the `CancellationToken`, and abandons the work if its `IsCan cellationRequested` property is `true`.

Cancellation support is not ubiquitous, because it's not always possible. Some operations simply cannot be cancelled. For example, once a message has been sent out over the network, you can't unsend it. Some operations allow work to be cancelled up until some point of no return has been reached. (If a message is queued up to be sent but hasn't actually been sent, then it might not be too late to cancel, for example.) This means that even when cancellation is offered, it might not do anything. So, when you use cancellation, you need to be prepared for it not to work.

Parallelism

The .NET class library includes some classes that can work with collections of data concurrently on multiple threads. There are three ways to do this: the `Parallel` class, Parallel LINQ, and TPL Dataflow.

The Parallel Class

The `Parallel` class offers three static methods: `For`, `Foreach`, and `Invoke`. The last of those takes an array of delegates and executes all of them, potentially in parallel. (Whether it decides to use parallelism depends on various factors such as the number of hardware threads the computer has, how heavily loaded the system is, and how many items you want it to process.) The `For` and `Foreach` methods mimic the C# loop constructs of the same names, but they will also potentially execute iterations in parallel.

Example 16-22 illustrates the use of `Parallel.For` in code that performs a convolution of two sets of samples. This is a highly repetitive operation commonly used in signal processing. (In practice, a fast Fourier transform offers a more efficient way to perform this work unless the convolution kernel is small, but the complexity of that code would have obscured the main subject here, the `Parallel` class.) It produces one output sample for each input sample. Each output sample is produced by calculating the sum of a series of pairs of values from the two inputs, multiplied together. For large data sets, this can be time consuming, so it is the sort of work you might want to speed up by spreading it across multiple processors. Each individual output sample's value can be calculated independently of all the others, so it is a good candidate for parallelization.

Example 16-22. Parallel convolution

```
static float[] ParallelConvolution(float[] input, float[] kernel)
{
    float[] output = new float[input.Length];
    Parallel.For(0, input.Length, i =>
    {
        float total = 0;
        for (int k = 0; k < Math.Min(kernel.Length, i + 1); ++k)
        {
            total += input[i - k] * kernel[k];
        }
        output[i] = total;
    });

    return output;
}
```

The basic structure of this code is very similar to a pair of nested `for` loops. I've simply replaced the outer `for` loop with a call to `Parallel.For`. (I've not attempted to parallelize the inner loop—if you make each individual step trivial, `Parallel.For` will spend more of its time in housekeeping work than it does running your code.)

The first argument, `0`, sets the initial value of the loop counter, and the second sets the upper limit. The final argument is a delegate that will be invoked once for each value of the loop counter, and the calls will occur concurrently if the `Parallel` class's heuristics tell it that this is likely to produce a speedup as a result of the work running in parallel. Running this method with large data sets on a multicore machine causes all of the available hardware threads to be used to full capacity.

It may be possible to get better performance by partitioning the work in more cache-friendly ways—naive parallelization can give the impression of high performance by maxing out all your CPU cores while delivering suboptimal throughput. However, there is a trade-off between complexity and performance, and the simplicity of the `Parallel` class can often provide worthwhile wins for relatively little effort.

Parallel LINQ

Parallel LINQ is a LINQ provider that works with in-memory information, much like LINQ to Objects. The `System.Linq` namespace makes this available as an extension method called `AsParallel` defined for any `IEnumerable<T>` (by the `ParallelEnumerable` class). This returns a `ParallelQuery<T>`, which will support the usual LINQ operators.

Any LINQ query built this way provides a `ForAll` method, which takes a delegate. When you call this, it invokes the delegate for all of the items that the query produces, and it will do so in parallel on multiple threads where possible.

TPL Dataflow

TPL dataflow is a .NET class library feature that lets you construct a graph of objects that perform some kind of processing on information that flows through them. You can tell the TPL which of these nodes needs to process information sequentially, and which are happy to work on multiple blocks of data simultaneously. You push data into the graph, and the TPL will then manage the process of providing each node with blocks to process, and it will attempt to optimize the level of parallelism to match the resources available on your computer.

The dataflow API, which is in the `System.Threading.Tasks.Dataflow` namespace (which you'll find in a NuGet package of the same name), is large and complex and could have a whole chapter to itself. Sadly, this makes it beyond the scope of this book. I mention it because it's worth being aware of for certain kinds of work.

Summary

Threads provide the ability to execute multiple pieces of code simultaneously. On a computer with multiple CPU execution units (i.e., multiple hardware threads), you can exploit this potential for parallelism by using multiple software threads. You can create new software threads explicitly with the `Thread` class, or you can use either the thread pool or a parallelization mechanism, such as the `Parallel` class or Parallel LINQ, to determine automatically how many threads to use to run the work your application supplies. Threads can also provide a way to execute multiple concurrent operations that do not need the CPU the whole time (e.g., waiting for a response from an external service), but it is often more efficient to perform such work with asynchronous APIs (where available). The Task Parallel Library (TPL) provides abstractions that are useful for both kinds of concurrency. It can manage multiple work items in the thread pool, with support for combining multiple operations and handling potentially complex error scenarios, and its `Task` abstraction can also represent inherently asynchronous operations. If multiple threads need to use and modify shared data structures, you will need to use the synchronization mechanisms offered by .NET to ensure that the threads can coordinate their work correctly.

CHAPTER 17

Asynchronous Language Features

C# provides language-level support for using and implementing asynchronous methods. Asynchronous APIs are often the most efficient way to use certain services. For example, most I/O is handled asynchronously inside the OS kernel, because most peripherals, such as disk controllers or network adapters, are able to do the majority of their work autonomously. They need the CPU to be involved only at the start and end of each operation.

Although many of the services offered by operating systems are intrinsically asynchronous, developers often choose to use them through synchronous APIs (i.e., ones that do not return until the work is complete). This is a waste of resources, because they block the thread until the I/O completes. Threads have overheads, and to get the best performance it's usually best to have a relatively small number of OS threads. Ideally, your application would have only as many OS threads as you have hardware threads, but that's optimal only if you can ensure that threads only ever block when there's no outstanding work for them to do. (Chapter 16 described the difference between OS threads and hardware threads.) The more threads that get blocked inside synchronous API calls, the more threads you'll need to handle your workload, reducing efficiency. In performance-sensitive code, asynchronous APIs are useful, because instead of wasting resources by forcing a thread to sit and wait for I/O to complete, a thread can kick off the work and then do something else productive in the meantime.

The problem with asynchronous APIs is that they can be significantly more complex to use than synchronous ones, particularly if you need to coordinate multiple related operations and deal with errors. This is why developers often chose the less efficient synchronous alternatives back in the days before any mainstream programming languages provided built-in support. In 2012, C# and VB brought such features out of the research labs, and since then many other popular languages have added analogous features (most notably JavaScript, which acquired a very similar-looking syntax in 2016). The asynchronous features in C# make it possible to write code that uses efficient asynchronous APIs while retaining most of the simplicity of code that uses simpler synchronous APIs.

The asynchronous features are also useful in some scenarios in which maximizing throughput is not the primary performance goal. With client-side code, it's important to avoid blocking the UI thread to maintain responsiveness, and asynchronous APIs provide one way to do that. The language support for asynchronous code can handle thread affinity issues, which greatly simplifies the job of writing highly responsive UI code.

Asynchronous Keywords: async and await

C# presents its support for asynchronous code through two keywords: `async` and `await`. The first of these is not meant to be used on its own. You put the `async` keyword in a method's declaration, and this tells the compiler that you intend to use asynchronous features in the method. If this keyword is not present, you are not allowed to use the `await` keyword. This is arguably redundant—the compiler produces an error if you attempt to use `await` without `async`. If it knows when a method's body is trying to use asynchronous features, why do we need to tell it explicitly? There are two reasons. First, as you'll see, these features radically change the behavior of the code the compiler generates, so it's useful for anyone reading the code to see a clear indication that the method behaves asynchronously. Second, `await` wasn't always a keyword in C#, so developers were once free to use it as an identifier. Perhaps Microsoft could have designed the grammar for `await` so that it acts as a keyword only in very specific contexts, enabling you to continue to use it as an identifier in all other scenarios, but the C# team decided to take a slightly more coarse-grained approach: you cannot use `await` as an identifier inside an `async` method, but it's a valid identifier anywhere else.

The `async` keyword does not change the signature of the method. It determines how the method is compiled, not how it is used.

So the `async` keyword simply declares your intention to use the `await` keyword. (While you mustn't use `await` without `async`, it's not an error to apply the `async` keyword to a method that doesn't use `await`. However, it would serve no purpose, so the compiler will generate a warning if you do this.) Example 17-1 shows a fairly typical example. This uses the `HttpClient` class to request just the headers for a particular resource (using the standard HEAD verb that the HTTP protocol defines for this purpose). It then displays the results in a UI control—this method is part of the codebehind for a UI that includes a `TextBox` named `headerListTextBox`.

Example 17-1. Using async and await when fetching HTTP headers

```
// Note: as you'll see later, async methods usually should not be void
private async void FetchAndShowHeaders(string url, IHttpClientFactory cf)
{
    using (HttpClient w = cf.CreateClient())
    {
        var req = new HttpRequestMessage(HttpMethod.Head, url);
        HttpResponseMessage response =
            await w.SendAsync(req, HttpCompletionOption.ResponseHeadersRead);

        headerListTextBox.Text = response.Headers.ToString();
    }
}
```

This code contains a single `await` expression, shown in bold. You use the `await` keyword in an expression that may take some time to produce a result, and it indicates that the remainder of the method should not execute until that operation is complete. This sounds a lot like what a blocking, synchronous API does, but the difference is that an `await` expression does not block the thread—this code is not quite what it seems.

The `HttpClient` class's `SendAsync` method returns a `Task<HttpResponseMessage>`, and you might be wondering why we wouldn't just use its `Result` property. As you saw in Chapter 16, if the task is not complete, this property blocks the thread until the result is available (or the task fails, in which case it will throw an exception instead). However, this is a dangerous thing to do in a UI application: if you block the UI thread by trying to read the `Result` of an incomplete task, you will prevent progress of any operations that need to run on that thread. Since a lot of the work that UI applications do needs to happen on the UI thread, blocking that thread in this way more or less guarantees that deadlock will occur sooner or later, causing the application to freeze. So don't do that!

Although the `await` expression in Example 17-1 does something that is logically similar to reading `Result`, it works very differently. If the task's result is not available immediately, the `await` keyword does not make the thread wait, despite what its name suggests. Instead, it causes the containing method to return. You can use a debugger to verify that `FetchAndShowHeaders` returns immediately. For example, if I call that method from the button click event handler shown in Example 17-2, I can put a breakpoint on the `Debug.WriteLine` call in that handler, and another breakpoint on the code in Example 17-1 that will update the `headerListTextBox.Text` property.

Example 17-2. Calling the asynchronous method

```
private void fetchHeadersButton_Click(object sender, RoutedEventArgs e)
{
    FetchAndShowHeaders("https://endjin.com/", this.clientFactory);
    Debug.WriteLine("Method returned");
}
```

Running this in the debugger, I find that the code hits the breakpoint on the last statement of Example 17-2 before it hits the breakpoint on the final statement of Example 17-1. In other words, the section of Example 17-1 that follows the await expression runs *after* the method has returned to its caller. Evidently, the compiler is somehow arranging for the remainder of the method to be run via a callback that occurs once the asynchronous operation completes.

 Visual Studio's debugger plays some tricks when you debug asynchronous methods to enable you to step through them as though they were normal methods. This is usually helpful, but it can sometimes conceal the true nature of execution. The debugging steps I just described were contrived to defeat Visual Studio's attempts to be clever, and instead to reveal what is really happening.

Notice that the code in Example 17-1 expects to run on the UI thread because it modifies the text box's Text property toward the end. Asynchronous APIs do not necessarily guarantee to notify you of completion on the same thread on which you started the work—in fact, most won't. Despite this, Example 17-1 works as intended, so as well as converting half of the method to a callback, the await keyword is handling thread affinity issues for us.

The C# compiler evidently performs some major surgery on your code each time you use the await keyword. In older versions of C#, if you wanted to use this asynchronous API and then update the UI, you would need to have written something like Example 17-3. This uses a technique I showed in Chapter 16: it sets up a continuation for the task returned by SendAsync, using a TaskScheduler to ensure that the continuation's body runs on the UI thread.

Example 17-3. Manual asynchronous coding

```
private void OldSchoolFetchHeaders(string url, IHttpClientFactory cf)
{
    HttpClient w = cf.CreateClient();
    var req = new HttpRequestMessage(HttpMethod.Head, url);

    var uiScheduler = TaskScheduler.FromCurrentSynchronizationContext();
    w.SendAsync(req, HttpCompletionOption.ResponseHeadersRead)
        .ContinueWith(sendTask =>
```

```
    {
        try
        {
            HttpResponseMessage response = sendTask.Result;
            headerListTextBox.Text = response.Headers.ToString();
        }
        finally
        {
            w.Dispose();
        }
    },
    uiScheduler);
}
```

This is a reasonable way to use the TPL directly, and it has a similar effect to Example 17-1, but it's not an exact representation of how the C# compiler transforms the code. As I'll show later, await uses a pattern that is supported by, but does not require, Task or Task<T>. It also generates code that handles early completion (where the task has already finished by the time you're ready to wait for it) far more efficiently than Example 17-3. But before I show the details of what the compiler does, I want to illustrate some of the problems it solves for you, which is best done by showing the kind of code you might have written back before this language feature existed.

My current example is pretty simple, because it involves only one asynchronous operation, but aside from the two steps I've already discussed—setting up some kind of completion callback and ensuring that it runs on the correct thread—I've also had to deal with the using statement that was in Example 17-1. Example 17-3 can't use the using keyword, because we want to dispose the HttpClient object only after we've finished with it.[1] Calling Dispose shortly before the outer method returns would not work, because we need to be able to use the object when the continuation runs, and that will typically happen a fair bit later. So I need to create the object in one method (the outer one) and then dispose of it in a different method (the nested one). And because I'm calling Dispose by hand, it's now my problem to deal with exceptions, so I've had to wrap all of the code I moved into the callback with a try block, and call Dispose in a finally block. (In fact, I've not even done a comprehensive job—in the unlikely event that either the HttpRequestMessage constructor or the call that retrieves the task scheduler were to throw an exception, the HttpClient would not get disposed. I'm handling only the case where the HTTP operation itself fails.)

---

[1] This example is a bit contrived so that I can illustrate how using works in async methods. Disposing an HttpClient obtained from an IHttpClientFactory is normally optional, and in cases where you new up an HttpClient directly, it's better to hang on to it and reuse it, as discussed in "Optional Disposal" on page 339.

Example 17-3 has used a task scheduler to arrange for the continuation to run via the `SynchronizationContext` that was current when the work started. This ensures that the callback occurs on the correct thread to update the UI. The `await` keyword can take care of that for us.

Execution and Synchronization Contexts

When your program's execution reaches an `await` expression for an operation that doesn't complete immediately, the code generated for that `await` will ensure that the current execution context has been captured. (It might not have to do much—if this is not the first `await` to block in this method, and if the context hasn't changed since, it will have been captured already.) When the asynchronous operation completes, the remainder of your method will be executed through the execution context.[2]

As I described in Chapter 16, the execution context handles certain contextual information that needs to flow when one method invokes another (even when it does so indirectly). But there's another kind of context that we may be interested in, particularly when writing UI code: the synchronization context (which was also described in Chapter 16).

While all `await` expressions capture the execution context, the decision of whether to flow synchronization context as well is controlled by the type being awaited. If you `await` for a `Task`, the synchronization context will also be captured by default. Tasks are not the only thing you can `await`, and I'll describe how types can support `await` in the section "The await Pattern" on page 729.

Sometimes, you might want to avoid getting the synchronization context involved. If you want to perform asynchronous work starting from a UI thread, but you have no particular need to remain on that thread, scheduling every continuation through the synchronization context is unnecessary overhead. If the asynchronous operation is a `Task` or `Task<T>` (or the equivalent value types, `ValueTask` or `ValueTask<T>`), you can declare that you don't want this by calling the `ConfigureAwait` method passing `false`. This returns a different representation of the asynchronous operation, and if you `await` that instead of the original task, it will ignore the current `Synchroniza tionContext` if there is one. (There's no equivalent mechanism for opting out of the execution context.) Example 17-4 shows how to use this.

---

2 As it happens, Example 17-3 does this too, because the TPL captures the execution context for us.

Example 17-4. ConfigureAwait

```
private async void OnFetchButtonClick(object sender, RoutedEventArgs e)
{
    using (HttpClient w = this.clientFactory.CreateClient())
    using (Stream f = File.Create(fileTextBox.Text))
    {
        Task<Stream> getStreamTask = w.GetStreamAsync(urlTextBox.Text);
        Stream getStream = await getStreamTask.ConfigureAwait(false);

        Task copyTask = getStream.CopyToAsync(f);
        await copyTask.ConfigureAwait(false);
    }
}
```

This code is a click handler for a button, so it initially runs on a UI thread. It retrieves the Text property from a couple of text boxes. Then it kicks off some asynchronous work—fetching the content for a URL and copying the data into a file. It does not use any UI elements after fetching those two Text properties, so it doesn't matter if the remainder of the method runs on some separate thread. By passing false to Config ureAwait and waiting on the value it returns, we are telling the TPL that we are happy for it to use whatever thread is convenient to notify us of completion, which in this case will most likely be a thread pool thread. This will enable the work to complete more efficiently and more quickly, because it avoids getting the UI thread involved unnecessarily after each await.

Various asynchronous APIs introduced in Windows as part of the UWP API return an IAsyncOperation<T> instead of Task<T>. This is because UWP is not .NET-specific, and it has its own runtime-independent representation for asynchronous operations that can also be used from C++ and JavaScript. This interface is conceptually similar to TPL tasks, and it supports the await pattern, meaning you can use await with these APIs. However, it does not provide ConfigureAwait. If you want to do something similar to Example 17-4 with one of these APIs, you can use the AsTask extension method that wraps an IAsyncOperation<T> as a Task<T>, and you can call ConfigureAwait on that task instead.

If you are writing libraries, then in most cases you should call Con figureAwait(false) anywhere you use await. This is because continuing via the synchronization context can be expensive, and in some cases it can introduce the possibility of deadlock occurring. The only exceptions are when you are doing something that positively requires the synchronization context to be preserved, or you know for certain that your library will only ever be used in application frameworks that do not set up a synchronization context. (E.g., ASP.NET Core applications do not use synchronization contexts, so it generally doesn't matter whether or not you call Con figureAwait(false) in those.)

Example 17-1 contained just one await expression, and even that turned out to be fairly complex to reproduce with classic TPL programming. Example 17-4 contains two, and achieving equivalent behavior without the aid of the await keyword would require rather more code, because exceptions could occur before the first await, after the second, or between, and we'd need to call Dispose on the HttpClient and Stream in any of those cases (as well as in the case where no exception is thrown). However, things can get considerably more complex than that once flow control gets involved.

Multiple Operations and Loops

Suppose that instead of fetching headers, or just copying the HTTP response body to a file, I wanted to process the data in the body. If the body is large, retrieving it is an operation that could require multiple, slow steps. Example 17-5 fetches a web page gradually.

Example 17-5. Multiple asynchronous operations

```
private async void FetchAndShowBody(string url, IHttpClientFactory cf)
{
    using (HttpClient w = cf.CreateClient())
    {
        Stream body = await w.GetStreamAsync(url);
        using (var bodyTextReader = new StreamReader(body))
        {
            while (!bodyTextReader.EndOfStream)
            {
                string line = await bodyTextReader.ReadLineAsync();
                bodyTextBox.AppendText(line);
                bodyTextBox.AppendText(Environment.NewLine);
                await Task.Delay(TimeSpan.FromMilliseconds(10));
            }
        }
    }
}
```

This now contains three `await` expressions. The first kicks off an HTTP GET request, and that operation will complete when we get the first part of the response, but the response will not be complete yet—there may be several megabytes of content to come. This code presumes that the content will be text, so it wraps the `Stream` object that comes back in a `StreamReader`, which presents the bytes in a stream as text.[3] It then uses that wrapper's asynchronous `ReadLineAsync` method to read text a line at a time from the response. Because data tends to arrive in chunks, reading the first line may take a while, but the next few calls to this method will probably complete immediately, because each network packet we receive will typically contain multiple lines. But if the code can read faster than data arrives over the network, eventually it will have consumed all the lines that appeared in the first packet, and it will then take a while before the next line becomes available. So the calls to `ReadLineAsync` will return some tasks that are slow, and some that complete immediately. The third asynchronous operation is a call to `Task.Delay`. I've added this to slow things down so that I can see the data arriving gradually in the UI. `Task.Delay` returns a `Task` that completes after the specified delay, so this provides an asynchronous equivalent to `Thread.Sleep`. (`Thread.Sleep` blocks the calling thread, but `await Task.Delay` introduces a delay without blocking the thread.)

 I've put each `await` expression in a separate statement, but this is not a requirement. It's perfectly legal to write expressions of the form `(await t1) + (await t2)`. (You can omit the parentheses if you like, because `await` has higher precedence than addition; I prefer the visual emphasis they provide here.)

I'm not going to show you the complete pre-`async` equivalent of Example 17-5, because it would be enormous, but I'll describe some of the problems. First, we've got a loop with a body that contains two `await` blocks. To produce something equivalent with `Task` and callbacks means building your own loop constructs, because the code for the loop ends up being split across three methods: the one that starts the loop running (which would be the nested method acting as the continuation callback for `GetStreamAsync`), and the two callbacks that handle the completion of `ReadLineA sync` and `Task.Delay`. You can solve this by having a local method that starts a new iteration and calling that from two places: the point at which you want to start the loop, and again in the `Task.Delay` continuation to kick off the next iteration. Example 17-6 shows this technique, but it illustrates just one aspect of what we're expecting the compiler to do for us; it is not a complete alternative to Example 17-5.

---

3 Strictly speaking, I should inspect the HTTP response headers to discover the encoding, and configure the `StreamReader` with that. Instead, I'm letting it detect the encoding, which will work well enough for demonstration purposes.

Example 17-6. An incomplete manual asynchronous loop

```
private void IncompleteOldSchoolFetchAndShowBody(
    string url, IHttpClientFactory cf)
{
    HttpClient w = cf.CreateClient();
    var uiScheduler = TaskScheduler.FromCurrentSynchronizationContext();
    w.GetStreamAsync(url).ContinueWith(getStreamTask =>
    {
        Stream body = getStreamTask.Result;
        var bodyTextReader = new StreamReader(body);

        StartNextIteration();

        void StartNextIteration()
        {
            if (!bodyTextReader.EndOfStream)
            {
                bodyTextReader.ReadLineAsync().ContinueWith(readLineTask =>
                {
                    string line = readLineTask.Result;

                    bodyTextBox.AppendText(line);
                    bodyTextBox.AppendText(Environment.NewLine);

                    Task.Delay(TimeSpan.FromMilliseconds(10))
                        .ContinueWith(
                            _ => StartNextIteration(), uiScheduler);
                },
                uiScheduler);
            }
        };
    },
        uiScheduler);
}
```

This code works after a fashion, but it doesn't even attempt to dispose any of the resources it uses. There are several places in which failure could occur, so we can't just put a single using block or try/finally pair in to clean things up. And even without that additional complication, the code is barely recognizable—it's not obvious that this is attempting to perform the same basic operations as Example 17-5. With proper error handling, it would be completely unreadable. In practice, it would probably be easier to take a different approach entirely, writing a class that implements a state machine to keep track of where the work has gotten to. That will probably make it easier to produce code that operates correctly, but it's not going to make it any easier for someone reading your code to understand that what they're looking at is really little more than a loop at heart.

No wonder so many developers used to prefer synchronous APIs. But C# lets us write asynchronous code that has almost exactly the same structure as the synchronous equivalent, giving us all of the performance and responsiveness benefits of asynchronous code without the pain. That's the main benefit of async and await in a nutshell.

Consuming and producing asynchronous sequences

Example 17-5 showed a while loop, and as you'd expect, you're free to use other kinds of loops such as for and foreach. However, foreach can introduce a subtle problem: what happens if the collection you iterate over needs to perform slow operations? This doesn't arise for collection types such as arrays or HashSet<T> where all the collection's items are already in memory, but what about the IEnumerable<string> returned by File.ReadLines? That's an obvious candidate for asynchronous operation, but in practice, it will just block your thread each time it needs to wait for more data to arrive from storage. And that's because the pattern expected by foreach simply doesn't support asynchronous operation. The heart of the problem is the method foreach will call to move to the next item—it expects the enumerator (often, but not always an implementation of IEnumerator<T>) to provide a MoveNext method like the one shown in Example 17-7.

Example 17-7. The non-async-friendly IEnumerator.MoveNext

```
bool MoveNext();
```

If more items are forthcoming but are not yet available, collections have no choice but to block the thread, not returning from MoveNext until the data arrives. To fix this, C# 8.0 introduces a new pattern. There are corresponding new types in .NET Core 3.0's class library and .NET Standard 2.1, shown in Example 17-8 (first introduced in Chapter 5), that embody this new pattern. As with the synchronous IEnumerable<T>, foreach doesn't strictly require these exact types. Anything offering members of the same signature will work.

Example 17-8. IAsyncEnumerable<T> and IAsyncEnumerator<T>

```
public interface IAsyncEnumerable<out T>
{
    IAsyncEnumerator<T> GetAsyncEnumerator(
        CancellationToken cancellationToken = default);
}

public interface IAsyncEnumerator<out T> : IAsyncDisposable
{
    T Current { get; }

    ValueTask<bool> MoveNextAsync();
}
```

Conceptually this is identical to the synchronous pattern: an asynchronous `foreach` will ask the collection object for an enumerator, and will repeatedly ask it to advance to the next item, executing the loop body with the value returned by `Current` each time, until the enumerator indicates that there are no more items. The main difference is that the synchronous `MoveNext` has been replaced by `MoveNextAsync`, which returns an awaitable `ValueTask<T>`. (The `IAsyncEnumerable<T>` interface also provides support for passing in a cancellation token, although an asynchronous `foreach` won't use that itself.)

To consume an enumerable source that implements this pattern, you must put the `await` keyword in front of the `foreach`. C# can also help you to implement this pattern: Chapter 5 showed how you can use the `yield` keyword in an *iterator* method to implement `IEnumerable<T>`, but you can also return an `IAsyncEnumerable<T>`. Example 17-9 shows both implementation and consumption of `IAsyncEnumerable<T>` in action.

Example 17-9. Consuming and producing asynchronous enumerables

```
using System;
using System.Collections.Generic;
using System.IO;
using System.Threading.Tasks;

namespace AsyncEnum
{
    internal static class Program
    {
        private static async Task Main(string[] args)
        {
            await foreach (string line in ReadLinesAsync(args[0]))
            {
                Console.WriteLine(line);
            }
        }

        private static async IAsyncEnumerable<string> ReadLinesAsync(string path)
        {
            using (var bodyTextReader = new StreamReader(path))
            {
                while (!bodyTextReader.EndOfStream)
                {
                    string line = await bodyTextReader.ReadLineAsync();
                    yield return line;
                }
            }
        }
    }
}
```

As this example shows, you can make the Main method of a C# program async. You must return either a Task or Task<int>. (The latter lets you produce a nonzero exit code if you need to.) The .NET runtime doesn't support asynchronous entry points, so the C# compiler will generate a hidden method that acts as the real entry point, which calls your asynchronous Main, and then blocks until the task it returns completes.

Since this language support makes creating and using IAsyncEnumerable<T> very similar to working with IEnumerable<T>, you might be wondering whether there are asynchronous versions of the various LINQ operators described in Chapter 10. Unlike LINQ to Objects, IAsyncEnumerable<T> implementations are not in the parts of the class library built into .NET or .NET Standard, but Microsoft does supply a suitable NuGet package. If you add a reference to the System.Linq.Async package, and add a using System.Linq; declaration, all the LINQ operators will be available on IAsyncEnumerable<T> expressions.

While we're looking at asynchronous equivalents of widely implemented types, we should look at IAsyncDisposable.

Asynchronous disposal

As Chapter 7 described, the IDisposable interface is implemented by types that need to perform some sort of cleanup promptly, such as closing an open handle, and there is language support in the form of using statements. But what if the cleanup involves potentially slow work, such as flushing data out to disk? .NET Core 3.0 and .NET Standard 2.1 introduce a new interface, IAsyncDisposable, for this scenario. As Example 17-10 shows, C# 8.0 adds support for it: you can put the await keyword in front of a using statement to consume an asynchronously disposable resource. (You can also put await in front of a using declaration.)

Example 17-10. Consuming and implementing IAsyncDisposable

```
using System;
using System.IO;
using System.Threading.Tasks;

namespace AsyncDispose
{
    class Program
    {
        static async Task Main(string[] args)
        {
            await using (var w = new DiagnosticWriter(@"c:\temp\log.txt"))
            {
                await w.LogAsync("Test");
```

```
            }
        }
    }

    class DiagnosticWriter : IAsyncDisposable
    {
        private StreamWriter fs;

        public DiagnosticWriter(string path)
        {
            fs = new StreamWriter(path);
        }

        public Task LogAsync(string message) => fs.WriteLineAsync(message);

        public async ValueTask DisposeAsync()
        {
            if (fs != null)
            {
                await fs.FlushAsync();
                fs = null;
            }
        }
    }
}
```

 Although the await keyword appears in front of the using statement, the potentially slow operation that it awaits happens when
execution leaves the using statement's block. This is unavoidable
since using statements and declarations effectively hide the call to
Dispose.

Example 17-10 also shows how to implement IAsyncDisposable. Whereas the synchronous IDisposable defines a single Dispose method, its asynchronous counterpart defines a single DisposeAsync method that returns a ValueTask. This enables us
to annotate the method with async. An async using statement will ensure that the
task returned by DisposeAsync completes at the end of its block before execution
continues. You may have noticed that we've used a few different return types for
async methods. Iterators are a special case, just as they are in synchronous code, but
what about these methods that return various task types?

Returning a Task

Any method that uses await could itself take a certain amount of time to run, so as
well as being able to consume asynchronous APIs, you will usually also want to
present an asynchronous public face. The C# compiler enables methods marked with
the async keyword to return an object that represents the asynchronous work in pro-

gress. Instead of returning void, you can return a Task, or you can return a Task<T>, where T is any type. This provides callers with a way to discover the status of the work your method performs, the opportunity to attach continuations, and if you use Task<T>, a way to get the result. Alternatively, you can return the value type equivalents, ValueTask and ValueTask<T>. Returning any of these means that if your method is called from another async method, it can use await to wait for your method to complete and, if applicable, to collect its result.

Returning a task is almost always preferable to void because with a void return type, there's no way for callers to know when your method has really finished, or to discover when it throws an exception. (Asynchronous methods can continue to run after returning—in fact, that's the whole point—so by the time you throw an exception, the original caller will probably not be on the stack.) By returning a task object, you provide the compiler with a way to make exceptions available and, where applicable, a way to provide a result.

Returning a task is so trivially easy that there's very little reason not to. To modify the method in Example 17-5 to return a task, I only need to make a single change. I make the return type Task instead of void, as shown in Example 17-11, and the rest of the code can remain exactly the same.

Example 17-11. Returning a Task

```
private async Task FetchAndShowBody(string url, IHttpClientFactory cf)
// ... as before
```

The compiler automatically generates the code required to produce a Task or Value Task object and set it into a completed or faulted state when the method either returns or throws an exception. And if you want to return a result from your task, that's also very easy. Simply make the return type Task<T> or ValueTask<T>, and then you can use the return keyword as though your method's return type were just T, as Example 17-12 shows.

Example 17-12. Returning a Task<T>

```
public static async Task<string> GetServerHeader(
    string url, IHttpClientFactory cf)
{
    using (HttpClient w = cf.CreateClient())
    {
        var request = new HttpRequestMessage(HttpMethod.Head, url);
        HttpResponseMessage response = await w.SendAsync(
            request, HttpCompletionOption.ResponseHeadersRead);

        string result = null;
        IEnumerable<string> values;
```

```
        if (response.Headers.TryGetValues("Server", out values))
        {
            result = values.FirstOrDefault();
        }
        return result;
    }
}
```

This fetches HTTP headers asynchronously in the same way as Example 17-1, but instead of displaying the results, this picks out the value of the first `Server:` header and makes that the result of the `Task<string>` that this method returns. As you can see, the `return` statement just returns a `string`, even though the method's return type is `Task<string>`. The compiler generates code that completes the task and arranges for that string to be the result. With either a `Task` or `Task<T>` return type, the generated code produces a task similar to the kind you would get using `TaskCom pletionSource<T>`, as described in Chapter 16.

 Just as the `await` keyword can consume any asynchronous method that fits a particular pattern (described later), C# offers the same flexibility when it comes to implementing an asynchronous method. You are not limited to `Task`, `Task<T>`, `ValueTask`, and `Val ueTask<T>`. You can return any type that meets two conditions: it must be annotated with the `AsyncMethodBuilder` attribute, identifying a class that the compiler can use to manage the progress and completion of the task, and it must also offer a `GetAwaiter` method that returns a type implementing the `ICriticalNotifyCompletion` interface.

There's very little downside to returning one of the built-in task types. Callers are not obliged to do anything with it, so your method will be just as easy to use as a `void` method, but with the added advantage that a task is available to callers that want one. About the only reason for returning `void` would be if some external constraint forces your method to have a particular signature. For example, most event handlers are required to have a return type of `void`. But unless you are forced to use it, `void` is not a recommended return type for an asynchronous method.

Applying async to Nested Methods

In the examples shown so far, I have applied the `async` keyword to ordinary methods. You can also use it on anonymous functions (either anonymous methods or lambdas) and local functions. For example, if you're writing a program that creates UI elements programmatically, you may find it convenient to attach event handlers written as lambdas, and you might want to make some of those asynchronous, as Example 17-13 does.

Example 17-13. An asynchronous lambda

```
okButton.Click += async (s, e) =>
{
    using (HttpClient w = this.clientFactory.CreateClient())
    {
        infoTextBlock.Text = await w.GetStringAsync(uriTextBox.Text);
    }
};
```

 This has nothing to do with asynchronous delegate invocation, the now-deprecated technique I mentioned in Chapter 9 for using the thread pool that used to be popular before anonymous methods and the TPL provided better alternatives.

The await Pattern

The majority of the asynchronous APIs that support the `await` keyword will return a TPL task of some kind. However, C# does not absolutely require this. It will `await` anything that implements a particular pattern. (This is how UWP applications are able to use `await` even though APIs in that framework do not return TPL tasks.) Moreover, although `Task` supports this pattern, the way it works means that the compiler uses tasks in a slightly different way than you would when using the TPL directly—this is partly why I said earlier that the code showing task-based asynchronous equivalents to `await`-based code did not represent exactly what the compiler does. In this section, I'm going to show how the compiler uses tasks and other types that support `await`, to better illustrate how it really works.

I'll create a custom implementation of the `await` pattern to show what the C# compiler expects. Example 17-14 shows an asynchronous method, `UseCustomAsync`, that consumes this custom implementation. It assigns the result of the `await` expression into a `string`, so it clearly expects the asynchronous operation to produce a `string` as its output. It calls a method, `CustomAsync`, which returns that implementation of the pattern. As you can see, this is not a `Task<string>`.

Example 17-14. Calling a custom awaitable implementation

```
static async Task UseCustomAsync()
{
    string result = await CustomAsync();
    Console.WriteLine(result);
}

public static MyAwaitableType CustomAsync()
{
```

```
    return new MyAwaitableType();
}
```

The compiler expects the await keyword's operand to be a type that provides a method called GetAwaiter. This can be an ordinary instance member or an extension method. (So it is possible to make await work with a type that does not support it innately by defining a suitable extension method.) This method must return an object or value, known as an *awaiter*, that does three things.

First, the awaiter must provide a bool property called IsCompleted. The code that the compiler generates for the await uses this to discover whether the operation has already finished. In situations where no slow work needs to be done (e.g., when a call to ReadAsync on a Stream can be handled immediately with data that the stream already has in a buffer), it would be a waste to set up a callback. So await avoids creating an unnecessary delegate if the IsCompleted property returns true, and it will just continue straight on with the remainder of the method.

The compiler also requires a way to get the result once the work is complete, so the awaiter must have a GetResult method. Its return type defines the result type of the operation—it will be the type of the await expression. (If there is no result, the return type is void. GetResult still needs to be present, because it is responsible for throwing exceptions if the operation fails.) Since Example 17-14 assigns the result of the await into a variable of type string, the GetResult method of the awaiter returned by the MyAwaitableType class's GetAwaiter must be string (or some type implicitly convertible to string).

Finally, the compiler needs to be able to supply a callback. If IsCompleted returns false, indicating that the operation is not yet complete, the code generated for the await expression will create a delegate that will run the rest of the method. It needs to be able to pass that to the awaiter. (This is similar to passing a delegate to a task's ContinueWith method.) For this, the compiler requires not just a method, but also an interface. You are required to implement INotifyCompletion, and there's an optional interface that it's recommended you also implement where possible called ICriticalNotifyCompletion. These do similar things: each defines a single method (OnCompleted and UnsafeOnCompleted, respectively) that takes a single Action delegate, and the awaiter must invoke this delegate once the operation completes. The distinction between these two interfaces and their corresponding methods is that the first requires the awaiter to flow the current execution context to the target method, whereas the latter does not. The .NET class library features that the C# compiler uses to help build asynchronous methods always flow the execution context for you, so the generated code typically calls UnsafeOnCompleted where available to avoid flowing it twice. (If the compiler used OnCompleted, the awaiter would flow context too.) However, on .NET Framework, you'll find that security constraints may prevent the use of

UnsafeOnCompleted. (.NET Framework had a concept of *untrusted code*. Code from potentially untrustworthy origins—perhaps because it was downloaded from the internet—would be subject to various constraints. This concept was dropped in .NET Core, but various vestiges remain, such as this design detail of asynchronous operations.) Because UnsafeOnCompleted does not flow execution context, untrusted code must not be allowed to call it, because that would provide a way to bypass certain security mechanisms. .NET Framework implementations of UnsafeOnCompleted provided for the various task types is marked with the SecurityCriticalAttribute, which means that only fully trusted code can call it. We need OnCompleted so that partially trusted code is able to use the awaiter.

Example 17-15 shows the minimum viable implementation of the awaiter pattern. This is oversimplified, because it always completes synchronously, so its OnCompleted method doesn't do anything. In fact, when used as the await pattern is meant to be used, the method will never be called, which is why I've made it throw an exception. However, although this example is unrealistically simple, it will serve to illustrate what await does.

Example 17-15. An excessively simple await pattern implementation

```
public class MyAwaitableType
{
    public MinimalAwaiter GetAwaiter()
    {
        return new MinimalAwaiter();
    }

    public class MinimalAwaiter : INotifyCompletion
    {
        public bool IsCompleted => true;

        public string GetResult() => "This is a result";

        public void OnCompleted(Action continuation)
        {
            throw new NotImplementedException();
        }
    }
}
```

With this code in place, we can see what Example 17-14 will do. It will call GetA waiter on the MyAwaitableType instance returned by the CustomAsync method. Then it will test the awaiter's IsCompleted property, and if it's true (which it will be), it will run the rest of the method immediately. The compiler doesn't know IsComple ted will always be true in this case, so it generates code to handle the false case. This will create a delegate that, when invoked, will run the rest of the method, and pass that delegate to the waiter's `OnCompleted` method. (I've not provided `UnsafeOn Completed` here, so it is forced to use `OnCompleted`.) Example 17-16 shows code that does all of this.

Example 17-16. A very rough approximation of what await does

```
static void ManualUseCustomAsync()
{
    var awaiter = CustomAsync().GetAwaiter();
    if (awaiter.IsCompleted)
    {
        TheRest(awaiter);
    }
    else
    {
        awaiter.OnCompleted(() => TheRest(awaiter));
    }
}

private static void TheRest(MyAwaitableType.MinimalAwaiter awaiter)
{
    string result = awaiter.GetResult();
    Console.WriteLine(result);
}
```

I've split the method into two pieces, because the C# compiler avoids creating a delegate in the case where `IsCompleted` is `true`, and I wanted to do the same. However, this is not quite what the C# compiler does—it also manages to avoid creating an extra method for each `await` statement, but this means it has to create considerably more complex code. In fact, for methods that just contain a single `await`, it introduces rather more overhead than Example 17-16. However, once the number of `await` expressions starts to increase, the complexity pays off, because the compiler does not need to add any further methods. Example 17-17 shows something closer to what the compiler does.

Example 17-17. A slightly closer approximation to how await works

```
private class ManualUseCustomAsyncState
{
    private int state;
    private MyAwaitableType.MinimalAwaiter awaiter;

    public void MoveNext()
    {
        if (state == 0)
        {
            awaiter = CustomAsync().GetAwaiter();
            if (!awaiter.IsCompleted)
```

```
        {
            state = 1;
            awaiter.OnCompleted(MoveNext);
            return;
        }
    }
    string result = awaiter.GetResult();
    Console.WriteLine(result);
    }
}

static void ManualUseCustomAsync()
{
    var s = new ManualUseCustomAsyncState();
    s.MoveNext();
}
```

This is still simpler than the real code, but it shows the basic strategy: the compiler generates a nested type that acts as a state machine. This has a field (`state`) that keeps track of where the method has got to so far, and it also contains fields corresponding to the method's local variables. (Just the `awaiter` variable in this example.) When an asynchronous operation does not block (i.e., its `IsCompleted` returns `true` immediately), the method can just continue to the next part, but once it encounters an operation that needs some time, it updates the `state` variable to remember where it is, and then uses the relevant awaiter's `OnCompleted` method. Notice that the method it asks to be called on completion is the same one that is already running: `MoveNext`. And this continues to be the case no matter how many `await`s you need to perform—every completion callback invokes the same method, the class simply remembers how far it had already gotten, and the method picks up from there.

I won't show the real generated code. It is borderline unreadable, because it contains a lot of *unspeakable* identifiers. (Remember from Chapter 3 that when the C# compiler needs to generate items with identifiers that must not collide with or be directly visible to our code, it creates a name that the runtime considers legal, but that is not legal in C#; this is called an *unspeakable* name.) Moreover, the compiler-generated code uses various helper classes from the `System.Runtime.CompilerServices` namespace that are intended for use only from asynchronous methods to manage things like determining which of the completion interfaces the awaiter supports and handling the related execution context flow. Also, if the method returns a task, there are additional helpers to create and update that. But when it comes to understanding the nature of the relationship between an awaitable type and the code the compiler produces for an `await` expression, Example 17-17 gives a fair impression.

Error Handling

The `await` keyword deals with exceptions much as you'd hope it would: if an asynchronous operation fails, the exception emerges from the `await` expression that was consuming that operation. The general principle that asynchronous code can be structured in the same way as ordinary synchronous code continues to apply in the face of exceptions, and the compiler does whatever work is required to make that possible.

Example 17-18 contains two asynchronous operations, one of which occurs in a loop. This is similar to Example 17-5. It does something a bit different with the content it fetches, but most importantly, it returns a task. This provides a place for an error to go if any of the operations should fail.

Example 17-18. Multiple potential points of failure

```
private static async Task<string> FindLongestLineAsync(
    string url, IHttpClientFactory cf)
{
    using (HttpClient w = cf.CreateClient())
    {
        Stream body = await w.GetStreamAsync(url);
        using (var bodyTextReader = new StreamReader(body))
        {
            string longestLine = string.Empty;
            while (!bodyTextReader.EndOfStream)
            {
                string line = await bodyTextReader.ReadLineAsync();
                if (longestLine.Length > line.Length)
                {
                    longestLine = line;
                }
            }
            return longestLine;
        }
    }
}
```

Exceptions are potentially challenging with asynchronous operations because by the time a failure occurs, the method call that originally started the work is likely to have returned. The `FindLongestLineAsync` method in this example will usually return as soon as it executes the first `await` expression. (It's possible that it won't—if the relevant resource is in the local HTTP cache, or if the `IHttpClientFactory` returns a client configured as a fake that never makes any real requests, this operation could succeed immediately. But typically, that operation will take some time, causing the method to return.) Suppose this operation succeeds and the rest of the method starts to run, but partway through the loop that retrieves the body of the response, the computer loses network connectivity. This will cause one of the operations started by ReadLineAsync to fail.

An exception will emerge from the await for that operation. There is no exception handling in this method, so what should happen next? Normally, you'd expect the exception to start working its way up the stack, but what's above this method on the stack? It almost certainly won't be the code that originally called it—remember, the method will usually return as soon as it hits the first await, so at this stage, we're running as a result of being called back by the awaiter for the task returned by ReadLineA sync. Chances are, we'll be running on some thread from the thread pool, and the code directly above us in the stack will be part of the task awaiter. This won't know what to do with our exception.

But the exception does not propagate up the stack. When an exception goes unhandled in an async method that returns a task, the compiler-generated code catches it and puts the task returned by that method into a faulted state (which will in turn mean that anything that was waiting for that task can now continue). If the code that called FindLongestLineAsync is working directly with the TPL, it will be able to see the exception by detecting that faulted state and retrieving the task's Exception property. Alternatively, it can either call Wait or fetch the task's Result property, and in either case, the task will throw an AggregateException containing the original exception. But if the code calling FindLongestLineAsync uses await on the task we return, the exception gets rethrown from that. From the calling code's point of view, it looks just like the exception emerged as it would normally, as Example 17-19 shows.

Example 17-19. Handling exceptions from await

```
try
{
    string longest = await FindLongestLineAsync(
        "http://192.168.22.1/", this.clientFactory);
    Console.WriteLine("Longest line: " + longest);
}
catch (HttpRequestException x)
{
    Console.WriteLine("Error fetching page: " + x.Message);
}
```

This is almost deceptively simple. Remember that the compiler performs substantial restructuring of the code around each await, and the execution of what looks like a single method may involve multiple calls in practice. So preserving the semantics of even a simple exception handling block like this (or related constructs, such as a using statement) is nontrivial. If you have ever attempted to write equivalent error handling for asynchronous work without the help of the compiler, you'll appreciate how much C# is doing for you here.

 The await does not rethrow the AggregateException provided by the task's Exception property. It rethrows the original exception. This enables async methods to handle the error in the same way synchronous code would.

Validating Arguments

There's one potentially surprising aspect of the way C# automatically reports exceptions through the task your asynchronous method returns. It means that code such as that in Example 17-20 doesn't do what you might expect.

Example 17-20. Potentially surprising argument validation

```
public async Task<string> FindLongestLineAsync(string url)
{
    if (url == null)
    {
        throw new ArgumentNullException("url");
    }
    ...
```

Inside an async method, the compiler treats all exceptions in the same way: none are allowed to pass up the stack as they would with a normal method, and they will always be reported by faulting the returned task. This is true even of exceptions thrown before the first await. In this example, the argument validation happens before the method does anything else, so at that stage, we will still be running on the original caller's thread. You might have thought that an argument exception thrown by this part of the code would propagate directly back to the caller. In fact, the caller will see a nonexceptional return, producing a task that is in a faulted state.

If the calling method immediately calls await on the return task, this won't matter much—it will see the exception in any case. But some code may choose not to wait immediately, in which case it won't see the argument exception until later. The common convention for simple argument validation exceptions is that if the caller has clearly made a programming error, we should throw an exception immediately, but this code doesn't do that.

If it's not possible to determine whether a particular argument is valid without performing slow work, you will not be able to conform to this convention if you want a truly asynchronous method. In that case, you would need to decide whether you would rather have the method block until it can validate all arguments, or have argument exceptions be reported via the returned task instead of being thrown immediately.

In cases where you want to throw this kind of exception straightaway (e.g., because it's being called from code that does not immediately `await` the result, and you'd like to discover the problem as soon as possible), the usual technique is to write a normal method that validates the arguments before calling an `async` method that does the work, and to make that second method either private or local. (You would have to do something similar to perform immediate argument validation with iterators too, incidentally. Iterators were described in Chapter 5.) Example 17-21 shows such a public wrapper method and the start of the method it calls to do the real work.

Example 17-21. Validating arguments for async methods

```
public static Task<string> FindLongestLineAsync(string url)
{
    if (url == null)
    {
        throw new ArgumentNullException("url");
    }
    return FindLongestLineCore(url);

    static async Task<string> FindLongestLineCore(string url)
    {
        ...
    }
}
```

Because the public method is not marked with `async`, any exceptions it throws will propagate directly to the caller. But any failures that occur once the work is underway in the local method will be reported through the task.

I've chosen to forward the `url` argument to the local method. I didn't have to, because a local method can access its containing method's variables. However, relying on that causes the compiler to create a type to hold the locals to share them across the methods. Where possible, it will make this a value type, passing it by reference to the inner type, but in cases where the inner method's scope might outlive the outer method, it can't do that. And since the local method here is `async`, it is likely to continue to run long after the outer method's stack frame no longer exists, so this would cause the compiler to create a reference type just to hold that `url` argument. By passing the argument in, we avoid this (and I've marked the method as `static` to indicate that this is my intent—this means the compiler will produce an error if I inadvertently use anything from the outer method in the local one). The compiler will probably still have to create an object to hold on to local variables in the inner method during asynchronous execution, but at least we've avoided creating more objects than necessary.

Singular and Multiple Exceptions

As Chapter 16 showed, the TPL defines a model for reporting multiple errors—a task's Exception property returns an AggregateException. Even if there is only a single failure, you still have to extract it from its containing AggregateException. However, if you use the await keyword, it does this for you—as you saw in Example 17-19, it retrieves the first exception in the InnerExceptions and rethrows that.

This is handy when the operation can produce only a single failure—it saves you from having to write additional code to handle the aggregate exception and then dig out the contents. (If you're using a task returned by an async method, it will never contain more than one exception.) However, it does present a problem if you're working with composite tasks that can fail in multiple ways simultaneously. For example, Task.WhenAll takes a collection of tasks and returns a single task that completes only when all its constituent tasks complete. If some of them complete by failing, you'll get an AggregateException that contains multiple errors. If you use await with such an operation, it will throw only the first of those exceptions back to you.

The usual TPL mechanisms—the Wait method or the Result property—provide the complete set of errors (by throwing the AggregateException itself instead of its first inner exception), but they both block the thread if the task is not yet complete. What if you want the efficient asynchronous operation of await, which uses threads only when there's something for them to do, but you still want to see all the errors? Example 17-22 shows one approach.

Example 17-22. Throwless awaiting followed by Wait

```
static async Task CatchAll(Task[] ts)
{
    try
    {
        var t = Task.WhenAll(ts);
        await t.ContinueWith(
                x => {},
                TaskContinuationOptions.ExecuteSynchronously);
        t.Wait();
    }
    catch (AggregateException all)
    {
```

```
        Console.WriteLine(all);
    }
}
```

This uses `await` to take advantage of the efficient nature of asynchronous C# methods, but instead of calling `await` on the composite task itself, it sets up a continuation. A continuation can complete successfully when its antecedent completes, regardless of whether the antecedent succeeded or failed. This continuation has an empty body, so there's nothing to go wrong, which means that the `await` will not throw here. The call to `Wait` will throw an `AggregateException` if anything failed, enabling the `catch` block to see all of the exceptions. And because we call `Wait` only after the `await` completes, we know the task is already finished, so the call will not block.

The one downside of this is that it ends up setting up a whole extra task just so we can wait without hitting an exception. I've configured the continuation to execute synchronously, so this will avoid scheduling a second piece of work via the thread pool, but there's still a somewhat unsatisfactory waste of resources here. A messier but more efficient approach would be to use `await` in the usual way, but to write an exception handler that checks to see if there were other exceptions, as shown in Example 17-23.

Example 17-23. Looking for additional exceptions

```
static async Task CatchAll(Task[] ts)
{
    Task t = null;
    try
    {
        t = Task.WhenAll(ts);
        await t;
    }
    catch (Exception first)
    {
        Console.WriteLine(first);

        if (t != null && t.Exception.InnerExceptions.Count > 1)
        {
            Console.WriteLine("I've found some more:");
            Console.WriteLine(t.Exception);
        }
    }
}
```

This avoids creating an extra task, but the downside is that the exception handling looks a little odd.

Concurrent Operations and Missed Exceptions

The most straightforward way to use `await` is to do one thing after another, just as you would with synchronous code. Although doing work strictly sequentially may not sound like it takes full advantage of the potential of asynchronous code, it does make much more efficient use of the available threads than the synchronous equivalent, and it also works well in client-side UI code, leaving the UI thread free to respond to input even while work is then in progress. However, you might want to go further.

It is possible to kick off multiple pieces of work simultaneously. You can call an asynchronous API, and instead of using `await` immediately, you can store the result in a variable and then start another piece of work before waiting for both. Although this is a viable technique, and might reduce the overall execution time of your operations, there's a trap for the unwary, shown in Example 17-24.

Example 17-24. How not to run multiple concurrent operations

```
static async Task GetSeveral(IHttpClientFactory cf)
{
    using (HttpClient w = cf.CreateClient())
    {
        w.MaxResponseContentBufferSize = 2_000_000;

        Task<string> g1 = w.GetStringAsync("https://endjin.com/");
        Task<string> g2 = w.GetStringAsync("https://oreilly.com");

        // BAD!
        Console.WriteLine((await g1).Length);
        Console.WriteLine((await g2).Length);
    }
}
```

This fetches content from two URLs concurrently. Having started both pieces of work, it uses two `await` expressions to collect the results of each and to display the lengths of the resulting strings. If the operations succeed, this will work, but it doesn't handle errors well. If the first operation fails, the code will never get as far as executing the second `await`. This means that if the second operation also fails, nothing will look at the exception it throws. Eventually, the TPL will detect that the exception has gone unobserved, which will result in the `UnobservedTaskException` event being raised. (Chapter 16 discussed the TPL's unobserved exception handling.) The problem is that this will happen only very occasionally—it requires both operations to fail in quick succession—so it's something that would be very easy to miss in testing.

You could avoid this with careful exception handling—you could catch any exceptions that emerge from the first `await` before going on to execute the second, for example. Alternatively, you could use `Task.WhenAll` to wait for all the tasks as a single operation—this will produce a faulted task with an `AggregateException` if anything fails, enabling you to see all errors. Of course, as you saw in the preceding section, multiple failures of this kind are awkward to deal with when you're using `await`. But if you want to launch multiple asynchronous operations and have them all in flight simultaneously, you're going to need more complex code to coordinate the results than you would do when performing work sequentially. Even so, the `await` and `async` keywords still make life much easier.

Summary

Asynchronous operations do not block the thread from which they are invoked, making them more efficient than synchronous APIs, which is particularly important on heavily loaded machines. This also makes them suitable for use on the client side, because they enable you to perform long-running work without causing the UI to become unresponsive. Without language support, asynchronous operations can be complex to use correctly, particularly when handling errors across multiple related operations. C#'s `await` keyword enables you to write asynchronous code in a style that looks just like normal synchronous code. It gets a little more complex if you want a single method to manage multiple concurrent operations, but even if you write an asynchronous method that does things strictly in order, you will get the benefits of making much more efficient use of threads in a server application—it will be able to support more simultaneous users, because each individual operation uses fewer resources—and on the client side, you'll get the benefit of a more responsive UI.

Methods that use `await` must be marked with the `async` keyword and should usually return one of `Task`, `Task<T>`, `ValueTask`, or `ValueTask<T>`. (C# allows a `void` return type, but you would normally use this only when you have no choice.) The compiler will arrange for this task to complete successfully once your method returns, or to complete with a fault if your method fails at any point in its execution. Because `await` can consume any `Task` or `Task<T>`, this makes it easy to split asynchronous logic across multiple methods, because a high-level method can `await` a lower-level `async` method. Usually, the work eventually ends up being performed by some task-based API, but it doesn't have to be, because `await` only demands a certain pattern—it will accept any expression on which you can invoke a `GetWaiter` method to obtain a suitable type.

CHAPTER 18

Memory Efficiency

As Chapter 7 described, the CLR is able to perform automatic memory management thanks to its garbage collector (GC). This comes at a price: when a CPU spends time on garbage collection, that stops it from getting on with more productive work. On laptops and phones, GC work drains power from the battery. In a cloud computing environment where you may be paying for CPU time based on consumption, extra work for the CPU corresponds directly to increased costs. More subtly, on a computer with many cores, spending too much time in the GC can dramatically reduce throughput, because many of the cores may end up blocked, waiting for the GC to complete before they can proceed.

In many cases, these effects will be small enough not to cause visible problems. However, when certain kinds of programs experience heavy load, GC costs can come to dominate the overall execution time. In particular, if you write code that performs relatively simple but highly repetitive processing, GC overhead can have a substantial impact on throughput.

As Microsoft's ASP.NET Core team worked to improve the performance of their web server framework, in early versions they frequently ran into hard limits due to GC overhead. To enable .NET applications to break through these barriers, C# 7.2 introduced various features that can enable dramatic reductions in the number of allocations. Fewer allocations means fewer blocks of memory for the GC to recover, so this translates directly to lower GC overhead. Version 3.0 of ASP.NET Core started making extensive use of these features. This version improves performance across the board, but for the simplest performance benchmark, known as *plaintext* (part of the TechEmpower suite of web performance tests), this release improves the request handling rate by over 25%.

In some specialized scenarios, the differences can be more dramatic. In 2019, I worked on a project that processed diagnostic information from a broadband provider's networking equipment (in the form of RADIUS packets). Adopting the techniques described in this chapter boosted the rate at which a single CPU core in our system could process the messages from around 300,000/s to about 7 million/s.

There is a price to pay, of course: these GC-efficient techniques add significant complication to your code. And the payoff won't always be so large—although ASP.NET Core 3.0 improves over the previous version on all benchmarks, only the simplest shows a 25% boost. The practical improvement will really depend on the nature of your workload, and for some applications you might find that applying these techniques delivers no measurable improvement. So before you even consider using them, you should use performance monitoring tools to find out how much time your code spends in the GC. If it's only a few percent, then you might not be able to realize order-of-magnitude improvements. But if testing suggests that there's room for significant improvement, the next step is to ask whether the techniques in this chapter are likely to help. So let's start by exploring exactly how these new techniques can help you reduce GC overhead.

(Don't) Copy That

The way to reduce GC overhead is to allocate less memory on the heap. And the most important technique for minimizing allocations is to avoid making copies of data. For example, consider the URL http://example.com/books/1323?edition=6&format=pdf. There are several elements of interest in here, such as the protocol (http), the hostname (example.com), or the query string. The latter has its own structure: it is a sequence of name/value pairs. The obvious way to work with a URL in .NET is to use the System.Uri type, as Example 18-1 shows.

Example 18-1. Deconstructing a URL

```
var uri = new Uri("http://example.com/books/1323?edition=6&format=pdf");
Console.WriteLine(uri.Scheme);
Console.WriteLine(uri.Host);
Console.WriteLine(uri.AbsolutePath);
Console.WriteLine(uri.Query);
```

It produces the following output:

```
http
example.com
/books/1323
?edition=6&format=pdf
```

This is convenient, but by getting the values of these four properties we have forced the Uri to provide four string objects in addition to the original one. You could imagine a smart implementation of Uri that recognized certain standard values for Scheme, such as http and that always returned the same string instance for these instead of allocating new ones, but for all the other parts, it's likely to have to allocate new strings on the heap.

There is another way. Instead of creating new `string` objects for each section, we could take advantage of the fact that all of the information we want was already in the string containing the whole URL. There's no need to copy each section into a new string, when instead we can just keep track of the position and lengths of the relevant sections within the string. Instead of creating a string for each section, we would need just two numbers. And since we can represent numbers using value types (e.g., `int`, or, for very long strings, `long`), we don't need any additional objects on the heap beyond the single string with the full URL. For example, the scheme (`http`) is at position 0 and has length 4. Figure 18-1 shows each of the elements by their offset and position within the string.

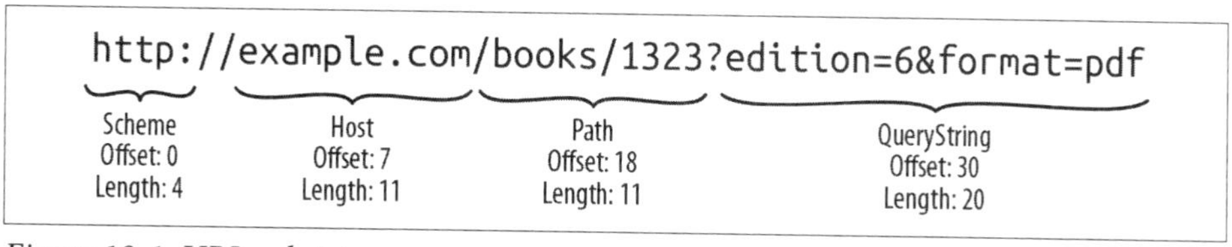

```
http://example.com/books/1323?edition=6&format=pdf
```

Scheme	Host	Path	QueryString
Offset: 0	Offset: 7	Offset: 18	Offset: 30
Length: 4	Length: 11	Length: 11	Length: 20

Figure 18-1. URL substrings

This works, but already we can see the first problem with working this way: it is somewhat awkward. Instead of representing, say, the `Host` with a convenient `string` object, which is easily understood and readily inspected in the debugger, we now have a pair of numbers, and as developers, we now have to remember which string they point into. It's not rocket science, but it makes it slightly harder to understand our code, and easier to introduce bugs. But there's a payoff: instead of five strings (the original URL and the four properties), we just have one. And if you're trying to process millions of events each second, that could easily be worth the effort.

Obviously this technique would work for a more fine-grained structure too. The offset and position (25, 4) locates the text 1323 in this URL. We might want to parse that as an `int`. But at this point we run into the second problem with this style of working: it is not widely supported in .NET libraries. The usual way to parse text into an `int` is to use the `int` type's static `Parse` or `TryParse` methods. Unfortunately, these do not provide overloads that accept a position or offset within a `string`. They require a string containing only the number to be parsed. This means you end up writing code such as Example 18-2.

Example 18-2. Defeating the point of the exercise by using Substring

```
string uriString = "http://example.com/books/1323?edition=6&format=pdf";
int id = int.Parse(uriString.Substring(25, 4));
```

This works, but by using `Substring` to go from our (offset, length) representation back to the plain `string` that `int.Parse` wants, we've allocated a new `string`. The whole point of this exercise was to reduce allocations, so this doesn't seem like progress. One solution might be for Microsoft to go through the entire .NET API surface area, adding overloads that accept offset and length parameters in any situation where we might want to work with something in the middle of something else (either a substring, as in this example, or perhaps a subrange of an array). In fact, there are examples of this already: the `Stream` API for working with byte streams has various methods that accept a `byte[]` array and also offset and length arguments to indicate exactly which part of the array you want to work with.

However, there's one more problem with this technique: it is inflexible about the type of container that the data lives in. Microsoft could add an overload to `int.Parse` that takes a `string`, an offset, and a length, but it would only be able to parse data inside a `string`. What if the data happens to be in a `char[]`? In that case you'd have to convert it to a string first, at which point we're back to additional allocations. Alternatively, every API that wants to support this approach would need multiple overloads to support all the containers that anyone might want to use, each potentially requiring a different implementation of the same basic method.

More subtly, what if the data you have is currently in memory that's not on the CLR's heap? This is a particularly important question when it comes to the performance of servers that accept requests over the network (e.g., a web server). Sometimes it is not possible to arrange for data received by a network card to be delivered directly into memory on .NET's heap. Also, some forms of interprocess communication involve arranging for the OS to map a particular region of memory into two different processes' address spaces. The .NET heap is local to the process and cannot use such memory.

C# has always supported use of external memory through *unsafe code*, which enables you to work with raw unmanaged pointers that work in a similar way to pointers in the C and C++ languages. However, there are a couple of problems with these. First, they would add yet another entry to the list of overloads that everything would need to support in a world where we can parse data in place. Second, code using pointers cannot pass .NET's type safety verification rules. This means it becomes possible to make certain kinds of programming errors that are normally impossible in C#. It may also mean that the code will not be allowed to run in certain scenarios, since the loss of type safety would enable unsafe code to bypass certain security constraints.

To summarize, it has always been possible to reduce allocations and copying in .NET by working with offsets and lengths, and either a reference to a containing string or array, or an unmanaged pointer to memory, but there was considerable room for improvement on these fronts:

- Convenience
- Wide support across .NET APIs
- Unified, safe handling of
  - Strings
  - Arrays
  - Unmanaged memory

But since C# 7.2, we've been able to use a type that addresses all three points: Span<T>. (See the next sidebar, "Support Across Language and Runtime Versions", for more information on how the features described in this chapter relate to C# language and .NET runtime versions.)

Support Across Language and Runtime Versions

You might be surprised that I've said that a particular version of C# (7.2) introduced a new type. Generally speaking, new types are defined in libraries so they're not tied to any particular version of C#, and superficially, it's true that Span<T> is just another type. It has been part of the core libraries that ship with .NET Core since v2.1, and there's a NuGet package, System.Memory, enabling you to use it in the .NET Framework. It's also available to any library that targets .NET Standard 2.1.

But while Span<T> is just another type, it requires C# 7.2 or later because it is defined as a ref struct. Older versions of C# do not support ref struct, so they are unable to use Span<T>.

Be aware that the effectiveness of the techniques in this chapter depends on which version of .NET you are using. Although the System.Memory NuGet package makes it possible to use the types discussed in this chapter in programs that run on the .NET Framework, you end up with a slightly different implementation than the one you will get when running the exact same code on .NET Core 2.1 or later. Starting with that version, .NET Core recognizes Span<T> and related types, and provides special optimizations. This is critical to the high performance offered by the features discussed in this chapter.

The latest version of the .NET Framework at the time of writing (version 4.8) lacks the Span<T> optimizations, and Microsoft has no plans to add them in future versions because the .NET Framework is superseded by .NET Core. Code using these techniques works correctly on .NET Framework, but if you want to reap the full performance benefits of these techniques, you'll need to run on .NET Core.

Representing Sequential Elements with Span<T>

The System.Span<T> value type represents a sequence of elements of type T stored contiguously in memory. Those elements can live inside an array, a string, a managed block of memory allocated in a stack frame, or unmanaged memory. Let's look at how Span<T> addresses each of the requirements enumerated in the preceding section.

A Span<T> encapsulates three things: a pointer or reference to the containing memory (e.g., the string or array), the position of the data within that memory, and its length.[1] To access the contents of a span, you use it much as you would an array, as Example 18-3 shows. This makes it much more convenient to use than ad hoc techniques in which you define a couple of int variables and have to remember what they refer to.

Example 18-3. Iterating over a Span<int>

```
public static int SumSpan(ReadOnlySpan<int> span)
{
    int sum = 0;
    for (int i = 0; i < span.Length; ++i)
    {
        sum += span[i];
    }
    return sum;
}
```

Since a Span<T> knows its own length, its indexer checks that the index is in range, just as the built-in array type does. And if you are running on .NET Core, the performance is very similar to using a built-in array. This includes the optimizations that detect certain loop patterns—for example, the CLR will recognize the code above as a loop that iterates over the entire contents, enabling it to generate code that doesn't need to check that the index is in range each time around the loop. In some cases it is even able to generate code that uses the vector-oriented instructions available in

---

[1] Depending on which version of .NET you're running on, the first two items may be combined. .NET Core does not store the pointer and offset separately: instead it just points directly to the data of interest. The version of Span<T> available for .NET Framework needs to maintain the pointer separately to ensure garbage collection handles spans correctly, because its CLR does not have the same modifications for supporting spans that .NET Core has.

some CPUs to accelerate the loop. (On .NET Framework, Span<T> is a little slower than an array, because its CLR does not include the optimizations that were added in .NET Core to support Span<T>.)

You may have noticed that the method in Example 18-3 takes a ReadOnlySpan<T>. This is a close relative of Span<T>, and there is an implicit conversion enabling you to pass any Span<T> to a method that takes a ReadOnlySpan<T>. The read-only form enables a method to declare clearly that it will only read from the span, and not write to it. (This is enforced by the fact that the read-only form's indexer offers just a get accessor, and no set.)

 Whenever you write a method that works with a span and that does not mean to modify it, you should use ReadOnlySpan<T>.

There are implicit conversions from the various supported containers to Span<T> (and also to ReadOnlySpan<T>). For example, Example 18-4 passes an array to the SumSpan method.

Example 18-4. Passing an int[] as a ReadOnlySpan<int>

```
Console.WriteLine(SumSpan(new int[] { 1, 2, 3 }));
```

Of course, we've gone and allocated an array on the heap there, so this particular example defeats the whole point of using spans, but if you already have an array to hand, this is a useful technique. Span<T> also works with stack-allocated arrays, as Example 18-5 shows. (The stackalloc keyword enables you to create an array in memory allocated on the current stack frame.)

Example 18-5. Passing a stack-allocated array as a ReadOnlySpan<int>

```
Span<int> numbers = stackalloc int[] { 1, 2, 3 };
Console.WriteLine(SumSpan(numbers));
```

Normally, C# won't allow you to use stackalloc outside of code marked as unsafe. The keyword allocates memory on the current method's stack frame, and it does not create a real array object. (Arrays are reference types, so they must live on the GC heap. A stackalloc expression produces a pointer type, because it produces plain memory without the usual .NET object headers. In this case, it would be an int*. You can only use pointer types directly in unsafe code blocks.) However, the compiler makes an exception to this rule if you assign the pointer produced by a stackalloc expression directly into a span. This is permitted because spans impose bounds checking, preventing undetected out-of-range access errors of the kind that normally make pointers unsafe. Also, the fact that Span<T> and ReadOnlySpan<T> are both ref struct types ensures that a span cannot outlive its containing stack frame, guaranteeing that the stack frame on which the stack-allocated memory lives will not vanish while there are still outstanding references to it. (.NET's type safety verification rules include special handling for spans.)

Earlier I mentioned that spans can refer to strings as well as arrays. However, we can't pass a string to this SumSpan for the simple reason that it requires a span with an element type of int, whereas a string is a sequence of char values. int and char have different sizes—they take 4 and 2 bytes each, respectively. Although an implicit conversion exists between the two (meaning you can assign a char value into an int variable, giving you the Unicode value of the char) that does not make a ReadOnly Span<char> implicitly compatible with a ReadOnlySpan<int>.[2] Remember, the entire point of spans is that they provide a view into a block of data without needing to copy or modify that data; since int and char have different sizes, converting a char[] to an int[] array would double its size. However, if we were to write a method accepting a ReadOnlySpan<char>, we would be able to pass it a string, a char[] array, a stackalloc char[], or an unmanaged pointer of type char* (because the in-memory representation of a particular span of characters within each of these is the same).

Since strings are immutable in .NET, you cannot convert a string to a Span<char>. You can only convert it to a ReadOnly Span<char>.

We've examined two of our requirements from the preceding section: Span<T> is easier to use than ad hoc storing of an offset and length, and it makes it possible to write a single method that can work with data in arrays, strings, the stack, or unmanaged memory. This leaves our final requirement: widespread support throughout .NET class libraries. As Example 18-6 shows, it is now supported in int.Parse, enabling us to fix the problem shown in Example 18-2.

---

2 That said, it is possible to perform this kind of conversion explicitly—the MemoryMarshal class offers methods that can take a span of one type and return another span that provides a view over the same underlying memory, but is interpreted as containing a different element type. But it is unlikely to be useful in this case: converting a ReadOnlySpan<char> to a ReadOnlySpan<int> would produce a span with half the number of elements, where each int contained pairs of adjacent char values.

Example 18-6. Parsing integers in a string using Span<char>

```
string uriString = "http://example.com/books/1323?edition=6&format=pdf";
int id = int.Parse(uriString.AsSpan(25, 4));
```

New overloads such as this one that accept a span where previously only a string or perhaps an array would be accepted are now very common. However, be aware that this is a work in progress. Span<T> is a relatively new type (it was introduced in 2018; .NET has been around since 2002), so there will inevitably be many third-party libraries that do not yet support it, and perhaps never will. Even Microsoft's own framework class libraries did not provide ubiquitous support for it in .NET Core 2.1, the first version to support Span<T>. However, it is becoming increasingly well supported, and the situation will only improve.

Utility Methods

In addition to the array-like indexer and Length properties, Span<T> offers a few useful methods. The Clear and Fill methods provide convenient ways to initialize all the elements in a span either to the default value for the element type, or a specific value. Obviously, these are not available on ReadOnlySpan<T>.

You may sometimes encounter situations in which you have a span and you need to pass its contents to a method that requires an array. Obviously there's no avoiding an allocation in this case, but if you need to do it, you can use the ToArray method.

Spans (both normal and read-only) also offer a TryCopyTo method, which takes as its argument a (non-read-only) span of the same element type. This allows you to copy data between spans. This method handles scenarios where the source and target spans refer to overlapping ranges within the same container.

Stack Only

The Span<T> and ReadOnlySpan<T> types are both declared as ref struct. This means that not only are they value types, they are value types that can live only on the stack. So you cannot have fields with span types in a class, or any struct that is not also a ref struct. This also imposes some potentially more surprising restrictions. For example, it means you cannot use a span in a variable in an async method. (These store all their variables as fields in a hidden type, enabling them to live on the heap, because asynchronous methods often need to outlive their original stack frame. In fact, these methods can even switch to a completely different stack altogether, because asynchronous methods can end up running on different threads as their execution progresses.) For similar reasons, there are restrictions on using spans in anonymous functions and in iterator methods. You use them in local methods, and you can even declare a ref struct variable in the outer method and use it from the nested one, but with one restriction: you must not create a delegate that refers to that local method, because this would cause the compiler to move shared variables into an object that lives on the heap. (See Chapter 9 for details.)

This restriction is necessary for .NET to be able to offer the combination of array-like performance, type safety, and the flexibility to work with multiple different containers. For situations in which this stack-only limitation is problematic, we have the Memory<T> type.

Representing Sequential Elements with Memory<T>

The Memory<T> type and its counterpart, ReadOnlyMemory<T>, represent the same basic concept as Span<T> and ReadOnlySpan<T>: these types provide a uniform view over a contiguous sequence of elements of type T that could reside in an array, unmanaged memory, or, if the element type is char, a string. But unlike spans, these are *not* ref struct types, so they can be used anywhere. The downside is that this means they cannot offer the same high performance as spans. (It also means you cannot create a Memory<T> that refers to stackalloc memory.)

You can convert a Memory<T> to a Span<T>, and likewise a ReadOnlyMemory<T> to a ReadOnlySpan<T>. This makes these memory types useful when you want something span-like, but in a context where spans are not allowed (e.g., in an asynchronous method).

 The conversion to a span has a cost. It is not massive, but it is significantly higher than the cost of accessing an individual element in a span. (In particular, many of the optimizations that make spans attractive only become effective with repeated use of the same span.) So if you are going to read or write elements in a Memory<T> in a loop, you should perform the conversion to Span<T> just once, outside of the loop, rather than doing it each time around. If you can work entirely with spans, you should do so since they offer the best performance. (And if you are not concerned with performance, then this is not the chapter for you!)

ReadOnlySequence<T>

The types we've looked at so far in this chapter all represent contiguous blocks of memory. Unfortunately, data doesn't always neatly present itself to us in the most convenient possible form. For example, on a busy server that is handling many concurrent requests, the network messages for requests in progress often become interleaved—if a particular request is large enough to need to be split across two network packets, it's entirely possible that after receiving the first but before receiving the second of these, one or more packets for other, unrelated requests could arrive. So by the time we come to process the contents of the request, it might be split across two different chunks of memory. Since span and memory values can each represent only a contiguous range of elements, .NET provides another type, ReadOnlySequence, to represent data that is conceptually a single sequence, but that has been split into multiple ranges.

 There is no corresponding Sequence<T>. Unlike spans and memory, this particular abstraction is available only in read-only form. That's because it's common to need to deal with fragmented data as a reader, where you don't control where the data lives, but if you are producing data, you are more likely to be in a position to control where it goes.

Now that we've seen the main types for working with data while minimizing the number of allocations, let's look at how these can all work together to handle high volumes of data. To coordinate this kind of processing, we need to look at one more feature: pipelines.

Processing Data Streams with Pipelines

Everything we're looking at in this chapter is designed to enable safe, efficient processing of large volumes of data. The types we've seen so far all represent information that is already in memory. We also need to think about how that data is going to get into memory in the first place. The preceding section hinted at the fact that this can be somewhat messy. The data will very often be split into chunks, and not in a way designed for the convenience of the code processing the data, because it will likely be arriving either over a network or from a disk. If we're to realize the performance benefits made possible by Span<T> and its related types, we need to pay close attention to the job of getting data into memory in the first place, and the way in which this data fetching process cooperates with the code that processes the data. Even if you are only going to be writing code that consumes data—perhaps you are relying on a framework such as ASP.NET Core to get the data into memory for you—it is important to understand how this process works.

The System.Io.Pipelines NuGet package defines a set of types in a namespace of the same name that provide a high-performance system for loading data from some source that tends to split data into inconveniently sized chunks, and passing that data over to code that wants to be able to process it *in situ* using spans. Figure 18-2 shows the main participants in a pipeline-based process.

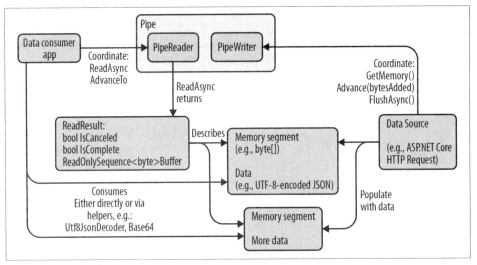

Figure 18-2. Pipeline overview

At the heart of this is the `Pipe` class. It offers two properties: `Writer` and `Reader`. The first returns a `PipeWriter`, which is used by the code that loads the data into memory. (This often doesn't need to be application-specific. For example, in a web application you can let ASP.NET Core control the writer on your behalf.) The `Reader` property's type is, predictably, `PipeReader`, and this is most likely to be the part your code interacts with.

The basic process for reading data from a pipe is as follows. First, you call `PipeR eader.ReadAsync`. This returns a task,[3] because if no data is available yet, you will need to wait until the data source supplies the writer with some data. Once data is available, the task will provide a `ReadResult` object. This supplies a `ReadOnlySe quence<T>`, which presents the available data as one or more `ReadOnlySpan<T>` values. The number of spans will depend on how fragmented the data is. If it's all conveniently in one place in memory, there will be just one span, but code using a reader needs to be able to cope with more. Your code should then process as much of the available data as it can. Once it has done this, it calls the reader's `AdvanceTo` to tell it how much of the data your code has been able to process. Then, if the `ReadRe sult.IsComplete` property is false, we will repeat these steps again from the call to `ReadAsync`.

An important detail of this is that we are allowed to tell the `PipeReader` that we couldn't process everything it gave us. This would normally be because the informa-

---

3 It is a `ValueTask<ReadResult>` because the purpose of this exercise is to minimize allocations. `ValueTask<T>` was described in Chapter 16.

tion got sliced into pieces, and we need to see some of the next chunk before we can fully process everything in the current one. For example, a JSON message large enough to need to be split across several network packets will probably end up with splits in inconvenient places. So you might find that the first chunk looks like this:

```
{"property1":"value1","prope
```

And the second like this:

```
rty2":42}
```

In practice the chunks would be bigger, but this illustrates the basic problem: the chunks that a `PipeReader` returns are likely to slice across the middle of important features. With most .NET APIs you never have to deal with this kind of mess because everything has been cleaned up and reassembled by the time you see it, but the price you pay for that is the allocation of new strings to hold the recombined results. If you want to avoid those allocations, you have to handle these challenges.

There are a couple of ways to deal with this. One is for code reading data to maintain enough state to be able to stop and later restart at any point in the sequence. So code processing this JSON might choose to remember that it is partway through an object, and that it's in the middle of processing a property whose name starts with "prope." But `PipeReader` offers an alternative. Code processing these examples could report with its call to `AdvanceTo` that it has consumed everything up to the first comma. If you do that, the `Pipe` will remember that we're not yet finished with this first block, and when the next call to `ReadAsync` completes, the `ReadOnlySequence<T>` in `ReadResult.Buffer` will now include at least two spans: the first span will point into the same block of memory as last time, but now its offset will be set to where we got to last time—that first span will refer to the `"prope` text at the end of the first block. And then the second span will refer to the text in the second chunk.

The advantage of this second approach is that the code processing the data doesn't need to remember as much between calls to `ReadAsync`, because it knows it'll be able to go back and look at the previously unprocessed data again once the next chunk arrives, at which point it should now be able to make sense of it.

In practice, this particular example is fairly easy to cope with because there's a type in the class library called `Utf8JsonReader` that can handle all the awkward details around chunk boundaries for us. Let's look at a real example.

Processing JSON in ASP.NET Core

Suppose you are developing a web service that needs to handle HTTP requests containing JSON. This is a pretty common scenario. Example 18-7 shows the typical way to do this in ASP.NET Core. This is reasonably straightforward, but it does not use any of the low-allocation mechanisms discussed in this chapter, so this forces ASP.NET Core to allocate multiple objects for each request.

Example 18-7. Handling JSON in HTTP requests

```
[HttpPost]
[Route("/jobs/create")]
public void CreateJob([FromBody] JobDescription requestBody)
{
    switch (requestBody.JobCategory)
    {
        case "arduous":
            CreateArduousJob(requestBody.DepartmentId);
            break;

        case "tedious":
            CreateTediousJob(requestBody.DepartmentId);
            break;
    }
}

public class JobDescription
{
    public int DepartmentId { get; set; }
    public string JobCategory { get; set; }
}
```

Before we look at how to change it, in case you're not familiar with ASP.NET Core, I will quickly explain what's happening in this example. The `CreateJob` method is annotated with attributes telling ASP.NET Core that this will handle HTTP POST requests where the URL path is `/jobs/create`. The `[FromBody]` attribute on the method's argument indicates that we expect the body of the request to contain data in the form described by the `JobDescription` class. ASP.NET Core can be configured to handle various data formats, but if you go with the defaults, it will expect JSON.

This example is therefore telling ASP.NET Core that for each POST request to `/jobs/create`, it should construct a `JobDescription` object, populating its `Depart mentId` and `JobCategory` from properties of the same name in JSON in the incoming request body.

In other words, we're asking ASP.NET Core to allocate two objects—a `JobDescrip tion` and a `string`—for each request, each of which will contain copies of information that was in the body of the incoming request. (The other property, `DepartmentId` is an `int`, and since that's a value type, it lives inside the `JobDescrip tion` object.) And for most applications that will be fine—a couple of allocations is not normally anything to worry about in the course of handling a single web request. However, in more realistic examples with more complex requests, we might then be looking at a much larger number of properties, and if you need to handle a very high volume of requests, the copying of data into a string for each property can start to cause enough extra work for the GC that it becomes a performance problem.

Example 18-8 shows how we can avoid these allocations using the various features described in the preceding sections of this chapter. It makes the code a good deal more complex, demonstrating why you should only apply these kinds of techniques in cases where you have established that GC overhead is high enough that the extra development effort is justified by the performance improvements.

Example 18-8. Handling JSON without allocations

```csharp
private static readonly byte[] Utf8TextJobCategory =
    Encoding.UTF8.GetBytes("JobCategory");
private static readonly byte[] Utf8TextDepartmentId =
    Encoding.UTF8.GetBytes("DepartmentId");
private static readonly byte[] Utf8TextArduous = Encoding.UTF8.GetBytes("arduous");
private static readonly byte[] Utf8TextTedious = Encoding.UTF8.GetBytes("tedious");

[HttpPost]
[Route("/jobs/create")]
public async ValueTask CreateJobFrugalAsync()
{
    bool inDepartmentIdProperty = false;
    bool inJobCategoryProperty = false;
    int? departmentId = null;
    bool? isArduous = null;

    PipeReader reader = this.Request.BodyReader;
    JsonReaderState jsonState = default;
    while (true)
    {
        ReadResult result = await reader.ReadAsync().ConfigureAwait(false);
        jsonState = ProcessBuffer(
            result,
            jsonState,
            out SequencePosition position);

        if (departmentId.HasValue && isArduous.HasValue)
        {
            if (isArduous.Value)
            {
                CreateArduousJob(departmentId.Value);
            }
            else
            {
                CreateTediousJob(departmentId.Value);
            }

            return;
```

```
        }

    reader.AdvanceTo(position);

    if (result.IsCompleted)
    {
        break;
    }
}

JsonReaderState ProcessBuffer(
    in ReadResult result,
    in JsonReaderState jsonState,
    out SequencePosition position)
{
    // This is a ref struct, so this has no GC overhead
    var r = new Utf8JsonReader(result.Buffer, result.IsCompleted, jsonState);

    while (r.Read())
    {
        if (inDepartmentIdProperty)
        {
            if (r.TokenType == JsonTokenType.Number)
            {
                if (r.TryGetInt32(out int v))
                {
                    departmentId = v;
                }
            }
        }
        else if (inJobCategoryProperty)
        {
            if (r.TokenType == JsonTokenType.String)
            {
                if (r.ValueSpan.SequenceEqual(Utf8TextArduous))
                {
                    isArduous = true;
                }
                else if (r.ValueSpan.SequenceEqual(Utf8TextTedious))
                {
                    isArduous = false;
                }
            }
        }

        inDepartmentIdProperty = false;
        inJobCategoryProperty = false;

        if (r.TokenType == JsonTokenType.PropertyName)
        {
            if (r.ValueSpan.SequenceEqual(Utf8TextJobCategory))
            {
```

```
                inJobCategoryProperty = true;
            }
            else if (r.ValueSpan.SequenceEqual(Utf8TextDepartmentId))
            {
                inDepartmentIdProperty = true;
            }
        }
    }

    position = r.Position;
    return r.CurrentState;
    }
}
```

Instead of defining an argument with a [FromBody] attribute, this method works directly with the this.Request.BodyReader property. (Inside an ASP.NET Core MVC controller class, this.Request returns an object representing the request being handled.) This property's type is PipeReader, the consumer side of a Pipe. ASP.NET Core creates the pipe, and it manages the data production side, feeding data from incoming requests into the associated PipeWriter.

As the property name suggests, this particular PipeReader enables us to read the contents of the HTTP request's body. By reading the data this way, we make it possible for ASP.NET Core to present the request body to us *in situ*: our code will be able to read the data directly from wherever it happened to end up in memory once the computer's network card received it. (In other words, no copies, and no additional garbage collectio˙ ɔverhead.)

The while loop in ͻreateJobFrugalAsync performs the same process you'll see with any code that reac˙ data from a PipeReader: it calls ReadAsync, processes the data that returns, and calls AdvanceTo to let the PipeReader know how much of that data it was able to process. We then check the IsComplete property of the ReadResult returned by ReadAsync, and if that is false then we go round one more time.

Example 18-8 uses the Utf8JsonReader type to read the data. As the name suggests, this works directly with text in UTF-8 encoding. This alone can provide a significant performance improvement: JSON messages are commonly sent with this encoding, but .NET strings use UTF-16. So one of the jobs that the simpler Example 18-7 forced ASP.NET to do was convert any strings from UTF-8 to UTF-16. On the other hand, we've lost some flexibility. The simpler, slower approach has the benefit of being able to adapt to incoming requests in more formats: if a client chose to send its request in something other than UTF-8—perhaps UTF-16 or UCS-32, or even a non-Unicode encoding such as ISO-8859-1—our handler could cope with any of them, because ASP.NET Core can do the string conversions for us. But since Example 18-8 works directly with the data in the form the client transmitted, using a type that only understands UTF-8, we have traded off that flexibility in exchange for higher performance.

Utf8JsonReader is able to handle the tricky chunking issues for us—if an incoming request ends up being split across multiple buffers in memory because it was too large to fit in a single network packet, Utf8JsonReader is able to cope. In the event of an unhelpfully placed split, it will process what it can, and then the JsonReaderState value it returns through its CurrentState will report a Position indicating the first unprocessed character. We pass this to PipeReader.AdvanceTo. The next call to PipeReader.ReadAsync will return only when there is more data, but its ReadResult.Buffer will also include the previously unconsumed data.

Like the ReadOnlySpan<T> type it uses internally when reading data, Utf8JsonReader is a ref struct type, meaning that it cannot live on the heap. This means it cannot be used in an async method, because async methods store all of their local variables on the heap. That is why this example has a separate method, ProcessBuffer. The outer CreateJobFrugalAsync method has to be async because the streaming nature of the PipeReader type means that its ReadAsync method requires us to use await. But the Utf8JsonReader cannot be used in an async method, so we end up having to split our logic across two methods.

> When splitting your pipeline processing into an outer async reader loop and an inner method that avoids async in order to use ref struct types, it can be convenient to make the inner method a local method as Example 18-8 does. This enables it to access variables declared in the outer method. You might be wondering whether this causes a hidden extra allocation—to enable sharing of variables in this way, the compiler generates a type, storing shared variables in fields in that type and not as conventional stack-based variables. With lambdas and other anonymous methods, this type will indeed cause an additional allocation, because it needs to be a heap-based type so that it can outlive the parent method. However, with local methods, the compiler uses a struct to hold the shared variables, which it passes by reference to the inner method, thus avoiding any extra allocation. This is possible because the compiler can determine that all calls to the local method will return before the outer method returns.

When using Utf8JsonReader, our code has to be prepared to receive the content in whatever order it happens to arrive. We can't write code that tries to read the properties in an order that is convenient for us, because that would rely on something holding those properties and their values in memory. (If you tried to rely on going back to the underlying data to retrieve particular properties on demand, you might find that the property you wanted was in an earlier chunk that's no longer available.) This defeats the whole goal of minimizing allocations. If you want to avoid allocations, your code needs to be flexible enough to handle the properties in whatever order they appear.

So the `ProcessBuffer` code in Example 18-8 just looks at each JSON element as it comes, and works out whether it's of interest. This means that when looking for particular property values, we have to notice the `PropertyName` element, and then remember that this was the last thing we saw, so that we know how to handle the `Number` or `String` element that follows, containing the value.

One strikingly odd feature of this code is the way it checks for particular strings. It needs to recognize properties of interest (`JobCategory` and `DepartmentId` in this example). But we can't just use normal string comparison. While it's possible to retrieve property names and string values as .NET strings, doing so defeats the main purpose of using `Utf8JsonReader`: if you obtain a `string`, the CLR has to allocate space for that string on the heap, and will eventually have to garbage collect the memory. (In this example, every acceptable incoming string is known in advance. In some scenarios there will be user-supplied strings whose values you will need to perform further processing on, and in those cases, you may just need to accept the costs of allocating an actual `string`.) So instead we end up performing binary comparisons. Notice that we're working entirely in UTF-8 encoding, and not the UTF-16 encoding used by .NET's `string` type. (The various static fields, such as `Utf8TextJobCategory` and `Utf8TextDepartmentId`, are all byte arrays created through `Encoding.UTF8` from the `System.Text` namespace.) That's because all of this code works directly against the request's payload in the form in which it arrived over the network, in order to avoid unnecessary copying.

Summary

APIs that break data down into the constituent components can be very convenient to use, but this convenience comes at a price. Each time we want some subelement represented either as a string or a child object, we cause another object to be allocated on the GC heap. The cumulative cost of these allocations (and the corresponding work to recover the memory once they are no longer in use) can be damaging in some very performance-sensitive applications. They can also be significant in cloud applications or high-volume data processing, where you might be paying for the amount of processing work you do—reducing CPU or memory usage can have a nontrivial effect on cost.

The `Span<T>` type and the related types discussed in this chapter make it possible to work with data wherever it already resides in memory. This typically requires rather more complex code, but in cases where the payoff justifies the work, these features make it possible for C# to tackle whole classes of problems for which it would previously have been too slow.

Index

S

Sample operator, 534
satellite resource assemblies, 564
Scan operator, 513
schedulers (Rx), 517-521
    built-in schedulers, 520
    ObserveOn extension method, 518
    passing schedulers explicitly, 519
    specifying, 518-520
    SubscribeOn extension method, 519
schedulers (thread-based tasks), 702
scope
    local variable instances, 43
    of variable, 40-44
    variable name ambiguity, 41-43
sealed classes, 292-294
sealed methods, 292-294
searching arrays, 218-225
seed, 453
Seek method, 616
Select operator
    data shaping and anonymous types, 438-439
    LINQ operators, 437-440
    projection and mapping, 440
selection statements, 44
SelectMany operator, 440-443, 503
self-contained applications, 548
Semaphore class, 687
semaphores, 687
sequence builders, Rx, 491-494
    empty, 491
    generate, 493
    never, 491
    range, 492
    repeat, 492
    return, 492
    throw, 492
sequence generation, LINQ, 471
sequence interfaces, 233-239
SequenceEqual operator, 459
sequences
    implementing, 239-246
    implementing IEnumerable<T> with itera-
        tors, 240-244
serialization, 645-654
    BinaryReader, BinaryWriter, BinaryPrimi-
        tives, 646
    CLR serialization, 647-648
    JSON.NET, 649-654

Utf8JsonReader, 759-761
server GC mode, 322
set operations, LINQ, 457
sets, 259-261
short weak reference, 314
simple name, 555
simple program, creating, 15-32
    adding a project to an existing solution, 17
    classes, 29
    namespaces, 25-29
    performing a unit test, 31
    program entry point, 30
    referencing external libraries, 19-21
    referencing one project from another, 18
    starting from scratch, 15-17
    writing a unit test, 21-25
simultaneous multithreading (SMT), 656
Single operator, 448
single-line comments, 52
single-precision numbers, 60
single-threaded apartment (STA), 605
slicing, 267
SMT (simultaneous multithreading), 656
Solution Explorer, 13
solutions (in Visual Studio), 13-14
    (see also simple program, creating)
sorted dictionaries, 258
sorted sets, 260
sorting arrays, 218-225
Span<T> type, 251, 748-752
SpinLock struct, 679-681
STA (single-threaded apartment), 605
stacks, 261
standards, 6-11
state, thread-local storage and, 660-662
statements, 44
STAThread attribute, 604
static classes, 110
static constructors, 141-145
static members, 108-110
static methods, 30
static typing, 34
Status property, 698
storage, thread-local, 660-662
Stream class, 614-623
    asynchronous operation, 620
    concrete types, 621
    copying, 618
    disposal, 619

unsafe code, 746
unspeakable names, 188, 398, 733
using declaration, 334
using directive, 25
using statement, 333, 725
Utf8JsonReader type, 759-761
UWP (Universal Windows Platform), 551

V

vacuous truth, 447
value type
    constraints, 203
    properties and mutable value types, 169-171
    unmanaged constraints, 203
    when to write, 127-131
ValueTask and ValueTask<T> types, 695
ValueTuple<T> type, 208
ValueType, 299
var keyword, 36-38
    positional pattern with, 98
    with variables holding LINQ queries, 421
var patterns, type patterns versus, 98
variables
    captured, 396-403
    declaring with var, 37
    in C# specification, 34
    local, 34-44
    local variable instances, 43
    name ambiguity, 41-43
    reference variables and return values,
        154-156
    scope, 40-44
verbatim string literals, 74-76
versioning
    assembly names, 558-561
    inheritance and library versioning, 286-292
    version numbers and assembly loading, 560
Virtual Execution System (VES), 7
virtual methods, 283-292
    abstract methods, 285
    hidden methods versus, 289
    inheritance and library versioning, 286-292
    interfaces versus, 285

Visual Basic, 6
Visual Studio
    #region and #endregion, 58
    adding a project to an existing solution, 17
    anatomy of a simple program, 15-32
    assemblies and, 539
    basics, 11-14
    constructor generation, 297
    creating a new program in, 15-17
    referencing external libraries, 19-21
    writing a unit test, 21-25
Visual Studio Code, 12
Visual Studio for Mac, 12

W

WaitHandle class, 684
weak references, 311-314
WER (Windows Error Reporting), 364
when clause, patterns with, 100
Where operator, 434-436
while loops, 91
whitespace, 53
Window operator, 510-514
windowing operators, 507-514
    Buffer operator, 507-510
    demarcating windows with observables, 513
    time-based overloads, 535
    Window operator, 510-514
Windows Error Reporting (WER), 364
workstation GC mode, 321
Write method, 616, 626

X

Xamarin, 8, 12
XML, 6

Z

zero, division by, 353
zero-argument constructors, 137-138
zero-like values, 205-206
Zip operator, 458

About the Author

Ian Griffiths works for endjin where he is a Technical Fellow. He lives in Hove, England, but can often be found on various developer mailing lists and newsgroups, where a popular sport is to see who can get him to write the longest email in reply to the shortest possible question. Ian is coauthor of *Windows Forms in a Nutshell*, *Mastering Visual Studio .NET*, and *Programming WPF*.

Colophon

The animal on the cover of Programming C# 8.0 is a gray crowned crane (*Balearica regulorum*). This bird's range extends in parts from Kenya and Uganda in the north into eastern South Africa, and they prefer to live in habitats such as open marshes and grasslands.

Adult birds stand 3 to 4 feet tall and weigh about 8 pounds. They are visually striking birds, with a gray body and pale gray neck, white and gold wings, a white face (with a red patch above), a black cap, a bright red throat lappet, and blue eyes. Topping all of this off (and giving them their name) is the distinctive spray of stiff gold filaments at the back of their heads.

Crowned cranes can live for up to 20 years in the wild, spending most of their waking hours stalking through the grass hunting for small animals and insects, as well as seeds and grains. They are one of only two types of crane to roost at night in trees, a feat made possible by a prehensile hind toe that allows them to grip branches. These birds produce clutches of up to four eggs; a few hours after hatching, the chicks are able to follow their parents, and the family together forages for food.

Social and talkative, crowned cranes group together in pairs or families, which at times combine into flocks of more than 100 birds. Like other cranes, they are well-known for their elaborate mating dancing, which includes elements such as short upward flights, wing flapping, and deep bows.

Despite their wide range, these birds are currently considered endangered, threatened by habitat loss, egg poaching, and pesticide use. Many of the animals on O'Reilly covers are endangered; all of them are important to the world.

The cover illustration is by Karen Montgomery, based on a black-and-white engraving from *Cassell's Natural History* (1896). The cover fonts are Gilroy and Guardian Sans. The text font is Adobe Minion Pro; the heading font is Adobe Myriad Condensed; and the code font is Dalton Maag's Ubuntu Mono.

O'REILLY®

There's much more where this came from.

Experience books, videos, live online training courses, and more from O'Reilly and our 200+ partners—all in one place.

Learn more at oreilly.com/online-learning